International Studies in Entrepreneurship

Series editors

Zoltan J. Acs, George Mason University, Fairfax, VA, USA
David B. Audretsch, Indiana University, Bloomington, IN, USA

More information about this series at http://www.springer.com/series/6149

Rui Baptista • João Leitão
Editors

Entrepreneurship, Human Capital, and Regional Development

Labor Networks, Knowledge Flows, and Industry Growth

Springer

Editors
Rui Baptista
Brunel Business School
Brunel University London
Kingston Lane, Uxbridge, UK

CEG-IST
Universidade de Lisboa
Lisbon, Portugal

João Leitão
Department of Management and Economics
University of Beira Interior
Covilhã, Portugal

CEG-IST
Universidade de Lisboa
Lisbon, Portugal

ISSN 1572-1922 ISSN 2197-5884 (electronic)
ISBN 978-3-319-38427-6 ISBN 978-3-319-12871-9 (eBook)
DOI 10.1007/978-3-319-12871-9
Springer Cham Heidelberg New York Dordrecht London

Springer is part of Springer Science+Business Media (www.springer.com)

Contents

Chapter 1
Introduction

Rui Baptista and João Leitão

1.1 Preface

Entrepreneurship is a sufficiently eclectic and multidimensional area of research to allow simultaneous approaches from a variety of scientific fields—from economics to sociology—using different levels and for different units of analysis, namely country, region, firm, and the individual. The relationship between entrepreneurship and the dynamics of endogenous growth has been well established (Audretsch et al. 2006; Acs et al. 2009), and so has its impact on regional employment growth (Fritsch and Mueller 2004; Baptista and Preto 2011).

After more than a decade of discussion reprising the Schumpeterian role of entrepreneurship in the context of endogenous growth theories, the main point that emerges is that not all entrepreneurship impacts growth in the same way. Impactful entrepreneurship requires an array of competences and behaviors from the entrepreneur in order to recognize opportunities in new ideas and converting those into innovations that enhance overall productivity, competitiveness, employment, and welfare. In order to have an impact on growth, entrepreneurship needs to add value, and not just appropriate existing value. More specifically, entrepreneurial change causes growth by combining factors of production in new, innovative ways, and using previously unused factors of production, thereby enhancing productivity.

New combinations of factors of production are brought about by entrepreneurial action in terms of new products and services, hiring of workers, process innovation.

R. Baptista (✉)
Brunel Business School, Brunel University London, Kingston Lane,
Uxbridge, UB8 3PH, UK

CEG-IST, Universidade de Lisboa, Av. Rovisco Pais, 1, Lisbon, 1050-001 Lisboa, Portugal
e-mail: rui.baptista@ist.utl.pt

J. Leitão
Department of Management and Economics, Universidade da Beira Interior,
Estrada do Sineiro, Covilhã, 6200-209 Covilhã, Portugal

CEG-IST, Universidade de Lisboa, Av. Rovisco Pais, 1, Lisbon, 1050-001 Lisboa, Portugal
e-mail: jleitao@ubi.pt

R. Baptista, J. Leitão (eds.), *Entrepreneurship, Human Capital, and Regional Development*, International Studies in Entrepreneurship 31,
DOI 10.1007/978-3-319-12871-9_1

Innovation generates knowledge flows to other competitors and companies in related industries, some of these flows occurring through the mobility of workers. Such mobility also serves, as documented by Phillips (2002), for new organizations to acquire the knowledge, competences, and routines of existing ones. Labor mobility provides new, innovative start-ups with the abilities required to organize and survive, and infuses incumbents with new ideas to facilitate restructuring and repurposing of old lines of business.

Human capital and its mobility within regions play, therefore, a fundamental role in the dynamics of entrepreneurship and economic growth. It is this role that provides the guiding question of this book. Human capital arises from three sources (Becker 1964): education, training and, perhaps most important for entrepreneurship, experience in organizations i.e., competences and routines that arise using technology, marketing, and finance in organizational contexts. Theories of human capital present knowledge as the stock of creative ideas that provide individuals with strengthened competences, behavioral characteristics, and cognitive skills allowing them to develop a more productive and efficient potential activity (Schultz 1963; Becker 1964; Mincer 1974). Faced with a scenario including a variety of potentially profitable opportunities, those individual possessing greater human capital are the ones more likely to recognize those opportunities, and mobilize and organize the resources necessary to implement and exploit them, leading to economic change.

Human capital has been subject to significant attention by researchers interested in uncovering the nature of its relationship with economic growth. However, most of the literature on this subject—which is critical for the economic, social, and financial sustainability of countries and regions—has been dominated by the neoclassical paradigm, thereby omitting the role played by a fundamental agent in the functioning of capitalist economies, i.e., the entrepreneur. The pioneering works of Lucas (1988) and Romer (1990), while recognizing the role of knowledge, eschewed all consideration of human capital and entrepreneurship. The so-called "Schumpeterian" models of endogenous growth (e.g., Aghion and Howitt 1992) focus on innovation as a product of R&D efforts, and not of entrepreneurial action. While the role of human capital (as it relates to training) is increasingly recognized as a determinant factor of long-term growth (Mulligan and Sala-i-Martin 1995; Bleaney and Nishiyama 2002), there is little or no consideration of human capital that is specific for entrepreneurship, or that emerges from organizational experience. That omission leads us to invite the reader of this book to revisit the seminal contributions of Schumpeter (1961) and Kirzner (1973), and Baumol (1968, 2002) who, while recognizing the exclusion of the entrepreneurship construct from the theories of economic growth, establish entrepreneurial action and capabilities as vital components of economic and social progress.

It is not easy to determine which specific aspects of human capital contribute more to entrepreneurial success. Davidsson and Honig (2003) indicate that the association between business performance and human capital may be confused with a set of other factors, namely persistence and professional experience. Cultural aspects can also moderate and blur this relationship. Lundström and Stevenson

(2001) point out that in the USA and some Western European countries, where there is a more favorable perception of critical factors such as risk, competition, and individualism, entrepreneurs will likely be more ambitious and the potential to enact economic change through entrepreneurship will likely be greater.

Differences in culture arise, however, between much smaller geographical units than countries. Such differences translate into institutions, firms, and individuals, and result in different dynamics for entrepreneurship and industrial development. The papers collected in this book add the regional element as a frame for the exploration of the dynamics of entrepreneurship and growth. The regional dynamics of industry growth are greatly influenced by employee mobility towards new firms. Successful incumbent firms can serve, usually unintentionally, as training grounds for their employees before they move on to work for, or indeed found new firms. By locating in close proximity to previous employers and hiring local workers with specific experience, in terms of the industry, entrepreneurs/founders strengthen the geographical differences between regions concerning the number and quality of companies.

The rich literature on geographical clusters which emerged from the seminal works of Porter (1990) and Krugman (1991) has mostly focused on economic and social mechanisms that arise from the benefits and costs or agglomeration: firms and industries are attracted to a region by pools of labor and supporting businesses; knowledge spillovers, networks and social capital. Only recently new work has emerged positioning entrepreneurship at the center of the cluster phenomenon. In a recent review, Chatterji et al. (2013) point to a variety of factors which are deemed to be spatial determinants of entrepreneurship, including the density of small businesses. Delgado et al. (2010) argue that the presence of related industries in a location fosters entrepreneurship by lowering the cost of starting a business, enhancing opportunities for innovation, and enabling better access to a more diverse range of inputs and complementary products. Entrepreneurship is gradually being recognized as occupying the center stage in the clustering phenomenon.

While by reprising the role of entrepreneurship in economic growth researchers revisited the works of Schumpeter, Kirzner, and Baumol, by bringing to the fore the role of entrepreneurship in the cluster phenomenon, researchers are now revisiting the work of Marshall (1922), Piore and Sabel (1984), Becattini (1989), and Markusen (1996) on industrial districts. Marshall's view of industrial districts can be extended to explore the nature of networks of business relationships and competences, institutional settings, and social and cultural characteristics of the regions where clusters originate. It seems clear that theoretical approaches that reduce the cluster phenomenon to the treatment of one critical variable—e.g., scale and transport costs, or knowledge spillovers—are unlikely to provide an explanation for cluster emergence and survival. It seems essential to integrate institutional settings, technology and production, and the life of the local community into a single model.

It is possible to suggest several paths towards deepening research on the role of entrepreneurship on the growth of regions. One can explore: (1) the motivations and effects associated with the high incidence of employee exchange between clients and suppliers; (2) the high degree of cooperation between competitors to reduce risk, stabilize the market and share innovation; (3) the disproportionate rates of employees involved in design and innovation activities; (4) the existence of strong business associations providing access to shared infrastructure, management academies, marketing initiatives, and technical and financial counseling; and (5) the strong commitment and efforts of local government in regulating and promoting the growth of core industries.

New research efforts should endeavor to achieve what the literature has arguably failed so far to do: provide policy makers and practitioners with critical information about which mechanisms lie behind cluster success, survival, and prosperity. The approaches presented in this book offer clues to what future work may explore when looking at entrepreneurship and regional growth. In terms of value added, this book contributes to the literature by suggesting answers to the following questions:

1. Is the growth and success of the cluster over time due to conjugating simple effects of concentration and transmission of business competences through spin-offs located in a given regional space?
2. Does increased density of job options outside the workplace contribute to increased mobility of human capital between firms located within clusters, and so improve coordination in the local labor market?
3. Do spin-offs benefit from hiring workers from successful incumbents, inasmuch as those workers are expected to perform better than other workers from different origins?

The book is divided in three parts: Part I—Entrepreneurship; Part II—Human Capital; and Part III—Regional Development. There follows a summarized review of the contributions contained in this edited volume, according to the structured design of the above-mentioned three parts.

In Part I on entrepreneurship, various theoretical and applied approaches are presented by a selection of prominent and young researchers whose visions enrich the current debate on the dimension of analysis situated at the individual level, i.e., the entrepreneur. They underline fundamentally the role of mobility, the relationship with the parent firm, the concentration of companies in one place, the experience and training of the productive work factor, as well as pointing out the importance of the geographical concentration of industries for new companies' viability, namely through direct recruitment from incumbent firms, which can result in the incubation of firms or projects, of the spin-off type, or in start-ups becoming autonomous, determining their evolutionary path and performance.

In Chap. 2, Maria do Rosário Cabrita, Cristina Cabrita, Florinda Matos, and María del Pilar Muñoz Dueñas approach the first dimension of analysis using the theory of intellectual capital as the pillar of analysis of regional development dynamics. Following a perspective based on knowledge, the authors argue that entrepreneurship can be thought of as a function of knowledge and attitude. Such a perspective proposes that there is one single dominant factor upon which the opportunity, the individual and the whole entrepreneurial process are based. This factor is knowledge as a property of individuals or organizations which are intelligent agents in their own right, and which are challenged to have a critical attitude in order to execute the entrepreneurial process. The authors expand their analysis to the regional dimension, by stating that concerning regions, their prosperity no longer lies in traditional assets such as cheap land and labor. Instead, regions' success is shaped by new categories of assets, such as skills, innovative firms, lifestyle amenities, cultural assets, and intellectual capital.

In Chap. 3, Nora Hesse explores the following question: How can the career paths of academic entrepreneurs influence university spin-off growth? In this line of reasoning, the author makes use of three literature streams, namely, the university status perspective, the human capital perspective, and the role identity perspective. The results obtained from the qualitative content analysis and extreme case analysis show that each university status comprises certain advantages and disadvantages. More human capital and a higher university status are not necessarily advantageous for long-term university spin-off growth. Instead, the willingness and ability for role identity change in terms of the degree of commitment to the entrepreneurial role is very important. With advancing university status, academic entrepreneurs have more difficulty in changing roles and leading the university spin-off with full commitment. Around one third of the academic entrepreneurs in the sample decided to continue their university career and work in the university spin-off at the same time on a part-time basis. Therefore, it is important to consider the career plans and growth intentions of an academic entrepreneur.

In Chap. 4, Eissa Alrumaithi, Maribel Guerrero, and Iñaki Peña explore the roles played by employee human capital and the work environment in the creation of organizational spin-offs. By adopting the human capital and corporate entrepreneurship approaches, a conceptual framework is proposed and tested by making use of data from the 2012 Spanish Adult Population Survey (Global Entrepreneurship Monitor, GEM). In the empirical approach a rare event model is used. The empirical evidence reveals the importance of specific human capital (entrepreneurship educational training) and the work environment (job autonomy) in determining an employee's propensity to become an intrapreneur and lead a spin-off "from" and "for" their employer. Moreover, a stronger moderation effect of job autonomy takes place in the relationship between entrepreneurship education and organizational spin-off creation. These new findings provide several implications in the sense that they could help employees, top managers, and policy makers to take into account the relevance of these individual and organizational factors when defining their strategic planning and decision-making processes.

In Chap. 5, Emeran Nziali and Alain Fayolle contribute to a better understanding of the construct of competitive advantage—and its related effects such as worker mobility—by investigating how far the resource that a spin-off already possesses constrains or determines the acquisition of subsequent ones. The authors consider both spin-offs and spin-outs as two distinct configurations of knowledge inheritance with the former differing from the latter in that it benefits from additional support of a financial or physical nature from its previous employer. Nevertheless, the authors explore the caveat found in the literature concerning the role played by knowledge inherited by entrepreneurs from the mother firm or industry and that of the founders leading the business creation process—namely her/his human capital. Thus, the authors hypothesize a greater preference for hiring coworkers when there is a greater inheritance of resources from a mother company. They rely on a dataset from the 2011 Global Entrepreneurship Monitor Survey and logit techniques to investigate the question. The main results reveal that human capital may moderate the deterministic effects of resource inheritance by weakening, maintaining, or strengthening the advantages that resource inheritance confers in hiring coworkers and early-stage performance by extension. In addition, having entrepreneurial experience helps spin-offs (but not spin-outs) to maintain the advantages of resource inheritance for those who say they possess it, and they tend to hire more coworkers than those who do not. In contrast with entrepreneurial experience and entrepreneurial skills, it is not clear whether educational level or having any experience as an employee sustains or weakens the effect inherited from business status.

In Chap. 6, Vera Rocha, Anabela Carneiro, and Celeste Varum compare the post-entry performance of pushed and pulled spin-offs, by using a rich matched employer–employee dataset. Moreover, the authors take into consideration a large number of start-up conditions that can affect spin-off survival and moderate the survival differences between necessity and opportunity spin-offs. In specific terms, the authors analyze whether start-up triggering conditions influence spin-offs' hazard rates. They control for industry and geographic relatedness to the incumbent firm, the decision to hire some coworkers who were previously employed by the parent firm and the general and specific human capital of spin-offs' founders. The empirical evidence reveals that unconditionally pushed spin-offs survive longer than those driven by other (i.e., pulled) factors. However, when the authors control for a larger number of observed differences between spin-offs, this survival bonus becomes insignificant. The results obtained also confirm that pushed spin-offs should not be overlooked, as they seem to play an important role in creating new jobs and absorbing a significant part of those workers displaced by the parent firm.

In Part II, the dimension of analysis relates to human capital, covering the influence of qualification, training, experience and the creativity of entrepreneurs, as well as the strategic dimension of exploration and absorption of external knowledge flows in the context of competitive market structures formed by a dominant base of micro, small and medium-sized firms.

In Chap. 7, Aurora Teixeira and Ricardo Castro assess the role played by human capital in its different forms in the performance of Portuguese spin-offs, including entrepreneurs' level and type of education, skills, experience, and network capabilities. The authors use a sample of 90 founders of 61 ASOs located in Portugal, associated with the University Technology Enterprise Network (UTEN). The main results reveal that among human capital dimensions, business expertise, most notably market knowledge, is the one affecting economic performance most in ASOs. Both the level and type of founders' formal education failed to significantly influence the economic performance of ASOs. The unemployed status of the founders (prior to creating the ASOs), formal contacts with the university, as well as undertaking R&D activities and internationalization emerged as critical positive determinants of economic performance in ASOs. Although some evidence exists on the relevance of university research excellence for the performance of ASOs, from this innovative research, an unambiguous result emerged regarding the university context: ASOs that exclusively resort to the services of Science Parks, Incubators, and TTOs outperformed the others.

In Chap. 8, Ugo Rizzo focuses on the influence of external knowledge via recruitment on ASO development. Considering what is stated in the reference literature on the importance of external knowledge for the development and growth of this type of firm, the author assesses the mechanisms by which such knowledge is internalized and the impact of such knowledge on firms' strategies and capacity development. The main results point out that ASOs' founding teams could decide whether to hire a surrogate entrepreneur or other managers, or hire external researchers, according to the specificities of their business and the market connections they developed during their academic activities. Moreover, when ASOs are created with specific ideas and purposes, hiring talented managers could speed up and focus the development path of the firm. Conversely, when ASOs are constituted with no clear-cut business ideas, or the initial idea needs to change because of market feedback, managers would be most useful when there is a lack of market connections. As for researchers, they seem to be useful mostly when the business needs to integrate different competences, and when the product becomes more standardized and less linked to cutting-edge academic research.

In Chap. 9, Dina Pereira and João Leitão address the still unexplored coopetition problematic, by making use of service firms' behavior in generating innovative services, to reveal their innovative performance and the dynamics of coopetition targeted at open innovation. The authors select a sample of 1,221 service firms that participated in the European Community Innovation Survey (CIS), 2008. A probit analysis is conducted for "knowledge-intensive service (KIS) firms" and "less-KIS firms." The main results reveal that coopetition arrangements between competing firms and the scientific community, and also firms' capacity to introduce innovations to the market, have a positive and significant influence on service firms' behavior in generating service innovations. Furthermore, the authors advocate that the effects of introducing process innovations inside the firm and the existence of internal R&D activities are of major significance for influencing positively the innovative behavior of service firms.

In Chap. 10, Rocío Aliaga-Isla compares how human capital influences two processes of entrepreneurship. With this purpose, the author analyses how Spaniards' general/specific human capital influences their likelihood of perceiving entrepreneurial opportunities and creating a business. A sample is collected from the Spanish Global Entrepreneurship Monitor—GEM, 2008 to perform a logistic regression analysis, in order to test several research hypotheses. The empirical findings reveal, on the one hand, that general human capital such as education is not significant for either perceiving entrepreneurial opportunities or creating a business. On the other hand, work experience, managerial business, and entrepreneurial training are positively associated with perceiving entrepreneurial opportunities and creating a business. In addition, the author reveals that specific types of human capital play different roles in entrepreneurship.

In Chap. 11, André Olim, Isabel Mota, and Sandra Silva analyze the impact of creativity on entrepreneurship. A multivariate linear regression analysis is applied, explaining new firm formation across Portuguese regions with explanatory variables that include both creativity and diversity indexes, innovation indicators, and the human capital dimension, as well as other control variables. The results show little evidence of the influence of creativity on the birth of new firms, while pointing to the relevance of agglomeration effects for new firms' formation and to the difficulty of immigrants in establishing a firm.

In Part III, the dimension of analysis concerns regional development, based on different empirical approaches related to the determinant factors of endogenous growth in different spatial units, giving special attention to approaches focused on the influence of firms' geographical concentration, as well as of firms' local and external environment and of the evolutionary path of industrial clusters on the growth of small and medium-sized enterprises. In the last two contributions, the analysis focuses on issues related to high-growth firms, namely factors that catalyze or restrict their growth, including intrinsic characteristics (age, size, capital structure, business governance, total productivity of factors, previous economic performance, business strategy, and R&D) and characteristics of a more extrinsic nature related to regional differences.

In Chap. 12, Murat Ali Dulupçu, Murat Karaöz, Onur Sungur, and Hidayet Keskin devote their attention to analysis and identification of the evolutionary trajectory of cluster policies and practices in Turkey. The authors analyzed the impact of international institutions on cluster policies, at different scales, and the role played by the shift of national policy towards regionalization. In operational terms, the authors characterize the adoption regime of cluster policies particularly through Regional Development Agencies (RDAs). They outline the possible dangers of unfiltered policy transfers in terms of cluster policies. In addition, disregarding regional features may lessen the impact of cluster policies. Alternatively, spending too much time on filtering could result in missing out on chances and high costs: the right combination of policy implications of clusters should be integrated in indigenous policy formulations.

In Chap. 13, Carlos Carreira and Luís Lopes implement a micro-level analysis in order to shed further light on the extent to which the local environment, namely agglomerations' economies and the regional knowledge base, has an effect on firms' productivity. Additionally, the authors investigate whether smaller firms are more dependent on the local environment than larger ones. To conduct the analysis, they use an unbalanced panel of Portuguese manufacturing firms covering the period 1996–2004. Controlling for endogeneity using the generalized method of moments estimator, the authors reveal that both localization and urbanization economies have a significant and positive effect on firm productivity, with the latter playing the most important role. Sectoral specialization economies are important for small and medium-sized firms, but not for large firms. However, larger firms, therefore those with higher absorptive capacity, benefit more from regional knowledge than smaller ones.

In Chap. 14, Carla Costa and Rui Baptista look at the history of the emergence of the molds and plastics industries in Portugal, finding that this history fits nicely with the accounts—originally proposed in Steven Klepper's various works—of new industries emerging from older, related industries, and regional clusters emerging from the mobility of specialized workers from successful incumbents to new firms created in the same regional environment.

In Chap. 15, Patrícia Bogas and Natália Barbosa address issues related to high-growth firms, by providing an empirical application to the Portuguese context. In doing so, the authors assess the impact of region-specific characteristics on the probability of the firm being high-growth. Using a sample of active firms registered in the *Quadros de Pessoal* database between 2002 and 2006, the empirical evidence obtained suggests that high-growth firms are not a random phenomenon and that region-specific characteristics determine significantly the probability of firms being high-growth. In particular, industrial diversity, services agglomeration, and the diversity of employees' qualifications in a region explain in a significant way the probability of a firm being high-growth.

In Chap. 16, Fløysand, Jakobsen, and Sánchez Hernández discuss the connection between changing ideas for regional policy formulation in Norway and Spain taking on a "scalar politics" framework. The analysis demonstrates that regional industrial policies are rooted in processes of downscaling in Norway and upscaling in Spain, while rescaling of regional policy away from being primarily a nationally controlled project is a universal concern. Another trend is that the policy instruments have become more homogeneous across communities and regions over the years.

Finally, in Chap. 17, Elsa Sarmento and Alcina Nunes aim to reveal who these fast-growing firms are and where they operate. These questions provide the foundation for an exploration into what the different policy choices are, engaging afresh with why and if they ought to receive support in the first place, raising the discussion as to when and how this could be provided and what the intended results could be. The authors use the *Quadros de Pessoal* dataset in order to provide a twofold measurement, according to employment and turnover growth criteria. The main results, applied to the Portuguese context, reveal a high proportion of SMEs in the population of fast-growing firms, the narrowing down of the difference between measurements according to employment and turnover criteria and the disproportionate amount of employment generated by the largest segment of fast-growing firms. Furthermore, the authors find that gazelles are outstanding job creators, having a disproportionately larger impact on job creation than high-growth firms. Accordingly, it is the rapid growth of a few large firms, combined with the entry of a higher number of firms of a greater average size that generates positive net job creation in Portugal. An open question deserves to be further explored, i.e., a deeper understanding of fast-growing firms ought to lead to adjustments in government policies, in order to foster their exceptional contribution to economic growth.

To conclude this introduction, the objective of this book is to bring together a number of innovative and ambitious contributions to the study of human capital, entrepreneurship, and growth, with a view to offering insights to policy makers on how to raise the innovative and entrepreneurial capacity of regions. We live today in a context of lack of credibility and trust in economic, financial, and political agents. Bank bailouts and rising inequality seem to signal that avenues to growth and wealth based on financial innovation are exhausted, or even discredited. In this context, small business and entrepreneurship become more than just another growth-enhancing mechanism, they provide a path for the regeneration of the industries and economies. Such path can only be walked with investment in knowledge creation, human capital formation, and ambitious entrepreneurial efforts.

Uxbridge and Fundão,
Rui Baptista
João Leitão

References

Acs ZJ, Braunerhjelm P, Audretsch DB, Carlsson B (2009) The knowledge spillover theory of entrepreneurship. Small Bus Econ 32:15–30

Aghion P, Howitt P (1992) A model of growth through creative destruction. Econometrica 60(2):323–351

Audretsch D, Keilbach M, Lehmann E (2006) Entrepreneurship and economic growth. Oxford University Press, New York

Baptista R, Preto MT (2011) New firm formation and employment growth: regional and business dynamics. Small Bus Econ 36:419–442

Baumol WJ (1968) Entrepreneurship in economic theory. Am Econ Rev 58:64–71

Baumol WJ (2002) The free-market innovation machine: analyzing the growth miracle of capitalism. Princeton University Press, Princeton

Becattini G (1989) Modelli di sviluppo. Il Mulino, Bologna

Becker G (1964) Human capital: a theoretical and empirical analysis, with special reference to education. University of Chicago Press, Chicago

Bleaney M, Nishiyama A (2002) Explaining growth: a contest between models. J Econ Growth 7(1):43–56

Chatterji A, Glaeser EL, Kerr WR (2013) Clusters of entrepreneurship and innovation (No. w19013). National Bureau of Economic Research, Cambridge

Davidsson P, Honig B (2003) The role of social and human capital among nascent entrepreneurs. J Bus Ventur 18(3):301–330

Delgado M, Porter ME, Stern S (2010) Clusters and entrepreneurship. J Econ Geogr 10(4):495–518

Fritsch M, Mueller P (2004) The effects of new business formation on regional development over time. Reg Stud 38:961–975

Kirzner I (1973) Competition and entrepreneurship. University of Chicago Press, Chicago

Krugman P (1991) Geography and trade. MIT, Cambridge

Lucas R (1988) On the mechanics of economic development. J Monet Econ 22:3–42

Lundström L, Stevenson A (2001) Patterns and trends in entrepreneurship/SME policy and practice in ten economies. Swedish Foundation for Small Business Research, Stockholm

Markusen A (1996) Sticky places in slippery space: a typology of industrial districts. Econ Geogr 72:293–313

Marshall A (1922) Principles of economics. Macmillan, London

Mincer J (1974) Schooling, experience, and earnings. Human behavior & social institutions no. 2. Columbia University Press, New York

Mulligan C, Sala-i-Martin X (1995) Measuring aggregate human capital. NBER working paper no. 5016, February 1995
Phillips DJ (2002) A genealogical approach to organizational life changes: the parent-progeny transfer among Silicon Valley law firms, 1946–1996. Adm Sci Q 47:474–506
Piore M, Sabel C (1984) The second industrial divide. Basic Books, New York
Porter M (1990) The competitive advantage of nations. Macmillan, London
Romer P (1990) Endogenous technological change. J Polit Econ 98(5):71–102
Schultz T (1963) The economic value of education. Columbia University Press, New York
Schumpeter J (1961) The theory of economic development: an inquiry into profits, capital, credit, interest, and the business cycle. OUP, New York. Translated from the German by Redvers Opie (1961)

Part I
Entrepreneurship

Chapter 2
Entrepreneurship Capital and Regional Development: A Perspective Based on Intellectual Capital

Maria Rosário Cabrita, Cristina Cabrita, Florinda Matos, and María del Pilar Muñoz Dueñas

Abstract The literature describes entrepreneurial process as a multidimensional and complex phenomenon. Most conceptual frameworks advocate that the entrepreneurship is a function of the opportunity and the individual entrepreneur, his or her characteristics and actions. A knowledge-based perspective suggests that entrepreneurship can be thought of as a function of knowledge and attitude. Such perspective proposes that there is one single dominant factor upon which the opportunity, the individual, and the whole entrepreneurial process are based. This factor is knowledge as a property of individuals or organizations which are intelligent agents in their own right, and which are challenged to have a critical attitude in order to execute the entrepreneurial process. Recent works on this research area suggest that there is a positive link between entrepreneurship, regional economic performance, and the creation of new firms and businesses. Regions are now facing rapidly evolving pressures from global economy. Regions prosperity no longer lies in traditional assets such as cheap land and labor. Instead, regions' success is shaped by new categories of assets, like skills, innovative firms, lifestyle amenities, cultural assets,

M.R. Cabrita (✉)
UNIDEMI, Department of Mechanical and Industrial Engineering, Faculty of Science and Technology, FCT, Universidade Nova de Lisboa, Caparica 2829-516, Portugal
e-mail: m.cabrita@fct.unl.pt

C. Cabrita
ISCTE-IUL Lisbon University Institute, Lisbon, Portugal
e-mail: cristinacabrita.arq@gmail.com

F. Matos
IC Lab Research Centre, ICAA—Intellectual Capital Accreditation Association, Rua dos Bombeiros Voluntários, 4 R/C-Esq, Santarém 2000-205, Portugal
e-mail: florinda.matos@icca.pt

M.P. Muñoz Dueñas
Departamento de Economía Financiera y Contabilidad, Facultad de Ciencias Económicas y Empresariales, Universidad de Vigo, Vigo, Spain
e-mail: pilar.munoz@uvigo.es

R. Baptista, J. Leitão (eds.), *Entrepreneurship, Human Capital, and Regional Development*, International Studies in Entrepreneurship 31,
DOI 10.1007/978-3-319-12871-9_2

and intellectual capital. Although, in the last years, many studies have investigated the knowledge factors grounding local development there are still gaps in the research that need to be filled for the definition of the theory pillars of an intellectual capital dimension of regional development dynamics. This chapter contributes to the literature on the role entrepreneurship plays in regional development, providing a holistic view of the knowledge-based entrepreneurial activity.

Keywords Entrepreneurship capital • Human capital • Intellectual capital • Regional development

2.1 Introduction

It is generally accepted in the literature that entrepreneurship is primarily a "regional event" (Feldman 2001). However, the study of entrepreneurship and new firm formation has also demonstrated that not all places are alike in their potential to generate new entrepreneurs. In the context of knowledge economy (KE), the entrepreneurial vitality of a region depends to a large extent on the capabilities to activate, develop, sustain, and manage knowledge dynamics and processes. The knowledge-based capital is a source of regional innovation capacity which supports that regions differ in: (1) the way they capture and retain talents (Florida 1995); (2) the extent of social network (Schiuma et al. 2008); and (3) the scale and quality of public infrastructures (Polenske 2004).

The knowledge-based economy has put the focus on the regional dimension of economic growth. It has also shifted development perspectives from output to input factors as production became more knowledge-based, calling for a better understanding of how firms, universities, and government institutions deploy their core resources and competencies and interact to accrue economic growth (Rodriguez and Viedma 2006). In this special context, entrepreneurship facilitates knowledge spillovers through the implication of start-ups and growth of new enterprises where their ideas are commercialized.

In the age of knowledge the key source of economic vitality and growth are intangible assets. They play a prominent role in enhancing competitiveness. Resources like intellectual capital (IC) are perceived as crucial factors especially for regional growth. It is widely accepted that territorial systems depend increasingly on their ability to master and develop knowledge resources. This issue has been largely investigated in the last decade (Edvinsson 2002; Tallman et al. 2004; Smedlund and Poyhonen 2005; Carrillo 2006; Martins and Viedma 2006; Lerro and Schiuma 2009). Recent literature on creative economy and knowledge-based urban development emphasizes the role of regions and cities in becoming basic "building blocks" for economic growth (Yigitcanlar 2009). Although the relevance of knowledge as source of innovation and competitiveness at regional and local level is recognized, most studies have focused attention on isolated knowledge components, rather than on a holistic view of the knowledge-based capital building a region's innovation capacity (Bounfour and Edvinsson 2005). This work aims to develop a framework that links entrepreneurship capital and regional development, where the intellectual capital perspective provides a holistic approach of the knowledge-based entrepreneurial activity.

This chapter is organized as follows. Section 2.2 discusses the different approaches to understanding entrepreneurship and presents the notion of entrepreneurship capital as a regional factor of production that attracts individuals. Section 2.3 develops a knowledge-based perspective on entrepreneurship. Then, providing a knowledge-based interpretation of entrepreneurial activity, links between entrepreneurship capital and regional development are pointed out, adopting a perspective based on intellectual capital.

2.2 Entrepreneurship and Entrepreneurial Capital

The term entrepreneurship has several levels of meaning, which makes it hard to reach a consensus about an appropriate definition. Nowadays, the entrepreneurship area comprehends a broad range of theories and approaches and has been studied in different ways and with several purposes. Academics from various fields of social sciences—notably economics, psychology, and sociology—have given contributions to this area (Casson 2010). There are, at least three approaches to understanding entrepreneurship: (1) the economic approach, which studies the functions of entrepreneurs in economy; (2) the psychological approach, which examines personal characteristics specific to entrepreneurs, and; (3) the social-behavioral approach, which stresses the influence of the social environment as well as personal attributes. Entrepreneurship is then multidisciplinary (Raposo et al. 2008), sometimes a fuzzy concept.

According to the OECD (1998), there are three ways how entrepreneurship can be measured. First, entrepreneurship involves a dynamic process in which new firms are starting up, existing firms are growing, and unsuccessful ones are restructuring or closing down. This approach is anchored on the notion of creative destruction (Schumpeter 1911/1934) and has been operationalized by start-up rates and survival rates. Second, entrepreneurship refers to new firms formation or small businesses. This is mostly measured by the self-employment or business ownership rate. Finally, entrepreneurship tends to be identified as innovation, which is mostly captured by R&D measures.

An interesting point in the literature is related to the *supply side* and the *demand side* of entrepreneurship. On the supply side, related to the "pool" of potential entrepreneurs, important perceptions include willingness, individual attributes, motivational factors, and perceived ability to become an entrepreneur. Education levels and the availability of entrepreneurship training programs are possible determinants of perceived skills. On the demand side, or "space for" entrepreneurship, there need to be opportunities for entrepreneurship, but equally entrepreneurs need to perceive opportunities to start a business (Kirzner 1973; Shane and Eckhardt 2003). The quantity and quality of perceived opportunities may be enhanced by regional and national conditions such as economic growth, population growth, culture, and national entrepreneurship policy. Thus, entrepreneurship is a result of endogenous and exogenous aspects.

Audretsch and Keilbach (2004) introduced the concept of entrepreneurship capital stressing those aspects of a region that are conducive to the creation of new business. The authors refer to entrepreneurship capital as a regional or spatial factor of production that attracts individuals willing to incur the risk of starting up a new business, and then expand their definition to include other factors that result from the interactions of these individuals (or entrepreneurs) at different levels of aggregation. Such other factors include informal networks at the group or team level, formal networks at the organizational level, and, finally, the regional milieu, which comprises, among other things, the business culture, supporting institutions, and institutional obstacles (Audretsch and Monsen 2008). The milieu, described as a system of regional institutions, rules, and practices that lead to innovation, is essentially a context for development. Several studies have been developed and empirically tested which demonstrate that: (1) entrepreneurship capital contributes to economic growth, over and above traditional forms of capital (e.g., physical, labor); (2) R&D intensive entrepreneurship capital has a greater long-term impact on long-term regional productivity; (3) high technology entrepreneurship capital impacts labor productivity growth (Audretsch and Keilbach 2004).

2.2.1 *Entrepreneurship Initiatives in the Context of Knowledge Economy*

Globalization is causing profound change in the economic structure of nations, regions, cities, industries, and firms. New technological advances have diminished transportation, telecommunications, and computational costs, increasing the ease of global flows of information.

In the context of KE wealth creation depends on the generation and exploitation of knowledge involving not only science and technology but also knowledge of practice required to create economic value. We are assisting to a shift from a managed economy to entrepreneurial economy both in OECD countries and developing countries. The impact of the knowledge-based era is pervasive and the shift to knowledge-based economic activity is said to be the driving force underlying the emergence of the entrepreneurial economy (Andersson et al. 2010).

Entrepreneurship has gained additional attention in the current economic crisis, as it is widely viewed as a key aspect of economic dynamism (Leitão et al. 2011). As globalization reshapes the international economic landscape and technological change creates greater uncertainty in countries' productive structures, entrepreneurship is believed to offer ways to help to meet new economic, social, and environmental challenges. As a response, national governments and international organizations such the Organization for Economic Co-operation and Development

(OECD) and the European Commission (EC) have increased their focus on entrepreneurship programs and initiatives. The World Economic Forum (WEF) and the EC, for example, are currently involved in advising governments and universities with a view to improving the strategies, structures, and practices aimed at implementing and developing entrepreneurship education (World Economic Forum 2009; European Commission 2012). Several initiatives also take place to promote the assessment of the national level of entrepreneurial activity. The global entrepreneurship monitor (GEM) http://www.gemconsortium.org/ is a research program that attempts to provide comparable measures of entrepreneurial activity at the national level. The entrepreneurship indicators program (EIP) launched by OECD in 2006 aims to build internationally comparable statistics on entrepreneurship and its determinants. In 2007, Eurostat joined forces with the OECD to create a joint OECD-Eurostat EIP in order to establish standard definitions and concepts as a basis for the collection of empirical data. The panel study of entrepreneurial dynamics (PSED) http://www.psed.isr.umich.edu/psed/home is a program designed to analyze how people start their businesses. More recently, The European Entrepreneurial Region (EER) initiative http://cor.europa.eu/en/takepart/eer/Pages/eer.aspx helps to identify and reward annually up to three, the regions with the most convincing and forward-thinking policy strategy granting an entrepreneurial label: "entrepreneurial region of the year." The aim of the initiative is to create dynamic, green, and entrepreneurial regions throughout Europe. At the same time entrepreneurship education is booming worldwide (Neck and Greene 2011). The OECD, for example, is currently involved in advising governments and universities with a view to improving the strategies, structures, and practices aimed at implementing and developing entrepreneurship education.

Beyond knowledge as the source of entrepreneurial opportunities, a matching of opportunities and resources to create value through new activity must take place. From the readings on the subject, we cannot determine today the exact nature of the next wave of entrepreneurship; however, it is known that it will require more creative, innovative, and entrepreneurial attitudes, skills, and behaviors.

2.3 A Knowledge-Based Perspective on Entrepreneurship

The study of the entrepreneur's role is well represented in the literature (Feldman 2001; Cuervo 2005; Audretsch and Monsen 2008). The literature describes entrepreneurial process as a multidimensional and complex phenomenon. As suggested by Audretsch (2003), the absence of a generally accepted definition of entrepreneurship reflects the multidimensionality of the concept, which involves uncertainty-bearing, innovation, opportunity-seeking, and enterprising individuals.

Many contributions to the field follows in literature, each elaborating on different entrepreneurial functions within the economy. History of economic thought on entrepreneurship is mainly anchored on two schools: (1) the German tradition based on Thünen (1826/1960) and Schumpeter (1911/1934), and (2) the Austrian school rooted in von Mises (1949) and Kirzner (1973). More recently is emerging in the literature a knowledge-based perception on the entrepreneurial phenomenon that centers the discussion around on how knowledge, together with individual ability, defines opportunity.

Schumpeter made significant contributions to the theory of entrepreneurship, stressing innovation and leadership as the main characteristics of entrepreneurship. The Schumpeterian entrepreneur causes waves of creative destruction by introducing "new combinations," which make current technologies and products obsolete. These "new combinations" include: (1) the creation of a new good or a new quality; (2) the creation of a new method of production; (3) the opening of a new market; (4) the capture of a new source of supply; and (5) the creation of a new organization or industry (Schumpeter 1934).

The Austrian tradition of entrepreneurship focuses on profit opportunities and the importance of competition. The key concept in Kirzner's notion of entrepreneurship is that entrepreneurs are behind the competitive behavior that drives the market process responding to opportunities rather than creating them.

Most conceptual frameworks focus on the individual entrepreneur and his or her characteristics and actions. Some authors (Venkataraman 1997; Shane and Venkataraman 2001), advocating an opportunity-based framework, argue that entrepreneurship is a function of the individual and the opportunity. They consider the individual and opportunity to be the essential elements of the entrepreneurial equation:

$$\text{Entrepreneurship} = f\left(\text{individual, opportunity}\right)$$

According to the authors, the key aspects of entrepreneurship are: (1) the sources of opportunities; (2) the process of discovery, evaluation, and exploitation of opportunities to introduce new goods and services, ways of organizing, markets, processes, and raw materials through organizing efforts that previously had not exist; (3) the set of individuals who discover, evaluate, and exploit them. An important point leading this discussion is the ontological assumption about whether opportunity is an endogenous or exogenous phenomenon. The Austrian school of economics (e.g., Kirzner 1997) considers opportunity as exogenous. Although the discovery process depends on the individual and the opportunity, the domain of entrepreneurship is quite narrow because opportunity is a specific possibility, situation, venture, or chance, which is not created by the entrepreneur. Kirzner (1997, p. 72) notes that "an entrepreneurial attitude is one which is always ready to be surprised, always ready to take the steps needed to profit by such motives." In the same line, Alvarez and Barney (2007) point out that the key to entrepreneurial success is a disposition to alertness for new opportunities and the ability to quickly act upon revealed opportunities.

In contrast to this, other scholars view the concept of opportunity as depending on the endogenous factors (e.g., Rindova and Fombrun 2001; Gartner and Carter 2003). They believe that opportunities are a product of individual entrepreneurial actions, or, perhaps more important, a product of collective action. The basic assumption is that entrepreneurs can shape their market and institutional environments, that they can create opportune changes in them, and in so doing, can construct their own context.

More recently, Ihrig et al. (2006) developed a knowledge-based perspective on entrepreneurship, suggesting that entrepreneurship can be thought of as a function of knowledge and attitude. Knowledge drives the process of discover and, in this sense, it is the enabling force of the entrepreneurial process. However, there are people who have the knowledge to start a new venture but never do so. Basically, the critical attitude is what the potential entrepreneur needs in order to finally start a new venture. The concept of critical attitude should not only consist of the "perceived desirability and the perceived feasibility" but also of the "emotional, intellectual, and physical energy to see a venture through to fruition" (Erikson 2002, p. 282). Then, the mathematical formula changes to this one:

$$\text{Entrepreneurship} = f\left(\text{knowledge, attitude}\right)$$

A perspective of entrepreneurship based on knowledge proposes that there is one single dominant factor upon which the opportunity, the individual, and the whole entrepreneurial process are based. This factor is knowledge as a property of individuals or organizations which are intelligent agents in their own right (Quinn 1992), and which are challenged to have a critical attitude in order to execute the entrepreneurial process. In the same vein, Forsman (2008) relates entrepreneurial success with three words: intention, ability, and opportunity. Prior knowledge feeds positive opportunity recognition. The entrepreneur's values, beliefs, and goals have an effect on which opportunities will be selected to be important for consideration.

Although there is no common definition to characterize the entrepreneur some agreements on the personal characteristics seem to exist (Beverland and Lockshin 2001; Raposo et al. 2008; Fayolle 2013). Most of the literature associates the following types of characteristics to entrepreneurs: individual attributes; risk taking; need for achievement; locus of control, self-confidence and optimism; profit motivation; creativity; and other motivational factors and personal values.

Entrepreneurship necessarily involves individuals and their response to economic opportunities (Shane and Eckhardt 2003). Not only is the source of opportunities important, but the nature of the individual recognizing and commercializing these opportunities. Knowledge influences the nature of entrepreneurship because it has an impact on opportunity recognition and exploitation. Opportunity recognition and exploitation refer to the ability to identify good ideas and transform them into businesses that generate income and add value. Both processes therefore depend on the abilities of individuals to acquire and process knowledge—their learning abilities. Entrepreneurial activity is then a function of the extent to which individuals recognize opportunity and possess the capacity, motivation, and skills to exploit it, reflected in start-up efforts and job formation.

2.4 Entrepreneurship Capital and Regional Development: A Perspective Based on Intellectual Capital

During the past decade, regional and national IC has been attracting an increasing amount of attention, not only from academics and managers, but also from national policy makers. A World Bank (1999) report points out that the adoption of policies to increase a nation's intellectual wealth can improve people's lives, besides giving them higher incomes. Bounfour and Edvinsson (2005) advert that only those countries with knowledge-intensive industries will be the winners in terms of future wealth creation.

Koenig (1997) argues that IC is usually considered to have two components: (1) the knowledge itself, and (2) the structure to maintain and distribute that knowledge appropriately. Although there is no widely accepted definition, at least three elements are common in almost all definitions: (1) intangibility; (2) knowledge that creates value; and (3) effect of collective practice. A well-known definition is the one proposed by Edvinsson and Malone (1997, p. 3): "intellectual capital is the knowledge applied to work to create value." In this sense, IC represents knowledge that creates value. Some attempts to operationalize the concept have emerged in the literature, classifying IC into the categories of human capital (HC), structural capital (SC), and relational capital (RC). Both at the micro and macro level several taxonomies have been described (Lin and Edvinsson 2011; Bontis 2004). The IC of a nation includes the hidden values of individuals, enterprises institutions, communities, and regions that are the current and potential sources for wealth creation. These hidden values are the roots for nourishment and the cultivation of future well-being.

Regional IC (RIC) is viewed as a capacity of a region to create wealth and intangible assets. Some authors have examined the knowledge-based capacity of a region examining the human capital, the structural capital and the social capital (Lerro and Schiuma 2009). For the purpose of this study we examine those three types of capital as the drivers of the knowledge-based entrepreneurial activity in a region.

2.4.1 Human Capital

Human capital refers to the know-how that characterizes the different actors operating within a region. It comprises both people and the region's capacity to make use of the human capital i.e., the opportunity for people to be creative and productive. Human capital includes those factors that are built upon or are reflective of know-how, both tacit and explicit, which individuals and more generally regional stakeholders possess and exercise. In some cases, the know-how may reside in the individuals; in other cases, the know-how may be collectively owned by region's stakeholders.

A wide range of empirical studies have documented the role of human capital in regional growth. Using a sample of United Kingdom between 1980 and 1998, Van Stel and Storey (2004) link the impact of employment growth and the creation of new business to specific public policies that supported entrepreneurship and found that the qualification of entrepreneurial or non-entrepreneurial region depends on the stock and the quality of the human capital of the region.

Education and experience have been identified as important measures of human capital. Education measures potential talent or skill, but occupation provides a potentially more robust measure of utilized skill—that is how human talent or capability is absorbed by and used by the economy. Education provides an underlying level of capability, but such capability has to be converted into productive work. Thus occupation is the mechanism through which education is converted into skill and labor productivity. At regional level, human capital also refers to quantity and quality of research (Feldman and Desrochers 2003), entrepreneurial skills, and inflow of external talents.

2.4.2 Structural Capital

Structural capital relates to infrastructures linked to regional culture, history, attitudes, norms, values, behaviors, image, and other cultural dimensions characterizing the regional systems (Cooke and Wills 1999; Iyer et al. 2005; Thurik 2009). According to Passow et al. (2005), reputation has also been considered a valuable, structural intangible asset that allows a region to achieve value targets.

2.4.3 Social Capital

Social capital has received an increased attention in the literature and has been studied at multiple levels, including the individual (Gratton and Ghoshal 2003), organizational (Nahapiet and Ghoshal 1998), and regional or national (Iyer et al. 2005). At the individual, social capital has been defined as the resources embedded in one's relationships with others. Social capital is about *who* one knows, and *how well* one knows (Gratton and Ghoshal 2003). At the organizational level, social capital refers to the value to an organization in terms of the relationships formed by its members for the purpose of engaging in collective action (Nahapiet and Ghoshal 1998). On a macro level, social capital has been analyzed in terms of its impact on the well-being of regions and nations.

Social capital comprises the knowledge assets mainly the result of the dynamic interdependencies linking regional actors related to the stakeholders' social dynamics taking place within a local system and include many components, such as, among others, values, culture, routines, behaviors, networking, identity, atmosphere, and so on.

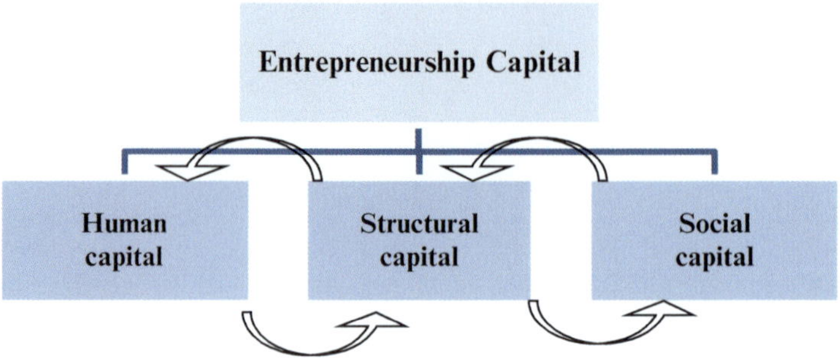

Fig. 2.1 Entrepreneurship capital: a knowledge-based perspective

While the knowledge-based development approach has the organization of the innovative production and the related support structure as the prime focus, the entrepreneurship approach pays attention to retaining and attracting talents for innovative production. A knowledge-based perspective on entrepreneurship capital refers to the overall intangibles—human, structural, and social—that a region can express, practically and potentially (Fig. 2.1).

These intangibles within a region operate as bundles of resources. Wealth is then created through complex dynamic exchanges between tangibles (money, goods, buildings, infrastructures) and intangibles (cognition processes, intelligence, culture, values, and emotions) where individuals, groups, or organizations engage in a value network by converting what they know, both individually and collectively, into tangible and intangible value.

The notion that entrepreneurship may constitute an important driver of economic growth is supported by a growing body of empirical evidence indicating a positive relationship between different measures of entrepreneurship and regional economic performance. Klapper (2006) found out a strong relationship between greater entrepreneurship and such factors as higher GDP per capita and greater financial development. Audretsch et al. (2006), with a sample of German region, estimated a production function and they found a positive relationship between entrepreneurship, capital venture, and regional economic growth. Mrabet et al. (2013) state that entrepreneurship capital measured in terms of start-up rate positively affects and boosts the economic performance.

The global knowledge economy highlights the role of regions as the appropriate "strategy sites of intervention" (Lagendijk 2000, p. 184) of every nation's economic growth, prosperity, and competitiveness. In this approach, regions appear as focal points for learning and knowledge creation in the new age of global, knowledge-intensive competition. The increasing role of the region and its potential for economic development are anchored in "untraded interdependencies" (Scott and Storper 2003) that take the form of conventions and informal rules and habits that coordinate economic actors under conditions of uncertainty, and thus foster and shape entrepreneurial, productive, and innovative activities.

Systematic innovation and competence-building are seen as key drivers of regions' development and competitiveness. Systematic innovation, supported by interactive learning and collective entrepreneurship, expands the regional knowledge base (Lundvall and Johnson 1994). From a regional development perspective, the driving forces behind economic growth are those able to enhance reciprocal understanding and mutual trust and enable tacit knowledge transmission (e.g., set of habits, routines, norms, and laws under which its people shape their beliefs, values, behaviors, and attitudes) among the agents of the regional economy (Martins and Viedma 2006).

During the innovation process—from the birth of a new idea through to the launch of a new product on the market—entrepreneurship capital (human, structural, and social) interacts with the other types of capital (physical, market, financial), putting each type to its highest and best use. The most effective (successful) entrepreneurs are those who can use their personal drive and energy to activate the entire network of capital.

The connectivity between entrepreneurship capital and regional development calls for a conceptual framework that recognizes the importance of human capital, structural capital, and social capital for regional economic growth. A perspective based on IC can help to frame the knowledge-based entrepreneurship approach, emphasizing the human, structural, and social capital as the main knowledge-based categories building the knowledge-based capital of a region, as depicted in Fig. 2.2.

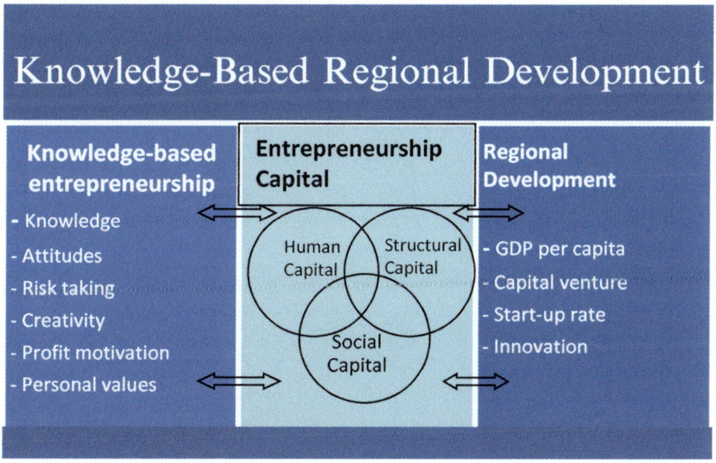

Fig. 2.2 A framework for knowledge-based regional development

2.5 Conclusions

In a globalized and strongly competitive world only regions with the ability to attract and keep intellectual capital can win.

Today the position regions are more than before determined by their competencies and skills to learn and develop themselves in a continuous process to cultivate some specific, differentiated and locally rooted knowledge, and to foster linkages with other knowledge pools in the world. Consequently, local initiatives and an enterprising disposition are becoming more and more important in regional competitiveness.

Entrepreneurship is a discipline with a knowledge-based theory. A person can learn and acquire the competencies of becoming an entrepreneur and start a venture and make it grow. However, in the context of KE, the entrepreneurial vitality of a region depends to a large extent on its capabilities to activate, develop, sustain, and manage knowledge dynamics and processes.

A perspective based on IC helps us to identify intangibles that drive the entrepreneurship capital within a region, where the key to wealth creation lies with the effectiveness of knowledge transfers and conversions. Human capital, structural capital, and social capital are the key drivers of the knowledge-based entrepreneurial activity in a region.

Acknowledgments We gratefully acknowledge the support given by UNIDEMI, R&D unit in Mechanical and Industrial Engineering in the Faculty of Science and Technology, FCT, New University of Lisbon, Portugal.

References

Alvarez SA, Barney J (2007) Discovery and creation: alternative theories of entrepreneurial action. Strateg Entrep J 1(11):11–26

Andersson T, Murley M, Formica P (2010) Knowledge-driven entrepreneurship: the key to social and economic transformation. Springer, New York

Audretsch D (2003) Entrepreneurship—a survey of the literature. Office for Official Publications of the European Communities, Luxembourg

Audretsch D, Keilbach M (2004) Entrepreneurship capital and economic performance. Reg Stud 38(8):949–959

Audretsch D, Monsen E (2008) Entrepreneurship capital: a regional, organizational, team and individual phenomenon. In: Mayson S, Barrett R (eds) International handbook of HRM and entrepreneurship. Edward Elgar, Cheltenham

Audretsch D, Keilbach M, Lehmann E (2006) Entrepreneurship and growth. Oxford University Press, New York

Beverland M, Lockshin L (2001) Organizational life cycles in small New Zealand wineries. J Small Bus Manag 39(4):354–362

Bontis N (2004) National intellectual capital index: a United Nations initiative for the Arab region. J Intellect Cap 5:13–39

Bounfour A, Edvinsson L (2005) Intellectual capital for communities. Elsevier Butterworth-Heinemann, Boston

Carrillo FJ (2006) Knowledge cities, 1st edn. Elsevier Butterworth-Heinemann, Boston
Casson M (2010) Entrepreneurship: theory, networks, history. Edward Elgar, Cheltenham
Cooke P, Wills D (1999) Small firms, social capital and the enhancement of business performance through innovation programmes. Small Bus Econ 13:219–234
Cuervo A (2005) Individual and environmental determinants of entrepreneurship. Int Entrep Manag J 1(3):293–311
Edvinsson L (2002) The knowledge capital of nations. Knowl Manag 5(7):27–30
Edvinsson L, Malone M (1997) Intellectual capital: realising your company's true value by finding its hidden brainpower. HarperCollins, New York
Erikson T (2002) Entrepreneurial capital: the emerging venture's most important asset and competitive advantage. J Bus Ventur 17:275–290
European Commission (2012) Effects and impact of entrepreneurship programmes in higher education. European Commission, Brussels
Fayolle A (2013) Personal views on the future of entrepreneurship education. Entrep Reg Dev Int J 25(7–8):692–701
Feldman MP (2001) The entrepreneurial event revisited: firm formation in a regional context. Ind Corp Change 10:861–891
Feldman M, Desrochers P (2003) Research universities and local economic development: lessons from the history of Johns Hopkins University. Ind Innov 10(11):5–24
Florida R (1995) Towards the learning region. Futures 27:527–536
Forsman H (2008) Business development success in SMEs: a case study approach. J Small Bus Enterp Dev 15(3):606–622
Gartner WB, Carter NM (2003) The language of opportunity. In: Steyaert C, Hjorth D (eds) New movements in entrepreneurship. Edward Elgar, London, pp 121–153
Gratton L, Ghoshal S (2003) Managing personal human capital: new ethos for the "volunteer" employee. Eur Manag J 21(1):1–10
Ihrig M, Knyphausen-Aufseβ D, O'Gorman C (2006) The knowledge-based approach to entrepreneurship: linking the entrepreneurial process to the dynamic evolution of knowledge. Int J Knowl Manag Stud 1(1/2):38–58
Iyer S, Kitson M, Toh B (2005) Social capital, economic growth and regional development. Reg Stud 39(8):1015–1040
Kirzner I (1973) Competition and entrepreneurship. University of Chicago Press, Chicago
Kirzner I (1997) Entrepreneurial discovery and the competitive market discovery process: an Austrian approach. J Econ Lit 35(1):60–85
Klapper L (2006) Entrepreneurship: how much does the business environment matter? Viewpoint series, note 313. Financial and Private Sector Development Vice Presidency, World Bank Group, Washington
Koenig MD (1997) Intellectual capital and how to leverage it. Bottom Line Manag Libr Financ 10(3):112–118
Lagendijk A (2000) Regional paths of institutional anchoring in the global economy. The case of the north-east of England and Aragón. In: Groenewegenen J, Elsner W (eds) An industrial policy agenda 2000 and beyond—new challenges to industrial policy. Kluwer, Dordrecht, pp 184–222
Leitão J, Lasch F, Thurik R (2011) Globalisation, entrepreneurship and regional environment. Int J Entrep Small Bus 12(2):129–138
Lerro A, Schiuma G (2009) Knowledge-based dynamics of regional development: the case of Basilicata region. J Knowl Manag 13(5):287–300
Lin C, Edvinsson L (2011) National intellectual capital: a comparison of 40 countries. Springer, New York
Lundvall B-Å, Johnson B (1994) The learning economy. J Ind Stud 1(2):23–42
Martins B, Viedma JM (2006) The region's intellectual capital benchmarking system: enabling economic growth through evaluation. J Knowl Manag 10(5):41–54
Mrabet A, Jebali L, Ellouze A (2013) Entrepreneurship capital and economic performance in MENA region: dynamic panel approach. J Emerg Trends Econ Manag Sci 4(1):71–79

Nahapiet J, Ghoshal S (1998) Social capital, intellectual capital, and the organizational advantage. Acad Manag Rev 23(2):242–267
Neck HM, Greene PG (2011) Entrepreneurship education: known worlds and new frontiers. J Small Bus Manag 49(1):55–70
Organization for Economic Co-operation and Development (1998) Fostering entrepreneurship. OECD, Paris
Passow T, Fehlmann R, Grahlow H (2005) Country reputation—from measurement to management: the case of Liechtenstein. Corp Reput Rev 7:309–326
Polenske KR (2004) Competition, collaboration and cooperation: an uneasy triangle in networks of firms and regions. Reg Stud 38(9):1021–1035
Quinn JB (1992) Intelligent enterprise: a new paradigm for a new era. Free, New York
Raposo M, Paço A, Ferreira J (2008) Entrepreneur's profile: a taxonomy of attributes and motivations of university students. J Small Bus Enterp Dev 15(2):405–418
Rindova VP, Fombrun CJ (2001) Entrepreneurial action in the creation of the specialty coffee niche. In: Schoonhoven CB, Romanelli E (eds) The entrepreneurship dynamic. Stanford University Press, California, pp 236–261
Rodrigues BM, Viedma JM (2006) The region´s intellectual capital benchmarking system: enabling economic growth through evaluation. J Knowl Manag 10(5):41–54
Schiuma G, Lerro A, Carlucci D (2008) The knoware tree and the regional intellectual capital index: an assessment within Italy. J Intellect Cap 9(2):283–300
Schumpeter J (1934) The theory of economic development: an inquiry into profits, capital, credit, interest and the business cycle. Harvard University Press, Cambridge
Scott AJ, Storper M (2003) Regions, globalization, development. Reg Stud 37(6–7):549–578
Shane S, Eckhardt J (2003) The individual-opportunity nexus. In: Acs Z, Audretsch D (eds) Handbook of entrepreneurship research: an interdisciplinary survey and introduction. Kluwer, Boston
Shane S, Venkataraman S (2001) Entrepreneurship as a field of research: a response to Zahra and Dess, Singh and Erikson. Acad Manage Rev 26(1):13–16
Smedlund A, Poyhonen A (2005) Intellectual capital creation in regions: a knowledge system approach. In: Edvinsson L, Bounfour A (eds) Intellectual Capital for Communities. Elsevier Butterworth-Heinemann, Boston
Tallman S, Jenkins M, Henry N, Pinch S (2004) Knowledge, clusters, and competitive advantage. Acad Manage Rev 29(2):258–271
Thurik R (2009) Entrepreneurship, economic growth and policy in emerging economies. UNUWIDER Research Paper. World Institute for Development Economic Research
Van Stel A, Storey D (2004) The link between firm births and job creation: is there a Upas tree effect? Reg Stud 38:893–909
Venkataraman S (1997) The distinctive domain of entrepreneurship research: an editor's perspective. In: Katz J, Brockhaus R (eds) Advances in entrepreneurship, firm emergence, and growth, vol 3. JAI, Greenwich, pp 119–138
von Mises L (1949) Human action. Yale University Press, New Haven
World Bank (1999) Knowledge for development. Oxford University Press, New York
World Economic Forum (2009) Educating the next wave of entrepreneurs. Unlocking entrepreneurial capabilities to meet the global challenges of the 21st century. World Economic Forum, Geneva
Yigitcanlar T (2009) Planning for knowledge-based urban development: global perspectives. J Knowl Manag 13(5):228–242

Chapter 3
Career Paths of Academic Entrepreneurs and University Spin-Off Growth

Nora Hesse

Abstract With regard to the perspectives of human capital, university status and role identity, I investigate how the career paths of academic entrepreneurs can influence university spin-off growth. The results from the qualitative content analysis and extreme case analysis show that each university status comprises certain advantages and disadvantages. Academic entrepreneurs are located in a trade-off. More human capital and a higher university status are not necessarily advantageous for long-term university spin-off growth. Instead, the willingness and ability for role identity change in terms of the degree of commitment to the entrepreneurial role is very important. Therefore, it is important to consider the career plans and growth intentions of an academic entrepreneur. In order to compensate certain disadvantages of different university statuses the formation of founding teams with complementary skills and university statuses should be promoted.

Keywords Academic entrepreneurs • Academic spin-offs • Academic start-ups • University career paths

3.1 Introduction

Universities are increasingly seen as engines for regional innovation and economic growth (Lawton Smith 2007; Etzkowitz 2008; Mustar et al. 2008). Some famous high-tech regions have evolved on the basis of universities, for example, Silicon Valley in California, Greater Boston in Massachusetts, or the Research Triangle in North Carolina (Saxenian 1983; Sternberg 1995). In these regions, university spin-offs are regarded as one important vehicle of knowledge transfer and commercialization from university to industry. Furthermore, empirical studies confirm that university spin-offs have a higher employment growth (Egeln et al. 2002; Czarnitzki

N. Hesse (✉)
Institute of Economic and Cultural Geography, Leibniz Universität Hannover, Schneiderberg 50, Hannover 30167, Germany
e-mail: hesse@wigeo.uni-hannover.de

R. Baptista, J. Leitão (eds.), *Entrepreneurship, Human Capital, and Regional Development*, International Studies in Entrepreneurship 31,
DOI 10.1007/978-3-319-12871-9_3

et al. 2014) and a higher survival rate (Lawton Smith and Ho 2006; Zhang 2009) compared to average firms. This benefits regional development and is therefore a key interest among policy makers.

The focus of this paper is on the individuals who are behind these processes, those academic entrepreneurs who develop great ideas at a university and decide to put them into practice. One famous example is the Stanford University Ph.D. Student Larry Page, who founded the internet search engine Google (Shane 2004). Academic entrepreneurs do not comprise a homogeneous group. Depending on the time they have spent in university before founding a university spin-off, they have been through different university career paths and so they can be students, research staff, or professors. The aim of this paper is to investigate how academic entrepreneurs' university career can affect university spin-off growth. For this purpose, research questions were derived from three conceptual perspectives: university status, human capital, and role identity.

The relationship between the career paths of entrepreneurs and growth intentions is still inconclusive. While some quantitative studies deny an influence (Kolvereid 1992; Birley and Westhead 1994) others empirically prove it (Cassar 2007). Obviously, this relationship can hardly be investigated by quantitative analysis, because career paths are quite complex. They extend over a long period of time and many career decisions are path dependent and interrelated, so that they can hardly be forced into predefined rigid independent variables (Kodithuwakku and Rosa 2002; Druilhe and Garnsey 2004). For these reasons, my empirical analysis is based on qualitative survey data from 87 academic entrepreneurs of two German universities. The analytical process relied on a qualitative content analysis and extreme case analysis.

This paper is structured as follows: First the three conceptual perspectives are discussed and two research questions are derived. After introducing the data and methods used in this paper, the empirical results of the qualitative content analysis and extreme case analysis are discussed. Finally, a conclusion is drawn including the contribution of the study to literature, implications for policy and further research as well as limitations.

3.2 Conceptual Framework

In order to comprehensively explain the relationship between academic entrepreneurs' career paths and subsequent university spin-off growth three streams of literature are relevant: the university status perspective, the human capital perspective, and the role identity perspective. The first and last perspectives were also selected by Ding and Choi (2011), who investigated the influence of scientists' career paths on their decision to create a venture or join a scientific board. The human capital perspective is for example also used by Müller (2006) for explaining the success of university spin-offs.

3.2.1 University Status Perspective

Founding a university spin-off is an outstanding event in the life of a scientist. Normally scientists reflect intensely before taking this step: if they want to take the risk, what they might lose, and what their social network would think about the decision. It is important to keep in mind that university spin-off creation is still considered to be a controversial behavior in certain universities and areas of studies in Germany (Dörre and Neis 2010). In contrast to the United States, the prospects of returning to academia after leaving university to start up a university spin-off are quite low in Germany (Wentland et al. 2011).

With advancing time in university, scientists are likely to climb up the university hierarchical ladder. Empirical studies prove that an individual's position in the status hierarchy (bottom-, middle-, and top-status) influences his conformity (see for example Phillips and Zuckerman 2001). It may therefore be reasonably assumed that a scientist's university status influences both the decision to create a university spin-off as well as subsequent university spin-off growth.

At the beginning of the university career, individuals have usually little to lose. They are open for new adventures and willing to take risks because they still do not belong to a specific social group where certain norms are expected. This freedom enables them to generate extraordinary innovations apart from social group norms (Phillips and Zuckerman 2001), which can be advantageous for university spin-off growth. However, this also leads to certain disadvantages. Low university status entrepreneurs do not possess a social network, which enables them to access resources and information easily. This might hinder university spin-off growth.

At the middle level of a university career, academics want to belong to a certain social group which makes them quite dependent on external expectations. The fear of disenfranchisement makes them act quite conservatively (Phillips and Zuckerman 2001). On the one hand they have already reached a certain status that they would risk, losing. On the other hand they have not gained the reputation and resources to an extent that gives them the security and freedom as is the case for high status entrepreneurs (Phillips and Zuckerman 2001). Nevertheless, it can be assumed that middle university status entrepreneurs possess more reputation than low university status entrepreneurs. This makes it easier for them to overcome the liability of newness (Garnsey 1998) and foster university spin-off growth. Also, they have a wider social network than low university status entrepreneurs, which also facilitates the access to relevant resources as long as the university spin-off matches existing social group norms (Phillips and Zuckerman 2001).

Individuals with a high university status, especially star scientists, usually possess good access to resources and information to be able to cope with and evaluate the risks connected with founding a university spin-off (Phillips and Zuckerman 2001). They enjoy a high level of reputation within their field and social network. This makes it easier for them to gain initial credibility, acquire funding, and attract customers (Shane 2004), which is advantageous for university spin-off growth. Following Phillips and Zuckerman (2001) it can be assumed that high university status entrepreneurs tend to exploit opportunities, which are in line with the norms of their social network.

In summary, with increasing university status, reputation and access to resources through the social network usually increase (Ding and Choi 2011), which in turn is advantageous for university spin-off growth.

3.2.2 Human Capital Perspective

According to the human capital theory, individuals are endowed with skills and knowledge and can increase their overall knowledge through investments in their human capital like schooling, on-the-job-training, searching for information, etc. (Becker 1975). Early in the academic life cycle, scientists invest in their human capital in order to gain scientific expertise in a specific subject. This usually happens through basic science research. After achieving important milestones scientists create a university spin-off to exploit their research results or specific competencies they have acquired in order to get financial returns on their human capital (Shane 2004; Ding and Choi 2011). This argument also received empirical support (Klofsten and Jones-Evans 2000).

In the field of entrepreneurship, investments in human capital are usually seen as an advantage in terms of a company's survival, growth, and profitability (Shane 2004; Stützer 2010; Parker 2005; Colombo and Grilli 2005). However, Lazear (2005) differentiates between employees and entrepreneurs. While employees tend to be specialists in their field, entrepreneurs should rather be a Jack-of-all-Trades. This means entrepreneurs have to combine different skills. Large investments in one special subject are an obstacle for becoming a successful entrepreneur. According to Lazear (2005), it is quite obvious that scientists obtain expertise in their field, but this kind of knowledge alone is not sufficient. Furthermore, large investments in human capital for example lead to a higher risk aversion and higher opportunity costs (Davidsson and Honig 2003). Especially in the context of university spin-offs a positive relationship between human capital acquisition in a university and a university spin-off's success is not inevitable (Mason et al. 2011; Helm and Mauroner 2007; Wennberg et al. 2011), because at a certain point in time the danger of a cognitive lock-in might develop (Murray and Häubl 2007).

The acquisition of scientific expertise in a university is strongly related to the specificity of the university knowledge applied in the university spin-off. Regarding the degree of knowledge, transferred literature distinguishes exploitation spin-offs, competence spin-offs, and academic start-ups (Bathelt et al. 2010; Egeln et al. 2002; Karnani and Schulte 2010). Exploitation spin-offs are based on concrete research results or novel methods, which at least one academic entrepreneur has developed at a university. Competence spin-offs emerged from specific knowledge or skills, which at least one academic entrepreneur has acquired in a university. The academic entrepreneur's specific competence enables him or her to develop the original idea further, oftentimes even independently from the university. By contrast, academic start-ups comprise only generic knowledge or skills, which at least one academic entrepreneur has acquired in a university (Egeln et al. 2002). An empirical study for Germany discovered that external stakeholders react more constrained to university spin-offs of high status inventors, who want to exploit research results. This is because firstly, exploitation spin-offs need a large team with various competencies. Therefore, the sales productivity is quite low in the first years. Secondly, standardization and economies of scale for exploitation spin-offs are difficult to achieve (Egeln et al. 2002).

3.2.3 Role Identity Perspective

Scientists and entrepreneurs have in principle two opposite value systems and academic entrepreneurs obviously operate within this area of tension (Szyperski and Klandt 1981). These opposite value systems are reflected in the scientists' and entrepreneurs' attitudes and behaviors. The respective mentality is firmly anchored in their minds and cannot be changed easily. This means that scientists have to shift their roles to become successful academic entrepreneurs (Jain et al. 2009). Chandler and Jansen (1992) for example identified three different roles a founder has to adopt: an entrepreneurial, a managerial, and a technical–functional role. Entrepreneurs act in a highly competitive market environment. They seek market success through profit orientation and market acceptance. In utmost contrast, scientists act in an environment far apart from economic constraints which gives them the opportunity to pursue independent research. They are used to writing applications for research projects to acquire funding and they are mainly interested in a technological success (Stephan and Levin 1996). German scientists improve their reputation mainly through own publications in highly specialized journals and secondly through teaching, whereas patenting, technology transfer and entrepreneurial activity are less important (Wentland et al. 2011). So if scientists transfer their academic habits to their new roles as entrepreneurs, they might fail to orientate to the market and to force economic success through identifying buyers and making marketing (Nörr 2010).

Erdös and Varga (2012) rightly state that empirical studies hardly consider the role of scientists as entrepreneurs. Adopting new roles is a difficult task especially for scientists, who pass through a long-term university career before founding a university spin-off. Due to the long and intense socialization process in a university (Ding and Choi 2011), they have another entrepreneurial attitude than students or doctoral students, who might have never planned to work for the university for a longer time and who did not internalize the university value system in such intensity (Mangematin 2000). Therefore, it can be generally expected, that doctors and professors have both a lower entrepreneurial and profit orientation. Therefore, they might create university spin-offs with less growth potential.

Scientists, who stayed in a university for a long time, identify themselves to such an extent with their academic role that they are able or not willing to change it even after founding a university spin-off. This persistence of identity can lead to the situation that the academic entrepreneur wants to stay in a university and run the university spin-off only part-time (Braun-Thürmann et al. 2010; Nicolaou and Birley 2003; Jain et al. 2009). Empirical evidence exists that it is important whether an academic entrepreneur has left the university to set up a company or not (Pirnay et al. 2003; Shane 2004). Heading the university spin-off only on a part-time basis bears the risk of reducing personal commitment and thereby growth expectations (Egeln et al. 2002; Doutriaux 1987).

3.2.4 Developing Research Questions

In the conceptual discussion the importance of an academic entrepreneur's career path for university spin-off growth was explained through three different perspectives. Career paths are quite complex, as the above described conceptual perspectives result in competing expectations for university spin-off growth (see Fig. 3.1). Furthermore, career paths extend over a long period of time and can contain breaks. For these reasons, it is appropriate to base the empirical analysis on a qualitative research design. Qualitative research generally focuses on analytical instead of

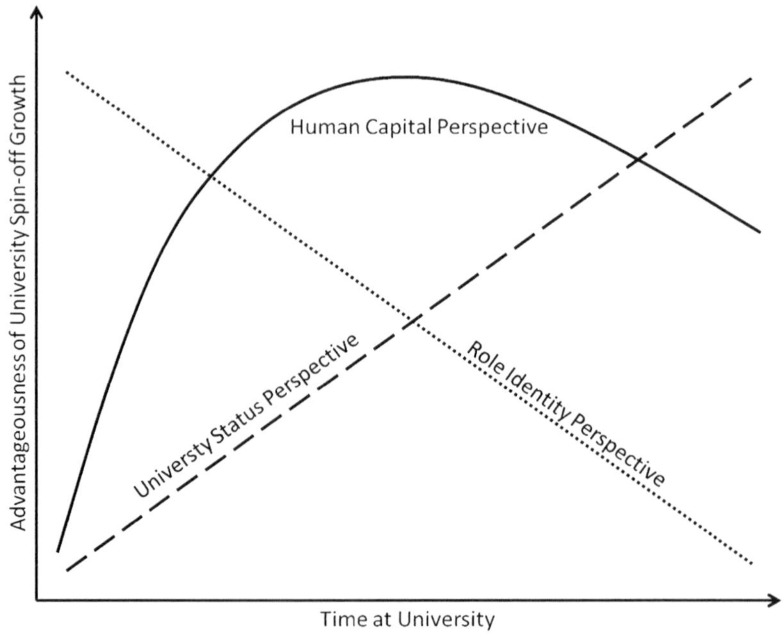

Fig. 3.1 Conceptual framework on the three perspectives of career paths. *Source*: Own illustration

statistical generalization (Miles and Huberman 1994). In the following analysis of the career paths of academic entrepreneurs I investigate:

1. How the university status, human capital, and role identity influence university spin-off growth.
2. How the university status, human capital, and role identity interact with each other.

3.3 Data and Methods

Different approaches for collecting and analyzing qualitative data exist (Bernard and Ryan 2009). With the means of a qualitative content analysis I first investigate how the university status, human capital, and role identity separately influence university spin-off growth. In order to determine university spin-off growth, I look at the number of employees. For this analysis I use the whole sample. Then I conduct a comparative analysis of selected extreme cases. I identify three academic entrepreneurs of high growth university spin-offs and three academic entrepreneurs of low growth university spin-offs with similar career paths and analyze their career paths in depth. In this way it is possible to show the importance and interaction of the three perspectives.

3.3.1 Defining Academic Entrepreneurs

Following Pirnay et al. (2003) and Smilor et al. (1990) I defined academic entrepreneurs as scientists or students who left a university to start a company or who founded (or co-founded) a company while still affiliated with a university to exploit their knowledge and/or skills acquired at university in a profit-making perspective. Accordingly, the companies created are called university spin-offs. In contrast to some other authors, who only consider technology-oriented university spin-offs in their studies (see for example Smilor et al. 1990), I take a broader view of knowledge transfer by including academic entrepreneurs of knowledge-intensive service companies (see for example also Rappert et al. 1999).

I analyze university spin-offs which were founded from 1980 until 2011. The time between leaving a university and the official business formation did not exceed a maximum of 3 years because this study investigates spin-offs based on university knowledge. The temporal boundary of a maximum of 3 years is a good compromise. On the one hand I avoid taking entrepreneurs into account, who gained significant knowledge in the private sector (Pirnay et al. 2003; Wennberg et al. 2011). On the other hand a sufficient time period is necessary for setting up a company, especially in high-tech sectors.

3.3.2 Data Collection and Sampling Approach

A wide range of literature already exists on top universities and regions like Silicon Valley in California, Greater Boston in Massachusetts, or the Research Triangle in North Carolina (Saxenian 1983; Sternberg 1995). In this paper, the cases were drawn from the two biggest universities in Lower Saxony, Germany with regard to the total number of students,[1] the number of students in subjects which are common for university spin-offs,[2] the number of scientific staff, and research expenditures (Kulicke et al. 2008). The two chosen universities, Hannover and Göttingen, are particularly suitable examples for German mid-range universities located in regions outside high-tech clusters. At this kind of university individual characteristics and career paths play an important role for university spin-offs, because only a weak entrepreneurial support structure exists.

Since the data on university spin-offs in Germany is far from being accurate, the data used in this paper was collected within the framework of a broader research project.[3] The current study should therefore also give an overview on university spin-off activities at the two chosen universities. For this reason a more comprehensive approach to data collection was chosen compared to other qualitative studies (Baker and Edwards 2012). In order to identify as many academic entrepreneurs as possible the total sample of university spin-offs for the two universities was composed as follows:

In the first step of data collection I had informal discussions with leaders of the technology transfer offices and employees of different economic development agencies in the two survey regions Hannover and Göttingen. I also asked the heads of all institutes of the two universities for information about university spin-offs by mail in order to avoid a bias for the benefit of university spin-offs which used advice on funding and financing matters. Furthermore, I initiated a search operation through the business network XING in order to capture any university spin-offs, which had contact neither with the current faculty staff nor with the technology transfer offices nor with employees of different economic development agencies.

The second step of data collection was a validation of all contacts I collected by e-mail and further internet searches. In many cases it was not clear if a business was from an academic entrepreneur according to our definition. In total, I obtained a list of 334 academic entrepreneurs. From this population, 152 academic entrepreneurs were asked for an interview. Sixty-five were unresponsive or did not agree to an interview. A sampling grid was used to ensure a heterogenic sample structure

[1] Leibniz Universität Hannover had 21,478 students and Georg-August-Universität Göttingen 26,381 students in the summer semester 2013 (Georg-August-Universität Göttingen 2013; Leibniz Universität Hannover 2013).

[2] These are the MINT subjects (mathematics, computer science, natural science and engineering) and medical science (Kulicke et al. 2008). MINT subjects are comparable with the STEM fields used in English that comprise science, technology, engineering and mathematics.

[3] See acknowledgements at the end of this chapter.

(Schreier et al. 2007; Bernard and Ryan 2009). The cases were equally distributed throughout the two basic categories: students or scientists.[4]

In the third step of data collection, I had semi-structured face-to-face interviews with 87 academic entrepreneurs (Bernard and Ryan 2009) during the period of September 2011 to January 2012. The face-to-face interviews usually took place in the respective company and ranged from 45 min to 2½ h in length.[5] The vast majority of interviews was openly recorded and directly transcribed.[6] Throughout the interviews, I asked open-ended questions pertaining to the chronological career path before the university spin-off as well as the phases of preparing, establishing, and developing the university spin-off (Vohora et al. 2004; Roberts and Malone 1996; Rasmussen 2011). During and after the interviews the interviewer took field notes. Furthermore, a post-interview questionnaire and information collected from the university spin-off websites and press articles augmented the data.

3.3.3 Data Coding and Analysis

In the first step, I conducted a qualitative content analysis with all 85 transcribed interviews (Mayring 2008; Gläser and Laudel 2009) which was supported by the qualitative data analysis software NVivo. Table 3.1 shows important factors derived from the three conceptual perspectives. In the qualitative content analysis these factors were considered.

In order to differentiate different university statuses I developed six categories which show the university status of every academic entrepreneur at the time of the university spin-off creation. The different university statuses are categorized as follows: (1) "Students" who were still studying at the university. (2) "Graduates" who founded the university spin-off after graduating from the university. (3) "Doctoral students" or research associates without a doctor's degree. (4) "Doctors" who had already achieved the doctoral degree and left the university. (5) "Postdoctoral fellows" who worked at a university after achieving the doctoral degree. In most cases the individuals were working on their habilitation.[7] (6) "Professors" including private lecturers, adjunct professors and emeriti. In this category the individuals had finished their habilitation.

[4] Although the cases were also equally distributed between the two chosen universities, I did not differentiate the academic entrepreneurs according to their parent university in this study, because this was only relevant for the research project. For the aim of this present study the parent university was not relevant.

[5] A few academic entrepreneurs were interviewed at neutral places or by telephone due to distance, space or scheduling problems.

[6] In a few cases a content protocol was written during the interview if the interviewee did not want to be recorded.

[7] Qualification phase after the doctorate for a teaching career in higher education.

Table 3.1 Coding frame for academic entrepreneurs' career paths

Conceptual perspectives	Important factors	Description	Examples
University status perspective	Reputation and access to resources through social network	Contacts to and recognition in scientific community and private economy	*"The professorial image helped me a lot at the beginning, but of course it also commits me to always do more than my competitors." (USO68)*
	Independence	Independence of university spin-off from parent university or dependency between university spin-off and parent university	*"The only risk, which is a problem in our private institute, is the moment where I would be absent. The company is quite dependent on my person, my name and the university context." (USO68)*
Human capital perspective	Scientific expertise and resulting knowledge transfer	Degree of specificity of the university knowledge applied, differentiating exploitation spin-offs, competence spin-offs, and academic start-ups	*It was definitely an exploitation of university know-how.* (*USO14*)
	Management skills	Mention of management skills acquired at university on-the-job, which were helpful for university spin-off	*"Fortunately, as a group leader, I had to do personal management, financial management and so on. I had a group of 15 people and I was fully responsible scientifically and financially." (USO02)*
Role identity perspective	Identification with entrepreneurial role	Occurrence of the desire to be self-employed differentiating before studies, during studies, during doctoral studies, after doctorate and later, directly with the idea	*"It actually came directly with the idea. Before I didn't have a plan like I have to be self-employed when I am 40 or so." (USO07)*
		Mention of difficulties concerning role identity change in terms of profit orientation, workload, etc.	*"I had to grow into this role as an entrepreneur. And it took some time." (USO33)*
	Commitment to university spin-off	Differentiation between left university and still works at university	*"When I founded the company, I actually quit the scientific career for myself." (USO17)*

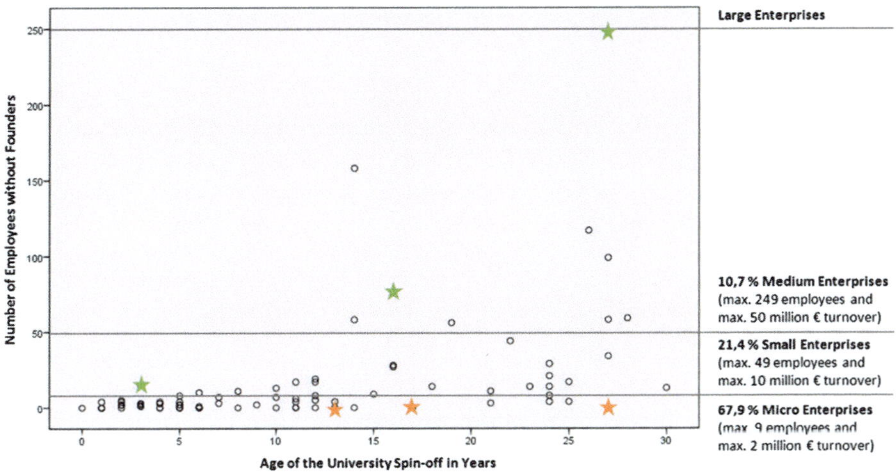

Fig. 3.2 Identification of extreme cases measured according to university spin-off size. *Note*: $N=85$. One case corresponds to one university spin-off. Number of employees is based on full-time equivalents. Categorization of enterprises in accordance with the Federal Bureau of Statistics (2013). Selected cases for extreme case study highlighted in *yellow* and *green*. *Source*: Own survey 2011

On the basis of the qualitative content analysis of all interviews, I conducted a comparative extreme case analysis in the second step. Therefore I identified three academic entrepreneurs of high growth university spin-offs and three academic entrepreneurs of low growth university spin-offs measured according to the increase of employees (see Fig. 3.2).[8] These six academic entrepreneurs are combined to three pairs with very similar career paths but very different university spin-off growth. This approach is especially useful for a contrasting comparison and an identification of the possible best practice. Although high growth university spin-offs are rather rare in our samples, they are of course the most favored by policy makers and most eligible for support because they have a high influence on regional economic growth. In contrast, low growth university spin-offs have a weak influence on regional economic growth but they occur more frequently and also contribute to regional economic diversity and innovation (Cohen and Klepper 1992). The selection of extreme cases shows more specifically how the career paths of academic entrepreneurs contribute to university spin-off growth.

[8] Firm's performance can be measured in many different ways. Common indicators used in literature are survival rate, employment growth, sales growth, productivity and credit rating (Helm and Mauroner 2011). This paper focuses on employment as a measure of performance because it has the most consistent positive correlation with other growth measures and is a key interest among policy makers (Wiklund 1998; Davidsson et al. 2007). Furthermore, it is less susceptible to fluctuations and a good indicator for the university spin-offs' overall assets (Gibcus and Stam 2012). Nevertheless, these propositions do not apply to all branches equally. Other definitions of university spin-off growth could lead to different results. Furthermore, university spin-off growth should not be equated with success, because success always depends on the respective business goals (Hayter 2010).

3.4 Results of the Qualitative Content Analysis

Based on the conceptual perspectives discussed above and by using a qualitative content analysis, I show how university status, human capital and role identity can affect university spin-off growth. The results for each conceptual perspective are explained in individual chapters and different university statuses are addressed.

3.4.1 Results from the University Status Perspective

In the following, I present the results concerning the expectation that academic entrepreneurs with a higher university status may be more likely to find a high growth university spin-off. I discuss the advantages and disadvantages of low, middle, and high university status entrepreneurs successively.

Low status university entrepreneurs who start a university spin-off, such as students and graduates, have low entry barriers. In accordance with the theoretical assumption, several of them reported that they were used to coping with little income anyway and were willing to take risks, as the following quotation of a graduate indicates: "Now we are studying and get along with little money. Now we can see what happens if we start a company with ideas which were brought to the university's attention but cannot carry out." (*USO08*). This quotation also indicates that students are still quite flexible, which is also in line with the theoretical assumption. At the beginning of a university career, an individual is also more willing to learn something new and to adapt to new situations quickly. Low status academic entrepreneurs have only little responsibility in their private and professional lives and have more freedom. On the other hand, some students and even graduates had to cope with legitimacy problems in the first years, as one student reports: "We had the image of a students' firm for many years. We had to fight for a long time. Especially the authorities did not take us seriously, although this was actually unfounded after a certain initial phase." (*USO04*). In some sectors, like information technology, a young, dynamic firm's image might not be an obstacle, but in other sectors, such as scientific and technical services, it is. Established scientists normally do not have to cope with such prejudices.

Middle university status entrepreneurs, such as doctoral students, also enjoy a high degree of freedom because in Germany they usually have part-time contracts. They can plan the rest of their time relatively freely, as this doctoral student states: "With a professor, who would have said: 'If you do not work on your thesis for 100 % I will dismiss you!', we would have had a problem." (*USO74*). Nevertheless, the triple burden of working in a university, writing a doctoral thesis and establishing a university spin-off is often a hard struggle for doctoral students. This struggle becomes even harder, the more successful a university spin-off becomes. As a result, it may take doctoral students longer to finish a thesis. In some cases they may quit their academic career, as one third of the doctoral students in the sample did. Nevertheless, having a doctoral degree of course bears several advantages which make it possibly worthwhile to finish a doctorate before founding a university spin-off. For example, customers often have a higher trust in the quality and reliability of a company and a doctoral degree can also open doors.

High university status entrepreneurs, such as postdoctoral fellows and professors, usually possess a high reputation. This makes it easier for them to gain legitimacy for a university spin-off. Yet these laurels in advance also oblige the academic entrepreneur to be more innovative and better than competitors, as this professor states: "The professorial image helped me a lot at the beginning, but of course it also commits me to always do more than my competitors. Of course I am expected to be a little more innovative, to perform a little bit better, have a bit better overview, and no standard concepts." (*USO68*). These high expectations of customers rapidly lead to high pressures. Furthermore, high status academic entrepreneurs usually think twice before founding a university spin-off, because they are afraid of putting their career and reputation at risk. This fear can also hinder high status academic entrepreneurs to become an entrepreneur with a full commitment.

The majority of university spin-offs founded by high status academic entrepreneurs are listed in the sector "scientific services," as mentioned before. This fact hinders the long-term growth of a company because the economic success of a university spin-off is strongly dependent on the academic entrepreneur's university status and can hardly be transferred to other persons, as this quotation underlines: "The only risk, which is a problem in our private institute, is the moment where I would be absent. The company is quite dependent on my person, my name and the university context. Therefore, it is hardly possible to say that the company would continue to exist without me in case I retire. It is an important factor that I have to appear everywhere. Even if my staff knows it better than I do, the people expect me to be there. Much is dependent on my image and the whole concept. I think it will continue quite well as long as I am fit." (*USO68*). This fact is a severe uncertainty factor for long-term university spin-off growth.

The results of the content analysis with a special focus on university status show that the reputation helps in terms of gaining legitimacy early on. This is especially useful at the beginning of the university spin-off but in the long run this can develop into a disadvantage because university spin-off growth is highly dependent on the academic entrepreneur's university status. The hypothesis that especially high status entrepreneurs create high growth university spin-offs cannot be confirmed. Instead it is important to decouple the university spin-off from the academic entrepreneur and the university in the long run to achieve high growth (Rasmussen and Borch 2010).

3.4.2 Results from the Human Capital Perspective

In the following, I present the results concerning the second expectation that increasing human capital and resulting knowledge transfer may have a diminishing marginal utility for university spin-off growth and may even become disadvantageous.

The focus is on human capital acquisition, firstly in terms of scientific expertise and the resulting knowledge transfer and secondly in terms of additional management skills acquired in a university.

Students and graduates, who discover a market gap and decide to exploit it, usually start up a university spin-off on the basis of the knowledge he or she acquired during studies. Transferring research results into practice plays a rather minor role at this low university status. Sometimes results of the diploma thesis or knowledge gained from the employment as a student assistant were implemented. However, in the majority of cases the identification of a market gap rather happened due to personal matters, social trends, experience and contacts from part-time jobs, internships or voluntary work. In these university spin-offs, only basic competencies acquired in studies are of importance.

Doctoral students, research associates (without a doctor's degree), and doctors acquire profound scientific expertise in a certain subject during doctoral studies and research projects. The majority discover a market gap based on their research activities. Projects with high practical relevance and close contact to industry partners have the highest potential to be transferred into practice and facilitate a market entry. Many doctoral students, research associates and doctors start up a university spin-off because the industry partners have a concrete demand for a product developed in a research project. However, there are also a handful of doctoral students, research associates and doctors who set up a business only on the basis of basic competencies they acquired in their doctoral studies and research projects.

Postdoctoral fellows and professors possess extensive scientific expertise in different research areas, because they researched different projects for many years. The majority of them discovered a market gap due to their research and consultant activities. Industry contacts of course are also very helpful and facilitate a market entry.

Figure 3.3 shows the different characteristics of knowledge transfer and the number of university spin-offs for the respective university status. The results show that the higher the university status the more scientific expertise is acquired and therefore the more university knowledge is transferred to the university spin-off. With advancing university status the trend shifts from academic start-ups over competence spin-offs to exploitation spin-offs. However, a positive influence of the degree of university knowledge transfer into the university spin-off on spin-off growth could not be determined for our sample. Positive extreme cases exist for both, university spin-offs based on the exploitation of research results as well as university spin-offs based on the application of competencies. The majority of the university spin-offs of postdoctoral fellows and professors are listed in the scientific service sector. This often hinders the long-term growth because the tacit knowledge applied and the profound scientific expertise makes the company very dependent on the academic entrepreneur and can hardly be transferred to other persons.

Besides scientific expertise, academics also gain management skills in a university which might be helpful for entrepreneurship as the interviewees reported. The skills varied according to the university status. In the following some examples are given.

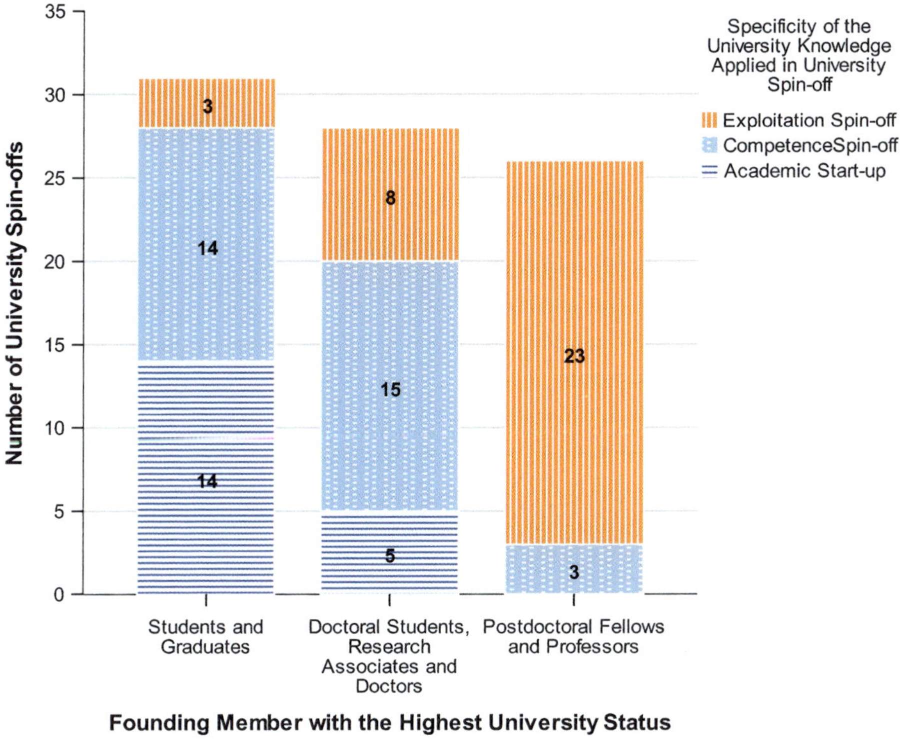

Fig. 3.3 Knowledge transfer and university status. Valid cases: 85. *Source*: USO survey 2011

Students and graduates do not only possess little scientific expertise but also only little working experience which is mostly based on student projects, internships, part-time jobs, or diploma theses. Accordingly, they have only little experience in project management. In the early phase of a university spin-off, they may have difficulties to estimate and control the complexity, duration, and cost of customer orders. This often results in a high workload for them at certain times and in the worst case in a noncompliance with time limits. This can lead to order cancellations from customers and severe image damage. However, such initial problems are not serious in most cases, so that university spin-offs develop well, as this quotation of a student shows: "Of course we only had little experience. Nobody of us was professionally experienced and of course we did not have a clue about how to start a firm. Everything was quite improvised, but it still worked anyway." (*USO04*). This quotation shows that youthful ease may help get over initial difficulties.

Doctoral students, research associates, and doctors have already acquired working experience in a university which is valuable for founding a university spin-off. Many of them already have experience in applying for, managing and evaluating research projects, as this quotation of a doctoral student shows: "Before, I made my living at the university with project applications, management, and evaluation.

Actually, this is a skill, which I could bring to the company. I simply know where I have to look for support offers. I am able to overview that quite quickly." (*USO33*).

Alongside the lower university status skills, postdoctoral fellows and professors are usually also responsible for personnel. Therefore, they attain valuable skills in personnel management as this postdoctoral fellow remarks: "Fortunately, as a group leader, I had to do personnel management, financial management and so on. I had a group of 15 people and I was fully responsible scientifically and financially." (*USO02*).

These additional skills acquired in a university are certainly advantageous but they do not seem to be crucial for long-term university spin-off growth. The vast majority of the interviewees had to initially cope with a lack of business knowledge. I could not identify any long-term advantage for academic entrepreneurs who already had prior management knowledge.

3.4.3 Results from the Role Identity Perspective

In the following, I present the results concerning the third expectation that difficulties with role identity change may increase with advancing time in a university and hinder university spin-off growth. Therefore, I address the statements made by long-standing university staff that concern the difficulties in role identity change.

More than one quarter of our interviewees stated that they did not develop the desire to start a business until they had a concrete business idea. Before that, they either never thought about becoming an entrepreneur or they did not even want to become an entrepreneur (see Fig. 3.4). Especially for academic entrepreneurs with a high university status, the desire for entrepreneurship only developed with a concrete business idea quite late in their university career and oftentimes on demand from industry. This finding indicates that many academic entrepreneurs were not prepared emotionally and mentally for their new role, which can cause difficulties especially during the initial years.

For example, a professor reported that it was difficult for him to get used to the stress and workload that managing a university spin-off entails: "I have to say that being self-employed means greater stress than being employed at the university. I would almost say twice as much (laughing). Well, our applied projects are of course not as complex as basic research, but we handle eight, nine, ten projects at the same time. Particularly, they all have a certain time schedule that we have to meet. It generates a huge pressure to do everything as expected. As a professor, I have also worked a lot. But it is something else when you simply say: 'That is a customer, who has to be served until a certain point. The results have to be presented and they have to be largely excellent.' With a professorship it is something else. They don't have the direct link of 'When I lose a customer, I will have less money next year.' For a professor this is completely different. Also the psychological pressure is not as high. If I screw something up as a professor, although nobody does it and nobody wants it and this harms my reputation, this does not affect my livelihood." (*USO68*).

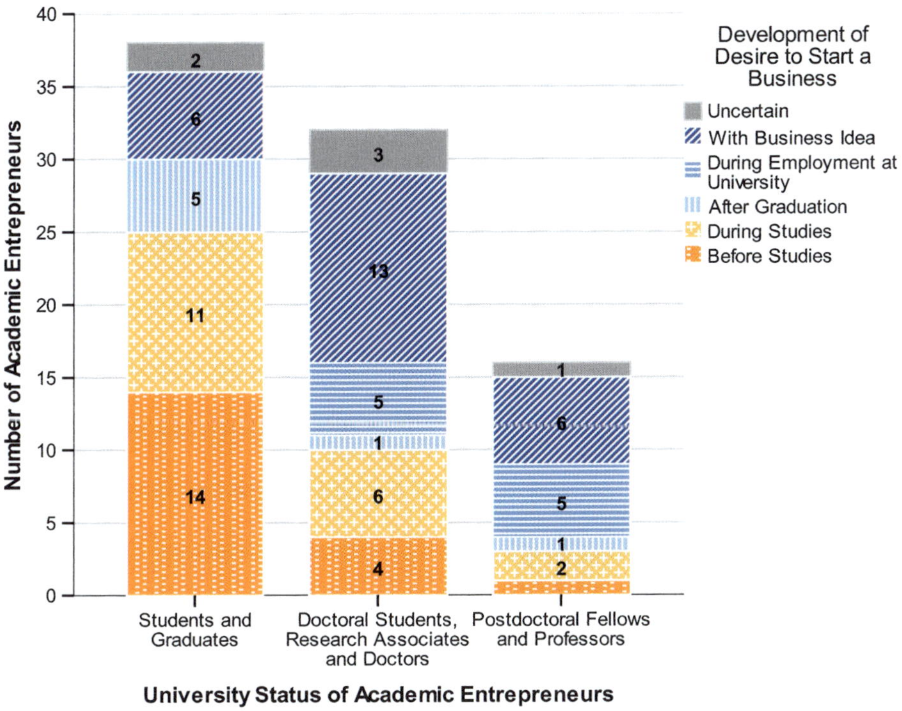

Fig. 3.4 Development of the desire to be self-employed. Valid cases: 86. *Source*: USO survey 2011

Another example for emerging difficulties due to different value systems between academia and the private sector is a lack of profit orientation. Individuals, who target a university career and already worked in university for long time, are usually not very profit oriented. They are rather driven by a scientific interest. This makes it difficult for them to run a university spin-off in the initial period. It takes them a while before they learn to change their viewpoint, as this professor vividly described: "You should not be too much of a geek and scientist who becomes obsessed with fiddling and loses sight of his targets. A crucial turning point for me was a banker who asked me right after starting the business: 'Why have you started the business? What was your motivation?' I had to think about what to answer, and things like self-fulfillment and having fun came to my mind. While I was thinking he said: 'Now don't start with self-fulfillment and it was so much fun. There is only one reason that you should have. Everything else doesn't count; otherwise you can pack up and go home. The only right to exist for a business is to earn money.' And he was right. It sounds so simple. In the beginning, it might also sound immoral, particularly if you tell this to a scientist. But he was right, I have to earn money. I have to evaluate everything I consider as a businessman; whether something comes out of it at the end of the day or whether it is only a little fun." (*USO41*).

With regard to the commitment to the entrepreneurial role, the academic entrepreneurs in our study can be divided into two groups. On the one hand there are

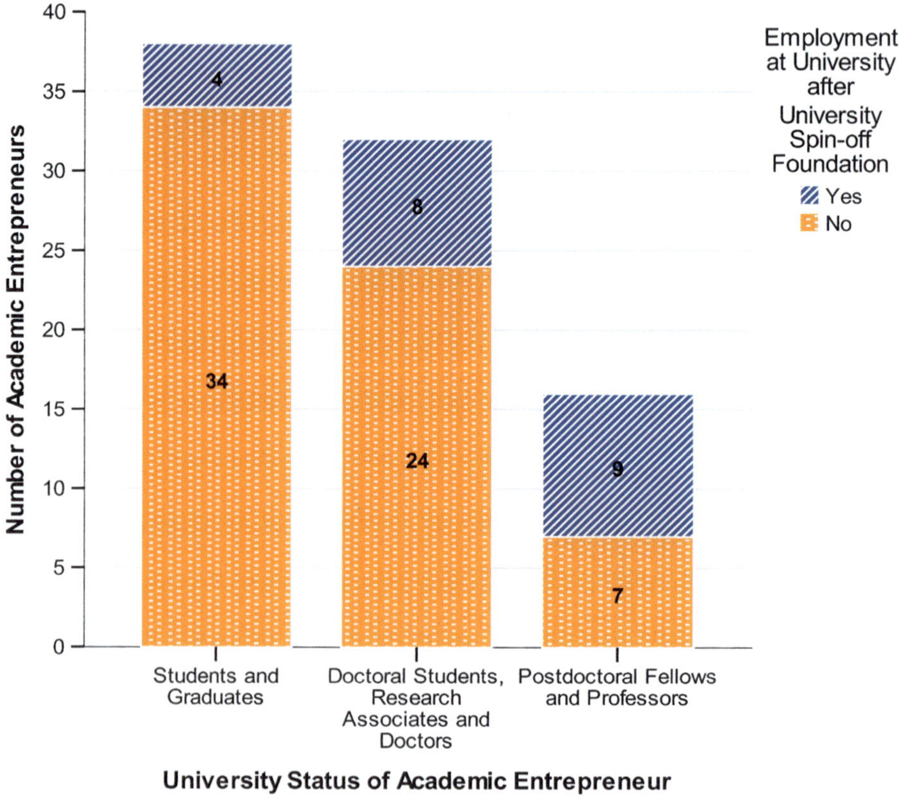

Fig. 3.5 Employment at university after university spin-off foundation. Valid cases: 86. *Source*: USO survey 2011

academic entrepreneurs who wanted to change their role and ended their university career for the university spin-off. On the other hand there are academic entrepreneurs who actually do not want to change roles and never leave the university. Around one third of the academic entrepreneurs in the sample decided to continue their university career and work in the university spin-off at the same time on a part-time basis (see Fig. 3.5). For some of these individuals the university career served solely to finance themselves in the initial years of business. However this career path can also be chosen because of opposite motives. For these individuals, the university career is the first choice. They never plan to be a full-time entrepreneur and leave university because they would rather do research and teaching. The question then is, why do these individuals startup a university spin-off in the first place. Individuals, who target a university career, see the university spin-off as a good opportunity either to finance their subsequent university career or to gain a reputation as a university professor later.

Many postdoctoral fellows in the sample decided to startup a university spin-off because they suffered from a lack of job security in the university due to part-time and fixed-term contracts. Usually postdoctoral fellows have almost no experience in the private sector but at the same time they are highly qualified and possess a mature personality. This makes it very difficult for them to find a subsequent job as a dependent employee in the private sector in case their contracts are not extended or they do not find a professorial chair after their habilitation. Therefore, they go on two separate tracks regarding their professional career. In the end, many of these kinds of academic entrepreneurs nevertheless stay in a university in the long run and their university spin-offs remain small for that reason. In contrast, the few postdoctoral fellows who left university immediately after foundation or after a transitional period have a good chance to establish big university spin-offs. Postdoctoral fellows who have discovered a market gap on the basis of their research projects and are disenchanted with the self-purpose of university research generally have a high growth potential because they are highly innovative and have a high commitment to their new role. However, a long development phase due to a low market maturity of the developed products or services often leads to high financing needs and delayed growth.

For the professors in the sample, the university career is definitely in first place and the university spin-off is of secondary importance. This lies in the nature of the chosen career paths. In engineering science professors usually start up a business because they can improve their reputation as well as research and teaching. Therefore, most professors do not start a university spin-off with a full commitment. More often professors are members of the founding team and support the university spin-off with scientific advice, financial capital, or reputation. Even if professors themselves generated the business idea they prefer to share the university spin-off with their employees, who then work with a full commitment, as this doctor reports about sharing the university spin-off with his professor: "We are three people in our company: Actually primarily me and the professor and another minority holder. I myself am actually responsible for the operating business, the rest is strategic advance, let's just put it this way." (*USO48*).

The results of the content analysis show that the role identity change from being a scientist to being an entrepreneur becomes increasingly difficult with longer working times in a university. Especially postdoctoral fellows and professors reported that they had trouble with this, whereas students and graduates who are at the beginning of their university careers, hardly ever described such problems. In contrast to management skills, the attitude towards entrepreneurship and adaption to a new value system are harder to learn. The socialization process, which takes place in a university, should therefore not be underestimated. As a result, with advancing time in a university and rising university status the commitment for an entrepreneurial role tends to decrease.

3.5 Results of Extreme Case Analysis

In this chapter I show the importance of and interaction between the three conceptual perspectives for selected cases. I identified three positive and three negative extreme cases in the samples in terms of university spin-off growth measured as the

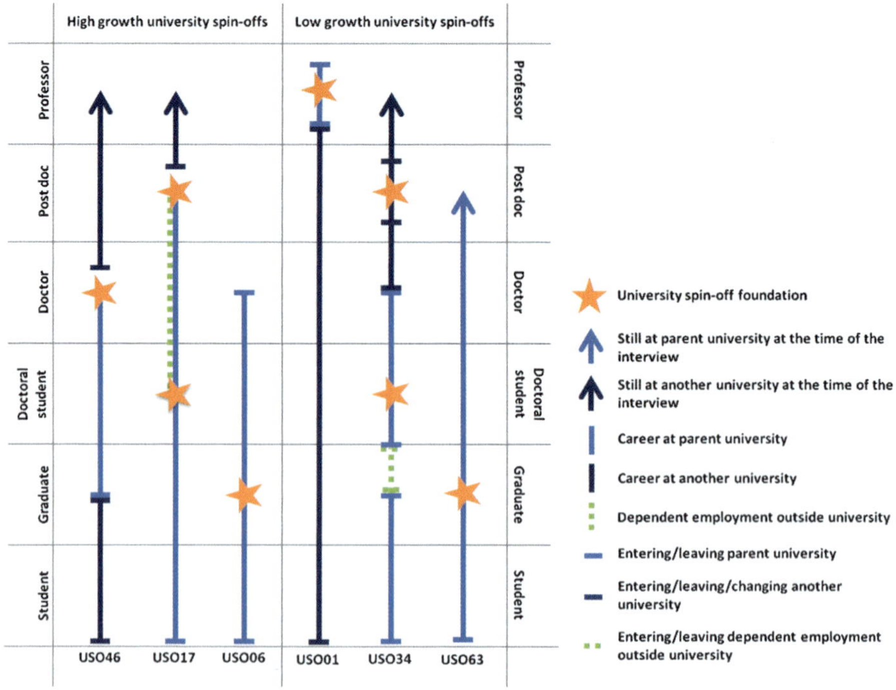

Fig. 3.6 Academic entrepreneurs' career paths. *Note*: Results of the extreme case analysis. Growth is measured by the average annual increase in employees from the year of university spin-off formation to 2011. Sampling Approach based on positive and negative extreme cases. *Source*: Own illustration, USO survey 2011

number of employees in 2011. I investigated their university career paths in depth in order to identify some patterns explaining the growth differences between high growth and low growth examples. They obviously vary considerably and it is clearly recognizable at a glance that a longer university career is not necessarily better for university spin-off growth (see Fig. 3.6).

In order to explain the importance of the willingness of role identity change, I compared the career paths of two academic entrepreneurs with the case numbers USO17 and USO34 (see Fig. 3.6). At first glance the interviewees have much in common. The two university spin-offs are founded in knowledge-intensive services and the academic entrepreneurs were still working at the university as professors at the time of the interview. They have both made prior experiences in the private sector, on the one hand through prior self-employment and on the other hand through dependent employment. They founded their second university spin-off after finishing the doctoral degree, which brought advantages for them at the beginning, as this quotation shows: "Of course my doctoral degree helped me solving practical problems like renting an office and convincing the landlord that I am absolutely able to pay the rent." (*USO17*). Nevertheless the university spin-offs' growth differs vastly.

The academic entrepreneur of the high growth university spin-off left the university when founding his second university spin-off. The decision to leave the university was not quite voluntary. He transferred a research project into the university spin-off and founded the university spin-off and became a full-time entrepreneur, because he had no future at his parent university at that time: “When I founded the company, I actually quit the scientific career for myself.” (*USO17*). Later he describes of the fear of risking his career: “I was scared of how my life would continue. My parents were very concerned and very disappointed with my decision. I actually wanted to become a scientist and professor and they were scared that my career is ending now.” (*USO17*). After some years he established a large scientific service company and then decided to continue his university career and finish his habilitation after all. In contrast, the academic entrepreneur of the low growth university spin-off left the university after graduation, but after a short time in the private industry he realized that he wished to pursue a university career. Although he is shaped entrepreneurially by his family, he returned to the university. He founded the two university spin-offs because they forwarded his university career. He never had the intention to leave university to be a full-time entrepreneur, although the demand situation would allow an expansion. “If I do the controlling for large projects, I will get a lot of money, but this is rather craft work for me. That does not bring me forward as a professor. Consulting in large projects, the provision of expert opinions is what helps me professionally.” (*USO34*).

A similar situation applies to the academic entrepreneurs with the case numbers USO06 and USO63 (see Fig. 3.6). The interviewee of the high growth university spin-off continued his university career by making his Ph.D. for a few years after foundation in order to have a secure income during the initial years. “We decided that I remain at the university and my partner leads the company with full commitment, so that we try to ensure a certain seed funding. I received a regular salary at the university, while my self-employed partner did not earn any money at that time. Therefore, we said that we share my salary.” (*USO06*). This way, he was also able to gain deeper knowledge and to expand his industry contacts. For the academic entrepreneur of the low growth university spin-off the opposite is the case. He founded the university spin-off right after his graduation in order to finance his university career and never wanted to be a full-time entrepreneur, as this quotation illustrates: “I lead my company as a part-time job and get money for that. It is nothing different than acquiring third party funding, because I see myself as a scientist in the first place. I still write scientific studies.” (*USO63*). Obviously, the university spin-off is a means to an end for him. A university spin-off founded because of this reason will hardly become a big company. The data shows quite clearly that university spin-offs, which are not managed by at least one founding member with full commitment, at least for the initial years, usually stay small (see also Fig. 3.6).

In order to explain the interaction and evolving disadvantages from scientific expertise, deriving knowledge transfer and university status, I compared the academic entrepreneurs with the case numbers USO01 and USO46 (see Fig. 3.6). The interviewees have in common that they founded exploitation spin-offs in the service sector. During their research projects they both acquired a good reputation and established a wide social network not only within the scientific community but also to partners in the private economy and industry. USO01 was a reputable professor in engineering with many contacts to industry. He founded the university spin-off in the sector of scientific services on a concrete demand from one of his industry partners. He did it because he was a luminary in his field and he saw a possibility to finance his doctoral students by the university spin-off. The business was going well until he retired from university and the institute was closed. Even after many successful years on the market, the dependency of the university spin-off on the institute, the professor's scientific expertise, and university status was still so high that the continuation of the business or the sale of the university spin-off to another professor was simply impossible. In contrast, the high growth academic entrepreneur USO46 acknowledged the danger of the dependence on university status and university. He founded the university spin-off after finishing his doctoral studies together with his professor in the consulting sector. At the beginning the professor's reputation helped him a lot, but the decoupling of the university spin-off from the university and his professor's reputation was very important for him. After some years on the market the professor retired progressively from the operative and even strategic business. The young doctor changed from the scientific role to the entrepreneurial role with full commitment. He managed the university spin-off on a full-time basis, and it has grown rapidly in its initial years. However, now the doctor received a call for a university chair. This will increase his reputation and financial situation. As a result, he plans to lead the university spin-off only on a part-time basis in future. Although he was aware of the importance to decouple the university spin-off from the parent university, he now plans to link it with his new university chair. He states that the employment increase will therefore most likely not exceed 15 employees, but he plans to raise outside funds.

The examples of the selected extreme cases show that a comprehensive consideration reveals the complex interaction between the three perspectives and thus allows further insights on how processes occur in reality. Although the academic entrepreneurs with a high university status state that they had advantages from the high reputation and their social network, these advantages are more important in the initial years. With advancing time on the market a high university status and profound scientific expertise even bears some risks for university spin-off growth. The decoupling of the university spin-off from the academic entrepreneur's university status seems to be very important for long-term university spin-off growth in terms of employment increase. No less important is the identification with the entrepreneurial role and the willingness to manage the company with full commitment at least in the initial years.

3.6 Conclusions

Referring to the title of this paper it can be stated that a longer university career is not necessarily better for subsequent university spin-off growth. The theoretical assumptions as well as the empirical results from the content analysis and extreme

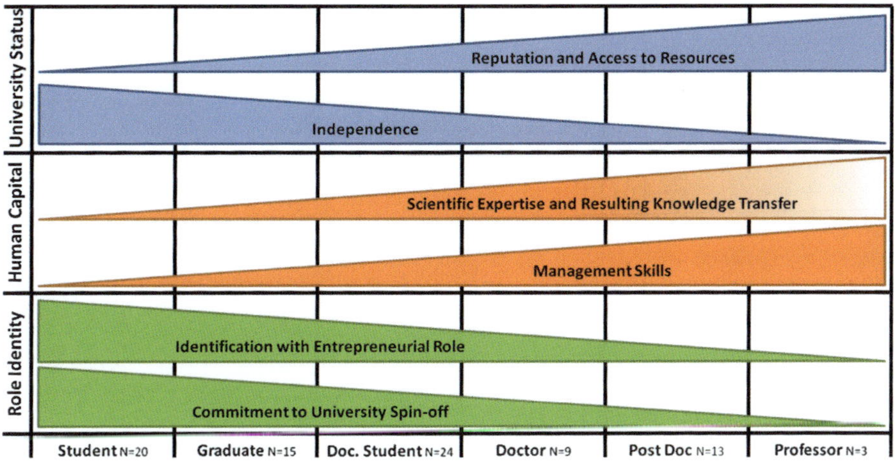

Fig. 3.7 Advantages of university career for university spin-off growth. *Note*: Summarized results of the content analysis. Fading color of the triangle "Scientific Expertise and Resulting Knowledge Transfer" demonstrates diminishing marginal utility. In principle, missing advantages may be counted as disadvantages, but each advantage may also entail a respective disadvantage as explained in the text. *Source*: Own illustration, USO survey 2011

case analysis show that each university status comprises certain advantages and disadvantages; summarized in Fig. 3.7. Academic entrepreneurs are located in a trade-off. With advancing university status the reputation and access to resources, the scientific expertise and resulting knowledge as well as the management competence of a person of course increases. Nevertheless, some examples show that a high degree of scientific expertise and the resulting knowledge transfer in connection with a high university status even develop into a disadvantage for long-term university growth due to a high dependency on the academic entrepreneur and on the university. Only for the role identity change the results are quite clear: With advancing university status, academic entrepreneurs have increased problems to change the roles and to lead the university spin-off with full commitment. Around one third of the academic entrepreneurs in the sample decided to continue their university career and work in the university spin-off at the same time on a part-time basis. These types of university spin-offs usually stay small (Nicolaou and Birley 2003; Doutriaux 1987). The willingness and ability for a role identity change in terms of commitment to the entrepreneurial role is very important for the growth intention of an academic entrepreneur and subsequent university spin-off growth. At least one founding member should work in the university spin-off with full commitment in the initial years. Overall, the results indicate that the cognitive ability and the social network of an academic entrepreneur are important to achieve university spin-off growth. However, the growth intentions also play a crucial role.

3.6.1 Research Implications

The study contributes to a better understanding of the career paths of academic entrepreneurs and the effects on university spin-off performance by using three different research perspectives: human capital (Becker 1975; Lazear 2005), university status (Phillips and Zuckerman 2001), and role identity (Jain et al. 2009; Merton 1973). The current study thereby also contributes to the existing literature on university spin-off development and performance because, in contrast to the existing literature, it considers the time at university as being important for the subsequent university spin-off performance.

Examining career paths is quite a complex task. They extend over a long period of time and include decisions which are path dependent and interrelated (Kodithuwakku and Rosa 2002; Druilhe and Garnsey 2004). The relationship between the career paths of entrepreneurs and growth intentions is therefore still ambiguous. While some quantitative studies deny an influence (Kolvereid 1992; Birley and Westhead 1994) others empirically prove it (Cassar 2007). The qualitative research design has thereby proven to be a great advantage for analyzing the career paths of academic entrepreneurs.

The results of this study show that the role identity change and the resulting growth intention of an academic entrepreneur have a crucial influence on university spin-off growth. Although some empirical studies in the recent past have suggested that entrepreneurial growth intentions are important for subsequent business growth (Gundry and Welsch 2001; Cassar 2007; Hermans et al. 2012; Stam et al. 2007; van Stel et al. 2010; Douglas 2013), this issue has hardly been considered in the field of academic entrepreneurship. Further research should therefore consider growth intentions as being important for university spin-off growth and investigate this relationship more in depth.

The results of this study furthermore show that only a minority of university spin-offs belongs to the group of high flyers and many lead a university spin-off on a part-time basis. Further research should therefore look at self-employment as a part-time job for scientists. This phenomenon has only received little attention in literature so far (Nicolaou and Birley 2003; Jain et al. 2009), although it might represent an untapped potential for the university and the region. Also, it should be investigated what kind of alternative benefits, apart from employment and profit, derive from university spin-offs once for the region and once for the university. Especially in the German context, this is of particular importance because German universities usually are not allowed to acquire shares in the university spin-offs and do not receive any financial benefit.

3.6.2 Policy Implications

On the basis of the results, the policy recommendation is that subsidies should not be dependent on a high degree of knowledge transfer or a high university status of the academic entrepreneur. Instead, it is of particular importance to consider the university status and career plans of an academic entrepreneur, in order to compensate particular disadvantages of different university statuses and to recognize an academic entrepreneur's growth intention. Furthermore, I recommend, to support, the formation of founding teams with complementary skills and university statuses (Breitenecker et al. 2011; Ensley and Hmieleski 2005). Students and doctoral students usually have a high willingness to learn. This might diminish the cognitive distance between professors and management graduates (Nooteboom et al. 2007). The professor's scientific expertise would be coupled with the students' risk disposition and flexibility. The graduates therefore could profit from the professor's reputation and far-reaching social networks. Nevertheless some problems might occur. Disputes can arise due to an imbalance between the professor and the students. Due to the different university statuses, collaboration at eye-level is difficult. A possible solution to avoid many problems in advance is to clarify the division of tasks and competence fields from the beginning. This empirical study describes some positive examples where professors are shareholders and scientific advisors, but the operating business is performed by graduates, so that both sides can benefit from each other.

3.6.3 Limitations

Although the present empirical study fills certain research gaps, one needs to consider the results in the context of limitations, which I address in the following. Firstly, limitations regarding the transferability of the results should be considered. The results are solely based on a sample within the German context, whereas both universities are located in the same federal state with comparable environments. Despite several reasons justifying this approach, it should be noted that the results are therefore hardly transferable to other regions or countries.

Secondly, the following data-related biases should be considered. The study is largely based on established university spin-offs. I only contacted those academic entrepreneurs who were still on the market at the time of the survey, although a large number of academic entrepreneurs do not succeed in establishing and running a university spin-off (Garnsey 1998). Furthermore, I only took private limited companies and corporations into account. Thus, a general success bias might exist. One could also assume some bias due to nonresponse. However, those academic entrepreneurs who did not respond to our contact request, could be either less or more successful. Some may be embarrassed, others could be too busy. I interviewed academic entrepreneurs ex-post. A retrospective study always tends to suffer from some kind of memory decay. There is a risk that outcomes are assigned to circumstances that did not in fact exist at that time.

Finally, the qualitative content analysis is only focused on the differences of university statuses and their influence on university spin-off growth. Nevertheless advantages and disadvantages exist, which many of our interviewees had in common: Generally all the university spin-offs in our sample are knowledge-intensive.

A relatively high amount of human capital can be assumed for all academic entrepreneurs in our sample. Independently from the university status, some academic entrepreneurs in the sample had prior entrepreneurial experience and therefore huge advantages. However, the vast majority of the interviewees had to cope with a lack of business knowledge. Because of the novelty of the products and services it was difficult to estimate market potential and costumer demand. Many of our sampled entrepreneurs had problems in entering the market.

Acknowledgments This work was prepared in the context of a research project "University spin-offs in Lower Saxony and their regional economic impact: empirical evidence from Hannover and Göttingen." It was funded from 2010 to 2013 by the Ministry for Science and Culture of Lower Saxony, grant no. AZ. 76202-17-5/09. My special thanks go to my research team members Rolf Sternberg and Arne Vorderwülbecke as well as the interviewees for sharing their stories and insights. Furthermore I would like to thank Jürgen Brünjes at the German Centre for Research on Higher Education and Science Studies (DZHW) and my other colleagues at the Institute of Economic and Cultural Geography of the Leibniz Universität Hannover as well as the discussants and participants at the DRUID Academy Conference 2013 and 53rd European Regional Science Association Congress for their valuable comments on an earlier draft.

References

Baker SE, Edwards R (2012) How many qualitative interviews is enough. National Centre for Research Methods Review Paper. http://eprints.ncrm.ac.uk/2273/4/how_many_interviews.pdf

Bathelt H, Kogler DF, Munro AK (2010) A knowledge-based typology of university spin-offs in the context of regional economic development. Technovation 30(9–10):519–532

Becker GS (1975) Human capital: a theoretical and empirical analysis, with special reference to education. Columbia University Press, New York

Bernard HR, Ryan GW (2009) Analyzing qualitative data: systematic approaches. Sage, Los Angeles

Birley S, Westhead P (1994) A taxonomy of business start-up reasons and their impact on firm growth and size. J Bus Ventur 9(1):7–31

Braun-Thürmann H, Knie A, Simon D (2010) Unternehmen Wissenschaft—Ausgründungen als Grenzüberschreitungen akademischer Forschung [Enterprise science—spin-offs as border-crossings of academic research]. Transcript, Bielefeld

Breitenecker RJ, Schwarz EJ, Claussen J (2011) The influence of team heterogeneity on team processes of multi-person ventures: an empirical analysis of highly innovative academic start-ups. Int J Entrep Small Bus 12(4):413–428

Cassar G (2007) Money, money, money? A longitudinal investigation of entrepreneur career reasons, growth preferences and achieved growth. Entrep Reg Dev 19(1):89–107

Chandler GN, Jansen E (1992) The founder's self-assessed competence and venture performance. J Bus Ventur 7(3):223–236

Cohen WM, Klepper S (1992) The tradeoff between firm size and diversity in the pursuit of technological progress. Small Bus Econ 4(1):1–14

Colombo MG, Grilli L (2005) Founders' human capital and the growth of new technology-based firms: a competence-based view. Res Policy 34(6):795–816

Czarnitzki D, Rammer C, Toole A (2014) University spin-offs and the "performance premium". Small Bus Econ 43(2):309–326

Davidsson P, Honig B (2003) The role of social and human capital among nascent entrepreneurs. J Bus Ventur 18(3):301–331

Davidsson P, Achtenhagen L, Naldi L (2007) What do we know about small firm growth? In: Parker S (ed) The life cycle of entrepreneurial ventures, vol 3. Springer, New York, pp 361–398
Ding W, Choi E (2011) Divergent paths to commercial science: a comparison of scientists' founding and advising activities. Res Policy 40(1):69–80. doi:10.1016/j.respol.2010.09.011
Dörre K, Neis M (2010) Das Dilemma der unternehmerischen Universität: Hochschulen zwischen Wissensproduktion und Marktzwang [The dilemma of the entrepreneurial university: universities between knowledge production and market pressure]. Edition Sigma, Berlin
Douglas EJ (2013) Reconstructing entrepreneurial intentions to identify predisposition for growth. J Bus Ventur 28(5):633–651
Doutriaux J (1987) Growth pattern of academic entrepreneurial firms. J Bus Ventur 2(4):285–297, doi:http://dx.doi.org/10.1016/0883-9026(87)90022-X
Druilhe C, Garnsey E (2004) Do academic spin-outs differ and does it matter? J Technol Transf 29(3):269–285
Egeln J, Gottschalk S, Rammer C, Spielkamp A (2002) Spinoff-Gründungen aus der öffentlichen Forschung in Deutschland: Kurzfassung; Gutachten für das Bundesministerium für Bildung und Forschung [Spin-offs from public research in Germany: summary; report for the Federal Ministry for Education and Research]. ZEW Dokumentationen
Ensley MD, Hmieleski KM (2005) A comparative study of new venture top management team composition, dynamics and performance between university-based and independent start-ups. Res Policy 34(7):1091–1105
Erdös K, Varga A (2012) The academic entrepreneur: myth or reality for increased regional growth in Europe? In: Erdös K, Varga A (eds) Creative knowledge cities: myths, visions and realities. Edward Elgar, Cheltenham, pp 157–181
Etzkowitz H (2008) The triple helix. University-industry-government. Innovation in action. Routledge, Madison
Federal Bureau of Statistics (2013) Kleine und mittlere Unternehmen (KMU) [Small and medium enterprises (SME)]. https://www.destatis.de/DE/ZahlenFakten/GesamtwirtschaftUmwelt/UnternehmenHandwerk/KleineMittlereUnternehmenMittelstand/KMUBegriffserlaeuterung.html. Accessed 1 May 2013
Garnsey E (1998) A theory of the early growth of the firm. Ind Corp Chang 7(3):523–556
Georg-August-Universität Göttingen (2013) Zahlen, Daten und Fakten [Numbers, data and facts]. http://www.uni-goettingen.de/de/24499.html. Accessed 31 Oct 2013
Gibcus P, Stam E (2012) Firm resources, dynamic capabilities, and the early growth of firms. Scales research reports, EIM Business and Policy Research, H201219
Gläser J, Laudel G (2009) Experteninterviews und qualitative Inhaltsanalyse: Als Instrumente rekonstruierender Untersuchungen [Expert interviews and qualitative content analysis: as instruments of reconstructing investigations]. VS Verlag, Wiesbaden
Gundry LK, Welsch HP (2001) The ambitious entrepreneur: high growth strategies of women-owned enterprises. J Bus Ventur 16(5):453–470
Hayter C (2010) In search of the profit-maximizing actor: motivations and definitions of success from nascent academic entrepreneurs. J Technol Transf 36(3):340–352
Helm R, Mauroner O (2007) Success of research-based spin-offs. State-of-the-art and guidelines for further research. Rev Manag Sci 1(3):237–270
Helm R, Mauroner O (2011) Soft starters, research boutiques and product-oriented firms: different business models for spin-off companies. Int J Entrep Small Bus 12(4):479–498
Hermans J, Vanderstraeten J, Dejardina M, Ramdani D, Stam E, van Witteloostuijn A (2012) Ambitious entrepreneurship: antecedents and consequences. Department of Economics Working Papers Series 1210, University of Namur, Namur
Jain S, George G, Maltarich M (2009) Academics or entrepreneurs? Investigating role identity modification of university scientists involved in commercialization activity. Res Policy 38(6):922–935. doi:10.1016/j.respol.2009.02.007
Karnani F, Schulte R (2010) Screening von Gründungspotenzialen—Kompetenz-Ausgründungen aus Hochschulen und Forschungseinrichtungen: Oder: Wie man Innovationspotenziale kartog-

raphiert. [Screening entrepreneurial potentials—competence spin-offs from universities and research institutions: or how one can map innovation potentials]. Lüneburger Beiträge zur Gründungsforschung, 7

Klofsten M, Jones-Evans D (2000) Comparing academic entrepreneurship in Europe—the case of Sweden and Ireland. Small Bus Econ 14(4):299–309

Kodithuwakku SS, Rosa P (2002) The entrepreneurial process and economic success in a constrained environment. J Bus Ventur 17(5):431–465

Kolvereid L (1992) Growth aspirations among Norwegian entrepreneurs. J Bus Ventur 7(3):209–222

Kulicke M, Schleinkofer M, Mallig N, Schönenbrücher J, Heiser C (2008) Rahmenbedingungen und Potenziale für Ausgründungen aus der Wissenschaft, Aktueller Stand im Kontext von EXIST–Existenzgründungen aus der Wissenschaft [Framework conditions and potentials for spin-offs from the science, current status in the context of EXIST business start-ups from the science]. Fraunhofer IRB, Stuttgart

Lawton Smith H (2007) Universities, innovation, and territorial development: a review of the evidence. Environ Plann C Govern Pol 25(1):98–114

Lawton Smith H, Ho K (2006) Measuring the performance of Oxford University, Oxford Brookes University and the government laboratories' spin-off companies. Res Policy 35(10): 1554–1568

Lazear EP (2005) Entrepreneurship. J Labor Econ 23(4):649–680

Leibniz Universität Hannover (2013) Studierendenstatistik Sommersemester 2013 [Statisticso on students summer semester 2013]. http://www.uni-hannover.de/imperia/md/content/strat_controlling/statistiken/allgemein/sommersemester_2013.pdf. Accessed 31 Oct 2013

Mangematin V (2000) PhD job market: professional trajectories and incentives during the PhD. Res Policy 29(6):741–756

Mason C, Tagg S, Carter S (2011) Does education matter? The characteristics and performance of business started by recent university graduates. In: Borch OJ, Fayolle A, Kyro P, Ljunggren E (eds) Entrepreneurship research in Europe: evolving concepts and processes, European research in entrepreneurship. Edward Elgar, Cheltenham, pp 13–33

Mayring P (2008) Qualitative Inhaltsanalyse: Grundlagen und Techniken [Qualitative content analysis: basics and techniques]. Beltz, Weinheim

Merton RK (1973) The sociology of science. Theoretical and empirical investigations. University of Chicago Press, Chicago

Miles MB, Huberman AM (1994) Qualitative data analysis: an expanded sourcebook. Sage, Thousand Oaks

Müller B (2006) Human capital and successful academic spin-off. ZEW discussion paper

Murray KB, Häubl G (2007) Explaining cognitive lock-in: the role of skill-based habits of use in consumer choice. J Consum Res 34(1):77–88

Mustar P, Wright M, Clarysse B (2008) University spin-off firms: lessons from ten years of experience in Europe. Sci Public Policy 35(2):67–80

Nicolaou N, Birley S (2003) Academic networks in a trichotomous categorisation of university spinouts. J Bus Ventur 18(3):333–359

Nooteboom B, Van Haverbeke W, Duysters G, Gilsing V, van den Oord A (2007) Optimal cognitive distance and absorptive capacity. Res Policy 36(7):1016–1034

Nörr M (2010) Spin-Offs: Wie Wissenschaftler zu Unternehmern werden. Anforderungen an den Gründer und das Transferobjekt [How scientists become entrepreneurs. Requirements on the founder and the transfer object]. Diplomica, Hamburg

Parker SC (2005) The economics of entrepreneurship: what we know and what we don't. Now Publishers, Boston

Phillips DJ, Zuckerman EW (2001) Middle-status conformity: theoretical restatement and empirical demonstration in two markets. Am J Sociol 107(2):379–429

Pirnay F, Surlemont B, Nlemvo F (2003) Toward a typology of university spin-offs. Small Bus Econ 21(4):355–369

Rappert B, Webster A, Charles D (1999) Making sense of diversity and reluctance: academic-industrial relations and intellectual property. Res Policy 28(8):873–890
Rasmussen E (2011) Understanding academic entrepreneurship: exploring the emergence of university spin-off ventures using process theories. Int Small Bus J 29(5):448–471. doi:10.1177/0266242610385395
Rasmussen E, Borch OJ (2010) University capabilities in facilitating entrepreneurship: a longitudinal study of spin-off ventures at mid-range universities. Res Policy 39(5):602–612. doi:10.1016/j.respol.2010.02.002
Roberts EB, Malone DE (1996) Policies and structures for spinning off new companies from research and development organizations. R D Manag 26(1):17–48
Saxenian A (1983) The genesis of Silicon Valley. Built Environ 9:7–17
Schreier M, Naderer G, Balzer E (2007) Qualitative Stichprobenkonzepte [Qualitative sampling concept]. In: Naderer G, Balzer E (eds) Qualitative Marktforschung in Theorie und Praxis. Gabler, Wiesbaden, pp 231–245
Shane S (2004) Academic entrepreneurship: university spinoffs and wealth creation (New Horizons in Entrepreneurship). Edward Elgar, Cheltenham
Smilor RW, Gibson DV, Dietrich GB (1990) University spin-out companies: technology start-ups from UT-Austin. J Bus Ventur 5(1):63–76
Stam E, Suddle K, Jolanda SJA, Andre van Stel A (2007) High growth entrepreneurs, public policies and economic growth. Jena Economic Research Papers, 2007(019)
Stephan P, Levin S (1996) Property rights and entrepreneurship in science. Small Bus Econ 8(3):177–188
Sternberg R (1995) Technologiepolitik und High-Tech Regionen: Ein internationaler Vergleich [Technology policy and high-tech regions: an international comparison]. LIT, Münster
Stützer M (2010) Human capital and social capital in the entrepreneurial process. Wirtschaftswissenschaftliche Fakultät, Friedrich-Schiller-Universität Jena, Jena
Szyperski N, Klandt H (1981) Wissenschaftlich-technische Mitarbeiter von Forschungs- und Entwicklungseinrichtungen als potentielle Spin-off-Gründer. Eine empirische Studie zu den Entstehungsfaktoren von innovativen Unternehmungsgründungen im Lande Nordrhein-Westfalen. [Scientific-technical staff of research and development institution as potential spin-off founders. An empirical study on the factors of development of innovative start-ups in the Land of North Rhine-Westphalia]. Westdeutscher, Opladen
van Stel A, Thurik R, Stam E, Hartog C (2010) Ambitious entrepreneurship, high-growth firms and macroeconomic growth. Scales Research Reports, EIM Business and Policy Research, H200911
Vohora A, Wright M, Lockett A (2004) Critical junctures in the development of university high-tech spinout companies. Res Policy 33(1):147–175
Wennberg K, Wiklund J, Wright M (2011) The effectiveness of university knowledge spillovers: performance differences between university spinoffs and corporate spinoffs. Res Policy 2011(40):1128–1143
Wentland A, Knie A, Simon D (2011) Warum aus Forschern keine Erfinder werden: Innovationshemmnisse im deutschen Wissenschaftssystem am Beispiel der Biotechnologie [Why scientists do not become inventors: innovation barriers in the German science system, the example of the biotechnology sector]. WZBrief Bildung, Wissenschaftszentrum Berlin für Sozialforschung, 17
Wiklund J (1998) Small firm growth and performance: entrepreneurship and beyond. Internationella Handelshögskolan, Jönköping
Zhang J (2009) The performance of university spin-offs: an exploratory analysis using venture capital data. J Technol Transf 34(3):255–285

Chapter 4
The Role of Employee's Human Capital and the Work Environment on the Creation of Organizational Spin-Offs: Evidence from Spain

Eissa Alrumaithi, Maribel Guerrero, and Iñaki Peña

Abstract Previous studies have recognized the relevance of certain individual (generic and specific human capital) and organizational (work environment) factors in the creation of new ventures from and for an existing organization. The objective of this exploratory study is to understand the roles of employee human capital and the work environment on the creation of organizational spin-offs. Adopting the human capital and the corporate entrepreneurship approaches, a conceptual framework was proposed and tested with data from the 2012 Spanish Adult Population Survey (Global Entrepreneurship Monitor, GEM). Due to the nature of the data and research objective, a rare event model was used for the analysis. Our results provide evidence about the relevant roles of specific human capital (entrepreneurship educational training) and the work environment (job autonomy) on the propensity that an employee becomes an intrapreneur and leads a spin-off "from" and "for" their employer. We also show that a stronger moderation effect of job autonomy takes place in the relationship between entrepreneurship education and organizational spin-off creation. In general, these results would help employees, top managers, and policy makers take into account the relevance of these individual and organizational factors when defining their strategic decisions/planning.

Keywords Corporate entrepreneurship • Corporate venturing • Organizational spin-off • Human capital • Organizational environment

E. Alrumaithi • M. Guerrero (✉) • I. Peña
Deusto Business School, Mundaiz 50, Donostia-San Sebastian, Spain
e-mail: maribel.guerrero@deusto.es

R. Baptista, J. Leitão (eds.), *Entrepreneurship, Human Capital, and Regional Development*, International Studies in Entrepreneurship 31,
DOI 10.1007/978-3-319-12871-9_4

4.1 Introduction

Previous studies on corporate entrepreneurship (CE) have shown the development and implementation of new ideas initiated within the boundaries of an existing organization (Hornsby et al. 2002), particularly, two streams of activities: internal (innovation, strategic renewal) and external (corporate venturing, joint venture, spin-off). In general, several scholars have recognized the relevance of this phenomenon in promoting sustainability, competitiveness, and added value for firms (Covin and Slevin, 1991). The recent global financial crisis was a strategic game-changer for most organizations. Severe resource constraints and unpredictable market conditions created significant challenges for organizational survival, let alone for growth through innovation and venturing activities. These conditions have fostered a greater need for a better understanding of the corporate entrepreneurial process. This paper adopts the perspective of venturing activities defined as the creation of new ventures "from" and "for" an existing organization (parent firm) based on ideas proposed by employees or top managers (Lindholm 1994; Parhankangas and Arenius 2003; Narayanan et al. 2009).

In the past decade, several individual (education, fear of failure, risk taking) and organizational factors (autonomy, organizational structure, etc.) have been examined (Sathe 1985; Covin and Slevin 1991; Rutherford and Holt 2007). Parker (2011) showed that human capital (generic and specific) is a relevant individual factor during the creation of new ventures and also helps to distinguish the main characteristics of independent new ventures from corporate ventures. Corporate entrepreneurship studies have evidenced certain work environment characteristics that increase/retard the propensity of corporate venturing activities within existing organizations (Zahra et al. 1999; Hornsby et al. 2002; de Jong et al. 2011). However, insights and research concerning determinant factors (work environment/human capital) of organizational spin-offs at individual levels are limited. Therefore, the main objective of this exploratory study is to understand the roles of employee human capital and the work environment on the creation of spin-offs "from" and "for" an existing organization.

Adopting the human capital and corporate entrepreneurship approach, a conceptual framework was proposed and tested using data from the 2012 Spanish Adult Population Survey (Global Entrepreneurship Monitor, GEM). A rare event statistical model with a sample of 5,274 full-time employees aged 30–60 years old was developed. In general, the results provide evidence about the relevant roles of specific human capital (entrepreneurship educational training) and the work environment (job autonomy) on the propensity that an employee becomes an intrapreneur and leads a spin-off from and for their employer. We also show that a stronger moderation effect of job autonomy takes place in the relationship between entrepreneurship education and organizational spin-off creation. Our introduction is followed by an explanation of the conceptual framework, in particular, the roles of human capital, the work environment, and the interaction effect of the work environment on the creation of the organizational spin-off. Then the methodological section presents the main characteristics of the sample, variables, and the model used in the statistical analysis. The following section outlines the main results. Finally, the paper ends with the conclusion and implications.

4.2 Theoretical Framework and Hypothesis

4.2.1 Human Capital

Scholars have studied in depth the importance of human capital in entrepreneurial ventures. They have proposed that human capital comprised of education, experience and skills plays a vital role in the entrepreneurial process (Oosterbeek et al. 2010). Human capital refers to skills and knowledge that individuals acquire through investments in schooling, on-the-job training, and other types of experience (Becker 1964). In other words, individuals with appropriate knowledge (education, skills, experience) are more able to identify and perceive economic opportunities for exploitation. According to Polanyi (1967), knowledge could either be explicit (know what) or tacit (know how). Explicit knowledge refers to information carried out in procedures, processes, formal written documents and educational institutions (Davidsson and Honig 2003). For example, a post-secondary degree is considered explicit knowledge carried out in an educational institution, whereas tacit knowledge includes "non-codified" activities such as experience obtained on the job (Davidsson and Honig 2003). Consequently, the integration of explicit and tacit knowledge is believed to facilitate individuals' decisions to act entrepreneurially. Early human capital literature proposed two streams of human capital schemes: generic and specific (Becker 1964). Generic human capital encompasses skills, knowledge, experience, and capabilities that are useful for management in existing organizations. Specific human capital encompasses skills, knowledge, experience, and capabilities obtained for special purposes, such as the development of a new venture. According to Parker (2011), these two types of human capital could explain the differences among entrepreneurs and intrapreneurs. In this paper, the generic human capital factor is analyzed via *higher education* and the specific human capital factor is analyzed via *entrepreneurship education*.

Generic human capital includes formal education. Prior studies have focused on the influence of education level on individuals' entrepreneurial activities (Sexton and Kent 1981; Brockhaus 1982; Gasse 1982). Those studies have shown a strong impact on individuals' capabilities that are necessary to identify and to exploit opportunities (Unger et al. 2011). Thus, educational attainment is connected to the decision and success of becoming self-employed, as well as the potential success (Delmar and Davidsson 2000). Following this perspective, previous studies have found positive relationships between education and proactive behaviors (LePine and Van Dyne 1998) and also with continuous improvement (Fuller et al. 2006). Educated people are more likely to be proactive and take risks to advance their careers. Entrepreneurial behaviors are generally associated with better job performances and appraisals, and the pursuit of opportunities makes the most out of individuals' human capital investments. Also, different levels of education (high school, college degree, master degree, and doctorate) could affect entrepreneurial activities distinctively. The effect of each educational level on entrepreneurship has been studied; however, there is no consensus in the findings (Evans and Leighton 1989;

Bellu et al. 1990; Davidsson 1995; Honig 1996; Gimeno et al. 1997; Reynolds 1997). As a result, there is contrasting evidence about how generic human capital impacts on an individual's entrepreneurship choice (Davidsson and Honig 2003; Grilo and Thurik 2008; Parker 2009). For the purpose of this exploratory study, the emphasis is on higher education (college degree). Blanchflower (2004) found that higher education has a positive impact on entrepreneurial activities. Indeed, Koellinger (2008) showed that higher education increases individuals' abstract thinking, curiosity, and strong interest to find general solutions to problems. For instance, Bosma et al. (2010) found that employees with this kind of knowledge are expected to participate or to be involved in the identification and development of entrepreneurial activities (new products/services, new business units, spin-offs) within the organization, particularly when they have perceived the support of their employers. Therefore, employees with higher education are more likely to create an organizational spin-off because the knowledge they accumulated makes them believe they have the capacity to do it. Consequently,

H1a: *Employees with a higher level of education are more likely to engage in the creation of organizational spin-offs than employees with a lower level of education.*

Specific human capital includes non-formal education, such as training courses to reinforce specific capabilities such as entrepreneurship (Gorman et al. 1997). Prior studies have shown that *entrepreneurship education* promotes entrepreneurial activities (Levie and Autio 2008). Also, policy makers have endorsed entrepreneurship through specific entrepreneurship educational platforms (European Commission 2006). Entrepreneurship education has been incorporated into the educational programs of many countries (Kuratko 2005; European Commission 2006). A key assumption is that entrepreneurship skills can be taught, and it has been shown in several investigations' findings that: (1) a positive effect has been measured in years of schooling on entrepreneur performance (Van der Sluis et al. 2006; Van der Sluis and Van Praag 2007) and (2) a positive/effective effect of business training has been measured in the performance of people who start their own business (Karlan and Valdivia 2011). The main debate has been focused on which type of educational level (middle school, high school and college) needs to incorporate entrepreneurship education programs in order to be more effective. Entrepreneurship education, therefore, would not have the same effects on all types of students. However, entrepreneurship training primes individuals to engage in entrepreneurial activities; the theory of planned behavior (Ajzen 1991) states that planned behaviors are intentional and thus are predicted by intention toward that behavior (Souitaris et al. 2007). Dyer and Dickinson (1994) suggested that specialized courses in entrepreneurship, or training programs about how to start a business, might give people the confidence to start their own business (Gorman et al. 1997). Under this point of view, employees enrolled in organizations with an entrepreneurial orientation and those who possess entrepreneurship education and training could apply this specific knowledge and expertise to engage into entrepreneurial activities within the organization (i.e., creation of organizational spin-offs). Therefore,

H1b: Employees with prior entrepreneurship education training are more likely to engage in the creation of organizational spin-offs than employees without entrepreneurship education training.

4.2.2 Work Environment

An adequate work environment is important to encourage, adopt, and create value through new business ideas or innovations inside existing organizations. In general, within organizations there are employees with innovative ideas, but only a few concepts are retained and exploited with the support of the employers. Previous studies have determined several factors that kill the spirit of innovation as well as several factors that provoke employees' willingness to bring forth their innovative ideas within and for parent firms (Zahra 1991; Zahra and Covin 1995; Zahra et al. 1999). In particular, these studies have shown the relevance of internal organizational factors such as incentive and control systems (Sathe 1985), organizational culture (Kanter 1985; Hisrich and Peters 1986), organizational structure (Covin and Slevin, 1991; Naman and Slevin 1993; Dess et al. 1999), and managerial support (Stevenson and Jarillo 1990). Thus, this exploratory study examines the impact of *job autonomy* on fostering organizational spin-off creations, in particular how these factors may help encourage employees to participate actively in the creation of organizational spin-offs for their employers.

Job autonomy is defined as the ability to determine independently how to perform a job or a task (Axtell et al. 2000), a personal initiative, and an idea implementation or problem solving (Bindl and Parker 2010). Therefore, job autonomy represents the degree of discretion given to employees to perform their jobs based on their timing and method and without criticizing employees when they commit mistakes (Kuratko et al. 1990; Hornsby et al. 1999, 2002). This scheme provides employees with the environment in which their personal initiatives, idea implementation, and problem solving are manifested (Bindl and Parker 2010). Interestingly, job autonomy is one of the core constructs in the assessment of an adequate climate that promotes corporate entrepreneurship (Hornsby et al. 1993, 2002). Previous studies have demonstrated that job autonomy is correlated with the number of ideas developed and implemented by higher-level managers within existing organizations. Moreover, at the individual level, previous studies have connected job autonomy with various elements of entrepreneurship activities (i.e., degrees of discretion might distract employees from focusing on exploring new innovative ideas). In general, the evidence suggests that employees with job autonomy participate actively in the development or implementation of entrepreneurial activities within organizations with an entrepreneurial orientation (Hornsby et al. 2002). Other studies have also concluded that employees with job autonomy demonstrate more innovative behavior and satisfaction (Axtell et al. 2000). Employees who perceive autonomy are more likely to generate, transfer, and exploit innovative ideas. As a consequence, these types of employees are considered a relevant intangible within existing organizations that could be responsible for the performance and the competitive advantage of their firms. Therefore, employees with job autonomy are expected to engage in organizational spin-off creation. Consequently,

H2a: *Employees who perceive job autonomy in the work context are more likely to engage in the creation of organizational spin-offs than employees who do not perceive autonomy at work.*

4.2.3 The Moderation Effect of the Work Environment

The creation of a new venture may be influenced by several organizational and individual factors. Undoubtedly, those factors could have both a direct and an indirect effect on the propensity to create a new venture. Based on previous studies, this paper also explores the moderation effect of the work environment (job autonomy) on the relationship between human capital (generic: higher education; specific: entrepreneurship education) and the creation of organizational spin-offs.

The moderation effect of the work environment on generic human capital: Previous sections presented several arguments regarding how generic human capital (higher education) and the work environment (job autonomy) would influence employees' decision to act entrepreneurially and on the active participation in the creation of organizational spin-offs for the parent firm. During their daily activities, employees with a higher level of education are individuals who possess the technical knowledge required to identify opportunities, linked or not with the core business of their employers, that later would be transformed into economic and social value for the organization (Hornsby et al. 2002; Arnold et al. 2007). In general, those employees might exploit these opportunities either on behalf of their organization (participating in the creation of new product/services, business unit or new organizations) or for themselves (becoming independent entrepreneurs). This decision would be mediated by the work environment. Undoubtedly, an adequate work environment that encourages and supports innovations and new business ideas persuades employees to participate actively within and for their organization (Parker 2011). Otherwise, employees would keep their innovative ideas for themselves and exploit them outside the organization, possibly even becoming rivals. Employees who have a higher level of education and perceive job autonomy during their daily work are more likely to promote potential economic opportunities than others. Therefore, the moderation effect of job autonomy on employees with a higher level of education provides to them the elements (satisfaction, authenticity, and self-efficacy) required to develop, implement, and lead the creation of organizational spin-offs with the support of parent firms (Rosso et al. 2010). As a consequence,

H3a: *Employees with a higher level of education, moderated by the perception of job autonomy, are more likely to engage in creating organizational spin-offs than employees with a lower level of education.*

The moderation effect of the work environment on specific human capital: As mentioned, entrepreneurship education provides individuals with the specific skills and knowledge that reinforce their confidence to start their own business (Dyer and Dickinson 1994). Parker (2009) argues that employees' specific human capital influences the development path of a new idea or the culmination of an innovation. Following this perspective, the perception of job autonomy could mediate that employees with this specific entrepreneurship training would be more creative, innovative, and proactive in the implementation and development of entrepreneurial activities within existing organizations (Axtell et al. 2000) and generate a higher added value for their organization (Nord et al. 1990; Harpaz and Fu 2002). In this context, the moderation effect of the work environment on entrepreneurship education enhances specific individuals' skills and personal incentives to participate in the creation of start-ups with the support of a parent firm. Therefore,

H3b: *Employees with entrepreneurship education, moderated by the perception of job autonomy, are more likely to engage in creating an organizational spin-off than employees without entrepreneurship education training.*

4.2.4 Conceptual Framework

Based on the previous literature review, Fig. 4.1 shows the conceptual model proposed in this paper. In summary, it is possible to identify the direct effect of both human capital (H1a & H1b) and organizational environment on the creation of organizational spin-offs (H2a), as well as the moderate effect that the work environment will produce on employees' human capital when they decide to participate or not in the creation and development of new start-ups "from" and "for" their employer (H3a & H3b).

4.3 Methodology

4.3.1 Sample

Data was collected from the 2012 Global Entrepreneurship Monitor (GEM) Adult Population Survey applied in Spain.[1] The GEM project is an international research program focused on the analysis of entrepreneurial activity around the world. In each country, representative samples of randomly selected adults (at least 2,000 per country) are surveyed every year to estimate the percentage of the adult population involved in firm start-ups. All research members of the project apply the same

[1] In 2012, in the Spanish questionnaire, the Basque Country Team added some questions that allow for the identification of employees involved in the creation of spin-offs for their employer.

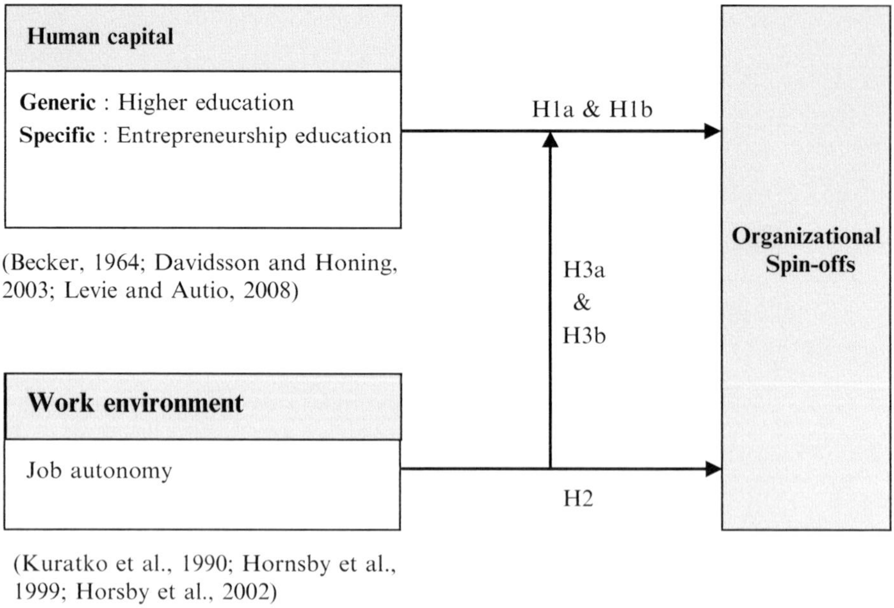

Fig. 4.1 Proposed conceptual framework

data-collecting methods in order to achieve comparable results (Reynolds et al. 2005). In total, the Spanish sample integrates 21,900 individuals aged 19–64 years. In this study, only 5,274 observations associated with full-time employees aged 30–60 years[2] were used.

4.3.2 Variables

The dependent variable *organizational spin-off* is a dummy variable that takes the value of 1 when a respondent is a full-time employee involved in the creation of an organizational spin-off (a new business created for and inside an existent organization); it takes the value 0 otherwise. Spin-off is a business creation grounded on a business idea developed within a parent firm being taken into a self-standing firm (Lindholm 1994; Parhankangas and Arenius 2003). The independent variables are divided into two sections: human capital and work environment. Based on Becker's ideas (1964), human capital is divided into generic and specific human capital. In this exploratory study, generic human capital is measured by *higher education*, a dichotomous variable that takes the value 1 if the employee holds a bachelor's degree and 0 otherwise (Blanchflower 2004). Specific human capital is measured by

[2] On average, the age of an entrepreneur in Spain is 37 years old. Therefore, we consider this age range to take into account the individuals with a higher propensity to becoming entrepreneurs.

the variable *entrepreneurship education*, a dummy variable that takes the value 1 if the respondent is taking a course or training on *entrepreneurship education* and 0 otherwise (Levie and Autio 2008). Work environment is measured by *job autonomy*, a binary variable that takes the value of 1 when the employee perceives that he/she has a higher level of decision making in the way of doing his/her work, and 0 otherwise (de Jong et al. 2011).

The control variables included in the analysis are *age* and *gender*. In this respect, Bosma et al. (2010) indicated that most of the individuals who are involved in early stage entrepreneurial activity are *middle-aged* individuals. Therefore, individuals of middle age are in a better position to manifest their competence into introducing new means to enhance productivity, profitability and firm creation. For the purpose of this exploratory study, individuals aged 30–60 years are selected to overcome self-selection biasness. Age is supposed to incorporate the positive effects of growing experience and the negative effects of declining uncertainty tolerance and desire to start a business (Bosma and Levie 2010). *Gender* is a dichotomous variable indicating whether the employee is male. It takes the value 1 if he is male and 0 otherwise. Some studies suggest that males tend to engage in entrepreneurial activities more than females (Reynolds et al. 2005).

4.3.3 Method of Analysis

Due to the nature of the data and dependent variable, a rare event relogit model was used to test our hypotheses. King and Zeng (2001a, b) developed a version of the relogit model to compute unbiased estimates. Relogit is an unbiased estimator that gives the user the choice between two bias correction techniques: prior correction and weight correction (Trapido 2004). Also, there is no value in relogit that corresponds to the maximum of the likelihood but always calculates robust standard errors. Robust standard errors, unlike the usual ones, are calculated without the assumption of independence across observations and result in more conservative estimates of coefficients' statistical significance. In general, three models were developed to test the hypotheses proposed. In Model 1, the effect of human capital (higher education and entrepreneurship education) on organizational spin-off creation was tested. Model 2 also includes the effect of work environment (job autonomy) on the creation of organizational spin-offs. Model 3 tested the moderation effect of the work environment on the relationship between human capital and organizational spin-off creation.

4.4 Results and Discussion

The data-descriptive statistics show that only 0.4 % of the sample size (5,274) reflects employees who created organizational spin-offs for their parent firms. And 26.7 % of the employees hold college degrees, whereas employees who received

Table 4.1 Rare events estimations

		Model 1	Model 2	Model 3
Human capital (H1a & H1b)	Higher education	–0.613 (0.388)	–0.511 (0.432)	0.368 (0.720)
	Entrepreneurship education	1.467*** (0.360)	1.172** (0.381)	–0.445 (1.094)
Work environment (H2)	Job autonomy		1.734*** (0.421)	1.084 (0.707)
Moderation effect (H3)	Job autonomy * higher education			–1.242 (0.895)
	Job autonomy * entrepreneurship education			2.373 (1.228)ᵗ
Control variables	Age	0.218 (0.231)	0.060 (0.244)	0.053 (0.245)
	Age^2	–0.002 (0.002)	–0.002 (0.002)	–0.002 (0.002)
	Gender	0.499 (0.393)	0.751 (0.450)ᵗ	0.772 (0.425)ᵗ
	Constant	–10.964 (5.190)	–8.002 (5.550)	–7.582 (5.504)
	Pseudo R^2	0.055	0.108	0.139

Note: ***$p \leq 0.001$, **$p \leq 0.01$, *$p \leq 0.05$, ᵗ$p \leq 0.1$

entrepreneurship education comprised 62.7 % of the entire sample size, which is the highest among all variables. The statistics also reveal that 46.4 % of the employees exercise job autonomy at their work, and 26.3 % perceive that their jobs are meaningful. Table 4.1 summarizes the main results.

4.4.1 Role of Human Capital and the Work Environment on Organizational Spin-Off Creation

The results show that the effect of higher education is negative but not statistically significant (Model 1). A possible explanation behind this result could be the opportunity costs for these employees represented by higher levels of human capital (*higher education*), which can impact whether they become an intrapreneur or pursue higher potential professional opportunities within existing organizations. In this case, the decision to act entrepreneurially would take a long time because individuals expect to accumulate knowledge and experience (Shane and Venkataraman 2000). Other explanations could be associated with the organizations' employee reward and compensation system (Klepper 2001; Freeman and Engel 2007). Therefore, there is not enough evidence to support the H1a, which states that employees with a higher level of education are more likely to engage in the creation of organizational spin-offs than employees with a lower level of education.

Regarding specific human capital, the variable *entrepreneurship education training* shows a positive and statistically significant effect (1.467; $p<0.001$). This implies that prior employees' entrepreneurship education contributes to their engagement in the creation of an organizational spin-off for an existing organization. For existing organizations with entrepreneurial orientations, that their employees possess these specific skills and knowledge represents important intangible resources for their rejuvenation, diversification, and sustainability. Therefore, prior entrepreneurship training impacts on the propensity of those individuals to participate in the creation of new ventures (Levie and Autio 2008), in particular the creation of organizational spin-offs for their employers. Based on that, we found evidence to support H1b. Regarding the work environment, *job autonomy* evidenced a positive and statistically significant effect (1.734; $p<0.001$) on the creation of organizational spin-offs (Model 2). This means that the Spanish employees who perceive they have job autonomy are more likely to actively lead the creation of spin-offs from and for their main employers than employees who do not perceive that they have job autonomy (providing support to H2a). Also, this result confirms that a certain degree of work discretion given to employees helps them to explore innovative projects that later could be transformed into new products/services or new ventures (Axtell et al. 2000). These results confirm evidence from previous studies in which job autonomy usually increases individuals' motivation, which consequently enhances employee probability to engage in entrepreneurial activities within existing organizations (Shane et al. 2003; Marvel et al. 2007; de Jong et al. 2011).

4.4.2 The Moderation Effect of the Work Environment

The moderation effect of the work environment (*job autonomy*) on the relationship between generic human capital (*higher education*) and the creation of an organizational spin-off is shown in Model 3 (Table 4.1). Similar to the results presented in Model 1, the effect of a higher level of education on the creation of organizational spin-offs, in this case mediated by job autonomy, is negative and statistically not significant. In other words, even though employees perceive a positive work environment, it does not reinforce their entrepreneurial behavior to participate actively in the creation of a spin-off for their employer. Based on these results, Spanish employees with a higher level of education may show a higher opportunity cost of becoming an intrapreneur than continue as an employee for the organization, which could be explained by the perception of opportunity cost (higher individual risk) influenced by the economical uncertainty (higher levels of unemployment). Based on that, there is not enough evidence to support the H3a stating that Spanish employees with a higher level of education, mediated by the perception of their work environment, are more likely to engage in the creation of organizational spin-offs than employees with a lower level of education.

On the other hand, the moderation effect of work environment (*job autonomy*) on the relationship between specific human capital (*entrepreneurship education training*) and the creation of an organizational spin-off is shown in Model 3 (Table 4.1). Interestingly, the moderation effect of job autonomy on the relationship between entrepreneurship education and the creation of an organizational spin-off is a positive effect and statistically significant (2.373; $p<0.100$). This implies that employees who have received entrepreneurship education training (i.e., have specific skills, abilities, and knowledge that reinforce their self-efficacy) and simultaneously perceive job autonomy (i.e., independence to take decisions in their daily activities) are more likely to become intrapreneurs and lead the development/creation of new venture from and for an existing organization (i.e., their employer or parent firm). This result confirms and complements the previous findings about the roles of entrepreneurship education (Davidsson and Honig 2003; Kuratko 2005; Van der Sluis et al. 2006; Van der Sluis and Van Praag 2007) and job autonomy (Axtell et al. 2000; Hornsby et al. 2002; Arnold et al. 2007; Rosso et al. 2010) on entrepreneurial activities. Therefore, this evidence supports H3b, which states that employees with entrepreneurship education, mediated by the perception of job autonomy, are more likely to engage in creating an organizational spin-off than employees without entrepreneurship education training.

4.5 Conclusions and Implications

On one hand, previous studies showed that human capital (generic and specific) was a relevant individual factor during the creation of independent new ventures and corporate ventures (Parker 2011). On the other hand, prior studies also found that certain work environment characteristics could increase/retard the propensity to engage in entrepreneurial activities (Zahra et al. 1999; Hornsby et al. 2002; de Jong et al. 2011). The main objective of this exploratory study is to understand the roles of employee human capital and the work environment on the creation of spin-offs "from" and "for" an existing organization. Modestly, this study contributes to the corporate entrepreneurship literature by exploring not only the direct but also the moderation effect of work environment on the relationship between human capital and the creation of organizational spin-offs. Our results show that under uncertainty economic conditions (i.e., the economic recession experienced in Spain), the opportunity cost of employees to participate actively in the development of entrepreneurial activities promoted by the employer (the support of an existing organization with an entrepreneurial orientation) would be influenced by their specific human capital (the skills, abilities, experience, and knowledge required to be entrepreneurs) and their perception of job autonomy (the motivation and independence of making their own decision). In other words, employees believe that they who do not feel confident about their skills, experience, and knowledge would prefer to explore new professional opportunities to be promoted within the organization.

This paper presents several limitations that allow for the further exploration of this phenomenon in future research. For instance, it is important to include other variables related to the work environment (i.e., individual rewards, salary, antiquity, etc.), organizational level (i.e., size, type, sector, etc.) and country level (i.e., economic conditions). A natural extension is to analyze the effect of several external environmental factors on the creation of organizational spin-offs (Miller 1983; Covin and Slevin 1991; Zahra 1991; Antoncic and Hisrich 2001). Moreover, it is relevant to explore the performance of these organizational spin-offs with respect to similar independent ventures (Klepper 2001). Finally, the main managerial implications for Spanish organizations with an entrepreneurial orientation will be to adopt training policies that reinforce the entrepreneurial skills of their employees as well as ensuring that the work environment provides more independence to those talented and entrepreneurial employees who are involved in the development of innovative/entrepreneurial projects. The implications for policy makers will be oriented to provide evidence about the relevance of entrepreneurship education training; therefore, it is important to provide not only entrepreneurship education at different levels of education but also incentives to those existing organizations with entrepreneurial orientation.

Acknowledgments A previous version of this paper was presented at the 2013 RENT Conference that took place at the University of Management and Economics in Vilnius, Lithuania on November 20–22. We are grateful to the anonymous reviewers for their helpful and constructive comments. Maribel Guerrero and Iñaki Peña acknowledge the funding received from Global Entrepreneurship Research Association (GERA), Basque Ministry of Education, Basque Government and SPRI Group (Saiotek 2012–2013).

4.6 Correlation Matrix

No	Variable	Mean	SD	1	2	3	4	5	6
1	Organizational spin-offs	0.004	0.070	1					
2	Higher education	0.464	0.498	−0.021ᵗ	1				
3	Entrepreneurship education	0.263	0.440	0.054***	0.053***	1			
4	Job autonomy	0.267	0.442	0.067***	0.015	0.079***	1		
5	Age	44.809	8.335	0.005	−0.068***	−0.081***	0.051***	1	
6	Gender	0.524	0.499	0.022ᵗ	−0.138***	0.010	0.037***		1

Note: ***$p \leq 0.001$, **$p \leq 0.01$, *$p \leq 0.05$, ᵗ$p \leq 0.1$

References

Ajzen I (1991) The theory of planned behavior. Organ Behav Hum Decis Process 50:179–211

Antoncic B, Hisrich RD (2001) Intrapreneurship: construct refinement and cross-cultural validation. J Bus Ventur 16:495–527

Arnold KA, Turner N, Barling J, Kelloway EK, McKee MC (2007) Transformational leadership and psychological well-being: the mediating role of meaningful work. J Occup Health Psychol 12:193–203

Axtell CM, Holman DJ, Unsworth KL, Wall TD, Waterson PE, Harrington E (2000) Shopfloor innovation: facilitating the suggestion and implementation of ideas. J Occup Organ Psychol 73(3):265–285

Becker GS (1964) Human capital. The University of Chicago Press, Chicago

Bellu R, Davidsson P, Goldfarb C (1990) Toward a theory of entrepreneurial behavior: empirical evidence from Israel, Italy, and Sweden. Entrep Reg Dev 2(2):195–209

Bindl UK, Parker SK (2010) Proactive work behaviour: forward-thinking and change-oriented action in organizations. In: APA handbook of industrial and organizational psychology, vol 2. American Psychological Association, Washington, DC, pp 567–598

Blanchflower DG (2004) Self-employment: more may not be better, no. w10286. National Bureau of Economic Research, Cambridge

Bosma NS, Levie J (2010) Global entrepreneurship monitor 2009. Executive report. Babson College, Babson Park

Bosma NS, Stam FC, Wennekers ARM (2010) Intrapreneurship: an international study. Scales, Utrecht University, Utrecht

Brockhaus RH (1982) The psychology of the entrepreneur. In: Kent CA, Sexton DL, Vespers ICH (eds) Encyclopedia of entrepreneurship. Prentice-Hall, Englewood Cliffs

Covin JG, Slevin D (1991) A conceptual model of entrepreneurship as firm behavior. Entrep Theory Pract 16(1):7–25

Davidsson P (1995) Determinants of entrepreneurial intentions. In: RENT IX conference, Piacenza, Italy

Davidsson P, Honig B (2003) The role of social and human capital among nascent entrepreneurs. J Bus Ventur 18(3):301–331

De Jong JPJ, Parker S, Wenneker S, Wu C (2011) Corporate entrepreneurship at the individual level: measurement and determinants. In: EIM research reports. EIM, Zoetermeer

Delmar F, Davidsson P (2000) Where do they come from? Prevalence and characteristics of nascent entrepreneurs. Entrep Reg Dev 12:1–23

Dess GG, Lumpkin GT, McGee JE (1999) Linking corporate entrepreneurship to strategy, structure, and process: suggested research directions. Entrep Theory Pract 23(3):85–102

Dyer FC, Dickinson JA (1994) Development of sun compensation by honeybees: how partially experienced bees estimate the sun's course. Proc Natl Acad Sci 91(10):4471–4474

European Commission (2006) Entrepreneurship education in Europe: fostering entrepreneurial mindsets through education and learning. In: Final proceedings of the conference on entrepreneurship education in Oslo

Evans D, Leighton L (1989) Some empirical aspects of entrepreneurship. Am Econ Rev 79:519–535

Freeman J, Engel JS (2007) Models of innovation: startups and mature corporations. Calif Manage Rev 50(1):94–119

Fuller JB, Marler LE, Hester K (2006) Promoting felt responsibility for constructive change and proactive behavior: exploring aspects of an elaborated model of work design. J Organ Behav 27:1089–1120

Gasse Y (1982) Elaborations on the psychology of the entrepreneur. In: Kent CA, Sexton DL, Vespers KH (eds) Encyclopedia of entrepreneurship. Prentice-Hall, Englewood Cliffs

Gimeno J, Folta T, Cooper A, Woo C (1997) Survival of the fittest? Entrepreneurial human capital and the persistence of underperforming firms. Adm Sci Q 42:750–783

Gorman G, Hanlon D, King W (1997) Some research perspectives on entrepreneurship education, enterprise education and education for small business management: a ten-year literature review. Int Small Bus J 15(3):56–77

Grilo I, Thurik AR (2008) Determinants of entrepreneurial engagement levels in Europe and the US. Ind Corp Change 17(6):1113–1145

Harpaz I, Fu X (2002) The structure of the meaning of work: a relative stability amidst change. Hum Relat 55:639–667

Hisrich RD, Peters MP (1986) Establishing a new business venture unit within a firm. J Bus Ventur 1(3):307–322

Honig B (1996) Education and self-employment in Jamaica. Comp Educ Rev 40(2):177–193
Hornsby JS, Naffziger DW, Kuratko DF, Montagno RV (1993) An interactive model of the corporate entrepreneurship process. Entrep Theory Pract 17(2):29–37
Hornsby JS, Kuratko DF, Montagno RV (1999) Perception of internal factors for corporate entrepreneurship: a comparison of Canadian and U.S. managers. Entrep Theory Pract 24(2):9–24
Hornsby JS, Kuratko DF, Zahra SA (2002) Middle managers' perception of the internal environment for corporate entrepreneurship: assessing a measurement scale. J Bus Ventur 17(3):253–273
Kanter RM (1985) Supporting innovation and venture development in established companies. J Bus Ventur 1:47–60
Karlan D, Valdivia M (2011) Teaching entrepreneurship: impact of business training on microfinance clients and institutions. Rev Econ Stat 93(2):510–527
King G, Zeng L (2001a) Logistic regression in rare events data. Polit Anal 9(2):137–163
King G, Zeng L (2001b) Explaining rare events in international relations. Int Organ 55(3):693–715
Klepper S (2001) Employee start-ups in high-tech industries. Ind Corp Change 10:639–674
Koellinger P (2008) Why are some entrepreneurs more innovative than others? Small Bus Econ 31(1):21–37
Kuratko DF (2005) The emergence of entrepreneurship education: development, trends, and challenges. Entrep Theory Pract 29(5):577–598
Kuratko D, Montagno RV, Hornsby J (1990) Developing an intrapreneurial assessment instrument for an effective corporate entrepreneurial environment. Strateg Manage J 11:49–58
LePine JA, Van Dyne L (1998) Predicting voice behavior in work groups. J Appl Psychol 83(6):853–868
Levie J, Autio E (2008) A theoretical grounding and test of the GEM model. Small Bus Econ 31(3):235–263
Lindholm Å (1994). The Economics of Technology-Related Ownership Changes. A study of innovativeness and growth through acquisitions and spin-offs. Chalmers University of Technology
Marvel MR, Griffin A, Hebda J, Vojak B (2007) Examining the technical corporate entrepreneurs' motivation: voices from the field. Entrep Theory Pract 31(5):753–768
Miller D (1983) The correlates of entrepreneurship in three types of firms. Manag Sci 29(7):770–791
Naman JL, Slevin DP (1993) Entrepreneurship and the concept of fit: a model and empirical tests. Strateg Manage J 14:137–153
Narayanan VK, Yang Y, Zahra SA (2009) Corporate venturing and value creation: a review and proposed framework. Res Policy 38(1):58–76
Nord WR, Brief AP, Atieh JM, Doherty EM (1990) Studying meanings of work: the case of work values. In: Brief A, Nord W (eds) Meanings of occupational work: a collection of essays. Lexington Books, Lexington
Oosterbeek H, van Praag M, Ijsselstein A (2010) The impact of entrepreneurship education on entrepreneurship skills and motivation. Eur Econ Rev 54(3):442–454
Parhankangas A, Arenius P (2003) From a corporate venture to an independent company: a base for a taxonomy for corporate spin-off firms. Res Policy 32(3):463–481
Parker SC (2009) The economics of entrepreneurship. Cambridge University Press, Cambridge
Parker SC (2011) Intrapreneurship or entrepreneurship? J Bus Ventur 26(1):19–34
Polanyi M (1967) The tacit dimension. Routledge and Kegan, London
Reynolds PD (1997) Who starts new firms? Preliminary explorations of firms-in-gestation. Small Bus Econ 9(5):449–462
Reynolds P, Bosma N, Autio E, Hunt S, De Bono N, Servais I, Chin N (2005) Global entrepreneurship monitor: data collection design and implementation 1998–2003. Small Bus Econ 24:205–231
Rosso BD, Dekas KH, Wrzesniewski A (2010) On the meaning of work: a theoretical integration and review. Res Organ Behav 30:91–127

Rutherford MW, Holt DT (2007) Corporate entrepreneurship: an empirical look at the innovativeness dimension and its antecedents. J Organ Chang Manag 20(3):429–446

Sathe V (1985) Managing an entrepreneurial dilemma: nurturing entrepreneurship and control in large corporations. In: Hornaday JA, Shils EB, Timmons JA, Vesper KH (eds) Frontiers of entrepreneurship research. Babson College, Wellesley

Sexton DL, Kent CA (1981) Female executives and entrepreneurs: a preliminary comparison. In: Proceedings of the entrepreneurship research conference

Shane S, Venkataraman S (2000) The promise of entrepreneurship as a field of research. Acad Manage Rev 25(1):217–226

Shane S, Locke EA, Collins CJ (2003) Entrepreneurial motivation. Hum Resour Manag Rev 13(2):257–279

Souitaris V, Zerbinati S, Al Laham A (2007) Do entrepreneurship programmes raise entrepreneurial intention of science and engineering students? The effect of learning, inspiration and resources. J Bus Ventur 22(4):566–591

Stevenson HH, Jarillo JC (1990) A paradigm of entrepreneurship: entrepreneurial management. Strateg Manage J 11(5):17–27

Trapido D (2004) Binding conflict: the competition-to-cooperation switch in firm dyads. Working paper

Unger JM, Rauch A, Frese M, Rosenbusch N (2011) Human capital and entrepreneurial success. A meta-analytical review. J Bus Ventur 26(3):341–358

Van der Sluis J, Van Praag CM (2007) Returns to education for entrepreneurs and employees: identification by means of changes in compulsory schooling laws. Working paper, University of Amsterdam, Netherlands

Van der Sluis J, Van Praag M, Van Witteloostuijn A (2006) Why are the returns to education higher for entrepreneurs than for employees? Working paper, University of Amsterdam, Netherlands

Zahra SA (1991) Predictors and financial outcomes of corporate entrepreneurship: an exploratory study. J Bus Ventur 6(4):259–285

Zahra SA, Covin JG (1995) Contextual influences on the corporate entrepreneurship–performance relationship: a longitudinal analysis. J Bus Ventur 10:43–58

Zahra SA, Nielsen AP, Bogner WC (1999) Corporate entrepreneurship knowledge and competence development. Entrep Theory Pract 23:169–189

Chapter 5
Early-Stage Businesses, Resource Inheritance, and Coworkers Hiring: The Moderating Role of Founder's Human Capital

Emeran Nziali and Alain Fayolle

Abstract The role of firm's resources or specifically knowledge in achieving sustained competitive advantage has been well established in strategic management literature. To strengthen their competitive advantage, extent or enrich their knowledge base, firms used to hire people embedding appropriate human capital. Whereas the nature of this competitive advantage has been largely investigated, it is not exactly the case for the processes or conditions through which firms used to construct it. This paper wants to contribute to a better understanding of how it is constructed by investigating, how far the resource that spinoff already has constrained, or determine the acquisition of next ones.

We are considering spinoffs and spinouts as two distinct configurations of knowledge inheritance with the former being different from the latter in that s(he) benefits from additional support of financial or physical nature from its previous employer. Nevertheless, nothing is clear on the respective role of knowledge the spinoffs/spinouts have inherited from mother firm or industry and that of the founders leading the business creation process—namely her/his human capital. We hypothesize a greater preference for coworkers hiring in case of greater inheritance of resources from a mother company. The propensity of spinoffs/spinouts to hire founders' previous coworkers should be greater than that of other entrants but moderating effect should be expected giving a relative importance to person who is hiring.

First results come with new evidences supporting old arguments of some resource-based views of scholars regarding the importance of resources that characterizes a firm and its position in terms of competitive advantage. These evidences are compelling for they suggest that the phenomenon already begin at firm's early stage and extends it on preoccupations of first hires. Other results are also interesting in understanding the contribution of the status of some new businesses in worker mobility, knowledge diffusion, competition between spinoffs/spinouts and mother firms, and in a certain sense cluster dynamics.

E. Nziali (✉) • A. Fayolle
EMLYON Business School, Écully, France
e-mail: NZIALI@em-lyon.com; fayolle@em-lyon.com

R. Baptista, J. Leitão (eds.), *Entrepreneurship, Human Capital, and Regional Development*, International Studies in Entrepreneurship 31,
DOI 10.1007/978-3-319-12871-9_5

Keywords Clusters dynamics • Coworkers • Human capital • Mobility • Spinoffs • Spinouts

5.1 Introduction

The role of firm's resources or specifically knowledge in achieving sustained competitive advantage and business performance has been well established in strategic management literature (Barney 1991; Decarolis and Deeds 1999, Argote and Ingram 2000). To strengthen their competitive advantage or extent or enrich their knowledge base, firms used to hire appropriate people embedding human capital. The hiring process depicting therefore a dimension of the knowledge competition firms are going through worker mobility, knowledge diffusion or cluster dynamics, are such resource related phenomenon for their effectiveness is partly fueled by the knowledge competition firms are experiencing in order to mobilize or capture appropriate human capital or knowledge bases to develop their competitive advantage.

Whereas the nature this competitive advantage has been largely investigated—through the internal analysis of firms' resources, for example—it is not exactly the case for the processes or conditions through which firms construct this advantage. Specific configurations are those where the acquisition of new resource is constrained by the existence of previous one. This is mostly observed in early-stage of business life where entrepreneurs do not have the legacy of resource strengths (Brush et al. 2001) so as to be involved in the collection of strategic ones and construct the competitive advantage. Reversely, in the case of effectiveness of this legacy there's not always a good assessment of the specific role of the entrepreneur. Evidences on the construct of competitive advantage in early-stage are rare but the actual interest in spinoffs or spinouts can provide the means to fill this gap by investigating how resource inheritance, founder's human capital and first hire are related.

This paper wants to contribute to a better understanding of the construct of competitive advantage—and its related effects such as worker mobility—by investigating how far the resource that a spinoff already has constrained or determine the acquisition of next ones. The strength of these inherited resources is to be related to the founder's human capital in early-stage hiring process. In fact resource inheritance happens when a founder having a previous experience as employee decides to rely on this later to create a new business. It can result from a disagreement between the founder and his former employer (Klepper 2007; Klepper and Thompson 2010) but also as a specific strategy when most appropriated for the development of the new business (Parker 2011). We are considering spinoffs and spinouts as two distinct configurations of knowledge inheritance with the former distinct from the latter in that it benefits from additional support of financial or physical nature from its previous employer (Koster and Wissen 2006; Bager et al. 2010).

Recent evidences on the role of spinoffs in clusters dynamics highlight the fact that they rely on their mother industry or firms as natural place to hire at early-stage experienced workers (Cheyre et al. 2013) in general previous founders' coworkers. Nevertheless, nothing is clear on the respective role of knowledge they have inherited from mother firm or industry and that of the founders leading the business creation process—namely her/his human capital. In addition, if one considers the largest domain of business performance, this role of founder's human capital has been investigated for early-stage business (Cooper et al. 1994; Colombo and Grilli 2010) but with less interest given to the resource and knowledge contexts surrounding the new firm.

We hypothesize a greater preference for coworkers hiring in case of greater inheritance of resources from a mother company. The propensity of spinoffs/spinouts to hire founders' previous coworkers should be greater than that of other entrants but moderating effect should be expected giving a relative importance to person who is hiring.

We rely on a data set from the 2011 Global Entrepreneurship Monitor's Survey and logit techniques to investigate the question. We seize it in a sample of 9,234 early-stage entrepreneurs of which 1,024 spinoff's founders from 52 countries declaring whether or not they are going to hire a previous coworker (HC). Declarations on coworkers hiring are complemented with that on various forms of human capital and additional controls.

The next section comes with a brief review of the relevant literature and the details of our hypotheses. The third section discusses the methodology and data whereas the fourth presents the results. The last section includes a discussion and conclusion.

5.2 Literature Review and Hypotheses

5.2.1 Resources Inheritance and Coworker Hiring

There's an agreement on how firms' resources should be related to their performance. Namely the former are expected to provide firm with competitive advantage required for the latter. In so far, new ventures inheriting some resources are supposed to have some advantage over those not inheriting. Two configurations of inheritance are generally mentioned referring either to the case an employee leaves his firm and create a new business or the one where the founder envisions the same but is working in collaboration with his/her employer, receiving additional support to launch the new business.

In this study, we assume a good hiring strategy is a necessary condition for new business performance due to the key role associated with human capital embedded in hired people. Support for this argument is easily founded in resource-based view literature (Penrose 1959; West and Noel 2009) or human resource management literature. There's a higher degree of exigency for new firms in early-stage hiring since they are in need of basic organizational knowledge which have to transit within their bosom (Wiklund and Shepherd 2003) so that hiring has to be to the height of the expected performance.

(a) Considering inheritance of knowledge bases by new firms
For their first hires, firms have to choose between unskilled employees—that have to be trained—or experienced ones. The first option as it is costly and time consuming is in general avoided unless if the new firm has no choice. In case of inheritance, and then of relatedness of the knowledge bases of the new firm with those of some incumbents, the hiring process is constrained, suggesting some competition between the new and old firms. The relatedness of knowledge bases is supposed to impact the hiring process in the sense that the two groups will target the same human capital bases, and compete in hiring similar workers, generally issued from the Mother Company or industry. Actual experienced workers and somehow founder's coworkers have to be candidates but, the former have to be the main for they are already in founder network (Johanisson 1998).

To approach the concept of knowledge inheritance we have distinguished between spinoffs, spinouts, and traditional entrepreneurship. The last one is distinct from the former for it is not explicitly related to the knowledge base of an incumbent or an experience of the founder as former employee. We hypothesize, because of knowledge inheritance, and then relatedness of knowledge bases that the new businesses will tend to hire more workers from their mother firm or industry than classic entrepreneurs will do. That is:

H1: Spinoffs and spinouts hire more founders' previous coworkers than classical entrepreneurs

(b) Receiving additional support from mother company
In spite of knowledge inheritance, some differences may still exist between inheriting new venturing firms due to the relative strategy they choose to set up the firm. Some of them should have received financial or physical support from mother firm (spinoff) and some others should not have received (spinout). We expect the additional support to impact the hiring process in the sense that beneficiaries endowed with more resources will have a greater advantage, increasing their capacity to hire.

One can argue that the close connection between the beneficiaries and the supporting firm can somehow come with some problems for hiring a coworker will strengthen the strategy of the new firm but dampen that of the mother company in the sense that the latter could experience a human capital loss. Nevertheless, we assume the benefit of some support from the mother company come with another message: it gives the means to the founder to hire workers and work with them as colleagues from the beginning in the early days of the business project or the gestation phase. In so far the coworker to be hired can therefore be supposed to work on this specific project but as entity of Mother Company which is supposed to end in spinoffs. Letting such employees go will probably dampen the mother firm performance but not more than the spinoff creation will do. We therefore expect the benefit of a financial or physical support to increase the degree of hire of a coworker.

H2: Spinoffs hire more founders' previous coworkers than spinouts do

5.2.2 Boundary Role of Human Capital

As we have mentioned earlier, this study does not seek to provide evidence of positive effects of resource inheritance on coworkers hiring only, but seeks to investigate the moderating effect of human capital on this advantage also. Specifically we are interested in whether resource inheritance effects can be heightened or dampened by founder's human capital.

In general, literature supports the thesis of a direct positive effect of founder's human capital or founding teams on firm performance. In these cases, performance refers either to firm growth (Colombo and Grilli 2010), profit, created employment and hazard out of business (Bosma et al. 2004) or start-up process completion (Davidsson and Honig 2003). As for previous direct effects, human capital of partners has also been found to have indirect and positive effect on profitability of firms (Hitt et al. 2001). In this last case authors argue that performance is attained through the construct of competitive advantage as it is the case in resource-based view, but supported by no evidence.

Regarding the degree of human capital impact, while some authors argue that it is overemphasized (Baum and Silverman 2004), others state that it constitutes one of the core factors in the entrepreneurial process (Haber and Reichel 2007). This disagreement manifests itself through the magnitude of coefficients and conceptualization of research. In their meta-analysis of the role of human capital in entrepreneurship, Unger et al. (2011) considers all these differences—type of human capital, performance measures, and the construct of their related studies—and still found positive and significant relations between human capital and performance but with many moderators. Two major forms of human capital were identified: investment (education/experience) and outcomes (knowledge/skills) but the former have been found to have lower effect on performance than the latter.

After defining human capital as skills and knowledge that individuals acquire through investments in schooling, on-the-job training, and other types of experience (Becker 1964), we will distinguish between those two categories of human capital attributes: investment and outcomes. Human capital investments include experiences such as education and work experience that may or not lead to knowledge and skills, whereas outcomes of human capital investments are acquired knowledge and skills.

Contrary to the other research emphasizing the degree of human capital, this study focus is on the possession of specific types. As far as early-stage hire may have to be considered as a condition for business performance, we expect the possession of any type of human capital to complement the effect of inheritance of resources. This complementing effect is so that not having this specific type of human capital will inhibit coworker hiring. We are interested in four types of human capital: education level, experience in entrepreneurship, previous employee experience, and entrepreneurial skills: the latter is considered as an outcome and the formers as human capital investment. We hypothesize:

H3: Founder's education level will moderate H1 and H2 such that the lower is the education level the higher is the weakening of positive effect issued from resource inheritance

H4: Founder's experience in entrepreneurship will moderate H1 and H2 such that an absence of entrepreneurial experience (relatively of possessing it) will weaken positive effects from resource inheritance

H5: Founder's experience as an employee will moderate H1 and H2 such that an absence of previous employee experience (relatively of having it) will weaken positive effects from resource inheritance

H6: Founder's entrepreneurial skills will moderate H1 and H2 such that a lack of entrepreneurial skills (relatively of possessing it) will weaken positive effects from resource inheritance

Hypotheses are summarized in the graph below.

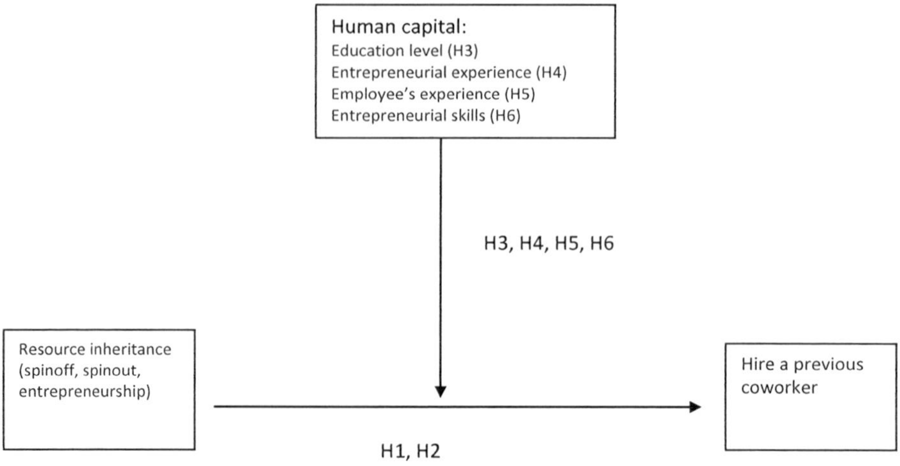

5.3 Method

5.3.1 Sample

To investigate how resource inheritance and human capital are related with coworkers hiring we have collected data from the 2011 cycle of Global Entrepreneurship Monitor's Survey. Originally it consists of a total of 162,724 respondents, spread on 55 countries[1] with each country encountering no less than 2,000 respondents. Seventeen thousand nine hundred and thirteen people of the total declared to be involved in early-stage entrepreneurial activity might it be the nascent (less than 3 months of existence) or the start-up phase (between 3 and 42 months).

Since specific types of entrepreneurship namely spinoff, spinout and start-up can be depicted it enables to formalize the height of resource inheritance. We split the pool of early-stage entrepreneurs accordingly, distinguishing first those whom the experience as employees was the basis for their business creation, and among them those who received some financial or physical support from their previous employer to launch their business. This group is distinct from another one composed of those who created a business with their own idea and received no support from their previous employer. We pay attention to the fact that all entrepreneurs were working or not before involving in the new business so that there should be or not some coworkers in their network. Their decision to hire or not one of them results from the degree they are not considering them as strategically useful to their business.

Entrepreneurs who didn't know if they received or not some support or who refused to answer were excluded from the data set. We did the same with their business ideas, how far it was related or not to that of their previous firms. This is necessary for a better quality of the sample so as to appreciate the degree to which entrepreneurs have or not to compete with their previous employer (or parent firm) for previous coworkers relying on their professional network.

Finally in spite of the choice of some people to be involved as spinoff or not, it remains that countries differ in the degree that they develop this activity broadly speaking. As a case point spinoff represents 29.4 % versus 1.8 % of total early-stage activity respectively in United Arab Emirates and in Guatemala. For we are interested in nascent and start-up stages of business development we consider that each stage has to be represented at country level (a rate different from zero), and no country has to display less than 5 % of spinoff in the total share of entrepreneurial activity; if not it does not have to remain in the sample. In so far we have excluded Belgium (no spinoff in nascent phase), Guatemala, and Bosnia-and-Herzegovina

[1] United Arab Emirates, Argentina, Australia, Bosnia and Herzegovina, Barbados, Bangladesh, Belgium, Brazil, Chile, China, Colombia, Czech Republic, Germany, Denmark, Algeria, Spain, Finland, France, Greece, Guatemala, Croatia, Hungary, Ireland, Iran, Jamaica, Japan, Korea, Lithuania, Latvia, Mexico, Malaysia, Nigeria, Netherlands, Norway, Panama, Peru, Pakistan, Poland, Portugal, Romania, Russia, Sweden, Singapore, Slovenia, Slovakia, Switzerland, Thailand, Turkey, Trinidad and Tobago, Taiwan, United Kingdom, United States, Uruguay, Venezuela, South Africa.

(no spinoff in start-up phase). At the end we obtained the sample, a total of 9,234 early-stage entrepreneurs of which 1,024 spinoff (11 %), 3,825 spinouts (41.2 %), and 4,435 classic new venturing (47.8 %).

5.3.2 *Dependent Variable*

5.3.2.1 Hire a Previous Coworker

The founder's hiring strategy is supposed to target only previous coworkers for they are the most experienced and embed human capital most appropriated for their business project. In so far, all respondents were asked if they have already hired, or planned to hire one of their previous coworkers. It is a binary variable which takes the value 1 in case of "yes" and 0 otherwise.

5.3.3 *Independent Variables*

Main independents are of two groups with the first one referring to the status of the new business in terms of resource inheritance and the second to human capital type.

5.3.3.1 New Business Status

Given that the new firm has the possibility to inherit both knowledge and additional support from mother firm, inherit only knowledge or not inherit at all, each new business is identified as one of these three types respectively spinoff (3), spinout (2), and classical new firm or start-up (1). The numbers in brackets are their respective codes in the variable with one being the referent category.

5.3.3.2 Human Capital

Four variables are considered for human capital: education level, previous experience as employee, some experience in entrepreneurship, and the fact to have or not the skills for entrepreneurship. As for the former variables these ones are issued from Global Entrepreneurship Monitor 2011 survey. Their attributes appear in the table below (Table 5.1). Educational level refers to the highest level of education reached by the respondent at the time of the survey; employee experience refers to the fact of being in employment in the period of the creation. To be considered as having an experience in entrepreneurship, the respondents have to declare to have participated in a setting up of a business or exit from a business in the last 12 months. Finally having or not entrepreneurial skills is a matter of self-assessment by the respondent.

Table 5.1 Data description

Variable	Description
Hire a coworker (HC)	=1 if the founders have already hired a coworker or is planning to do so, 0 otherwise
New business status (NBS)	=1 if classical new firm, 2 for spinout, and 3 for spinoff
Education level	Preprimary education (0), primary education or first stage of basic education (1), lower secondary or second stage of basic education (2), (upper) secondary education (3), post-secondary non-tertiary education (4), first stage of tertiary education (5), second stage of tertiary education (6)
Entrepreneurial skills	=1 if the respondent declares having the knowledge, skills, and experience required to start a business, otherwise
Entrepreneurial experience	=1 if the past 12 months the founder has closed, shut down a business, or done anything to help start a business, 0 otherwise
Employee experience	=1 if the founders declares to be in employment when creating the business
Age	Age of the respondent: a continuous variable
Gender	=1 if female and 0 otherwise
Income	Income categories: low (first third: lowest) middle (medium level); upper (third third)
Technology sector	=1 if medium or high technology sector, =0 for no/low technology sector
Country level development category	Factor driven (1); efficiency driven (2); innovation driven (3)

5.3.4 Control Variables

We consider five controls related to both individual characteristics—such as gender, age, and income level—and context variables such as the technological appraisal of the sector of creation and the country category of development (Table 5.1).

The effect of age on performance is contrasted; on one hand seniors are supposed to be less efficient than younger individuals but due to the time they spent working they are supposed to have more resources—that is means for performance—than them. The key should rest in the consideration of performance but in any consideration, having already considered resource inheritance hiring more coworkers should be perceived as a contribution to it. As for age one of the keys for the appreciation of gender effect on performance will reside in the understanding of performance (Cliff 1998) but hiring coworker seems to be critical stage. The income level of founder is supposed to impact positively the business performance. Finally technological characteristics of an entering industry might also explain the more or less growth expectations and may be performance (Sandberg and Hofer 1987).

5.4 Results

We provide in Table 5.2 cross values (and ratios) of new business status (NBS) or resource inheritance with that of coworkers hired. It suggests that spinoffs come with the smallest number (1,022) but the highest rate of coworkers hired (69 %) contrary to classic new firms which are in the greatest number (4,832) but the lowest share of respondents declaring to hire coworkers (29 %).

Table 5.3 (below) displays intercorrelations of all the variables we described and some of them are notable. For example the correlation between the dependant hire a coworker (HC) and the main explicative NBS is negative suggesting that the ranking of categories between HC and NBS are globally inverted; each of the three NBS has to be associated with different behaviors in terms of coworker hiring. In spite of the difference in their internal structure, the height of the coefficient remains high (0.25) and meaningful denoting a net effect and the importance in considering the link between the two variables. The value of this coefficient is the highest of all intercorrelations with NBS—followed by that entrepreneurial experience—confirming our intuition to consider it as the main explicative so as to investigate the moderating effect of human capital additionally.

Since the correlation of Entrepreneurial experience and NBS comes with a high and positive value (0.10) it appears as the most interesting attribute of human capital to examine. Nevertheless, it remains low (independent) so as the intercorrelations with the three other human capital variables. Finally, the intercorrelations (exception of those mentioned above) between all the independent are very low, suggesting these variables can be included simultaneously in regressions while avoiding problems of multicollinearity.

To test our hypothesis, we have run logistic regressions with SPSS and several problems—such as multicollinearity among the independent variables, zero cells for a dummy-coded independent variable because all of the subjects have the same value for the variable, etc. and "complete separation" whereby the three groups in the dependent event variable can be perfectly separated by scores on one of the independent variables—can occur without being detected. In general they produce large standard errors (over 2) for the variables included in the analysis and very often produce very large *B* coefficients as well. As it appears in Tables 5.4 and 5.5 below, none of the standard errors or *B* coefficients is excessively large, so there is no evidence of a numeric problem with the analysis.

Table 5.2 Spinoff, spinout, and their degree of founder's coworker hiring

		No		Yes		Total	
		Number	%	Number	%	Number	%
New business status	Classic new firms	3,146	71	1,286	29	4,432	48
	Spinouts	1,991	52	1,831	48	3,822	41
	Spinoffs	314	31	708	69	1,022	11
	Total	5,451	59	3,825	41	9,276	100

Table 5.3 Correlations[a]

Variables	1	2	3	4	5	6	7	8	9
1. Hiring a coworker									
2. New business status	−0.25**								
3. Education level	−0.01	−0.03**							
4. Entrepreneurial experience	0.10**	0.05**	0.02*						
5. Entrepreneurial skills	−0.02**	0.02**	0.03**	0.08**					
6. Employee experience	−0.00	−0.04**	−0.04**	0.03**	−0.01				
7. Technological sector	−0.02*	0.00	0.10**	0.02	0.01	−0.00			
8. Country group	−0.08**	−0.01	0.25**	−0.14**	0.01	−0.07**	0.08**		
9. Gender	0.09**	−0.08**	0.04**	−0.04**	−0.04**	−0.01	−0.08**	0.00	
10. Income	−0.04**	−0.01	0.24**	0.04**	0.08**	−0.03**	0.04**	0.01	−0.07**

[a]Tau of Kendall; $*p<0.05$; $**p<0.01$

Table 5.4 Coworkers hiring; knowledge inheritance and human capital

Variables	*B*	Erreur std.	Wald	Signif.	Exp(*B*)
Age	−0.001	0.002	0.425	0.514	0.999
[NBS = 1]	−0.428	0.182	5.518	0.019	0.652
[NBS = 2]	0.355	0.183	3.771	0.052	1.426
[NBS = 3]	1.301	0.193	45.357	0.000	3.674
[e.experience = 0]	0.612	0.056	119.967	0.000	1.844
[e.skills = 0]	−0.173	0.067	6.662	0.010	0.841
[educlevel = 0]	0.258	0.182	2.004	0.157	1.295
[educlevel = 1]	−0.148	0.173	0.736	0.391	0.862
[educlevel = 2]	−0.103	0.142	0.522	0.470	0.903
[educlevel = 3]	−0.010	0.126	0.007	0.933	0.990
[educlevel = 4]	−0.123	0.131	0.873	0.350	0.885
[educlevel = 5]	−0.077	0.126	0.371	0.542	0.926
[em.experience = 0]	0.190	0.096	3.907	0.048	1,209
[gender = 0]	−0.342	0.052	42,875	0.000	0.710
[sector = 0]	−0.129	0.108	1.434	0.231	0.879
[CAT_GCR2 = 1]	−0.673	0.102	43.336	0.000	0.510
[CAT_GCR2 = 2]	−0.172	0.055	9.753	0.002	0.842
[Income = 33]	−0.414	0.081	25.855	0.000	0.661
[Income = 3,467]	−0.050	0.056	0.771	0.380	0.952
−2 log-vraisemblance	8308.335	Pseudo R-deux de Nagelkerke	0.159	Spécif. Modèle (Khi-Chi-deux)	965.307

Table 5.5 Moderating effects of entrepreneurial skills on new business status

Variables	*B*	Erreur std.	Wald	Signif.	Exp(*B*)
[NBS = 1] × [educlevel = 0]	−0.395	0.206	3.689	0.055	0.674
[NBS = 1] × [educlevel = 1]	−1.045	0.232	20.204	0.000	0.352
[NBS = 1] × [educlevel = 2]	−0.703	0.136	26.745	0.000	0.495
[NBS = 1] × [educlevel = 3]	−0.533	0.082	41.986	0.000	0.587
[NBS = 1] × [educlevel = 4]	−0.614	0.102	36.240	0.000	0.541
[NBS = 1] × [educlevel = 5]	−0.801	0.084	91.842	0.000	0.449
[NBS = 1] × [educlevel = 6]	−0.658	0.178	13.760	0.000	0.518
[NBS = 2] × [educlevel = 0]	0.398	0.209	3.620	0.057	1.489
[NBS = 2] × [educlevel = 1]	0.224	0.181	1.536	0.215	1.251
[NBS = 2] × [educlevel = 2]	0.031	0.123	0.063	0.802	1.031
[NBS = 2] × [educlevel = 3]	0.134	0.082	2.675	0.102	1.144
[NBS = 2] × [educlevel = 4]	−0.051	0.097	0.273	0.601	0.951
[NBS = 2] × [educlevel = 5]	0.217	0.084	6.721	0.010	1.242
[NBS = 2] × [educlevel = 6]	0.151	0.179	0.711	0.399	1.162
[NBS = 3] × [educlevel = 0]	1.593	0.317	25.215	0.000	4.918
[NBS = 3] × [educlevel = 1]	0.879	0.314	7.827	0.005	2.408
[NBS = 3] × [educlevel = 2]	1.145	0.226	25.744	0.000	3.142
[NBS = 3] × [educlevel = 3]	0.917	0.138	43.820	0.000	2.501
[NBS = 3] × [educlevel = 4]	1.047	0.179	34.303	0.000	2.848
[NBS = 3] × [educlevel = 5]	1.158	0.173	44.994	0.000	3.182
[NBS = 3] × [educlevel = 6]	1.527	0.423	13.028	0.000	4.605
−2 log-vraisemblance	8,291.506				
Pseudo R-deux de Nagelkerke	0.162				
Spécif. Modèle (Khi-Chi-deux)	982.136				

We have also checked the Likelihood Ratio Tests and Parameter Estimates. The variables "age" and "technological sector" were not really significant in explaining differences of new businesses in hiring coworkers for simple regression without interactions (Table 5.4). They have not been reintroduced in following regressions concerned with interaction variables (Table 5.5). Tables 5.4 and 5.5 below display the main results.

Regarding hypotheses, H1 predicted a greater impact on HC for spinoffs/spinouts than classic new ventures whereas H2 has specified that when considering additional support spinoffs received, the effect of the latter is the greatest.

As it is shown in Table 5.4, after accounting for our controls, we found significant and positive effects of spinoff (1.301) and spinouts (0.355). A new firm benefiting from spinoff status increases the likelihood that the founder will hire a coworker by approximately 267 and 43 % for spinouts: the two are related by a multiplicative number greater than 6 confirming H2. In contrast a business creation made through a classic canal—that is without any type of resource inheritance—decreases this likelihood of 35 % which value is lower than any of the two that we have with spinoffs or spinouts as suggested by H1.

To realize our moderation tests, each human capital variable has to interact with NBS in subsequent and different regressions including additional controls to. Tables 5.5 and 5.6 below display the output for interacting variables only and other statistics associated (properties) with the related regression.

The education level variable enters the regression significantly with most variables when interacting with spinoff (NBS=3) and classic entrepreneurship (NBS=1). These interacting variables have the statistically significant relation to distinguish founders which hire coworkers from those who do not. One can first observe that the general structure of the results parallels those we obtained without interaction (a trend of hiring coworkers for spinoff/spinout and not to hire them for classic). Nevertheless, the results are noticeable for lowest (educlevel=0) educated. In the case of spinoffs and spinouts the increase in likelihood to hire a coworker is respectively 392 % and 49 % which are the highest inside each category. For the classic entrepreneur, the decrease is only 33 % (one of the smallest). Out of the spinoff group where the second rank—in hiring coworkers—is occupied by the most educated (educlevel=6) with the other categories, this place is occupied by categories of various education levels such as the second for spinout (educlevel=2) and the third for classic entrepreneurs (educlevel=3). Since H3 was expecting education level variable to moderate H1 and H2 such that when education level is the lowest, the positive effect from resource inheritance will have to be weakened at the highest, H3 is not verified. In other words, it is not clear whether having an educational level confers any distinct advantage in strengthening or maintaining the effect from resource inheritance.

To examine H4 entrepreneurial experience variable is interacting with NBS and the results are reported in the third panel of Table 5.6. The general structure of the results is remaining the same as in earlier results in the sense coefficients from spinoffs are globally greater than the others but inside each category of NBS the results are more confused with entrepreneurs not having entrepreneurial experience (e.experience=0) having the greater trend to hire coworker. For example, when we

Table 5.6 Moderating effects of entrepreneurial skills, employees, and entrepreneurial experience

Variables	*B*	Erreur std.	Wald	Signif.	Exp(*B*)
Moderating effects of entrepreneurial skills on new business status (*Model 1*)					
[NBS = 1] × [e.skills = 0]	−0.727	0.102	51.073	0.000	0.483
[NBS = 1] × [e.skills = 1]	−0.689	0.062	123.877	0.000	0.502
[NBS = 2] × [e.skills = 0]	−0.151	0.107	1.998	0.158	0.860
[NBS = 2] × [e.skills = 1]	0.131	0.060	4.720	0.030	1.140
[NBS = 3] × [e.skills = 0]	0.809	0.186	18.930	0.000	2.246
[NBS = 3] × [e.skills = 1]	1.084	0.094	131.577	0.000	2.955
−2 log-vraisemblance	8,316.311	Pseudo R-deux de Nagelkerke	0.158	Spécif. Modèle (Khi-Chi-deux)	957.331
Moderating effects of employee experience on new business status (*Model 2*)					
[NBS = 1] × [em. experience = 0]	−0.661	0.141	21.866	0.000	0.516
[NBS = 1] × [em. experience = 1]	−0.649	0.061	113.191	0.000	0.522
[NBS = 2] × [em. experience = 0]	0.440	0.155	8.041	0.005	1.553
[NBS = 2] × [em. experience = 1]	0.104	0.059	3.086	0.079	1.110
[NBS = 3] × [em. experience = 0]	1,736	0.344	25.524	0.000	5.673
[NBS = 3] × [em. experience = 1]	1,036	0.090	132.101	0.000	2.819
−2 log-vraisemblance	8,314.195	Pseudo R-deux de Nagelkerke	0.158	Spécif. Modèle (Khi-Chi-deux)	959.447
Moderating effects of entrepreneurial experience on new business status (*Model 3*)					
[NBS = 1] × [e. experience = 0]	0.091	0.077	1.381	0.240	1.095
[NBS = 1] × [e. experience = 1]	−0.736	0.064	133.792	0.000	.479
[NBS = 2] × [e. experience = 0]	0.660	0.079	68.995	0.000	1.935
[NBS = 2] × [e. experience = 1]	0.144	0.062	5.425	0.020	1.154
[NBS = 3] × [e. experience = 0]	1.028	0.171	36.226	0.000	2.795
[NBS = 3] × [e. experience = 1]	1.212	0.096	160.128	0.000	3.360
−2 log-vraisemblance	8,293.299	Pseudo R-deux de Nagelkerke	0.161	Spécif. Modèle (Khi-Chi-deux)	980.343

are considering spinouts, the likelihood of hiring a coworker increases 15 % when having an entrepreneurial experience (e.experience = 1), whereas 93 % when not having. In contrast, in case of spinoff, it seems that the increase in likelihood to hire a coworker is greater in case of entrepreneurial experience (260 %) than in case of absence (179 %). The absence of entrepreneurial experience weakens the advantage from resource inheritance in case of spinout and classic entrepreneurship but not for spinoff which are strengthened. H4 should be considered as partially verified.

The interaction of employee experience and NBS appears in Table 5.6 (second panel). The order of effects issued from degree of resource inheritance still parallels the original one but it appears—in subcategories—that those who declare to have created their firms when in employment tend to have a lower likelihood on coworkers recruiting. H5 is not verified.

The interaction of entrepreneurial skills variable and NBS appears in the first panel of Table 5.6. It suggests that each status of new firm maintains the advantages issued from knowledge inheritance even in subcategories, where entrepreneurs with entrepreneurial skills tend to have greater likelihood of coworker hiring than those who do not. In fact in case of spinoff, spinout or classical entrepreneurship not having entrepreneurial skills (e.skills = 0) decreases the likelihood of hiring a coworker compared with having those skills (e.skills = 0). H6 is verified.

5.5 Discussion and Conclusion

The results of this study are significant for different reasons. First they come with new evidence supporting old arguments of some resource-based views of scholars regarding the importance of resources that characterizes a firm and its position in terms of competitive advantages. This evidence is compelling for it suggests that the phenomenon already begins at firm's early stage and extends it on preoccupations of first hires.

Equally important are the results concerned with human capital. Whereas some of our hypotheses regarding their moderating role are not verified (H5), others are partially (H3, H4) or totally verified (H6). They suggest that human capital may moderate the deterministic effects of resource inheritance by weakening, maintaining, or strengthening the advantages that resource inheritance confers in hiring coworkers and early-stage performance by extension. As a case point, having entrepreneurial skills helps to sustain the positive effects issued from resource inheritance (H6) in the sense that those who declare having these skills tend to hire more coworkers and more experienced workers than those who do not.

Having entrepreneurial experience helps spinoffs (but not spinouts) in maintaining the advantages of resource inheritance for those who declare possessing it tend to hire more coworkers than those who do not. In contrast of entrepreneurial experience and entrepreneurial skills, it is not clear whether educational level or having any experience as an employee sustains or weakens the effect inherited from business status.

These results are interesting for understanding the contribution of the status of some new businesses in worker mobility, knowledge diffusion, competition between spinoffs/spinouts and mother firms, and in a certain sense cluster dynamics. In so far, worker mobility has been considered as one of the key mechanisms through which knowledge diffuses and then of plants' performance (Boschma et al. 2009) and, spinoff/spinout one of the main vector behind labor mobility (Cheyre et al. 2013). However few works are concerned with establishing this specific trait comparatively to classic entrants. By investigating the specific case of hiring previous coworkers of new firm founder, this study comes with evidences that at early-stage of the new firms there's a hierarchy between respectively spinoff, spinout, and classic entrepreneurs.

This hierarchy in mobilizing coworkers informs a better knowledge of the origins of competition some incumbents (and mother firms) are exposed to. In so far, the more there's an inheritance in terms of knowledge related to that of an incumbent and the more the founder is endowed with entrepreneurial skills and experience the greater is the likelihood of this competition to be established.

The main limitations of this study are to be considered as created by the specific context of this research that is, the focus on early-stage of the life of the firm and interest in the hire of a specific group of employees: founder's previous coworkers. In fact, the more the spinoff progresses in the development of its own knowledge base, the more it may substantially differ from the mother firm, taking the competition to new territories with other incumbents. Finally, the fact that the likelihood of hiring previous coworkers is the lowest for classic entrepreneurs, does not mean that they have less impact on worker mobility and knowledge diffusion but that they are less concerned with coworker hiring since their knowledge bases are not related with that of incumbents.

References

Bager T, Ottósson H, Schott T (2010) Intrapreneurs, entrepreneurs and spin-off entrepreneurs: similarities and differences. Int J Entrep Small Bus 10(3):339–358

Baker T, Aldrich H (1994) Friends and strangers: early hiring practices and idiosyncratic jobs. In: Bygrave W, Birley S, Churchill NC, Gatewood E, Hoy F, Keeley RH, Wetzel WE Jr (eds) Frontiers of entrepreneurship research. Center for Entrepreneurial Studies, Babson College, Wellesley, pp 75–87

Barney JB (1991) Firm resources and sustained competitive advantage. J Manag 17:99–120

Baum JAC, Silverman BS (2004) Picking winners or building them? Alliance, intellectual, and human capital as selection criteria in venture financing and performance of biotechnology start-ups. J Bus Ventur 19:411–436

Becker GS (1964) Human capital. Columbia University, New York

Boschma R, Eriksson R, Lindgren U (2009) How does labour mobility affect the performance of plants? The importance of relatedness and geographical proximity. J Econ Geogr 9(2): 169–190

Bosma NS, van Praag CM, Thurik AR, de Wit G (2004) The value of human and social capital investments for the business performance of startups. Small Bus Econ 23:227–236

Brush G, Greene G, Hart M (2001) From initial idea to unique advantage: the entrepreneurial challenge of constructing a resource base. Acad Manag Exec 15(1):64–78
Cheyre C, Klepper S, Veloso F (2013) Spinoffs and the mobility of US merchant semiconductor inventors. Manag Sci (Forthcoming)
Cliff J (1998) Does one size fit all? Exploring the relationship between attitudes towards growth, gender, and business size. J Bus Ventur 13(6):523–542
Colombo M, Grilli L (2010) On growth drivers of high-tech start-ups: exploring the role of founders' human capital and venture capital. J Bus Ventur 25(6):610–626
Cooper AC, Gimeno-Gascon FJ, Woo CY (1994) Initial human and financial capital as predictors of new venture performance. J Bus Ventur 9:371–395
Davidsson P, Honig B (2003) The role of social and human capital among nascent entrepreneurs. J Bus Ventur 18:301–331
Decarolis DM, Deeds DL (1999) The impact of stocks and flows of organizational knowledge on firm performance: an empirical investigation of the biotechnology industry. Strateg Manag J 20:953–968
Franco A, Filson D (2006) Spin-outs: knowledge diffusion through employee mobility. RAND J Econ 37:841–860
Guido B, Klepper S (2009) Heritage and agglomeration: the Akron tire cluster revisited. Econ J 119:705–733
Haber S, Reichel A (2007) The cumulative nature of the entrepreneurial process: the contribution of human capital, planning and environment resources to small venture performance. J Bus Ventur 22(1):119–145
Hitt M, Biermant L, Shimizu K, Kochhar R (2001) Direct and moderating effects of human capital on strategy and performance in professional service firms: a resource-based perspective. Acad Manag J 44(1):13–28
Johanisson B (1998) Personal networks in emerging knowledge-based firms: spatial and functional patterns. Entrep Reg Dev 10:297–312
Klepper S (2007) Disagreements, spinoffs, and the evolution of detroit as the capital of the U.S. automobile industry. Manag Sci 53:616–631
Klepper S, Sleeper S (2005) Entry by spinoffs. Manag Sci 51:1291–1306
Klepper S, Thompson P (2010) Disagreements and intra-industry spinoffs. Int J Ind Organ 28:526–538
Koster S, Wissen L (2006) Inherited resources and company support as a basis for new firm formation. A taxonomy of founding types: start-ups, spin-outs, and spin-offs. In: Karlsson C, Johansson B, Stough R (eds) Entrepreneurship and dynamics in a knowledge-economy. Routledge, New York
Lécuyer C (2006) Making Silicon Valley. MIT, Cambridge
Parker S (2011) Intrapreneurship or entrepreneurship? J Bus Ventur 26(1):19–34
Penrose ET (1959) The theory of the growth of the firm. Wiley, New York
Sandberg W, Hofer C (1987) Improving new venture performance: the role of strategy, industry structure, and the entrepreneur. J Bus Ventur 2(1):5–28
Unger JM, Rauch A, Frese M, Rosenbuch N (2011) Human capital and entrepreneurial success: a meta-analytical review. J Bus Ventur 26(3):341–358
West G, Noel T (2009) The impact of knowledge resources on new venture performance. J Small Bus Manag 47(1):1–22
Wiklund J, Shepherd DA (2003) Knowledge-based resources, entrepreneurial orientation, and the performance of small and medium-sized businesses. Strateg Manag J 24(13):1307–1314
Winter SG (1987) Knowledge and competence as strategic assets. In: Teece DJ (ed) The competitive challenge. Harper and Row, New York, pp 159–184
Woo C, Willard G, Beckstead S (1989) Spin-offs: what are the gains? J Bus Strateg 10(2):29–32
Woo C, Willard G, Daellenbach U (1992) Spin-off performance: a case of overstated expectations? Strateg Manag J 13:433–447

Chapter 6
Where Do Spin-Offs Come From? Start-Up Conditions and the Survival of Pushed and Pulled Spin-Offs

Vera Rocha, Anabela Carneiro, and Celeste Varum

Abstract Although previous research shows that spin-offs are among the most successful firms in an industry, outperforming de novo entrants, few studies consider the heterogeneity of corporate spin-offs in relation to firm performance or survival. Against this backdrop, the objective of the present chapter is twofold. First, this study aims to add to our knowledge on the relationship between spin-off type and firm survival using a comprehensive matched employer-employee dataset from Portugal. After controlling for their different start-up conditions—namely regarding initial hiring schemes, business-owners' characteristics, and the industrial and geographical relatedness to the parent firm—and a set of firm, industry, and macroeconomic characteristics, we found no significant survival differences between opportunity and necessity spin-offs. Second, based on the findings, we suggest that necessity spin-offs have not received the attention they deserve. Not only do necessity spin-offs perform an important role in the dynamics of competitive markets, by offering a possible solution for recently displaced individuals, but they also create new jobs and help to prevent the depreciation of workers' human capital.

Keywords Corporate spin-offs • Entrepreneurship • Firm survival • Displacement • Labor mobility • Human capital

V. Rocha (✉)
Faculdade de Economia, Universidade do Porto, CEF.UP, CIPES, and Copenhagen Business School (INO), Rua Dr. Roberto Frias, Porto 4200-464, Portugal
e-mail: verarocha@fep.up.pt

A. Carneiro
Universidade do Porto and CEF.UP, Porto, Portugal
e-mail: anacar@fep.up.pt

C. Varum
Universidade de Aveiro, GOVCOPP, and DEGEI, Aveiro, Portugal
e-mail: camorim@ua.pt

R. Baptista, J. Leitão (eds.), *Entrepreneurship, Human Capital, and Regional Development*, International Studies in Entrepreneurship 31,
DOI 10.1007/978-3-319-12871-9_6

6.1 Introduction

For a long time corporate spin-offs—commonly defined as start-ups founded by a former employee of an existing firm—were documented to have great comparative advantages and to perform better than de novo entrants (Franco and Filson 2006; Agarwal et al. 2011; Muendler et al. 2012; Andersson and Klepper 2013). By being understood as a particular form of labor mobility through which knowledge is more easily transferred from an incumbent firm (Klepper and Sleeper 2005; Boschma et al. 2009), and by benefiting from parent firm's contacts and network ties (Agarwal et al. 2004), spin-offs are comparatively better endowed with specific resources and informational advantages that make them better able to overcome the so-called liability of newness (Phillips 2002).

More recently, researchers called for further attention to the heterogeneity of corporate spin-offs, and a line of research has been exploring the distinction between opportunity (pulled) and necessity (pushed) entrepreneurship applied to spin-off activities (e.g., Buenstorf 2009; Bruneel et al. 2013; Dick et al. 2013).[1] Opportunity spin-offs (or pulled spin-offs) are defined as spin-offs triggered by the discovery of a promising entrepreneurial opportunity. In contrast, necessity spin-offs (or pushed spin-offs) are defined as spin-offs triggered by events that adversely affect the parent firm and render future employment at this firm less attractive or even impossible. Hence, necessity spin-offs are very often launched by employees of incumbent firms to escape deteriorating job conditions.

While the importance of pulled-induced spin-offs has increasingly been recognized in recent years, the role of pushed-induced spin-offs has been far overlooked (Buenstorf 2009). Moreover, in spite of the interest upon spin-offs' performance, there is scant research addressing the type of spin-off in relation to its growth or survival prospects. The few studies that exist have found pulled spin-offs to outperform their pushed counterparts (e.g., Eriksson and Kuhn 2006; Muendler et al. 2012; Andersson and Klepper 2013), though the results often offer limited generalization due to the small samples of analyzed firms (e.g., Buenstorf 2009; Bruneel et al. 2013).

Against this backdrop, the contribution of the present chapter is twofold. First, differences and similarities between opportunity spin-offs and necessity spin-offs are further explored using a large longitudinal matched employer-employee dataset for Portugal. It has been possible to identify and follow over 50,000 spin-offs created between 1992 and 2007, so our study is both innovative and rare on this regard. In particular, we analyze if start-up triggering conditions influence spin-offs' hazard rates. Industry and geographic relatedness to the incumbent firm, the decision of hiring some coworkers who were previously employed by the parent firm, and the general and specific human capital of spin-offs' founders are also controlled for.[2] Surprisingly, our results show that unconditionally pushed spin-offs survive longer

---

[1] Note that the distinction between opportunity and necessity spin-offs is solely based on the triggering event driving the actual decision to start the new firm.

[2] "Incumbent firm" and "parent firm" will be used interchangeably throughout the chapter and should be understood as synonymous.

than those driven by other (i.e., pulled) factors. However, as we control for a larger number of observed differences between spin-offs, this survival bonus becomes insignificant. Second, our analysis confirms that pushed spin-offs should not be overlooked, as they seem to play an important role in creating new jobs and absorbing a significant part of those workers displaced by the parent firm.

To the best of our knowledge, this is one of the first studies to compare the post-entry performance of pushed and pulled spin-offs, using a rich matched employer-employee dataset, and to take into consideration a large number of start-up conditions that can both affect spin-off survival and moderate the survival differences between necessity and opportunity spin-offs. Finally, while most of the literature concerned with spin-offs has restricted their attention to high-tech spin-offs spawned by successful surviving parent firms (e.g., Klepper and Sleeper 2005; Franco and Filson 2006; Agarwal et al. 2011), our study covers all spin-offs established in all industries during the time span under analysis. Finally, we provide empirical evidence for a European economy in which entrepreneurship may play an important role, taking into account the large number of bankruptcies and the significant increase in unemployment rates observed over the most recent years in Portugal, as a result of the severe economic crisis.

The chapter is organized as follows. Section 6.2 briefly reviews the main literature concerned with pushed-pulled spin-off performance. Section 6.3 presents the data, the criteria adopted to identify pushed and pulled spin-offs and the empirical strategy. Section 6.4 provides a preliminary description of the sample, in order to highlight the main sources of observed differences between the two types of spin-offs. Section 6.5 presents and discusses our empirical results. Section 6.6 concludes.

6.2 Prior Literature

Not all spin-offs arise from the identification of an opportunity by some employee(s), or from some strategic action of incumbent firms—which frequently seed spin-offs to develop new technologies, to serve new markets, to create complementarities, or to focus on their core business (Parhankangas and Arenius 2003; Iturriaga and Cruz 2008). Spin-offs also emerge from necessity. Adverse developments in the incumbent firm such as firm closure or massive downsizing, bankruptcy, changes in management or a takeover may push an employee (or a few of them) to leave and create their own company (e.g., Von Greiff 2009; Bruneel et al. 2013).

Not surprisingly, the role of pushed-induced spin-offs has been far overlooked until recently (Buenstorf 2009). Over the last few decades, most of the western economies have suffered extensive worker displacements (Von Greiff 2009), a phenomenon that has been even more exacerbated by the recent economic crisis and the consequent large number of firm closures (ILO 2013). Now, more than ever, with entrepreneurship being proposed as one of the possible routes to exit the crisis (OECD 2013), pushed spin-offs deserve the attention of both scholars and policy-makers, given their potential role in absorbing some of the unemployment generated by declining parent firms.

Moreover, few studies consider the heterogeneity of corporate spin-offs in relation to firm performance or survival (Buenstorf 2009; Cabral and Wang 2009; Muendler et al. 2012; Andersson and Klepper 2013; Bruneel et al. 2013). As regards the relative performance of the two types of spin-offs, opportunity spin-offs may have the comparative advantage of being based on a unique, newly discovered business opportunity and a more controlled timing of entry. Moreover, pulled spin-offs may keep strong parent-progeny relationships after entry, which can give them the access to important information, resources, markets, and technologies, as well as sources of credibility, legitimacy, reputation, and identification of opportunities (Hitt et al. 2001; Phillips 2002; Eriksson and Kuhn 2006). By preserving some links with their parent firms, pulled spin-offs may thus maintain the advantages associated with being small, while utilizing the existing assets of a larger corporation (Parhankangas and Arenius 2003; Wallin and Dahlstrand 2006). The same is not possible for necessity spin-offs, particularly for those prompted by the closure of the parent firm. This is expected to result in a more distinctive performance of opportunity spin-offs relative to necessity spin-offs.

Cabral and Wang (2009) propose that spin-offs generating from surviving incumbents outpace spin-offs originating from dying parents because the former are typically founded by individuals with high entrepreneurial talent, whereas those leaving dying firms often form their own business to escape from unemployment, regardless of their entrepreneurial ability. The same expectations are shared by Bruneel et al. (2013).

From a different perspective, the literature also suggests the existence of a significant positive correlation between parent and spin-off performances so more successful incumbents tend to produce more successful spin-offs (see Cabral and Wang 2009; Bruneel et al. 2013). In the same line of thought, spin-offs driven by pushed-nature factors (e.g., closures of incumbent firms) are likely to perform worse (e.g., Eriksson and Kuhn 2006; Muendler et al. 2012).

However, while the linkages established between pulled spin-offs and their parent firms may provide them some comparative advantages, parental influence can also generate inertia, dependence, and resistance to change (Wallin and Dahlstrand 2006; Ferriani et al. 2012). In contrast, necessity spin-offs may become more autonomous and responsive to the overall environment by being forced to strive in the market without similar support. Furthermore, those creating their own company as a way to escape unemployment—despite their possibly lower entrepreneurial ability (Cabral and Wang 2009)—may become comparatively more attached to their business (see, for instance, Block and Sandner 2009; Rocha et al. 2013) and may have lower performance thresholds than those creating a spin-off to explore an identified opportunity. The latter may have more ambitious goals and consequently give up earlier and close down the firm if such performance thresholds are not attained (Gimeno et al. 1997; McCann and Folta 2012).

Accordingly, a deep understanding of post-entry performance of necessity and opportunity spin-offs is still lacking. Besides, most of the empirical studies conducted so far have either been based on specific industries and/or relied on very small samples of spin-offs, thus offering limited generalization of their results (see Buenstorf (2009), who analyzed 48 spin-offs in the German laser industry; Cabral and Wang (2009), whose study was applied to about 780 firms in the US automobile industry; or Bruneel et al. (2013), who relied on 46 spin-offs in Flanders).[3]

Furthermore, pushed and pulled spin-offs are probably different in a variety of aspects, so analyzing whether performance differences persist after taking into account specific spin-offs' characteristics and start-up conditions could improve our knowledge about necessity and opportunity spin-offs' post-entry behavior. Industry and geographical relatedness to the incumbent firm, the presence of "movers" from the parent firm in the spin-offs' workforce, and entrepreneurs' human capital are three dimensions that, according to the literature, are believed to affect spin-off performance and that could either amplify or mitigate the performance differences between pushed and pulled spin-offs. Thus, these aspects should also be accounted for when comparing the two types of spin-offs, as discussed in more detail throughout the chapter.

6.3 Data and Methodological Issues

6.3.1 Data

The empirical study reported in this chapter is based upon data from *Quadros de Pessoal* (hereafter, QP), a large longitudinal linked employer-employee dataset from the Portuguese Ministry of Employment. All firms in the private sector employing at least one wage earner are legally obliged to fill in this annual survey and provide information about each of its establishments and workers. Requested data at the firm-level include employment, sales, industry, ownership, location, among others. At the individual-level, QP has information about each worker's age, education, gender, qualifications, wages, occupational category, tenure, number of hours worked, and type of contract. All firms, establishments, and workers are identified with a unique identification number, so they can be followed and matched over time. Accordingly, QP dataset provides very rich information both on firms and workers, not only allowing the identification of entries and exits (of firms and

[3] To the best of our knowledge, the most comprehensive studies conducted so far were those by Eriksson and Kuhn (2006) for Denmark, for the period 1981–2000, Muendler et al. (2012) for Brazil, for the period 1995–2001, and Andersson and Klepper (2013) for Sweden, for the period 1993–2005. These three studies analyzed the survival of new firms, distinguishing (pushed and pulled) spin-offs from the other start-up firms. However, the former restricted their analysis to firms with a maximum size of ten employees, and none of them have information on particular start-up conditions that possibly moderate the survival gap among firms, as entrepreneurs' characteristics or spin-offs' proximity to the parent firm. All of them are also especially concerned with the differences between (pushed/pulled) spin-offs and other de novo entrants, thus paying less attention to the differences in the performance of pushed and pulled spin-offs.

individuals), but also making it possible to track individuals' trajectories and transitions across firms, industries, and locations.

Raw QP files are available for the period 1986–2009.[4] Entries of new firms are identified by the first time (year) a firm is recorded in QP files. Firm exit is identified by the moment a firm ceases to answer the survey. We have required an absence of the firm from the files larger or equal to 2 years in order to identify its definite closure.[5,6] For this reason, in our subsequent analysis we use data only until 2007, so the last year we can identify firm exits is 2007. Data for 2008 and 2009 are only used to check the presence or absence of firms in QP files.

6.3.2 Identification of Pulled and Pushed Spin-Offs

We started by identifying all start-up firms entering over the period of 1992–2007 (excluding 2001), whose business-owner(s) (BOs) was/were in paid employment in $t-1$ or $t-2$ and who left the previous employer.[7] For spin-offs founded by two or more BOs in each year t, we have required that all of them were employed in the same incumbent firm, and that all of them had left their previous employer immediately before (in $t-1$ or $t-2$) engaging in the creation of the new start-up firm.

We have then classified these spin-offs as "pushed" or "pulled" according to the situation of the incumbent firm by the time of the employees' exit (see Table 6.1). Those spin-offs founded by individuals who come from a firm that either closed or

[4] There is a gap for the particular years of 1990 and 2001 in the worker-level files, for which no information was gathered at the individual-level.

[5] A temporary exit may occur for a number of reasons other than cessation of activity, a very likely reason being that the data were not received in the Ministry of Employment before the date when the recording operations were closed. Accordingly, firms that were temporarily absent from the files for 1 year were not considered to have definitely closed—that is, firms that were in the files in years $t-1$ and $t+1$ were considered to be active in year t even if they were not actually in the file. The firms' record was amended for that year—for time-varying variables (e.g., employment), we have computed the average of those variables in years $t-1$ and $t+1$ (see, for instance, Mata and Portugal (2002), who adopted similar procedures). Therefore, for a closure to be recorded in $t-1$, a firm has to be absent from the file in t, $t+1$, and in all the subsequent years.

[6] In this study, exit is defined as firm closure. Despite the comprehensiveness of QP dataset, it does not allow the distinction between different modes of exit. For the particular cases of exits due to mergers or acquisitions, prior studies (e.g., Geroski et al. 2010) have documented that less than 1 % of the total number of liquidations in Portugal has been due to mergers or acquisitions, thus suggesting that our inability to identify mergers in QP is not likely to affect our results.

[7] Due to the missing data at the worker-level for 2001, we are not able to identify the BO(s) of firms entering this year. As our classification of spin-offs into "pushed" or "pulled" requires detailed information about the origin of BO(s) founding the firm, entries occurring in 2001 had to be excluded. For firms entering before 2001 and active in 2001, we adopted particular procedures to fill in the missing values of firm-level variables related to the characteristics of the workforce in that particular year (e.g., the share of female workers in the firm in 2001), by computing the mean values of adjacent years. Similar procedures were adopted by previous studies on firm survival, also using QP dataset (e.g., Geroski et al. 2010; Mata and Portugal 2002).

Table 6.1 Criteria to identify pushed and pulled spin-offs

The employee i leaves the firm **A** ("parent/incumbent firm") in $t-1$ or $t-2$ and becomes BO in the new spin-off firm **B** in t	+	Firm **A** closes down in the same year of employee's exit	=	Firm **B** is classified as a pushed spin-off
		Firm **A** suffers a significant downsizing (≥30 % of the workforce) in the same year of employee's exit	=	
		Firm **A** continues operating after the employee's exit, without significant downsizing	=	Firm **B** is classified as a pulled spin-off

suffered a significant downsizing are classified as "pushed spin-offs." In such a case, the creation of the spin-off may actually be a response of some employees to an adverse development in the parent firm, being possibly closer to necessity spin-offs.[8] The remaining spin-offs were classified as "pulled spin-offs," which may include either corporate spin-offs that are the result of opportunities exploited by an incumbent firm—"incumbent-backed spin-offs" (Bruneel et al. 2013)—or spin-offs initiated by one or more employees who identify an opportunity and decide to explore it independently of their employer—"opportunity spin-offs" (Buenstorf 2009).

A total of 50,656 spin-offs established over the period of 1992–2007 (excluding 2001) were thus identified—18,390 pushed spin-offs and 32,266 pulled spin-offs. Out of these, 49 % operated in the same 2-digit industry of the parent firm. By distinguishing pushed from pulled spin-offs, this share changes to 62 % and 42 %, respectively. Regarding spin-offs' location and their geographic proximity to the parent firm, 53 % of spin-offs (65 % of all pushed and 46 % of all pulled spin-offs) were located in the same municipality of the parent firm. Both industry and geographic relatedness to the parent firm will, hence, be controlled for in all our estimations.

6.3.3 Empirical Model and Variables

To study which factors may affect the survival of spin-offs and to test whether the survival differences of pushed and pulled spin-offs are significant, we employ discrete time duration models. We follow each spin-off from the moment of entry to its last record in QP files, which may either correspond to their closure or to the last year of available information about the firm—right-censored cases.

[8] In some cases, the creation of a new firm immediately after the closure of the previous employer may not be a "true" spin-off driven by pushed-nature factors, but a restructuring of the same firm. We tried to identify those cases by taking into account the tenure of the coworkers, hired at the moment of entry. Pushed spin-offs hiring coworkers (i.e., workers coming from the parent firm) who present long tenures (larger than 2 years) are probably a reorganization of the incumbent firm, rather than a necessity spin-off created by one of the employees (or few of them). This was the case for about 900 pushed spin-offs, which were excluded from the analysis.

We estimate a piecewise constant hazard model, where exit rates are assumed to be constant within each interval but allowed to be different at particular intervals of some years. Such a flexible (nonparametric) modeling has been recognized to be preferred in order to avoid serious misspecifications of the functional form of baseline hazard rates. Moreover, such flexible baseline hazard function makes an attractive model with which to combine a specific heterogeneity assumption (e.g., Cameron and Trivedi 2005:620). Accordingly, following usual conventions (e.g., Meyer 1990), the estimated model corresponds to Prentice and Gloeckler (1978) model incorporating a gamma mixture distribution to control for firm-level unobserved heterogeneity (see also Jenkins 1995).

Formally, for each spin-off i, the probability of exit at discrete time t_j, $j = 1, 2, \ldots$, given survival until time t_j, is defined as

$$h_{ij} = 1 - \exp\left\{-\exp\left[\gamma(t) + X_i(t)'\beta + \log(\varepsilon_i)\right]\right\}, \tag{6.1}$$

where h_{ij} is the hazard rate of spin-off i after surviving for exactly j years; $\gamma(t)$ is a set of indicator variables for different duration intervals, thus describing the pattern of duration dependence in spin-offs' exit rates; $X_i(t)$ is a vector of time dependent and independent variables which are expected to impact on spin-offs' survival; β is a vector of unknown parameters to be estimated and ε_i is a Gamma distributed random variable with unit mean and variance $\sigma^2 = v$. Conveniently, the survivor function for this model has a closed form expression (see Meyer (1990) for details), and hence so does the log-likelihood function, which may be written as follows:

$$L(\gamma,\beta,\sigma^2) = \sum_{i=1}^{N} \log \left\{ \begin{array}{l} \left[1 + \sigma^2 \cdot \sum_{j=0}^{t_j - 1} \exp\left\{\gamma(t) + X_i(t)'\beta\right\}\right]^{-\sigma^{-2}} \\ -c_i \left[1 + \sigma^2 \cdot \sum_{j=0}^{t_j} \exp\left\{\gamma(t) + X_i(t)'\beta\right\}\right]^{-\sigma^{-2}} \end{array} \right\}$$

where c_i is an indicator variable, assuming the value 1(0) whenever the spin-offs' spell is complete (right-censored).

Vector $X_i(t)$ includes our central variable—the type of spin-off (pushed or pulled)—and other aspects along which firms differ and that are likely to affect their hazard rates. Start-up conditions are some of those aspects, so we need to account for them. In particular, parent–spin-off relatedness (in terms of industry and location), the presence of "movers" from the parent firm in the spin-offs' new hires, and entrepreneurs' human capital are three dimensions that are expected to influence spin-off survival, and that possibly affect—by alleviating or amplifying—the survival differences between pushed and pulled spin-offs.

Parent–spin-off relatedness has been mostly analyzed at the industry-level, as many studies defined spin-off companies as new firms founded by former employees in the same (usually high-tech) industry (e.g., Agarwal et al. 2004; Klepper and Sleeper 2005; Franco and Filson 2006). However, subsequent studies have shown that many spin-offs neither operate in high-tech industries, nor in exactly the same industry of the parent firm (e.g., Eriksson and Kuhn 2006; Muendler et al. 2012). The same applies to the region where spin-offs locate. The larger the industry-level similarity the more likely it is the inheritance of routines and the transfer of resources from the parent firm. However, it is also a "local affair" (Boschma and Frenken 2011:296), as knowledge transfers and labor mobility are believed to be more successful when the relatedness is greater (at the industry and geographical levels) between firms (e.g., Sapienza et al. 2004; Malmberg and Power 2005; Boschma et al. 2009).

The mobility of workers from the parent firm to the spin-off also constitutes one of the most important mechanisms through which routines, procedures, knowledge, and various forms of capital may be transferred (Helfat and Lieberman 2002; Audretsch and Keilbach 2005; Franco and Filson 2006). Accordingly, firms hiring these "coworkers" (i.e., employees who move from the parent firm to the new spin-off) at the moment of entry are believed to be better able to reduce the initial uncertainty in the market and to have a comparative advantage over other firms (Song et al. 2003; Leung et al. 2006; Tzabbar et al. 2013). Furthermore, both knowledge transfers (embodied in coworkers) and knowledge spillovers (conditional on, for instance, coworkers' accumulated experience in the parent firm) may aid spin-off performance (Agarwal et al. 2011), and perhaps attenuate the differences between pushed and pulled spin-offs. In fact, although pushed spin-offs originating from dying firms cannot maintain any relationship with their parents, worker flows from the parent firm may be a particularly important resource for these firms, helping them to overcome the liability of newness, besides reinforcing their potential role in reducing unemployment and preventing the devaluation of human capital of those who have lost their job due to unfavorable environments in the parent firm (Buenstorf 2009).

Finally, entrepreneurs' characteristics are also increasingly recognized to significantly influence new venture performance. Entrepreneurial talent of spin-offs' founders—being multidimensional (Unger et al. 2011; Mayer-Haug et al. 2013) and mainly embodied in entrepreneurs' general and specific human capital—has been shown to be particularly important during firm infancy and to improve the survival of new firms (e.g., Delmar and Shane 2006). As some differences between the founders of pushed and pulled spin-offs may exist, some of them unobserved (Cabral and Wang 2009), this issue should not be neglected. However, many studies have been unable to control for these potential differences among firms due to data restrictions (e.g., Muendler et al. 2012; Andersson and Klepper 2013).

Hence, vector $X_i(t)$ includes indicator variables for the industrial and regional parent–spin-off relatedness, an indicator variable for the presence of coworkers hired at the start-up, the human capital of the BO(s) (namely education, industry-specific experience and entrepreneurial experience),[9] some spin-offs' characteristics (including start-up size, workforce characteristics, location and a set of indicator

[9] For spin-offs founded by two or more BOs, we consider their average human capital (in particular, the average number of schooling years, the average number of years of experience in the 2-digit industry, and the average number of years of entrepreneurial experience acquired in the past).

variables for firm age, as a way to flexibly analyze the duration dependence of firm exit rates), and a final set of control variables related to the industry, regional, and macroeconomic environment.

6.4 Pushed and Pulled Spin-Offs in Portugal: What the Data Tell Us

Figures 6.1 and 6.2 illustrate the relative importance of spin-offs in the Portuguese economy. The former depicts the share of both types of spin-offs in the total number of new firm entries identified in QP data. Over 30 % of the new firms created in recent years are spin-offs.

Spin-offs also account for an increasing share of the total employment created by new firms (Fig. 6.2). In the most recent years, spin-offs accounted for more than one third of the jobs created by new entrants, with pushed and pulled spin-offs assuming a similar relative importance each.

The figures also reveal that pushed spin-offs should not be overlooked. In the beginning of the period under analysis, pulled and pushed spin-offs accounted respectively, for about 18 % and 9 % of total new entries in the private sector. By 2007, the corresponding shares were already 21 and 13 %. Pushed-nature spin-offs assume a more evident role in terms of jobs created.

Table 6.2 shows the importance of pushed and pulled spin-offs in different industries. Retail trade absorbs over 20 % of all spin-offs. There is also significant spin-off activity in Construction, Restaurants and Hotels, Wholesale Trade, as well as Real State and Business Services.

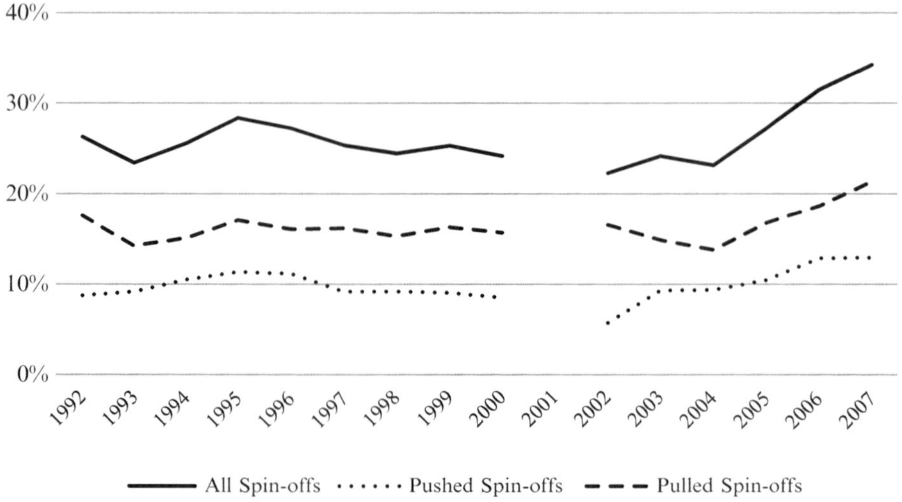

Fig. 6.1 Number of spin-offs on total number of new entries

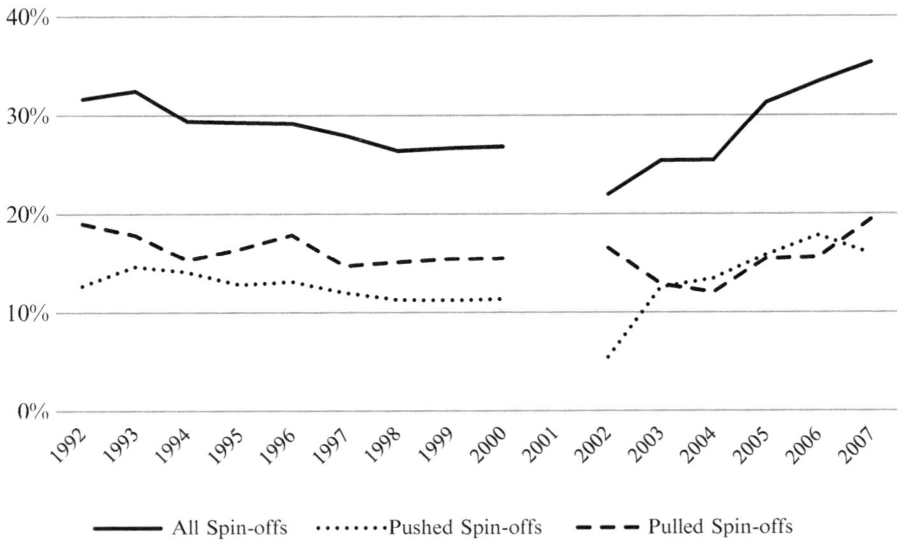

Fig. 6.2 Relative importance of spin-offs in the employment created by new firms

In some industries, spin-offs emerge more often in the same industry of the parent firm (notably in Textile Manufacturing Industry and Construction—about 15 % and 37 % of all spin-offs operating in the same industry of the parent firm belong to those industries, respectively). In contrast, spin-offs in Services (e.g., Wholesale Trade or Real State and Business Services) are less frequently related with the parent's former industry.

These patterns suggest that industry-specific knowledge may be relatively more important to enter into some particular industries than into others. Starting a business—either driven by opportunity or necessity—in certain industries (especially in Manufacturing) may require some prior specific knowledge about the industry in order to reduce uncertainty and risk. The lack of specific knowledge about the industry may be understood as less problematic to enter in other industries (possibly in Trade and some particular Services).

Figure 6.3 plots pushed and pulled spin-offs' survival patterns. Table 6.3 complements this analysis, by presenting the survival rates of both groups of firms for selective periods of time, according to the industry and geographic relatedness to the incumbent firm. These results show that, unconditionally (i.e., without controlling for any observed or unobserved differences between firms), pushed spin-offs survive longer than their pulled counterparts. These differences remain statistically significant across the several subsamples described in Table 6.3, except for spin-offs located in a different municipality of the parent firm—in that case, pulled spin-offs seem to outpace those entrepreneurial firms driven by more pushed-nature factors.

As expected, hazard rates are lower for those spin-offs more closely related to the parent firm—i.e., both for those remaining in the same region and those operating in the same industry of the parent firm. Nonetheless, these first statistics suggest that

Table 6.2 Distribution of spin-offs by industries (2-digit) (%)

	Pulled Spin-offs			Pushed Spin-offs		
	Pulled spin-offs	Pulled spin-offs operating in the same industry of the parent firm	Pulled spin-offs operating in a different industry from that of the parent firm	Pushed spin-offs	Pushed spin-offs operating in the same industry of the parent firm	Pushed spin-offs operating in a different industry from that of the parent firm
(11) Agriculture and hunting	1.11	0.78	1.35	1.10	1.12	1.07
(12) Forestry and logging	0.25	0.14	0.32	0.23	0.22	0.26
(13) Fishing	0.04	0.03	0.05	0.03	0.00	0.09
(29) Other mining	0.17	0.13	0.20	0.25	0.25	0.25
(31) Manufacture of food, beverages, and tobacco	1.41	1.60	1.28	1.68	1.69	1.66
(32) Textile, wearing apparel, and leather industries	3.98	7.12	1.69	5.49	7.72	1.85
(33) Manufacture of wood and wood products, including furniture	1.10	1.14	1.07	1.81	2.11	1.32
(34) Manufacture of paper and paper products, printing, and publishing	1.10	1.29	0.96	1.06	1.17	0.87
(35) Manufacture of chemicals and chemical, petroleum, coal, rubber, and plastic products	0.35	0.34	0.36	0.34	0.30	0.40

(36) Manufacture of nonmetallic mineral products, except products of petroleum and coal	0.84	1.06	0.67	0.98	1.16	0.70
(37) Basic metal industries	0.07	0.02	0.11	0.09	0.04	0.18
(38) Manufacture of fabricated metal products, machinery, and equipment	3.54	4.54	2.81	4.08	4.55	3.33
(39) Other manufacturing industries	0.97	1.10	0.88	1.54	1.43	1.72
(41) Electricity, gas, and steam	0.02	0.00	0.03	0.01	0.00	0.03
(42) Water works and supply	0.01	0.00	0.02	0.03	0.01	0.06
(50) Construction	13.16	17.23	10.18	16.15	19.74	10.31
(61) Wholesale trade	10.11	8.16	11.53	10.40	8.45	13.58
(62) Retail trade	22.34	21.93	22.64	21.98	20.95	23.65
(63) Restaurants and hotels	12.54	11.84	13.05	11.52	11.41	11.70
(71) Transport and storage	4.99	5.75	4.44	4.55	5.06	3.71
(72) Communication	0.24	0.07	0.35	0.20	0.08	0.38
(81) Financial institutions	0.49	0.24	0.66	0.30	0.20	0.45

(continued)

Table 6.2 (continued)

	Pulled Spin-offs			Pushed Spin-offs		
	Pulled spin-offs	Pulled spin-offs operating in the same industry of the parent firm	Pulled spin-offs operating in a different industry from that of the parent firm	Pushed spin-offs	Pushed spin-offs operating in the same industry of the parent firm	Pushed spin-offs operating in a different industry from that of the parent firm
(82) Insurance	0.17	0.16	0.17	0.11	0.04	0.22
(83) Real state and business services	15.49	10.98	18.77	11.57	9.02	15.71
(91) Public administration and defense	2.72	2.77	2.69	1.93	1.84	2.08
(92) Sanitary and similar services	0.15	0.07	0.21	0.08	0.05	0.13
(93) Social and related community services	0.42	0.24	0.55	0.27	0.20	0.40
(94) Recreational and cultural services	0.84	0.34	1.22	0.64	0.27	1.25
(95) Personal and household services	1.39	0.93	1.73	1.58	0.92	2.65
Total (%)	100.00	100.00	100.00	100.00	100.00	100.00

Values in percentage. Industries are classified according to the international classification of economic activities (ISIC-Rev.2, 2-digit). Industries 21—Coal Mining, 22—Crude Petroleum and Natural Gas Production, 23—Metal Ore Mining, and 96—International and Other Extra-Territorial Bodies are not included in Table 6.2, given that no spin-offs were identified in these industries

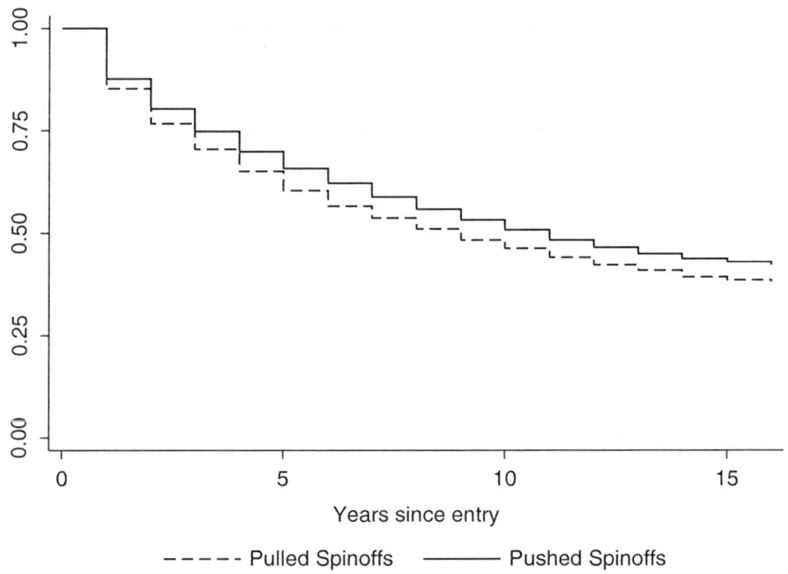

Fig. 6.3 Kaplan-Meier survivor function of pushed and pulled spin-offs

Table 6.3 Comparative survival rates of pushed and pulled spin-offs, according to the proximity to the parent firm

Years since entry	Industry-level (2d) proximity				Geographic proximity[a]			
	Same industry		Different industry		Same region		Different region	
	Pushed	Pulled	Pushed	Pulled	Pushed	Pulled	Pushed	Pulled
1	0.8915	0.8713	0.8528	0.8399	0.9254	0.9269	0.3693	0.4407
5	0.6852	0.6336	0.6147	0.5838	0.7075	0.6800	0.1433	0.1794
10	0.5310	0.4993	0.4727	0.4367	0.5483	0.5237	0.0903	0.1153
15	0.4489	0.4196	0.3971	0.3606	0.4628	0.4361	0.0739	0.0926

[a]"Same region" means that the spin-off is located in the same municipality of the parent firm. Portugal had 308 municipalities in 2007

geographical distance has a larger negative impact on spin-offs' survival prospects than industry-level distance. Note that more than 80 % of the spin-offs established in a region different from that of the incumbent firm closed down 5 years after entry; the corresponding exit rate for those establishing close to the incumbent firm (i.e., in the same municipality) was about 30 %. Entering in an industry different from that of the parent firm also seems to penalize spin-offs in terms of survival. However, the data show that even 15 years after entry about 36–40 % of spin-offs operating in a different 2-digit industry remained active.

Finally, Table 6.4 provides further descriptive statistics for pushed and pulled spin-offs, now taking into account their main distinctions at the firm- and industry-levels. Our data reveal that hiring coworkers is a much common practice among

Table 6.4 Descriptive statistics for pushed and pulled spin-offs (Portugal, 1992–2007)[a]

	All spin-offs		Same 2-d sector		Different 2-d sector		Same region		Different region	
	Pushed	Pulled	Pushed	Pulled	Pushed	Pulled	Pushed	Pulled	Pushed	Pulled
N	18,390	32,266	11,359	13,501	7,031	18,765	11,872	14,804	6,518	17,462
Workers' mobility										
Hire coworkers (%)	0.376	0.145	0.480	0.243	0.208	0.075	0.457	0.211	0.228	0.090
Human capital of the BO(s)										
Schooling years	8.067	8.857	7.662	8.294	8.721	9.262	7.636	8.420	8.851	9.228
Industry (2-d) experience (years)	2.703	1.942	4.039	4.114	0.545	0.379	2.973	2.310	2.213	1.629
Entrepreneurial experience (years)	1.457	1.267	1.496	1.335	1.394	1.219	1.526	1.370	1.331	1.180
Firm-level controls										
Start-up size (no. employees in logs)	1.163	0.975	1.273	1.090	0.985	0.893	1.230	1.021	1.041	0.936
College workers (%)	0.076	0.122	0.061	0.098	0.099	0.139	0.056	0.101	0.112	0.139
Female workers (%)	0.350	0.351	0.340	0.331	0.366	0.366	0.359	0.361	0.333	0.343
Employees' age <25 years old (%)	0.183	0.195	0.186	0.208	0.178	0.186	0.188	0.205	0.176	0.187
Employees' age: [25–34] (%)	0.376	0.399	0.369	0.399	0.389	0.399	0.365	0.398	0.394	0.400
Employees' age: [35–54] (%)	0.389	0.364	0.390	0.355	0.386	0.371	0.390	0.354	0.387	0.373

Employees' age ≥55 (%)	0.052	0.042	0.055	0.038	0.047	0.044	0.057	0.043	0.043	0.040
Urban location (%)	0.396	0.411	0.387	0.401	0.410	0.418	0.366	0.373	0.450	0.444
Number of BOs	1.420	1.290	1.480	1.341	1.322	1.253	1.487	1.342	1.297	1.245
Industry and regional controls[b]										
Minimum efficient scale	3.658	3.507	3.836	3.764	3.371	3.322	3.758	3.630	3.475	3.402
Industry growth (%)	0.040	0.044	0.032	0.035	0.053	0.051	0.038	0.040	0.043	0.048
Churn rate in the 2-d sector (%)	0.241	0.246	0.240	0.244	0.243	0.247	0.240	0.247	0.243	0.245
Churn rate in the region (county) (%)	0.242	0.243	0.244	0.244	0.241	0.243	0.241	0.240	0.245	0.246
Primary sector (%)	0.016	0.015	0.015	0.011	0.016	0.019	0.016	0.016	0.015	0.015
Manufacturing (%)	0.167	0.130	0.197	0.176	0.121	0.097	0.197	0.158	0.115	0.107
Energy & construction (%)	0.158	0.128	0.193	0.168	0.101	0.100	0.150	0.133	0.171	0.124
Services (%)	0.659	0.726	0.595	0.645	0.762	0.784	0.637	0.693	0.699	0.754

[a]Excluding 2001

[b]*Minimum Efficient Scale*: median number of employees in the 2-digit industry in each year; *Industry growth*: annual percentage change in 2-digit employment; *Churn rate in the 2-d sector*: ratio (entries + exits)/total number of firms in the 2-d sector, by year; *Churn rate in the region*: ratio (entries + exits)/total number of firms in the county, by year

pushed than among pulled spin-offs: almost 38 % of all pushed spin-offs hire some other workers who were employed in the parent firm; such hiring scheme is observed in less than 15 % of pulled spin-offs. These hires of coworkers at the start-up are even more significant among spin-offs located geographically close to, and remaining in the same industry of, the parent firm.

Regarding the general and specific human capital of the founders, the statistics show that pulled spin-offs' BOs are, on average, more educated, while pushed spin-offs' founders are relatively more endowed with specific human capital (namely, industry-specific and entrepreneurial experience).

At the firm-level, we observe that pushed spin-offs enter at a relatively larger scale than their pulled counterparts—which may be achieved, in part, by hiring some workers from the parent firm—while pulled spin-offs present a larger share of highly educated individuals. Despite being less remarkable, the differences related to spin-offs' location in urban areas, or to their workforce composition (regarding workers' gender and age), will also be controlled for in our estimations.

Following prior studies on firm survival (e.g., Mata and Portugal 1994; Audretsch and Mahmood 1995; Honjo 2000), we will also control for the overall competitive environment at the industry and regional levels, by taking into account the minimum efficient scale and the growth rate of the industry, as well as the churn/turnover rate of the industry and the region where each spin-off is located.

6.5 Empirical Results

6.5.1 Spin-Offs Survival

In Table 6.5, we present the results obtained from the estimation of several specifications of the discrete time hazard model with gamma frailty described in Sect. 6.3.3. Specification 1 only includes as explanatory variables an indicator variable distinguishing pushed from pulled employee spin-offs. The results confirm the conclusion already advanced by the preliminary analysis of spin-offs' survival rates, presented and discussed in the previous section: without controlling for any other observed differences between firms, pushed spin-offs are about 22 % less likely to close down operations and exit the market than pulled spin-offs $(1-\exp(-0.2506)=0.2217)$. Unobserved heterogeneity is now controlled for and shown to be statistically significant.

In the second specification, we control for the industrial and geographical relatedness to the parent firm. The results confirm that both measures of relatedness significantly reduce spin-offs' exit rates. Even so, pushed spin-offs are estimated to have, on average, 15 % lower hazards, regardless the industry and the region where they are located.

The third specification controls for the presence of coworkers hired from the parent firm. Spin-offs seem to strongly benefit from the presence of these workers,

Table 6.5 Empirical results for the discrete time proportional hazard model (Portugal, 1992–2007)[a]

	(1)	(2)	(3)	(4)	(5)	(6)
Type of spin-off						
Pushed spin-off	−0.2506*** (0.0187)	−0.1671*** (0.0187)	−0.0565*** (0.0191)	−0.0631*** (0.0193)	−0.0341* (0.0175)	−0.0244 (0.0159)
Same 2-d industry of the parent firm		−0.2572*** (0.0180)	−0.1478*** (0.0184)	−0.0724*** (0.0232)	0.0068 (0.0211)	−0.0142 (0.0194)
Same region of the parent firm		−0.2689*** (0.0151)	−0.2557*** (0.0150)	−0.2572*** (0.0151)	−0.2140*** (0.0149)	−0.2220*** (0.0144)
Workers' mobility						
Hire coworkers			−0.5243*** (0.0225)	−0.5064*** (0.0230)	−0.2704*** (0.0236)	−0.2148*** (0.0214)
Human capital of the BO(s)						
Schooling years				−0.0226*** (0.0021)	−0.0175*** (0.0022)	−0.0070*** (0.0020)
Industry (2-d) experience				−0.0268*** (0.0041)	−0.0358*** (0.0039)	−0.0301*** (0.0036)
Entrepreneurial experience				−0.0751*** (0.0092)	−0.0429*** (0.0084)	−0.0313*** (0.0078)
Firm-level controls						
Start-up size					−0.1650*** (0.0126)	−0.2167*** (0.0123)
College workers					−0.3350*** (0.0391)	−0.3108*** (0.0372)
Female workers					0.1282*** (0.0204)	0.1417*** (0.0202)
Employees' age: [25–34][b]					0.0122 (0.0334)	0.0832** (0.0324)

(continued)

Table 6.5 (continued)

	(1)	(2)	(3)	(4)	(5)	(6)
Employees' age: [35–54][b]					−0.0879*** (0.0329)	0.0202 (0.0317)
Employees' age ≥55[b]					0.0047 (0.0494)	0.1574*** (0.0469)
Urban location					0.1316*** (0.0164)	0.1287*** (0.0149)
Number of BOs					−0.3746*** (0.0167)	−0.3261*** (0.0153)
Firm age = [2, 3][c]					−0.1424*** (0.0217)	−0.1315*** (0.0204)
Firm Age = [4, 5][c]					−0.1865*** (0.0336)	−0.2106*** (0.0300)
Firm age = 6+[c]					−0.2474*** (0.0498)	−0.2773*** (0.0430)
Industry, regional and macroeconomic environment						
Minimum efficient scale						0.0276*** (0.0071)
Industry growth						−0.3202*** (0.0656)
Churn rate in the 2-d industry						0.3686*** (0.0139)

Churn rate in the region						0.2345*** (0.0135)
Primary sector[d]						−0.5874*** (0.0727)
Energy and construction[d]						−0.0518 (0.0333)
Services[d]						−0.1585*** (0.0331)
Crisis periods						0.1281*** (0.0217)
Constant	−1.8098*** (0.0144)	−1.5739*** (0.0175)	−1.5638*** (0.0174)	−1.2480*** (0.0287)	−0.8188*** (0.0462)	−2.5202*** (0.0702)
Number of observations	256,384	256,384	256,384	256,384	256,384	256,384
Log likelihood	−77628.37	−77349.67	−77073.15	−76945.68	−76291.40	−75248.99
Unobserved heterogeneity	1.1480***	1.0531***	1.0117***	1.0446***	0.6067***	0.2674***

"Crisis Periods" is equal to 1 for years 1993 and 2003, 0 otherwise. "Unobserved heterogeneity" at the bottom of the table refers to gamma variance, which is always statistically significant. *, ** and *** mean significant at 10 %, 5 % and 1 %, respectively
[a]Excluding 2001. Reference categories: [b]Employees' age <25; [c]Firm age = 1; [d]Manufacturing

as they may be a channel for knowledge transfers, consequently reducing uncertainty and mitigating the so-called liability of newness (Song et al. 2003; Audretsch and Keilbach 2005; Agarwal et al. 2004, 2011). These results also suggest that part of the relative survival advantages shown by pushed spin-offs are related to their larger endowments of these particular human resources: according to specification 3, pushed spin-offs are only 5–6 % less likely to exit than their pulled counterparts.

In specification 4, we include the variables related to general and specific human capital of the founder(s). As expected, BOs' education and specific experience significantly contribute to reduce the hazard rates of their firms. Specification 5 adds a set of firm-level control variables that, according to prior studies on firm survival (see, for instance, the survey by Manjón-Antolín and Arauzo-Carod 2008), are expected to influence firm exit rates. The final specification (in the last column) also controls for industry, regional, and macroeconomic environment.

A larger start-up size and a more educated workforce are both found to be associated to lower hazard rates, while location in a large urban area is found to increase the risk of exit. A larger share of female workers is also linked with higher hazard rates, in line with prior studies that found that firms tend to be more productive if their workforces have a lower fraction of female workers (e.g., Haltiwanger et al. 2007). Firms with younger workforces also seem to have, on average, lower hazards. Spin-offs founded by more than one BO also present longer lifetimes and thus lower exit rates than spin-offs founded by a single BO. A larger founding team actually helps to reduce the liability of newness, through the share of risks and resources (e.g., financial and human capital resources). Results also show that hazard rates decrease with firm age, which confirms that spin-offs' exit rates present negative duration dependence (see also Geroski et al. 2010; Andersson and Klepper 2013).

When controlling for all these firm-level characteristics, the survival differences between pushed and pulled spin-offs become minor and weakly significant. The similarities between the spin-off and the parent firm at the industry-level also become unimportant after taking into account all these observed differences among firms. Survival advantages arising from geographic proximity to the parent firm, in turn, remain highly significant throughout the several specifications.

Finally, when industry, regional, and macroeconomic environment are also taken into consideration, the survival gap initially detected between the two groups of spin-offs actually vanishes and becomes statistically insignificant. Industries where the minimum efficient scale is larger shift firm exit rates upward, and so do industries and regions where entry and exit rates are higher—and where turbulence and competition also tend to be stronger (Santarelli and Vivarelli 2007).[10] In contrast, industry growth rate—potentially signaling better industry conditions and profit opportunities—reduces exit rates (see also Honjo 2000). In line with prior studies, hazard rates are higher during more recessive periods (e.g., Varum and Rocha 2012).

In sum, the results show that, as we control for a larger number of sources of observed heterogeneity between firms, the survival differences between pushed and

[10] As entry and exit rates are typically positively and significantly correlated (Geroski 1995), we control for the churn rate of the industry and the region where each spin-off is located.

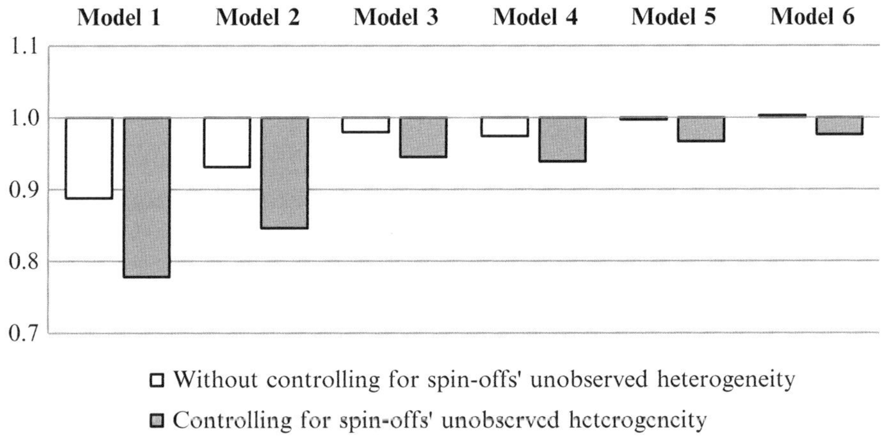

Fig. 6.4 Estimated hazard ratio of pushed spin-offs relative to pulled spin-offs

pulled spin-offs gradually fade away. Moreover, significant unobserved heterogeneity persists throughout the estimations. In Fig. 6.4, we illustrate and compare the estimated hazard ratio of pushed spin-offs relatively to their pulled counterparts, with and without controlling for firm-level unobserved heterogeneity.

The results show that, not only do the hazard differences vanish as we control for a larger set of observed characteristics of firms, industries and the overall environment surrounding spin-offs, but also those estimated differences are moreover larger when taking into account spin-offs' unobserved heterogeneity. In other words, pushed spin-offs seem to have some observed characteristics that help them to overcome the potential disadvantages or weaknesses that we might expect them to present by being driven by more pushed-nature factors (for instance, the presence of coworkers—and, consequently, the possible knowledge advantages that may derive from their presence—the region-specific experience, the industry-specific and entrepreneurial experience of their founders), as well as unobserved characteristics that reinforce those survival differences and that favor them against pulled spin-offs.

Entrepreneurs' motivations may be part of those unobserved differences. Pushed spin-offs are triggered by more unfavorable environments at the parent firm, namely by contexts of collective dismissals. Accordingly, their creation may constitute the response of their founders to their unemployment situation. The founders of pulled spin-offs may actually have other type of motivations when establishing their firms—probably less driven by the necessity and more driven by some opportunity, possibly being less autonomous and less independent from the parent firm. The founders of pushed spin-offs, instead, are expected (and forced) to be more self-sufficient and may become more attached to their firms, thus being more resilient in the market, which may contribute to increase the survival span of those pushed-type spin-offs.

6.5.2 *The Quantity and Quality of Workers' Mobility*

The literature on spin-offs' performance has been highlighting the need to consider both the relative quantity and the quality of labor moving from the parent firm to the spin-off. The better the quality of those workers moving from one firm to another—in terms of education, ability, or experience—the more valuable may their presence be in the spin-off. In this section, we extend the previous analysis in order to study the characteristics of coworkers hired at entry in more detail, and how they may influence spin-off survival.

From Fig. 6.5, we confirm that hiring workers previously employed in the parent firm is a most common practice among pushed spin-offs (recall Table 6.4). Besides, the relative importance of these individuals is higher in the subsample of pushed spin-offs among those firms hiring at least one coworker at the moment of their entry. On average, 44 % of the pushed spin-offs' workforce at entry was composed by coworkers; in pulled spin-offs, they accounted, on average, to 38 % of the initial labor force.[11]

Figure 6.6 shows the relative importance of those coworkers, subsequently hired by new spin-offs, in the total workforce of the parent firm in the year of spin-offs' founder exit. On average, pushed (pulled) spin-offs absorb 37 % (21 %) of the parent firm's workforce. This also reveals the significant role played by pushed

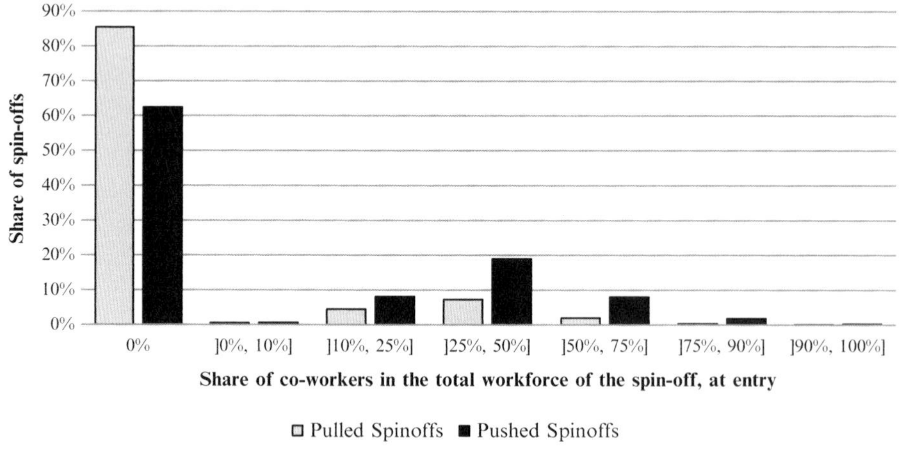

Fig. 6.5 Relative importance of coworkers in total spin-off workforce, at entry (Portugal, 1992–2007, Excluding 2001)

[11] Regarding the qualifications of coworkers in the parent firm, the great majority of them occupied middle or low-ranked positions. Overall, 52 % (54 %) of coworkers employed by pushed (pulled) spin-offs were qualified or highly qualified professionals in the parent firm, and 40 % (38 %) had lower qualifications (e.g., less qualified or nonqualified professionals, or apprentices).

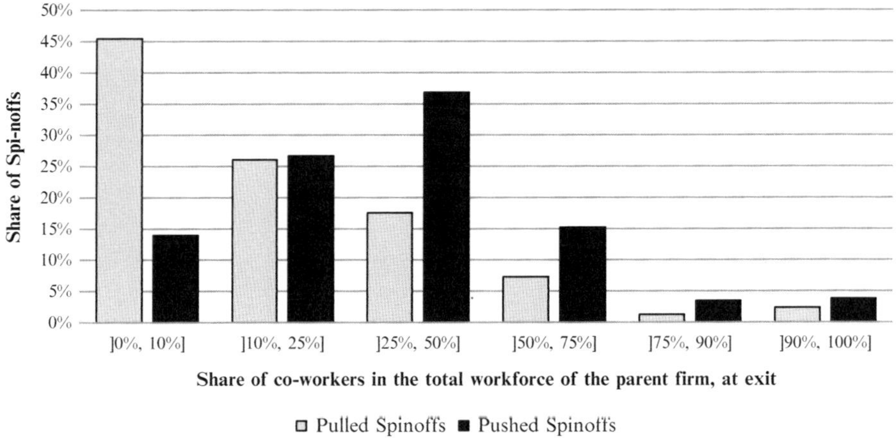

Fig. 6.6 Relative importance of coworkers in total parent firm workforce, at the moment of spin-offs' founders' exit (Portugal, 1992–2007, Excluding 2001). Spin-offs with no coworkers are excluded

spin-offs in generating new jobs for those who recently became unemployed, due to parent firm closure or downsizing.

Table 6.6 provides some descriptive statistics about the coworkers employed by pushed and pulled spin-offs, overall and according to the parent–spin-off relatedness at the industry and geographic levels. Some remarkable patterns arise from the analysis of the data: first, the mobility of coworkers is more significant between more related firms (either at the industry-level or in geographic terms) (cf. Table 6.4); second, coworkers employed by pushed spin-offs have, on average, accumulated a somewhat longer experience in the parent firm, have lower education levels, earned lower hourly wages at the parent firm and are, on average, slightly older than those employed by pulled spin-offs.

We have then extended our previous estimations in order to evaluate how the relative quantity and quality of coworkers influence spin-offs' hazards. Departing from the global specification presented in Table 6.5, we have replaced the indicator variable "Hire coworkers" by the set of variables summarized in Table 6.6, in order to, first, measure the relative importance of coworkers in the total spin-offs' workforce and, second, proxy the general and specific human capital of these workers. We summarize the main results in Table 6.7.

In the first specification we evaluate the effect of the relative quantity of coworkers in the total spin-off workforce. The results suggest that firms with a larger proportion of coworkers among their employees will have lower hazard rates. This confirms that a stronger presence of these workers in the new firm may reduce the liability of newness, moderate the initial uncertainty, and reinforce potential knowledge transfers from the parent firm to the spin-off.

In the second specification, we replace this variable by the four proxies of coworkers' human capital—education, work experience accumulated in the parent firm (i.e., tenure), age, and previous hourly wage in the parent firm. Although each

Table 6.6 Description of coworkers moving from the parent firm to the employee spin-off (Portugal, 1992–2007)[a]

	All spin-offs		Same 2-d industry		Different 2-d industry		Same region		Different region	
	Pushed	Pulled	Pushed	Pulled	Pushed	Pulled	Pushed	Pulled	Pushed	Pulled
Share of coworkers from the parent firm in the spin-offs' workforce, at entry (%)[b]	0.165	0.055	0.213	0.092	0.089	0.028	0.205	0.082	0.094	0.031
Average tenure accumulated by coworkers in the parent firm (months)[c]	53.53	52.45	53.17	51.09	54.86	55.61	54.96	55.17	48.29	47.06
Average schooling of coworkers (years)[c]	6.296	6.891	6.152	6.596	6.830	7.571	6.169	6.615	6.760	7.437
Average hourly wage of coworkers in the parent firm (euros)[c]	2.847	3.250	2.787	3.071	3.074	3.665	2.712	2.926	3.343	3.892
Average age of coworkers (years)[c]	35.18	34.06	35.23	34.13	34.98	33.90	35.14	34.31	35.33	33.56

[a]Excluding 2001
[b]Mean values for all spin-offs (i.e., those hiring coworkers and those with no coworkers)
[c]Mean values for the subsample of spin-offs with at least one worker hired from the parent firm

Table 6.7 The effect of relative quantity and quality of coworkers on spin-offs' survival (Portugal, 1992–2007)[a]

	(1)	(2)	(3)
Pushed spin-off	−0.0245 (0.0159)	−0.0297* (0.0159)	−0.0255 (0.0160)
Share of coworkers at entry	−0.4161*** (0.0452)		−0.1754** (0.0690)
Average schooling of coworkers		−0.0114** (0.0044)	−0.0066* (0.0039)
Average tenure of coworkers in the parent firm		−0.0018*** (0.0003)	−0.0016*** (0.0003)
Average age of coworkers		−0.0010 (0.0010)	
Average hourly wage of coworkers in the parent firm		0.0045 (0.0053)	
Number of observations	256,384	256,384	256,384
Log likelihood	−75257.40	−75242.05	−75239.48
Unobserved heterogeneity	0.2589***	0.2785***	0.2795***

All these specifications include all the variables of model 6 (in Table 6.5). The results obtained for those variables were not qualitatively different from those reported in Table 6.5, so we omit them to save space, being available upon request

*, ** and *** mean significant at 10 %, 5 % and 1 %, respectively

[a]Excluding 2001

of them is found to reduce the hazard rates of spin-offs (when included in intermediate specifications, not reported here), only coworkers' education and tenure in the parent firm remain statistically significant when included all together in the same specification.

Finally, specification (3) controls for both the relative quantity of coworkers and their "quality." The effect of the relative quantity of coworkers is now lower in magnitude, but still significant. Regarding the variables measuring the human capital of these workers, the experience accumulated in the parent firm seems to be the most relevant source of human capital for the firm (the effect is statistically significant at the 1 % level). This suggests that coworkers' specific human capital is a particularly valuable asset to new spin-offs hiring these workers. The longer the workers were employed at the parent firm, the greater their knowledge of routines and procedures might be, and the resultant knowledge spillovers (Wezel et al. 2006; Agarwal et al. 2011). This result also works in favor of pushed spin-offs, whose coworkers are, on average, slightly more experienced than those hired by their pulled counterparts.

6.6 Concluding Remarks

In this study we have used a large longitudinal matched employer-employee dataset covering all firms in the Portuguese private sector, which has allowed us to identify a total of 50,656 spin-offs entering from 1992 to 2007 (18,390 pushed spin-offs and 32,266 pulled spin-offs). Discrete time hazard models, incorporating a gamma mixture distribution to control for firm-level unobserved heterogeneity, were employed to study how different the survival prospects of those two groups of spin-offs are. Additionally, we have tried to uncover some of the factors that may help to explain these differences, by taking into account the parent–spin-off relatedness at the industry and geographic levels, the presence of coworkers, and BOs' human capital.

The empirical analysis revealed that, unconditionally, pushed spin-offs have lower exit rates than pulled counterparts. However, as we control for spin-offs' unobserved heterogeneity and several sources of observed differences between firms, the survival gap tends to vanish and becomes negligible. Specific knowledge of the region, the presence of coworkers (and especially the tenure they acquired in the parent firm), as well as BOs' general and specific human capital seem to contribute to explain part of the survival differences initially found between pulled and pushed spin-offs. In addition, pushed spin-offs seem to have unobserved characteristics that reinforce the differences and favor their apparent survival bonus over pulled spin-offs. Entrepreneurs' motivations, besides their relatively lower ambitions and performance thresholds, may be part of those unobserved differences that contribute for a longer survival time of pushed spin-offs.

Our analysis also reveals that pushed spin-offs are important employers, so their significance should not be ignored. By the end of the period studied, they were responsible for over 15 % of all the jobs created by new entrants in the private sector, similarly to pulled spin-offs. Moreover, they also assume an important role in the absorption of part of those workers who were recently displaced by the parent firm.

Overall, the results thus highlight the potentially important role that entrepreneurship, and pushed spin-offs in particular, may play in the market, by creating new jobs, hiring unemployed individuals, and hence allowing the reutilization of their competences and preventing the depreciation of their human capital. Under the widespread context of economic crisis in many European countries, marked by an unusually large number of bankruptcies and massive layoffs, spin-offs of a more pushed-nature may become more prominent in the near future, by working as a possibly successful solution to unemployment. For Portugal in particular, where job losses have become a recurrent bottleneck over the last years, our results suggest that entrepreneurship—under the form of necessity spin-offs—may play a particularly relevant role and constitute a potential answer to the increasing unemployment rates.

Acknowledgements We acknowledge GEE–MEE (Gabinete de Estratégia e Estudos—Ministério da Economia e do Emprego) for allowing the use of *Quadros de Pessoal* dataset. The first author also acknowledges FCT (Fundação para a Ciência e Tecnologia) for financial support through the doctoral grant SFRH/BD/71556/2010. CEF.UP—Center for Economics and Finance at the University of Porto is funded by Programa Compete—POFC (Fundação para a Ciência e Tecnologia and European Regional Development Fund); project reference: PEst-OE/EGE/UI4105/2014.

References

Agarwal R, Echambadi R, Franco AM, Sarkar MB (2004) Knowledge transfer through inheritance: spin-out generation, development and survival. Acad Manage J 47(4):501–522
Agarwal R, Campbell B, Franco AM, Ganco M (2011) What do I take with me: the impact of transfer and replication of resources on parent and spin-out performance. Center for Economic Studies, U.S. Census Bureau Working Papers, Working Paper No. 11-06, Washington, DC
Andersson M, Klepper S (2013) Characteristics and performance of new firms and spinoffs in Sweden. Ind Corp Change 22(1):245–280
Audretsch DB, Keilbach M (2005) The mobility of economic agents as conduits of knowledge spillovers. In: Fornahl D, Zellner C, Audretsch DB (eds) The role of labour mobility and informal networks for knowledge transfer, International Studies in Entrepreneurship, vol 6. Springer, Dordrecht, pp 8–25
Audretsch DB, Mahmood T (1995) New firm survival: new results using a hazard function. Rev Econ Stat 77(1):97–103
Block J, Sandner P (2009) Necessity and opportunity entrepreneurs and their duration in self-employment: evidence from German micro data. J Ind Competition Trade 9(2):117–137
Boschma R, Frenken K (2011) The emerging empirics of evolutionary economic geography. J Econ Geogr 11(2):295–307
Boschma R, Eriksson R, Lindgren U (2009) How does labour mobility affect the performance of plants? The importance of relatedness and geographical proximity. J Econ Geogr 9(2):169–190
Bruneel J, de Velde EV, Clarysse B (2013) Impact of the type of corporate spin-off on growth. Entrep Theory Pract 37(4):943–959
Buenstorf G (2009) Opportunity spin-offs and necessity spin-offs. Int J Entrepreneurial Venturing 1(1):22–40
Cabral L, Wang Z (2009) Spin-offs: theory and evidence from the early U.S. automobile industry. Federal Reserve Bank of Kansas City, Research Working Paper No. 08-15, Kansas City
Cameron AC, Trivedi PK (2005) Microeconometrics—methods and applications. Cambridge University Press, Cambridge
Delmar F, Shane S (2006) Does experience matter? The effect of founding team experience on the survival and sales of newly founded ventures. Strateg Organ 4(3):215–247
Dick JMH, Hussinger K, Blumberg B, Hagedoorn J (2013) Is success hereditary? Evidence on the performance of spawned ventures. Small Bus Econ 40(4):911–931
Eriksson T, Kuhn JM (2006) Firm spin-offs in Denmark 1981-2000—patterns of entry and exit. Int J Ind Organ 24(5):1021–1040
Ferriani S, Garnsey E, Lorenzoni G (2012) Continuity and change in a spin-off venture: the process of reimprinting. Ind Corp Change 21(4):1011–1048
Franco AM, Filson D (2006) Spin-outs: knowledge diffusion through employee mobility. Rand J Econ 37(4):841–860
Geroski P (1995) What do we know about entry? Int J Ind Organ 13(4):421–440
Geroski PA, Mata J, Portugal P (2010) Founding conditions and the survival of new firms. Strateg Manage J 31(5):510–529
Gimeno J, Folta TB, Cooper AC, Woo CY (1997) Survival of the fittest? Entrepreneurial human capital and the persistence of underperforming firms. Adm Sci Q 42(4):750–783
Haltiwanger JC, Lane JI, Spetzer JR (2007) Wages, productivity and the dynamic interaction of business and workers. Labour Eon 14(3):575–602
Helfat CE, Lieberman MB (2002) The birth of capabilities: market entry and the importance of pre-history. Ind Corp Change 11(4):725–760
Hitt M, Ireland R, Camp S, Sexton D (2001) Introduction to the special issue 'Strategic entrepreneurship: entrepreneurial strategies for wealth creation'. Strateg Manage J 22(6–7):479–491
Honjo Y (2000) Business failure of new firms: an empirical analysis using a multiplicative hazards model. Int J Ind Organ 18(4):557–574

ILO (2013) Global employment trends 2013—recovering from a second jobs dip. Int Labor Office, Geneva
Iturriaga FL, Cruz NM (2008) Antecedents of corporate spin-offs in Spain: a resource-based approach. Res Policy 37(6–7):1047–1056
Jenkins SP (1995) Easy estimation methods for discrete-time duration models. Oxf Bull Econ Stat 57(1):129–138
Jovanovic B (1982) Selection and the evolution of industry. Econometrica 50(3):649–670
Klepper S, Sleeper S (2005) Entry by spinoffs. Manage Sci 51(8):1291–1306
Leung A, Zhang J, Wong PK, Foo MD (2006) The use of networks in human resource acquisition for entrepreneurial firms: multiple "fit" considerations. J Bus Venturing 21(5):664–686
Malmberg A, Power D (2005) How do (firms in) clusters create knowledge? Ind Innov 12(4): 409–431
Manjón-Antolín MC, Arauzo-Carod JM (2008) Firm survival: methods and evidence. Empirica 35(1):1–24
Mata J, Portugal P (1994) Life duration of new firms. J Ind Econ 42(3):227–245
Mata J, Portugal P (2002) The survival of new domestic and foreign-owned firms. Strateg Manage J 23(4):323–343
Mayer-Haug K, Read S, Brinckmann J, Dew N, Grichnik D (2013) Entrepreneurial talent and venture performance: a meta-analytic investigation of SMEs. Res Policy 42(6–7):1251–1273
McCann BT, Folta TB (2012) Entrepreneurial entry thresholds. J Econ Behav Organ 84(3): 782–800
Meyer BD (1990) Unemployment insurance and unemployment spells. Econometrica 58(4): 757–782
Muendler M, Rauch JE, Tocoian O (2012) Employee spinoffs and other entrants: stylized facts from Brazil. Int J Ind Organ 30(5):447–458
OECD (2013) Entrepreneurship at a glance 2013. OECD Publishing, Paris
Pakes A, Ericsson R (1998) Empirical implications of alternative models of firm dynamics. J Econ Theory 79(1):1–45
Parhankangas A, Arenius P (2003) From a corporate venture to an independent company: a base for a taxonomy for corporate spin-off firms. Res Policy 32(3):463–481
Phillips DJ (2002) A genealogical approach to organizational life changes: the parent-progeny transfer among Silicon Valley law firms, 1946-1996. Adm Sci Q 47(3):474–506
Prentice R, Gloeckler L (1978) Regression analysis of grouped survival data with application to breast cancer data. Biometrics 34(1):57–67
Rocha V, Carneiro A, Varum CA (2013) Entrepreneurship dynamics: entry routes, business-owner's persistence and exit modes. CEF.UP Working Paper No. 2013-10, Porto
Santarelli E, Vivarelli M (2007) Entrepreneurship and the process of firms' entry, survival and growth. Ind Corp Change 16(3):455–488
Sapienza HJ, Parhankangas A, Autio E (2004) Knowledge relatedness and post-spin-off growth. J Bus Venturing 19(6):809–829
Song J, Almeida P, Wu G (2003) Learning-by-hiring: when is mobility more likely to facilitate interfirm knowledge transfer? Manage Sci 49(4):351–365
Tzabbar D, Aharonson BS, Amburgey TL (2013) When does tapping external sources of knowledge result in knowledge integration? Res Policy 42(2):481–494
Unger JM, Rauch A, Frese M, Rosenbusch N (2011) Human capital and entrepreneurial success: a meta-analytical review. J Bus Venturing 26(3):341–358
Varum CA, Rocha V (2012) The effect of crises on firm exit and the moderating effect of firm size. Econ Lett 114(1):94–97
Von Greiff J (2009) Displacement and self-employment entry. Labour Econ 16(5):556–565
Wallin MW, Dahlstrand AL (2006) Sponsored spin-offs, industrial growth and change. Technovation 26(5–6):611–620
Wezel FC, Cattani G, Pennings JM (2006) Competitive implications of interfirm mobility. Organ Sci 17(6):691–709

Part II
Human Capital

Chapter 7
Economic Performance of Portuguese Academic Spin-Offs: Does the Human Capital of Founders Matter?

Aurora A.C. Teixeira and Ricardo Castro

Abstract Most existing literature on spin-offs deals with factors affecting the emergence of these firms and not so much with what influences their economic outcomes. Moreover, the role of human capital as a potential booster of economic performance in spin-offs has been neglected or analyzed rather superficially. This chapter aims at assessing the role that human capital plays on the performance of Portuguese spin-offs in its different forms, including the entrepreneurs' level and type of education, skills, experience, and network capabilities. Using a sample of 90 founders of 61 Academic Spin-Offs (ASOs) located in Portugal, associated with the University Technology Enterprise Network (UTEN), it was found that among human capital dimensions, business expertise, most notably market knowledge, was the one that affected economic performance the most in ASOs. Both the level and type of formal education of the founders failed to significantly influence the economic performance of ASOs. The unemployment status of the founders (prior to creating the ASOs), formal contacts with university, as well as the undertaking of R&D activities and internationalization emerged as critical positive determinants of economic performance in ASOs. Although some evidence exists on the relevance of university research excellence for the performance of ASOs, a univocal result emerged regarding the university context: ASOs that exclusively resort to the services of Science Parks, Incubators, and TTOs outperformed the others.

Keywords Human capital • Academic spin-offs • Economic performance

A.A.C. Teixeira (✉)
Faculdade de Economia, CEF.UP, Universidade do Porto,
INESC TEC, OBEGEF, Porto, Portugal
e-mail: ateixeira@fep.up.pt

R. Castro
Faculdade de Economia, Universidade do Porto, Porto, Portugal
e-mail: 110481023@fep.up.pt

R. Baptista, J. Leitão (eds.), *Entrepreneurship, Human Capital, and Regional Development*, International Studies in Entrepreneurship 31,
DOI 10.1007/978-3-319-12871-9_7

7.1 Introduction

For a considerable period of time, human capital has been considered a key factor for the countries' economic growth (Lucas 1988; Romer 1990). Macro level studies have considered, in general, that human capital is the amount of formal education that each individual possesses (Mincer 1958; Schultz 1960). This concept, however, encompasses not only formal education but a set of activities related to people that is likely to influence the individual's future income. These activities include formal education, training, on-the-job training, improving health care in general, and other types of informal education, which could improve the efficiency of individuals (Becker 1962).

Although not examined in depth, at micro level, more specifically, at the level of the firms, human capital has also been identified as a lever for economic performance in firms (Davidsson and Honig 2003; Shane and Khurana 2003; Walter et al. 2006; Alvarez and Rodriguez 2011). In this case, human capital might refer to the entrepreneurs' level of formal education (Colombo and Grilli 2009; Gimmon and Levie 2010), training (Gimeno et al. 1997; Colombo and Grilli 2010; Ganotakis 2012), social networks (Davidsson and Honig 2003; Shane and Khurana 2003; Walter et al. 2006; Alvarez and Rodriguez 2011), or average human capital of firms, with regard to the level of education, training, and experience of the firms' collaborators (Teixeira 2002).

Even though there is a vast literature on the relevance of human capital for firm performance taking either the human capital of entrepreneurs (Colombo and Grilli 2009; Gimmon and Levie 2009; Ganotakis 2012) or collaborators as isolated factors of performance, analyses integrating both the human capital of entrepreneurs and collaborators as interacting explanatory factors are scarce. The majority of existing studies tends to focus on the influence of human capital on SMEs (Soriano and Castrogiovanni 2012), large companies (Hitt et al. 2001), population in general (Davidsson and Honig 2003; Alvarez and Rodriguez 2011), or start-ups (Gimmon and Levie 2010; Okamuro et al. 2011). There is still a limited understanding of how the different dimensions of human capital influence the economic performance of ASOs (O'Shea et al. 2005; Karlsson and Wigren 2012). It is likely that, contrarily to other types of firms, the relevance of the entrepreneurs' human capital on the performance of ASOs involves dimensions (for instance, type of education, level of industrial-related experience) often neglected by existing literature.

Nowadays, ASOs play a major role in society as they transform new scientific discoveries into business opportunities (Grandi and Grimaldi 2005; O'Shea et al. 2005; Walter et al. 2006). A spin-off company can be defined as a new company that was established by transferring "core technology" and founders from a parent organization. It is considered a mechanism for technology transfer because it is usually formed to commercialize technology that originated in a public Research and Development (R&D) laboratory, a university, or a private company (Carayannis et al. 1998). A University Spin-Off (USO) or Academic Spin-Off (ASO) involves the transfer of a core technology from an academic institution to a new company, where the founding member(s) may include the academic inventor(s) (O'Shea et al. 2008).

Although there are several interesting studies on ASOs, most of them focus on the factors that propel their emergence, and not so much on their economic performance after they are created. Some recent studies analyzing ASOs located in developed countries, such as Sweden and the USA, investigate how legitimacy, social, and human capital influence the university employees' propensity to launch start-ups (O'Shea et al. 2005; Karlsson and Wigren 2012). Some studies on ASOs in Portugal have been recently released, but they focus on the general determinants of performance (Teixeira and Grande 2013) or on the determinants of the internationalization speed in such firms (Teixeira and Coimbra 2014). They do not assess in detail the impact that the different dimensions of human capital of entrepreneurs and firms have on the economic performance of these firms.

This study aims at filling this gap by investigating the impact of human capital, in its various dimensions, on the economic performance of ASOs. It contributes to the literature that analyzes this type of companies by studying the determinants of their performance, focusing on their development process and not solely on their emergence. Additionally, it contributes to a broader literature on the performance determinants of firms, specifying the different dimensions of the entrepreneurs' human capital.

To address this chapter's goal, quantitative and causality methods are used on a sample of 90 founders of 61 ASOs out of a population of 116 Portuguese university spin-offs created in the last 10 years and associated with entities belonging to the University Technology Enterprise Network (UTEN).[1]

The present chapter is organized as follows: Sect. 7.2 reviews the relevant literature, specifying the main concepts and the key determinants of economic performance in firms. Section 7.3 presents the methodological considerations and the data used in the analysis. Section 7.4 presents the empirical results, and the Conclusions provide the main results, limitations, and policy implications of the findings.

7.2 Main Determinants of Performance in ASOs: A Review of the Literature

In a context where governments seek to promote knowledge-based activities, while reducing public expenditure, universities are seen as entities capable of supporting the creation of knowledge economies that generate large economic benefits (Sarkar 2010; Wright et al. 2012). Universities were created in order to produce exclusive science and technology, knowledge, and qualified workers (O'Shea et al. 2005). However, their mission was to expand and today they are important instruments of technological transfer and economic growth (Klofsten and Jones-Evans 2000;

[1] UTEN is a network of professional Technology Transfer Offices (TTOs) focused on the commercialization and internationalization of Portuguese Science and Technology.

Wright et al. 2012). It is known that one of the mechanisms of transferring knowledge from university to the market is creating Academic Spin-Offs (ASOs). These firms are created specifically with the objective of exploiting technological knowledge originating within universities, and according to some authors they provide important contributions to economic growth and technological innovation (Grandi and Grimaldi 2005; Wright et al. 2012).

The group of factors that determine and influence the performance of ASOs is very wide, similarly to those affecting other types of firms, such as SMEs. In general, these studies categorize the determinants of firm performance into three main groups: entrepreneurs (Davidsson and Honig 2003; Shane and Khurana 2003; Walter et al. 2006; Alvarez and Rodriguez 2011), firms (O'Shea et al. 2005; Colombo and Grilli 2009), and context (Colombo and Grilli 2009; Gimmon and Levie 2010) related factors.

7.2.1 Determinants Related to Entrepreneurs

7.2.1.1 Factors Related to Human Capital

Business opportunities depend on prior knowledge such as information about technological or market developments, or market inefficiencies (Shane 2000) that create opportunities for introducing new products, processes, or strategies (Alvarez and Rodriguez 2011). The ability to identify business opportunities is a cognitive task that allows some individuals, but not others, to discover entrepreneurial opportunities (Shane and Venkataraman 2000). Entrepreneurial activity depends on the interaction between the characteristics of the opportunities and of the people who exploit them (Casson 2005). Thus, opportunities are objective, but the perception of opportunity is subjective (Casson 2005). These opportunities do not appear in the absence of human action, and are rather created through the efforts of individuals (Freeman 1982).

The human capital theory states that education or training provides individuals with greater cognitive capacity, making workers more productive and efficient (Mincer 1958; Schultz 1960; Becker 1962). The same theory also states that companies have an economic incentive to invest in human capital, expecting to obtain higher future profits derived from higher levels of productivity with regard to wages paid (Becker 1962). If (business) opportunities arise, individuals with more or higher human capital quality should identify them better than those with less human capital (Davidsson and Honig 2003). Formal education is a component of human capital that may help accumulate explicit knowledge that can provide skills that are useful for entrepreneurs to create businesses (Alvarez and Rodriguez 2011). Nevertheless, human capital is not only made up of knowledge provided by formal education but it also includes knowledge acquired through experience and practical learning (Davidsson and Honig 2003).

The technology that the new spin-off will exploit and the characteristics of the founders are fundamental for the new company, since they largely represent the entire purpose of creating the new firm. Prior research has indicated that the founders' human capital tends to enhance the economic performance of the new spin-off (Okamuro et al. 2011; Karlsson and Wigren 2012).

Alvarez and Rodriguez (2011) studied the factors that influence the discovery of business opportunities, focusing on human capital, social capital, and gender, which they believe are key factors for maximizing the discovery of business opportunities. The authors confirm the influence that human capital has on the discovery of opportunities was consistent with previous research (Shane 2000; Davidsson and Honig 2003). This acknowledges that formal education contributes to the accumulation of knowledge, which gives entrepreneurs useful skills to create businesses (Alvarez and Rodriguez 2011). Other dimensions besides formal education, such as skills and experience, were also pointed out as key factors to discover business opportunities (Shane and Venkataraman 2000; Alvarez and Rodriguez 2011) and related to firm performance (Ganotakis 2012). In fact, Gimeno et al. (1997) found that both the level of education and management experiences were positively related to a firm's economic performance.

The literature is somewhat conflicting when it comes to the influence that academic degrees have on venture creation, survival, and performance (Gimmon and Levie 2010). There are various studies on the relationship between new venture performance and education levels, indicating that research-focused individuals have a lower propensity to start businesses, and therefore a researcher is valued based on academic production, while an entrepreneur is valued based on market results (Roberts 1991; Karlsson and Wigren 2012). Karlsson and Wigren (2012) studied the way human capital influences employees' start-up propensity in Sweden. These authors demonstrate that tacit knowledge, such as being able to help a colleague to start a business, has a positive impact on the creation of start-ups. Additionally, the academic position of the individual had a negative correlation with business start-ups.

Also related to the emergence of start-ups, Roberts (1991) proposed an inverted U relationship between the technology flow from an advanced research and development "source organization" to a newly founded firm and the level of education. The author found that performance, measured by the flow of technology transferred, increases up to Master's Degree level and then drops at PhD level. Assuming that the factors behind emergence also matter for subsequent performance, it is possible to state that:

Hypothesis 1: There is a nonlinear relation between the founders' level of formal education and the economic performance of ASOs.

In order to build a successful company, it is fundamental to have knowledge on business, product development and production, as well as on the market (Gimeno et al. 1997; Colombo and Grilli 2010; Ganotakis 2012). Business management expertise provides specific human capital on the aspects of business that are relevant to create a spin-off company, which includes skills such as selling, finance, sales, technology, logistics, marketing, organization, and communication (Shane 2003). The study conducted by Ganotakis (2012) measured human capital through the entrepreneurial founding team's formal education, which was divided into general education, technical education, and business education. The author realized that the specific human capital of the entrepreneur, especially associated with business/managerial, sector-specific, and commercial skills are the key factors to manage a firm, and to identify appropriate markets for the product/service, resulting in a significant performance increase in a firm; however, general education fails to significantly cause an impact on performance.

In a recent study, Colombo and Grilli (2009) found a significant correlation between the founders' number of years of economic or management education and firm growth, and a weaker effect of technology education. Earlier, Almus and Nerlinger (1999) found that new ventures with entrepreneurs with vast engineering and technical skills have shown higher levels of growth. Entrepreneurs with highly advanced/specialized technological expertise are likely to possess knowledge generated by R&D, and this knowledge can lead them to exploit leading edge technologies, and therefore introduce new and technologically complex, innovative products/services to a market (Ganotakis 2012), thus increasing firm performance.

Thus, it is suggested that:

Hypothesis 2: The type of human capital of an ASO founder influences the spin-offs' economic performance.

Start-ups are commonly small companies with scarce initial resources, where human capital and complementary resources brought by founders are the main competing advantages (Shane and Stuart 2002; Shane 2004).

Penrose (1959) presented the concept of a firm as a bundle of resources. The author provides a theory for effective management of a firm's resources, productive opportunities, and diversification strategy. She suggests that firms develop advantages from market imperfections and create economic value due to the effective and innovative management of resources, and it is this heterogeneity of resources that gives each firm its unique character (Kor and Mahoney 2004). From the concept of the resource-based view, firms gain and sustain competitive advantage by deploying valuable resources (Barney 1986). The life cycle of technology is frequently short, which leads to increasingly accelerated product development (Wu 2007). Consequently, technological start-ups face volatile environments, in which competing technologies appear frequently and thus survival and performance are not assured.

The resources and abilities brought to the firm by the entrepreneur are crucial for the performance and include the core resources of the entrepreneur, such as specialized knowledge (Amit and Schoemaker 1993), financial capital (Brush et al. 1997), and managerial ability (Collis 1991).

Therefore, the following hypothesis is proposed:

Hypothesis 3: The type of resource the founder brings to the new venture influences economic performance.

The professional experience of the individual is key when founding the firm (Haveman and Cohen 1994), which influences the entrepreneur's expectations concerning the new company. According to several studies, work experience (Gimmon and Levie 2010; Soriano and Castrogiovanni 2012), entrepreneurial expertise (Shane and Khurana 2003), and previous knowledge in a particular industry (Shane 2000; Okamuro et al. 2011) enhance the ability to discover and sustain entrepreneurial opportunities. This is related to the importance of market knowledge, defined as organized and structured information about the market, which includes the knowledge of a company's upstream (suppliers) and downstream (customers) partners and competitors (Lee and Habte-Giorgis 2004). Entrepreneurs with previous industry experience will have a better knowledge of any underdeveloped technological and marketing opportunity in that specific sector, which may provide good potential for market exploitation (Shane 2000).

In the specific case of ASOs, oftentimes the inventors of new technology do not have industry experience since their careers have been mostly academic, connected to research or teaching activities (Karlsson and Wigren 2012). Studies have shown that ASOs founded by a team that involves both the inventor and people with significant industry experience are likely to perform better than other university spin-offs (Doutriaux and Barker 1995). Therefore, the spin-offs will perform better if their management team incorporates individuals with industry experience (Walter et al. 2006).

Accordingly, it is possible to state that:

Hypothesis 4: The professional experience and status of the ASO founders influence their economic performance.

The Triple Helix argument suggests that the interaction involving university-industry-government is fundamental in leveraging innovation in a knowledge-based society where the university is considered the source of new knowledge and technology, the industry represents the source of production activities, and the government is the source of contractual relations (Etzkowitz 2003).

Various companies base their activities on R&D and innovation only if they receive government funds (Zawislak and Dalmarco 2010), and for that reason the government is an important part of that tripod (universities-firms-government), essentially because it is responsible for the laws, policies, and funds that may regulate and enhance academic spin-offs.

There are several forms of support provided by governmental agencies and other organizations to newly created firms. This can be considered a competitive advantage (Lee et al. 2001) to leverage the economic performance of firms, not only from the national top-down level, but also from the local bottom-up level, often in collaboration with other organizations in civil society (Etzkowitz 2003). Specifically, many governments have introduced an increasing range of policies encouraging the involvement of universities in technology transfer (D'Este and Patel 2007). By reducing the possible risk effects that are common during the early stage of a start-up, increased levels of network capabilities protect the new ventures from environmental threats (Lee et al. 2001).

University–industry knowledge transfer refers to various interactions at different levels, involving the exchange of knowledge and technology between universities and firms (Bodas Freitas et al. 2013), which can be designated as the third mission of universities and are the very mechanisms for generating technological spillovers (D'Este and Patel 2007). The main purpose of university-industry relations is to complement company resources by producing highly qualified scientific knowledge (Zawislak and Dalmarco 2010). These interactions include various types of equity or contract-based relationships between universities and industry, the commercialization of intellectual property and employment interactions (Bodas Freitas et al. 2013). Nevertheless, there is empirical evidence that shows that relationships, such as personnel mobility, informal contacts, consulting relationships, and joint research projects, represent a very important role in the transfer of knowledge between university and industry (D'Este and Patel 2007; Cohen et al. 2002).

There are various studies focusing on university–industry interactions (Rothaermel et al. 2007; D'Este and Iammarino 2010); nevertheless, these studies focus on the institutional mode and few of them analyze informal interactions (Bodas Freitas et al. 2013). It is presumed that most interactions with individual academics are informal, which is difficult to measure, if they are not explicitly formalized in personal contractual interactions.

The network relations of academic spin-off founders with university and government provide companies with a variety of resources, such as market information, ideas, social support, venture funding, and financial resources, which help improve their performance (Walter et al. 2006). Network capability allows a firm to associate its own assets to those of other firms by building relationships, and it is a mechanism for anticipating market opportunities (Pérez and Sánchez 2003).

A study conducted by Shane and Stuart (2002), which used data from 134 firms founded to exploit MIT-assigned inventions during the 1980–1996 period, focuses on the role of the founders' social capital and on how initial resource endowments affect the performance of new ventures. The study demonstrates that university spin-offs, where entrepreneurs have direct and indirect relationships with venture investors, are most likely to receive venture funding and are less likely to fail. The researchers concluded that the social capital of the firm's founders represents an important benefaction.

There is evidence of a positive and significant relationship between the social networks of the entrepreneurs and the potential for discovering opportunities to create businesses (Alvarez and Rodriguez 2011). This confirms the idea that individuals integrated in dense social networks are more willing to cooperate and have a higher degree of trust, and therefore they have a greater access to large amounts of information, which can lead to the discovery of new entrepreneurial opportunities (Davidsson and Honig 2003; Shane and Khurana 2003; Alvarez and Rodriguez 2011).

Hirai et al. (2012) examined the effect that external advice networks have on the performance of university spin-offs (measured by a factor analysis using the variables of sales volume, employment and competitive capabilities), by studying 79 Japanese university spin-offs. The researchers found a significantly positive relationship where more nonredundancy in a university spin-off external advice network is associated with superior venture performance.

Therefore, it is proposed that:

Hypothesis 5: The level and type of network capabilities of ASO founders influence the firm's economic performance.

7.2.1.2 Other Entrepreneur-Related Factors

Studies have demonstrated that firms founded by a team present a better performance in terms of growth, as opposed to firms founded by a single person. This happens because the potential individual know-how deficits are compensated by other members of the founding team (Eisenhardt and Schoonhoven 1990). An earlier study by Eisenhardt and Schoonhoven (1990) focused on the characteristics of the founding top-management team. Involving a sample of 92 newly founded US semiconductor firms in Silicon Valley, the study found that the combination of size, heterogeneity, and joint experience of the founding top-management team was significantly correlated with firm growth. Therefore, the following hypothesis is proposed:

Hypothesis 6: ASOs with a higher number of founders are more likely to present a better economic performance than the remaining ASOs.

The commitment of the entrepreneurs to the company is indicative of the amount of human resources devoted to the venture. Firms created by "fake" entrepreneurs, that is, those who see the venture as a "hobby," tend to present a lower performance than that achieved by full-time entrepreneurs (Doutriaux and Barker 1995). Therefore, the following hypothesis is proposed:

Hypothesis 7: ASOs whose founders are committed full time to the ASOs are more likely to perform better economically than the remaining ASOs.

7.2.2 Determinants Related to Firm

Several factors related to the characteristics and resources of firms are likely to influence the performance of a company (Shrader and Simon 1997), most notably: how the spin-offs emerge (Colombo and Grilli 2010), export and innovation capabilities (Lee and Habte-Giorgis 2004), and company size (Lee and Habte-Giorgis 2004).[2]

Since in ASOs the technology is rarely market-ready, the source of creation of the firm is crucial, because the knowledge surrounding the technology is necessary

[2] Age and size of the firms are typically included as important determinants of firm performance. This work does not include such variables as ASOs are mainly very small and young firms. Instead, the size of the founding team was included, as well as information on whether the firm exports or not, which might be considered "instrumental" variables of size and age, respectively.

to modify or adapt the technology and associated products/services to meet customer requirements (Di Gregorio and Shane 2003). Therefore, the following hypothesis is proposed:

Hypothesis 8: ASOs whose source of creation is associated to firms are more likely to perform better economically than the remaining ASOs.

Innovation has been identified for a very long time as a critical lever for economic performance in firms (Lee and Habte-Giorgis 2004; O'Shea et al. 2008; Carmona et al. 2012). It involves input-related activities, such as Research and Development (R&D), and measurable outputs, including patents and other intellectual property right mechanisms that have the potential for generating income and new products and services (Lee et al. 2001). This input and output bundle is often recognized as the firm's technological capabilities. Lee et al. (2001) define technological capabilities as a firm's competitive advantage, which include technological knowledge, namely patents and production skills. These capabilities become even more central in technological start-ups (Shrader and Simon 1997).

The technological capability, viewed as patents, is an important core competence for new ventures to gain market acceptance and to accomplish long-term competitive advantages and performance, especially because high-tech industries are progressively more innovative and competitive (Zahra et al. 2006). In fact, according to a study conducted by Lee et al. (2001), which focused on 137 Korean start-ups, it was found that the number of patents, utility models, and designs registered on the Korean Patents are proxies to the firms' technological capabilities and positively and statistically significant to their performance (sales variation for 2 years).

In addition, business R&D is essential to gain competiveness in the market. Studies have shown that firms that invest in R&D tend to experience higher growth than firms that do not. This happens because R&D is crucial for product and process innovation, improving the performance of firms that use innovation as a strategy (Lee and Habte-Giorgis 2004). Since not all innovations are patentable, and some firms have a lower propensity to secure patents, the intensity of R&D expenditure can be used as an alternative to assess innovation dynamics in firms (Yang et al. 2010). Therefore, the following hypothesis is proposed:

Hypothesis 9: Innovative ASOs are more likely to perform better economically than the remaining ASOs.

Exports are likely to have a positive impact on firm performance as firms can take advantage of a growing market abroad (Teixeira and Grande 2013). However, few studies demonstrate the direct linkage between ASO exports and performance. While studying manufacturing firms in the USA, Lee and Habte-Giorgis (2004) found that exports have a significant and positive influence on the economic performance of firms. Therefore, the following hypothesis is proposed:

Hypothesis 10: Exporting ASOs are more likely to perform better economically than the remaining ASOs.

7.2.3 Determinants Related to Context

Resources and capabilities may provide a university with advantages in technology transfer processes (O'Shea et al. 2005; Powers and McDougall 2005). Gras et al. (2008) categorize five types of resources and capabilities related to universities: human capital (researchers), stock of (theoretical and applied—publications and patents) knowledge, policies and strategies, resources and capabilities of TTOs, and support measures provided by universities for new academic entrepreneurs and spin-offs.

Existing studies demonstrated that the size and nature of financial resources allocated to universities influence the performance of ASOs, suggesting that a greater proportion of industry-level funding is associated with higher levels of technology transfer (O'Shea et al. 2005).

There is evidence of a significant correlation between the quality of university researchers and spin-off performance (Zucker et al. 1998; O'Shea et al. 2005; Powers and McDougall 2005). Powers and McDougall (2005) have shown that human capital related to individuals from higher quality academic institutions create spin-offs to capture the revenue generated by their intellectual capital. This suggests that it may be easier for academics from top tier universities to assemble resources to create start-ups due to their increased credibility (DiGregorio and Shane 2003). O'Shea et al. (2005) also found a significant correlation between the quality of university researchers and spin-off activity. Another explanation for the spin-off rate is that a highly ranked university increases chances to obtain funding from investors, since it is believed that technologies created in higher quality universities are better than in less prominent universities (DiGregorio and Shane 2003). Albeit the university patenting pool does not guarantee that a university developing technology will be transformed into a product/service—and ultimately implemented on the market (Powers and McDougall 2005)—it represents a safety measure for potential economic value in the future. While Powers and McDougall (2005) found that university patenting is not a prediction of spin-off activity, O'Shea et al. (2005) uncovered a positive correlation between the number of university patents and spin-off activity. Additionally, some authors believe that spin-off activity can be encouraged or inhibited according to the different policies and strategies of universities regarding technology transfer (Di Gregorio and Shane 2003). The excellence of university R&D centers is likely to reflect such idiosyncrasies. Therefore, the following hypothesis is proposed:

Hypothesis 11: The characteristics and quality of Host Universities influence the economic performance of ASOs.

Incubators and other related science and technology infrastructures, in particular science parks and TTOs, are viewed as a support environment for start-ups. These may include shared office spaces, a pool of shared support services to reduce overhead costs, professional business support and network provision, with professional business support being the most relevant function provided by the incubator (Bergek and Norrman 2008). Thus, since most university technologies are embryonic, it is necessary to develop them until they can be put on the market; therefore, the existence of incubators, science parks, and TTOs can influence spin-off activity and performance by providing an adequate environment for business development (DiGregorio and Shane 2003). Although Di Gregorio and Shane (2003) and O'Shea et al. (2005) failed to uncover a significant effect of the presence of university-affiliated incubators/science parks/TTOs on start-up rates, it is possible to state that:

Hypothesis 12: ASOs that resort to technology transfer support from TTOs and other science and technology infrastructures outperform the remaining ASOs.

The "milieu innovateur" corresponds to a set of formal and informal relationships that are established in delimited territorial spaces involving the different economic and social agents, forms of production, and even a specific culture (Camagni 1991). Certain sectors tend to agglomerate spatially (Stuart and Sorenson 2003) because the environment of firms plays a role in the innovation process, both in terms of static efficiency (i.e., increases the efficiency of technologies already in use) and in terms of dynamic efficiency (by reducing the uncertainty that characterizes the processes of innovation and imitation, favoring the development of collective learning processes) (Camagni 1991). Then, since economic, legal, and cultural environments influence businesses activity, the geographic location of the universities and the activity sector are likely to influence the creation and performance of the spin-off (DiGregorio and Shane 2003).

O'Shea et al. (2008) suggest that the knowledge infrastructure of a region is a key factor in spin-off activity, and Maine et al. (2010) found significant evidence suggesting that specialized cluster effects are associated with higher growth rates for young biotech firms. Therefore, the following hypotheses are proposed:

Hypothesis 13: ASOs located in highly economically developed regions outperform the remaining ASOs.

Hypothesis 14: The activity sector of the ASO is likely to influence its economic performance.

7.3 Methodological Considerations

Given that the University Technology Enterprise Network (UTEN) is the only source in Portugal that gathers information on the ASOs linked to each Portuguese public university, this assessment uses these ASOs as the target population. Data on the firms and context were gathered and provided by Aurora Teixeira and Marlene Grande, who have been responsible within UTEN for several studies on ASOs (Teixeira and Grande 2013). The distribution of ASOs by Portuguese public universities is depicted in Table 7.2 (in Appendix).

A new questionnaire was created on entrepreneur features and implemented through a direct email survey (between March and June 2013), which was sent to all founders of the 116 ASOs studied previously by Aurora Teixeira and Marlene

Grande. This new founder questionnaire was designed to contain extensive and detailed information on the human capital characteristics of each founder, such as education, experience, and social capital. By the end of the survey period, responses from 61 firms (out of the 116 firms) had been obtained, representing 90 founders (out of 302), which correspond to response rates of respectively, 53 % (in terms of number of firms) and 30 % (in terms of number of founders).

The questionnaire has been organized into seven sections. Each question of the questionnaire makes it possible to obtain the proxies for the relevant variables, which are then used for testing the hypotheses provided in Sect. 7.2.

The first section includes the demographic characteristics of founders, such as name, gender, and time dedicated to the company. The second section describes the founders' level of education (less than high school, high school, bachelor's, degree, master's, and PhD) and the respective area of education (sciences and health, exact sciences, social sciences, computer science, economic/managerial, and engineering). The third section refers to the three most important complementary training obtained. Choices included technological, business/administration, and human resources/behavioral/leadership. The fourth section includes the resources brought by each founder to the firm at the date of its formation: capital, market knowledge, technological, marketing and sales, business contacts, and organization management. The fifth section explores the professional experience prior to the formation of the firm by sector (banking/insurance/consultancy, biotechnology, construction, electrical engineering, mining/metals and minerals, food industry, aircraft industry, automotive industry, footwear industry, pharmaceutical industry, maritime industry, mechanical industry, furniture, chemicals, health, information technology and communication, textiles and clothing, and tourism) and type of organization (micro company, less than 10 workers), small company (between 10 and 49 workers), medium business (between 50 and 249), large business (more than 250 workers), multinational. The sixth section explores the employment status at the time the current company was created: unemployed, company owner (company exists, company bankrupt, company sold), employee, self-employed, and student. The seventh section studies the social capital of the founder, the relationship between social capital and university spin-off performance has not been studied properly (Hirai et al. 2012). The assumption explored here is that the entrepreneurs' social capital contributes to the performance of the new venture, defining two types of relationships at the date the ASO was established. First, the formal linkages are defined as if the founder had at least two contacts per year, including contracts, projects between organizations and the company. Second, informal linkage is defined as if the founder had at least two contacts per year, including personal relationships and/or established through common interests with a more social character. This study focused on the formal and informal relations with University, Industry, and Government. In addition, the specific type of industry (micro, small, medium, large, multinational) and type of Government (national, local. European) of both formal and informal relations are described in detail.

Based on the literature review performed, the econometric specification to be estimated comprises three main groups of determinants: (1) those related to the founder(s) (formal level of education, area and complementary education, resources brought to the company at the date of its formation, previous experience and employment status at the time of the creation of the ASO, level and type of network capabilities, number of founders, and founders' commitment to the ASO); (2) those related to the ASO (source of creation, innovation, internationalization); and (3) contextual factors (university characteristics, TTO support, regional factors, and sector of the ASO). In algebraic terms, the general econometric specification that is used to test the hypotheses put forward stands as follows:

$$
\begin{aligned}
& \textit{Economic performance}_i = \hat{\beta}_0 + \\
\text{Entrepreneurs' related determinants} & \left\{
\begin{aligned}
& +\hat{\beta}_1 \textit{Formal level of education} + \hat{\beta}_2 \textit{Area of education} + \\
& +\hat{\beta}_3 \textit{Resources brought to the company at the date of its formation} + \\
& +\hat{\beta}_4 \textit{Previous experience and employment status} + \\
& +\hat{\beta}_5 \textit{Level and type of network capabilities} + \hat{\beta}_6 \textit{Number of founders} + \\
& +\hat{\beta}_7 \textit{ founders committed} +
\end{aligned}\right. \\
\text{Firms' related determinants} & \left\{ +\hat{\beta}_8 \textit{ Source of creation} + \hat{\beta}_9 \textit{ Innovation} + \hat{\beta}_{10} \text{ Internationalization} + \right. \\
\text{Contextual determinants} & \left\{ +\hat{\beta}_{11} \textit{ University} + \hat{\beta}_{12} \textit{ TTo} + \hat{\beta}_{13} \textit{ Region} + \hat{\beta}_{14} \textit{ Sector} + \hat{e}_i \right.
\end{aligned}
\tag{1}
$$

where i is the subscript for each founder and e_i is the sample error term.

The proxies related to the determinants of economic performance (i.e., the model's independent variables) are described in Table 7.3 (in Appendix), together with the study's main hypotheses.

7.4 Empirical Results

7.4.1 Descriptive Results

Similarly to Ganotakis (2012), economic performance is measured by annual sales per individual employed, including founders (in FTE). In 2011, a respondent ASOs had on average 20.4 thousand EUR in sales per capita, with some ASOs presenting no sales at all, and the ASO with the highest sales per capita reaching 122.82 thousand EUR. This does not compare very favorably to the situation of Portuguese SMEs. In fact, the turnover per capita observed in an average SME in Portugal was around 89.6 thousand EUR (reference year 2009, Source: INE), which is much higher than the evidence by ASOs in our sample.

Looking at the percentiles of sales per capita, it was found that ASOs that are below the percentile 50, the "Low performers," registered sales per capita below 8.9 thousand EUR. "Medium performers" had sales per capita between 8.9 and 34.7 thousand EUR (percentile 75) and "High performers" (upper percentile) registered sales per capita above 34.7 thousand EUR.

On average, the team of founders of a Portuguese ASO includes approximately 3 individuals, with the time committed to the venture being quite high (78 %) (Table 7.4, in Appendix).

In several studies on ASOs it has been found that founders are highly qualified academically (Colombo and Delmastro 2002; Colombo and Piva 2012; Karlsson and Wigren 2012). Portuguese ASO founders are also highly educated individuals, with 27.8 % having a master's degree and about one third with a PhD. This is almost twice the proportion found in start-ups in general (IAPMEI 2007). Thus, in Portugal ASO founders are much more qualified in formal terms than their start-up counterparts (less than one quarter of these founders have a university degree, and only 0.6 % have a PhD).

Almus and Nerlinger (1999) found that ASOs with entrepreneurs specialized in technical areas, such as engineering and science, showed higher levels of growth (growth is measured as employment numbers, at least at two different points in time).

The majority of the respondent founders are graduated in Engineering (42.2 %), 15.6 % in Computer Science. Only 11.1 % graduated in Economics or Management. Nevertheless, 36.7 % of the founders did some kind of complementary course on business-related subjects. For technological complementary formal education, the corresponding figure is 28.9 %. A relatively low share of founders (16.7 %) has complementary education on human resources/behavioral/leadership issues. In line with the arguments by Colombo and Piva (2012), the ASO founders possess a large amount of technical and scientific competencies.

Technological knowledge and capital are the most frequent resources brought by the founders to their ASOs, with 86 % and 78 % of the founders, respectively, claiming to have brought such resources to the firm by the time of its establishment. Other resources brought by 42 %/37 %/32 % of the founders are business contacts/market knowledge/organizations management. It is possible to observe that marketing and sales are the less frequent resources brought by (18 %) founders to the firm.

According to the study by Colombo and Piva (2012), on average, the founders of ASOs have greater experience with R&D, but are less experienced in industry, both in technical and commercial positions. In term of sectors, 26 % of the founders had previous experience in the ICT sector, 24 % in the University or R&D sector, and 11 % in industry.

A quite balanced proportion of founders claimed to have past professional experience in firms from different sizes (39 % in large, 24 % in micro, and 21 % in small and medium firms).

The founders' social capital in terms of (formal and informal) business contacts is quite high, with more than 80 % claiming that in the last year they have established regular formal and informal contacts with the University, Industry, Government, or other entities.[3] More specifically, about half of the respondents said to have established formal contacts with Industry, and 29 % with Multinational firms. It was observed that 87 % of the founders had formal contacts and 83 % had informal contacts. It was also found that 49 % of the founders had *formal contacts with*

[3] It is considered a formal contact if the founder has at least two contacts per year, including contracts and projects between organizations and the firm. Conversely, informal contacts occur when the founder has at least two contacts per year with the organization, including personal relationships and/or established through common interests, with a more social character.

Industry, 17 % had *Formal contacts with Government*, and 29 % had *Informal contacts with Industry—Multinational*.

In terms of firm characteristics, 22 % of the founders state that ASOs were created outside the university (Table 7.4, in Appendix). Although a significant proportion of the founders (51 %) are linked to ASOs that conducted R&D activities in the period 2008–2011, a quite low percentage (14 %) registered patents in the same period. Over 40 % of founders are linked to ASOs that export. In 2009, Portugal had 348,552 micro, small, and medium enterprises (SMEs). From these, 10 % of the total were exporting SMEs. Thus, it is important to mention that although this number is very low, turnover represented 40.0 % of the total SMEs activity in 2009 (INE 2011). The turnover per capita observed in the total SMEs was around 89.8 thousand EUR, and 39 thousand EUR below SME exporters.

On average, ASOs, whose source of creation is external to the university, perform R&D activities and export tend to outperform their remaining counterparts.

In 2010, universities associated with the respondent founders have registered 6 international patents per thousand researchers (c.f. Table 7.4, in Appendix). In terms of scientific production disseminated internationally, the ASO founders are associated with universities that produced, on average, 2.9 articles indexed in the WOS/ISI per researcher in the period 2000–2007, where 54 % of their research centers are classified as Very Good or Excellent by the Portuguese Foundation for Science and Technology (FCT).

In terms of region characteristics, on average the respondent founders are associated with ASOs located in relatively developed NUTs III regions (presenting a per capita purchasing power index 10 points above the national average). Approximately one quarter of the founders are linked to ASOs that benefited from TTOs or other S&T infrastructure support. Only this latter variable is statistically correlated with the ASOs' economic performance, reflecting that in bivariate terms the ASOs that resort to TTOs/S&T support perform relatively worse than the remaining.

7.4.2 Causality Analysis: Determinants of Economic Performance in ASOs

Seven different models were estimated in accordance with the hypotheses specified (Table 7.1). These models reveal a good quality of fit, with more than 60 % of the variance of firm sales per capita explained by the variables included in the models. All the groups of determinants considered—entrepreneurs, firms, or context—are relevant for explaining economic performance in ASOs.

In terms of human capital, it was found that, for the sample considered, the founder's level of formal education is not significant in any of the models (thus, *H1* is not corroborated). Nevertheless, this is in line with some extant studies (e.g., Roberts 1991; Ganotakis 2012; Karlsson and Wigren 2012). In that sense, the concept presented by Roberts (1991) and Ganotakis (2012) of an inverted U relationship between the formal education level and the ASO performance was not clear in this study. This lack of statistical significance of the education level of ASO founders

Table 7.1 Determinants of ASOs economic performance: econometric models: estimation results

Determinant group			Hypothesis		Proxy for the independent variable	Model 1	Model 2	Model 3	Model 4	Model 5a	Model 5b	Model 6
Entrepreneurs' related determinants	Human capital	Education level	*H1: Founders' formal education level*		Master	0.161	0.133	-0.004	0.140	0.173	0.040	0.037
					PhD	0.178	0.130	0.243	0.288	0.551	0.162	0.133
		Education type	*H 2: Type of human capital*	*H2a: Advanced/specialized technological expertise*	Engineering degree	0.270	0.245	0.275	0.278	0.271	0.264	0.236
				H2b: Complementary education in Business/ Administration	Complementary Business/ Administration training	-0.567*	-0.508	-0.538*	-0.482	-0.409	-0.504	-0.474
		Resources	*H3: Resource the founder brings*	*H3a: Capital*	Capital	-0.059	-0.105	-0.074	-0.091	-0.101	-0.125	-0.155
				H3b: Market knowledge	Markets Knowledge	0.675**	0.716**	0.628*	0.723**	0.715**	0.695**	0.723**
				H3c: Business contacts	Business Contacts	-0.251	-0.219	-0.245	-0.305	-0.280	-0.300	-0.251
		Professional experience	*H4: Professional experience and status*	*H4a: Prior experience*	Professional experience	-	-	-0.009	-	-	-	-
				H4b: Prior experience in the same industry	Same industry experience	0.375	0.394	0.352	0.339	0.334	0.333	0.350
				H4c:Previous industry experience	Professional experience in Industry	-	-	0.444	-	-	-	-
				H4d: Previous University or R&D experience	Professional experience in University or R&D	-	-	-0.274	-	-	-	-
				H4e: Previous experience in large or Multinational	Large	0.316	0.317	-	0.098	0.167	0.134	0.118
					Multinational	-	-	-0.672	-	-	-	-
				Hypothesis 4f: ASOs founders' prior status employment situation is likely to influence the economic performance of ASOs	Self-employ or company other	0.141	0.131	0.218	-	-	-	-
					Self-employed	-	-	-	0.675	0.762	0.779	0.790
					Unemployed	-	-	-	10.041*	0.926*	10.138**	10.127**
					Employee	-	-	-	0.330	0.262	0.362	0.359
					Is a company Owner: still exists	-	-	-	0.791	0.727	0.836	0.799
Entrepreneurs' related determinants	Human capital	Networks	*H 5: Network capabilities*	*H5a: Formal linkages*	Formal contacts	-	-	-	-	-0.334	-	-
				H5b: Formal linkages with University; Industry; Government	Formal contacts with University	0.347	0.349	0.467	0.608*	0.782	0.743*	0.747*
					Formal contacts with Industry	0.048	0.057	0.090	0.081	0.121	0.214	0.180
					Formal contacts with Government	-0.006	0.005	-0.087	-0.166	0.516	-0.035	0.034
					Formal contacts with Industry - Multinational	-	-	-	-	0.463	-	-
					Formal contacts with Government - National	-	-	-	-	-10.161*	-	-
				H5c: Informal linkages with University; Industry; Government	Informal contacts with University	-	-	-	-	-	-0.161	-0.133
					Informal contacts with Industry	-	-	-	-	-	-0.208	-0.151
					Informal contacts with Government	-	-	-	-	-	-0.215	-0.280
	Other factors	Number of founders	*H6: Size of founders' team*		Number of founders (in ln)	0.385	0.369	0.354	0.272	0.198	0.323	0.292
		Full time equivalent of founder	*H7: Commitment*		Full time equivalent of the founder to the company (in ln)	0.087	0.089	0.027	0.068	0.100	0.111	0.080

(continued)

Table 7.1 (continued)

(…)

Determinant group		Hypothesis		Proxy for the independent variable		Model 1	Model 2	Model 3 Model 4	Model 5a	Model 5b	Model 6
Firms' related determinants	Source of creation	*H8: Source of creation*		Source creation of the firm is external to the university	-0.069	-0.131	0.021	-0.050	-0.188	-0.051	-0.101
	Innovation	*H9: Innovation*	*H9a: Patents*	If the firm has patents between the year of 2008 - 2011	-0.905*	-0.856*	-0.824*	-0.792*	-0.674	-0.847*	-0.757
			H9b: R&D	If the firm has R&D between the year of 2008 - 2011	10.725***	10.750	10.606***	10.644***	10.650***	10.627***	10.637***
	Internationalization	*H10: Exporter*		If the firm exports	0.555**	0.499*	0.593	0.639**	0.708***	0.616**	0.579**
Contextual determinants	University characteristics	*H11: Host University characteristics*	*H11a: Certified scientific research and scientific publications)*	Scientific pool of knowledge (WOS publications per researcher) (2000-2007) (in ln)	-	0.368	-	-	-	-	0.463
			H11b: Pool of advanced applied/ commercialized knowledge (patents)	International patent pool per 1000 researchers (2010) (in ln)	-	-0.122	-	-	-	-	-0.079
			H11c: Research excellence	Proportion of Research units classified with 'Excellent' or 'Very Good' by the FCT	0.015	0.015	0.018*	0.015	0.011	0.012	0.011
	University technology transfer office support	*H12: Technology transfer support*	*H12a: Science park*	Science park	10.723***	10.793***	10.763***	10.711***	10.845***	10.527***	10.657***
			H12b: Incubator	Incubator	0.853***	0.821**	0.803**	0.864***	0.854***	0.738**	0.738**
			H12c: TTO	TTO	10.734***	10.627**	10.558**	10.643**	10.858***	10.316*	10.342*
	Region	*H13: Region*		Index of purchasing power per NUT III regions (in ln)	10.510**	10.317*	10.574**	10.592**	10.705**	10.658**	10.450*
	Sector	*H14: Sector of activity (Default: ICT)*		Energy sector	20.069	20.098***	20.016***	10.957***	20.178***	10.943***	20.007***
				Bio sector	0.080	0.082	-0.104	-0.012	0.053	0.059	0.043
				Micro sector	0.575	0.682	0.934	0.550	0.201	0.599	0.718
				Agri-food sector	0.977*	0.931*	0.719	0.469	0.695	0.573	0.535
				Consulting sector	20.284***	20.281***	20.816***	10.942***	10.932***	10.753**	10.803**
				Constant	-90.411	-80.783	-90.394	-100.003	-100.513	-100.156	-90.524
				Adjusted R2	**0.632**	**0.626**	**0.627**	**00.641**	**0.649**	**0.628**	**0.620**

Grey cells identify relative high correlation

Note: (***) (**) (*) statistically significant at (1 %) (5 %) (10 %)

might, to a large extent, be explained by the fact that ASO entrepreneurs are in their vast majority highly educated individuals.

Although Ganotakis (2012) and Almus and Nerlinger (1999) have found that ASOs whose entrepreneurs had high engineering and technical skills showed higher levels of growth, in this analysis the type of human capital (proxied by engineering degrees and complementary business education) failed, in general, to have a significant impact on the ASOs' economic performance. Thus, *H2* was not verified. In particular, complementary education in Business/Administration (*H2b*), when significant, emerged negatively related to economic performance, which contrasts with the evidence found by Colombo and Grilli (2009).

The importance of managerial capabilities obtained through formal education is somehow demystified here; instead, the study highlights the relevance of other sources of business knowledge acquired, namely through experience, which are often neglected in comparison with formal business knowledge acquired through formal education. This type of informal managerial capabilities is reflected in our models by the market knowledge brought by the founder to the ASOs (*H3b*), which is evidence of a significant and positive relation to economic performance in all models (at 5 % significance level).

Other resources brought by the founder, namely capital (*H3a*) or business contacts (*H3c*), failed to have an impact on ASO performance.

Professional experience has been seen as a key factor for firm performance (*H4*). In the case presented here, and contrasting with existing studies (Shane 2000; Okamuro et al. 2011; Ganotakis 2012), the various proxies of professional experience, most notably the entrepreneurs' experience in the same sector (prior to founding the ASO), are not statistically significant. It might be that the experience effect is captured largely, as referred above, by the founder's past market knowledge and prior occupational status.

The evidence collected indicates that the prior employment status of the founder is relevant for explaining economic performance in ASOs. In particular, ASOs whose founders were unemployed previously to the creation of the ASO, compared to those who were employed, present, on average, a higher economic performance (*H4i*). Thus, unemployment spells do not necessary "condemn" individuals to necessity or unsuccessful business venturing. This is an interesting finding, which is in disagreement with the commonly accepted idea that entrepreneurship induced by necessity is associated with low(er) performance in new ventures, comparatively to those induced by opportunity (Lumpkin and Katz 2009).

An important dimension of the founders' human capital is their social networks. The estimations suggest that ASOs whose founders establish regular formal contacts with Universities managed to achieve higher economic performances, whereas those that establish regular formal contacts with national government show lower performance. Thus, the type of formal contacts established is important (*H5b*).

When it comes to the other factors related to the entrepreneur, namely the size of the founders' team (*H6*) and the founders' commitment to the ASO (*H7*), although the estimates are positive, none of them has had a significant influence on the performance of ASOs. This is somehow at odds with the findings by Eisenhardt and Schoonhoven (1990), who found a significant positive correlation between the size of the team and firm growth, and by Doutriaux and Barker (1995), who suggest that firms created by part-time entrepreneurs presented a lower performance than those created by full-time entrepreneurs.

In terms of firm-related determinants, the findings suggest that the source for firm creation does not influence performance (*H8*) as conveyed in the study by Colombo and Grilli (2010), while innovation capabilities (*H9a,b*) and the internationalization propensity of ASOs significantly influence their economic performance. Specifically, evidence shows that ASOs that conducted R&D activities in the period 2008–2011 or that exported by 2011 are more productive, which corroborates *H9b* and *H10*, and is in accordance with the literature (Lee and Habte-Giorgis 2004; Teixeira and Grande 2013). Further evidence suggests that ASOs with patents in 2008–2011 reveal lower per capita sales (failing to validate *H9a*). This latter finding contrasts with that of Lee et al. (2001), although this study measured firm performance by 2 years sales variation and not per capita sales. It might be that in the case of the Portuguese ASOs patents represent a cost and do not yet yield any return due to their recent application/registration.

The contextual determinants are critical for the economic performance of ASOs, most notably the existing support in terms of technology transfer, the region's development level and the sector in which the ASOs operates.

Albeit Powers and McDougall (2005) found that there was a strong relation between faculty quality (measured by the total number of citations that each university received) and ASO performance (measured by the number of start-ups created), our estimations failed to find a significant relation between a university's pool of knowledge (i.e., WOS publications per researcher) and ASO performance (rejecting *H11a*). In the same line of Powers and McDougall (2005), it was found that the university's patent portfolio is not significantly related to ASO performance (thus *H11b* is not corroborated).

The only university features that proved to have some influence on the economic performance of ASOs is research excellence, that is, the proportion of R&D centers that were classified by the government science evaluation body, the FCT (*Fundação para a Ciência e a Tecnologia*), as "Very Good" or "Excellent" (thus, *H11c* receives middle support).

Interestingly, the support received by ASOs in the technology transfer process, through university science parks (*H12a*), incubators (*H12b*), or TTOs (*H12c*) emerged as an important factor for economic performance in ASOs. Thus, *H12* receives strong support. Comparatively to the situation of combined science parks-incubators-TTO support (or no support at all),[4] those ASOs that claimed to resort exclusively to one of the technology transfer support mechanisms present higher levels of sales per capita. Even though the findings by Di Gregorio and Shane (2003) and O'Shea et al. (2005) suggested that the presence of a university incubator has no significant impact on start-up activity, our results clearly show that these S&T infrastructures are critical for ASO performance.

[4] Almost all surveyed ASOs stated that they have received some kind of support, exclusively or combined.

The development of the local industrial basis and the existence of positive regional spillover effects implicitly incorporated in region's per capita purchasing power have a significant impact on the performance of ASOs. The corroboration of *H13* confirms the importance of a strong regional basis for new businesses to survive and endure (Pfeifer and Sarlija 2010).

Finally, this study suggests that the sector of activity is important for the performance of ASOs (Gadenne 1998), which corroborates *H14*. Firms that operate in the Energy/Environment/Sustainability, Consulting, and Agri-food sectors present, on average, with all the remaining factors being constant, higher productivity levels comparatively to those operating in the ICT/Software/Digital Media sector. Contrarily, the Bio/Pharmaceutical or Medical devices/diagnosis, and Microelectronics/Robotics sectors show no relation to ASO performance.

7.5 Conclusions

The emphasis on academic entrepreneurship increased recently for policy makers and university leaders. Viewed as solution for an unstable economy and society as a result of globalization (Wright et al. 2012), academic entrepreneurship is also believed to promote increased employment and innovation (O'Shea et al. 2005).

The aim of this study was to extend our understanding of the determinants of economic performance in Academic Spin-Offs (ASOs), considering three groups of determinants—entrepreneurs, firms, and context—and focusing and reflecting on the several dimensions of the founders' human capital. The main research question was: "Does the human capital of founders matter for economic performance in Portuguese ASOs?".

To address this research question, this study analyzed a sample of 90 founders from 61 ASOs created in 1997 or afterwards, located in Portugal and associated with entities within the University Technology Enterprise Network (UTEN).

More specifically, this study investigated the effect that general and specific human capital of founders of Portuguese ASOs have on the economic performance (measured by sales per capita) of those firms, as well as the combination of skills that need to exist in a founding team to promote high performance levels. The results of this analysis contribute to the existing literature in a number of ways.

The extant empirical studies on this topic primarily focus on ASO start-up rate and survival, neglecting the subsequent factors that influence the companies' economic performance, namely the human capital of ASO founders. This study also addresses the scarcity of research on how different dimensions of human capital influence the economic performance of ASOs (O'Shea et al. 2005; Karlsson and Wigren 2012; Ganotakis 2012), providing a theoretical debate on the existence of different types of human capital of founders that are likely to influence company performance.

An interesting finding of this study was that although high levels of education level and technical education had a positive impact, these were statistically nonsignificant for ASO performance. Moreover, the complementary business/

administration obtained by formal education, when significant, was negatively related to ASO performance, which contrasts with the extant literature (for instance, Colombo and Grilli 2009). Interestingly, other types of business expertise acquired, especially by informal paths, most notably market knowledge, caused more impact on the company performance than managerial capabilities acquired in formal education.

A thought-provoking result contrary to the literature (for instance, Lumpkin and Katz 2009) emerged in this study: the ASO founders that were unemployed at the moment the ASO was created presented higher economic performances when compared to those who presented other employment statuses (such as employees, self-employed, business owners).

Formal contacts with university, as well as the undertaking of R&D activities and internationalization, emerged as critical determinants of economic performance in ASOs. Moreover, research of excellence in universities also contributes (albeit in a smaller extent) to ASO performance. The results found further uncover the strong role played by the university technology support infrastructures, most notably Science Parks, Incubators, and TTOs, on the performance of Portuguese ASOs, especially when the ASOs used each type of support exclusively, as opposed to combining diverse supports. Finally, the fact that ASOs located in highly developed regions managed to present higher performances demonstrates the importance of regional spillovers, in line with Pfeifer and Sarlija (2010).

Some of the results found have important policy implications. For instance, being an exporting firm is significantly and positively related to economic performance. Thus, policies that allow access to international business intelligence services and market prospect knowledge will for sure contribute to the long-term sustainability of ASOs. This might be coupled with innovation policies directed toward more specialized incubating and technology transfer services by the university technology support infrastructures, most notably Science Parks, Incubators, and TTOs, anchored in the internationalization of ASOs.

The formal contacts with university are critical determinants of economic performance in ASOs. Therefore, intensifying the interactions and connections between the agents (universities, research centers, laboratories research, and technological infrastructures) and ASOs should contribute to the formation of a true innovation system, geared toward competitiveness and sustainable learning. This might be achieved through active employment policies that foster formal human resource immersion of TTOs/Science Parks/Incubators staff in business firms and temporary training periods for ASO staff.

As usual in empirical scientific research, the small size of the sample that was used undermines an adequate assessment of some of the dimensions of the founders' human capital. An in-depth, qualitative account of the founders' background would also be an important complement to the quantitative study undertaken and would make it possible to uncover the mechanisms through which tacit knowledge, informal, and social linkages interact within the team of founders and influence ASO performance. Such endeavor is likely to constitute an interesting and challenging path for future research.

Appendix

Table 7.2 Distribution of the population of ASOs by TTO and University (reference year: 2013)

Associated university	UTEN partner associated to technology transfer	Target ASOs [founders]	Respondent ASOs [founders]	Effective response rate ASOs [founders], in %	% of total response rate ASOs [founders]
ISCTE	INDEG	1 [1]	1 [1]	100.0 [100.0]	1.6 [1.1]
U. Algarve/ U. Évora	CRIA	12 [22]	8 [12]	66.7 [54.5]	14.8 [15.6]
	Sines Tecnopólo	1 [2]	1 [2]	100.0 [100.0]	
U. Aveiro	UATEC	8 [30]	3 [3]	37.5 [10.0]	4.9 [3.3]
U. Beira Interior	Parkurbis	5 [8]	1 [1]	20.0 [12.5]	3.3 [2.2]
	UBI GAPPI	2 [6]	1 [1]	50.0 [16.7]	
U. Coimbra	IPN	6 [15]	2 [2]	33.3 [13.3]	6.6 [10.0]
	OTIC-UC	4 [16]	2 [7]	50.0 [43.8]	
U. Lisboa	IMM	2 [8]	1 [1]	50.0 [12.5]	1.6 [1.1]
U. Madeira	Gapi Madeira	1 [2]	1 [2]	100.0 [100.0]	1.6 [2.2]
U. Minho	Avepark	3 [6]	1 [1]	33.3 [16.7]	13.1 [11.1]
	Avepark and Spinpark	3 [14]	1 [1]	33.3 [7.1]	
	Avepark and TecMinho	1 [2]	1 [1]	100.0 [50.0]	
	Avepark. Spinpark and TecMinho	1 [1]	1 [1]	100.0 [100.0]	
	Spinpark and TecMinho	1 [3]	1 [3]	100.0 [100.0]	
	TecMinho	10 [30]	3 [3]	30.0 [10.0]	
U. Nova Lisboa	FCT-UNL	3 [6]	2 [3]	66.7 [50.0]	8.2 [6.7]
	FCT-UNL and Madan Parque	3 [10]	2 [2]	66.7 [20.0]	
	Madan Parque	7 [11]	1 [1]	14.3 [9.1]	
U. Porto	INESC Porto	6 [21]	4 [5]	66.7 [23.8]	37.7 [41.1]
	UPIN	2 [3]	2 [3]	100.0 [100.0]	
	UPTEC	25 [67]	15 [27]	60.0 [40.3]	
	UPTEC/UPIN	2 [6]	2 [2]	100.0 [33.3]	
U. Técnica Lisboa	Inovisa	2 [3]	1 [1]	50.0 [33.3]	6.6 [5.6]
	Taguspark	1 [1]	1 [1]	100.0 [100.0]	
	TT@IST	4 [8]	2 [3]	50.0 [37.5]	
Total		116 [302]	61 [90]	52.6 [29.8]	100.0 [100.0]

Table 7.3 Hypothesis and proxies for the independent variables

Determinant group	Hypothesis				Proxy for the independent variable
Entrepreneurs' related determinants	Human capital	Education level	*Hypothesis 1: There is a nonlinear relation between founders' formal education level and ASOs economic performance*		Master (dummy: yes: 1; no: 0)
					PhD (dummy: yes: 1; no: 0)
		Education type	*Hypothesis 2: The type of human capital of ASO' founder influence this latter economic performance*	*H2a: Advanced/specialized technological expertise*	Engineering degree (dummy: yes: 1; no: 0)
				H2b: Complementary education in Business/Administration	Complementary business/administration training (dummy: yes: 1; no: 0)
		Resources	*Hypothesis 3: The type of resource the founder brings to the new venture influences this latter economic performance*	*H3a: Capital*	Capital (dummy: yes: 1; no: 0)
				H3b: Market knowledge	Market knowledge (dummy: yes:1; no:0)
				H3c: Business contacts	Business contacts (dummy: yes: 1; no: 0)
		Professional experience	*Hypothesis 4: The professional experience and status of ASOs' founders influence ASOs economic performance*	*H4a: Prior experience*	Professional experience (dummy: yes: 1; no: 0)
				H4b: Prior experience in the same industry	Same industry experience (dummy: yes: 1; no: 0)
				H4c: Previous industry experience	Professional experience in industry (dummy: yes: 1; no: 0)
				H4d: Previous University or R&D experience	Professional experience in University or R&D (dummy: yes: 1; no: 0)
				H4e: Previous experience in large or Multinational	Large (dummy: yes: 1; no: 0)
					Multinational (dummy: yes: 1; no: 0)
				H4f: ASOs founders' prior status employment situation is likely to influence the economic performance of ASOs	Self-employ or company other (dummy: yes: 1; no: 0)
					Self-employ (dummy: yes: 1; no: 0)
					Unemployed (dummy: yes: 1; no: 0)
					Employee (dummy: yes: 1; no: 0)
					Is a company owner (dummy: yes: 1; no: 0)

	Human capital	Networks	*Hypothesis 5: The level and type if network capabilities of ASOs founder influence the firm's economic performance*	*H5a: Formal linkages*	Formal contacts (dummy: yes:1; no: 0)
				H5b: Formal contacts with University, Industry and Government	Formal contacts with University (dummy: yes: 1; no: 0)
					Formal contacts with Industry (dummy: yes: 1; no: 0)
					Formal contacts with Government (dummy: yes:1; no:0)
					Formal contacts with Industry—Multinational (dummy: yes:1; no:0)
					Formal contacts with Government—National (dummy: yes:1; no:0)
				H5c: Informal contacts with University, Industry and Government	Informal contacts with University (dummy: yes:1; no:0)
					Informal contacts with Industry (dummy: yes:1; no:0)
					Informal contacts with Government (dummy: yes:1; no:0)
	Other factors	Number of founders	*Hypothesis 6: ASOs with higher number of founders are more likely to have better economic performance than the remaining ASOs.*		Number of founders (in ln)
		Full time equivalent of founder	*Hypothesis 7: ASOs whose founders are full-time committed to the ASOs are more likely to have a better economic performance than the remaining ASOs.*		Full time equivalent of the founder to the company (in ln)

(continued)

Table 7.3 (continued)

Determinant group	Hypothesis			Proxy for the independent variable
Firms' related determinants	Source of creation	*Hypothesis 8: ASOs whose source of creation of the company has a relation to firms are more likely to have a better economic performance than the remaining ASOs.*		Source creation of the firm is external to the university (dummy: yes:1; no:0)
	Innovation	*Hypothesis 9: Innovative ASOs are more likely to have a better economic performance than the remaining ASOs.*	*H9a: Patents*	If the firm has patents between the year of 2008–2011 (dummy: yes: 1; no: 0)
			H9b: R&D	If the firm has R&D between the year of 2008–2011 (dummy: yes: 1; no: 0)
	Internationalization	*Hypothesis 10: Exporting ASOs are more likely to have a better economic performance than the remaining ASOs*		If the firm exports (dummy—1: yes; 0: no)
Contextual determinants	University characteristics	*Hypothesis 11: Host University characteristics and quality influence the economic performance of ASOs*	*H11a: Certified scientific research and scientific publications*	Scientific pool of knowledge (WOS publications per researcher) (2000–2007) (in ln)
			H11b: Pool of advanced applied/commercialized knowledge (patents)	International patent pool per 1,000 researchers (2010) (in ln)
			H11c: Research excellence	Proportion of Research units classified with "Excellent" or "Very Good" by the FCT
	University technology transfer office support	*Hypothesis 12: ASOs that resort to technology transfer support from TTOs and other science and technology infrastructures outperform the remaining ASOs*	*H12a: Science park* *H12b: Incubator* *H12c: TTO*	Science park (dummy: yes: 1; no: 0) Incubator (dummy: yes: 1; no: 0) TTO (dummy: yes: 1; no: 0)

	Region	*Hypothesis 13: ASOs located in higher economic developed regions outperform the remaining ASOs*	Index of purchasing power per NUT III regions (in ln)
	Sector	*Hypothesis 14: The sector of activity of the ASO is likely to influence its economic performance*	Energy sector (1 when the ASO belongs to the energy sector)
			Bio sector (1 when the ASO belongs to the bio sector)
			Micro sector (1 when the ASO belongs to the micro sector)
			Agri-food sector (1 when the ASO belongs to the agri-food sector)
			Consulting sector (1 when the ASO belongs to the Consulting sector)

Table 7.4 Descriptive statistics for the dependent variable and entrepreneurs' related factors

			Mean	Min	Max	Correlation Coefficient[a]	Sig. (2-tailed)
	Dependent variable	0. Sales per capita (th. €)	20.4	0	122.8	-	-
Human capital	Maximum level of formal education	1. Master	0.300	0	1	0.045	0.615
		2. PhD	0.278	0	1	-0.152	0.090*
	Type of formal education	3. Economic/ Managerial	0.111	0	1	0.000	1.000
		4.: Engineering	0.422	0	1	0.147	0.102*
		5. Computer science	0.156	0	1	-0.186	0.038**
	Complementary education	6. Technological	0.289	0	1	0.005	0.957
		7. Business	0.367	0	1	0.008	0.926
		8. Human Resources / Behavioural / Leadership	0.167	0	1	-0.027	0.768
	Resources brought to the company at the date of its formation	9. Capital	0.778	0	1	-0.095	0.289
		10. Markets knowledge	0.367	0	1	0.229	0.011***
		11. Technological	0.856	0	1	0.031	0.728
		12. Marketing and sales	0.178	0	1	0.037	0.677
		13. Business contacts	0.422	0	1	0.118	0.189
		14. Organizations Management	0.322	0	1	0.066	0.461
	Previous Experience	15. Has professional experience	0.811	0	1	-0.017	0.847
		16. Same sector as ASO	0.400	0	1	0.233	0.010**
		17. Sector: ICT	0.267	0	1	0.223	0.013**
		18. Sector: University or R&D	0.244	0	1	-0.195	0.030**
		19. Sector: Industry	0.111	0	1	0.086	0.340
		20. Type organization: Micro	0.244	0	1	0.052	0.559
		21. Type organization: Small	0.211	0	1	0.089	0.320
		22. Type organization: Medium	0.211	0	1	-0.046	0.610
		23. Type organization: Large	0.389	0	1	0.123	0.173
		24. Type organization: Multinational	0.0889	0	1	-0.029	0.747
	Employment status	25. Self-employed or company owner	0.256	0	1	0.080	0.372
		26. Student or scholarship	0.233	0	1	-0.242	0.007***
		27. Unemployed	0.089	0	1	0.109	0.223
		28. Employee	0.422	0	1	0.073	0.414
		29. Self-employed	0.144	0	1	0.010	0.908
		30. Company owner: company exists	0.078	0	1	0.043	0.631
	Social capital	31. Network Capabilities	0.933	0	1	-0.101	0.263
		32. Formal contacts	0.867	0	1	0.024	0.787
		33. Informal contacts	0.833	0	1	-0.167	0.063*
		34.Formal contacts with University	0.744	0	1	-0.052	0.562
		35. Formal contacts with Industry	0.489	0	1	0.081	0.365
		36. Formal contacts with Government	0.167	0	1	-0.001	0.987

(continued)

Table 7.4 (continued)

(...)

			Mean	Min	Max	Correlation Coefficient[(a)]	Sig. (2-tailed)
Human capital	Social capital	37.Formal contacts with Industry: Large	0.211	0	1	-0.104	0.246
		38.Formal contacts with Industry: Multinational	0.122	0	1	0.065	0.466
		39.Formal contacts with Government: National	0.100	0	1	-0.065	0.471
		40.Informal contacts with University	0.722	0	1	-0.110	0.221
		42. Informal contacts with Industry	0.578	0	1	-0.063	0.480
		42. Informal contacts with Government	0.189	0	1	-0.148	0.100*
Other factors		43. Number of Founders (no.)	2.8	1	9	-0.127	0.114
		44. FTE (full time equivalent), in %	78.9	5	100	0.274	0.001***
Firms' related factors		45. Source creation of the firm: External to the university	0.222	0	1	0.177	0.049**
		46. Has Patents in 2008 - 2011	0.144	0	1	-0.104	0.248
		47. Performed R&D activities in 2008-2011	0.511	0	1	0.431	0.000***
		48. Exporter	0.422	0	1	0.291	0.001***
Contextual factors		49. University international patent pool (number of international registered patents per 1000 researchers), 2010	5.82	0.000	20.60	0.005	0.956
		50. University Scientific pool of knowledge (publications indexed in WOS/ISI per researcher, 2000-2007)	2.90	.097	4.487	-0.063	0.435
		51. Proportion of Research units with Very Good or Excellent by FCT	0.538	0.00	0.869	0.032	0.689
		52. ASO resort to TTO/other S&T infrastructure support	0.244	0	1	-0.361	0.000***
		53. Science park	0.167	0	1	0.193	0.032**
		54. Incubator	0.411	0	1	0.172	0.056*
		55. TTO	0.056	0	1	0.026	0.769
		56. Per capita purchasing power index of the NUT III region where the firm is located (2009)	110.8	76.7	145.3	0.085	0.288
		57. ICT sector	0.51	0	1	-0.020	0.822
		58. Energy sector	0.13	0	1	0.229	0.011*
		59. Bio sector	0.20	0	1	-0.296	0.001**
		60. Micro sector	0.044	0	1	0.215	0.017*
		61. Agri-food sector	0.067	0	1	-0.012	0.896
		62. Consulting sector	0.044	0	1	0.045	0.614

Grey cells identify relative high correlation coefficients between independent variables and the dependent variable sales per capita

Note: *N*?=?90; (***) (**) (*) statistically significant at (1 %) (5 %) (10 %)

[a]We use Kendall-tau, which is a nonparametric correlation coefficient that can be used to assess and test correlations between non-interval scaled variables. Nevertheless, results do not differ substantially from those obtained with Pearson correlation coefficient

References

Almus M, Nerlinger E (1999) Growth of new technology based firms: which factors matter? Small Bus Econ 13:141–154

Alvarez N, Rodriguez V (2011) Discovery of entrepreneurial opportunities: a gender perspective. Ind Manag Data Syst 111(5):755–775

Amit R, Schoemaker P (1993) Strategic assets and organizational rent. Strateg Manag J 14:33–46

Barney J (1986) Strategic factor markets: expectations, luck, and business strategy. Manag Sci 32(10):1231–41

Becker G (1962) Investment in human capital: a theoretical analysis. J Polit Econ 70:9–49

Bergek A, Norrman C (2008) Incubator best practice: a framework. Technovation 28:20–28

Bodas Freitas I, Geuna A, Rossi F (2013) Finding the right partners: institutional and personal modes of governance of university–industry interactions. Res Policy 42:50–62

Brush C, Greene P, Hart M, Edelman L (1997) Resource configurations over the life cycle of venture. In: Frontiers of entrepreneurship research, 1997: Proceedings of the 17th annual entrepreneurship research conference, pp 315–329

Camagni R (1991) Local Milieu, uncertainty and innovation networks: towards a new dynamic theory of economic space. In: Camagni R (ed) Innovation networks: spatial perspectives. Belhaven Press, London

Carayannis E, Rogers E, Kurihara K, Allbritton M (1998) High-technology spin-offs from government R&D laboratories and research universities. Technovation 18(1):1–11

Carmona P, Momparler A, Gieure C (2012) The performance of entrepreneurial small and medium-sized enterprises. Serv Ind J 32(15):2463–2487

Casson M (2005) The individual-opportunity nexus: a review of Scott Shane: a general theory of entrepreneurship. Small Bus Econ 24:423–430

Cohen W, Nelson R, Walsh J (2002) Links and impacts: the influence of public research on industrial R&D. Manag Sci 48:1–23

Collis D (1991) A resource based analysis of global competition: the case of the bearings industry. Strateg Manag J 12:49–68

Colombo M, Delmastro M (2002) How effective are technology incubators? Evidence from Italy. Res Policy 31(7):1103–1122

Colombo M, Grilli L (2009) A capital partnership: how human and venture capital affect the growth of high-tech start-ups. Strateg Chang 18:231–239

Colombo MG, Grilli L (2010) On growth drivers of high-tech start-ups: exploring the role of founders' human capital and venture capital. J Bus Ventur 25(6):610–626

Colombo M, Piva E (2012) Firms' genetic characteristics and competence-enlarging strategies: a comparison between academic and non-academic high-tech start-ups. Res Policy 41(1):79–92

D'Este P, Iammarino S (2010) The special profile of university–business research partnerships. Pap Reg Sci 89(2):335–50

D'Este P, Patel P (2007) University-industry linkages in the UK: what are the factors determining the variety of interactions with industry? Res Policy 36(9):1295–1313

Davidsson P, Honig B (2003) The role of social and human capital among nascent entrepreneurs. J Bus Venturing 18:301–31

Di Gregorio D, Shane S (2003) Why do some universities generate more start-ups than others? Res Policy 32(2):209–227

Doutriaux J, Barker M (1995) The university-industry relationship in science and technology. Industry Canada Occasional Papers. Industry Canada, Ottawa, p 11

Eisenhardt K, Schoonhoven C (1990) Organizational growth: linking founding team, strategy, environment, and growth among U.S. semiconductor ventures. Adm Sci Q 35:504–529

Etzkowitz H (2003) Innovation in innovation: the triple helix of university-industry-government relations. Soc Sci Inf 42(3):293–337

Freeman J (1982) Organizational life cycles and natural selection processes. Res Organ Behav 4:1–32

Gadenne D (1998) Critical success factors for small business: an inter-industry comparison. Int Small Bus J 17(1):36–56
Ganotakis P (2012) Founders' human capital and the performance of UK new technology based firms. Small Bus Econ 39:495–515
Gimeno J, Folta T, Cooper A, Woo C (1997) Survival of the fittest? Entrepreneurial human capital and the persistence of underperforming firms. Adm Sci Q 42(4):750–783
Gimmon E, Levie J (2009) Instrumental value theory and the human capital of entrepreneurs. J Econ Issues 43(3):715–732
Gimmon E, Levie J (2010) Founder's human capital, external investment, and the survival of new high-technology ventures. Res Policy 39(9):1214–1226
Grandi A, Grimaldi R (2005) Academics organizational characteristics and the generation of successful business ideas. J Bus Venturing 20:821–845
Gras J, Galiana Lapera D, Solves I, Jover A, Sancho J (2008) An empirical approach to the organisational determinants of spin-off creation in European universities. Int Entrep Manag J 4(2):187–198
Haveman H, Cohen L (1994) The ecological dynamics of careers: the impact of organizational founding, dissolution, and merger on job mobility. Am J Sociol 100:104–52
Hirai Y, Watanabe T, Inuzuka A (2012) Empirical analysis of the effect of Japanese university spinoff's social networks on their performance. Tech Forecasting Soc Chang 80(6):1119–1128
Hitt M, Bierman L, Shimizu K, Rochhar R (2001) Direct and moderating effects of human capital on strategy and performance in professional service firms: a resource-based perspective. Acad Manage J 44(1):13–28
IAPMEI (2007) Observatório da Criação de Empresas — Relatório 2007, IAPMEI - Agência para a Competitividade e Inovação, Lisbon
INE (2011) Estudos sobre Estatísticas Estruturais das Empresas — 2007–2009, Instituto Nacional de Estatística, Lisbon
Karlsson T, Wigren C (2012) Start-ups among university employees: the influence of legitimacy, human capital and social capital. J Technol Transfer 37(3):297–312
Klofsten M, Jones-Evans D (2000) Comparing academic entrepreneurship in Europe—the case of Sweden and Ireland. Small Bus Econ 14:299–309
Kor Y, Mahoney J (2004) Edith Penrose's (1959) contributions to the resource-based view of strategic management. J Manag Stud 41(1):183–192
Lee J, Habte-Giorgis B (2004) Empirical approach to the sequential relationships between firm strategy, export activity, and performance in U.S. manufacturing firms. Int Bus Rev 13: 101–129
Lee C, Lee K, Pennings J (2001) Internal capabilities, external networks and performance: a study on technology-based ventures. Strateg Manag J 22:615–640
Lucas R (1988) On the mechanics of economic development. J Monet Econ 22:3–42
Lumpkin G, Katz J (2009) Advances in entrepreneurship, firm emergence and growth, vol 11. Emerald Group Publishing Limited, Bingley
Maine M, Shapiro M, Vining R (2010) The role of clustering in the growth of new technology-based firms. Small Bus Econ 34(2):127–146
Mincer J (1958) Investment in human capital and personal income distribution. J Polit Econ 66:281–302
O'Shea R, Allen T, Chevalier A, Roche F (2005) Entrepreneurial orientation, technology transfer and spinoff performance of U.S. universities. Res Policy 34:994–1009
O'Shea R, Chug H, Allen E (2008) Determinants and consequences of university spinoff activity: a conceptual framework. J Technol Transfer 33:653–666
Okamuro H, Kato M, Honjo Y (2011) Determinants of R&D cooperation in Japanese start-ups. Res Policy 40(5):728–738
Penrose E (1959) The theory of the growth of the firm. Wiley, New York
Pérez M, Sánchez A (2003) The development of university spin-offs: early dynamics of technology transfer and networking. Technovation 23:823–831

Pfeifer S, Sarlija N (2010) The relationship between entrepreneurial activities, national and regional development and firm efficiency-Global entrepreneurship Monitor (GEM)-based evidence from Croatia. J Entrep 19(1):23–41
Powers J, McDougall P (2005) University start-up formation and technology licensing with firms that go public: a resource-based view of academic entrepreneurship. J Bus Venturing 20:291–311
Roberts E (1991) The technological base of the new enterprise. Res Policy 20(4):283–97
Romer P (1990) Endogenous technological change. J Polit Econ 98:S71–S102
Rothaermel F, Agung S, Jiang L (2007) University entrepreneurship: a taxonomy of the literature. Ind Corp Chang 16(4):691–791
Sarkar S (2010) Empreendedorismo e Inovação. Escolar Editora, Lisboa
Schultz T (1960) Capital formation by education. J Polit Econ 68:571–583
Schumpeter J (1939) Business cycles. A theoretical, historical and statistical analysis of the capitalist process. McGraw-Hill Book Company, New York
Schumpeter J (1943) Capitalism, socialism and democracy, 5ª edição (2003). Routledge, New York
Shane S (2000) Prior knowledge and the discovery of entrepreneurial opportunities. Organ Sci 11:448–69
Shane S (2001) Technological opportunities and new firm creation. Manag Sci 47(2):205–220
Shane S (2003) A general theory of entrepreneurship: the individual-opportunity nexus. Edward Elgar Press, Northhampton
Shane S (2004) Encouraging university entrepreneurship. The effect of the Bayh–Dole Act on university patenting in the United States. J Bus Venturing 19(1):127–151
Shane S, Khurana R (2003) Bringing individuals back in: the effects of career experience on new firm founding. Ind Corp Chang 12:519–543
Shane S, Stuart T (2002) Organizational endowments and the performance of university start-ups. Manag Sci 48(1):154–170
Shane S, Venkataraman S (2000) The promise of entrepreneurship as a field of research. Acad Manage Rev 25:217–26
Shrader R, Simon M (1997) Corporate versus independent new ventures: resource, strategy and performance differences. J Bus Venturing 12:47–66
Soriano D, Castrogiovanni G (2012) The impact of education, experience and inner circle advisors on SME performance: insights from a study of public development centers. Small Bus Econ 38:333–349
Stuart T, Sorenson O (2003) The geography of opportunity: spatial heterogeneity in founding rates and the performance of biotechnology firms. Res Policy 32(2):229–253
Teixeira AAC (2002) On the link between human capital and firm performance. A theoretical and empirical survey. FEP Working Papers n° 121, November 2002
Teixeira AAC, Coimbra C (2014) The determinants of the internationalization speed of Portuguese University spin-offs: an empirical investigation. J Int Entrep 12:270–308, forthcoming
Teixeira AAC, Grande M (2013) Determinants of the economic performance of Portuguese academic spin-offs: do science and technology infrastructures and support matter? FEP Working papers no. 502, Sept 2013
Walter A, Auer M, Ritter T (2006) The impact of network capabilities and entrepreneurial orientation on university spin-off performance. J Bus Venturing 21:541–567
Wright M, Mosey S, Noke H (2012) Academic entrepreneurship and economic competitiveness: rethinking the role of the entrepreneur. Econ Innov New Technol 21:429–444
Wu L (2007) Entrepreneurial resources, dynamic capabilities and start-up performance of Taiwan's high-tech firms. J Bus Res 60:549–555
Yang C, Lin H, Li H (2010) Do R&D spinoffs have higher R&D productivity? Evidence from Taiwanese electronics firms. Ind Innov 17(3):285–307
Zahra A, Sapienza J, Davidsson P (2006) Entrepreneurship and dynamic capabilities: a review, model and research agenda. J Manag Stud 43(4):917–955
Zawislak P, Dalmarco G (2010) The silent run: new issues and outcomes for university-industry relations in Brazil. J Technol Manag Innov 6(2):66–82
Zucker L, Darby M, Armstrong J (1998) Geographically localized knowledge: spillovers or markets? Econ Inq 36(1):65–86

Chapter 8
Recruitment Processes and Capability Development in Academic Spin-Offs: An Exploratory Work

Ugo Rizzo

Abstract This work focuses on the influence of external knowledge via recruitment on the development of academic spin-off (ASO) firms, that is those businesses that are generated by academic staff and are based on results of research conducted within the university. Given the importance of external knowledge for these firms to develop and grow it is important to understand the mechanisms by which such knowledge is internalized and the impact of such knowledge on the firms' strategies and capability development. This work, by means of a multiple case study research, seeks to shed light on the issue with respect to recruitment processes. Results show that hiring managers and researchers from the external environment is a response to some particular situations. The consequences of these recruitment strategies are also analyzed.

Keywords Academic founders • CEO • External knowledge • Knowledge internalization • Networks

8.1 Introduction

This work focuses on the influence of external knowledge on the development of academic spin-off (ASO) firms, that is those businesses that are generated by academic staff based on results of their research conducted within the university. These firms act as bridges between university and industry allowing academic knowledge to reach the market as a product (e.g., Fontes 2005) and are considered important for the economic environment because of their positive impact on the processes of technological change and economic development (Vincett 2010).

U. Rizzo (✉)
Department of Economics and Management, University of Ferrara,
via Voltapaletto 11, Ferrara 44121, Italy
e-mail: ugo.rizzo@unife.it

R. Baptista, J. Leitão (eds.), *Entrepreneurship, Human Capital, and Regional Development*, International Studies in Entrepreneurship 31,
DOI 10.1007/978-3-319-12871-9_8

Innovation scholars have clearly highlighted how to innovate and maintain competitive advantage firms cannot rely entirely on internal knowledge sources and have to refer to the external environment. To this end several works highlighted how important it is to combine existing and external knowledge in order to stimulate innovation capabilities (Kogut and Zander 1992; Turner and Fern 2012; Rosenkopf and Nerkar 2001) and that grounding business activity on integration of different knowledge bases is positively correlated with performance (Rosenkopf and Almeida 2003; Song et al. 2003).

Among the variety of strategies by which external knowledge is internalized by firms, such as networks, alliances, and mergers (Rosenkopf and Almeida 2003; Song et al. 2003; Paruchuri and Eisenman 2012), hiring personnel represents one of the main channels by which to upgrade and diversify the firm's knowledge base (Song et al. 2003). Although managers and experienced personnel are among the main channels by which firms extend their knowledge base with positive effects on performance (Kraatz and Moore 2002; Song et al. 2003; Paruchuri and Eisenman 2012) it has also been shown how the hiring of new graduates may have positive impacts if their background is broader compared to the core business of the firm in which they are hired (Rizzo et al. 2013a).

In this work we seek to explore the influence that the knowledge acquired by ASO firms via the recruitment of personnel has on its capability development. More specifically we concentrate on the pattern of recruitment of both managers and employees in a sample of ASO firms and explore how such external knowledge impact on the capabilities of firms, therefore ultimately on its growth strategies.

By defining capabilities as those organizational constructions that ultimately impact on firm strategies (Dosi et al. 2000; Eisenhardt and Martin 2000; Helfat and Winter 2011), this study investigates how talented managers and researchers hired from the industrial world affect the process of growth and development of ASO firms. The issue has been poorly explored at the level of ASO firms and seems particularly interesting because of the scarce average growth performances these firms show (Lambert Review 2003).

This work is structured as follows: in Sect. 8.2 an analysis of the conceptual framework and literature review on the areas explored in this thesis and an outline of the argument are put forward. In Sect. 8.3 we describe the methodology, the data collection, and the analysis of the case studies undertaken in order to test the conjecture delineated. Finally a concluding section is provided.

8.2 Theoretical Framework: External Knowledge Internalization via Recruitment and ASO Firms

Economics and management literature on ASO firms have explored the advantages and disadvantages of hiring a *surrogate entrepreneur* in some depth (e.g., Franklin et al. 2001; Clarysse and Moray 2004). One of the main advantages of hiring a surrogate entrepreneur, and of employing managers of various backgrounds from the industrial world, lies in shifting the focus of the firm toward market requirements. Several studies in fact highlighted the fact that a main obstacle to the development of an ASO firm lies in the lack of entrepreneurial capabilities and market understanding in the team of academic founders.

It has been shown how academics often seek to focus more on technical issues rather than on market needs when creating a venture (Chiesa and Piccaluga 2000; Ramaciotti and Rizzo 2014). This can mean that there may be a lack of attention paid to the formation of relationships with the external environment which are necessary in order to provide the venture with the required supporting tools needed for it to develop (Radosevich 1995). Moreover there is a related desire for academics to remain employed at university and to continue their career there (Doutriaux 1987; Chiesa and Piccaluga 2000; Rizzo 2014).

Although such identified constraints faced by academics who become entrepreneurs may undermine the capability of the team to grow into a successful venture, literature does not strongly agree as to whether hiring a surrogate entrepreneur is always the best choice. Clarysse and Moray (2004) find that coaching the academic entrepreneur may be a better solution: this may be particularly true when the knowledge to be exploited is of a high degree of tacitness. On the contrary Franklin et al. (2001) find that the surrogate entrepreneur may overcome several constraining factors and therefore may represent a preferred solution.

Generally, however, the effects of hiring an experienced manager seem to be regarded as producing positive output in the development of ASO firms. Studies found that acquiring managers from the external environment improves the USO firm's performance (e.g., Bjørnåli and Gulbrandsen 2010). Among the competences that these managers bring into the firm are important improvements to the networking assets of the ASO firms, especially with respect to the financial needs the ASO firms usually face, especially at the very early stage of their development.

The positive effects obtained through the acquisition of external knowledge by means of the hiring of managers are also well known with respect to new firms which are not spin-offs. Several studies highlight the centrality of manager capabilities and experience in order for the firm to improve its innovation and productive performances (Boeker 1997). Rao and Drazin (2002, p. 503) show how hiring talented managers positively affects the routines and capabilities of "newer and poorly connected firms" and allows these firms to enhance their innovation capabilities.

Although the internalization of external knowledge by means of hiring has been mostly studied in respect to the effects of managers, more recent investigations have also focused on the effect of hiring non-managers, especially technical personnel, that is engineers and researchers (Rosenkopf and Almeida 2003; Tzabbar et al. 2013). These studies found that hiring new and possibly experienced engineers is particularly beneficial for the innovation capabilities of a company when the knowledge brought in by the new engineers is different from the core competence of the hiring firm (Song et al. 2003). More specifically it has been noted how the diversification and broadening of the competences within the firm, and especially in the R&D department or in the functions related to the innovation processes, tend to lead to an upgrade of the skills base of the firm with consequent improvement in its routines and capabilities (Song et al. 2003; Murmann 2013; Rizzo et al. 2013a).

When we consider the ASO firms, the effects in terms of knowledge acquisition derived from hiring personnel of a non-managerial level have not been investigated, at least to our knowledge. Some studies identified two main mechanisms of hiring technical personnel in ASO firms: the recruitment of personnel from the parent organization or by means of recruitment agencies, that is from the external environment (Rizzo 2015). These studies highlighted the fact that it may be common practice for a new ASO firm to hire engineers or researchers from the research group from which the ASO was spun-off: in fact the specific competences needed by the ASO firms may only be available, given their tacitness and specificities, in the group of research from which the ASO was spun-off.

However it may also be arguable that such highly specific competences may be particularly valuable at the very beginning of the start-up development, and become less and less important as the firm starts to grow and becomes an established firm in the market place (Rizzo et al. 2013b). On the contrary loosening ties with the parent organization is considered to be vital for many ASO firms (Doutriaux 1987) as new technology based firms need to focus less on technological development and more on market needs as times goes by Raffa et al. (1996).

A study on the difference in performance between ASO firms and other high tech start-ups revealed that ASO firms tend to take off some years later compared to average start-ups. However after about 5 years on average, they tend to catch up and possibly to outperform the average start-up (Vendrell-Herrero and Ortín-Ángel 2014). These different development paths may be due to the need to adapt commercially valuable research results to a market product. This study contributes to this literature by investigating the capability development processes that allow the spin-off to reach significant growth performance.

This work represents an exploratory study that seeks to investigate the effect that hiring both managers and employees from the external environment have on the ASO firms capability development with respect to the coaching of scientists as entrepreneurs and managers, and hiring employees from the parent organization. More specifically we investigate why ASO teams of founders decide to rely on one system of hiring and not another, and how such choices affect the capability development of these firms.

8.3 Research Design

8.3.1 Data and Methodology

The aim of this work is to explore whether ASOs behave differently and how, in terms of capability development in respect to their recruitment strategies. Given the 5 years converging interval between ASOs and other start-ups (Vendrell-Herrero and Ortín-Ángel 2014), we mostly concentrated on ASO development during the 5 years after constitution. Grounding on the literature presented above we can derive

Table 8.1 Framework of reference for the analysis: ASOs' typologies

		Managers	
		Surrogate entrepreneur/ managers	Coached scientists
Researchers	Recruitment agencies	External knowledge based ASO	External researchers based ASO
	Parent organization	External manager based ASO	Internal knowledge based ASO

four typologies of ASO firms, as detailed in Table 8.1. At one extreme we have ASO firms that employ a surrogate entrepreneur and/or hire managers from the industrial world and at the same time do not recruit their technical employees from the parent organization: we named this type of firm as "external knowledge based ASO."

At the other extreme we have the ASO whose CEO and managers are academic scientists and which employ their researchers from the parent organization: we labelled these firms as "internal knowledge based ASO." In between we have two typologies of ASOs, one in which managers come from the external environment and employees from the parent organization ("external manager based ASO"), and one in which employees come from the external environment and the entrepreneur and the managers are coached scientists ("external researchers based ASO").

Given the exploratory nature of this work, as the investigation regards dynamic processes, and as the research questions we seek to ask are in the *why* and *how* form, we develop a multiple case study research (Yin 1994; Eisenhardt 1989). We thus conducted ten face to face interviews in ten ASO firms. We sought to create a heterogeneous sample of cases (Eisenhardt 1989). ASOs interviewed therefore belong to various different sectors and were selected from two different countries: Italy and the UK. These two countries are appropriate for an understanding of the heterogeneity of ASO firms because in the former the process has been in place for longer and it has developed greater experience in dealing with the phenomenon; on the other hand the two countries are different in terms of institutions, that is of intended as social technologies (Nelson and Sampat 2001): the UK, compared to Italy, displays a wider set of institutions such as a developed venture capitalist market, higher levels of private funding to universities, and so on.

The firms selected were generated by universities of the Emilia-Romagna region in the north of Italy, and from the universities of the Greater Manchester region in UK. Both regions perform well in Europe in terms of innovative activities and technology transfer indicators. They show analogous levels of GDP, personnel involved in science and technology and in the high tech sectors, expenditure in R&D and patent applications to the EPO. All these indicators show these two regions to be above the European average levels (Hollanders et al. 2009).

The best performing ASOs in each region were selected according to the data collected through TTOs and university websites. We selected the best performing firms according to various indicators identified via websites, chamber of commerce information, databases such as the Bureau van Dijk and so on. The indicators on which we provide a selection are: turnover volume and growth rate, number of employees, number of patents and presence, and amount of Venture Capital and Business Angel funds. Moreover we made sure, with the help of TTOs staff, to select cases according to the four typologies previously described. We therefore made sure we selected firms that belong to each of the categories above identified, in which at least one firm is Italian and one English in each group. Finally we ensured to triangulate our data once the case studies were developed in order to strengthen the validity of the analysis (Yin 1994).

The face to face interviews were based on a very much open ended questionnaire: questions were developed according to the specificities of each case study. However the final objective was clear, and regarded the understanding of the reasons why certain recruitment choices were made and which effects were produced in terms of firms' capabilities. We therefore sought to speak to at least one of the founders. We did this in all but two cases where we spoke to a manager who had entered the firm very soon after its creation. Finally, to avoid data misinterpretation, an independent colleague visualized the coded material.

8.3.2 Data Analysis

The data analysis seeks to understand the impact on the capabilities of the ASO firms through its recruiting strategies, both of managers and of researchers-employees. Table 8.2 synthetically describes the firms' characteristics and their recruitment strategies.

The firms in the configuration "external knowledge based ASO" all employed a surrogate entrepreneur from the very beginning and in the space of a few years they also hired at least another manager from the industrial world. The main impact of these managers on the firm's functioning concerns the set of relations with different market actors, among which the most important regard the connection with venture capitalists (VC) and private investors. These managers provided the firm with a market focus, and in two of the three cases led to weakening of ties with the university in just a couple of years. In one case the head office was moved to another region of the country after the fourth year. Firm C is the one which weakened ties with universities more slowly as the technological development of the product still needed some specific research input 4 years after constitution. However the role of external knowledge, especially of managers, is largely recognized, as in a period of 3 years four managers from the external environment entered the company. Those managers provided various input to the ASO development. An example of how they impacted is given by the statement of one of them referring to the technological development of the product:

> The technology has not changed much from the initial idea. What changed has been the direction about processes and materials to use. The target applications have been re-prioritised so as to focus on some products first and larger markets later when the market is more mature: we had a change of strategy. These changes were given by market feedback:

Table 8.2 Sample firms characteristics and recruitment strategies

Firm	Business activity	Country	Recruitment strategy configuration
Firm A	Biopharmaceutical company active in the discovery and development of fully proprietary therapeutics for the treatment of neuropathic pain	Italy	External knowledge based ASO
Firm B	Molecular diagnostics concerned with respiratory fungal infection	UK	External knowledge based ASO
Firm C	Design and production of breakthrough printing technology based on nanotechnology	UK	External knowledge based ASO
Firm D	Assistance in clinical investigations to institutional, non-profit, and private sponsors	Italy	External manager based ASO
Firm E	The core technology of the firm is a mathematical algorithm for process control, and the core product is software for monitoring applications and control systems	UK	External manager based ASO
Firm F	Carrying out R&D related to the chemistry of the solid state drugs	Italy	External researchers based ASO
Firm G	Prototypes and services related to human–machine interaction	Italy	External researchers based ASO
Firm H	Active in the building services sector and currently especially concerned with energy issues. The firm has two main activities: software production and provision of consultancy services	UK	External researchers based ASO
Firm I	Physical diagnostic technologies applied to electrical equipment	Italy	Internal knowledge based ASO
Firm J	Business psychology company producing specific software and offering consultancy services	UK	Internal knowledge based ASO

> Scott [sale and marketing director: hired 2 years after constitution], when he came in, analysed the opportunities available, the viability and applications commercially. He talk to technology partners, analysts and he build up a body of knowledge and he went back in history of the company to see what worked and what not.

Although this firm remained attached to university research, the R&D function developed within the firm remained of a more applied nature, and a few years after constitution the recruitment strategy started to refer to the entire market. In other words, for the firms of this group, shifting the business from a research project to a market product and breaking away from the university led the R&D activity to become less specific. As a consequence the competences required were more diffused and the recruiting process could be conducted on a wider platform. The point made by a manager of Firm B is exemplary:

> We select the best we find, no matter where they graduated

The group of firms belonging to the "external manager based ASO" group basically benefited from the same advantages of bringing into the firm a set of valuable connections with market actors and the knowledge of the market requirements. For example the team of founders of Firm D understood quite soon after constitution that the idea of business they envisaged was not feasible with their assets at hand. Less than 1 year after constitution they hired a surrogate entrepreneur in the CEO role. This figure brought in a set of connections and knowledge of clients and partners that allowed Firm C to take off in very short time. The CEO said:

> I had knowledge of the market. I had worked in both other service firms as this one, and also in pharmaceutical companies. I knew what to do in order to make a good clients-customers relation work, and I also knew the environment in which to move.

The business basically remained the same, at least for the initial years, but the number of clients rapidly expanded. Firm E, similarly, thanks to the managing director (also a founder) who came from industry, was able to create a set of partners to work with in order to get feedback in the product development phases. Moreover the managing director was also particularly important at the very beginning in pushing the business to make use of various consulting services while developing the initial product up to a proper level to be sold on the market.

The configuration "external researchers based ASO" includes three firms in which the entrepreneur and the main firms managers were all academics. For example Firm F was set up in order to create a channel through which to direct the large number of research contracts that were entering the research department of the scientist entrepreneur. The founder stated that they hired employees from the external environment and not from the parent organization because

> It is useful in order to broader our perspective on new products development [...] We needed to expand the business and diversify. We needed to shift our focus and be able to offer pharmaceutical firms a higher set of services, so to speak, to shift toward a more applied research type of product. [...] We needed different competences on which to base the product development. [...] We [founders] are all materials chemists, so we employed some general chemists, a couple of graduates in pharmacy, and a couple of graduates in chemistry and pharmaceutical technologies.

It therefore emerges that Firm F chose to internalize different competences in order to amplify the sphere of business. Conversely Firm G was created from an interdisciplinary department, and the business is based on the fusion of different type of competences. The two founder entrepreneurs include an industrial engineer and a communication science graduate. The business in fact regards the production of human–machine interaction prototypes and a considerable part of the production concerns ergonomics. When we consider the engineering side of the business the influence of different competences is vital, and recruitment was carried out from different departments. Among various electronics and mechanical engineers an important role was played by the mechatronics engineers that started to enter the firm a couple of years after its constitution:

> We really like these types of engineers. [...] I am not saying that they brought in some particular competences that we had not at all before. However they clearly made us to potentiate those competences.

Similarly Firm H is a very flexible company that expanded in several direction of business. The new recruitments were mostly driven by the need to include different competences within the firm. These new competences therefore were the tool in order to drive the firms evolution.

The fourth group regards the "internal knowledge based ASO." The main point of our interests is to understand the reasons behind the choices and how capabilities were developed. Firm I was created on the basis of 20 years of research activities, which had made the research group of the scientist entrepreneur internationally recognized. This prestige allowed the entrepreneur to possess important knowledge of market requirements:

> The CEO was the most brilliant PhD student of professor X [founder entrepreneur] and the one who was responsible for finding clients. The fame of professor X however played a fundamental role in this activity.

The business developed in a somewhat disorganized way, without even a strictly defined mission from the very beginning. However the strong competences of the founders allowed progressive growth and expansion. In 10 years the firm becomes a multinational company with subsidiaries in several countries around the world. As a consequence for the first 6–7 years all engineers came from the parent department, and the business definition and consolidation mostly driven by the famous scientist entrepreneur.

Firm L,[1] similarly to Firm I, shaped a core business only after some years of being on the market. This lag may be a symptom of acquiring the market knowledge needed to run a business. However, once again the specific application of competences of a high degree of tacit knowledge, required the scientists to become entrepreneurs. Capabilities were developed through time again thanks to the networking assets of the scientists:

> Some work come to us and allowed us to keep the business running for some years without developing a core business

The capability development of this firm is based on the slow process of market understanding shown by scientist entrepreneurs in identifying a core business. For the first 6 years the business concerned itself with the provision of consultancy services related to business psychology. In this interval of time employees were mostly Ph.D. students and post-doctoral fellows of the two scientist entrepreneurs. Again the tacitness of the knowledge needed to conduct the business ground this choice of employee selection. The interviews therefore reveal that the process of capability development, as may be expected, is slower in those firms which belong to the "internal knowledge based ASO": although the tacitness of the business we found in the case studies play a role, the market understanding seems to represent a main reason for this slowness.

---

[1] We must specify that among the founders of Firm L there was a manager with previous experience from the TTO of the university, and that in the first 5 years another manager was hired. However we included Firm L in this group because the role of the two scientists entrepreneurs was far more influential on the development, growth and strategic choices of the ASO.

As we saw from the information collected from the analysis we can see how recruiting strategies affect the capability development of firms. More specifically we saw how they are mechanisms of overcoming knowledge constraints. Recruiting external personnel in order to overcome these constraints seem to be particularly relevant in those cases in which the business idea is clear from the very beginning and the knowledge required for growth is not highly specific. Moreover we saw how hiring managers has an important impact on the strategies of ASO firms mostly because they make the firm adopt a pure market focus and because they are an important source of market connections. On the contrary recruiting researchers from the external environment impacts on the capabilities of firms because it allows entrepreneurs and managers to respond to their business expansion or diversification strategies.

8.4 Concluding Thoughts

This exploratory work has sought to investigate the capability development process taking place in the early stages of ASO development in relation to the recruitment strategies adopted by the firms. In particular we sought to comprehend how managers from the external environment and researchers from outside the parent department impact on the innovation capabilities and growth strategies of the firms. As external knowledge is fundamental to firms' development, and given the difficulties that ASO firms have in taking off, the comprehension of how capabilities are developed thanks to the recruitment strategies seems to remain a poorly explored issue which therefore justified an exploratory qualitative work.

The main findings of this work regard the impact that different types of external knowledge acquired via recruitment have on capability development of ASOs. We saw how surrogate entrepreneurs and managers tend to shape the business according to specific market objectives: they shape firms strategies developing the path to follow given the available resources and the objective to reach. Conversely the influence of researchers on the capability of firms mainly affect the capabilities of reaching some pre-defined objective identified by the managers, either they are coached or surrogate.

Moreover we have seen the influence of managers and surrogate entrepreneur on enlarging the networking assets of the firms, making the provision of financing capital and other types of market connections possible. On the other hand the firms coaching the entrepreneur in our sample of selected successful ASOs were already endowed with proper networking assets. However, they needed, on average, more time to shape the business and identify a core business. This seems to be particularly true for those firms in the "internal knowledge based ASO" configuration, which needed some time to find the proper core business—that is of a high level of tacitness. In these cases and in the ASOs of the configuration "external researchers based ASO" we saw how the knowledge of partners and potential customers was developed during the academic times, and this allowed these firms to survive the time necessary to identify a core business and at the same time receive market feedback.

This exploratory work therefore seems to indicate that ASO team of founders could decide whether to hire a surrogate entrepreneur or other managers, or hire external researchers, according to the specificities of their business and the market connections they developed during their academic activities. Moreover when ASO are created with specific ideas and purposes, hiring talented managers could speed up and focus the development path of the firm. Conversely, when the ASO is constituted with no clear cut ideas of business, or the initial idea needs to change because of market feedback, managers would be most useful when there is a lack of market connections. With respect to the researchers, they seem to be useful mostly when the business needs to get shaped on the integration of different competences, and when the product becomes more standardized and less linked to edge academic research.

This work provides a first exploration of a complex issue. The case study analysis therefore is justified in order to shed light on an unknown sector. However this work is not free of limitations. First of all generalizing our results has to be done with caution: we in fact selected only very successful ASOs, and the same questions addressed to less successful ASOs could lead to a deeper knowledge of the pros and cons and the contexts in which it is preferable to hire external managers and researchers rather than coaching the scientists and hiring researchers from the parent organization.

Once the insights of this work are confirmed and the categorization developed in our theoretical framework prove to be useful, further research would be needed in order to test pros and cons of the different recruitment decisions, and to link such decision to the characteristics of firms and their performances. The findings of these researches could also lead to important policy implications, on the one hand directed toward TTOs about how to manage the ASOs they generate, and, on the other hand to founders of ASOs giving them insights into how to set their growth and development strategies.

References

Bjørnåli ES, Gulbrandsen M (2010) Exploring board formation and evolution of board composition in academic spin-offs. J Technol Transf 35:92–112

Boeker W (1997) Executive migration and strategic change: the effect of top manager movement on product market entry. Adm Sci Q 42:213–236

Chiesa V, Piccaluga A (2000) Exploitation and diffusion of public research: the case of academic spin-off companies in Italy. R&D Manag 30:329–339

Clarysse B, Moray N (2004) A process study of entrepreneurial team formation: the case of a research-based spin-off. J Bus Ventur 19:55–79

Dosi G, Nelson RR, Winter SG (eds) (2000) The nature and dynamics of organizational capabilities. Oxford University Press, Oxford

Doutriaux J (1987) Growth patterns of academic entrepreneurial firms. J Bus Ventur 2:285–297

Eisenhardt KM (1989) Building theories from case study research. Acad Manag Rev 14:488–511

Eisenhardt KM, Martin JA (2000) Dynamic capabilities: what are they? Strateg Manag J 21(Special Issue):1105–1121

Fontes M (2005) The process of transformation of scientific and technological knowledge into economic value conducted by biotechnology spin-offs. Technovation 25:339–347
Franklin SJ, Wright M, Lockett A (2001) Academic and surrogate entrepreneurship in university spin-out companies. J Technol Transf 26:127–141
Helfat CE, Winter SG (2011) Untangling dynamic and operational capabilities: strategy for the (n) ever-changing world. Strateg Manag J 32:1243–1250
Hollanders H, Tarantola S, Loschky A (2009) Regional innovation scoreboard. http://www.proinno-europe.eu
Kogut B, Zander U (1992) Knowledge of the firm, combinative capabilities, and the replication of technology. Organ Sci 3(3):383–397
Kraatz MS, Moore JH (2002) Executive migration and institutional change. Acad Manag J 45:120–143
Lambert Review (2003) Lambert review of business—university collaboration. UK HM Treasury
Murmann JP (2013) The coevolution of industries and important features of their environments. Organ Sci 24:58–78
Nelson RR, Sampat BN (2001) Making sense of institutions as factor shaping economic performance. J Econ Behav Organ 44:31–54
Paruchuri S, Eisenman M (2012) Microfoundations of firm R&D capabilities: a study of inventor networks in a merger. J Manag Stud 49:1509–1535
Radosevich R (1995) A model for entrepreneurial spin-offs from public technology sources. Int J Technol Manag 10:879–893
Raffa M, Zollo G, Caponi R (1996) The development process of small firms. Entrep Reg Dev 4:359–371
Ramaciotti L, Rizzo U (2014) The determinants of academic spin-off creation by Italian universities. R&D Manag. doi: 10.111/radm.12105
Rao H, Drazin R (2002) Overcoming resource constraints on product innovation by recruiting talent from rivals: a study of the mutual fund industry, 1986–94. Acad Manag J 45:491–507
Rizzo U (2014) Why do scientists create academic spin-offs? The influence of the context. J Technol Transf, forthcoming
Rizzo U (2015) Entrepreneurial opportunity recognition and exploitation in academic spin-offs. In: Bonnet J, Dejardin M, de Lema DGP (eds) Exploring the entrepreneurial society. Institutions, Behaviors and Outcomes, Edward-Elgar, London
Rizzo U, Freddi D, Ramaciotti L (2013a) The impact of new scientific knowledge on firms routines and capabilities. The case of mechatronics. Paper presented at the R&D management conference 2013, Manchester, UK
Rizzo U, Nicolli F, Ramaciotti L (2013b) The development process of new technology-based firms. Int J Entrep Innov Manag 17(4–6):352–369
Rosenkopf L, Almeida P (2003) Overcoming local search through alliances and mobility. Manag Sci 49(6):751–766
Rosenkopf L, Nerkar A (2001) Beyond local search: boundary spanning, exploration and impact in the optical disc industry. Strateg Manag J 22:287–306
Song J, Almeida P, Wu G (2003) Learning-by-hiring: when is mobility more likely to facilitate interfirm knowledge transfer? Manag Sci 49(4):351–365
Turner SF, Fern MJ (2012) Examining the stability and variability of routine performances: the effects of experience and context change. J Manag Stud 49:1407–1434
Tzabbar D, Aharonson BS, Amburgey LT (2013) When does tapping external sources of knowledge results in knowledge integration. Res Policy 42:481–494
Vendrell-Herrero F, Ortín-Ángel P (2014) University spin-offs vs other NTBFs: total factor productivity differences at outset and evolution. Technovation 34(2):101–112
Vincett PS (2010) The economic impacts of academic spin-off companies, and their implications for public policy. Res Policy 39:736–747
Yin RK (1994) Case study research: design and methods, 3rd edn. Sage, London

Chapter 9
Coopetition and Open Innovation: An Application to KIS vs. Less-KIS Firms

Dina Pereira and João Leitão

Abstract This paper tackles in an innovative way the issue on coopetition, by making use of service firms' behavior in generating innovative services, to reveal their innovative performance and the dynamics of coopetition targeted at open innovation. For this purpose, we use a dataset of 1,221 service firms that participated in the European Community Innovation Survey (CIS), 2008. A probit analysis is conducted for "knowledge-intensive service (KIS) firms" and "less-KIS firms" and, the results reveal that coopetition arrangements between competing firms and scientific community, and also firms' capacity to introduce innovations into the market, have a positive and significant influence on service firms' behavior to generate service innovations. Furthermore, this study also reveals that the effects of introducing process innovations inside the firm and the existence of internal R&D activities are of major significance for influencing positively the innovative behavior of service firms.

Keywords Absorptive capacity • Coopetition • Innovation • Knowledge-intensive services

9.1 Introduction

As a means of fostering innovation, firms, and other institutions make use of the so-called coopetition, this being a compound of strategic cooperation and competition among rivals (Rusko 2011). When dealing with emerging technologies, characterized by uncertainty regarding market opportunities, firms opt for strategic coopetition (Garraffo 2002).

Several authors analyzed the strategic use of coopetition by firms dealing with emerging technologies (Brandenburger and Nalebuff 1996; Gomes-Casseres 1996;

D. Pereira (✉) • J. Leitão
Department of Management and Economics, Universidade da Beira Interior, Estrada do Sineiro, Covilhã 6200-209, Portugal

CEG-IST, Universidade de Lisboa, Av. Rovisco Pais, 1, Lisboa 1050-001, Portugal
e-mail: dina@ubi.pt

R. Baptista, J. Leitão (eds.), *Entrepreneurship, Human Capital, and Regional Development*, International Studies in Entrepreneurship 31,
DOI 10.1007/978-3-319-12871-9_9

Harbison and Pekar 1998). Others focused on the benefits of coopetition (Bagshaw and Bagshaw 2001; Garraffo 2002; Chien and Peng 2005; Rusko 2011).

The risks of opportunistic behavior emerging from coopetition were the object of analysis (Nieto and Santamaria 2007), as well as the importance of coopetition, especially when it comes to developing incremental innovations in high-tech industries (Abernathy and Clark 1985; Fjelstad et al. 2004; Ritala and Hurmelinna-Laukkanen 2009). The risks of appropriability regarding intellectual property (IP) and knowledge ownership in coopetition alliances were studied by a set of scholars (Seung and Russo 1996; Rammer 2002; Blomqvist et al. 2005; Dagnino and Rocco 2009; Escribano et al. 2009).

This article presents a contribution to previous studies, by using service firms' behavior in generating innovative services, to unveil their innovative performance and the impact of the dynamics of coopetition targeted at open innovation. In this vein, we conduct a probit analysis to the determinant factors of service firms' behavior to generate innovative products/services influenced by policies targeted at driving innovative behavior among firms, scientific community and competitors, spurring firm's absorptive capacity and forming collaboration schemes with competitive partners increasing the pace of innovative performance.

It contributes to the empirical literature on research and development (R&D) management by adopting a different perspective from prior work and complementing earlier studies deepening the understanding of the behavioral process of creating innovation, under the framework of coopetition and open innovation. A set of service firms is analyzed, since this economic activity sector is considered an adequate laboratory for assessing the role played by coopetition in fostering open innovation in highly turbulent and competitive environments, especially by contrasting "knowledge-intensive service (KIS) firms" and "less-knowledge-intensive services (LKIS) firms."

Authors like Muller and Zenker (2001), Miozzo and Grisham (2006) refer that KIS firms are gaining an important position in the market, assuming to be one of the major forces of the economic activity. Previously, and according to Boden and Miles (2000) and Wood (2006), these firms were grouped on "other services," but due to several changes in their production processes, the role of ICT technologies, the human capital force in economic growth, and the implementation of the knowledge-based society, the role of these firms is increasingly taking a central position in economy.

Regarding Merino and Rubalcaba (2012), as KIS firms are considered one of the major sources of structural change in the advanced economies, they have increased their relative share of importance in the European economy by 30 % since 1979, achieving 33 % of the employment force (37 % in the United States) in 2004 and 35 % of value added (39 % in the United States). The impact of KIS firms is derived from their capacity to generate and diffuse localized knowledge, to facilitate and adopt technological, organizational, social, and other typologies of innovation.

The determinant factors of the innovative behavior of service firms are analyzed, by making use of the data available in the European CIS Survey, 2008.

The remainder of this article is structured as follows. Section 9.2 develops the theoretical underpinnings, drawn from the literature on coopetition and open innovation and innovative products and services. Section 9.3 presents the empirical approach. Section 9.4 refers to the analysis, main results, and discussion. Finally, the article concludes and presents limitations, implications for policy-makers, and guidelines for practitioners engaged in strategic cooperation oriented to create innovation.

9.2 Theoretical Framework and Hypotheses

9.2.1 *From Coopetition to Open Innovation: Is It Important to Implement Process Innovations?*

According to Luo et al. (2007), the coopetition concept was introduced in the 1980s by Raymond Noorda and became the subject of several studies during the 1990s, namely the issue of dyadic coopetition (Bengtsson and Kock 2000, 2003) or multi-faceted coopetition (Amburgey and Rao 1996; Tsai 2002; Luo and Slotegraaf 2006).

Brandenburger and Nalebuff (1996) consider coopetition as an alternative way to perform in business, as distinct from competition, strategically used by firms that deal with emerging technologies in innovation networks.

In the view of Bagshaw and Bagshaw (2001) coopetition allows better performance for the firms involved than competitive arrangements, as by strategically managing cooperation and competition, the relationship can evolve through controlled behavior by partners and rivals.

Coopetitive relations call our attention for the concept of open innovation, which, according to Chesbrough (2003), derives from the process of ideas that appear from internal and/or external sources as well as technology can enter in the process at different stages and projects can flow to the market in multiple ways (through outlicensing, cooperative arrangements, a spin-off company or through the marketing and sales channels of the firm). Chesbrough et al. (2006), present the concept of open innovation which can be understood as the use of inflows and outflows of knowledge in order to foster internal innovation and to develop the markets for external use of innovation. In this sense, firms can and should make use of external knowledge and internal and external paths to the market while developing their own technology.

9.2.2 *From Coopetition to Open Innovation: The Role of Absorptive Enablers*

Achieving higher absorptive capacity increases the pace of engaging in coopetition and enables innovativeness (Ritala and Hurmelinna-Laukkanen 2009). Cohen et al. (2000) studied this process using the framework based on the concept of firm's absorptive capacity. This concept refers to the identification of valuable knowledge in the environment, the capacity to assimilate it and align it with existing knowledge stocks and finally exploit it in internal R&D activities to achieve successful innovation.

Zahra and George (2002) analyzed the concept of absorptive capacity as a dynamic capability, creating a model of the components, antecedents, contingencies, and outcomes of absorptive capacity. Their model was innovative because they substituted the component of "recognizing the value" with "acquisition" and relocated the influence of appropriability regimes. Additionally, these scholars enlarged the model with the transformation concept that follows the assimilation component, activation triggers, and social integration mechanisms, and divided absorptive capacity into "potential" absorptive capacity and "realized" absorptive capacity. The process of transformation gives firms the capacity to develop changes in existing processes to be able to absorb new knowledge, assimilating it by means of interpretation and comprehension within existing cognitive structures.

Regarding that statement, Todorova and Durisin (2007) proposed that firms cannot transform their knowledge assets when they are not able to assimilate them. Furthermore, Zahra and George (2002) distinguish between potential absorptive capacity and realized absorptive capacity. The first has to do with acquisition and assimilation of new external knowledge by reconfiguring the resource base and deploying capacities, while the second deals with transformation and exploitation of new external knowledge by developing new products and processes. Potential absorptive capacity without realized capacity does not produce an effect on the firm's competitive advantage.

In addition, the authors identified the activation triggers, social integration mechanisms, and appropriability regimes acting as key contingencies. Social integration mechanisms help to lower the barriers between assimilation and transformation, increasing absorptive capacity, which is understood, by the proposed model, as being a dynamic capacity involving a set of organizational routines (e.g., social interactions) and processes. The ability to learn and absorb depends on the capacity to value external knowledge (Zahra and George 2002).

According to Rothaermel and Alexandre (2009), the greater the firm's absorptive capacity the greater its ability to fully capture the benefits resulting from flexibility in technology sourcing. Furthermore, the ability to recognize and exploit knowledge flows varies from one firm to another, resulting in unequal benefits acting as a competitive advantage. This absorptive capacity varies according to the firm's existing enablers, like knowledge stock embedded in its processes, people, and products.

Several authors point out that the main benefit derived from collaboration between competitors is the creation of completely new products (Tether 2002; Quintana-Garcia and Benavides-Velasco 2004).

Ritala and Hurmelinna-Laukkanen (2009) state that coopetition helps to develop incremental innovation in current products and services, being an effective mode of generating new innovations especially in high-tech industries. Furthermore, patents are used, as stated by Carayol and Roux (2007) and Ma and Lee (2008), to establish collaborative technological relationships between firms and their stakeholders.

The studies of Brandenburger and Nalebuff (1996), Dussauge et al. (2000) and Tether (2002) deal with the association between firms' innovative capacity and the coopetition arrangements they enter to generate value added and increase productivity.

Several scholars (Zahra and George 2002; Todorova and Durisin 2007; Rothaermel and Alexandre 2009; Kostopoulos et al. 2011) devoted their studies to analyze the impact of introducing process innovations inside the firm, which can be either in the production process or in the organizational structure, embracing R&D positioning, such as fostering open innovation channels and absorptive capacity on the firm's behavior to generate innovations. Thus:

H1: The introduction of process innovations inside the firm has a positive and significant impact on the firm's behavior to generate product/service innovations.

As Cohen and Levinthal (1989) defend, the firm's knowledge base plays the role of both innovation and absorption, since its tendency to assimilate external knowledge creates an incentive to invest in R&D. Gambardella (1992) also states that firms with better in-house R&D programs are more able and prepared to absorb external scientific information. Other authors analyzed the determinant role of the firm's absorptive capacity in exploiting the alliances it establishes (Arora and Gambardella 1994; Zahra and George 2002). In this line, having an internal R&D strategy makes the firm more prone to deal with coopetition relations and to get involved in open innovation channels and mechanisms.

The positive and significant impact of firms' investment in R&D activities performed inside the firm was also the subject of multiple studies, such as those of Cassiman and Veugelers (2006) and Li (2011). These authors point to the major importance of the firm's investing in its basic R&D intensity, and of increasing the firm's in-house R&D performance. In coopetition, controlling knowledge flows during joint R&D activities involves some risk, this being a critical issue in reaching success in strategic alliances oriented towards innovation activities embracing competitors. The risks of appropriability in a strategic alliance can be higher when partners are direct competitors (Park and Russo 1996). Appropriability methods can be of two types, formal and informal (Rammer 2002). Formal methods are the legal forms of protection such as patents, copyrights, and trademarks, to prevent others from using the firm's patents and knowledge embedded in them, despite allowing the competing firm to access patent knowledge and learn from it. Informal methods include secrecy, complex design, and lead time. In this sequence, we present the following hypothesis:

H2: The performance of R&D activities inside the firm has a positive and significant impact on the firm's behavior to generate product/service innovations.

Bergek and Bruzelius (2010) point out the interest of patent data as an indicator of collaborative technological activity. The association of several international inventors suggests the existence of international cooperation (Carayol and Roux 2007; Ma and Lee 2008). In addition, patents can indicate the emergence of an international trend in a certain technological field, which in turn can contribute to reveal the evolutionary pathway in terms of collaborative development oriented to technological innovation (Archambault 2002).

Chen and Chen (2011) state that patents protecting product/service innovations are one of the firm's important intangible assets, in the sense that they can provide additional revenue to be generated towards product commercialization.

The introduction of innovations into the market was also subject of several studies, for instance Tether (2002) and Quintana-Garcia and Benavides-Velasco (2004) that concluded that the main benefit derived from collaboration between competitors is the creation of completely new products. Belderbos et al. (2004) analyzed the relation between cooperative R&D and firm performance, focusing on the gains for the competitiveness of the firm derived from efficiency improvements. Ritala and Hurmelinna-Laukkanen (2009) focused on the significant effect of introducing innovations in the market on the innovative capacity of the firm, stating that coopetition develops incremental innovation in current products and services, being an effective mode of launching innovations in the market, especially in high-tech industries. In this vein, we formulate Hypothesis 3 as follows:

H3: The introduction of innovations into the market has a positive and significant impact on the firm's behavior to generate product/service innovations.

9.2.3 From Coopetition to Open Innovation: The Role of Coopetion Schemes

Belderbos et al. (2004) defend that R&D cooperation between competitors generates incremental efficiency gains. On the contrary, Nieto and Santamaria (2007) argue that coopetition does not favor innovation, since it can promote opportunistic behavior and minimize trust among rivals.

Establishing strategic partnerships between different firms in innovation projects to share risks, costs, and expertise has also become an important pattern in innovation management, of interest to both scholars and practitioners (Chesbrough 2003; Huston and Sakkab 2006; Enkel et al. 2009; Gassmann et al. 2010). This pattern results in coopetition, funded on strategic cooperation with competitors in innovation initiatives. Achieving higher absorptive capacity and forming collaboration schemes with competitive partners increase the pace of engaging in coopetition and imitation, especially when dealing with incremental innovations, being fundamental here the emphasis on protection (Ritala and Hurmelinna-Laukkanen 2009).

The area of patent protection is extremely important in achieving competitive advantage, since it protects patent assignees from imitation and supports the internal use of technologies (Aoki and Schiff 2008). Thus, strategic management of the patent portfolio is also important to achieve benefits and obtain competitive advantage (Grindley and Teece 1997).

Li (2011) examined the sources of external technology, absorptive capacity, and innovation capacity in Chinese state-owned high-tech firms, analyzing three types of investment to acquire technological knowledge in determining firms' innovation capacity, namely: in-house R&D; importing foreign technology; and purchasing domestic technology. He concluded that importing foreign technology only promotes innovation if in-house R&D is also conducted. Nevertheless, domestic technology purchases, such as patent licensing, have a favorable direct impact on innovation. The study also finds that absorptive capacity is determined by the source or nature of the external knowledge.

Kostopoulos et al. (2011) explore the role of absorptive capacity as a mechanism to identify and translate external knowledge inflows into tangible benefits, and also as a vehicle to achieve greater innovation and time-lagged financial performance. The authors suggest that external knowledge inflows, by using coopetition arrangements and collaborative relationships, are directly related to absorptive capacity and indirectly related to innovation.

The determinant factor of establishing coopetition arrangements between competing firms for the firm's capacity to create innovations, either in products or in services was analyzed by multiple scholars. Brandenburger and Nalebuff (1996) and Garraffo (2002) studied the establishment of strategic cooperation arrangements with competitors in firms of emerging technologies. Bengtsson and Kock (2000, 2003) focused on the dyadic coopetition as being a dyadic relationship, since competition is related to output activities such as distribution, services, product development and marketing, and cooperation deals with input activities, like R&D, buying, logistics and processing raw materials. In between the two, there are midstream activities, like production. Bagshaw and Bagshaw (2001) state that coopetition allows better performance for the firms involved than competitive arrangements, as by strategically managing cooperation and competition, the relationship can evolve through controlled behavior by partners and rivals. Belderbos et al. (2004) defend that R&D cooperation between competitors generates incremental efficiency gains. Also, Chien and Peng (2005) state that interorganizational relationships evolve into a social structure of coopetition, becoming a tool for cooperation and also for competition, acting at multiple levels, such as firms, strategic business units, departments, and task groups.

Jong and Marsili (2006) proposed a typology of coopetition arrangements, namely: (1) exchanges of patents and knowledge; (2) collaborative R&D activities; (3) strategic alliances for setting new standards; and (4) collaborative agreements to integrate established firms. These types of coopetition arrangements determine the firm's ability to compete in the marketplace and to implement the portfolio of a firm's coopetition activities that evolves over time. In addition, the authors refer that when dealing with firms that work on radical innovations, definition of new standards, or new converging technologies, coopetition is carried out for sizing market opportunities related to radical innovations, setting new standards, and/or integrating established firms through converging technologies.

Ritala and Hurmelinna-Laukkanen (2009) state that coopetition helps to develop incremental innovation in current products and services, being an effective mode of generating new innovations, especially in high-tech industries. Rusko (2011) defends that one of the main motivations for competitors to engage in strategic cooperation arrangements is based on the creation of greater value or benefit, in order to improve economic performance. Vasudeva and Anand (2011) studied firms facing technological discontinuities and their use of alliance portfolios to gather knowledge flows. They subdivide absorptive capacity into "latitudinal" and "longitudinal" components. The first corresponds to the use of diverse knowledge and the second is distant knowledge. Their findings suggest that a firm with a moderate latitudinal absorptive capacity, which is equivalent to medium diversity in its portfolio, has a high propensity for optimal use of knowledge. Thus we hypothesize:

H4: The set of coopetition relationships established between the firm and competing firms has a positive and significant impact on the firm's behavior to generate product/service innovations.

As mentioned by Dagnino and Rocco (2009), when coopetition occurs between public and private competitors, for instance between universities and industrial partners, in the challenging task of knowledge production, two critical situations can arise: coopetition for publications and coopetition for IPRs. To overcome these problematic issues, the previous authors suggest three strategies to mitigate the competitive pressure between university and industry, namely the sequencing and sanitizing of data and joint patents. The first implies the strategic management and sequential processes of first patenting and then publishing. The second concerns the removal of data that shall not be published, in order to avoid risks when patenting. The third corresponds to the collaborative patenting of knowledge, sharing rights and duties in the patent process. Firms usually regard this type of coopetition strategy as disadvantageous, preferring exclusive rights in order to commercialize technology freely.

The impact of relationships with the scientific community as being of major importance in generating firms' innovative performance has warranted the attention of several researchers, for example, Cockburn and Henderson (1998), Li (2011), Kostopoulos et al. (2011) and Vasudeva and Anand (2011). Thus, we formulate the following hypothesis:

H5: The set of coopetition relationships established between the firm and scientific community has a positive and significant impact on the firm's behavior to generate product/service innovations.

Based on the literature review, a conceptual model is proposed, to explore the relationships between the firm's behavior to generate product/service innovations and the determinant factors, namely, the introduction of process innovations inside the firm, the performance of R&D activities inside the firm, the introduction of innovations into the market, the coopetition relationships established between the firm and competing firms, and the coopetition relationships established between the firm and scientific community as shown in Fig. 9.1.

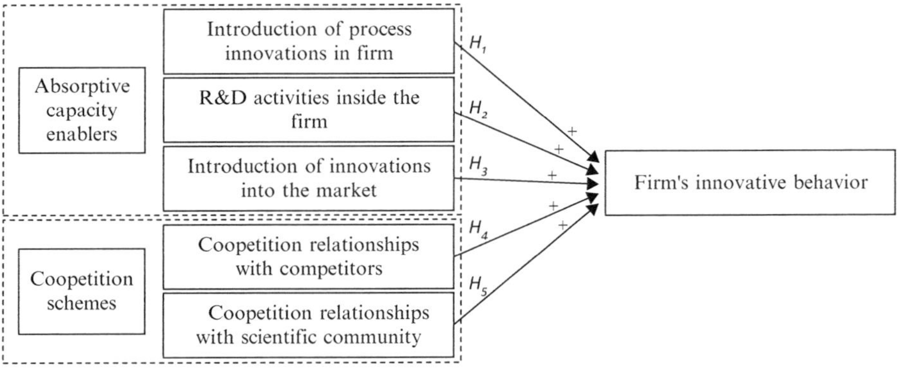

Fig. 9.1 Innovative behavior of firms and coopetition and open innovation strategies: conceptual model. *Source*: Authors

9.3 Methodology

9.3.1 Dataset, Method, and Dependent Variable

The present paper intends to analyze the determinant factors of the service firms' behavior to generate product and service innovations, by making use of the data available in the European CIS Survey, 2008, for Portuguese firms. For the present study we only gathered data from Portuguese firms, for which it was granted access from the Portuguese Science and Technology Foundation.

The data available is used to produce two subsamples related to service firms. Following the standard OECD sector classification based on NACE, the total sample is divided into "KIS firms" and "LKIS firms."

The sample has 1,221 respondent service firms, considering all firms in the analysis since they are all statistically valid. The subsamples of "KIS firms" and "LKIS firms" are submitted to a probit regression to estimate the probability associated with the different determinant factors of service firms' innovative behavior.

The dependent variable used is product/service innovation (1 for a firm that has carried out product/service innovation and 0 otherwise), which refers to the firm having generated and introduced into the market a new or improved product or service, with respect to its capacities or potential ease of use, parts or subsystems. The binary dependent variable suggests the use of a probit model for estimation purposes. The dependent variable was used as a proxy to assess the innovative behavior of firms, revealing pro-innovation behavior, according to the data available on the CIS survey. In addition, all the independent variables are also binary.

9.4 Empirical Findings

9.4.1 Descriptive Statistics

In the Figs. 9.2 and 9.3 we present a set of descriptive statistics for the dataset consisting of 1,221 service firms, which is a large sample and is a real asset for achieving representativeness. Approximately 60 % of firms are KIS firms, and almost 92 % are large firms. In Fig. 9.2 it may be observed that 26 % of the service firms have developed product/service innovations, authorship percentages for process innovations being distributed as follows: 30 % by the firm itself; 16 % by the firm in cooperation with other firms, and the remaining by other forms.

Almost 35 % of the service firms perform inside R&D activities and approximately 20 % acquire outside R&D activities. About 17 % acquire other external knowledge (such as patents, copyrights, and other unprotected knowledge) and 17 % introduce new products/services into the market (see Fig. 9.3).

9.4.2 Probit Estimation Results

Probit regressions were run on the service dataset separately, by considering two subsamples according to the NACE Eurostat classifications classification for "KIS firms" and "LKIS firms."

In accordance with Rubalcaba and Kox (2007) and compatible with NACE, KIS includes various business service activities, having as main input the highly sophisticated knowledge of its workforce, namely computer services, R&D services, and management consultancy, which can include telecommunications and financial, transport, or professional services.

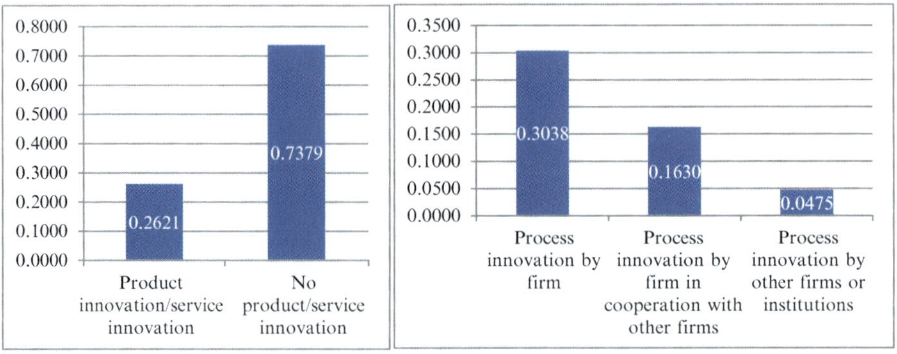

Fig. 9.2 Composition of service sample by product innovation performance and process innovation authorship

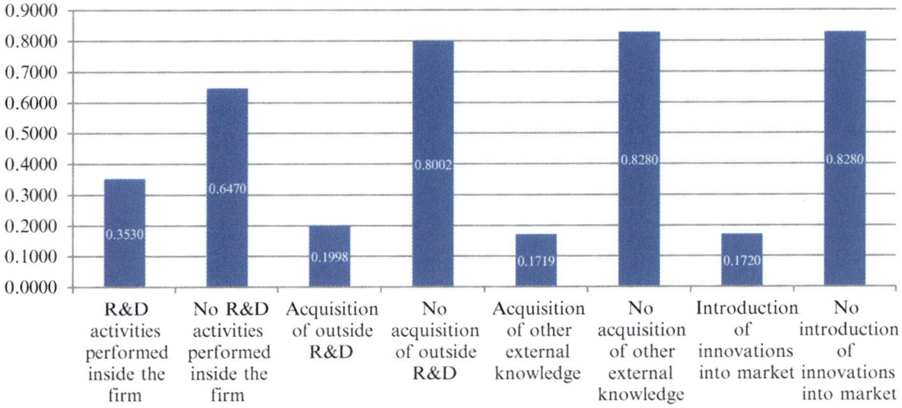

Fig. 9.3 Composition of service sample by R&D activities

Regarding the set of results presented in Table 9.1, and particularly the "all firms" column, we conclude that for the 1,221 service firms under analysis, the likelihood ratio chi-square of 356.21 with a p-value of 0.0000 confirms that our model as a whole is statistically significant. The last two columns show the probit regressions disaggregated into service subgroups—"KIS firms" and "LKIS firms."

The introduction of process innovations into the firm, either by the firm itself (a) or the firm in cooperation with others (b), presents a positive and significant association with the behavior to generate innovation (at 1 % significance). Besides this, the set of R&D activities performed inside the firm (c) has also a positive and significant impact on the dependent variable (at 1 % significance).

The fact that the service firm does not introduce innovations into the market (d) has a negative and significant effect on the behavior to generate product/service innovation (at 1 % significance), giving an association between the generation of innovation and its subsequent market introduction.

Also negative is the impact of the inexistence of cooperative relationships in terms of R&D (e) on the dependent variable (at 1 % significance), a public partner (f) being the preferred type of partner in cooperative relationships, this dummy variable having a positive and significant impact (at 1 % significance).

Cooperative relationships between the service firm and European competitors (g) and European universities (h) present a positive and significant association with the firm's behavior to generate innovation (the first at 1 % significance and the second at 5 % significance).

The set of cooperation agreements with a significant, though negative, impact on the firm's behavior to generate innovations, either product type or service type, are with American competing firms (i) and European laboratories (j).

The dummy variable of SME (k) has a negative and significant impact on the "LKIS firm's" behavior to generate innovations, meaning that the fact that this type of firm is a SME, impacts in a negative way on its capacity to generate innovations.

Table 9.1 Results of probit regressions for service firms

Product/service innovation	All firms	KIS firms	LKIS firms
Large firm	0.2917284[a]	–	–
SME	–	–0.024813	–0.71954[b] (k)
Process innovation by firm (a)	0.6788217[b]	0.6425258[b]	0.8003994[b]
Process innovation by firm in cooperation with other firms (b)	0.4931047[b]	0.579551[b]	0.5354501[b]
Process innovation by other firms or institutions	0.4324939[b]	0.314317	0.4787559
R&D activities performed inside the firm (c)	0.5340988[b]	0.4726756[b] (c1)	0.6925766[b] (c2)
Acquisition of outside R&D	–	0.2268566	–
No acquisition of outside R&D	–0.2870978[b]	–	–0.0354656
Introduction of innovations into market (m)	0.5200406[b]	–	–
No introduction of innovations into market (d)	–	–0.8073311[b] (d1)	0.0673119
Firm did not cooperate in R&D (e)	–0.8041166[b]	–1.037.318[b] (e1)	–0.5045445
Public partner (f)	–3.605.851	0.7028044[b] (f1)	–4.005.418
Private partner	4.071.048[b]	–	4.335.834[b] (l)
Firm cooperated with competitors in EU (g)	0.5535745[a]	1.375.734[b] (g1)	0.7578617
Firm cooperated with competitors in US (i)	–1.003.039[c]	–1.929.241[b] (i1)	–1.308.725
Firm cooperated with laboratories in PT	0.3690016	0.318485	0.9656868[a] (n)
Firm cooperated with laboratories in EU (j)	–1.708.198[c]	–2.208.943[b] (j1)	–
Firm cooperated with universities in EU (h)	0.7373061[a]	1.217.358[c] (h1)	0.2346324
Observations	1,221	746	475
Log likelihood	–526.22295	–318.34736	–190.09896
Pseudo R^2	0.2453	0.2957	0.1907

Note: The table only contains variables with values of significant impact
[a]Significant at 10 %
[b]Significant at 1 %
[c]Significant at 5 %

R&D activities carried out inside the service firm (e) also show a positive and significant association with the firm's generation of innovations (at 1 % significance), adding the fact that for "LKIS firms," private partners (l) show a positive and significant association with the firm's product/service innovations (at 1 % significance).

The major considerations to be pointed out when comparing results for the subsamples of "KIS firms" and "LKIS firms" are the fact that introduction of process innovations in the firm, either by the firm itself (a) or the firm cooperating with other firms (b) presents a positive and significant association with the firm's behavior to generate innovations.

Carrying out R&D activities inside the service firm (c) reveals a positive and significant effect on the firm's behavior to generate innovations, also for both subsamples (c1 and c2).

Considering the introduction of innovations into the market (m), it has a positive and significant effect on the dependent variable for the "all firms" sample and in the opposite direction, the non-introduction of innovations (d) has a negative and significant impact on the dependent variable, for the subsample of "KIS firms" (d1), assuming to be of extreme importance for KIS firms to generate and diffuse innovations into the market.

Another important effect on the behavior of "KIS firms" to generate innovation is derived from the R&D cooperation of these firms, justified in the present study by the significant and negative impact of the KIS firms' non-cooperation in R&D (e1) in their capacity to generate product/service innovation. For "KIS firms," the major positive and significant effect of R&D cooperation comes from public partners (f1). Nevertheless, for "LKIS firms" this effect is due to private partners (l).

The major impacting scientific community stakeholders for "KIS firms" on their innovative capacity comes from EU competitors (g1) and EU universities (h1), in a positive way, and US competitors (i1) and EU laboratories, in a negative manner (j1). As for "LKIS firms" the Portuguese laboratories (n) are the only external scientific community stakeholders that affect positively the innovativeness of these type of firms.

9.4.3 Research Hypotheses and Discussion

Taking into consideration Hypothesis 1, proposing a positive and significant effect of the introduction of process innovations in the service firm on its behavior to generate innovation, we find a significant and positive association for both subsamples under analysis. Thus, we fail to reject H1. These results are aligned with previous studies, for instance Zahra and George (2002), Todorova and Durisin (2007), Rothaermel and Alexandre (2009) and Kostopoulos et al. (2011) whose works concluded for a positive influence of introducing process innovations inside the firm on the firm's behavior to generate innovations, either in the form of innovative production processes, differentiated organizational schemes, or strategic redefinition of R&D positioning.

In what concerns Hypothesis 2 proposing a significant and positive impact of performing R&D activities inside the service firm on its behavior to generate product/service innovation, we confirm a positive and significant effect, failing to reject H2. This is also coherent with previous literature. As so, Cohen and Levinthal (1989) and Gambardella (1992) stated that in-house R&D programs and internal investment in R&D activities performed inside the firm are beneficial for generating an innovative capacity in firms. Other scholars also in line with these findings are Arora and Gambardella (1994), Zahra and George (2002), Cassiman and Veugelers (2006) and Li (2011).

For the Hypothesis 3, which defends a positive and significant impact of the introduction of innovations into the market on the firm's behavior to generate innovation, we verified a positive and significant effect, when considering the "all firms" sample, and so, we fail to reject H3. For the "KIS firms" and "LKIS firms" subsamples such effect is not observed. This positive effect was also found in previous studies of Tether (2002), Quintana-Garcia and Benavides-Velasco (2004), Belderbos et al. (2004) and Ritala and Hurmelinna-Laukkanen (2009) which denoted a positive impact of firms that introduce innovative products/services on the market and their innovative behavior. Nevertheless, the present study goes further and found that when disaggregating the sample for "KIS" and "LKIS firms," the impact effect is not significant, being only detected for "all firms." However if we look at the effect of not introducing innovations into the market, such effect reveals to be negative for "KIS firms," which justifies that this type of firms' innovative capacity is affected when they don't launch new products/services.

Considering Hypothesis 4 arguing for a positive and significant association between the set of coopetition relationships with service firm's competitors and its behavior to generate product/service innovation, we obtained a positive and significant effect for European competitor relationships, for the "all firms" sample and the "KIS firms" subsample, leading us to fail to reject H4. In addition, we can point out a significant, though negative, impact of US coopetition relations on the service firm's behavior to generate innovations, both in the "all firms" sample and the "KIS firms" subsample, and so we partially fail to reject H4. Previous scholars (Brandenburger and Nalebuff 1996; Bengtsson and Kock 2000, 2003; Bagshaw and Bagshaw 2001; Garraffo 2002; Belderbos et al. 2004; Chien and Peng 2005; Jong and Marsili 2006; Ritala and Hurmelinna-Laukkanen 2009; Rusko 2011; Vasudeva and Anand 2011) also defended a determinant effect of the establishment of coopetition arrangements between competing firms and their capacity to generate innovative products and services. As we go beyond these studies and disaggregate the coopetition relationships in national (i.e., Portuguese), European, and American competitors we found particular discrepancies between "KIS firms" and "LKIS firms," being "KIS firms" capacity to generate innovations significantly affected by European coopetition arrangements in a positive manner and by US parties, although negatively.

Finally, for Hypothesis 5, proposing a positive and significant effect of coopetition relationships among firms and the scientific community on the service firm's behavior to generate product/service innovation, we confirm a positive and significant impact of European universities for the "all firms" sample and the "KIS firms" subsample, and so we fail to reject H5. Furthermore, we also detect a significant but negative effect of coopetition relationships, particularly analyzing the impact of European laboratories in the "all firms" sample and the "KIS" subsample, on the dependent variable. Therefore, we also partially fail to reject H5 for the "all firms" sample and the "KIS firms" subsample. In this scenario, we are aligned with other studies, namely the ones of Cockburn and Henderson (1998), Li (2011), Kostopoulos et al. (2011) and Vasudeva and Anand (2011) which concluded for a positive and significant impact of settling relationships with the scientific community to spur the firms' innovative performance. It's important to stress the disaggregated effects of "KIS firms" and "LKIS firms" and typology of partner (laboratories, consultants, and universities), for which the impacting effect of cooperating with scientific community is significant and positive for "KIS firms" only when considering European universities and negative when dealing with European laboratories. For "LKIS firms" the only effect is seen in the positive and significant impact of relations with Portuguese laboratories.

9.5 Concluding Remarks, Implications, Limitations, and Future Research

The introduction of process innovations in the firms' internal organization and procedures and the practice of internal R&D activities are of major importance for the service firm's behavior to create new products/services, for the "all firms" sample and for "KIS firms" and "LKIS firms" subsamples.

Regarding the dummy variable of introduction of innovations into the market, this only reveals a significant and positive effect in the service firms' dataset as a whole.

Moreover, in what concerns the set of coopetition relationships between the service firms and competitors, only European competitors show a positive and significant impact on the dependent variable. However, for "LKIS firms" this effect is not observed.

Taking into consideration the impact of the set of coopetition relationships between firms and the scientific community, the major finding is related with the significant effect of coopetition agreements with European laboratories on the innovative behavior, although it is revealed to be negative both for the "all firms" sample and the "KIS firms." For its turn, a positive and significant effect is also detected but with European universities, in what concerns the "all firms" sample.

As concluded above, all the three hypotheses concerning the absorptive capacity enablers are determinant factors for the firm's capacity to generate innovations. Summing up, both hypotheses linked with coopeting schemes reveal that it's of extreme importance for firms to get involved in coopetition arrangements in order to perform better in generating innovations. For both and regarding "KIS firms," we confirmed the importance of coopetition schemes with European competing firms and European universities, fact that is possibly related with public policies targeted at promoting cooperation platforms supported by European frameworks in order to boost innovativeness of firms.

Since public policies play a crucial role in fostering innovative capacities, it is important that policy-makers understand the determinants of service firms' behavior to generate innovative products and services, and their effects on innovative performance, the generation of net value added and economic benefits.

In terms of policy implications arising from the present study, it is suggested that public policies should be guided towards the creation and consolidation of open innovation flows and towards fostering coopetition strategies between service firms and the scientific community, securing formal channels and mechanisms targeted at minimizing appropriability risks.

By making use of firms' behavior to generate innovation in order to reveal their innovative performance and the dynamics of coopetition public policies oriented to open innovation, the present study can give insights to those who manage innovation policy orientations, since knowledge of the set of determinant factors of firms' innovative behavior can be helpful in drawing up guidelines to foster and properly manage the open innovation workflows between service firms and their stakeholders, and then developing the capacity to generate and transfer new products to market.

Overall, the results of this analysis may provide helpful starting points for practitioners (either in service firms or coopetition stakeholders) who wish to estimate the directions of their organization's R&D projects, through coopetition arrangements with partners, in order to enhance the efficiency of technology transfer flows, and consequently stimulate the creation, diffusion, and regulation of defensive mechanisms to be used as routines by the service firms involved.

The main limitation of the present study is the lack of information on firms' innovative capacity when trying to access data on patenting behavior and other IP rights, such as copyrights and trademarks. This is also the main limitation of the database used in this study, the European CIS Survey, 2008, with the quasi-inexistence of data regarding firms' IP performance, considering additional data on patents, copyrights, and other IP rights, since the only reference to innovative products or services generated inside and by the firm that can or cannot be protected via IP formal mechanisms is the variable of product/service innovation.

In this connection, avenues for future research should be focused on the factors that motivate service firms to behave alternatively by implementing R&D corporate strategies, based on coopetition patenting initiatives, technological surveillance, or forecasting projects. This way, the service firms' behavior based on patenting strategies and their characteristics, which influence their coopetition arrangements, deserve to be further explored, by examining the entrepreneurial profile of the founder and management team.

References

Abernathy W, Clark K (1985) Innovation: mapping the winds of creative destruction. Res Policy 14:3–22

Amburgey T, Rao H (1996) Organizational ecology: past, present and future directions. Acad Manage J 39(5):1265–1286

Aoki R, Schiff A (2008) Promoting access to intellectual property: patent pools, copyright collectives and clearinghouses. R&D Manag 38(2):189–204

Archambault E (2002) Methods for using patents in cross-country comparisons. Scientometrics 54(1):15–30

Arora A, Gambardella A (1994) Evaluating technological information and utilizing it: scientific knowledge, technological capability, and external linkages in biotechnology. J Econ Behav Organ 24:91–114

Bagshaw M, Bagshaw C (2001) Co-opetition applied to training—a case study. Ind Commer Train 33(4/5):175–177

Belderbos R, Carree M, Lokshin B (2004) Cooperative R&D and firm performance. Res Policy 33:1477–1492

Bengtsson M, Kock S (2000) Coopetition in business networks—to cooperate and compete simultaneously. Ind Mark Manag 29:411–426
Bengtsson M, Kock S (2003) Tension in co-opetition. Academy of Marketing Science Annual Conference, Washington, DC, 28–31 May
Bergek A, Bruzelius M (2010) Are patents with multiple inventors from different countries a good indicator of international R&D collaboration? The case of ABB. Res Policy 39:1321–1334
Blomqvist K, Hurmelinna P, Seppanen R (2005) Playing the collaboration game right—balancing trust and contracting. Technovation 25:497–504
Boden M, Miles I (2000) Services and the knowledge-based economy. Continuum, London
Brandenburger AM, Nalebuff BJ (1996) Co-opetition. Currency, Doubleday, New York
Carayol N, Roux P (2007) The strategic formation of intra-individual collaboration networks. Evidence from co-invention patterns. Ann Écon Stat 87(88):275–301
Cassiman B, Veugelers R (2006) In search of complementarity in the innovation strategy: internal R&D and external knowledge acquisition. Manag Sci 52:68–82
Chen Y, Chen B (2011) Utilizing patent analysis to explore the cooperative competition relationship of the two LED companies: Nichia and Osram. Tech Forecasting Soc Chang 78:294–302
Chesbrough H (2003) Open innovation: the new imperative for creating and profiting from technology. Harvard Business School Press, Boston
Chesbrough H, Vanhaverbeke W, West J (2006) Open innovation: researching a new paradigm. Oxford University Press, New York
Chien T, Peng T (2005) Competition and cooperation intensity in a network—a case study in Taiwan simulator industry. J Am Acad Bus 7:150–155
Cockburn I, Henderson R (1998) Absorptive capacity, coauthoring behavior, and the organization of research in drug discovery. J Ind Econ 46(2):157–183
Cohen W, Levinthal D (1989) Innovation and learning: the two faces of R&D. Econ J 99: 569–596
Cohen W, Nelson R, Walsh J (2000) Protecting their intellectual assets: appropriability conditions and why US manufacturing firms patent (or not). NBER working paper, no. 7552
Dagnino G, Rocco E (2009) Coopetition strategy: theory, experiments and cases. Routledge, New York
Dussauge P, Garrette B, Mitchell W (2000) Learning from competing partners: outcomes and durations of scale and link alliances in Europe, North America and Asia. Strateg Manag J 21:99–126
Enkel E, Gassmann O, Chesbrough H (2009) Open R&D and open innovation: exploring the phenomenon. R&D Manag 39(4):311–316
Escribano A, Fosfuri A, Tribó J (2009) Managing external knowledge flows: the moderating role of absorptive capacity. Res Policy 38:96–105
Fjelstad AD, Becerra M, Narayanan S (2004) Strategic action in network industries: an empirical analysis of the European mobile phone industry. Scand J Manag 20:173–196
Gambardella A (1992) Competitive advantages from in-house basic research. Res Policy 21:391–407
Garraffo F (2002) Types of coopetition to manage emerging technologies. In: Second annual conference, innovative research in management, Stockholm
Gassmann O, Enkel E, Chesbrough H (2010) The future of open innovation. R&D Manag 40(3):213–221
Gomes-Casseres B (1996) The alliance revolution. Harvard University Press, Cambridge
Grindley P, Teece D (1997) Managing intellectual capital: licensing and cross-licensing in semiconductors and electronics. Calif Manage Rev 39:8–41
Harbison K, Pekar P (1998) Smart alliances. Jossey-Bass, San Francisco
Huston L, Sakkab N (2006) Connect and develop. Harv Bus Rev 84(3):58–66
Jong J, Marsili O (2006) The fruit flies of innovations: a taxonomy of innovative small firms. Res Policy 35:213–229
Kostopoulos K, Papalexandris A, Papachroni M, Ioannou G (2011) Absorptive capacity, innovation, and financial performance. J Bus Res 64(12):1335–1343

Li X (2011) Sources of external technology, absorptive capacity, and innovation capability in Chinese state-owned high-tech enterprises. World Dev 39(7):1240–1248

Luo X, Slotegraaf R (2006) Cross-functional coopetition: the simultaneous role of cooperation and competition within firms. J Mark 70(2):67–80

Luo X, Rindfleisch A, Tse DK (2007) Working with rivals: the impact of competitor alliances in financial performance. J Mark Res 44:73–83

Ma Z, Lee Y (2008) Patent application and technological collaboration in inventive activities: 1980–2005. Technovation 28(6):379–390

Merino F, Rubalcaba L (2012) Are knowledge-intensive services highly concentrated? Evidence from European regions. Tijdschr Econ Soc Geogr 104(2):1467–9663

Miozzo M, Grisham D (2006) Knowledge intensive business services. Edward Elgar, Cheltenham

Muller E, Zenker A (2001) Business services as actors of knowledge transformation: the role of KIBS in regional and national innovation systems. Res Policy 30:1501–1516

Nieto M, Santamaria L (2007) The importance of diverse collaborative networks for the novelty of product innovation. Technovation 27(6–7):367–377

Park S, Russo M (1996) When competition eclipses cooperation: an event history analysis of joint venture failure. Manag Sci 42(6):875–890

Quintana-Garcia C, Benavides-Velasco C (2004) Cooperation, competition, and innovative capability: a panel data of European dedicated biotechnology firms. Technovation 24(12):927–938

Rammer C (2002) Patente Und Marken Als Schutzmechanismen Für Innovationen. Studien Zum Deutschen Innovationssystem, 11-2003, Mannheim

Ritala P, Hurmelinna-Laukkanen P (2009) What's in it for me? Creating and appropriating value in innovation-related coopetition. Technovation 29(12):819–828

Rothaermel F, Alexandre M (2009) Ambidexterity in technology sourcing: the moderating role of absorptive capacity. Organ Sci 20(4):759–780

Rubalcaba L, Kox H (2007) Business services in European economic growth. Palgrave-MacMillan, London

Rusko R (2011) Exploring the concept of coopetition: a typology for the strategic moves of the Finnish forest industry. Ind Mark Manag 40(2):311–320

Seung P, Russo M (1996) When competition eclipses cooperation: an event history analysis of joint venture failure. Manag Sci 42(6):875–890

Tether BS (2002) Who co-operates for innovation, and why: an empirical analysis. Res Policy 31(6):947–967

Todorova G, Durisin B (2007) Absorptive capacity: valuing a reconceptualization. Acad Manage Rev 32(3):774–786

Tsai W (2002) Social structure of coopetition within a multiunit organization, competition and intraorganizational knowledge sharing. Organ Sci 13(2):179–190

Vasudeva G, Anand J (2011) Unpacking absorptive capacity: a study of knowledge utilization from alliance portfolio. Acad Manage J 54(3):611–623

Wood P (2006) The regional significance of knowledge-intensive services in Europe: Kisinn and After. Innovation 19:51–66

Zahra S, George G (2002) Absorptive capacity: a review, reconceptualization, and extension. Acad Manage Rev 27(2):185–203

Chapter 10
Does Human Capital Impact Differently the Opportunity Perception and the Business Creation? The Case of Spain

Rocío Aliaga-Isla

Abstract The current study analyzes how Spaniard's general/specific human capital influences their likelihood of perceiving entrepreneurial opportunities and creating a business. The analysis pivots around the comparison of two processes which are part of entrepreneurship. Data from the Spanish Global Entrepreneurship Monitor—GEM of 2008 are used. Logistic regression analysis is performed to test several theoretical hypotheses. Findings revealed that general human capital such as education is not significant for both perceiving entrepreneurial opportunities and creating a business. However, work experience, managerial business, and entrepreneurial training are positively significant to perceive entrepreneurial opportunities and to create a business. This research reveals that specific types of human capital play different roles in entrepreneurship. The contribution of this paper is to compare how the human capital influences upon two processes of entrepreneurship.

Keywords General and specific human capital • Opportunity perception • Business creation

10.1 Introduction

Entrepreneurship is a major driver of economic growth in the countries. Entrepreneurship is present in the political agenda and in academic arenas. Several scholars have researched about the first step of entrepreneurship, "the discovery" of entrepreneurial opportunities (Arenius and Clercq 2005; Baron and Ensley 2006; Baron 2004, 2006; Fiet 1996, 2007). In the same sense, business creation has been

---

R. Aliaga-Isla (✉)
Business Economics Department, Autonomous University of Barcelona,
Edificio B Campus de la UAB, CP. 08193, Bellaterra (Cerdanyola del Valles),
Barcelona, Spain
e-mail: rociodelpilar.aliaga@e-campus.uab.cat

R. Baptista, J. Leitão (eds.), *Entrepreneurship, Human Capital, and Regional Development*, International Studies in Entrepreneurship 31,
DOI 10.1007/978-3-319-12871-9_10

researched by academicians (Arenius and Minniti 2005; Bergmann and Sternberg 2007; Davidsson and Honig 2003; Liñán et al. 2011; Wennekers et al. 2005). These studies have analyzed several variables to understand the behavior of the entrepreneur as well the factors that influence the discovery and the business creation. However, analysis of both processes together is lacking. It means, analyze the discovery of entrepreneurial opportunities and business creation using the same data. It will show if the factors influence in different way both processes.

As mentioned above, entrepreneurship is a process that implies recognizing that the perception of entrepreneurial opportunities is the first step and the milestone of entrepreneurship. This means that the existence of opportunities plays an important role in this process of business creation (Shane 2003). According to Shane (2003) and Venkataraman (1997) individual firstly identifies an opportunity to exploit it or not. In general some prior studies on the perception of entrepreneurial opportunities and business creation have highlighted the importance of several resources such as the prior knowledge (Shane 2000), the alertness attitude of individuals (Kirzner 1973), and the network-based approach and human capital (Arenius and Clercq 2005), among others (Arenius and Minniti 2005; Shepherd and DeTienne 2005; Ucbasaran et al. 2008).

Among all the resources the individual possesses, the human capital factors have long been argued to be a critical resource for perceiving entrepreneurial opportunities and for creating a business. To analyze the different factors of human capital that affect these two processes is important in the extent that it allows us to know what human capital attributes are relevant for perceiving and for creating a business by Spaniards. Literature shows that general and specific human capital plays a role because of the constantly increasing knowledge-intensive in several environments (Unger et al. 2011). Human capital is important because it is the assets that individuals acquired through their investment in schooling, on the job, and in other kinds of experiences (Rauch and Rijsdijk 2013), so human capital is an idiosyncratic resource. Moreover, literature shows that general and specific human capital exist (Becker 1962; Rauch and Rijsdijk 2013; Weisberg 1996) and it has impacted differently upon the perception of entrepreneurial opportunities and business creation.

In this study, I aim to contribute to the existing literature analyzing two processes of entrepreneurship—the perception of entrepreneurial opportunities and the business creation by Spaniards—linked to human capital theory. To analyze the influence of general and specific human capital upon the perception of entrepreneurial opportunities and business creation, the Spanish Global Entrepreneurship Monitor—GEM of 2008 data is used. This database has information of Spaniards' characteristics which have allowed me to classify them in general and specific human capital. This human capital can influence on perceiving opportunities and business creation (Shane and Venkataraman 2000). In effect, some authors have stated that well-educated people will be more likely to perceive and exploit entrepreneurial opportunities. Information and skills that education and experiences provide is relevant to improve the entrepreneurial judgment by enhancing the analytic ability to recognize opportunities and then, create a business.

Education and experiences are known as general human capital, which constitute the prior knowledge of individuals, which is acquired over time (Hayek 1945; Venkataraman 1997). Also, managerial-business experience and entrepreneurial training (Amaral et al. 2011; Arribas and Vila 2007) are considered as specific human capital, while controlling for their demographic characteristics. In general, our results reveal different impacts of specific and general human capital upon the perception of entrepreneurial opportunities and business creation by Spaniards.

Contributions of this study are as follows: I shall focus on the analysis of Spaniards' human capital, general and specific, related to the perception of entrepreneurial opportunities and business creation. To conduct this analysis I have used data collected in the same period of time, so it allows me to see the Spaniard's behavior related to both processes, the perception of entrepreneurial opportunities and business creation. In certain way, this kind of analysis is a novelty because it is not usual, there are many studies focusing only on one of the two processes.

The paper proceeds as follows. The next section is dedicated to the theoretical framework related to the human capital theory highlighting general and specific human capital. Moreover, a literature review is conducted related to the perception of entrepreneurial opportunities and business creation. Section 10.3 presents the methodology and technique used for data analysis. Section 10.4 is devoted to empirical findings, Sect. 10.5 presents the discussion and conclusion and Sect. 10.6 is dedicated to present implications and future research lines.

10.2 Theoretical Framework

10.2.1 General and Specific Human Capital

The human capital theory is related to the acquisition of education and experiences by individuals. This resource provides individuals with knowledge that increase their cognitive abilities to perform activities in any field. The theory assumes that more human capital is better because it can influence individuals in the choice of careers or even in attitudes towards engaging themselves in entrepreneurial activities (Lucas 1978). However, human capital has dimensions that have been classified as general and specific human capital. For instance, Becker (1962) has distinguished between general and specific human capital. Becker highlighted that general human capital is related to skills and knowledge which could be transferable. His argument is based on the general and specific training, where specific training increases productivity in the firms and general training increases the marginal productivity in the firms. After the Becker's definition, concepts related to general (GHC) and specific human capital (SHC) came out in management (Weisberg 1996). In this sense, in the following sections, a literature review is developed related to human capital linked to the perception of entrepreneurial opportunities and business creation.

10.2.2 Human Capital and the Perception of Entrepreneurial Opportunities

Entrepreneurship is a process that begins with the perception of entrepreneurial opportunities, and after that, the individual should exploit it or not (Shane 2003). The perception of entrepreneurial opportunities is based on the approach of the Austrian economy. Kirzner (1973) suggests that only some may recognize specific opportunities in a given time, given that people have different idiosyncrasies and experiences of personal life. Shane and Venkataraman (2000) highlight that the perception of entrepreneurial opportunities could be performed using the cognitive properties and characteristics that one possesses. Moreover, Shane and Venkataraman (2000) point out that the possession of information is crucial, then the possession in terms of quantity relies completely on the experiences that individuals have had. For example, one can acquire information while he/she is studying, in a job, in the neighborhood where the individual lives or in the country where he/she is living, or elsewhere. Consequently, all these resources that an individual acquires constitute the idiosyncratic general and specific human capital which influences in the perception of entrepreneurial opportunities (Venkataraman 1997).

In this manner, the perception of entrepreneurial opportunities was studied by few authors, who used human capital as a factor to explain such process. Westhead et al. (2009) conducted a study that focused on opportunity identification by habitual and novice entrepreneurs who had prior business experience. This study compares the number of opportunities that both habitual and novice entrepreneurs had identified; data were collected in Great Britain. The identification of opportunities was based on information that both groups looked for and human capital was considered as a control variable. Education was used as a proxy of human capital.

Arenius and Clercq (2005) studied opportunity recognition under the focus of the network-based approach. The authors examined the effect of being embedded in different social networks and how it influences in the perception of opportunities. In this case, human capital is used as a variable to explain differences and it was a proxy of education of individuals. The sample used for the study was from Belgium and Finland Global Entrepreneurship Monitor—GEM of 2002.

In addition, the identification of opportunities has been studied considering the general and specific human capital (Ucbasaran et al. 2008). The authors studied the effect of general human capital versus specific human capital upon the identification of entrepreneurial opportunities. Education and work experience were considered as GHC, and business ownership experience, managerial capabilities, entrepreneurial capabilities, and technical capabilities were considered as SHC. Data were collected in 2000 of founders and owners of businesses, which were in sectors like agriculture, forestry and fishing, production, construction, and services located in Great Britain. The main finding showed that SHC variables have stronger relationship with the number of opportunities identified than GHC variables.

The identification of opportunities has also been explained using the prior knowledge approach and the potential financial reward (Shepherd and DeTienne 2005).

The authors remarked that prior knowledge could be gained through education, which facilitates the accumulation of new knowledge. This variable was measured as a prior knowledge of customers. Data were collected from students of a US university.

10.2.3 Human Capital and Business Creation

Some authors have used GHC related to the personal characteristics of the entrepreneur that are not directly related to his/her role in the business (Arribas and Vila 2007). So, formal education (Shepherd and Wiklund 2005) and work experience are considered as being GHC (Arribas and Vila 2007). Education is a common structure that provides individuals with skills and knowledge to deal with changes in economic environments (Arribas and Vila 2007; Davidsson and Honig 2003; Hatch and Dyer 2004). Despite education is a dimension of general human capital, some studies have found positive effect upon the probability to engage in entrepreneurial activities (Lucas 1978). In contrast, other authors have found negative effect upon entrepreneurship (Koellinger et al. 2007; Minniti and Bygrave 2003). Specifically, when tertiary education is analyzed some results showed that individuals have less chance to engage as entrepreneurs rather than those with primary or secondary education (Amaral and Baptista 2007). In the same sense, Bates (1990) found a positive relationship between higher education and business start-up in the service sector.

Work experience is also considered part of GHC and has usually been defined as the number of years involved in any work. For example, individuals that worked in managerial positions, those that create a business and those who worked in sectors such as trades and sales acquired different experience than those who worked as clerks, machine operators, and laborers, among others (Davidsson and Honig 2003). Therefore, this variance of experiences is not captured in the way of defining the work experience of individuals.

On the other hand, SHC is related to professional and training experiences (Arribas and Vila 2007). Some studies have used specific human capital related to skills and knowledge which is less transferable (Gimeno et al. 1997). The accumulation of SHC takes place in the job as well as in nonformal education, such as specific training courses. Some studies have considered vocational studies for referring to specific courses which are not formal education (Davidsson and Honig 2003). Usually, training courses are oriented to specific groups of people who are in a vulnerable situation (Awogbenle and Chijiote 2010).

Policy-makers believe that the level of entrepreneurship can be reached through education, especially with entrepreneurial education (Oosterbeek et al. 2010), both formal and nonformal. In this sense, entrepreneurial formation, nonformal, could be had in the private, public, or third sector (ONGs), and it is designed in modules of short duration. Most times this formation arises under the initiative of governments looking at the structure and necessity of skills in the local economy and market.

Also, entrepreneurial formation provides knowledge and skills to individuals. When the individual has some kind of entrepreneurial formation, he/she intends to reinforce and enlarge his/her knowledge to create a business (Neck and Greene 2011) or to improve the performance of his/her business. This argument is consistent with the limited scope of applicability that specific human capital has as a characteristic (Cooper et al. 1994; Ucbasaran et al. 2008). This means that entrepreneurial formation is oriented to develop specific skills and knowledge surrounding the business, but this specific knowledge loses its value outside of its particular domain.

Furthermore, the ownership experience is considered another dimension of SHC (Gimeno et al. 1997). This kind of experience provides individuals with knowledge and skills related to business (Spender 1996), and allows them the perception of opportunities in the same sector or even in another. These individuals manage specific knowledge of the market and deal with suppliers and customers. In the same branch, we could have the manager of the business, who despite not being the owner, deals with all aspects of the business and knows the market as well as the owner. Furthermore, the acquisition of managerial skills facilitates the perception of entrepreneurial opportunities (Westhead et al. 2009).

Some studies have found positive effect of entrepreneurial experience upon entrepreneurial intentions (Kolvereid and Isaksen 2006). For example, serial entrepreneurs, who are endowed with entrepreneurial-specific human capital has more probabilities for engaging in entrepreneurial activities (Ucbasaran et al. 2003; Westhead et al. 2005). In the same sense, individuals with previous managerial experience probably have acquired skills and abilities to pursue entrepreneurial opportunities (Eckhardt and Shane 2003; Gimeno et al. 1997). For example, serial and novice entrepreneurs were compared and the findings showed that previous experience in managing a business is important for managing other businesses, showing positive effect on reentering entrepreneurship (Ucbasaran et al. 2006). Furthermore, regarding general and specific human capital, Amaral et al. (2011) have found that specific dimensions of human capital play different roles. For example, dimensions of general human capital influenced negatively upon the hazard of becoming a serial entrepreneur. In contrast, dimensions of specific human capital influenced positively on the time to reentering entrepreneurship. Considering the theoretical framework related to human capital linked to the perception of opportunities and business creation, the following hypotheses are proposed:

H1a: Higher level of education increases the likelihood to perceive entrepreneurial opportunities

H1b: Higher level of education increases the likelihood to engage in business creation

H2a: Work experience increases the likelihood to perceive entrepreneurial opportunities

H2b: Work experience increases the likelihood to engage in business creation

H3a: Managerial-business experience increases the likelihood to perceive entrepreneurial opportunities

H3b: Managerial-business experience increases the likelihood to engage in business creation

H4a: The acquirement of entrepreneurial training increases the likelihood to perceive entrepreneurial opportunities

H4b: The acquirement of entrepreneurial training increases the likelihood to engage in business creation

10.3 Methodology

10.3.1 Data

To accomplish the objective of this study, the database of GEM—Global Entrepreneurship Monitor was used. The Global Entrepreneurship Monitor was founded by Babson College and London Business School in 1999, with the aim of analyzing issues related to entrepreneurship and its influence in economic growth. This database has been assembled to facilitate the research across nations through the comparison of topics related to entrepreneurship and the level of entrepreneurial activity (Reynolds et al. 2005).

Data used for this study come from the Spanish GEM for the year 2008. These data is a large stratified random sample of the Spanish population. The sample is stratified by 17 Spanish autonomous communities plus two autonomous cities Ceuta and Melilla. Respondents were contacted by telephone using randomized direct dial technique by a leading professional market investigation and public opinion service firm and monitoring by GEM consortium. Telephone numbers corresponding to different municipalities were random obtained from the annually updated "España Office V5.2" database of fixed and mobile telephones.

10.3.2 Variables

Variables selected for our study are detailed in Table 10.1. This Table shows Spanish GEM database of 2008 contains 30,879 observations from which cases without information have been dropped to avoid bias in the results.

10.3.2.1 Dependent Variables

Perception of opportunities: it was asked to respondents "in the next 6 months, will there be good opportunities for starting a business." This variable is measured as binary variable assuming value 1 if the individual perceives opportunities and 0 otherwise. Our data showed that the level of perceiving opportunities is 26 %.

Table 10.1 Descriptive statistics of variables

Variable	Definition	*N*	Mean	Std. dev.
Perception of opportunity	1 = yes, 0 = no	23,553	0.267	0.442
Business creation	1 = yes, 0 = no	30,879	0.068	0.251
More than 12 years of education	1 = yes, 0 = no	30,775	0.271	0.444
Work experience	1 = yes, 0 = no	30,879	0.731	0.443
Managerial-business Experience	1 = yes, 0 = no	30,879	0.119	0.323
Entrepreneurial formation	1 = yes, 0 = no	30,879	0.214	0.410
Gender	1 = male, 0 = female	30,879	0.501	0.500
Age	18–64 years	30,879	41.591	12.326

Business creation: it is a variable that captures two groups of individuals. Therefore, individuals involved in start-up effort and those that manage and own a business that is up to 42 months old are considered as business creation. This variable is measured as binary assuming value 1 if the individual is involved in business creation effort and 0 otherwise. Our data showed that the level of business creation is 6.8 %.

10.3.2.2 Independent Variables

Education: the GEM project uses the variable "maximum education attainment" to measure the level of education of individuals. All respondents interviewed gave their maximum level of education at the time of the survey. This variable was transformed in binary assuming 1 for individuals that have more than 12 years of education and 0 otherwise. Table 10.1 shows that 27 % of individuals have more than 12 years of education.

Work experience: was coded as binary variable assuming value 1 for individuals with active work status and 0 otherwise. According to our descriptive statistics, 73 % of individuals are active working. As it was explained in the theoretical framework work experience is part of general human capital, in this sense I am using this variable as proxy of work experience.

Managerial-business experience: Spanish GEM database considers the variable "owns or manages a business" which measures skills acquired by individuals. The values of this variable are 1 for individuals who acquired this kind of experience and 0 otherwise. Our data show that 12 % of individuals have this kind of experience.

Entrepreneurial training: This variable is determined by the answers of individuals who answer the question "have received some entrepreneurial training in his life." This variable is binary assuming 1 if the individual had entrepreneurial training and 0 otherwise. In Table 10.1 is observed that the level of entrepreneurial training of individuals is 21 %.

10.3.2.3 Control Variables

These variables are introduced with the objective to control some outcomes of the predictable variables related to the perception of entrepreneurial opportunities as well as the business creation. I considered "gender" important for our study, this variable is binary and has the value 1 = male and 0 otherwise. The proportion of male is (50.1 %) similar compared to female. An individual's "age" is another factor considered and is expressed in years between 18 and 64. Table 10.1 shows that the average of the individuals' age is 41 years old. Finally, Spanish regions were considered to capture some differences in opportunity sets across the country as well as in the business creation.

10.3.3 Econometric Methodology

As the dependent variables are discrete, it may use ordinal least square regression—OLS—to test the hypotheses. Nonetheless, this kind of model has certain econometric problems, such as ε does not have a Gaussian distribution, ε's variance is not constant, it is heteroskedastic and may predict probability values beyond the binomial values (1, 0) (Greene 2000). Considering that explained before, the hypotheses related to opportunity perception and business creation are tested using the logistic regression model.

The odds of perceiving entrepreneurial opportunities versus those who have not perceived opportunities; and the odds of creating a business versus those who have not created a business are estimated:

$$Y_{ij} = \beta_{0ij} + \beta_{1ij} X_{1ij} + \cdots + \beta_{kij} X_{kij} + \varepsilon_{kij}$$

where Y is the odds (in log form) of perceiving opportunities and creating a business for an individual i living in a specific Spanish region j. $\chi_{1ij},\ldots,\chi_{kij}$ are binary variables representing the general/specific human capital and control variables, and finally ε_{kij} represents the error term.

10.4 Empirical Findings

10.4.1 Human Capital and the Perception of Entrepreneurial Opportunities by Spaniards

Table 10.2 shows the models for the perception of entrepreneurial opportunities by Spaniards. Model 4 includes variables related to general and specific human capital. Table 10.2 also shows that some control variables are significant in all models. In Model 4 was found that men are more likely to perceive entrepreneurial opportunities than

Table 10.2 Logistic regression for perception of entrepreneurial opportunities

Variables	Model (1) Control	Model (2) GHC	Model (3) SHC	Model (4) Full
General human capital				
More than 12 years of education (H1a)		0.976 (0.033)		0.971 (0.033)
Work status (H2a)		1.165*** (0.041)		1.139*** (0.041)
Specific human capital				
Entrepreneurial Training (H3a)			1.227*** (0.043)	1.227*** (0.043)
Managerial-business experience (H4a)			1.131*** (0.049)	1.093** (0.048)
Control variables				
Gender	1.363*** (0.0406)	1.322*** (0.04)	1.349*** (0.04)	1.316*** (0.04)
Age	0.995*** (0.00122)	0.995*** (0.0012)	0.996*** (0.0012)	0.995*** (0.001)
Autonomous communities				
Andalusia (ref.)				
Aragon	1.960*** (0.161)	1.957742*** 0.162339	1.958*** (0.161)	1.958*** (0.162)
Asturias	1.128 (0.097)	1.134355 0.098234	1.115 (0.096)	1.123 (0.097)
Balearic Islands	1.651*** (0.165)	1.638435*** 0.165007	1.652*** (0.165)	1.642*** (0.165)
Canary Islands	1.287*** (0.108)	1.288871*** 0.109585	1.283*** (0.108)	1.286*** (0.109)
Cantabria	1.821*** (0.18)	1.838497*** 0.182841	1.829*** (0.181)	1.848*** (0.183)
Castila and Leon	1.102 (0.094)	1.105901 0.095413	1.101 (0.094)	1.106 (0.095)
Castilla la Mancha	0.694*** (0.063)	0.6997716*** 0.064019	0.696*** (0.063)	0.702*** (0.064)
Catalonia	1.911*** (0.157)	1.908589 *** (0.158)	1.908*** (0.157)	1.908*** (0.158)
Valencian Community	1.309*** (0.11)	1.314*** (0.111)	1.311** (0.11)	1.318*** (0.111)
Extremadura	1.543*** (0.154)	1.547*** (0.155)	1.538*** (0.153)	1.546*** (0.155)
Galicia	1.549*** (0.129)	1.552*** (0.13)	1.546*** (0.129)	1.552*** (0.13)
Madrid	1.275*** (0.108)	1.278*** (0.108)	1.264*** (0.107)	1.269*** (0.108)
Murcia	1.243** (0.106)	1.254*** (0.107)	1.243** (0.106)	1.255*** (0.107)
Navarra	1.339*** (0.116)	1.335*** (0.116)	1.328*** (0.115)	1.328*** (0.115)

(continued)

Table 10.2 (continued)

Variables	Model (1) Control	Model (2) GHC	Model (3) SHC	Model (4) Full
Country Basque	1.496*** (0.126)	1.501*** (0.127)	1.500*** (0.126)	1.508*** (0.127)
La Rioja	1.396*** (0.142)	1.396*** (0.143)	1.391*** (0.142)	1.395*** (0.143)
Ceuta	1.329** (0.172)	1.346** (0.175)	1.337** (0.173)	1.354** (0.176)
Melilla	0.931 (0.125)	0.931 (0.125)	0.936 (0.126)	0.936 (0.126)
N	23,553	23,467	23,553	23,467

Odds ratios are reported. Standard errors in parentheses
$*p<0.1$, $**p<0.05$, $***p<0.01$

are women. Also, results showed that older people tend to perceive entrepreneurial opportunities than do younger ones.

Analyzing general human capital, it was found that the relationship between education and the perception of entrepreneurial opportunities is not significant in Models 2 and 4. In this sense, no support was found for Hypothesis 1a. Hypothesis 2a states that individuals who have work experience are more likely to perceive entrepreneurial opportunities than are those without this experience. The findings, in Model 4 support this hypothesis; there is a significant relationship between the work experience of individuals and the perception of entrepreneurial opportunities.

In turn, regarding specific human capital, Hypothesis 3a states that individuals who possess managerial-business experience are more likely to perceive entrepreneurial opportunities than are those individuals without this experience. Significant relationship was found between managerial-business experience and the perception of entrepreneurial opportunities in Model 4 while in Model 3 the results show stronger relationship between these variables. Therefore, Hypothesis 3a found support. Hypothesis 4a indicates that individuals with entrepreneurial training are more likely to perceive entrepreneurial opportunities than are those individuals without this training. The findings support this hypothesis; there is a significant relationship between entrepreneurial training and the perception of entrepreneurial opportunities.

10.4.2 Human Capital and Business Creation by Spaniards

Table 10.3 reports the outcomes of logistic regression analysis related to the business creation in Spain. Regarding the analysis of the variables related to general human capital, our results show that education is not significant for creating a business by Spaniards. Therefore, H1b not found support. Nonetheless, work experience seems to play an important role for creating a business. Results show that the relationship between work experience and business creation is significant. It means that Spaniards who had work experience are more likely to create a business than those who do not have any. Therefore, H2b found support.

Table 10.3 Logistic regression for business creation

	Model (1)	Model (2)	Model (3)	Model (4)
Variables	Control	GHC	SHC	Full
General human capital				
More than 12 years of education (H1b)		1.013 (0.050)		1.081 (0.055)
Work status (H2b)		1.765*** (0.057)		1.274*** (5.804)
Specific human capital				
Entrepreneurial training (H3b)			1.238*** (0.066)	1.210*** (0.065)
Managerial-business experience (H4b)			8.501*** (0.418)	5.996*** (0.297)
Control variables				
Gender	1.369*** (0.062)	1.047 (0.048)	1.245*** (0.059)	1.054 (0.050)
Age	0.988*** (0.0018)	0.985*** (0.002)	0.981*** (0.001)	0.978*** (0.002)
Autonomous communities				
Andalusia (ref.)				
Aragon	1.198 (0.145)	1.122 (0.138)	1.215 (0.154)	1.163 (0.149)
Asturias	0.907 (0.116)	0.851 (0.111)	0.816 (0.109)	0.774** (0.105)
Balearic Islands	0.942 (0.147)	0.840 (0.133)	0.927 (0.151)	0.858 (0.141)
Canary Islands	1.021 (0.127)	0.955 (0.121)	1.065 (0.139)	1.016 (0.134)
Cantabria	1.152 (0.171)	1.084 (0.163)	1.181 (0.183)	1.132 (0.177)
Castila and Leon	0.811 (0.107)	0.773 (0.103)	0.762** (0.105)	0.743** (0.103)
Castila la Mancha	1.005 (0.126)	0.987 (0.127)	0.995 (0.131)	0.988 (0.132)
Catalonia	1.047 (0.130)	0.958 (0.121)	1.047 (0.136)	0.988 (0.130)
Valencian Community	1.031 (0.128)	0.978 (0.124)	1.015 (0.132)	0.984 (0.130)
Extremadura	1.039 (0.158)	0.969 (0.150)	0.881 (0.141)	0.846 (0.136)
Galicia	1.119 (0.138)	1.056 (0.132)	1.091 (0.140)	1.052 (0.137)
Madrid	1.252 (0.150)	1.160 (0.142)	1.261** (0.159)	1.195 (0.152)
Murcia	0.910 (0.117)	0.920 (0.120)	0.868 (0.116)	0.883 (0.120)

(continued)

Table 10.3 (continued)

Variables	Model (1) Control	Model (2) GHC	Model (3) SHC	Model (4) Full
Navarra	0.918 (0.120)	0.826 (0.109)	0.851 (0.116)	0.798 (0.110)
Basque Country	1.038 (0.130)	0.954 (0.121)	1.055 (0.138)	0.999 (0.132)
La Rioja	0.956 (0.150)	0.866 (0.138)	0.860 (0.141)	0.815 (0.134)
Ceuta	0.767 (0.166)	0.699 (0.155)	0.784 (0.176)	0.729 (0.167)
Melilla	0.505 (0.129)	0.464 (0.119)	0.526 (0.138)	0.500 (0.132)
N	30,879	30,775	30,879	30,775

Odds ratios are reported. Standard errors in parentheses

*$p<0.1$, **$p<0.05$, ***$p<0.01$

Results of specific human capital analysis report that the relationship between entrepreneurial training and business creation is significant for Spaniards. In terms of the role of managerial-business experience, results showed that this experience is also significant for creating a business by Spaniards. This result suggests that Spaniards who possess managerial-business experience increase the odds of creating a business compared to their counterparts who do not possess this kind of experience. Therefore, Hypothesis 4b found support.

Finally, in terms of the control variables, it is found that gender is not statistically significant for business creation by Spaniards. Furthermore, it was found a significant relationship between age and business creation. This relationship showed that older people are more likely to create a business as compared to their older counterparts.

Considering results from Tables 10.2 and 10.3, I conclude that the perception of entrepreneurial opportunities and business creation is impacted in similar way. For both steps of entrepreneurship specific human capital seems more relevant than general human capital, excluding work experience.

10.4.3 Robustness Check of the Models

Some tests were carried out to assess the goodness of fit of the models. For our models, the Model χ^2 test is considered. The Model χ^2 test compares observed values with theoretical or expected values. It is the difference between the $-2\text{Log}\,L$ of the fitted model and the $-2\text{Log}\,L$ of the null hypothesis model. This test was used in some studies for the same purposes (Arenius and Clercq 2005; Li 2001). Also, in Table 10.4 is showed the Pseudo R^2 which indicates the variance explained by our models. And finally, the overall hit rate is considered in order to test whether the addition of the predictor variables led to a significant improvement of the model.

Table 10.4 Robustness check of the models

	Perceiving opportunities	Business creation
Model χ^2		
Control variables	408.28 (20)***	121.78 (20)***
GHC	425.54 (22)***	1,397.55 (22)***
SHC	451.23 (22)***	1,846.87 (22)***
Full	463.66 (24)***	2,633.26 (24)***
Pseudo R^2		
Control variables	0.0079	0.0149
GHC	0.0912	0.0156
SHC	0.1202	0.0165
Full	0.1719	0.0170
Overall hit rate		
Control variables	73.27	93.19
GHC	73.22	93.18
SHC	73.27	93.19
Full	73.22	93.18

Table shows χ^2 values with degrees of freedom in parenthesis
*Significant at 95 %, **significant at 99 %

10.5 Conclusion and Discussion

On the basis of the above findings, logistic regression was used to predict the propensity of perceiving entrepreneurial opportunities and creating a business by Spaniards. To do that, Spanish GEM data of 2008 were used. Some variables related to general and specific human capital were considered, in order to analyze the likelihood of these variables upon the perception of entrepreneurial opportunities as well as business creation. The discussion of this study is based on the comparison of results with other studies that focused separately on the perception of opportunities and business creation.

Interestingly, in the outcomes of this study general human capital showed that education is not significant for perceiving entrepreneurial opportunities and creating a business by Spaniards. These results are consistent with Storey (1994) who detects an inverse relationship between educational attainment and firm formation. Moreover, Ucbasaran et al. (2008) analyzed the influence of several levels of education upon the identification of entrepreneurial opportunities. For instance, respondents who reported a postgraduate degree as their higher level of education were weekly associated with an increased probability of identified opportunities. In the same vein, Marvel (2013) studied types of knowledge and experience of new technology entrepreneurs who had been searching for an opportunity to compare to those who identified an opportunity. Results showed that education was not statistically significant to search opportunities. Gruber et al. (2012) examined how several types of pre-entry human capital shape the identification of market opportunities for emerging technology firms. Results showed that educational specialization is not relevant for opportunity identification. Despite same studies showed negative relationship of education upon business perception and business creation, it is found that education also has a positive relationship upon the perception of entrepreneurial opportunities and business creation (Davidsson and Honig 2003; Kolstad and Wiig 2013). It could be possible that education influences in a way in the different institutional environments. For this reason, results of this study will be taken with caution.

Regarding the other component of general human capital, work experience resulted important for perceiving entrepreneurial opportunities and for creating a business by Spaniards. I have provided several arguments to explain the positive effect of work experience in the process of perceiving entrepreneurial opportunities. Several indicators of work experience have been operationalized, as it was mentioned before, for this study work experience indicate whether the individual was working or not. It means, they had a relationship with a specific market and sector, which increase their likelihood of perceiving opportunities as well as the business creation attitude. In this sense, these results showed that work experience of individuals is more relevant than is education for perceiving opportunities and creating a business in Spain. These results are consistent with previous studies that found that work experience is associated with the ability to become self-employed and to create new business (Bates 1990; Gimeno et al. 1997). Moreover, higher levels of work experience were significantly associated with an increased probability of perceiving more opportunities (Ucbasaran et al. 2008). This result makes sense, if an individual has more experience in a specific sector he/she is able to lead with particularities of such sector, so he/she may create a firm and/or may perceive specific opportunities.

Regarding specific human capital, I found that entrepreneurial training is significant and has a positive effect on the perception of entrepreneurial opportunities and business creation by Spaniards. This result is consistent with previous studies (Davidsson and Honig 2003). In this sense, I may affirm that entrepreneurial training is relevant to engage in entrepreneurial activities. Therefore, training classes or/and courses help new entrepreneurs to solve issues related to information, legal, procedural, marketing, and strategy to start their business.

Managerial-business experience, as was mentioned before, is the experience that the individual acquired by managing or owning a business. Managerial business experience is significant for perceiving entrepreneurial opportunities and creating a business by Spaniards. Results of this study are consistent with previous studies that showed that this experience is relevant for perceiving and creating a business. For instance, Gruber et al. (2012) has tested the effects of entrepreneurial and management experience upon the identification of opportunities for emerging technology firms finding positive and statistically significant effects. Moreover, Ucbasaran et al. (2008) tested the effects of some variables related to human capital specifically the business ownership experience upon the identification of entrepreneurial opportunities. Results showed that individuals with ownership experience increases the likelihood of pursuing more opportunities.

To summarize, these results show that some factors of general and specific human capital are more significant than others. For instance, work experience is more relevant than is education for perceiving entrepreneurial opportunities and creating a business by Spaniards. And, entrepreneurial training resulted in a very significant relationship to perceive opportunities and to create a business by Spaniards as compared to managerial-business experience which was relevant for both processes, too. I should consider that these results shed light and portray the case of Spaniards engaged in the process of perceiving entrepreneurial opportunities and creating a business.

10.6 Implication and Future Research Lines

The perception of opportunities is important to create a business, as mentioned by Shane and Venkataraman (2000). In this study, I analyzed the human capital—general and specific—of Spaniards who are involved in entrepreneurial activities.

The novel contribution of this study is to shed some light when comparing two processes of entrepreneurship, the perception of entrepreneurial opportunities and the business creation by Spaniards. So, this study let to know the human capital of Spaniards and how it influences in the perception of opportunities and business creation. This information could be useful for policy makers in order to promote self-employment to decrease the rate of unemployment and the pay of unemployment security in Spain.

Furthermore, a key point in our results was the entrepreneurial training factor which was significant in both processes the perception of entrepreneurial opportunities and business creation by Spaniards. Thereby, if entrepreneurial training influences the perception of entrepreneurial opportunities and business creation, more entrepreneurial training could be implemented targeting Spaniards entrepreneurs.

Acknowledgments I thank Professor Yancy Vaillant for providing me the Spanish Global Monitor Entrepreneurship data.

References

Amaral A, Baptista R (2007) Transitions of paid employment to entrepreneurship: an empirical study for Portugal. In: Dowling MJ, Schmude J (eds) Entrepreneurship in Europe: new perspectives. Edward Elgar, Cheltenham

Amaral AM, Baptista R, Lima F (2011) Serial entrepreneurship: impact of human capital on time to re-entry. Small Bus Econ 37(1):1–21

Arenius P, Clercq DD (2005) A network-based approach on opportunity recognition. Small Bus Econ 24(3):249–265

Arenius P, Minniti M (2005) Perceptual variables and nascent entrepreneurship. Small Bus Econ 24(3):233–247
Arribas I, Vila JE (2007) Human capital determinants of the survival of entrepreneurial service firms in Spain. Int Entrep Manag J 3(3):309–322
Awogbenle C, Chijiote I (2010) Youth unemployment: entrepreneurship development programme as an intervention mechanism. Afr J Bus Manag 46:831–835
Baron RA (2004) Potential benefits of the cognitive perspective: expanding entrepreneurship's array of conceptual tools. Acad Manag Perspect 19(2):169–172
Baron R (2006) Opportunity recognition as pattern recognition: how entrepreneurs "connect the dots" to identify new business opportunities. Acad Manag Perspect 20(1):104
Baron RA, Ensley MD (2006) Opportunity recognition as the detection of meaningful patterns: evidence from comparisons of novice and experienced entrepreneurs. Manag Sci 52(9): 1331–1344
Bates T (1990) Entrepreneur human capital inputs and small business longevity. Rev Econ Stat 72(4):551–559
Becker GS (1962) Investment in human capital: a theoretical analysis. J Polit Econ 70(5):9–49
Bergmann H, Sternberg R (2007) The changing face of entrepreneurship in Germany. Small Bus Econ 28(2/3):205–221
Cooper A, Gimeno-Gascon F, Woo C (1994) Initial human and financial capital as predictors of new venture performance. J Bus Ventur 9(5):371–395
Davidsson P, Honig B (2003) The role of social and human capital among nascent entrepreneurs. J Bus Ventur 18(3):301–331
Eckhardt J, Shane S (2003) Opportunities and entrepreneurship. J Manag 29(3):333–349
Fiet J (1996) The informational basis of entrepreneurial discovery. Small Bus Econ 8(6):419–430
Fiet J (2007) A prescriptive analysis of search and discovery. J Manag Stud 44(4):592–611
Gimeno J, Folta T, Cooper A, Woo C (1997) Survival of the fittest? Entrepreneurial human capital and the persistence of underperforming firms. Adm Sci Q 42(4):750–783
Greene WJ (2000) Econometric analysis, 4th edn. Prentice Hall, Upper Saddle River
Gruber M, MacMillan IC, Thompson JD (2012) From minds to markets how human capital endowments shape market opportunity identification of technology start-ups. J Manag 38(5): 1421–1449
Hatch NW, Dyer JH (2004) Human capital and learning as a source of sustainable competitive advantage. Strateg Manag J 25(12):1155–1178
Hayek F (1945) Use of knowledge in society. Am Econ Rev 1(4):519–530
Kirzner I (1973) Competition and entrepreneurship. University of Chicago Press, Chicago
Koellinger P, Minniti M, Schade C (2007) "I think I can, I think I can": overconfidence and entrepreneurial behavior. J Econ Psychol 28(4):502–527
Kolstad I, Wiig A (2013) Is it both what you know and who you know? Human capital, social capital and entrepreneurial success. J Int Dev 25(5):626–639
Kolvereid L, Isaksen E (2006) New business start-up and subsequent entry into self-employment. J Bus Ventur 21(6):866–885
Li P (2001) Immigrants' propensity to self-employment: evidence from Canada. Int Migr Rev 35(4):1106–1128
Liñán F, Rodríguez-Cohard JC, Rueda-Cantuche JM (2011) Factors affecting entrepreneurial intention levels: a role for education. Int Entrep Manag J 7(2):195–218
Lucas RE (1978) On the size distribution of business firms. Bell J Econ 9(2):508–523
Marvel MR (2013) Human capital and search-based discovery: a study of high-tech entrepreneurship. Entrep Theory Pract 37(2):403–419
Minniti M, Bygrave W (2003) Global entrepreneurship monitor: 2003 executive report. Babson College, Babson Park
Neck H, Greene P (2011) Entrepreneurship education: know worlds and new frontiers. J Small Bus Manag 49(1):55–70
Oosterbeek H, van Praag M, Ijsselstein A (2010) The impact of entrepreneurship education on entrepreneurship skills and motivation. Eur Econ Rev 54(3):442–454

Rauch A, Rijsdijk SA (2013) The effects of general and specific human capital on long-term growth and failure of newly founded businesses. Entrep Theory Pract 37(4):923–941

Reynolds P, Bosma N, Autio E, Hunt S, De Bono N, Servais I, Chin N (2005) Global entrepreneurship monitor: data collection design and implementation 1998–2003. Small Bus Econ 24(3):205–231

Shane S (2000) Prior knowledge and the discovery of entrepreneurial opportunities. Organ Sci 11(4):448–469

Shane S (2003) A general theory of entrepreneurship: the individual-opportunity nexus. Edward Elgar, Cheltenham

Shane S, Venkataraman S (2000) The promise of entrepreneurship as a field of research. Acad Manage Rev 25(1):217–226

Shepherd DA, DeTienne DR (2005) Prior knowledge, potential financial reward, and opportunity identification. Entrep Theory Pract 29(1):91–112

Shepherd DA, Wiklund J (2005) Entrepreneurial small businesses: a resource-based perspective. Edward Elgar, Cheltenham

Spender J (1996) Making knowledge the basis of a dynamic theory of the firm. Strateg Manag J 17(Winter):45–62

Storey DJ (1994) Understanding the small business sector. Cengage Learning EMEA, Andover

Ucbasaran D, Wright M, Westhead P (2003) A longitudinal study of habitual entrepreneurs: starters and acquirers. Entrep Reg Dev 15(3):207–228

Ucbasaran D, Westhead P, Wright M (2006) Habitual entrepreneurs. Edward Elgar, Cheltenham

Ucbasaran D, Westhead P, Wright M (2008) Opportunity identification and pursuit: does an entrepreneur's human capital matter? Small Bus Econ 30(2):153–173. doi:10.1007/s11187-006-9020-3

Unger JM, Rauch A, Frese M, Rosenbusch N (2011) Human capital and entrepreneurial success: a meta-analytical review. J Bus Ventur 26(3):341–358

Venkataraman S (1997) The distinctive domain of entrepreneurship research: an editor's perspective. In: Katz J, Brockhaus R (eds) Advances in entrepreneurship, firm emergence and growth, vol 3. JAI, Greenwich, pp 119–138

Weisberg J (1996) Differential teamwork performance: the impact of general and specific human capital levels. Int J Manpow 17(8):18–29

Wennekers S, van Wennekers A, Thurik R, Reynolds P (2005) Nascent entrepreneurship and the level of economic development. Small Bus Econ 24(3):293–309

Westhead P, Ucbasaran D, Wright M, Binks M (2005) Novice, serial and portfolio entrepreneur behavior and contributions. Small Bus Econ 25(2):109–132

Westhead P, Ucbasaran D, Wright M (2009) Information search and opportunity identification: the importance of prior business ownership experience. Int Small Bus J 27(6):659–680

Chapter 11
The Influence of Creativity on Entrepreneurship: The Portuguese Case

André Olim, Isabel Mota, and Sandra T. Silva

Abstract Literature shows that a high level of new firm creation significantly contributes to regional economic performance and is a clear sign of a thriving economy; hence, the understanding of the factors promoting new firm formation is crucial for economic development. Typically, literature has shown the influence of several variables such as the unemployment rate or the population density on firms' birth rate. A more recent approach has been suggesting that creativity is one of the factors promoting new firm formation and, thus, economic growth. Richard Florida's *The Rise of the Creative Class* (2002) was a seminal contribution for the recognition of the importance of creative people, creative industries, creative economies, and, thus, creativity. Many authors, inspired by this contribution, have been undertaking theoretical and empirical studies to analyze the role of creativity in economics. The aim of this chapter is to follow such contributions, discussing the impact of creativity on entrepreneurship in Portugal. A multivariate linear regression analysis is applied, explaining new firm formation across Portuguese regions with explanatory variables that include both creativity and diversity indexes, innovation indicators and the human capital dimension, as well as other control variables. Our results show little evidence of the influence of creativity on the birth of new firms, while pointing to the relevance of agglomeration effects for new firms' formation and to the difficulty of immigrants in establishing a firm.

Keywords Entrepreneurship • Creativity • Panel data

A. Olim (✉)
Faculdade de Economia, Universidade do Porto, Rua Dr. Roberto Frias, Porto 4200-464, Portugal
e-mail: 110481014@fep.up.pt

I. Mota • S.T. Silva
Faculdade de Economia, CEF.UP, Universidade do Porto, Rua Dr. Roberto Frias, Porto 4200-464, Portugal
e-mail: imota@fep.up.pt; sandras@fep.up.pt

R. Baptista, J. Leitão (eds.), *Entrepreneurship, Human Capital, and Regional Development*, International Studies in Entrepreneurship 31,
DOI 10.1007/978-3-319-12871-9_11

11.1 Introduction

A high level of new firm creation significantly contributes to regional economic performance and is a clear sign of a thriving economy; therefore, understanding the factors promoting new firm formation is crucial for economic development (Lee et al. 2004). While traditional literature has shown the influence of several variables such as the unemployment rate, population density, industrial structure, human capital, availability of funding and entrepreneurial characteristics on new firm formation and regional economic development, a more recent approach by authors such as Florida (2002, 2003) has been suggesting that creativity is one of the main factors promoting new firm formation and, thus, innovation and economic growth.

Some characteristics boost an entrepreneurial-favorable climate and promote the innovative abilities of the human capital, i.e., creativity. But is it true that creative and diverse regions attract a more innovative and entrepreneurial human capital, thus encouraging new firm formation? In a nutshell, is there a direct and positive relationship between entrepreneurship and creative and diverse regions?

The importance of creativity for entrepreneurship cannot be ignored or taken lightly. Thus, how does creativity in its various dimensions and intertwined causes perform in promoting entrepreneurship in a European country such as Portugal? The main goal of this work is to understand the relation between creativity and entrepreneurship in the Portuguese context, taking into account the effect of creativity in new firm formation after controlling for other determinants of firms' birth.

This study will undertake a multivariate linear regression analysis. The dependent variable will be new firm formation (measured by data obtained from *Instituto Nacional de Estatística—Sistema de Contas Integradas das Empresas*) at the NUTS 3 level, for the comprising period of 2004–2010. The explanatory variables will be composed by both creativity and diversity indexes, innovation indicators and a human capital dimension, controlling for other variables (such as cost variables, agglomeration economies, and market dimension).

11.2 Literature Review

11.2.1 Main Concepts of Creativity

Florida (2003) points out that economists and geographers accept economic growth as a regional mechanism driven by, and spreading from, specific regions, cities, or even neighborhoods. He also points out that a more powerful theory of city and regional growth has been emerging since the early 1990s, postulating that people are the driving force behind regional growth, a perspective known as the "human capital" theory of regional development. The ground-breaking work by Jacobs (1969, 1984) made theorists note the ability of cities to attract creative people and thus spur economic growth. While previous economic growth theories and models were developed upon nations and huge economic blocks, now emerges a more regional sense and dimension of economic growth. Theories and models such as Solow's growth model (Solow 1957), or the endogenous growth theories, take into account labor, human capital, innovation, and knowledge as significant contributors to economic growth at the nationwide level (e.g., Romer 1986, 1990; Lucas 1988; Aghion and Howitt 1992), but fail to recognize the small and all-important contributions made at the regional level. Namely, they fail to account for the contribution of entrepreneurship brought about by creativity. Authors like Richard Florida aim directly at this purpose (i.e., entrepreneurship and creativity); in his book *The Rise of the Creative Class*, Florida (2002) points to a correlation between a region's economic development and its share of creativity (measured by the tolerance towards diversity, the capacity to invent or improve technology and the richness of public amenities).

Florida develops his theories on regional development and the creative class on the previous works of both Jacobs and Lucas. Jacobs (1969) first stressed the role of cities and regions in the transfer and diffusion of knowledge, noting that as the scale and diversity of the cities increase, so do the connections between economic actors, leading to the generation of new ideas and innovations. Lucas (1988) further developed these notions, identifying the role of human capital externalities in economic development. He also highlighted the clustering effect of human capital, embodied with the knowledge factor. Finally, he recognized the role of great cities, which concentrate human capital and information, creating knowledge spillovers and becoming engines of economic growth. Because cities reduce the cost of knowledge transfer, ideas move more quickly, leading to a faster rise of new knowledge. Florida (2003) argues that locations with a greater number of talented people thrive and are better suited to attract more talent. But his perspective differs from the usual human capital theories. Florida's perspective differs from those in respect to two things: first, it identifies a type of human capital—creative people—as key to economic growth; and, second, it identifies the underlying factors that shape the location decisions of those people—in relation to innovation, diversity, and tolerance. Thus, Florida (2003) introduces the notion of a "creative class" composed by those that engage in tasks whose function is to create meaningful new forms. He divides this creative class into two groups: first, the core of the creative class—scientist and engineers, university professors, poets and novelists, artists, entertainers, actors, designers and architects, as well as the thought leadership of modern society (non-fiction writers, editors, cultural figures, think-tank researchers, analysts, and other opinion-makers)—, and, second, the "creative professionals" who work in a wide range of knowledge-based occupations in high-tech sectors, financial services, the legal and health-care professions and business management. Additionally, Florida et al. (2008a) find that human capital and the creative class have complementary roles in regional development.

Florida stresses creativity as a fundamental and intrinsic human characteristic, since all human beings are creative and all are potential members of the creative class. Moreover, Florida introduces his 3Ts of economic development as the key to understanding the new economic geography of creativity and its effects on economic outlines: technology, talent, and tolerance. Technology is defined as a function of both innovation and high-technology concentrations in a region; talent as those people with a bachelor's degree and above; and tolerance as openness, inclusiveness, and diversity to all ethnicities, races, and life patterns. Only locations with all three critical and intertwined factors will score high in creativity and quantity of members belonging to the creative class. Lee et al. (2010) have the same opinion, arguing that innovation is a joint product of human capital and the diversity and openness of a local.

But not all agree with Florida's 3Ts. For instance, Pratt (2008) outlines the fact that technology, talent, and tolerance are mere proxies and while the numbers of Florida's analysis might look convincing, the underlying concepts are woolly. He goes on to point out that the 3Ts depend on the definition chosen, on the variables used, and on their relationship with the target variables. However, he is not against the definition of a creative class itself as a means to explain regional economic growth; he just criticizes the conceptualization process. Unlike Pratt, though, some detractors do not accept Florida's creative class theory at all (Vorley et al. 2008). Peck (2005) is one of such derogatory works. Peck calls Florida's argument in *The Rise of the Creative Class* both straightforward and rather elusive. He goes on to say that the production of authentic neighborhood cultures through deliberate public-policy interventions (following Florida's approaches) is a daunting, if not infeasible, task, even though Florida has voiced about how some cities have oversimplified his ideas. Malanga (2004) says that the best-performing cities on measures like employment and population growth, or the rate of formation of high-growth companies, are not creative capitals (such as San Francisco or New York), but low-tax, business-friendly cities defined as creative losers (like Las Vegas and Memphis), while Glaeser and Saiz (2004) find that skilled cities are growing because they are becoming more economically productive when compared to less skilled cities, and not because these cities are becoming more attractive places to live.

Despite these criticisms, Cohendet et al. (2010) believe that the work initiated by Florida has set the background for an emerging field of research, opening a large agenda for studies on creativity. Nonetheless, these authors find a limitation in Florida's work: he often considers who the creative people are, rather than what they really do; his suggestions are more a necessary condition for having a creative city through the accumulation of talents belonging to the creative mass, rather than a comprehensive vision of the actual processes that lead an urban milieu to be more creative-oriented. Hence, instead of the anatomy of the creative class proposed by Florida, Cohendet et al. (2010) propose an anatomy of the creative city and an understanding of the emergence and formation of creative processes in those particular local ecologies of knowledge. The result is a division of the creative city in three different layers: the upperground, the middleground and the underground. The upperground is characterized by formal institutions such as cultural firms or institutions whose specific role is to bring creative ideas to the market. The middleground is the level where the work of communities is decisive in designing the grammars of use and other common platforms necessary for knowledge transmission and learning that precedes innovation in those geographically bounded innovative environments. Finally, the underground is constituted by creative individuals such as artists or other knowledge works, individuals not immediately linked to the commercial and industrial world. Hospers (2003) has little doubt that cities are the locations where knowledge, creativity, and innovation thrive. He finds that cities that develop clever and original strategies on a local scale have the opportunity to grow to become competitive, creative cities. For Hospers, creative cities have been a phenomenon belonging to every era; throughout history there have been various types: technological-innovative, cultural-intellectual, cultural-technological, and technological-organizational. Technological-innovative cities are birthplaces for new technological developments or, sometimes, real technological revolutions, for which America's Silicon Valley is an example. Cultural-intellectual cities are those where culture (e.g., figurative and performing arts) and science bloom in a period of tension between the established conservative order and a small group of innovative-minded radicals—this generation gap produces creativity reactions on the part of artists, philosophers, and intellectuals. Such an example, of "creative revolution," is Florence during the Renaissance. Cultural-technological cities are a merger of the major characteristics of the previous two types of creative cites: technology and culture go hand in hand, for which the film industry of Hollywood is an example. Lastly, technological-organizational cities are those where local actors find original solutions to problems stemming from large-scale urban life, like the supply of water for the population, the need of infrastructure, transport and housing—an example is Rome under Caesar (aqueducts) or London in the 1980s (re-structure of the Docklands). Even though Hospers says it is impossible to predict when and where a creative city will emerge he identifies the factors that can increase the chances of developing urban creativity and thus contributing to an urban knowledge economy: concentration (of population), diversity (extending Florida's notion further), and instability (as an extra condition for urban creativity). Notwithstanding, he stresses that creative cities cannot be constructed from the scratch: the roots of creativity must be already there, lying in the existing, historically developed urban environment. In a nutshell, policy-makers can only foster the chances for the emergence of urban creativity (Hospers and Dalm 2005).

Pratt (2008) extends the concept of creativity, applied before to creative cities, to creative industries. According to him, it was not until the late 1990s that the term "creative industries" was put to use, after the UK Creative Industries Task Force produced the first mapping document (DCMS 1998), which defined creative industries as including several activities such as advertising, antiques, architecture, crafts, design, fashion, film, leisure, software, music, performing arts, publishing, software, TV, and radio. Pratt goes on to point out that the term cultural industries had been previously used to refer to a similar domain of policy and activity by authors like O'Connor (2004) and Garnham (2005), but it was a rather amorphous one that sometimes was indicative of commercial activities, sometimes not.

Just like Hospers (2003) said, creative cities derive from roots of creativity already present (historically). Hartley (2005) claims that creative industries are a consequence of local history, and so they vary geographically, depending on heritage and circumstance.

But none of the above, i.e., creative cities and creative industries, can come into existence without the observance of a creative economy. Peters and Besley (2008) state that the notion of a "creative economy" has been around since the early 1990s, first introduced by John Howkins. Howkins (2001) defines creative economy not merely in terms of the concepts of creativity, culture, heritage, knowledge, information, innovation, or in terms of the performing arts, publishing, etc., but rather more broadly as an economy where a person's ideas, not land or capital, are the most important input and output. Peters and Besley (2008) focus that Howkins' account of the creative economy that emerges from different literatures, mainly the Schumpeter's "creative destruction" and his account of entrepreneurship. The study points out that the creative economy, broadly conceptualized, links the primacy of ideas in both arts and sciences in a more embedded and social framework of entrepreneurship. In a nutshell, the UNCTAD's (2008) report on *The challenge of assessing the Creative Economy* defines creative economy as the interface between creativity, culture, economics, and technology, expressed in the ability to create and circulate intellectual capital, with the potential to generate income, jobs, and export earnings, while at the same time promoting social inclusion, cultural diversity, and human development.

11.2.2 On Creativity and Entrepreneurship

Through creative cities, creative industries, and creative economies, a surge is expected in entrepreneurship and the thriving of new innovative firms. Schumpeter's "creative destruction" theory is perhaps the first and most prominent and coherent account of entrepreneurship.[1] Schumpeter, as noted by Peters and Besley (2008), provided an account of entrepreneurship and the role and significance of the entrepreneur who, through innovation, led the gales of "creative destruction," making old ideas, technologies and skills obsolete, serving as the source of progress and improvement in the standard of living. For Schumpeter, the entrepreneur is the individual carrying out new combinations, introducing new products or processes, identifying new export markets or sources of supply, even creating new types of organization. His vision is somewhat of the entrepreneur as a hero, as someone

[1] The concept of entrepreneurship first came into light centuries ago, but with different meanings. Kyrö (1996) points that in the seventeenth century the French verb "entrependre," meaning being able to bring off some project or activity, began to be applied. Richard Cantillon (1755) was one of the first authors linking the broad concept of entrepreneurship with economics. Additionally, the timeless Adam Smith (1776), in his *Wealth of Nations*, designates entrepreneurs as those reacting to variations in the economy, while John Stuart-Mill (1848) stresses entrepreneurship as the point of origin of a private firm.

motivated by the dream and the will to found a private kingdom, the will to conquer, to prove oneself superior to others, and ultimately by the joy of creating (Peters and Besley 2008).

McClelland (1961) establishes three levels encouraging individual entrepreneurship: the need for achievement, the need for affiliation and the need for power. The need for achievement refers to an individual's desire of some significant accomplishment, his/her need of competitive success. Second, the need for affiliation is stated as an individual's need of belonging and sense of involvement within a social group. Lastly, the need for power is viewed as the necessity of control and influence, the prevailing of one's ideas and the augmenting of one's status. Combined, these three psychological human needs and motivational processes are crucial to the individual's financial growth and, consequently, to the entrepreneurial activity. Nonetheless, Peters and Besley (2008) stress the importance of shifting away from the figure of the lone and heroic individual who is willing to take risks towards entrepreneurship as the model for a society or as a set of infrastructural conditions enabling creativity. Drucker (1985) argues that entrepreneurship is not an economic end in itself and that the entrepreneur does not need to show any particular trait of personality; rather, he needs only a self-commitment on innovation. Leadbeater and Oakley (2001) call the knowledge entrepreneurship a structured activity, instead of merely a flash of individual genius, built in six stages: creation, sensing, packaging, mobilizing, acting, and exiting. Thus, the basic unit of entrepreneurship is not the individual per se but teams or partnerships providing tight networks in distinctive industry clusters. Also, Leadbeater and Oakley suggest that the most powerful forces driving entrepreneurship are technological change and knowledge creation, cultural change, economic changes and the willingness of financial markets and investors to sanction risk taking. To this regard, Johannisson (1984) says that entrepreneurial culture is defined as a social context where entrepreneurial behavior is encouraged.

Sternberg (1988) defines entrepreneurship as a form of creativity—labelled as business or entrepreneurial creativity—because new businesses are often original. Lee et al. (2004) divide academic approaches on entrepreneurship into two major categories: the first one on entrepreneurs (and the reasons why an individual decides to become one and start a new firm) and the second one on regional variations in firm formation (looking at structural variations in geographical areas).

As noted above, the approaches on entrepreneurs take into account the psychological characteristics of the individual. But there are also other types of characteristics that can turn an individual into an entrepreneur: Yoon (1997) suggests that immigrants are more likely to become entrepreneurs because they are systematically excluded from employment that offers suitable wages, job security, and career opportunities, while Evans and Leighton (1989) find that men with more financial resources and more confidence in their own ability are more likely to be self-employed.

The question that now arises is if creativity powers entrepreneurship, i.e., new firm formation.

11.2.3 Empirical Studies on Creativity and Entrepreneurship

In the previous section, several theories of entrepreneurship and creativity were highlighted. Within this framework one of the most prominent effects that emerges is that creativity spurs new firm formation (after controlling for traditional determinants of entrepreneurship). But when the results of empirical studies are taken into account, does creativity and, to some extent, creative cities, creative industries, and creative economies still matter as a determinant of new firm formation?

Several studies can be highlighted as an evidence of creativity's effect and importance (see Table 11.1). Lee et al.'s (2004) study shows that, in general, new firm formation is indeed associated with creativity and that the most open and creative regions (regarding diversity and talent), by attracting more human capital, achieve a more dynamic entrepreneurship. The main goal of this study was to determine whether connections exist between regional social characteristics, human capital and new firm formation in several urban areas of the United States of America (through the use of data provided by Metropolitan Statistical Areas [SMAs], Primary MSAs [PMSAs] and Labour Market Areas [LMAs]). Using bivariate correlation analysis and multivariate ordinary least square (OLS) analysis, new firm formation (data from Longitudinal Establishment and Enterprise Microdata [LEEM] on firm births per one million people) was explained by a measure of creativity (Bohemian Index—the proportion of bohemians and other artistically creative people), a measure of diversity (Melting Pot Index—the percentage of the population that is foreign born—and Diversity (or Gay) Index—the concentration of same-sex male unmarried partners in the population), a measure of human capital (the percentage of adults in the population with a bachelor's degree and above), a patent variable, the income growth rate, and the population growth rate. Mainly, the authors found that new firm formation is strongly associated with creativity when controlling for the traditional variables suggested in the literature. Firm formation is most closely associated with the Bohemian Index and positively and significantly associated with the Diversity Index, but insignificantly with the Melting Pot Index. It is also strongly associated with human capital, but only moderately associated with patents and reasonably with income change. Finally, it is highly correlated with population growth.

Donegan et al. (2008) undertake a similar study, exploring the relationships between the presence of the creative class (individuals reflecting some degree of creativity) and regional economic performance. Again, the sample of multivariate regression models was drawn from SMAs, where metropolitan economic performance (measured as the percentage change in jobs, percentage change in per capita personal income and the instability of jobs) was explained by a measure of talent (Creative Class Index—the percentage of MSA workforce in super-creative core[2]

[2] According to Florida (2002), the super-creative core is defined as: computer and mathematical occupations; architecture and engineering occupations; life, physical, and social science occupations; education, training, and library occupations; and arts, design, entertainment, sports, and media occupations.

Table 11.1 Main empirical studies on creativity and entrepreneurship

Author(s)	Main goal	Sample	Methodology	Dependent variables	Explanatory variables		Main findings
Lee et al. (2004)	Determine whether connections exist among regional social characteristics, human capital and new firm formation	Sample 1: Metropolitan Statistical Areas (SMAs)/Primary MSAs (PMSAs) Period: 1994–1996 Sample 2: Labour Market Areas (LMAs) Period: 1997–1998 United States of America	Bivariate correlation analysis Multivariate Ordinary Least Squares (OLS) analysis	New firm formation (Firm births per one million people)	*Creativity*	- Bohemian Index: % of bohemians and other artistically creative people	Regions that are open, creative and attract human capital enjoy a more dynamic entrepreneurship
					Diversity	- Melting Pot Index: % of the population that is foreign born	
						- Gay Index: concentration of same-sex male unmarried partners in the population	
					Human Capital	- % of adults in the population with a bachelor's degree and above	
					Income Growth rate		
					Population Growth rate		
Florida et al. (2008b)	Examine the relationships between talent, technology and regional development	Sample: 31 Chinese provincial-level regions in mainland China Period: 2004	Structural equation models (SEM), estimated with maximum likelihood (LM)	Regional Development (GDP per capita)	*Talent*	- Human Capital: individuals with a college or higher-level degree - Creative Class: % of professional and technical workers within the local population	- The relationship between the distribution of talent and technology and between the distribution of talent and regional economic performance is weak in China - The presence of universities and the actual stock of talent are strongly related - Tolerance plays an important role in the distribution of talent and technology in China
					Technology	- High technology: location quotient of the value added for high-tech industries - Patents: officially approved patents per capita	
					Regional institutions and cultural factors	- University: number of university students standardized by local population - Tolerance: Hukou index	

(continued)

Table 11.1 (continued)

Author(s)	Main goal	Sample	Methodology	Dependent variables	Explanatory variables		Main findings
Rutten and Gelissen (2008)	Investigate whether differences in creativity and diversity are a good predictor of differences in regional wealth	Sample: 94 European regions Period: 1998–2001 NUTS-2 level	Ordinary least squares (OLS) regression	Level of regional economic development (GDP per capita)	*Technology*	- In novation: number of patents per million inhabitants for each region - High-tech: investments in R&D of a region's private firms as a % of that region's GDP	- Regional differences in diversity are directly related to differences in regional wealth - The synergetic effect of technology and talent on the level of regional wealth depends on the degree of diversity that resides within regions - Creativity and diversity deserve a more prominent place in economic geography
					Talent	- Human capital: % of the workforce with a bachelor's degree or higher - Share of knowledge-intensive services (KISs) occupations in the total workforce	
					Diversity	- Melting Pot: the % of non-nationals in the population (Eurostat data) - Tolerance index: average score across regions of the number of times each respondent agreed to having a member of gays, gypsies, Jews, or Muslims as their neighbor (by the European Values Survey (EVS) 1999) - Bohemian values: composite index (EVS 1999)	

Donegan et al. (2008)	Explore the relationships between the presence of the creative class and regional economic performance	Sample: U.S. metropolitan areas (SMAs) Period: 1994–2003	Multivariate regression models	Metropolitan economic performance: - % change in jobs - % change in per capita personal income	*Talent*	- Creative class index: % of MSA workforce in super-creative core and creative professional occupations - Bohemian index: location quotient for artistically creative people in MSA	- Indicators of human capital and industry composition perform as well or better than talent, tolerance and technology in explaining both job and income growth and job instability at the metropolitan level
					Tolerance	- Melting pot index: % of foreign-born people in MSA - Gay index: location quotient for males who identify as gay	
					Technology	- Tech-pole: multiplicative combination of: the MSA's high-tech industrial output as a percentage of total US high-tech industrial output; and the MSA's location quotient of high-tech industrial output	
					Human Capital	- % of adults with bachelor's degrees	
					Industry Mix	- Share of a region's total earnings from manufacturing - Share of earnings from business services - Share of earnings from sole proprietorships	
Boschma and Fritsch (2009)	Analyze the regional distribution of the creative class and its impact at the economic regional level	Sample: 500 regions of 7 European countries (Denmark, England and Wales, Finland, Germany, the Netherlands, Norway, and Sweden) Period: 2002 NUTS 3 level	Descriptive statistics Multivariate estimation models (Spatial Error Models)	Regional population share of employees in creative occupations	*Regional culture*	- Bohemian Index: share of regional population in bohemian occupations - Openness Index: share of foreign-born people	- Strong empirical evidence that the creative class is unevenly distributed across Europe - Evidence of a positive relationship among creative class occupation, employment growth and entrepreneurship at the regional level
					Regional facilities	- Public provision index: share of the labor force working in public health care and public education - Cultural opportunity index: share of the workforce that is active in cultural and recreational activities	
					Region's economic performance	Annual employment growth rate	
					Population density		

(continued)

Table 11.1 (continued)

Author(s)	Main goal	Sample	Methodology	Dependent variables	Explanatory variables		Main findings
Qian (2010)	Investigate the geographic distribution of talent and its association with innovation, entrepreneurship and regional economic performance in China	Sample: China's provincial-level data (31 provinces of mainland China) Period: 1997–2004	Descriptive analysis Correlation analysis Regression analysis (OLS)	Talent: - Human capital index: number of people with a college or higher-level degree divided by the local population of 15 years old and older Creativity index: proportion of professional and technical personnel among the local population	*Market factors*	- Average wage - Wage change - Employment Change	- The single most important contributor to the talent distribution in China is the presence of universities - Wage levels, service amenities and openness also contribute to talent attraction but to different extents - Human capital, outweighing the creative class, exhibits positive effects on innovation, entrepreneurship and regional economic performance
					Amenities	- Service amenities	

					Openness	- Hukou index: proportion of population without local Hukou or registration	- Openness may play an important role in regional innovative activity, consistent with Florida's theory on diversity
					University	- University students divided by local population	
					City index	- Proportion of urban population in total population	
					Innovation	- Innovation index: officially granted patents per capita - High-tech index: location quotient of the value added in high-tech industries	
					Entrepreneurship	- Number of new established firms divided by the employed population	
					Regional economic performance	- GDP per capita	
Audretsch et al. (2010)	Investigate the determinants of entrepreneurial activity in German regions	Sample: 97 German regions Period: 1998–2005 NUTS 3 level	Regression analysis (OLS)	Regional entrepreneurship (start-ups per 10,000 inhabitants)	*Control variables*	- Regional unemployment rate: number of unemployed as a % of regional labor force - Population density: inhabitants per square kilometer in the German planning regions	- Regions with a high level of knowledge provide more opportunities for entrepreneurship than other regions - Diversity has a positive impact on technology oriented start-ups
					Knowledge variables	- RD: share of R&D workers in total employment - HQ: share of highly qualified employees in total employment	- Diversity of people is more conducive to entrepreneurship than the diversity of firms
					Diversity measures	- Index of fractionalization: probability that two randomly selected individuals in a community belong to the same group - Theil index - Modified Herfindahl index	- Regions characterized by a high level of knowledge and cultural diversity form an ideal breeding ground for technology oriented start-ups

(continued)

Table 11.1 (continued)

Author(s)	Main goal	Sample	Methodology	Dependent variables	Explanatory variables		Main findings
Kerimoglu and Karahasan (2011)	Determine if regions specializing in creative strategic sectors have rapid productivity growth will experience faster growth and concentration of talent with positive and significant impact on regional economic performance	Sample: 17 Autonomous Communities of Spain Period: 1996–2004 (INE, SABI, IVIE)	Static non-spatial panel data model GLS estimator	Regional economic performance: - Volume of regional employment - Value added in industrial and service oriented production - GDP of Autonomous Communities	*Occupational attainment*	- Employment in talent-based occupations (% of employment)	- Talent is unevenly dispersed among the regions of Spain and this has severe impact on the differences between the economic activity levels, measured by employment volume, industry and service value added and finally regional GDP
					Educational attainment	- Employment with bachelor's degree and above (% of employment)	- Talent is a vital element of the regional differences
Kerimoglu and Karahasan (2012)	Investigate the spatial distribution of creative capital and its connection with regional disparities	Sample: Spanish provinces Period: 1996–2004 SABI database	Exploratory spatial data tools Moran's I LISA	Spatial dispersion of creative capital	Creative capital: high-tech, knowledge intensive services, real estate, architecture and engineering, research and development, advertising and market research, professional, scientific and technical activities, financial and insurance activities, other creative activities such as publishing, software publishing, telecommunications, and computer programming occupations		- There is an unequal structure for creative capital - Creative employment is spatially dependent across the territory of Spain - Provinces with high creative capital have relatively high per capita income in Spain - There is strong and significant impact of the creative capital endowments on the regional differences in Spain

Piergiovanni et al. (2012)	Examine the importance of creativity, new business formation, Intellectual Property Rights (IPR) activities and other factors in determining regional growth	Sample: 103 Italian provinces Period: 2001–2006 (NUTS 3)	Regression analysis (OLS)	Relative growth rate of value added (*per province*)	*Creativity*	- Growth rate of the number of firms in creative industries - Share of creative firms in the population of all non-agriculture firms active in the region - Number of university faculties per resident population	- Positive effect of the increase in the number of firms operating in creative industries, of the net entry, and of a greater provision of leisure amenities on regional economic growth - The share of legal immigrants is found to have a positive impact on employment growth
				Relative growth rate of employment (*per province*)	*New business formation*	- Net entry rate of firms	
					IPR activities	- Incremental growth of the stock of trademarks and registered designs & models by province - Number of trademarks and registered designs & models in the respective province - Incremental growth of the stock of patents and utility patents - Number of patents and utility patents in the respective province	
					Provision of amenities	- Number of restaurants per capita - Number of movie theatre tickets per capita	
					Migration	- Share of legal immigrants per 1,000 resident population	
					Educational attainment	- Employment with bachelor's degree and above (% of employment)	

(continued)

Table 11.1 (continued)

Author(s)	Main goal	Sample	Methodology	Dependent variables	Explanatory variables		Main findings
Berggren and Elinder (2012)	Investigate how tolerance, as measured by attitudes toward different types of neighbors, affects economic growth	Sample: 54 countries from Asia, Latin America, the EU, North America and transition countries Period: 1998–2007	Fixed-effects panel-data analysis	Average annual growth in real GDP per capita	*Tolerance homosexuals*	- Share of the population that does not pick "homosexuals" in answer to the question: "On this list are various groups of people. Could you please mention any that you would not like to have as neighbors?"—World Values Survey (WVS)	- Tolerance toward homosexuals is negatively related to growth - Robust results are not found for tolerance toward people of a different race, but the sign of the estimated coefficients is positive, suggesting that the inclusion of people irrespective of race makes good use of productive capacity
					Tolerance race	- Share of the population that does not pick "people of a different race" in answer to the same question (WVS)	
					Alternative education measures	- Enrol: gross enrolment rate in secondary education - Cognitive skills: average test scores in math and science in primary and secondary school	

and creative professional occupations—and Bohemian Index—the location quotient for artistically creative people in MSA), a measure of tolerance (Melting Pot Index—the percentage of foreign-born people in MSA—and Gay Index—the location quotient for males who identify themselves as gay), a measure of technology (the Tech-pole—the multiplicative combination of the MSA's high-tech industrial output as a percentage of total US high-tech industrial output and the MSA's location quotient of high-tech industrial output), a measure of human capital (the percentage of adults with bachelor's degrees) and, finally, a measure of the industry mix (the relative fraction of a region's total earnings from manufacturing, from business services and from sole proprietorships). The parallels between the two studies are interesting, with the second one showing that indicators of human capital and industry composition perform as well as, or better than, talent, tolerance, and technology in explaining metropolitan job and income growth and job instability.

Hence, it seems that Lee et al. (2004) and Donegan et al. (2008) differ, with the latter considering that Richard Florida's 3Ts are poor predictors of metropolitan job and income growth and that attracting the creative class is no substitute for traditional strategies. However, Donegan et al. (2008) stress that the presence of the creative class in a region is not a disadvantage; rather, along with Florida's indices, it provides regions with a starting point for analyzing and harnessing their existing occupational strengths.

Boschma and Fritsch (2009) also analyze the creative class (in addition, its regional distribution) and its impact at the economic regional level by studying 500 regions of seven European countries (Denmark, England and Wales, Finland, Germany, the Netherlands, Norway, and Sweden) at NUTS 3 level. Through descriptive statistics and multivariate estimation models, they test the regional population share of employees in creative occupations in regard to regional culture (measured by the Bohemian Index—the share of regional population in bohemian occupations—and the Openness Index—the share of foreign-born people), regional facilities (measured by the Public provision index—the share of the labor force working in public health care and public education—and the Cultural opportunity index—the share of the workforce that is active in cultural and recreational activities), the region's economic performance (measured by the annual employment growth rate) and population density. Their findings, in line with Lee et al.'s (2004) study for the United States, indicate a positive relationship between creative class occupation, employment growth, and entrepreneurship at the regional level in those seven European countries. Moreover, they stress strong empirical evidence that the creative class is unevenly distributed across Europe.

Before Boschma and Fritsch (2009), Rutten and Gelissen (2008) analyze 94 European regions to investigate if differences in creativity and diversity were a good predictor of differences in regional wealth. Adapting much of Florida's explanatory variables to the European context, they estimate an OLS regression to determine the level of regional economic development (measured by GDP per capita) with technology measures (one of innovation—the number of patents per million inhabitants for each region—and one of high-tech—the investments in R&D of a region's private firms as a percentage of that region's GDP), talent measures (the percentage of the workforce with a bachelor's degree or higher—human capital—and the share of knowledge-intensive services (KISs) occupations in the total workforce), and diversity measures (the Melting Pot index—percentage of non-nationals in the population—, the tolerance index—by the 1999 European Values Survey[3] (EVS)—and bohemian values—composite index). Their findings prove that regional differences in diversity are directly related to differences in regional wealth and that the synergetic effect of technology and talent on the level of regional wealth depends on the degree of diversity that resides within regions. Lastly, they stress that creativity and diversity deserve a more prominent place in economic geography.

Some countries in Europe are studied separately. For instance, Audretsch et al. (2010) take data from 97 German regions at the NUTS 3 level to investigate the determinants of entrepreneurial activity. Trough regression analysis (OLS) they attempt to explain regional entrepreneurship (measured as the number of start-ups per 10,000 inhabitants) with some knowledge variables (the share of R&D workers in total employment and the share of highly qualified employees in total employment) and some diversity measures (the index of fractionalization, the Theil index, and the modified Herfindahl index), controlling for the regional unemployment rate (the number of unemployed as a percentage of the regional labor force) and the population density (number of inhabitants per square kilometer in the German planning regions). The results show that regions with a high level of knowledge provide more opportunities for entrepreneurship than other regions. Furthermore, diversity is shown to have a positive impact on technology-oriented start-ups, while diversity of people is proven to be more conducive to entrepreneurship than the diversity of firms. Finally, regions characterized by a high level of knowledge and cultural diversity are found to form an ideal breeding ground for technology-oriented start-ups.

Piergiovanni et al. (2012), on the other hand, examine the importance of creativity, new business formation, Intellectual Property Rights (IPR) activities, and other factors in determining regional growth in 103 Italian provinces at the NUTS 3 level. They relate the relative rate of growth of value added per province and the relative rate of growth of employment per province—as dependent variables—with creativity (measured by the growth rate of the number of firms in creative industries, the share of creative firms in the population of all active non-agriculture firms in the region and the number of university faculties per resident population), new business formation (measured by the net entry rate of firms), IPR activities (measured by the growth of the number of trademarks and registered designs & models by province, the incremental growth of the stock of patents and utility patents and the number of patents and utility patents in the respective province), provision of amenities (measured by the number of restaurants per capita and the number of movie theatre tickets per capita), and, finally, migration (measured by the share of legal immigrants

[3] The European Values Study is a large-scale, cross-national, and longitudinal survey research program on basic human values, providing insights into the ideas, beliefs, preferences, attitudes, values and opinions of citizens all over Europe since 1981 (http://www.europeanvaluesstudy.eu/).

per 1,000 resident population) as explanatory variables. The results show the positive effect on regional economic growth of the increase in the number of firms working at the level of creative industries, the positive effect on regional economic growth of the net entry of firms and the positive effect on regional economic growth of a greater provision of leisure amenities. Furthermore, the share of legal immigrants is found to have a positive impact on employment growth. Again, creativity, spurring creative industries, is proven a valuable determinant not only in terms of new firm formation but also in terms of regional economic growth.

Kerimoglu and Karahasan (2011) looked at Spain to determine if regions specializing in strategic sectors that are creative and have rapid productivity growth would experience faster growth and concentration of talent with positive and significant impact on regional economic performance. With a sample of 17 Autonomous Communities of Spain (INE, SABI, IVIE), they carry out a static non-spatial panel data model and a Generalized Least Squares (GLS) estimation. The dependent variable, regional economic performance, is measured by the volume of regional employment, the value added in industrial and service oriented production and the GDP of the Autonomous Communities. One of the explanatory variables, occupational attainment, is measured by employment in talent-based occupations (percentage of overall employment); another explanatory variable—educational attainment—is measured by employment associated with a bachelor's degree and above (percentage of total employment). Additionally, two control variables are included: the percentage of employment in manufacturing industries and the percentage in service industries. The main findings are that talent is a vital element of regional differences. As in Boschma and Fritsch's (2009) work, talent, and thus the creative class, is found to be unevenly dispersed among the regions of Spain. This has a strong impact on the differences between economic activity levels, measured by employment volume, industry and service value added, and regional GDP.

A second study by Kerimoglu and Karahasan (2012) investigates the spatial distribution of creative capital in Spain (using the SABI database for Spanish provinces), while adding its connection with regional disparities. The uneven structure of creative capital is stressed once again. Moreover, creative employment is revealed to be spatially dependent across the territory, as provinces with high creative capital have relatively high per capita income; also, a strong and a significant impact of creative capital endowments on regional differences is found. These findings come from exploratory spatial data tools, Moran's I and local indicators of spatial association (LISA); the spatial dispersion of creative capital is documented by analyzing the creative capital consisting of high-tech, knowledge intensive services, real estate, architecture and engineering, research and development, advertising and market research, professional, scientific and technical activities, financial and insurance activities, other creative activities such as publishing, software publishing, telecommunications, and computer programming occupations.

Outside of Europe and the United States, regions are outgrowing rankings of new firm formation. Such a region is the People's Republic of China. Hence, Florida et al. (2008b) examine the relationships between talent, technology, and regional development in 31 Chinese provincial-level regions in mainland China. By means of Structural Equation Models (SEM) with Maximum Likelihood (LM) estimation, the authors try to explain regional development (measured by GDP per capita) through talent (measured by human capital—individuals graduating with a college or higher-level degree—and the creative class—the proportion of professional and technical workers within the local population), technology (measured by high technology—the location quotient of the value added for high-tech industries—and patents—officially approved patents per capita) and regional institutions and cultural factors (measured by the number of university students standardized by local population and the Hukou index[4] for tolerance—as an alternative to the Gay index, since statistical data on gays are not available in China). What they find is that the presence of universities and the actual stock of talent are strongly related and that tolerance plays an important role in the distribution of talent and technology. However, they find a weak relationship between the distribution of talent and technology and the distribution of regional economic performance.

Similarly, Qian (2010) looks at China to investigate the geographic distribution of talent and its association with innovation, entrepreneurship, and regional economic performance for the same 31 provinces of mainland China. Employing descriptive analysis, correlation analysis and regression analysis (OLS), Qian attempts to describe talent (measured by the human capital index—those holding a college or higher-level degree divided by the local population of 15 year olds and older—and the creativity index—the proportion of professional and technical personnel among the local population) in relation to market factors (average wage, wage change and employment change), service amenities, the level of openness (measured by the Hukou index—the proportion of population without local Hukou or registration), universities (measured by the number of university students as a proportion of local population), the city index (the proportion of the urban population in the total population), innovation (measured by the innovation index—the officially granted patents per capita—and the high-tech index—location quotient of the value added in high-tech industries), entrepreneurship (measured by the number of new firms established divided by the employed population), and the regional economic performance (given by GDP per capita). Qian finds that the single most important contributor to talent distribution in China is the presence of universities. Wage levels, service amenities and openness also contribute to talent attraction, but to different extents. The author further finds that human capital, outweighing the creative class, exhibits positive effects on innovation, entrepreneurship, and regional economic performance. Consistently with Florida's theory of diversity, openness may play an important role in regional innovative activity.

[4]The Hukou index of openness is defined as the proportion of the population without a locally registered Hukou. Those with a locally registered Hukou are always permanent residents and receive local economic, social and political benefits, such as social welfare, education and voting rights. Those who live in a jurisdictional area without a local Hukou, however, are always "marginal" workers or visitors. If a large proportion of the population of a region does not have a locally registered Hukou, this indicates that a large proportion of the population is from outside the region.

In another line of work, Baron and Tang (2011) find that creativity has a positive and significant effect on founding entrepreneurs when investigating the joint effect, on firm-level innovation, of two variables pertaining to entrepreneurs: their positive affect[5] and creativity. Thus, creativity is related to firm-level innovation. Their inferences come from surveys mailed to and answered by 99 entrepreneurs in several south-eastern states of the United States (Alabama, Georgia Louisiana, Mississippi, and Tennessee). Some other data comes from archival industry data and statistical tests are also applied. Berggren and Elinder (2012), on the other hand, find that tolerance toward homosexuals is negatively related to growth. They investigate how tolerance, measured by attitudes toward different types of neighbors, affect economic growth in 54 countries from Asia, Latin America, the EU, North America and transition countries through a fixed-effects panel-data analysis.

Other empirical works examine creativity and its impact on entrepreneurship, but in a different scope of this article's purpose. For instance, Hackler and Tech (2008) explore whether the proposition of the creative class theories that there is crucial link between new firm formation and a region's creative milieu also explains the level and intensity of women, Hispanic, and Black business ownership. Their findings stress that opportunity structures, which may be positive and negative structural factors that influence the entry of minority groups into entrepreneurship, explain better the dynamics for these entrepreneurs, who in turn benefit from a regional environment that builds human capital and skill base, enabling access to a variety of financial resources, and facilitates market access.

Stolarick and Florida (2006) aim at determining the connections between individuals of the creative class that may create innovation and spillovers. The authors determine that these connections are possible and can have a positive impact on innovative and total business activity across the region. Acs and Megyesi (2009) assess the potential of transforming a traditionally industrial region into a creative economy in Baltimore, USA, through an independent and comparable study of seven similar industrial regions. Their findings show that Baltimore can develop further capabilities to pull creative talent from its surrounding area.

Also, the growth of industrialized urban regions is highly dependent on a region's ability to transform into creative knowledge economies. Williams and McGuire (2010) examine the effect of culture on national innovation and prosperity in 63 countries (industrialized, in development and in transition), from 1996 to 2004. Their findings suggest that culture influences economic creativity at the nationwide level and that innovation implementation explains some of the variation in prosperity across countries.

[5] Positive affect has been found to influence many aspects of cognition and behavior, including those directly relevant to activities that entrepreneurs perform in launching new ventures. Positive affect was measured using the 10-item scale from the Positive and Negative Affect Schedule (PANAS) developed and validated by Watson et al. (1988). The PANAS scale has been used to assess respondents' general feelings and emotions (i.e., how they feel on average).

11.3 Methodology

As pointed out before, the main goal of this work is to understand the influence of creativity on entrepreneurship in the Portuguese economy. For that purpose, we followed an empirical assessment taking into account the effect of creativity in new firm formation. Our econometric model can be described as follows:

$$\mathrm{NF}_{it} = \beta_1 + \beta X_{it} + u_{it} \tag{11.1}$$

where i represents the ith cross-section unit (NUTS 3 regions) (i=1, …, 26), t represents time (t=1, …, 7), NF_{it} is the dependent variable and describes the number of new firms per 1,000 inhabitants for region i at time t, β_1 is the common intercept, β is the vector of coefficients associated with the explanatory variables, X_{it} is the vector of explanatory variables for region i at time t, and u_{it} is the random term for region i at time t.

Both the dependent and the explanatory variables (encompassing creativity, diversity and innovation variables, as well as control variables) were gathered from *Instituto Nacional de Estatística* (INE)—*Sistema de Contas Integradas das Empresas*—considering the Nomenclature of Territorial Units for Statistics at the level 3 (NUTS 3) as our geographic unit.[6]

The vector of explanatory variables was composed by:

11.3.1 *Creativity Index*

EBA_{it}—Employees in bohemian activities by total population. This variable captures the openness of a region to talent and creativity; it measures a region's artistic creativity and intellectual dynamism. It is expected to be positively associated with new firm formation (e.g., Lee et al. 2004; Boschma and Fritsch 2009).

11.3.2 *Diversity Indexes*

FPV_{it}—Foreign people who requested a Portuguese visa per 100 inhabitants. Because immigrants usually lack skills, resources, and networks, they tend to be more self-employed than non-immigrants; therefore, this variable is expected to be

[6] Portugal has 30 NUTS 3: *Alto Trás-os-Montes*, *Ave*, *Cávado*, *Douro*, *Entre Douro e Vouga*, *Grande Porto*, *Minho-Lima*, *Tâmega*, *Baixo Mondego*, *Baixo Vouga*, *Beira Interior Norte*, *Beira Interior Sul*, *Cova da Beira*, *Dão-Lafões*, *Médio Tejo*, *Oeste*, *Pinhal Interior Norte*, *Pinhal Litoral*, *Pinhal Interior Sul*, *Serra da Estrela*, *Grande Lisboa*, *Península de Setúbal*, *Alentejo Central*, *Alentejo Litoral*, *Alto Alentejo*, *Baixo Alentejo*, *Lezíria do Tejo*, *Algarve*, *Açores* and *Madeira* (INE 2002). We exclude *Pinhal Interior Sul*, *Serra da Estrela*, the Island of *Açores* and the Island of *Madeira* since the number of new firms during the period 2004–2010 was quite small.

positively related with the birth of new firms (Lee et al. 2004). Notwithstanding, authors like Clark and Drinkwater (2000) point to a potential negative association between these variables since language barriers lower self-employment probabilities. Bulla and Hormiga (2011) also stress out financing difficulties, barriers, and excessive bureaucracy as factors preventing immigrant entrepreneurship. Hence, the expected sign for this variable is not clear.

$SMFP_{it}$—Share of marriages between foreign and Portuguese people by total marriages. This measure intends to capture some level of openness and tolerance, which is supposed to have a positive effect on entrepreneurship at the regional level (Boschma and Fritsch 2009).

11.3.3 Innovation Index

RD_{it}—Share of annual R&D expenditure on GDP. R&D expenditure is often used as a proxy for innovation, and we expect to observe a positive association with the birth of new firms (e.g., Rutten and Gelissen 2008; Audretsch et al. 2010).

11.3.4 Human Capital Index

HC_{it}—Number of adults with a bachelor's degree per 1,000 inhabitants. People with higher educational attainment tend to found new business more often than those with less educational attainment (Lee et al. 2004). Education is expected to have a positive influence on entrepreneurship (Donegan et al. 2008).

11.3.5 Control Variables

Market size: $GDPpc_{it}$—GDP per inhabitant, with an expected positive effect on firms formation (Cheng and Kwan 2000).

Agglomeration economies: $FIRMS_{it}$—Number of firms per 1,000 inhabitants, which is expected to be positively related with firms birth rate (Becker et al. 2011).

Land cost: PD_{it}—Population density (inhabitants/km^2), which is expected to have a negative association on firms formation (Figueiredo et al. 2002).

Labor cost: LC_{it}—Total expenditure with employees over total, which is supposed to have a negative effect on entrepreneurship (Kittiprapas and McCann 1999).

This work undertook the estimation of a balanced panel data, where the same cross-section data is surveyed over time.

When estimating panel data we must choose between a fixed effects model (FEM) or a random effects model (REM). FEM assumes that the independent variables are fixed across observation units and that the fixed effects are computed from the differences within each unit across time. The REM produces more efficient estimates since it includes information not only across individual units but also across time periods. However, the estimates of the random effects are consistent only if unit-specific effects are not correlated with the other explanatory variables. Since this is not usually true, FEM tends to be a reasonable choice (Greene 2011). Specific tests for this choice are shown bellow in Table 11.3.

Considering that the common intercept changes across regions, but that the slope coefficients do not, FEM can be implemented by applying dummy variables to the common intercept. Hence, Eq. (11.1) is rewritten as:

$$\mathrm{NF}_{it} = \beta_1 + \alpha D_{i-1} + \beta X_{it} + u_{it} \tag{11.2}$$

where i represents the ith cross-section unit (NUTS 3 regions) (i=1, …, 26), t represents time (t=1, …, 7), β_1 is the fixed effect for one of the regions, $D_{i\text{-}1}$ is a vector of dummy variables, each one corresponding to the remainder i-1 regions, and α is the constant associated to each dummy variable that should be added (+) or subtracted (-) to β_1.

In Table 11.2, we present the geographic distribution of the number of new firms per 1,000 inhabitants. As it can be observed, the region of *Algarve* presents the highest annual average of new firms, immediately followed by *Grande Lisboa. Grande Porto* comes in third place. This is no surprise since these geographic units are also the country's most important metropolitan areas, equipped with international airports, ports, and railway stations, and characterized by the presence of Portugal's major national and foreign companies. The standard deviation between regions is not very preeminent and even regions located in Portugal's inland, characterized by relatively slow economic and demographic growth, are fairly close to the annual averages of other regions.

Additionally, we analyzed the correlation between all proposed explanatory variables. We signal in Table 11.3 some situations for which the correlation is high. In order to exclude potential multicollinearity, we propose distinct specifications for the estimation of the econometric model, avoiding the combination of explanatory variables that are significantly correlated.

We now present, in Table 11.4, the estimation results with a panel least squares with cross-section and period fixed effects. As mentioned above, we considered different specifications for our model by allowing different combinations of control and explanatory variables.

Table 11.2 Geographic distribution of new firms from 2004 to 2010

NUTS 3	Designation	New firms per 1,000 inhabitants (2004–2010) (annual average)
1	*Portugal Mainland*	*14.99*
111	*Minho-Lima*	11.12
112	*Cávado*	13.02
113	*Ave*	11.38
114	*Grande Porto*	16.11
115	*Tâmega*	9.63
116	*Entre Douro e Vouga*	12.33
117	*Douro*	10.83
118	*Alto Trás-os-Montes*	10.97
161	*Baixo Vouga*	13.89
162	*Baixo Mondego*	14.91
163	*Pinhal Litoral*	14.29
164	*Pinhal Interior Norte*	10.35
165	*Dão-Lafões*	11.11
168	*Beira Interior Norte*	9.91
169	*Beira Interior Sul*	11.26
16A	*Cova da Beira*	10.93
16B	*Oeste*	14.54
16C	*Médio Tejo*	11.21
171	*Grande Lisboa*	20.21
172	*Península de Setúbal*	16.32
181	*Alentejo Litoral*	15.91
182	*Alto Alentejo*	11.93
183	*Alentejo Central*	14.06
184	*Baixo Alentejo*	12.87
185	*Lezíria do Tejo*	13.18
150	*Algarve*	21.03

Source: INE, Sistema de Contas Integradas das Empresas (2004–2010)

Table 11.3 Correlation matrix between explanatory variables

	EBA	FIRMS	FPV	GDP	HC	LC	PD	RD	SMFP
EBA	1.000								
FIRMS	0.6757	1.0000							
FPV	0.3890	0.4120	1.0000						
GDP	0.7352	0.7880	0.2968	1.000					
HC	0.3205	0.2167	0.0730	0.2146	1.0000				
LC	0.3038	–0.2682	–0.2491	–0.0865	–0.3117	1.0000			
PD	0.6787	0.2820	0.0725	0.5095	0.2489	0.0977	1.0000		
RD	0.48318	0.3085	0.1392	0.3334	0.5438	0.0557	0.4337	1.0000	
SMFP	*0.7188*	0.7288	0.4098	0.6084	0.0916	-0.4209	0.3319	0.1704	1.000

Table 11.4 Estimation results for alternative specifications: panel least squares with cross-section and period fixed effects (2004–2010)

Explanatory variables	Model I	Model II	Model III
Constant	13.29340 (0.0000)***	–21.76753 (0.0008)***	0.906319 (0.9095)
EBA_{it}	0.105657 (0.7734)		
FPV_{it}	–1.097741 (0.0036)***	–0.426795 (0.1596)	–0.801694 (0.0305)**
$SMFP_{it}$			11.96930 (0.0283)**
RD_{it}	11.23201 (0.6324)	–1.438049 (0.9409)	–18.41952 (0.4349)
HC_{it}	0.062148 (0.0885)*	–0.033985 (0.1721)	–0.030629 (0.3628)
$GDPpc_{it}$			0.059670 (0.0086)***
$FIRMS_{it}$		0.298344 (0.0000)***	
PD_{it}		0.022472 (0.2957)	0.028526 (0.3589)
LC_{it}	3.68E–07 (0.4189)	–1.11E-06 (0.0019)***	–9.95E-08 (0.7945)
Summary of statistics/specifications			
R^2	0.950917	0.970977	0.955951
Adjusted R^2	0.938731	0.963520	0.944246
S.E. of regression	0.799560	0.616964	0.762730
Sum squared residual	92.69790	54.81289	83.19122

Notes: (1) significance level at 1 % (***), 5 % (**) and 10 % (*); *p*-value in (). (2) Estimations made under White-diagonal standard error correction for valid statistic inference with an autoregressive component

11.4 Findings/Results

From Table 11.4 it is possible to verify that all three model specifications have a very good global fit, with an adjusted R^2 around 95 %.

The estimated results for Model I suggest little evidence of the influence of creativity on the birth of new firms. A 1 % point increase in FPV_{it} decreases NF_{it} by 1.09 % points, *ceteris paribus*. As pointed out before, only locations with technology, talent, and tolerance will score high in terms of creativity and quantity of members belonging to the creative class (e.g., Florida 2004, Lee et al. 2010). Since FPV_{it} aims at capturing the tolerance of Portuguese people in relation to foreign-born, Model I might be suggesting that tolerance has little impact on the creation of new firms. Nevertheless, the results of Model I for FPV_{it} could also being pointing that immigrants face some constraints with regards to new firm formation, either language barriers, bureaucracy restraints or other kind of impediments, as Clark and

Drinkwater (2000) and Bulla and Hormiga (2011) predicted. Additionally, Model I predicts a positive and statistically significant influence of HC_{it} on firm formation.

In Model II, the agglomeration variable $FIRMS_{it}$ has a significant and positive impact on the birth of new firms, suggesting the importance of agglomeration economies for the emergence of new firms, while LC_{it} has a negative significant effect with an estimated impact near zero.

The variable $GDPpc_{it}$ has a significant and positive impact on the birth of new firms in Model III, once more sustaining the relevance of agglomeration effects for new firms' formation. As in Model I, there is a negative and significant effect of FPV_{it}. Despite this effect of FPV_{it}, $SMFP_{it}$, which is a proxy for openness and tolerance that is expected to have a positive effect on entrepreneurship at the regional level (Boschma and Fritsch 2009), has a very significant impact on NF_{it}: an increase in this variable by 1 % point increases NF_{it} by 11.9 % points, *ceteris paribus*. Therefore, with regards to tolerance, the results of this model seem to be in line with the literature.

All other explanatory variables are not statistically significant and/or in line with the expected sign proposed by the literature in any of our model specifications. Estimations for variables aiming at capturing, respectively, talent and technology, EBA_{it} and RD_{it}, are not statistically significant. This means that our results do not sustain evidence that a region's artistic creativity and intellectual dynamism is important for the emergence of new firms, as some of the contributions from the literature previously revised sustained (e.g., Lee et al. 2004; Boschma and Fritsch 2009). The same occurs for the proxy on human capital. Although commonly recognized in the literature as having a positive influence on entrepreneurship (Donegan et al. 2008) since people with higher educational attainment are more business-oriented than those with less education attainment (Lee et al. 2004), HC_{it} emerges with a negative impact. Finally, population density is also statistically insignificant.

Next, we present in Table 11.5 the results of the tests implemented in order to sustain our choice for cross-section and period fixed effects. Running our regression

Table 11.5 FEM tests – alternative specifications

Cross-section and period fixed-effects tests/specifications	Model I	Model II	Model III
Cross-section *F stat* (*p-value*)	24.520323 (*0.000*)	15.718201 (*0.000*)	12.328742 (*0.000*)
Cross-section χ^2 *stat* (*p-value*)	301.020771 (*0.000*)	239.530390 (*0.000*)	209.137507 (*0.000*)
Period *F stat* (*p-value*)	55.637887 (*0.000*)	44.692661 (*0.000*)	38.269640 (*0.000*)
Period χ^2 *stat* (*p-value*)	217.418345 (*0.000*)	191.389113 (*0.000*)	174.302984 (*0.000*)
Cross-section/Period *F stat* (*p-value*)	41.790607 (*0.000*)	30.117932 (*0.000*)	22.460228 (*0.000*)
Cross-section/Period χ^2 *stat* (*p-value*)	417.875265 (*0.000*)	366.316892 (*0.000*)	322.082549 (*0.000*)

using NF_{it} as the dependent variable over the selected explanatory variables and a constant term, we tested for the nature of fixed effects under FEM for both cross-section and period effects. The results confirm the choice for FEM with both cross-section and period fixed effects. For all model specifications, and for a confidence level of 95 %, the two statistic values for cross-section F and cross-section X^2 ratios, as well as the associated *p-values*, allow us to strongly reject the null hypothesis that the cross-section effects are redundant. Relatively to the period effects, the two corresponding statistic values and the associated *p-values* also allows to strongly reject the null hypothesis that the period effects are redundant. Finally, cross-section/period F and X^2 ratios conduct to a clear rejection of the null hypothesis that all effects are redundant.

11.5 Conclusions

Firm formation is undoubtedly essential to sustain a high regional economic performance. Each region must consider and make available the necessary conditions to promote the birth of new firms. As a nation, more than considering and making available the necessary conditions, policies must be taken to promote new firm formation and regional economic development. Traditional literature has been putting in evidence the effect of variables such as the unemployment rate, population density, industrial structure, human capital, availability of funding, and entrepreneurial characteristics on new firm formation. A new line of study has been proposing a new variable to capture such effect: creativity. Authors like Florida (2002, 2003) go as further as to say that creativity is one of the main factors promoting the birth of new firms. Florida argues that places with a greater number of talented people thrive and are better suited to attract more talent. He even presents the notion of a "creative class" composed by those that engage in tasks whose function is to create meaningful new forms, while also introducing his 3Ts of economic development—technology, talent and tolerance—as significant keys to identify an economic geography of creativity.

The main goal of this work was to understand the relation between creativity and entrepreneurship in the Portuguese context. Previous studies have shown that a positive relation between creativity and entrepreneurship is possible (e.g., Lee et al. 2004; Boschma and Fritsch 2009; Audretsch et al. 2010; Piergiovanni et al. 2012).

By means of a multivariate linear regression analysis, we estimated three different model specifications that aimed at capturing the influence of creativity on entrepreneurship in the Portuguese context. We obtained data from *Instituto Nacional de Estatística—Sistema de Contas Integradas das Empresas* to create one dependent variable (NF_{it}), five explanatory variables (EBA_{it}, FPV_{it}, $SMFP_{it}$, RD_{it}, and HC_{it}), and four control variables ($GDPpc_{it}$, $FIRMS_{it}$, PD_{it}, and LC_{it}).

The explanatory variables aimed at capturing the effects of Florida's 3Ts as well as other keys to identify an economic geography of creativity suggest in the revised literature. The results suggested that, however, the influence of creativity on entrepreneurship is not clear in the Portuguese context. Our three model specifications showed little evidence of the influence of creativity on the birth of new firms, while pointing to the relevance of agglomeration effects for new firms' formation.

An interesting result is that of the explanatory variable FPV_{it}. Composed by foreign people who requested a Portuguese visa per 100 inhabitants, it intended to capture immigrants' impact on entrepreneurship. Lee et al. (2004) suggested that immigrants tend to be more self-employed than non-immigrants because they usually lack skills, resources and networks, while Clark and Drinkwater (2000) and Bulla and Hormiga (2011) stressed that they might face difficulties in establishing a firm in the receiving country because of language barriers, financing difficulties, and excessive bureaucracy. Our results point that the troubles anticipated by Clark and Drinkwater (2000) and Bulla and Hormiga (2011) might be happening in the Portuguese case, preventing immigrants from establishing new firms in Portugal. Therefore, we believe that policies intending to reduce bureaucracy and financing difficulties should be considered.

Additionally, the variable $SMFP_{it}$, which intends to measure the openness and tolerance of a region, is shown to have a positive and significant impact on firm formation, along with the proxy for the human capital.

All into account, our results cannot allow us to either support the theories that creative and diverse regions attract more innovative and entrepreneurial human capital, thus encouraging new firm formation, as some authors propose (e.g., Florida 2002, 2003; Hospers 2003; Lee et al. 2004, 2010; Boschma and Fritsch 2009; Cohendet et al. 2010; and Piergiovanni et al. 2012), or refute them, as other authors do (e.g., Malanga 2004; Glaeser and Saiz 2004; Peck 2005; Pratt 2008; Vorley et al. 2008; and Donegan et al. 2008). Rather, it suggests that other factors may promote the birth of new firms. Such factors could either be creativity-related (e.g., human capital, tolerance) or not (e.g., agglomeration variables).

As future research, we intend to (1) explore other proxies for creativity and innovation that may explain the formation of new firms, (2) investigate the effect of creativity in the creation of high-tech firms, and finally, (3) search for the potential association between creativity-related policies and entrepreneurship policies.

References

Acs ZJ, Megyesi MI (2009) Creativity and industrial cities: a case study of Baltimore. Enterp Reg Dev 21(4):421–439

Aghion P, Howitt P (1992) A model of growth through creative destruction. Econometrica 60(2):323–351

Audretsch D, Dohse D, Niebuhr A (2010) Cultural diversity and entrepreneurship: a regional analysis for Germany. Ann Reg Sci 45:55–85

Baron RA, Tang J (2011) The role of entrepreneurs in firm-level innovation: joint effects of positive affect creativity, and environmental dynamism. J Bus Ventur 26:49–60

Becker K, Kronthaler F, Wagner K (2011) The entrepreneurship potential within Swiss regions—a comparison based on cluster analysis. In: Raposo M, Smallbone D, Balaton K, Hortovanyi L (eds) Entrepreneurship, growth and economic development. Edward Elgar, Cheltenham

Berggren N, Elinder M (2012) Is tolerance good or bad for growth? Public Choice 150(1–2):283–308
Boschma RA, Fritsch M (2009) Creative class and regional growth: empirical evidence from Severn countries. Econ Geogr 85(4):391–423
Bulla FJM, Hormiga E (2011) Highly-skilled Colombian immigrants in Spain: do they have to return home to start up in business? Educ Train 53(5):449–461
Cantillon R (1755) Essay on the nature of Commerce (trans: Higgs H (1931)). Macmillan, London
Cheng LK, Kwan YK (2000) What are the determinants of the location of foreign direct investment? The Chinese experience. J Int Econ 51(2):379–400
Clark K, Drinkwater S (2000) Pushed out or pulled in? Self-employment among ethnic minorities in England and Wale. Labour Econ 7(5):603–628
Cohendet P, Grandadam G, Simon L (2010) The anatomy of the creative city. Ind Innov 17(1):91–111
DCMS (Department of Culture, Media and Sport) (1998) Creative industries mapping document. DCMS, London
Donegan M, Drucker J, Goldstein H, Lowe N, Malizia E (2008) Which indicators explain metropolitan economic performance best? Traditional or creative class. J Am Plann Assoc 742(2):180–195
Drucker PF (1985) Innovation and entrepreneurship. Heinemann, London
Evans DS, Leighton LS (1989) Some empirical aspects of entrepreneurship. Am Econ Rev 79:519–535
Figueiredo O, Guimarães P, Woodward D (2002) Home-field advantage: location decisions of Portuguese entrepreneurs. J Urban Econ 52:341–361
Florida R (2002) The rise of the creative class: and how it's transforming work, leisure, community and everyday life. Basic Books, New York
Florida R (2003) Cities and the creative class. City Community 2(1):3–19
Florida R, Mellander C, Stolarick K (2008a) Inside the black box of regional development—human capital, the creative class and tolerance. J Econ Geogr 8(5):615–649
Florida R, Mellander C, Qian H (2008b) Creative China? The university, tolerance and talent in Chinese regional development. In: Working paper series in economics and institutions of innovation, no. 145. CESIS—Centre of Excellence for Science and Innovation Studies, Royal Institute of Technology, Stockholm
Garnham N (2005) From cultural to creative industries: an analysis of the implications of the "creative industries" approach to arts and policy making in the United Kingdom. Int J Cult Policy 11:15–30
Glaeser EL, Saiz A (2004) The rise of the skilled city. Brookings-Wharton Papers on Urban Affairs, vol 5, pp 47–94
Greene WH (2011) Econometric analysis, 7th edn. Prentice Hall, Upper Saddle River
Hackler D, Meyer H (2008) Diversity, entrepreneurship, and the urban environment. J Urban Aff 30(3):273–307
Hartley J (2005) Creative industries. Blackwell, Oxford
Hospers G (2003) Creative cities in Europe—urban competitiveness in the knowledge economy. Intereconomics 38(5):260–269
Hospers GJ, Dalm R (2005) How to create a creative city? The view points of Richard Florida and Jane Jacobs. Foresight 7(4):8–12
Howkins J (2001) The creative economy: how people make money from ideas. Allen Lane, London
INE (2002) Nomenclature of territorial units for statistics. Lisboa
Jacobs J (1969) The economy of cities. Random House, New York
Jacobs J (1984) Cities and the wealth of nations. Random House, New York
Johannisson B (1984) A cultural perspectives on small business—local climate. Int Small Bus J 2(4):32–43
Kerimoglu E, Karahasan C (2011) Geography of talent and regional differences in Spain. In: IREA Working Papers Series, 2011/7. Research Institute of Applied Economics, University of Barcelona, Barcelona

Kerimoglu E, Karahasan BC (2012) Location patterns of creative capital and regional disparities in Spain. In: IREA Working Papers Series, 2012/02. Research Institute of Applied Economics, University of Barcelona, Barcelona
Kittiprapas S, McCann P (1999) Industrial location behavior and regional restructuring within the fifth "tiger" economy: evidence from the Thai electronics industry. Appl Econ 31:37–51
Kyrö P (1996) The points of transition in reforming the understanding and meaning of entrepreneurship. Acad Enterp 2(1):70–93, European Edition
Leadbeater C, Oakley K (2001) Surfing the long wave: knowledge entrepreneurship in Britain. Demos, London. http://www.demos.co.uk/files/Surfingthelongwave.pdf. Accessed 5 April 2013
Lee S, Florida R, Acs ZJ (2004) Creativity and entrepreneurship: a regional analysis of new firm formation. Reg Stud 38(8):879–892
Lee S, Florida R, Gates G (2010) Innovation, human capital, and creativity. Int Rev Publ Admin 14(3):13–24
Lucas R Jr (1988) On the mechanics of economic development. J Monet Econ 22(1):3–42
Malanga S (2004) The curse of the creative class. City JA 14(1):36–45
McClelland DC (1961) The achieving society. Van Nostrand, Princeton
O'Connor J (2004) Cities, culture and the "transitional economies": developing cultural industries in St. Petersburg. In: Scott AJ, Power D (eds) Cultural industries and the production of culture. Routledge, London, pp 37–53
Peck J (2005) Struggling with the creative class. Int J Urban Reg Res 29:740–770
Peters MA, Besley T (2008) Academic entrepreneurship and the creative economy. Thesis Eleven 94(1):88–105
Piergiovanni R, Carree M, Santarelli E (2012) Creative industries new business formation and regional economic growth. Small Bus Econ 39:539–560
Pratt AC (2008) Creative cities: the cultural industries and the creative class. Geogr Ann B Hum Geogr 90(2):107–117
Qian H (2010) Talent creativity and regional economic performance: the case of China. Ann Reg Sci 45:133–156
Romer PM (1986) Increasing returns and long run growth. J Polit Econ 94(5):1002–1037
Romer PM (1990) Human capital and growth: theory and evidence. Carn-Roch Conf Ser Public Policy 32(1):251–286
Rutten R, Gelissen J (2008) Technology, talent, diversity and the wealth of European regions. Eur Plan Stud 16(7):985–1006
Smith A (1776) An inquiry into the nature and causes of the wealth of nations. Modern Library, New York
Solow RM (1957) Technical change and the aggregate production function. Rev Econ Stat 39:312–320
Sternberg RJ (1988) A three-facet model of creativity. In: Sternberg RJ (ed) The nature of creativity: contemporary psychological perspectives. Cambridge University Press, Cambridge, pp 125–147
Stolarick K, Florida R (2006) Creativity connections and innovation: a study of linkages in the Montréal Region. Environ Plan A 36:1799–1817
Stuart-Mill J (1848) The principles of Political Economy: with some of their applications to social philosophy. Parker, London
UNCTAD (2008) Creative economy report. The challenge of assessing the creative economy: towards informed policy-making, DITC/2008/2
Vorley TR, Mould OM, Smith HL (2008) Introduction to geographical economies of creativity, enterprise and the creative industries. Geogr Ann Ser B Hum Geogr 90(2):101–106
Watson D, Clark LA, Tellegen A (1988) Development and validation of brief measures of positive and negative affect: the PANAS scales. J Pers Soc Psychol 54:1063–1070
Williams LK, McGuire SJ (2010) Economic creativity and innovation implementation: the entrepreneurial drivers of growth? Evidence from 63 countries. Small Bus Econ 34:391–412
Yoon I (1997) On my own: Korean businesses and race relations in America. University of Chicago Press, Chicago

Part III
Regional Development

Chapter 12
Cluster(ing) Policies in Turkey: The Impact of Internationalization or the Imitation of Internationals

Murat Ali Dulupçu, Murat Karaöz, Onur Sungur, and Hidayet Ünlü

Abstract Having a highly centralized administrative system, Turkey's development policies have been managed and directed by the central ministries which led to further state dependency in the local and avoid the self-evolution of regional policy making capacity. Thus the premature nature of regional development in Turkey, by and large, necessitates top-to-down approaches that enforced a unique trajectory of regionalization process instead of self-emerging regionalism. In the absence of augmented development tools and policy design, the cluster policies found a robust environment to grow. In other words the localities seek for the easiest and popular way toward development, and clusters have been perceived as the imitable regional development policy by many organizations and localities with a little questioning if they are appropriate for their localities or not. Surprisingly, known by only a few of the scholars, Turkey hosts one of the oldest clusters, now known as a touristic destination called as the Grand Bazaar in Istanbul which dates back to fifteenth century—the Ottoman period—exhibits cluster characteristics when there was no awareness about clusters. However by the establishment of the Republic with a strong central government to keep the nation and country intact, the regional structures inherited from the Ottoman Empire lost their ground. The recent emerge of cluster policies in Turkey is parallel to the acceleration of regional development particularly after the

M.A. Dulupçu (✉) • H. Ünlü
Department of Economics, Süleyman Demirel University, Isparta, Turkey
e-mail: mdulupcu@yahoo.com; hunlu32@hotmail.com

M. Karaöz
Department of Econometrics, Akdeniz University, Antalya, Turkey
e-mail: mkaraoz@gmail.com

O. Sungur
Department of Economics, Mehmet Akif Ersoy University, Burdur, Turkey
e-mail: onur_sungur@yahoo.com

R. Baptista, J. Leitão (eds.), *Entrepreneurship, Human Capital, and Regional Development*, International Studies in Entrepreneurship 31,
DOI 10.1007/978-3-319-12871-9_12

2000s, mainly due to the EU accession process. Even the visit of Michael Porter's team to Turkey is a strong evidence of internationalization of national cluster policies. In this line the chapter tries to illustrate the international dimension in the development of cluster policies in Turkey. To do so it discusses the brief history of absence(ness) of regional development policies in Turkey and recent efforts to regionalize. In this regard the policy shifts towards clusters in various public policy documents are examined and the efforts by the international and local organizations for developing clusters in various parts of the country are shown.

Keywords Cluster policies • Concentration • Cooperation • Innovation systems • Regional development agencies

12.1 Introduction

While clusters are everywhere as a redeemer among the regional development tools, the evolution of clusters exhibits unique characteristics in the different geographies. The extensive literature on clusters consists of pros and cons yet the cons seem to be weak depending on rising populism and interest on regional development policy (Diez 2001; Asheim et al. 2006; Boschma and Kloosterman 2005). It is not an exaggeration to say that "the rise of clusters" is positively correlated with so-called *Silicon Valleyism*, a hope for various regions and localities either to create or to gain more competitiveness (Nolan 2003; Šarić 2011). While many commentators argue that this interest on regions and clusters is a part of restructuring in capitalism (Lovering 1999) some others point out differences in development levels and cultures (Ruokolainen 2011; Cooke and Lazzeretti 2008; Hospers and Beugelsdijk 2002). Whatever the theoretical background, clusters are utilized by the national and local policy makers as well as international institutions aiming at promotion of economic development, and Turkey is not an exception.

The trajectory of emerge and evolution of clusters in Turkey shares an almost similar pattern with the history of regional economic development in Turkey. Being late, in other words lagging behind in terms of adaptation to the recent wave of regional development, cluster policy came into the agenda parallel to regionalization efforts which have been mostly initiated by the acquis of the EU. This situation is basically because of the strong centralism in policy making and unitary concerns which avoid the bottom-to-up decision-making process. For that reason the EU has been utilized as an anchor by the many Turkish governments to accelerate transformations which had been otherwise could not find enough advocates and supporters to take necessary steps to transform the country. The inherited premature nature of regional policy making led to hegemony of the national development planning leaving little room for alternative regional development tools until the 2000s. Correspondingly clustering as policy tool stuck in this national dominancy and the other tools for regional development could not be developed until the 2000s when the EU accepted to open membership negotiations at least symbolically. Then, the evolution of cluster policies could not be examined and explained without understanding the evolution of regional policies in Turkey.

Current approaches to regional economic development draw upon diverse theoretical fields and concepts but there is some agreement as to the importance of clusters. Various researchers from a wide range of disciplines stress the role of interrelational structure of different sectors to perform concentration in producing a range of goods and services (Malmberg 1996; Gordon and McCann 2000; Fan and Scott 2003; Ellison et al. 2010). In this regard, clusters refer to interconnected companies and institutions in a particular field that encompasses an array of linked industries in a locality that serves as a source of competitiveness through cooperation (Porter 1998). This kind of so-called *coopetition* (cooperation + competition) is becoming more vital in the global market where firms and localities have to face with an increasing competition fostered by high mobility. Thus, the rapid change both in technologies and markets (innovations) as well as government policies has induced firms and localities to take collective actions to enhance their capacity to adapt and respond to uncertainty (Lundvall 1998), and clusters is the one of the main routes to collective action. Of course, it is an oversimplification to make a single definition of clusters. As types and classification may differ, the policy inspiration and implication also differ. That is to say clusters mainly may emerge through: (1) self-forming, (2) interaction with the others, (3) imposed by the others. Regard to the Turkish experience, the last two policy formations are commonly observed as will be discussed in the following pages.

Surprisingly, known by only a little the scholars, Turkey hosts one of the oldest clusters, now known as a touristic destination called as the Grand Bazaar (Armatlı Köroğlu et al. 2009; Özelçi Eceral et al. 2009; Güzey et al. 2010) in Istanbul which dates back to fifteenth century—the Ottoman period—exhibits cluster characteristics when there was no awareness about clusters. However by the establishment of the Republic with a strong central government to keep the nation and country intact, the regional structures inherited from the Ottoman Empire lost their ground. As mentioned above, the current emerge of cluster policies in Turkey is parallel to the acceleration of regional development policies, particularly after the 2000s. Even the visit of Michael Porter's team to Turkey (www.competitiveturkey.org) is a strong evidence of internationalization of national cluster policies. There is no apparent categorization of Turkish cluster policies yet we can distinguish the following:

1. National cluster policies led by the central organizations
2. International cluster policies imposed by the international organizations
3. Local cluster policies inspired from the internationals but initiated locally to catch up other localities without strong and appropriate regional base for self-emerging clusters

This study has a few intertwined goals. The paper mainly aims to analyze and identify the evolution of cluster policies and practices in Turkey. The impact of the international institutions on cluster policies could be observed at different scales.

However, this embedded impact could not be isolated from national policy shift toward regionalization. Thus we start with analyzing the past and recent efforts to regionalize in Turkey. Next we discuss the public policy and policy formations towards clusters at various scales and in various public and governmental organizations. Thirdly, the paper tries to illustrate how international organizations effect and shape domestic cluster policies, particularly the EU. Fourthly, we examine local and regional enthusiasms to adapt cluster policies particularly through the regional development agencies (RDAs). The final section concludes.

12.2 Background of Regional and Local Policymaking in Turkey

One can easily trace how economic development policies are centrally formulated, planned, controlled, and implemented since the foundation of the Republic of Turkey. This centralism is related to highly bureaucratic nature of the Ottoman Empire which had been transferred from Byzantine (Kılıçbay 1995; Kongar 1999; Ortaylı 2002). The result of this historical heritage was a dominant central budgetary control that increased locals' expectation from the central administration (Kalaycıoğlu 1997), which led to further state dependency. In other words, localities highly depend on central government decisions instead of making their own decision, at least in economic issues. And handling problems of the economic development in such a large country—in terms of geography and population—through central policies limited the rational implementations of development policies. Obviously the overarching goal of all the industrial and development policies, determined by the central government, has been industrialization along with westernization. This so-called *top-to-bottom westernization perspective* is also proved by Turkey's membership to the Organization of Economic Cooperation and Development (OECD), the Council of Europe and the North Atlantic Treaty Organization (NATO) and as well in its negotiation process for full membership to the EU (Park 2000). In this line one can regard the transplantation of territorial administrative system from Byzantine as the first significant step towards westernization (Ortaylı 2002).

Despite its aspiration for westernization, the unique trajectory of economic development has differentiated Turkey from both western (i.e., the EU) and central European (i.e., the former communist bloc) countries. On the one hand, throughout the economic history of Turkey, liberalism and private economic activities had been welcomed except depression and war periods; on the other hand, the state had been often regarded as the "nanny state" due to lack of extensive capital formation that assumed to be the key driving force of economic development. This dichotomy-based nature of Turkish economic development along with domestic and geographical political instability created a larger space for the state to both assume and play an important role in economic and social life. The liberal policy measures of the early 1980s, which had been undertaken against the post-oil shock, were even insufficient to alleviate the existing prolonged statism in economic planning and decision-making. From the 1980s and onwards, liberalization of the economy has transformed import substitution regime to export-led industrialization without eliminating existing statism. Ultimately, the liberal policies had only restructured the market economy and increased its openness (Bulutay 1995; Kazgan 1994; Öniş 1995; Öniş and Karataş 1994; Öniş and Ercan 2001; Buğra 2003a, b; Buğra and Keyder 2006; Keyder 2000; Insel 1996, 2005).

The bureaucratic and state-centered policymaking can also be seen in the policies of the State Planning Organization (SPO—named as the Ministry of Development in 2011), founded in 1960, or in its Five Year Development Plans (FYDP). The Turkish Development Plans, the most functional current plan type, which have their legal foundations in the Constitution, have the characteristics of providing compulsory measures to the public sector and guidelines to the private sector. In this regard, the SPO aims to lay down development targets and assist the related government units in the decision-making process for economic and social development and natural resources management; and to regulate and direct state aid for development. It also prepares annual and public investment programs, and approves all public investment projects as well as those proposed by municipalities for financing by either domestic or foreign resources. Obviously, handling such critical functions and planning 81 provinces through a single central organization, which itself often suffers from a lack of personnel and finance, is difficult. This structure itself can be seen as an evidence of how centralized economic development planning in Turkey is (Dulupçu et al. 2004; Soyak 2003, 2004, 2005; DPT 1996; Güler 1996). In this atmosphere the SPO ultimately sees centrally led and controlled regional economic development as an activity designed only for less-developed provinces and clusters as a way to gain competitiveness could not be put forward for a long time.

However, one can rationalize centrally planned regional development by putting forward the high degree of disparities among the geographical regions and the provinces in Turkey. For the SPO, the easiest way to approach the regional economic development has been the generalization of regional problems under the regional disparities approach. In fact, the planning approach based on regional disparities took place in all FYDPs (between 1962 and 2013 nine plans were prepared). As it can be seen in Table 12.1, from the first plan to the last one, regional disparities have always been among the main problem to be dealt with. However, one cannot see an integrated policy approach to regional development throughout the planning periods on the whole, except for the 8th and ongoing 9th Development Plans, which employed strategic and participatory principles and approaches of planning at least in a limited manner (DPT 1962, 1967, 1972, 1978, 1984, 1989, 1995, 2000, 2006).

The priority attributed to the regional disparities, of course, was not the sole problem in regional development. The organization and formulation of the regional policies by the SPO also reflected the "absence" of a regional administrative body in regional economic development since the SPO did not have any regional or

Table 12.1 Regional policies in development plans

Plans	Principles	Approaches and policies	Targets	Instruments
1st DP (1963–1967)	– Increasing influence of economic development on the regions	– Regional planning	– Balanced urbanization and regional public service and income distribution	– Financial incentives
	– Regional economic integration	– Growth poles (e.g., East Marmara, Çukurova, Antalya, Zonguldak)	– Investment efficiency	– Alternative measures depending on investment in less favored regions
2nd DP (1968–1972)	– Focusing on population problems stemmed from rapid urbanization	– Regional or/and provincial planning	– Balanced interregional development	– Tax reductions
			– Balanced (social equity) distribution between regions	– Financial incentives toward private investments
		– Indirect regional planning	– Investment efficiency	– Pilot projects
				– Keban Dam Project (Second biggest dam in Turkey)
3rd DP (1973–1977)	– Alleviation of regional disparities	– Sectoral and provincial planning	Same as in the second plan	– Financial incentives
	– Development of particular less favored regions			– Industrialization programmes for less favored regions
				– Inventory of local assets
				– Provincial planning
				– Sectoral planning
				– “Packet projects”
				– Priority Provinces for development

4th DP (1979–1983)	– Mobilization of all resources to solve regional problems	– Empowerment of inter-sectoral and interregional connections	– Development of geographically less favored regions	– Interest rate reductions for investments
			– Regional and sectoral mutual dependency	– Various financial aids
			– Spatial organization	– To publish necessary measures for various sectors and regions
				– "Packet projects"
				– Investments in provinces and regions
				– Çukurova urban development project
				– The Southeastern Anatolian Project (DPT-JICA)
5th DP (1985–1989)	– To accelerate development rationalization of resource using in less favored and sectorally high potential regions	– Direct regional planning, including studies of regional affects of projects (proposal of 16 functional regions)	– Regionally balanced development depending on social equity	– Scheduling of regional development tables for determination of potential resources
				– Choosing relevant investments according to abovementioned tables
				– To provide infrastructures for industrial projects predetermined in line with prioritized regions and relevant sectors
				– Financial aids for investments in Priority Provinces for development
				– The SAP

(continued)

Table 12.1 (continued)

Plans	Principles	Approaches and policies	Targets	Instruments
6th DP (1990–1994)	– Integration of social, administrative, legal and financial dimensions for implementation	– Planning at regional and subregional level	– Balanced growth in regions	– Increasing the amount of available financial resources for Priority Provinces for development and state support
	– Adaptation of statistical system in line with the EU and international standards		– Supporting subdistricts to prevent migration from villages towards cities	– Incentives for private sector in Priority Provinces for development and establishment of a special fund for this aim
				– Industrial districts
				– The SAP
7th DP (1996–2000)	– Integration of sectoral and spatial analysis	– Regional and subregional projects	– Rationalization of both demographic change and migration	– To continue the implementation of Priority Provinces for development
	– Sectoral specialization of cities	– Mobilization of regionally embedded competences	– To analyze metropolitan problems in a separate category	– Emergency Support Programme to East and South-east Anatolia
	– City planning	– Sustainable development	– Policy development for housing problems	– The SAP
	– Alleviation of regional disparities		– Regional disparities	– Legal measures
	– Strengthening competitiveness			– Housing projects
				– Supporting SMEs in Priority Provinces for development
				– Zonguldak-Bartın-Karabük Regional Development Plan, the Eastern Black Sea Project, the East Anatolia Project
8th DP (2001–2005)	– Participatory planning	– Regional planning from a strategic perspective	– Enhancing competitiveness	– SME's supports

	– Sustainability	– Clustering	– Local entrepreneurship and mobilization of local resources	– EU funds
	– Rationalization in the use of resources	– Provincial development plans	– Regional disparities	– First comprehensive regional plans
	– Adaptation to the EU regional development policies			– Human capital investments
				– The SAP
				– The EAP
				– The EBSP, etc.
9th DP (2007–2013)	– Participatory planning	– Regional Development Agencies	– Enhancing competitiveness	– The RDAs
	– Sustainability	– Regional planning from a strategic perspective	– Local entrepreneurship and mobilization of local resources	– Diversification of Incentive Systems
	– Rationalization in the use of resources	– Clustering	– Regional disparities	– SME's supports
	– Adaptation to the EU regional development policies	– Provincial development plans (ending within the period of 9th plan)	– Integration to global economy	– EU funds
	– Introduction of recent regional development instruments	– Innovation systems	– Knowledge-based economy	– Regional development plans by the RDAs
	– Expansion of plan span from 5 to 7 years in line with the EU regulations	– Entrepreneurship		– The SAP
				– The EAP
				– The EBSP
				– Konya Plain Project
				– Giant public investment project such as Canal Istanbul, and High Speed Train Projects
				– Technoparks and incubation centers

Source: Various development plans; DPT (2000); OECD (1986, p. 5); OECD (1988, p. 8); Gül et al. (2013)

provincial offices. That is to say the SPO and its planning approach reflected the unitary, centralized, and statist traditions common in Turkey.

The priority given to the regional disparities, the rapid urbanization, a lack of regional administrative body, and decentralized policymaking approach shape the efforts and processes of the regional development planning in Turkey. As a result of centrally (top-to-bottom) prepared and implemented FYDPs, the provinces cannot lay out plans through collaboration and participation, and implement them. Besides, there is not an embedded tradition of local economic development planning. In general, the state and its field agencies are regarded as the sole engine of development by the local people. This is self-evident in local or provincial public expectations. Thus, these conditions, on the one hand, reduce public participation in regional development planning; and on the other hand, they help rationalize interventionist and centralistic approaches of the administration (Ertugal 2005).

However the EU has strong impacts (Lagendijk et al. 2009; Sobacı 2009) on regional policies since the 2000s. The very first regionalization occurred during 2004–2006 by the Preliminary National Development Plan (DPT 2003) which had been prepared for the sake of the EU funding. Following the implementation of this plan, Turkey for the first time faced with regional bodies responsible for regional development. The law numbered 5449 was enacted on 25 January 2006 and provided for a legal framework for establishing regional development agencies (Official Gazette 2006). Regional development agencies have been established in all 26 NUTS II regions throughout Turkey. The RDAs are defined as separate local–regional administration units, but national coordination among the RDAs is to be done by the Ministry of Development (former SPO). The main objectives of the RDAs are to invigorate and support local and regional potential for economic development, to organize economic development, and related research and education activities in their respective regions, to enhance the cooperation among public, civic, and private sectors, to enable an efficient and suitable utilization of public resources, and, among others. Ironically, there is a hesitation in using the word "regional" in the RDAs as a result of the fear from separatist movement and centralism heritage, and thus the RDAs are solely called as the DAs (development agencies) in Turkey.

Each RDA has developed a regional development plan with strategic perspective. The agencies are given responsibilities to strengthen the cooperation among public sector, private sector, and NGOs and to ensure the effective utilization of resources at local level. Correspondingly mobilizing local potential by the DAs will lead to acceleration of regional development, ensuring sustainability and reducing inter and intra regional disparities.

The introduction of the RDAs to existing centralized development planning is obviously a challenge that raises new forms of tensions between the center and the region. For the center getting used to losing the power and authority creates an environment where the government and the bureaucrats are afraid of making mistakes which would possibly have deeper impacts to the success of governmental policies. For the region, the issue is more complex at least for two main aspects. First, the regions would not have experienced to plan and control regional development before the establishment of the RDAs. This, in turn, raises many concerns about planning capacity of the RDAs. Second, the regional development plans exclusively depend on strategic planning. However, it is becoming a more complex issue to reach distant targets in a rapidly moving global and knowledge-based economy. In such innovative environment the regions are supposed to be a vehicle to accelerate any society's capacity to adapt to the new changes, but in Turkish bureaucracy the strategic planning is often reduced to participatory planning which neglects possible scenarios in an interrelated world. For instance, a region clearly depends on the other to some extent and thus planning should include the others' responses. This turns us to a basic dilemma: less regional capacity produces similar plans and similar plans do not help to produce further capacity.

The scenery regarding regional development, cluster policies perceived as a key to solve most of the regional problems, often beyond the limits of the exact clusters. A simple web research on the local newspapers about clusters shows us that due to its popularity, clusters are attributed miracle powers which could cure almost everything (for such exaggerated news, for example, see Sanayi Gazetesi 2012a, b; İşim 2010).

12.3 The Beginning and the Initial Reflections on Public Policy Documents

In Turkey, compared to the European counterparts, it can be said that not only the clusters and clustering policies but also the quality of regional policies are premature. Thus one can expect that it will take a certain period of time to go beyond the inherited understanding of strong central economic development. However, gaining official candidate status for the EU in 1999 and opening membership negotiations in 2005 has accelerated the regionalization process with a hope that strong regional administrative and economic structures would further assist to catch up the EU countries' level of prosperity (EC 2005a, b, c). To clarify, the impact of the EU process has been utilized by the government to transform two problematic areas, amongst others: further democratization and real regionalization for the first time. And clustering policy could not be analyzed without an internationalization argument (Jessop 1991, 1993, 2001).

Taken the absence of capacity of regional policy making into consideration, naturally the main strategy, employed by the central governments, has been increasing awareness and widening training about clusters since the 2000s. However, the first critical step was not taken by the government instead a business NGO took the lead role.

The very first step towards clusters was the establishment of competitive advantage of Turkey (CAT) platform in 1999, a civil arena for increasing awareness and researches on clusters. Correspondingly, a macro level clustering perspective was accepted by the platform due to insufficient capacities at the regional scale (Bulu and Eraslan 2004, p. 161). Of course, this choice is not accidental. In order to create an appropriate atmosphere, relevant stakeholders should be well informed and the macro level cluster perspective serves to this specific atmosphere.

The CAT was first started with the assistance of Michael Porter's team by the private sector representatives (Tansug 2009) and later various governmental institutions, universities, and NGOs joined the platform. The main departure point in this platform was to determine the competitive industries in the country and assign certain business professionals who would be responsible for the development of clusters in their respective sector. In this line, clusters-related activities were initiated not from a regional development perspective instead from a macro industrial approach based on increasing (and creating) competitiveness. So the internationalization of policies, the EU impact on Turkey, paved way to top-to-bottom clustering understanding from the very first stage. As this approach has been matured, the CAT platform turned into an association, titled International Competitiveness Research Institute. Some of the activities covered in this period by the platform are:

- Particular business firms, universities, banks, professional associations, and the media discussed and began to understand what could be role of clusters for Turkey.
- Using Porter's framework, the platform tried to distinguish potential competitive industries and initiate respective clustering processes. For instance, in this line, in a famous touristic destination in Istanbul, namely Sultanahmet, a pilot clustering study successfully finalized.
- Academic partners of the platform supervised master and doctoral thesis concerning clusters, wrote articles in media, shot TV programmes as well.
- Having the advantage of being first, the platform had bid for some EU funded projects and took a lead role clustering projects particularly in the least developed eastern and southeastern regions of the country. On the other hand, the CAT (later the institute) became the first address for the local authorities or business association who want to learn about or implement clustering approach.

Apart from the CAT there have been many different efforts both at the central and regional level concerning clusters. However, the evolution of cluster policies in Turkey cannot be separately evaluated from the evolution of regional development policies as pointed previously. Until the 9th Development Plan which was prepared accordingly the EU budgetary periods (for 2007–2013) employed a more participatory approach, there had been no concrete agenda concerning the clusters in public policy documents. The 9th Development Plan can be regarded as a turning point yet it heavily tried to transcend so-called *to alleviate regional disparities* approach that has been effective since the establishment of the SPO in 1960. The 9th Plan instead focuses on increasing regional competitiveness which gave path to clusters as a nexus of sectoral and regional policies (DPT 2006). Likewise the CAT, the central planning took competitiveness and also innovation as gateway to cluster policies. Once again regions have to face with "clusterize" approach likewise "regionalize."

The very first public policy that strongly emphasizes clusters is the SME's Strategy and Action Plan prepared by the Ministry of Industry for the sake of adaptation to the EU procedures in 2004 (Alsaç 2010). Although all of the five strategic fields (DPT 2007) have not directly mentioned clustering, the action plan pointed out the importance of supporting local clusters. The revised version of this document in 2007 accepted clusters as a tool to increase the competitiveness of the SMEs and explicitly announced that in the following periods clusters would be supported under the responsibility of Ministry of Industry.

The recent Medium-Term Programmes prepared by the Ministry of Economy for 2009–2011 and 2012–2014 both stress the role of clusters in economic development. The 2009–2011 programme, referring to 9th Development Plan, stresses that the regional clusters (DPT 2008) would be developed in particular areas where they have potential innovative and productive capacity and cooperation among SMEs. The 2012–2014 programme, being rather comprehensive compared to the preceding, concentrates on two axes: developing innovation and R&D through increasing university–business collaboration and prioritizing local and indigenous dynamics for creating and supporting clusters (DPT 2011).

There are some other central ministries and public institution which also underlined the importance of clusters in their strategy and policy documents. However on the ground, there is no concrete formulation and financial means to support clusters. The existing financial supports given by different ministries are more concentrated on networking and agglomeration of SMEs rather than clustering. For example, Ministry of Industry utilized the concept of Organized Industrial Zones which is supported through incentive of input cost reduction and land allocation. On the other hand, the KOSGEB, the SMEs supporting public institution, co-finances certain equipment and laboratory investments which would be commonly used at least by five firms (KOSGEB 2003). The technoparks and technology incubation centers are also perceived as business-academia networking platforms thus regarded as appropriate arenas for clustering. Unfortunately none of these fundamental supporting mechanisms is directly linked to clustering, at least in contemporary understanding of clusters.

So what the policy makers are trying to reach in terms of cluster creating and developing seems to be confusing in several aspects. First of all, anchoring the EU for regional transformation must be transcended to sustain what is achieved in clustering. Not surprisingly, as will be discussed in the following section, the local response to cluster policy has been also internationally induced. To reach a certain level of understanding in the perception of clustering, one can tolerate top-to-bottom policies but the need to shift to bottom-to-up policies is becoming clear, otherwise two potential threats will emerge: to reduce clusters into agglomeration and difficulties to sustain existing efforts and structures concerning clusters.

Secondly, there is no clear distinction of scales which further confuses the perception clusters. It is observed that the terms of local–national–sectoral–regional clusters could be used even in the same public policy document. This has led to a third dilemma: different ministries are using different tools to create clusters and there is no clear policy coordination. Consequently it causes duplication of many activities and misunderstanding among ministerial bureaucrats. Actually the main problem lies behind the central approach to clusters which to some extent neglects the uniqueness of localities which are the non-replicable qualities of competitive advantage (Porter 2009; EC 2009; Deimel et al. 2009).

Table 12.2 The relevance of other policy fields with cluster policies in policy documents

Policy fields	Relation to clustering policies	Reflections on policy documents
Regional development policies	Agglomerations, activating local dynamics and potentials	9th Development Plan, medium term programme, law on RDAs, regional competitiveness operational programme by Ministry of Industry
Industrialization policies	Clustering as tool for strengthening cooperation among firms in a particular value chain	Industry policy, medium-term programme, regional competitiveness operational programme by the Ministry of Industry
Science and technology policies	Regional innovation strategies and cooperative interactions for innovation	Regional innovation strategy plan and various documents by The Scientific and Technological Research Council of Turkey
SME's support policies	Increasing relations and cooperation among the SMEs for rising competitiveness	SME's strategy and action plan, 9th Development Plan
Foreign trade policies	Export-focused policy for high value added and competitive economy	Export strategic plan by the Undersecretariat of foreign trade, law No. 1994, medium-term programme
Agricultural policies	Establishing agricultural producers unions for creating clusters	Agricultural strategy
		SME's strategy and action plan
Tourism policies	Establishing infrastructure unions for tourism, supporting R&D and triple helix	Tourism strategy, 9th Development Plan
Labour policies	Increasing the quality of workforce	Labour market strategy, 9th Development Plan, laws No. 3146 and 1985
Education and training	Supporting vocational training and education to increase the quality of workforce for SMEs which are in particular cluster	Laws No. 3308 and 1986 prepared by the Ministry of Education

Source: DTM (2009, p. 33)

Although the recent literature contains variety of clusters, from contemporary to distant ones, the starting point in Turkish cases depends on competitiveness thus on sectoral basis. Contrary, the policy documents mix up the varieties of clusters, neglects "spontaneous" types instead prefers "policy-driven" type of clusters (Chiesa and Chiaroni 2005; Su and Hung 2009).

Table 12.2 summarizes the confusing status of clusters in various policy fields. The recentness of clusters and clustering policies pretend an increasing role to clusters without strong sound in legislations and public policy documents. Actually many documents refer to clusters but do not take necessary actions and step to realize what it argued in these documents. Naturally agglomerations have found strong legislative framework as a result of inherited centralism. For example while laws on Organized Industrial Zones, Free Trade Zones, Specialized Organized Industrial Zones and Technoparks have a legislative background, cluster policies seem to be stuck within the intentions mentioned in various policy documents. In fact, as will be seen in the following section, cluster policies have been specified through projects funded by different sources. This situation, arguably, has advantages and disadvantages. It is advantageous since legislative regulations impose a top-to-bottom approach which creates a single framework for all. On the negative side, project-based clustering efforts may suffer from lack of local and regional capacity on project management and regional development arise concerns about sustainability of clusters. Of course, we have to keep in mind the relationship between capitalist restructuring and cluster in Turkey which questions articulation of production systems at different levels.

12.4 The Impact of International Perspective on Domestic Clusters

Although national policy formation relatively seems independent from international policy perspective, the lack of regional capacity along with premature regional development policy making caused seemingly countrywide spread of cluster policy. This was seemingly because of misunderstanding of what clusters mean: it was first perceived as either agglomeration or as simple industrial concentration by various localities and their respective representatives (such as the leaders of chambers of commerce and industry or provincial governors) from the different parts of the country. Due to exploitation of the EU membership as an anchor for the domestic transformation, the foremost international impacts raised by the EU are the acquis and accession funding. Although the EU does not impose compulsorily a change in regional development administration system in the accession process, the various country reports on Turkey (for example, CEC 2001, 2004; European Council 2001; EC 2005d) by the EU explicitly criticizes the poor capacity of regional development and highly recommends the establishment of regional development agencies (Dulupçu and Sungur 2006). Nonetheless throughout the negotiations the agencies were established as aforementioned. However the EU funding was utilized to initiate not only new understanding of regional policy in the country but also for the dissemination of clusters as an instrument for regional development.

The most well-known EU funded (through Pre-Accession Financial Instrument for Turkey) clustering project is "Development of a Clustering Policy for Turkey" which began to be prepared by the Ministry of Economy in 2005. The title of the project hosted the ironical nature of perception of clusters in the eyes of bureaucrats: clusters are somehow should be planned and developed nationally in order to initiate local development. This 2-year lasted project officially began in 2007 and had a couple of main purposes which were actually beyond the limits of the project:

to design a clustering policy to support sustainable development which includes economic, social, and environmental dimensions and to increase export capacity of the country by gaining competiveness. To realize this purpose the project aimed to increase cooperation among the SMEs, to develop innovative actions, to create economies of scale, to promote inward investment, to find out the policies to determine the need for infrastructure to increase regional and national competitiveness. Obviously to realize such critical aims through a single project was an overexpectation. Nonetheless, the project ultimately tried to raise awareness without actual intervention. Of course it would be unfair to heavily criticize hence it followed-up formal project cycle with limited time and budget.

This six million euro cost project consists of three main components. The first component is about creating capacity for national clustering policy and implementation. Thus includes training of mostly central and to some extent regional personnel of different institutions, and study visits to successful regions. The second component is relatively important because it aimed to create a strategy document: national clustering strategy, a white book. In the third component, the project has determined the macro cluster mapping at the national level and empirically determined 32 cluster categories through some statistical studies and highlighted the potential development of 10 clusters. Each cluster has its theme, as the Table 12.3 below shows it explicitly (Bouget 2011). So this leading project reflects top-to-bottom understanding and makes Turkey a good geography to analyze and study all fashionable concepts and theories regarding regional studies (Park 2000).

A complementary project titled "SME Networking and Cluster Project" (co-financed by the EU and Turkish Government) in 2007 and started in 2011 and due to end in 2013 aimed to create sectoral cooperation based on clustering approach within the same geographical area as well as among different localities. Of course, the lack of informative background once again necessitated training in different levels and contexts. Being more specific and concentrated compared to aforementioned macro level project, this project aimed to analyze regional dynamics, to determine existing and potential sectors for regional cooperation, to augment

Table 12.3 Potential clusters by themes in development of a clustering policy for Turkey Project

Themes	Clusters
Innovation and entrepreneurship	Mersin processed food
	Ankara Software
Inter-actor network creation	Ankara machinery
	Denizli-Uşak home textiles
Cluster formation	Konya automotive parts and components
	Muğla Yacht building
Factor conditions	Manisa electrical and electronic appliances
	Marmara automotive
Cluster basis	Eskişehir-Bilecik-Kütahya ceramics
	İzmir organic food

Source: Bouget (2011, p. 4)

cooperation networks and knowledge sharing among firms, and—with a hope—to integrate some firms to international value chain. The leading role is given to Ministry of Industry thus main shareholders are chosen from the representatives of business sectors such as chambers of commerce and export associations. In this line five provinces are selected to initiate the programme, namely Samsun, Trabzon, Çorum, Kahramanmaraş, and Gaziantep where clustering information centers are supposed to be established. The perspective embedded in the project highly depends on awareness on clusters and networking possibilities including cluster business development and internationalization guidelines. Finally in abovementioned provinces clustering studies have been initiated in their relevant sectors, such as shoemaking in Gaziantep, medical equipment in Samsun and shipbuilding in Trabzon.

One of most profound ongoing studies concerning regional development is in Southeastern Anatolia, relatively least prosperous part of the country, has a component regarding cluster development. The largest public infra- and super-structure development project of the Turkish Republic, namely the GAP (Southeastern Anatolia Project), also utilizes clustering policies as a tool to foster regional development. The clustering development component is co-financed through the EU and the UNDP and concentrated on Şanlıurfa, Diyarbakır, and Adıyaman provinces and corresponding sectors, organic farming, marble, and textile industry respectively.

Among the other EU financed cluster projects, Istanbul Fashion and Textile clustering project has a distinctive role yet it is the very first (initiated in 2003) and large scale project in the country and served as a role model to other localities and institutions (for more information see Gülcan et al. 2011; Alsaç 2010). The project inclusively departs from the transfer of international know-how and run by a consortium consist of leading European fashion centers. The first phase was aimed at expertise sharing through technical consulting among the SMEs in the textile and clothing sector, at local, national, and European levels (Akgüngör et al. 2012), where second phase of the project directly targeted to create a cluster for the textile SMEs in Istanbul.

Apart from nationally programmed clustering projects there are some locally planned and run projects through the EU funding. These efforts radically differ from the abovementioned projects yet they are inspired from the local expectations and tried to bid for the EU money. However, the localities and local institutions generally tried to finance their clustering efforts through international funding (mostly the EU). Naturally this has led a clustering understanding at the global scale often neglecting the uniqueness of localities. To be mentioned, in Mersin food and agricultural industries, in Bursa transportation sector, in Eskişehir aviation sector are financed through 7th Framework Programme, and textile in Diyarbakır and automotive components in Konya are financed through EU-Turkey Chambers Partnership Grant Scheme (Fig. 12.1).

These examples show that internationally financed clustering efforts can be generalized under two main categories. On the one hand, clustering policies are formulated at the national scale by the related ministries, on the other some regions tried to express their enthusiasm towards cluster. The projects under the first category are not exactly designed to create actual clusters, instead to raise awareness and to

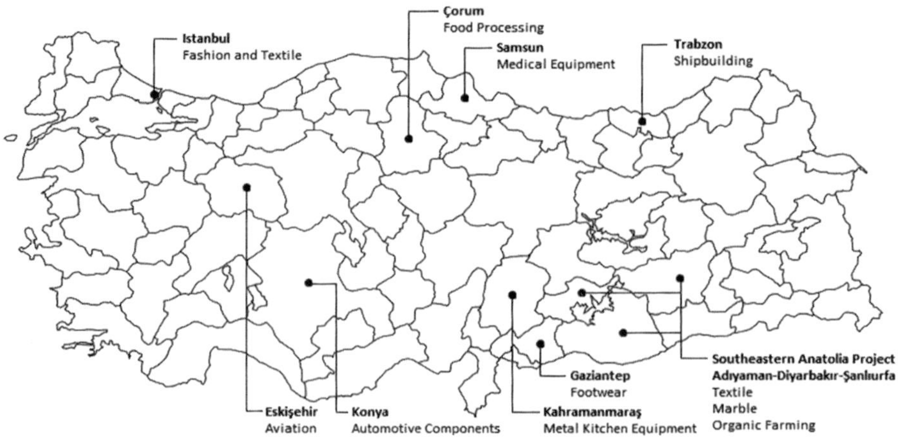

Fig. 12.1 Internationally financed regional clustering projects in various provinces in Turkey Source: Adapted from Öz (2004, p. 53)

inform the representatives of bureaucrats and business world. The only exception is Istanbul Fashion and Textile clustering project which covers the most developed region of the country not only in terms of income but also technologically and socially. Thus it was relatively close to the understanding of what the literature argues. As a result of the nationalization and centralization of clustering perspective in Turkey, the governments throughout the period always focused on certain regions, generally the least developed part of the country. It is not an exaggeration to say that the cluster policies at various scales were formulated within the limits of Keynesian understanding. So somehow "to clusterize" became a part of regional development policy making. The national perspective naturally targeted at underdeveloped regions where the lack of capacity at the local scale necessitates top-to-bottom imposition.

Under the second category, the absence of related financial means led localities to bid for the EU funding. Clearly, these projects came from the developed parts of the country. However, the international dimension of the projects contains basic dilemma: international cooperation eases knowledge transfer on the one hand, on the other hand the regions have to operate within the limits of project management and consultants' perspective. Many cluster projects for that reason tried to relate their projects with the funding area although the terms of conditions of the many project calls are not directly related to cluster development. Of course, the poor national level regional development financing might be accused for such attempts. As an answer to poor support programme to clusters, the government initiated sectoral and regional support programme which also contains various incentives for clusters in 2012 where cluster policies found a legislative base (Official Gazette 2012). In this programme, tax reduction supports are increased 5–10 % than already applied in the current region for the investments in organized industrial zones and sectoral collaboration investments for cluster development. Likewise, insurance premium supports are extended for 1–3 years for the investments in organized industrial zones and sectoral collaboration investments in supported regions. However, there is no clear definition about which initiatives could be accepted as "cluster." Shortly, in this specific programme, the availability of clusters increases the advantages of support programme to firms. However the absence of no clear definition of clusters in the support programme led to creation of many business associations which of most are entitled as "x sectoral cluster association." So having an association name that includes cluster is perceived as an enough criteria for utilizing the advantages of the support programme by many localities. More interestingly nearly all advantages of the support programme are cost reducing incentive without having a real base for sustaining and fostering the clusters.

Consequently the efforts to "clusterize" are diverse have limited theoretical and practical background. However the establishment of the RDAs created a hopeful expectation for more realistic and sustainable clusters with an embedded regional and local perspective. Is it the case?

12.5 The RDAs and Clusters: How Do They Formulize at the Local Level?

After years of coalition having a single-headed government since 2002 with a relatively strong political and public support helped Turkey to stabilize its macroeconomic indicators. This macro achievement entered into a new phase with the establishment of the RDAs aiming to transfer the macro achievements to meso and micro levels. However, the RDAs are designed in line with the EU regulations with a hope to fasten adaptation to utilize Structural Funds when the full membership would be achieved. Thus ontologically the cluster policies of the RDAs are strongly connected to European perspective on regional development. In this process, unfortunately, clustering became somehow biding for projects. In other words, clusters found a strong room in regional projects in order to be financed. Therefore almost all RDAs prioritized "creating and supporting clusters" in their regional development plans which have been used as a guideline in programming.

A quick analysis of clustering projects financed by the RDAs led us to a simple categorization (see websites of various Turkish RDAs for detailed information, for example, BAKA, BEBKA, DOKA, MARKA, and GEKA):

- Base industries: Traditionally some regions have leading sectors, often agglomerated. Some projects targeted at turning agglomerations into clusters to increase competitiveness of relevant industries to survive under price competition.
- Potentials: Under this category, the projects tried to support or initiate previously undervalued industries either due to lack of financial supports or misprioritization.
- New sectors: To create more innovative environment, many regions are trying to emphasize high-tech industries such as IT, advanced medical and bioscience (Table 12.4).

Table 12.4 RDAs' cluster projects: some examples

Cluster category	Cluster development (and region)	Diagnosing cluster possibilities network (and region)
Base industries		Wood industry—West Mediterranean
		Tourism—Antalya
		Livestock—Burdur
		Mining—Burdur
		Steel and iron—Osmaniye
Potentials	Medical—Ankara	Ceramics—Bursa
	Medical—Samsun	Yacht—Bodrum
	Medical—İzmir	Tourism—Karaman
New sectors	IT—Ankara	Home appliance—Merzifon
	Fashion—İzmir	

Since the establishment of RDAs, nearly 50 projects, financed by the Turkish RDAs, reflect the enthusiasm towards creating clusters. Although budgets, dimensions, and methodologies may differ, the sectoral basis seems more dominant compared to regional basis. Only a few of the projects aimed to develop clusters while most of them tried to analyze cluster relations and networking possibilities. The ironic point is that until the establishment of the RDAs there had been no real project finance regarding clusters. This situation reveals an important question: if clustering had been so significant why none of the local authorities and business did support clusters from their own budgets? The answer lies behind the public policy documents which redeems clusters because of the international impose mainly by the EU. Put differently, as a result of long lasting centrally designed regional development policies, regions are always seeking for a guide (orders and models) and open to be shaped by external forces.

The response from the regions to cluster initiatives could be assessed as an effort to understand what the cluster really means. A closer look to the details of the RDA-financed projects show us that projects are mainly concerning training about clusters and developing strategies for cluster developing. Because of lack of capacity at the regional level, many project owners seek for international consultants to assist their efforts, a problem which has heavily criticized by Lovering seminal paper (Lovering 1999).

Consequently imitating the internationals became the basic formulation of cluster studies at regional level. However, it is not possible to say that the clustering has been supported in a systematic way in Turkey. In addition, the basic weaknesses and deficiencies in Turkish business and work culture are also seen on clustering. It can't be said that the Turkish firms would be successful on clustering "spontaneously," due to the unwillingness and failure in collaboration, cooperation, and joint ventures, and more importantly regionalization. For this reason, clustering in Turkey usually has emerged as "policy-driven." There is a lack of both social and intellectual capital on "spontaneous" clustering and this lack is tried to be eliminated with imitation and policy-driven clustering approaches.

12.6 Conclusion

The consensus, that ability and capacity of regions could foster economic development while enhancing more informal, institutional, and social interactions, is now finding more adherents from a rich variety of theoreticians and practitioners as well as equally question marks. One of the big issues is how to accommodate regions of developing countries—like Turkey—into this regional revitalization. And clusters are perceived as the fundamental way to fit into the regional development puzzle by Turkish governmental and nongovernmental organizations particularly through the inspiration and impact of international bodies.

Turkey, inspired by the formal EU candidacy status, has committed herself to a series of changes following the Helsinki Summit including regionalization which paved way to many projects on clusters. The regional playground in Turkey, in this context, has been faced with a challenge from "four pillars." The first comes from the global restructuring capitalism and reconfiguration of the state such as the RDAs, the second pillar is the EU accession and the Republic's Europeanization target as an interconnected process, the third is shaped by disarticulated politics often manifested in populism and the last one is that of statism and centralism—the dual workhouse of the traditional Turkish development policy.

There are clear dangers that unfiltered policy transfers might be at best ineffective and at worst harmful and this also applies to cluster policies. In addition disregarding the subnational features may lessen the impact of cluster policies. Alternatively spending too much time on filtering could result in missing out chances and high cost: a right combination of policy implications of clusters should be integrated to indigenous policy formulations.

Economic development and its planning at the local and regional levels requires fostering participatory public policy-making processes and a culture of initiative taking and participation among local people; and continuing support of central government, its local officials, and local public leaders, and other related civic, private, and public actors (Gül 2003). However, on the one hand the continuing habits of centralized bureaucratic structure, on the other relatively weak capacity of local public and private actors have the potential to limit the success clusters in Turkey. Similarly the efforts of the RDAs to develop clusters look quite mechanistic rather than functional and flexible. In order to avoid dead-end cluster policies, the local and regional either business or public leaders must understand the rationale behind clusters. Otherwise, regions would be inactive partners of the regional policy, and the cluster projects and programmes would turn into centrally imposed development plans, as they have always been.

References

Akgüngör S, Kuştepeli Y, Gülcan Y (2012) An overview on industry clusters and the impact of related variety on regional performance in Turkey. Eur Rev Ind Econ Policy (5). http://revel.unice.fr/eriep/index.html?id=3533
Alsaç F (2010) Clustering approach as a regional development tool and a cluster support model proposal for Turkey. Planning Expertise Thesis, State Planning Organization
Armatlı Köroğlu B, Özelçi Eceral T, Uğurlar A (2009) The story of a jewelry cluster in Istanbul metropolitan area: grand bazaar (Kapalıçarşı). GUJS 22(4):383–394
Asheim B, Cooke P, Martin R (2006) The rise of the cluster concept in regional analysis and policy: a critical assessment. In: Asheim B, Cooke P, Martin R (eds) Clusters and regional development: critical reflections and explorations. Routledge, London, pp 1–19
Boschma RA, Kloosterman RC (eds) (2005) Learning from clusters: a critical assessment from an economic-geographical perspective. Springer, Dordrecht
Bouget N (2011) Country report—Turkey, European Cluster Observatory, Deliverable D24-2
Buğra A (2003a) Piyasa Ekonomisi Macerası: Dün ve Bugün. Birikim Dergisi 170/171:10–20
Buğra A (2003b) Devlet—Piyasa Karşıtlığının Ötesinde. İletişim Yayınları, Istanbul
Buğra A, Keyder Ç (2006) Sosyal Politika Yazıları. İletişim Yayınları, Istanbul
Bulu M, Eraslan I (2004) Kümelenme Yaklaşımı. In: Saglam I (ed) Çağdaş Yönetim Yaklaşımları: İlkeler Kavramlar ve Yaklaşımlar. Beta Basım Yayım Dağıtım, Istanbul
Bulutay T (1995) Employment, unemployment and wages in Turkey. DIE-ILO, Ankara
CEC (Commission of the European Communities) (2001) 2001 Regular report on Turkey's progress towards accession, Brussels
CEC (Commission of the European Communities) (2004) 2004 Regular report on Turkey's progress towards accession, Brussels
Chiesa V, Chiaroni D (2005) Industrial clusters in biotechnology: driving forces, development processes and management practices. Imperial College Press, London
Cooke P, Lazzeretti L (2008) Creative cities, cultural clusters and local economic development. Edward Elgar, Cheltenham
Deimel M, Plumeyer C, Theuvsen L, Ebbeskotte C (2009) Regional networking as a competitive advantage? Empirical results from German pig production. Paper prepared for presentation at the 113th EAAE seminar 'A resilient European food industry and food chain in a challenging world', Greece, 3–6 Sept 2009
Diez MA (2001) The evaluation of regional innovation and cluster policies: towards a participatory approach. Eur Plann Stud 9(7):907–923
DPT (1962) 1st FYDP. DPT, Ankara
DPT (1967) 2nd FYDP. DPT, Ankara
DPT (1972) 3rd FYDP. DPT, Ankara
DPT (1978) 4th FYDP. DPT, Ankara
DPT (1984) 5th FYDP. DPT, Ankara
DPT (1989) 6th FYDP. DPT, Ankara
DPT (1995) 7th FYDP. DPT, Ankara
DPT (1996) Devlet Planlama Teşkilatı ile İlgili Mevzuat. DPT, Ankara
DPT (2000) 8th FYDP. DPT, Ankara
DPT (2003) Preliminary National Development Plan 2004–2006, Ankara
DPT (2006) 9th DP. DPT, Ankara
DPT (2007) KOBİ Stratejisi ve Eylem Planı 2007–2009, Ankara
DPT (2008) Bölgesel Gelişme, 9. Kalkınma Planı Özel İhtisas Komisyonu Raporu. DPT, Ankara
DPT (2011) Orta Vadeli Program 2012–2014, Ankara
DTM—Dış Ticaret Müsteşarlığı (2009) Beyaz Kitap: Türkiye İçin Kümelenme Politikasının Geliştirilmesi, Ankara
Dulupçu MA, Sungur O (2006) Adaptation problem of Turkey to the regional policies within the process of the EU membership: dilemmas and opportunities. International conference on the

changes and transformations in the socio-economic and political structure of Turkey within the EU negotiations, Dumlupınar University, Kütahya, 16–18 Mar, pp 297–316
Dulupçu MA, Gül H, Okçu M (2004) A new regional and local perspective for economic development in Turkey: illusion or reality? Paper presented at the 5th European urban and regional studies conference, Poland, 9–12 Sept 2004
EC (European Commission) (2005a) Proposal for a council decision—on the principles, priorities and conditions contained in the accession partnership with Turkey, Brussels, 9 Sept 2005
EC (European Commission) (2005b) Turkey 2005 Progress Report, Brussels, 9 Sept 2005
EC (European Commission) (2005c) Communication from the Commission–2005 enlargement strategy paper, Brussels, 9 Sept 2005
EC (European Commission) (2005d) Turkey 2005 Progress Report, Brussels
EC (European Commission) (2009) Constructing regional advantage: principles—perspectives—policies. European Commission Directorate-General for Research, Brussels
Ellison G, Glaeser EL, Kerr WR (2010) What causes industry agglomeration? Evidence from coagglomeration patterns. Am Econ Rev 100:1195–1213
Ertugal E (2005) Europeanisation of regional policy and regional governance: the case of Turkey. Eur Polit Econ Rev 3:18–53
European Council (2001) Turkey: 2000 accession partnership, Brussels
Fan CC, Scott AJ (2003) Industrial agglomeration and development: a survey of spatial economic issues in East Asia and a statistical analysis of Chinese regions. Econ Geogr 79(3):295–319
Gordon IR, McCann P (2000) Industrial clusters: complexes, agglomeration and/or social networks? Urban Stud 37(3):513–532
Gül H (2003) 'Ekonomik Kalkınmada Yerel Alternatifler', Cumhuriyetimizin 80. Yılında Kentsel Ekonomik Araştırmalar Sempozyumu (KEAS), Pamukkale Üniversitesi, 10–12 Eylül, Denizli
Gül H, Okçu M, Dulupçu MA (2013) Regional and local perspectives in economic development in Turkey. In: Kamalak I, Gül H (eds) Turkey in the new millennium. A critique of political, social and economic transformations, içinde (Der. İhsan Kamalak ve Hüseyin Gül). Lambert Academic, pp 263–309
Gülcan Y, Akgüngör S, Kuştepeli Y (2011) Knowledge generation and innovativeness in Turkish textile industry: comparison of Istanbul and Denizli. Eur Plann Stud 19(7):1229–1243
Güler BA (1996) Yeni Sağ ve Devletin Değişimi. TODAİE Yayınları, Ankara
Güzey Y, Taşseven O, Elifoğlu H (2010) Jewelry cluster in grand bazaar in Istanbul. 2nd jewel—jewellery design and education symposium (UMTTES2010), Kütahya, Turkey, pp 184–193
Hospers G, Beugelsdijk S (2002) Regional cluster policies: learning by comparing? Kyklos 55(3):381–402
http://www.competitiveturkey.org/version3/capsept00.html
Insel A (1996) ÖDP'nin Ekonomi Politikaları Üzerine. Birikim Dergisi 103:20–24
Insel A (2005) Neo-Liberalizm. Sena Ofset, Istanbul
İşim (2010) Tufan Geliyor, Küme Kurun! http://www.isim.org.tr/tr/duyurular-etkinlikler/duyurular/171-ziya-burhanettin-guvenc-tufan-geliyor-kume-kurun.html
Jessop B (1991) Regulation theory, post-Fordism and the state: more than a reply to Werner Bonefeld. In: Bonefeld W, Holloway J (eds) Post-Fordism and social form: a Marxist debate on the post-Fordist state. Macmillan, London
Jessop B (1993) Toward a Schumpeterian workfare state? Preliminary remarks on post-Fordist political economy. Stud Polit Econ 40:7–39
Jessop B (ed) (2001) Regulation theory and crisis of capitalism. Edward Elgar, Aldershot
Kalaycıoğlu E (1997) Decentralization and good governance. Paper presented at the Mediterranean development forum on 'Fiscal Decentralization', Marrakesh, 12–14 May
Kazgan G (1994) Yeni Ekonomik Düzende Türkiye'nin Yeri. Altın Kitapları, Istanbul
Keyder Ç (2000) Türkiye'de Devlet ve Sınıflar. İletişim Yayınları, Istanbul
Kılıçbay MA (1995) Benim Polemiklerim. İmge Kitabevi, Ankara
Kongar E (1999) 21. Yüzyılda Türkiye. Remzi Kitabevi, Istanbul
KOSGEB (2003) KOSGEB Destekleri Yönetmeliği, Ankara

Lagendijk A, Kayasu S, Yaşar S (2009) The role of regional development agencies in Turkey—from implementing EU directives to supporting regional business communities? Eur Urban Reg Stud 16(4):383–396
Lovering J (1999) Theory led by policy: inadequacies of the 'new regionalism' (illustrated from the case of Wales). Int J Urban Reg Res 23:379–395
Lundvall B-Å (1998) The learning economy: challenges to a economic theory and policy. In: Nielsen K, Johnson B (eds) Institutions and economic change: new perspectives on markets, firms and technology. Edward Elgar, Cheltenham
Malmberg A (1996) Industrial geography: agglomeration and local milieu. Prog Hum Geogr 20(3):392–403
Nolan CE (2003) Hamilton county's comparative and competitive advantages: business and industry clusters, community compass special research report 3–6. Hamilton County Regional Planning Commission, Cincinnati
OECD (1986) Documentation for the review of regional problems and policies in Turkey. Directorate for Science, Technology and Industry, England
OECD (1988) Regional problems and policies in Turkey. OECD, Paris
Official Gazette (2006) Kalkınma Ajanslarının Kuruluşu, Koordinasyonu ve Görevleri Hakkında Kanun, 8 Feb 2006, Number: 26074
Official Gazette (2012) Yatırımlarda Devlet Yardımları Hakkında Karar, 19 June 2012, Number: 28328
Öniş Z (1995) The limits of neoliberalism: towards a reformulation of development theory. J Econ Issues 25:97–119
Öniş Z, Ercan M (2001) Turkish privatization: institutions and dilemmas. Turk Stud 2:109–134
Öniş Z, Karataş C (1994) Dünyada Özelleştirme ve Türkiye. TÜSES Yayını, Istanbul
Ortaylı İ (2002) İmparatorluğun En Uzun Yılı. İletişim Yayınları, Istanbul
Özelçi Eceral T, Armatlı Köroğlu B, Uğurlar A (2009) Kuyumculuk Kümeleri: Istanbul Kapalıçarşı ile Dünya Örneklerinin Karşılaştırmalı Değerlendirmesi. Ekononomik Yaklaşım 20(70):121–143
Park B (2000) Turkey's European Union Candidacy: from Luxembourg to Helsinki—to Ankara. International Studies Association 41st annual convention, Los Angeles, CA, 14–18 Mar
Porter ME (1998) Clusters and new economics of competition. Harv Bus Rev 76(6):77–90
Porter ME (2009) The competitive advantage of nations, states and regions. Advanced Management Program, April
Ruokolainen O (2011) Strategic development of the regional cultural economy: four forms of cultural capital. University of Tampere Research Unit for Urban and Regional Development Studies, SENTE Working Papers 33/2011
Sanayi Gazetesi (2012a) Kümelenme Türkiye'yi Uçurur. http://www.sanayigazetesi.com.tr/roportaj/kumelenme-turkiyeyi-ucurur-h2631.html. Accessed 3 Oct 2012
Sanayi Gazetesi (2012b) Cari Açığın İlacını Buldu: Kümelenme. http://www.sanayigazetesi.com.tr/osb/cari-acigin-ilacini-buldu-kumelenme-h1543.html. Accessed 13 Mar 2012
Šarić S (2011) Competitive advantages through clusters: an empirical study with evidence from China. Springer, Wiesbaden
Sobacı Z (2009) Regional development agencies in Turkey: are they examples of obligated policy transfer? Public Org Rev 9(1):51–65
Soyak A (2003) Economic planning in Turkey: is there a need for the state planning organization? Doğuş Üniversitesi Dergisi 4:167–182
Soyak A (2004) Ulusaldan Uluslarüstüne İktisadi Planlama ve Türkiye Deneyimi. Der Yayınları, Istanbul
Soyak A (2005) Ertelenen 9. Kalkınma Planı Ve Türkiye'de Planlamanın Geleceği Üzerine Bir Not. Bilim ve Ütopya Dergisi 136:45–47
Su Y, Hung L (2009) Spontaneous vs. policy-driven: the origin and evolution of the biotechnology cluster. Technol Forecast Soc Change 76(5):608–619
Tansug MA (2009) Türkiye'nin İlk Kümelenme Analiz ve Geliştirme Çalışması: Sultanahmet Bölgesi Turizm Sektörü Kümelenme Projesi. Çerçeve Dergisi 17(51):62–67

Chapter 13
Are Small Firms More Dependent on the Local Environment than Larger Firms? Evidence from Portuguese Manufacturing Firms

Carlos Carreira and Luís Lopes

Abstract This paper analyzes the impact on firm-level total factor productivity of both agglomeration economies and regional knowledge base, using an unbalanced panel of Portuguese manufacturing firms covering the period 1996–2004. Controlling for the endogeneity using the difference generalized method of moments estimator, we found that both localization and urbanization economies have a significant and positive effect on firm productivity, with the latter playing the most important role. Sectoral specialization economies are important for small and medium firms, but not for large firms. However, larger firms, therefore those with higher absorptive capacity, profit more from regional knowledge than smaller ones.

Keywords Agglomeration economies • Regional knowledge • Total factor productivity (TFP) • Small firms • Firm-level studies

13.1 Introduction

The study of spatial agglomeration of both production activities and knowledge base is important to understand their contribution for local and, consequently, national economic growth. Notwithstanding the tendency to reducing transaction costs, there has been observed an increasing propensity for firms to agglomerate their activities in certain regions with economic impact on employment level, wages, knowledge, productivity, and economic growth.

The theories of the location of economic activities are microeconomic in their essence, which means that the empirical studies should use firm-level data. However, the unavailability of large microeconomic datasets has favored empirical investigations at the aggregate rather than micro-level. Even in the cases of micro-level

C. Carreira • L. Lopes (✉)
Faculdade de Economia/GEMF, Universidade de Coimbra, Coimbra, Portugal
e-mail: ccarreir@fe.uc.pt; perlopes@fe.uc.pt

R. Baptista, J. Leitão (eds.), *Entrepreneurship, Human Capital, and Regional Development*, International Studies in Entrepreneurship 31,
DOI 10.1007/978-3-319-12871-9_13

researches, given that productivity growth at firm- or plant-level is generally not available, most of earlier studies use proxies such as employment and wage growth—under the assumptions that there is a national labor market and that labor is homogeneous, then productivity growth will result in proportional employment gains through shifts in labor demand (see, for example, Glaeser et al. 1992; Henderson et al. 1995; Combes 2000).

In this paper, we implement a micro-level analysis in order to shed further light on the extent to which the local environment, namely agglomeration economies and regional knowledge base, has an effect on firms' productivity. Additionally, we also investigate whether smaller firms are more dependent of local environment than larger ones. To conduct the analysis, we will use an unbalanced panel of Portuguese manufacturing firms covering the period 1996–2004.

This paper makes two main contributions to the economic literature. Even though agglomeration economies and regional knowledge base encompass a large number of studies, to our awareness, there has been no research that assesses the role of these two productivity sources together. Furthermore, there is scarce evidence on the effect of local environment on firms' total factor productivity (TFP), especially across firms' size.

The paper proceeds as follows. After a brief review of the background literature in the next section, Sect. 13.3 presents the empirical model and the dataset. Section 13.4 evaluates the effects of agglomeration economies and regional knowledge base on firm productivity through firm size. Section 13.5 offers some brief concluding remarks.

13.2 Theory and Selected Empirical Findings

The location of economic activity within the models of the new economic geography is endogenously determined through the interaction between two forces: the "centripetal" forces that attract economic agents to the same location and the "centrifugal" forces that push them apart (Krugman 1998). Externalities, a key concept developed by Marshall, are the most important centripetal force, as they are central to explain why production activities tend to agglomerate in certain regions.[1] The rationale is that, in the process of choosing its spatial location, a firm looks for the proximity of other firms due to the benefits they can get. Glaeser et al. (1992) identifies three sources of externalities:

- Marshall-Arrow-Romer (MAR)—after the three pioneering contributions of Marshall (1890/1961), Arrow (1962), and Romer (1986)—or localization externalities, which are related to intra-industry economies arising from the regional concentration of firms in the same industry (i.e., sectoral specialization). Firms have advantages in being located near others belonging to the same industry because the geographical concentration of an industry can increase the variety of

[1] Krugman (1998) identifies as the main centrifugal forces the immobile factors (e.g., certain land and natural resources), the high land rents and the external diseconomies (such as congestion).

intermediate goods available (at lower prices) as well as the dimension of final goods demand, can attract a large labor force with the skills demanded by that industry and can spread a great specialized knowledge level (namely via informal channels).

- Jacobs or urbanization externalities, which are connected to inter-industry economies arising from the variety of regional economic activities (Jacobs 1969). A sectoral diversity in a given region can stimulate a more diverse client base protecting firms from volatile demand, can create a vast spectrum of locally available inputs easing their switching in case of scarcity or a rise in prices and can disseminate a more assorted knowledge base increasing the possibility of discovering new products or production processes.
- Porter or competition externalities, which are related with competition intensity within a region. Competition stimulates both production and adoption of innovations and, consequently, improves firms' performance (Porter 1990). Porter externalities are similar to MAR externalities, but unlike earlier, it is local competition and not local monopoly that stimulates a faster search and adoption of innovations.

As it is possible to see, the theories that underlie externalities are microeconomic in essence, which means that empirical studies should use firm-level data. Given that until recently data on firms' productivity was generally not available, most of the studies used proxies. Glaeser et al. (1992), for example, using a dataset of 170 USA cities, between 1956 and 1987, find that MAR externalities have a negative impact on employment growth, while Jacobs and Porter economies positively affect it. Glaeser et al. (1992) approach has been replicated by other authors using both employment and wage growth as a dependent variable (see Cingano and Schivardi 2004, for a brief survey). However, the results of these researches are to some extent puzzling. Using 1991 Italian census data, Cingano and Schivardi (2004) show that, taking local employment growth as the dependent variable, the specialization effect is negative and variety effect has a significant and positive impact, in line with Glaeser et al.'s results, while using firm-level-based TFP indicators, the specialization effect is reversed and becomes positive, and neither sectoral variety nor the degree of local competition has any effect. Cingano and Schivardi (2004) question the conclusions of previous empirical works arguing that they suffer from serious "identification problems" when interpreted as evidence of dynamic externalities, since the chain of causality from agglomeration economies to employment growth could be reversed—the use of employment or wages growth at firm-level as dependent variable is based on the (unlikely) assumption that productivity growth will result in proportional employment gains through shifts in labor demand (see, for example, Glaeser et al. 1992; Henderson et al. 1995; Combes 2000).

Therefore, since externalities imply a change in output not fully accounted for by a change in inputs, TFP would be a better measure of performance. Martin et al. (2011) show that French plants from 1996 to 2004 benefit in terms of TFP growth from localization economies, but not from urbanization economies. They do not find any consistent pattern for local competition. An explanation can be that competition incentives firms to invest in R&D, but if the succession of innovations is rapid, the returns from R&D are low, which will reduce the R&D investment and, as a consequence, the innovations. In the case of the USA plants, over the period 1972–1992, Henderson (2003) finds that localization economies only have strong positive effects on TFP in high-tech not in mechanical industries. He also finds little evidence of urbanization economies.

Another interesting strand of economic geography research, favored by the flourishing endogenous growth theories, has pointed out that localized knowledge and technology spillovers matter for innovative activity, which is consequently shaped by space and concentrated in certain areas (see, for example, Scott 1988; Feldman 1994; Acs 2002; Johansson and Lööf 2008; Bronzini and Piselli 2009). In particular, it is argued that proximity to the knowledge base can encourage the circulation of ideas and the transmission of knowledge, thanks to face-to-face contacts and social interaction, which in turn facilitates innovation (Storper and Venables 2004; see Audretsch and Feldman 2005, for a review of theoretical and empirical studies). The knowledge-transfer environment in which a firm is embedded can also play a key role in explaining productivity differential between firms located in different geographic areas (Amesse and Cohendet 2001)—for example, *knowledge intensive business services* (KIBS) are crucial to disseminate knowledge across the region and to support firms' innovative activity (Muller and Zenker 2001).

Looking at the firm size, in general small firms could be expected to be more dependent on the local environment than larger firms (Henderson 2003; Andersson and Lööf 2011). Indeed, they are less able than large firms to internalize innovative inputs and to provide complementary activities that may facilitate innovation (Feldman 1994).

On the whole, despite the fact that the literature on agglomeration economies and regional knowledge base encompass a large body of studies, to our awareness, there has been no empirical research that assesses the role of these two productivity sources together. In fact, if both factors affect productivity and interact with each other and if one these factors is omitted, estimations of elasticity can be biased. Moreover, there is scarce evidence on effect of local environment across firms' size. We will try to fill this gap by assessing the role of both agglomeration economies and regional knowledge base effects in enhancing the TFP by firm size.

13.3 Empirical Methodology

13.3.1 The Dataset

To conduct our empirical analysis, we use an unbalanced panel of Portuguese manufacturing firms covering the period 1996–2004. The raw data is drawn from the combination of two statistical data sources, both run by the Portuguese Statistical Office (INE): *Inquérito às Empresas Harmonizado* (IEH), an annual business survey with information on both the input requirements and the output level; and *Ficheiro de Unidades Estatísticas* (FUE) which contains a variety of firm characteristics (activity, number of employees, age, and location) of all Portuguese firms, critical to compute spatial agglomeration variables. The longitudinal dimension of the panel, required for our analysis, was constructed using firm's unique identification code.

The unit of production considered is thus the firm. Each firm is assigned to a given region (at NUTS3 level, definition of 2002) through a spatial identification code. Thus, the first drawback of the data is that multi-plant firms may affect our results if their different plants are located in different regions. We note, however, that the different plants of corporations are often registered as distinct legal entities, thus the multi-plant phenomena impact on results may be small.

The IEH survey comprises all firms operating in Portugal with more than 100 employees, plus a representative random sample of firms with less than 100 employees.[2] For the purpose of this paper, the following filters were applied: firstly, due to lack of good data, firms with less than 20 employees were eliminated from the estimation sample[3]; secondly, firms located in the island regions (i.e., Madeira and Azores) were excluded; thirdly, given the number of observations, those firms operating in the manufacture of tobacco products (CAE 16) and manufacture of coke, refined petroleum products, and nuclear fuel (CAE 23) were also excluded; finally, firms with missing observations or unreasonable values (negative values and outliers) were dropped from the estimation sample. For each industry, we define as an outlier a firm for which the log difference between an input and the output is in the top and bottom one percentile of the respective distribution. As a result of all these procedures, we have, for the period 1996–2004, an unbalanced panel of 8,074 firms and a total of 32,003 (year-firm) observations.

13.3.2 Empirical Model and Variables

The main purpose of our analysis is thus to shed further light on the extent to which the local environment has an impact on productivity. In the past few years the study of this issue has greatly shifted from aggregated regional level towards the understanding of the operation of micro units (Stephan 2011; Ottaviano 2011). Accordingly, the general model that we use for our empirical analysis is a firm-level Cobb–Douglas production function—we assume that each firm is located in a given region r and operates in a given industry j[4]

$$Y_{it} = A_{it} K_{it}^{\alpha_j} L_{it}^{\beta_j} M_{it}^{\theta_j} \tag{13.1}$$

[2] The sample is representative of the Portuguese sector disaggregation (at three-digit level), both in terms of employment size and sales.

[3] We note that firms with less than 20 employees represent about 71 % of Portuguese manufacturing firms, but only 16 % of total employment (average over the period; source: OECD database).

[4] We omit subscripts j and r to simplify the notation except when it causes ambiguity.

where Y_{it} is the real gross output of the *i*th firm and year *t* (located in region *r* and operating in industry *j*), and K_{it}, L_{it}, and M_{it} are capital, labor, and material (intermediate) inputs, respectively; A_{it} is the TFP. We allow for the coefficients α_j, β_j, and θ_j to vary across industries. Given the regulation of the Portuguese labor market, we cannot assume perfect competition hypothesis, so neither constant returns to scale. The advantage is that, we disentangle TFP changes from production-scale effects, otherwise attributed to TFP.

The *gross output* is given by the sum of total revenues from sales, services rendered, and production subsidies. It is deflated by the producer price index at the three-digit level. The *labor* input is a 12-month employment average. *Materials* include the cost of materials and services purchased and were deflated by the GDP deflator. *Capital stock* is measured as the book value of total net assets (excluding financial investments and cash stock).

We assume that TFP of firm *i* is driven not only by firm's knowledge, but also by both agglomeration economies and regional knowledge base

$$A_{it} = \left(R_{it}\right)^{\gamma}\left(S_{it}^{jr}\right)^{\varphi}\left(Z_{it}^{jr}\right)^{\phi} \tag{13.2}$$

where R_{it} is the firm's knowledge stock in year *t*, S_{it}^{jr} is a vector of covariates that reflects the potential for spatial agglomeration economies of industry *j* in region *r*, and Z_{it}^{jr} is a vector of covariates that proxies regional knowledge base.

We assume as a proxy for firm's stock of knowledge the inverse of firm's size times its age

$$\text{FKNOW}_{it} = \frac{1}{L_{it} \cdot \text{Age}_{it}} \tag{13.3}$$

The rationale is that older and larger firms often command more resources and have higher managerial experience (Jovanovic 1982). The firm's knowledge returns are assumed nonlinear and decreasing. The index (13.3) ranges between close to zero (high level of knowledge), when firm is very large and old, and one (low level of knowledge), if it had only one employee and 1 year old—in our case, since we have imposed a censoring level of 20 employees, the maximum value is 0.05.

As discussed in Sect. 13.2, three kinds of advantages of the proximity for economic agents (agglomeration economies) can be distinguished: localization, urbanization, and competition economies. The localization (or sectoral specialization) economies are measured, for each firm, as the share of other employees working in the same industry (at the two-digit level) within a region (Combes 2000)[5]

$$\text{LOC}_{it}^{jr} = \frac{L_t^{jr} - L_{it}}{L_t^{r} - L_{it}} \tag{13.4}$$

with $L_t^{jr} = \sum_{i \in J^{jr}} L_{it}$ and $L_t^{r} = \sum_{i \in I^{r}} L_{it}$, where J^{jr} and I^r are the set of firms belonging to industry *j* in region *r* and whole region *r*, respectively, in year *t*.

[5] Since we subtract *i*th firm's employment, LOC are firm-specific.

The urbanization (or sectoral diversity) economies are proxied by the inverse of the Herfindahl–Hirschman index of industry concentration based on the employment share of the different industries (at the two-digit level), except the respective industry *j*, in a region (Henderson et al. 1995; Combes 2000)

$$\mathrm{URB}_t^{jr} = \frac{1}{\mathrm{HR}_t^{jr}} \tag{13.5}$$

with $\mathrm{HR}_t^{jr} = \sum_{g \neq j \wedge g \in G^r} \left[L_t^{gr} / \left(L_t^r - L_t^{jr} \right) \right]^2$, where G^r is the set of industries in region *r*. The measure of industrial diversity (13.5) ranges between 1 (minimum value), when all other manufacturing employment in the region is concentrated in a single industry, and $J^r - 1$ (maximum value) if it is uniformly distributed across all (other) industries. As pointed out by Combes (2000), the value of this indicator is not directly linked with the previous one of industrial specialization. In fact, if the regional employment is highly concentrated in a given industry and the several remaining industries have approximately the same size, the values of both indexes (concentration and diversity) for this industry are high.

To measure the degree of competition inside each industry at local level (competition externalities), we use the inverse of the Herfindahl–Hirschman index of regional employment concentration

$$\mathrm{COMP}_t^{jr} = \frac{1}{\mathrm{HJ}_t^{jr}} \tag{13.6}$$

with $\mathrm{HJ}_t^{jr} = \sum_{i \in J^{jr}} \left(L_{it} / L_t^{jr} \right)^2$. The higher is the employment share of firm *i*, therefore lesser uniform distribution of employment across firms, the lower is COMP_t^{jr}. The index also tends to increase with the number of firms.

Taking into account the theories of innovation and technological diffusion outlined in Sect. 13.2, we consider two kinds of factors through which regional innovative environment might impact on firm's productivity: knowledge transfer and knowledge base. Some economic agents such as those that operating in KIBS play a crucial role in disseminating knowledge through the region and supporting firms' innovative activity. We represent the capacity of transfer knowledge as the number of employees working in KIBS sector in the region.[6] In order to capture the effect of knowledge base, we distinguish two sources: regional R&D employment (RD) and the number of higher degree establishments in a region (UNIV)—the role of universities in innovation has been highlighted by various studies, such as Fritsch and Slavtchev (2007) and Cassia et al. (2009).

[6] According to *European Monitoring Centre on Change*, KIBS comprises the following CAE-rev2.1 divisions: (CAE 72) computer and related activities, (CAE 73) research and experimental development, and (CAE 74) other business activities.

13.3.3 Estimation Strategy

We adopt the so-called two-step approach. We firstly estimate the factor elasticity parameters of the following (log) Cobb–Douglas production function for each two-digit industry

$$y_{it} = a + \alpha^j k_{it} + \beta^j l_{it} + \theta^j m_{it} + u_{it} \tag{13.7}$$

where lower-case letters denote the log upper-case variables of Eq. (13.1), to compute firm-level (log) TFP

$$\hat{a}_{it} = y_{it} - \hat{\alpha}^j k_{it} - \hat{\beta}^j l_{it} - \hat{\theta}^j m_{it} \tag{13.8}$$

In the estimation of Eq. (13.1), we control for macroeconomic shocks by including year dummy variables. Additionally, we assume $u_{it}=\omega_{it}+\eta_{it}$, with ω_{it} denoting a firm-specific unobserved component and η_{it} a residual term uncorrelated with input choices. Ordinary least-squares (OLS) estimation of Eq. (13.7) produces inconsistent estimates due to the likely presence of simultaneity and selection bias: the simultaneity bias arises because input demands are also determined by firm's knowledge of its productivity level, which makes ω_{it} correlated with the observed inputs; the selection bias is generated by endogenous exit, as smaller firms, with lower capital intensity, are more likely to exit. Assuming that ω_{it} is time invariant, Eq. (13.7) can be estimated using the least square dummy variable approach or the within transformation.[7] Consistency of the fixed effect model requires, however, strictly exogeneity of the included regressors, a nonrealistic assumption (Griliches and Mairesse 1998). To overcome this problem, we estimate Eq. (13.7) using the generalized method of moments (GMM) methodology for 20 separate industries (at two-digit level). In particular, we employ the Arellano and Bond (1991) one-step difference GMM (GMM-DIF) estimator, which transforms the panel data model in first differences to remove the individual effects and then uses lagged levels of the dependent variable and the predetermined variables as instruments for the endogenous differences.[8]

We then estimate (in the log form) the model (13.2)

$$\begin{aligned} a_{it} = \gamma_0 + \gamma_1 \text{fknow}_{it} + \varphi_1 \text{loc}_{it}^{jr} + \varphi_2 \text{urb}_t^{jr} + \varphi_3 \text{comp}_t^{jr} \\ + \phi_1 \text{kibs}_t^r + \phi_2 \text{univ}_t^r + \phi_3 \text{rd}_t^r + \upsilon_{it} \end{aligned} \tag{13.9}$$

where the residual term is given by $\upsilon_{it}=\mu_i+\varepsilon_{it}$. We cannot disentangle firm and regional fixed effects with this formulation, but that does not affect the estimation. Since all covariates are expressed in logarithms, the estimated coefficients can be interpreted as elasticity parameters.

[7] The random effects model is rejected in favor of the presence of fixed effects by both Hausman and robust Hausman tests at the 1 % significance level (see Wooldrige 2002).

[8] Regressions were performed using the Stata, *xtabond2* procedure (Roodman 2009). The results presented in the paper are robust to fixed-effects (Olley and Pakes 1996; Levinsohn and Petri 2003) and GMM-System methods. These results are available from the authors upon request.

Regarding Eq. (13.9), we note that it is subject to two main sources of endogeneity: unobserved heterogeneity and simultaneity bias. In fact, some regional characteristics (e.g., public infrastructures, local climate, natural resources, etc.) that are not taken into account in this econometric model can affect the propensity to agglomerate, while at the same time agglomeration influences these regional characteristics—in other words, υ_{it} is correlated with the independent variables. Additionally, self-selection of the more productive firms also creates a simultaneity problem. Higher productivity in larger markets (or denser areas) may not be due to agglomeration economies (learning effect); it might instead be due to the fact that high-productivity firms are more likely to be attracted to these advantageous markets (selection effect).[9] In other words, because more productive firms are likely located in larger/denser regions, average firm productivity in these regions should be higher even if there are negligible agglomeration economies, which means that OLS estimates might be biased (Baldwin and Okubo 2006; Melitz and Ottaviano 2008; Andersson and Lööf 2011; Saito and Gopinath 2009). To deal with the endogeneity problem, we estimate the model using again the GMM-DIF procedure. Industry and regional dummies were also included in the estimation.

As discussed in Sect. 13.2, it can be expected that the role of local environment can be different across firms of different sizes. In order to investigate this, we will split the sample into three size classes: firms with 20–100, 100–250, and 251 or more employees (small, medium, and large firms, respectively). The thresholds are those used by the OECD, except for large firms—in Portugal, there are only a few firms with more than 500 employees, the OECD threshold.

13.3.4 Summary Statistics

Tables 13.1 and 13.2 report the summary statistics and the correlations matrix, respectively, of the main variables used in our estimations. Most variables exhibit strong variability, as shown by the large values of standard deviations respective to their mean (Table 13.1). Even if between variations account for a large part of this heterogeneity, within standard-deviation has a nonnegligible role in its explanation. The mean manufacturing firm in the estimation sample has 122 employees and produce 9,812,000€.

The correlation matrix reveals that, as expected, there is a statistically significant (at 5 %) and negative correlation between TFP and FKNOW—recall that lower values of variable mean higher level of knowledge—and a statistically significant and positive correlation between TFP and both spatial agglomeration and regional knowledge covariates, except in the case of URB (Table 13.2). The correlation between the regional knowledge covariates (i.e., KIBS, RD, and UNIV) is rather high, which should cause multicollinearity problems in the regressions. Given that, the two explanatory variables that measures the knowledge input available in the region, RD and UNIV, are replaced by their product (i.e., RKNOW = RD × UNIV).

[9] In the Portuguese case, larger markets and denser areas are highly correlated.

Table 13.1 Descriptive statistics, 1996–2004

		Mean	Std. dev.			Min	Max
Variable	Obs	Overall	Overall	Between	Within	Overall	Overall
(a) Firm-specific							
$Y\,(10^3€)$	32,003	9,812	39,822	29,437	8,382	118	2,076,602
$K\,(10^3€)$	32,003	9,927	35,903	29,689	10,685	28	2,019,021
L	32,003	122	236	185	47	20	7,455
$M\,(10^3€)$	32,003	6,934	32,795	23,938	6,002	11	1,699,340
TFP	32,003	40.9	29.6	29.2	6.8224	7.0	702.8
FKNOW	31,960	0.0015	0.0023	0.0030	0.0009	0.00	0.048
(b) Regional level							
LOC	32,003	0.1428	0.1406	0.1427	0.0213	0.00	0.805
URB	32,003	7.0256	3.0239	3.0009	0.6114	1.23	13.316
COMP	32,003	37.4	46.3	52.0	8.7	1.0	272.5
KIBS	32,003	17,239	35,589	32,548	9,774	24	143,322
RD	32,003	2,166	3381	3,163	688	0	11,991
UNIV	32,003	25.3	32.7	31.4	5.2	0	97

Figure 13.1a displays the distribution of sample firms across the 28 NUTS3 regions. The map shows a high concentration of firms in the North, mainly not only in the regions of Grande Porto, Ave, and Baixo Vouga, but also in the region of Grande Lisboa. Figure 13.1b highlights the spatial distribution of the weighted average of the TFP level. As can be seen, the regions of Minho-Lima, Ave, Cova da Beira, Pinhal Interior Norte, and Pinhal Litoral show the highest values of TFP.[10]

13.4 How Large Are the Local Environment Effects Across Size Classes?

The key results of GMM-DIF estimation of model (13.9) are presented in Table 13.3—the factor elasticity estimates for each industry, used in the second-step to compute firm-level TFP, are in Appendix Table 13.4. The Appendix Table 13.5 summarizes the key coefficient estimates of model (13.9) using ordinary least-squares estimators. Column (1) of Table 13.3 summarizes the main coefficient estimates for the overall sample, while columns (2)–(4) show the results by size classes. The validity of GMM-DIF estimates depends on the absence of second-order serial autocorrelation and on the choice of the appropriate set of instruments. This is indeed the case, since, as expected, the Arellano–Bond AR(1) test shows a negative first-order serial correlation, while the AR(2) test indicates that residuals are seemingly free from second-order serial correlation. Moreover, the null hypothesis of the Hansen test that the overall instruments are valid is not rejected in all four regressions. We note that the Hansen and Sargan tests for over-identifying restrictions show opposite results; however, the Sargan test should be interpreted with care, since the model allows for heteroskedasticity rendering the test baseless.

[10] See NUTS3 regions in Fig. 13.2.

Table 13.2 Correlation across covariates (pooled yearly values), 1996–2004

	Y	*K*	*L*	*M*	TFP	FKNOW	LOC	URB	COMP	KIBS	RD
K	0.83*	1									
L	0.63*	0.57*	1								
M	0.93*	0.79*	0.58*	1							
TFP	0.05*	0.06*	0.09*	0.03*	1						
FKNOW	−0.11*	−0.12*	−0.20*	−0.09*	−0.06*	1					
LOC	−0.04*	−0.04*	0.02*	−0.04*	0.06*	−0.02*	1				
URB	0.09*	0.09*	0.05*	0.08*	−0.01	−0.05*	−0.35*	1			
COMP	−0.05*	−0.06*	−0.00	−0.05*	0.29*	0.00	0.49*	−0.27*	1		
KIBS	0.08*	0.08*	0.05*	0.06*	0.04*	−0.06*	−0.19*	0.53*	−0.05*	1	
RD	0.08*	0.09*	0.05*	0.06*	0.05*	−0.06*	−0.22*	0.62*	−0.05*	0.98*	1
UNIV	0.07*	0.08*	0.05*	0.06*	0.04*	−0.06*	−0.27*	0.71*	−0.06*	0.88*	0.93*

Note: * denotes statistical significance at the 0.05 level

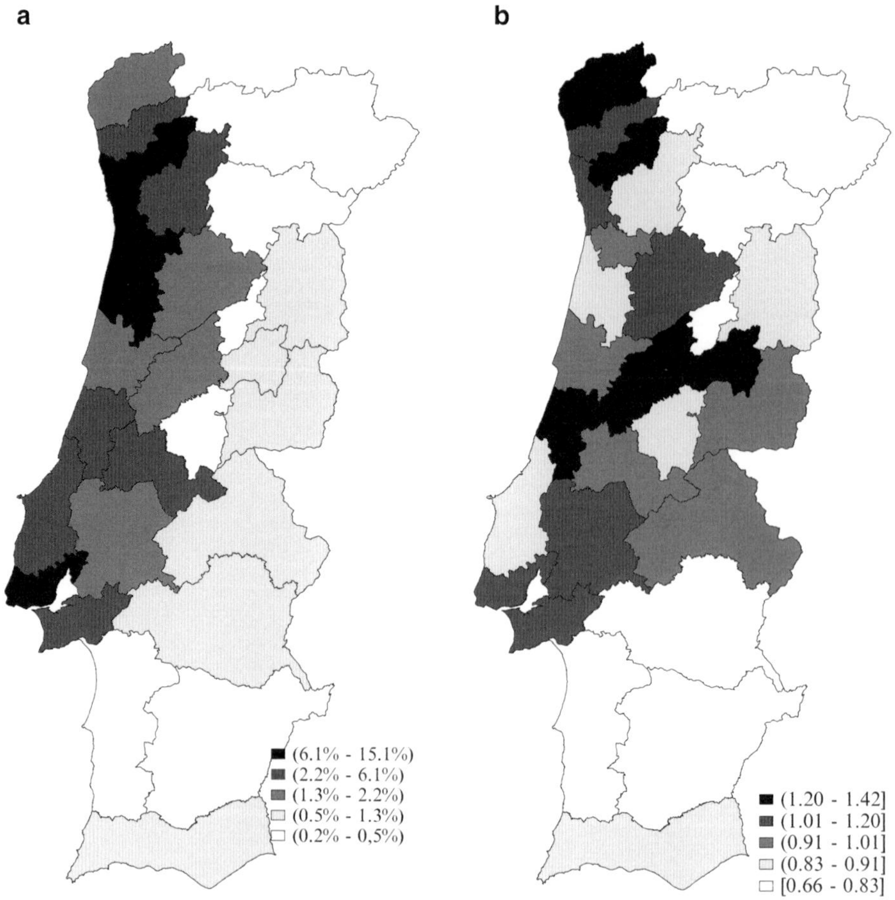

Fig. 13.1 Number of firms and TFP by NUTS3 regions. (**a**) Number of firms (percentage of total). (**b**) Total factor productivity (quintiles)

13.4.1 Overall Sample Analysis

Looking at the estimated parameters in column (1) of Table 13.3, firm's stock of knowledge (FKNOW) has a statistically significant (at 5 %) and virtual impact on firm's productivity—an increase in knowledge implies that the corresponding index reduces, then increasing the productivity—but it is far to explain all productivity gains. Localization (LOC) and urbanization (URB) economies also positively impact (at the 1 % significance level) on the firm's productivity, while no effects of the degree of local competition (COMP) are found at conventional significance levels. In particular, increasing by 1 % the share of other employees working in the same industry region, *ceteris paribus*, increases the TFP of a firm by 0.0068 %. In the case of the employment share of the other industries in the region, the corresponding increment in the TFP is 0.0751 %. These results seem to point out a superiority of sectoral diversity (urbanization) economies.

Table 13.3 Results of GMM-DIF regression

Firm size				
Variable	Overall (1)	Small (2)	Medium (3)	Large (4)
FKNOW	−0.0690** (0.0271)	0.0017 (0.0470)	−0.2943*** (0.0474)	−0.0991*** (0.0352)
LOC	0.0068*** (0.0025)	0.0065* (0.0038)	0.0087** (0.0042)	0.0006 (0.0036)
URB	0.0751*** (0.0191)	0.0773*** (0.0248)	0.0083 (0.0341)	0.0744** (0.0361)
COMP	0.0023 (0.0066)	0.0026 (0.0091)	0.0092 (0.0096)	0.0008 (0.0131)
KIBS	0.0078** (0.0033)	0.0127** (0.0050)	−0.0034 (0.0055)	0.0184*** (0.0064)
RKNOW	0.0241*** (0.0041)	0.0195*** (0.0054)	0.0141** (0.0061)	0.0318*** (0.0111)
No. of observations	11,015	5,368	3,958	2,107
No. of firms	2,922	1,827	1,046	478
No. of instruments	49	42	31	44
i. AR(1) and Prob(z)	−6.33 0.000	−2.52 0.012	−6.53 0.000	−6.02 0.000
ii. AR(2) and Prob(z)	1.95 0.051	1.64 0.101	0.07 0.948	0.73 0.468
iii. Sargan test and Prob(z)	274.89 0.000	81.26 0.000	0.48 0.785	115.97 0.000
iv. Hansen test and Prob(z)	4.93 0.177	0.00 1.000	0.86 0.651	7.02 0.319

Notes: The table summarizes the key coefficient estimates for four different regressions of model (13.9). GMM-DIF denotes the Arellano–Bond one-step difference GMM estimator. All regressions include industry and regional dummies. Variables are in logarithmic form (except in the case of the dummy variables). Robust standard errors are given in parentheses. ***, **, and * denote statistical significance at the 0.01, 0.05, and 0.10 levels, respectively

For its part, regional knowledge also seems to play a key role on firms' TFP gains. In fact, both the number of employees working in KIBS sector-region and regional knowledge base have a positive impact (significance at 5 % and 1 %, respectively) on the productivity—increasing KIBS (RKNOW) by 1 %, all else equal, increases the TFP by 0.0078 (0.0241) %.

13.4.2 Differences Across Firms' Size

We now refine our analysis splitting the sample into three size classes—small, medium, and large firms, respectively, columns (2), (3), and (4) of Table 13.3—, considering that agglomeration economies and regional knowledge might have heterogeneous impact across firms. In related works, Martin et al. (2011) and Henderson (2003) find that small firms benefit more from agglomeration economies than larger ones.

Looking at the estimated parameters of agglomeration variables, our first finding is that small and medium firms benefit from localization economies, while at the same time large firms do not benefit from this sectoral specialization. However, we also find that localization economies are stronger for medium than small firms, contrary to the expected. A second finding is that there is a significant and positive relationship between sectoral diversity and productivity for small and large firms, but stronger for the smaller ones. Finally, the impact of regional knowledge (KIBS and RKNOW) seems to be higher for large firms than small firms. One explanation for this unexpected finding can be that small firms have not accumulated enough knowledge to absorb external (regional) knowledge ("absorptive capacity of firms," after Cohen and Levinthal 1989).

Also surprisingly, while firm's internal knowledge has a significant (at 1 %) expected effect on the productivity level of medium and large firms, it does not seem to impact on the productivity of small firms. A possible explanation for this unexpected finding can be that sample partition created a homogeneous group of (small) firms which have not yet accumulated enough internal knowledge to impact on productivity.

13.5 Conclusion

This study focuses on the extent to which the local environment has an impact on productivity across firms' size, using an unbalanced panel of Portuguese manufacturing firms covering the period 1996–2004. We assume that both agglomeration economies and regional knowledge have a positive impact on firms' TFP. Additionally, smaller firms are more dependent of local environment than larger firms.

Our econometric estimates confirm the conjecture that the agglomeration economies and regional knowledge base seem to be important to explain productivity gains at firm-level. In particular, we found that both localization and urbanization economies have a significant and positive effect on firms' TFP, with the latter playing the most important role. Sectoral specialization economies are important for small and medium firms, but not for large firms. However, larger firms, consequently, those with higher absorptive capacity, profit more from regional knowledge than smaller ones.

Overall, this paper contributes to a better understanding of the economic mechanisms and, consequently, may contribute to the implementation of the adequate regional policies to enhance economic growth. Our findings imply that fostering productivity could require different instruments across firms' size. Regional specialization seems to be a worthwhile policy to promote productivity gains of small firms. To help small firms to benefit from regional knowledge base, policy makers could promote the creation of internal knowledge inside of these firms' type.

Several issues remain in question, which should deserve our attention in the future, namely the unexpected results for the localization economies and firm's internal knowledge within the small firms.

13.6 Appendix

Table 13.4 Production function elasticities by industry

Industry	α	β	θ
Food products and beverages	0.031* (0.017)	0.053* (0.029)	0.759*** (0.031)
Textiles	0.026 (0.024)	0.156*** (0.035)	0.712*** (0.022)
Wearing apparel	0.146*** (0.021)	0.421*** (0.087)	0.457*** (0.023)
Leather and leather products	0.079*** (0.027)	0.202*** (0.055)	0.714*** (0.032)
Wood and wood products	0.011 (0.021)	0.100*** (0.039)	0.720*** (0.023)
Pulp, paper, and paper products	0.099*** (0.035)	0.140* (0.072)	0.676*** (0.046)
Publishing and printing	0.058*** (0.020)	0.143*** (0.048)	0.656*** (0.028)
Chemical and chemical products	0.030 (0.021)	0.124*** (0.029)	0.770*** (0.025)
Rubber products	0.003 (0.057)	0.107 (0.097)	0.636*** (0.064)
Plastics products	0.001 (0.025)	0.103* (0.056)	0.710*** (0.037)
Other nonmetallic mineral products	0.027 (0.022)	0.116*** (0.034)	0.736*** (0.025)
Basic metals	0.023 (0.029)	0.270*** (0.063)	0.731*** (0.029)
Fabricated metal products	0.091** (0.036)	0.216*** (0.036)	0.627*** (0.038)
Machinery and equipment	0.079*** (0.029)	0.300*** (0.053)	0.632*** (0.024)
Electrical and optical equipment	0.068** (0.031)	0.104*** (0.040)	0.742*** (0.028)
Motor vehicles, trailers, and semi-trailers	0.025 (0.027)	0.147*** (0.042)	0.736*** (0.031)
Other transport equipment	0.067 (0.085)	0.220* (0.119)	0.590*** (0.079)
Furniture, manufacturing n.e.c., and recycling	0.124*** (0.038)	0.075** (0.035)	0.698*** (0.029)

Notes: Arellano and Bond (1991) one-step difference GMM estimates of Eq. (13.9). α, β, and θ denote capital, labor, and material elasticities, respectively. All regressions include year dummies. Robust standard errors are given in parentheses. ***, **, and * denote statistical significance at the 0.01, 0.05, and 0.10 levels, respectively

Table 13.5 Results of OLS and FE

Variable	Pooled OLS				FE			
	Overall (1)	Small (2)	Medium (3)	Large (4)	Overall (5)	Small (6)	Medium (7)	Large (8)
FKNOW	–0.019*** (0.002)	–0.006*** (0.002)	0.006 (0.003)	–0.009*** (0.003)	–0.051*** (0.007)	–0.046*** (0.012)	–0.081*** (0.014)	–0.054*** (0.017)
LOC	0.001 (0.001)	0.001 (0.002)	0.000 (0.002)	0.002 (0.002)	0.002 (0.002)	0.006* (0.003)	0.006 (0.005)	–0.003 (0.005)
URB	0.005 (0.008)	0.003 (0.013)	0.018 (0.013)	0.029 (0.023)	0.059*** (0.016)	0.045** (0.023)	0.067** (0.032)	0.057* (0.034)
COMP	0.004 (0.002)	0.007** (0.003)	0.006 (0.004)	–0.015*** (0.005)	0.000 (0.006)	–0.013 (0.008)	0.008 (0.010)	–0.009 (0.01)
KIBS	0.010*** (0.003)	0.011*** (0.004)	0.008** (0.004)	0.016** (0.007)	0.011*** (0.003)	0.007 (0.005)	0.006 (0.005)	0.020*** (0.006)
RKNOW	0.015*** (0.004)	0.010* (0.005)	0.026*** (0.006)	0.029*** (0.010)	0.025*** (0.004)	0.014** (0.006)	0.030*** (0.007)	0.041*** (0.011)
No. of observations	14,882	7,803	4,972	2,107	14,882	7,803	4,972	2,107
R^2	0.950	0.943	0.956	0.962	0.847	0.672	0.480	0.308

Notes: The table summarizes the key coefficient estimates of Eq. (13.9). OLS and FE denote ordinary least-squares and fixed effects (within) estimators. All regressions include industry and regional dummies. Variables are in logarithmic form (except in the case of the dummy variables). Robust standard errors are given in parentheses. ***, **, and * denote statistical significance at the 0.01, 0.05, and 0.10 levels, respectively

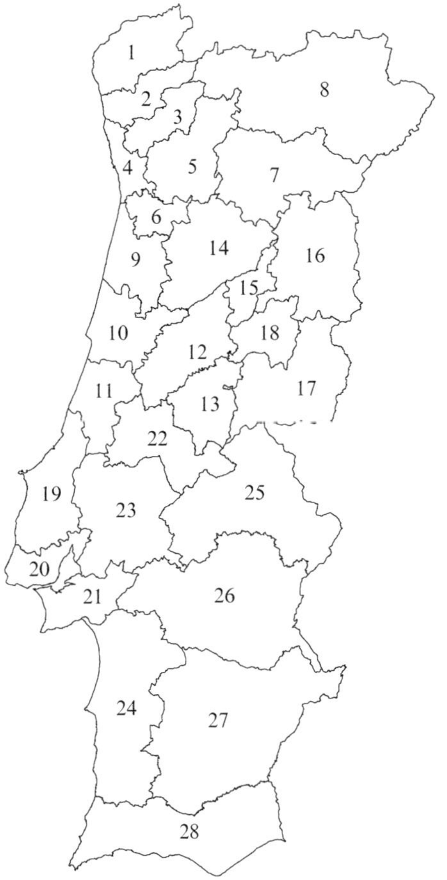

Fig. 13.2 NUTS3 regions of mainland Portugal

References

Acs Z (2002) Innovation and the growth of cities. Edward Elgar, Cheltenham

Amesse F, Cohendet P (2001) Technology transfer revisited from the perspective of the knowledge-based economy. Res Policy 30:1459–1478

Andersson M, Lööf H (2011) Agglomeration and productivity: evidence from firm-level data. Ann Reg Sci 46(3):601–620

Arellano M, Bond S (1991) Some tests of specification for panel data: Monte Carlo evidence and an application to employment equations. Rev Econ Stud 58:277–297

Arrow KJ (1962) The economic implications of learning by doing. Rev Econ Stud 29:155–173

Audretsch DB, Feldman MP (2005) Knowledge spillovers and the geography of innovation. In: Henderson V, Thisse JF (eds) Handbook of urban and regional economics: cities and geography, vol 4. North-Holland, Amsterdam, pp 2713–2739

Baldwin RE, Okubo T (2006) Heterogeneous firms, agglomeration and economic geography: spatial selection and sorting. J Econ Geogr 6:323–346

Bronzini R, Piselli P (2009) Determinants of long-run regional productivity with geographical spillovers: the role of R&D, human capital and public infrastructure. Reg Sci Urban Econ 39:187–199
Cassia L, Colombell A, Paleari S (2009) Firms' growth: does the innovations system matter? Struct Chang Econ Dyn 20(3):211–220
Cingano F, Schivardi F (2004) Identifying the sources of local productivity growth. J Eur Econ Assoc 2(4):720–742
Cohen WM, Levinthal DA (1989) Innovation and learning: the two faces of R&D. Econ J 99(397):569–596
Combes P (2000) Economic structure and local growth: France 1984-1993. J Urban Econ 47: 329–355
Feldman MP (1994) The geography of innovation. Kluwer Academic, Boston
Fritsch M, Slavtchev V (2007) Universities and innovation in space. Ind Innov 14:201–218
Glaeser E, Kallal H, Sheikman J et al (1992) Growth in cities. J Polit Econ 100(6):1126–1152
Griliches Z, Mairesse J (1998) Production functions: the search for identification. In: Strøm S (ed) Econometrics and economic theory in the 20th century: the Ragnar Frisch centennial symposium. Cambridge University Press, Cambridge, pp 169–203
Henderson JV (2003) Marshall's scale economies. J Urban Econ 53:1–28
Henderson JV, Kuncoro A, Turner M (1995) Industrial development of cities. J Polit Econ 103:1067–1090
Jacobs J (1969) The economy of cities. Vintage, New York
Johansson B, Lööf H (2008) Innovation activities explained by firm attributes and location. Econ Innov New Technol 17(6):533–552
Jovanovic B (1982) Selection and the evolution of industry. Econometrica 50(3):649–670
Krugman P (1998) What's new about the new economic geography? Oxf Rev Econ Policy 14(2):7–17
Levinsohn J, Petri A (2003) Estimating production functions using inputs to control for unobservables. Rev Econ Stud 70:317–342
Marshall A (1890/1961) Principles of economics, 9th edn. Macmillan, London
Martin P, Mayer T, Mayneris F (2011) Spatial concentration and plant-level productivity in France. J Urban Econ 69:182–195
Melitz MJ, Ottaviano GIP (2008) Market size, trade, and productivity. Rev Econ Stud 75(1): 295–316
Muller E, Zenker A (2001) Business services as actors of knowledge transformation: the role of KIBS in regional and national innovation systems. Res Policy 30:1501–1516
Olley GS, Pakes A (1996) The dynamics of productivity in the telecommunications equipment industry. Econometrica 64(6):1263–1297
Ottaviano G (2011) 'New' new economic geography: firm heterogeneity and agglomeration economies. J Econ Geogr 11(2):231–240
Porter ME (1990) The competitive advantage of nations. Macmillan, London
Romer PM (1986) Increasing returns and long-run growth. J Polit Econ 94:1002–1037
Roodman D (2009) How to do xtabond2: an introduction to difference and system GMM in Stata. Stata J 9(1):86–136
Saito H, Gopinath M (2009) Plants' self-selection, agglomeration economies and regional productivity in Chile. J Econ Geogr 9:539–558
Scott AJ (1988) New industrial spaces. Pion, London
Stephan A (2011) Locational conditions and firm performance: introduction to the special issue. Ann Reg Sci 46:487–494
Storper M, Venables AJ (2004) Buzz: face-to-face contact and the urban economy. J Econ Geogr 4:351–370
Wooldrige JM (2002) Econometric analysis of cross section and panel data. MIT, Cambridge

Chapter 14
Organizational Heritage and Entrepreneurship: Steven Klepper's Theories Reflected in the Emergence and Growth of the Plastic Molds Industry in Portugal

Carla Costa and Rui Baptista

Abstract This paper reviews the history of the emergence of the molds and plastics industries in Portugal, finding that this history fits nicely with the accounts—originally proposed in Steven Klepper's various works—of new industries emerging from older, related industries, and regional clusters emerging from the mobility of specialized workers from successful incumbents to new firms created in the same regional environment. In addition, it addresses the role played by entrepreneurship, spinoffs, and the transmission of organizational competences from successful incumbents to new firms through the mobility of specialized workers played in the evolution of the two referred industries.

Keywords Agglomeration economies • Organizational heritage • Industry clusters • Molds • Plastics

---

This paper is dedicated to the memory of Steven Klepper, a close friend and a mentor.

C. Costa
School of Business and Economics, Maastricht University,
LN Maastricht, The Netherlands
e-mail: c.dorosariocosta@maastrichtuniversity.nl

R. Baptista (✉)
Brunel Business School, Brunel University London, Kingston Lane Uxbridge, UB8 3pH, UK

CEG-IST, Universidade de Lisboa, Av. Rovisco Pasi 1, Lisbon, 1050-001 Lisboa, Portugal
e-mail: rui.baptista@ist.utl.pt

R. Baptista, J. Leitão (eds.), *Entrepreneurship, Human Capital, and Regional Development*, International Studies in Entrepreneurship 31,
DOI 10.1007/978-3-319-12871-9_14

14.1 Introduction

This paper presents a brief historical account of development of the Portuguese industry of molds for plastic injection, focusing specifically on the role played by entrepreneurship, spinoffs, and the transmission of organizational competences from successful incumbents to new firms through the mobility of specialized workers played in the evolution of the two industries. The account suggests that, at least during the first decades of industrial development, mobility of key personnel from incumbents to new firms locating close to the parent firms played a far greater role than any mechanism associated with agglomeration economies/externalities, in line with the theories proposed by Steven Klepper.

Examples of extreme regional growth like Silicon Valley, where firm competiveness and employment growth in the semiconductor industry was very high in the second half of the twentieth century, motivate interest in clusters as models of successful economic development (Chatterji et al. 2013), potentially replicable elsewhere. Studies of highly concentrated industry clusters (Saxenian 1994; Lécuyer 2006) offer arguments stating that firms accrue benefits from agglomeration. Once firms in an industry begin to congregate in a specific region, such advantages will attract more companies into the region. The evidence compiled about clusters is broadly consistent with the existence of benefits from agglomeration associated with firm growth (Rosenthal and Strange 2004) and innovation (Baptista and Swann 1998).

A more recent line of work focuses on the role played by spinoffs[1] and, more broadly, the transmission of capabilities from parent firms to independent startups. In seminal works, Klepper (2008) and Buenstorf and Klepper (2009, 2010) propose that the offspring of the better firms inherit more capabilities and, therefore, become superior performers. Since new entrepreneurs tend not to venture far from their geographic origins, the best spinoffs locate near the best parents, leading to a buildup of superior firms in a region. Such a process does not strictly require the existence of any advantages associated with agglomeration.

This paper examines the emergence and growth of the Portuguese industry of plastic injection molding. Molds are metal parts used in plastic injection to shape plastic parts that are used as inputs in many industries. Molded plastic products are pervasive in today's economy, being used in industries such as consumer packaged goods, chemicals, electronics, automobiles, communications, drug delivery devices, and packaged food products, to name but a few. Each plastic component of a product requires one mold that is unique, made to order under the specifications of the customer for the resulting plastic part. Nowadays molds apply different materials technologies, optics, and information technologies in a technologically complex product often with tolerances of only a few microns (for precision molds). The mold can then be used to inject plastic resins to yield millions of identical plastic components by the plastics industry (Sopas 2001).

[1] The definition of "spinoffs" follows Klepper (2002), i.e., de novo firms whose founder(s) worked previously in the same industry.

The Portuguese plastic injection molding industry is recognized by the U.S. International Trade Commission as "one of the world's principal producers of precision molds for the plastics industry" (Fravel et al. 2002). Mold-making is strongly agglomerated, mostly in one region—Marinha Grande—located outside the main metropolitan centers of Lisbon and Oporto. Agglomeration occurred historically since the first few firms in the molds industry chose to locate in the same region, in a process similar to that experienced by the US automotive industry in Detroit and the semiconductor industry in Silicon Valley (Klepper 2007, 2010; Kowalski 2012).

14.2 Agglomeration vs. Heritage

Industry agglomeration is recognized as a prevailing characteristic associated with industrial growth, and there have been several attempts to explain it, originating from a variety of fields. Of these theories, the one that has gained most traction over decades of research is the explanation based on the existence of agglomeration economies, or externalities. Three fundamental factors are commonly invoked to explain clustering due to agglomeration economies. First, some regions may have natural advantages for firms in particular industries, causing entrants to cluster there. Second, pecuniary economies related to transportation costs and scale effects, as featured in new economic geography models (Krugman 1991a; Krugman and Venables 1995), may cause entrants to cluster near consumers and suppliers to their industry. Thirdly, and crucially, production, or supply-side externalities, may induce entrants to cluster (Marshall 1890; Porter 1990; Krugman 1991b). Supply-related factors drive companies to locate near their competitors, related industries, and suppliers: pooling of the labor market, supply of specialized inputs, and technological spillovers facilitate access to specialized workers, key inputs, and knowledge relevant for production, organization, and marketing.

Labor pooling agglomeration economies may derive from the reduction of uncertainty for the workers, who could move to a nearby company if demand decreases for their employer (Marshall 1890). Industry agglomeration may also increase the incentives for specialized suppliers to locate in the same region as their customers, and this proximity could bring benefits to the industry in terms of transportation costs (as modeled in Fujita et al. 1999), and knowledge flows (Porter 1990). Finally, technological spillovers are often referred in terms of the close presence of suppliers of ideas such as competitors, firms in related industries, as well as universities and other research institutions.

The extent of agglomeration in any one region is limited by various forces, including transportation costs, more intense price competition among more closely located firms, decreasing returns to scale as some inputs are increased relative to those that are fixed, and congestion costs. This implies that agglomeration economies would benefit the companies located in the region up to the point where congestion costs[2] begin to outweigh those benefits and the agglomerated region's performance declines.

There is a long tradition in regional and urban economics of modeling industry agglomerations as the result of Marshallian externalities. The micro-foundations of these externalities are reviewed in Duranton and Puga (2004) and empirically tested by Henderson (2003) and LaFountain (2005). Beginning with Krugman (1991b), a stream of literature known as the New Economic Geography has emerged to model agglomeration. However, the significance of agglomeration economies is hard to ascertain empirically (Glaeser and Gottlieb 2009).

An alternative, though not mutually exclusive view of the regional clustering of industries emerged from the work by Steven Klepper and coauthors. This view sustains that the clustering of entry is caused by the combination of entrants tending to locate close to their geographic roots and the uneven regional distribution of potential entrants (Klepper 2008, 2010; Buenstorf and Klepper 2009; Carias and Klepper 2010).

According to this view, new entrants need pre-entry organizational knowledge to compete (Phillips 2002; Helfat and Lieberman 2002). An important source of pre-entry capabilities is experience acquired by employees who later decide to leave and create independent spinoffs in the same or a related industry. These employees act as conduits for the industry and firm specific knowledge of incumbents to spill over to new firms, while incumbents inadvertently act as training grounds for new entrepreneurs. Agarwal et al. (1998) and Klepper (2007, 2008) argue that the success of new organizations is fundamentally shaped by knowledge inherited from industry incumbents that was accumulated by their founders throughout their careers. Founding teams serve as conduits for the transmission of incumbent knowledge and routines on to new firms.

Incumbent firms in an industry can be an important source of entrants in the form of employees leaving to found their own firms in the same industry. A large variety of studies have shown that entrants commonly locate close to where their founders previously worked and/or were born. Such studies arise from urban economics (Figueiredo et al. 2002), economics of entrepreneurship (Michelacci and Silva 2007), as well as sociology and management (Dahl and Sorenson 2009, 2012) and propose explanations associated with better access to human (skilled and educated workers), social (local network ties), and physical capital (sources of financing) in the region of origin. This finding has been dubbed "home field advantage" by Figueiredo et al. (2002), as entrepreneurs find it easier to exploit local sources of skilled labor, capital, and key inputs (Carias and Klepper 2010; Dahl and Sorenson 2009, 2012).

Buenstorf and Klepper (2009, 2010) propose a view, called heritage theory, which features the inheritance of organizational competence as the principal force underlying industry clustering. According to this view, clustering of an industry in a region begins with one firm (for instance, Oldsmobile in the case of the automotive industry in Detroit, or Goodrich in the case of the tire industry in Akron) and its

[2] Mills (1967) pointed out that agglomeration leads to diseconomies driven by congestion costs associated with land prices.

initial influence spreading to other regional producers, similar to the conventional agglomeration economics account. However, the subsequent growth of the regional cluster is attributed to an endogenous process in which incumbent firms involuntarily spawn independent spinoffs. As they try to enhance their own performance through technological innovation and improved organizational processes, successful industry incumbents inadvertently function as training grounds for their employees, allowing them to acquire the skills needed to start ventures of their own. This is part of a broader process in which firms differ in their competence. Through employee learning these competences are transferred to spinoffs. Employees become better and acquire more useful knowledge as prospective spinoff founders by working in superior incumbent firms. This increases the likelihood of spinoff formation from these firms as well as the performance of the ensuing spinoffs. Therefore, spinoffs stemming from the best founding or early firm in a region do better than those that do not. Like other new firms, spinoffs mostly locate where they originate, causing the spinoff dynamics to reinforce the existing geographical differences in birth potential for new entrants, both in number and quality.

Steven Klepper's views arguably motivated urban researchers to focus more on the role played by entrepreneurship in the industry agglomeration process. For instance, Glaeser et al. (2010a) proposed a model to test several possible origins for this stylized fact and found empirical support for the work of Chinitz (1961), who claimed that the supply of entrepreneurs differs across space. Glaeser et al. (2010b) argue that in regions with a higher supply of entrepreneurs—because there are more small firms—those entrepreneurs tend to locate their ventures in the same region. Golman and Klepper (2013) explain the role of entrepreneurship in cluster growth by associating it with the market opportunities generated by innovation led by the incumbents. The authors model cluster growth by spinoff formation associated with the discovery of new submarkets through innovation, showing that clustering may result from the self-reinforcing dynamics generated by innovation leading to spinoffs. This process would not require the presence of agglomeration economies.

14.3 The Inception and Early Evolution of the Portuguese Plastic Molds Industry

The Portuguese plastic molds industry is mostly clustered around the Marinha Grande region. This region, far outside the main administrative and industrial centers of Lisbon and Oporto, includes three adjacent *concelhos*[3] (Marinha Grande, Leiria, and Alcobaça). The region has an area totaling 1,160 km^2.

Molds are vital inputs for industries producing consumer goods. When a mold has deficiencies, these are likely to induce delays in the introduction of new products

[3] *Concelho* is the Portuguese administrative division for a region with a city council (i.e., analogous to a US county). Currently there are 278 *concelhos* in continental Portugal, with an average area of 320 km^2.

resulting in significant losses to the molds customer. Given the specificities of such intensely engineered products, they can be quite expensive and take a long time to manufacture—between 10 and 20 weeks, 12 on average (Silva 1996; Sopas 2001). Production requires intense communication with the customer and with possible subcontractors in order to minimize misunderstandings and consequent corrections, thus providing strong incentives for customers to establish long-term relationships with specific molds producers (Sopas 2001).

14.3.1 Prehistory

The early location of the Portuguese plastic molds industry is closely associated with the presence of precursor industries: glass and glass molds. The close relationship between new industries and their technological and market predecessors is a phenomenon well documented by Klepper and Simons (2000), who argue that an important pre-entry factor influencing firms' decisions and their future performance is their proximity to a precursor industry. These authors suggest that firm capabilities are critically shaped by their industrial antecedents. Klepper (2002) notes that early entrants often choose to locate in regions where precursor industries were already located. This was the case, for instance, of early firms in the automotive industry, which evolved from manufacturers of bicycles, engines, carriages, and wagons.

The first record of the presence of a glass factory in Marinha Grande region dates from around 1747 when the Irishman John Beare re-located the glass factory he owned in Coina (close to Lisbon) to Marinha Grande (Gomes 1990). He aimed to locate closer to an abundant supply of the main raw materials involved in glass production: sand and firewood (to fuel the glass furnace). Marinha Grande was indeed not far from the sea and it was located in the center of Leiria's pine forest, a dense forest several hundreds of years old, which belonged to the Portuguese Crown. In addition, the region had good access to transportation by boat and by land, to facilitate the shipping of final products and raw materials (Gomes 1990). However, the glass company faced considerable opposition from the administration of the protected pine forest, displeased by the large and careless consumption of wood, and was eventually closed down.

In 1769, the Portuguese King José I invited an English industrialist, William Stephens, who owned a lime furnace in Lisbon, to restart the glass factory (Barosa 1993). Stephens accepted the king's generous conditions[4] and turned "Real Fábrica de Vidros" (Royal Glass Factory) into a successful glass factory that had a very strong impact in the region. The factory required specialized workers knowledgeable about glassworks and a few were recruited from Italy, England, Ireland, and Belgium. These craftsmen would then teach the Portuguese apprentices their art and

[4] The King granted Stephens free use of the wood from his forest, a large loan without interest and a waiver on the imports tariff for the raw materials and export tariff for the glass products to sell, among other benefits (Barosa 1993).

this process eventually led to the creation of a large specialized workforce in the region (the industry involved mainly artisanal production processes).

William and later his brother John James managed the factory until 1826. By then the presence of this factory had induced the creation of many other small glass and crystal companies in the region, and the buildup of a mass of specialized glass-workers. These workers became symbols of the proletariat and unionism thrived in the region like nowhere else in the country. It was said that Marinha Grande was the home of the glass industry's "aristocratic proletariat" and there are reports of a long-standing tradition of solidarity and complicity among neighbors that was very unusual elsewhere (Henriques et al. 1991).

Even if there were many glass companies in the area, by 1920 there was only one small glass molds producer in Marinha Grande. The "Real Fábrica" ordered molds from abroad—Germany and Austria (Gomes 1998). This dependence from outside regions implied long delivery time and high priced molds. In 1925, one young tool-maker working at "Real Fábrica" since 1923, named Aires Roque, asked the manager's permission to create a molds workshop and, together with a highly skilled lathe operator, António Santos, produced the first die-casting mold for glass in Marinha Grande using chromium and steel (Henriques et al. 1991). While the two men left Marinha Grande to spend time learning while working for companies in other regions (Oliveira de Azeméis and Lisboa), there was never a question of Abrantes and Roque locating their workshop anywhere but in Marinha Grande.

In 1936 the plastics industry emerged in the region, starting the production of *bakelite* lids for perfume bottles at Nobre & Silva, the first plastics company to locate in Marinha Grande[5] (Gomes 1998). The company soon became a client of the molds manufacturers, starting to order a different type of molds for plastic pressing, which at the time used similar mechanical principles to the glass molds (Callapez 2000). Soon, the workshop named after Aires Roque, but eventually managed by his half-brother Aníbal Abrantes, started experimenting with molds for *bakelite* (Beira et al. 2004). Aníbal Abrantes' enthusiastic experiments were probably a way to escape a demand crisis in the glass molds market. Remarkably, these experiments were the origin of a disagreement between the two brothers that took them towards separate paths (Gomes 1990). While Aires Roque stayed with glass molds, Aníbal Abrantes pursued the course of plastic molds.[6]

In 1946 thermoplastics were introduced in the market for the first time, a new class of polymers that turns liquid when heated and freezes to a solid glassy state when cooled. This product could therefore be manufactured using plastic injection techniques (Gomes 1998). That same year, Aníbal Abrantes bought his brother's share in the workshop and started in Marinha Grande the first Portuguese company

---

[5] Nobre & Silva was the second plastics company to operate in the country and the first to locate in Leiria, close to Marinha Grande. The first company to produce plastic products was SIPE—Sociedade Industrial de Produtos Eléctricos had been created in 1935 in Dafundo to produce *bakelite* products for the electric industry.

[6] Klepper and Thompson (2010) propose a model of spinoffs generated by strategic disagreements which fits this event rather well.

(named after himself: A.H.A.) to produce the more resistant steel molds for plastic injection (Gomes 1998). Soon the company gained more clients as more plastics companies emerged nearby in Leiria but also further north (Gomes 1998). Benefiting from the economic expansion that followed the end of WWII the company and the industry prospered.

A.H.A. played a fundamental role in the industry's development as it became a center for worker training and networking. A.H.A. was the place many future entrepreneurs took their first steps in plastic molds manufacture, and where a network of personal contacts among workers was started.

A.H.A. also innovated significantly in the organization of work. While in the rest of the world plastic molds were still produced with artisanal processes, this company introduced division of labor. This permitted worker specialization along the production process (Vieira 2007). Neto (1999) explains that the inexistence of traditional toolmakers in Portugal—who would be locked into traditional ways—when the industry appeared (in the early 1940s) made it easier to innovate by organizing work in new ways.

14.3.2 The Spinoff Process and the Industry's Early Growth

As other molds companies were founded by workers leaving A.H.A., a large number of young workers were trained in specialized areas of mold manufacturing, many of whom later left their employer to start their own companies, often taking some of their colleagues with them after on-the-job learning periods that varied between 4 and 6 years[7] (Beltrão 1985). Hence, A.H.A. paved the way for the spawning of a large number of entrepreneurial small companies. Since plastic molds are highly specialized products developed based on customer specifications, economies of scale were of little relevance for the organization of the industry. Moreover, the specialized nature of the custom-fit products also meant that new firms could emerge without entering into direct competition with incumbents, so there was little scope for non-compete agreements or other competition-reduction practices, which facilitated the proliferation of new startups specialized in different parts of the production process, a pattern we can still find in the industry today (Vieira 2007).

This spinoff process was similar to what occurred at the genesis of the semiconductor, automotive, and tire industries in the USA (Buenstorf and Klepper 2009, 2010; Klepper 2007, 2010). In all these cases, it is possible to trace the origin of the majority of firms to a very small group of parent companies. Similar to the semiconductor and automotive cases, employees, often in small groups, left the early companies where they learned about the technology and the production process and accessed commercial connections that would help them create a new company. The mobility of people became common within the industry, and it became a tradition to

[7]From 4 to 6 years, as mentioned by Pedro F (1985) Enquadramento Histórico da Indústria de Moldes. In: I Congresso da Indústria de Moldes, Marinha Grande, pp 19–24.

preserve an agreeable atmosphere among old and new entrepreneurs. The industry grew from this repeated process of intra-industry spinoffs (Gomes 2005; Sopas 2001).

The movement of these key pioneers is historically reported as the driver of entrepreneurship and competitiveness, as well as of cluster growth in Marinha Grande in the first years of the industry. People who worked together or were trained together established long-term relationships that at some point in time would lead to the creation of new molds companies. Several entrepreneurs became owners of more than one company in the industry (Gomes 2005).

Although at its inception the industry relied on local customers, as early as 1957 the exports to the US market became regular, pioneered by A.H.A. Abrantes arranged a contract with an international agent, Tony Jongenelen, a Dutch with contacts in both European and US plastics producers (many of these were friends that fled to the USA after WWII). The first mold exported was used for the production of a doll sold in 1954 to a company in the UK, Holloway Plastics (Beltrão 1987).

The high quality and low price of the Portuguese molds (Beira et al. 2004) soon allowed the Portuguese companies to start exporting almost all of its production, mostly to the USA. Prospective clients started to visit the region in order to buy molds directly, and to work with the local companies on the development of specialized, custom-fit molds. Gradually, the Portuguese plastic molds industry became an international player (Gomes 2005).

14.3.3 A Second Growth Spurt and the Benefits of Agglomeration

The increased demand for electronics products based in plastics from the IT and automobile industries would lead, from the late 1970s, to a second, much larger, growth spurt, a time when new molds companies would emerge "overnight," often in improvised facilities, working for as much as 18 h a day, 7 days in the week (Henriques et al. 1991). Some companies would get quotations requests just because they were located in Marinha Grande (Sopas 2001). Competitiveness was aided by low wages and the rolling devaluation of Escudo against the Dollar (an IMF-mandated policy aiming to correct Portugal's trade deficit).

During this second growth spurt, spinoffs were championed by workers either from commercial departments (with knowledge about markets and customers) or design departments (working closely with customers to ensure conformity to their needs), and not by skilled operators. This trend drove the industry further into vertical disintegration, with fewer companies involved in all the value-adding activities, and more companies specialized only in parts of the process, such as design, expert production, or marketing (Oliveira 1996).

It is only during this second growth spurt that evidence of agglomeration economies is suggested by this research into the history of the industry. While local spinoffs remained the primary and almost exclusive process generating successful startups, it is clear that location in Marinha Grande facilitated random contacts of customers attracted by the concentration of specialized firms. Industry agglomeration may also have produced a demonstration effect due to the presence of successful companies in the region that could contribute to lowering the perceived entrepreneurial risk and stimulate further entry through imitation (a non-Marshallian agglomeration externality). Entrepreneurs in the molds industry mentioned that their colleagues' success were often an incentive to their decision to pursue their own businesses (Sopas 2001).

Companies reported advantages to locating in Marinha Grande related to the easier access to subcontracts from other producers in the region or from traders inside the region (Sopas 2001). However it can be argued that these advantages are also linked to the fact that the entrepreneurs were previously working in the region and in the same industry so these are not strictly Marshallian agglomeration economies.

14.4 Conclusion

It is easy to observe from this short historical account that the emergence and growth of the Portuguese molds industry closely resembles many of the key theoretical propositions developed by Steven Klepper and his coauthors over time about spinoffs, industry evolution and location. Specifically:

1. The inception of the industry is closely associated with the local presence precursor industries from which it inherited knowledge and competences: glass and glass molds, a relationship found by Klepper and Simons (2000) to predict future industry growth.
2. The birth of the first firm is associated with a spinoff arising from a disagreement between partners about which markets and technology choices to pursue, in the form modeled by Klepper and Thompson (2010).
3. The growth of the industry is dominated by involuntary spinoffs, with incumbents inadvertently serving as training grounds for skilled workers to develop technical and organizational knowledge, as well as social capital, as found by Klepper (2001, 2007, 2008).
4. The geographical clustering of the industry emerged not as a result of natural advantages or Marshallian agglomeration economies, but from the deliberate choice of spinoff founders to locate close to their parent companies, starting with the very first firm locating next to the predecessor industry's incumbents, in the manner postulated by Buenstorf and Klepper (2009, 2010), and Klepper (2008, 2010).
5. Subsequent cluster growth was dominated by spinoffs arising from the detection of new opportunities associated with innovation, commercialization, and design occurring in the absence of agglomeration economies, as predicted by Golman and Klepper (2013).

This paper has attempted to provide evidence of how a specific industry—plastic molds in Portugal—fits a variety of predictions and findings from Steven Klepper's research by providing a short historical account. Steven's contribution to the understanding of industry dynamics and evolution extends far and wide, and has had a fundamental impact in a variety of disciplines, including industrial organization, entrepreneurship, innovation studies, organizational ecology, and evolutionary economics.

For policy makers, Steven's research indicates that the main driver for successful entrepreneurship, as well as cluster emergence and growth, is linked to the spinoff phenomenon, implying that policies looking to seed local entrepreneurship and enhance regional development should look to encourage the establishment of high quality incumbents and facilitate the spinoff process by removing institutional and legal obstacles. Examples of such actions would be policies preventing the enforcement non-compete clauses in labor contracts and promoting an entrepreneurship-supportive environment.

References

Agarwal R, Echambadi R, Franco AM, Sarkar MB (2004) Knowledge transfer through inheritance: spin-out generation, development, and survival. Acad Manag J 47(4):501–522

Baptista R, Peter Swann GM (1998) Do firms in clusters innovate more? Res Policy 27:525–540

Barosa J (1993) *Memórias da Marinha Grande*, 3rd ed. Marinha Grande: Marinha Grande Municipality

Beira E, Crespo C, Gomes N, Menezes J (2004) Dos Moldes À Engenharia Do Produto, a Trajectória De Um Cluster. In: Heitor MH, Brito J, Rollo M (eds) Momentos De Inovação E Engenharia Em Portugal No Século XX. D. Quixote, Lisboa, pp 394–421

Beltrão VH (1985) Enquadramento Histórico da Indústria de Moldes. I Congresso da Indústria de Moldes, Marinha Grande, pp 13–15

Beltrão VH (1987) ...'E Se Mais Mundos Houvera'.... II Congresso da Indústria de Moldes, Marinha Grande, pp 57–61

Buenstorf G, Klepper S (2009) Heritage and agglomeration: the Akron tyre cluster revisited. Econ J 119:705–733

Buenstorf G, Klepper S (2010) Why does entry cluster geographically? Evidence from the US tire industry. J Urban Econ 68:103–114

Callapez ME (2000) Os plásticos em portugal—a origem da industria transformadora. Editorial Estampa, Lisbon

Carias C, Klepper S (2010) Entrepreneurship, the initial labor force, and the location of new firms. Working paper

Chatterji A, Glaeser E, Kerr WR (2013) Clusters of entrepreneurship and innovation. NBER working paper series 19013 (May)

Chinitz B (1961) Contrasts in agglomeration: New York and Pittsburgh. Am Econ Rev 51(2):279–289

Dahl M, Sorenson O (2009) The embedded entrepreneur. Eur Manag Rev 6(3):172–181

Dahl MS, Sorenson O (2012) Home sweet home: entrepreneurs' location choices and the performance of their ventures. Manag Sci 58(6):1059–1071

Duranton G, Puga D (2004) Micro-foundations of urban agglomeration economies. In: Henderson JV, Thisse JF (eds) Handbook of regional and urban economics. Elsevier, Amsterdam, pp 2063–2117

Figueiredo O, Guimarães P, Woodward D (2002) Home-field advantage: location decisions of Portuguese entrepreneurs. J Urban Econ 52(2):341–361

Fravel D, Lenchitz H, Colby-Oizumi H, DeSapio V, Fan Q, Greene W, Sykes A et al (2002) Tools, dies, and industrial molds: competitive conditions in the United States and selected foreign markets. US International Trade Commission, Washington, DC
Fujita M, Krugman P, Venables A (1999) The spatial economy. MIT, Cambridge
Glaeser E, Gottlieb JD (2009) The wealth of cities: agglomeration economies and spatial equilibrium in the United States. J Econ Lit 47(4):983–1028
Glaeser E, Rosenthal SSS, Strange WCC (2010a) Urban economics and entrepreneurship. J Urban Econ 67(1):1–14
Glaeser E, Kerr WR, Ponzetto GAM (2010b) Clusters of entrepreneurship. J Urban Econ 67(1):150–168
Golman R, Klepper S (2013) Spinoffs and clustering. Carnegie Mellon Mimeo (11 April), pp 1–40
Gomes SA (1990). Nótula Documental Sobre as Origens da Indústria Vidreira na Marinha Grande (1747-1768). Rev Port Hist 25:291–299. GEPE—Ministerio da Economia, Lisbon
Gomes JS (1998) Indústria dos Moldes em Portugal: Trajectórias Empresariais de Sucesso. GEPE—Ministério da Economia, Lisbon
Gomes N (2005). A Indústria Portuguesa dos Moldes para Plásticos — História, Património e a sua Musealização. GEPE — Ministério da Economia, Lisbon
Helfat C, Lieberman M (2002) The birth of capabilities: market entry and the importance of prehistory. Ind Corp Change 11:725–760
Henderson J (2003) Marshall's scale economies. J Urban Econ 53(1):1–28
Henriques MC, Silva R, Laranjeira S (1991) Entre os Vidros e os Moldes: Marinha Grande, um Espaço de Industrialização. Sociol Probl Prát 10:197–218
Klepper S (2001) Employee start-ups in high-tech industries. Ind Corp Change 10:639–674
Klepper S (2002) The capabilities of new firms and the evolution of the US automobile industry. Ind Corp Change 11:645–666
Klepper S (2007) Disagreements, spinoffs, and the evolution of Detroit as the capital of the U.S. automobile industry. Manag Sci 53(4):616–631
Klepper S (2008) The geography of organizational knowledge. Mimeo Carnegie Mellon University
Klepper S (2010) The origin and growth of industry clusters: the making of Silicon Valley and Detroit. J Urban Econ 67(1):15–32
Klepper S, Simons K (2000) Dominance by birthright: entry of prior radio producers and competitive ramifications in the U.S. television receiver industry. Strateg Manag J 21:997–1016
Klepper S, Thompson P (2010) Disagreements and intra-industry spinoffs. Int J Ind Organ 28(5):526–538
Kowalski J (2012) Industry location shift through technological change—a study of the US semiconductor industry (1947-1987). Carnegie Mellon University, Pittsburgh
Krugman P (1991a) Increasing returns and economic geography. J Polit Econ 99(3):483–499
Krugman P (1991b) Geography and trade. MIT, Cambridge
Krugman P, Venables A (1995) Globalization and the inequality of nations. Q J Econ 110(4):859–880
LaFountain C (2005) Where do firms locate? Testing competing models of agglomeration. J Urban Econ 58(2):338–366
Lécuyer C (2006) Making Silicon Valley: innovation and the growth of high tech, 1930-1970. MIT, Cambridge
Marshall A (1890) Principles of economics: an introductory volume. Macmillan, London
Michelacci C, Silva O (2007) Why so many local entrepreneurs? Rev Econ Stat 89:615–633
Mills ES (1967) An aggregative model of resource allocation in a metropolitan area. Am Econ Rev 57(2):197–210
Neto H (1999) A Indústria de Moldes. Fortunas & Negócios no. 84, Lisbon, page 76
Oliveira L (1996) Plataformas De Competitividade, Potencialidades E Emprego: Radiografia Aos Sectores Dos Moldes E Do Vidro. In: Estudo Socioeconómico Da Marinha Grande E Área Envolvente: Avaliação De Potencialidades. OEFP, Lisboa, pp 99–121
Phillips D (2002) A genealogical approach to organizational life changes: the parent-progeny transfer among Silicon Valley law firms, 1946-1996. Adm Sci Q 47:474–506

Porter M (1990) The competitive advantage of nations. Macmillan, London
Rosenthal SSS, Strange WCC (2004) Evidence on the nature and sources of agglomeration economies. In: Henderson JV, Thisse JF (eds) Cities and geography, vol 4. Elsevier, New York, pp 2119–2171
Saxenian A (1994) Regional advantage: culture and competition in Silicon Valley and route 128. Harvard University Press, Cambridge
Silva G (1996) Estratégias Genéricas De Porter: O Caso Da Indústria Portuguesa De Moldes. Univerdade de Coimbra, Portugal
Sopas L (2001) 'Born' exporting in regional clusters: preliminary empirical evidence. In: Berry M, McDermott M, Taggart J (eds) Multinationals in a new era. Palgrave, Hampshire
Vieira F (2007) Distritos industriais e inovação: o sector dos moldes em Portugal. Universidade do Minho, Portugal

Chapter 15
High-Growth Firms: What Is the Impact of Region-Specific Characteristics?

Patrícia Bogas and Natália Barbosa

Abstract This chapter analyzes high-growth firms in Portugal and aims at assessing the impact of region-specific characteristics on the probability of the firm being high-growth. Using a sample of active firms registered in the database *Quadros de Pessoal* between 2002 and 2006, the result suggests that high-growth firms is not a random phenomenon and that the region-specific characteristics determine significantly the probability of the firm being high-growth. In particular, industrial diversity, services agglomeration, and diversity of employees' qualifications in a region explain in a significant way the probability of a firm being high-growth.

Keywords High-growth firms • Regional-specific characteristics

15.1 Introduction

High-growth firms have attracted the attention and interest of researchers due to its important contribution to economic growth. This group of firms has higher levels of productivity than average and, according to literature, it also contributes in a disproportionate way to employment growth (BERR 2008). A high-growth firm is not a random phenomenon. Instead, it is linked with a set of factors, behaviors, strategies, and decisions that differentiate those firms to others (Barringer et al. 2005). For this reason, early studies analyze the determinants that have impact on high-growth, as Moreno and Casillas (2007) and Garcia and Puente (2012) to Spain, Falkenhall and Junkka (2009) to Sweden, and Hözl (2011) to Austria. However, these studies focus on firm- and industry-specific characteristics.

Although geographic location might influence firm's performance, little is known about the relationship between region-specific characteristics and the process of firm growth. Audretsch and Dohse (2007) and Barbosa and Eiriz (2011) are two

P. Bogas (✉) • N. Barbosa
University of Minho, Braga, Portugal
e-mail: patriciabogas@hotmail.com; natbar@eeg.uminho.pt

R. Baptista, J. Leitão (eds.), *Entrepreneurship, Human Capital, and Regional Development*, International Studies in Entrepreneurship 31,
DOI 10.1007/978-3-319-12871-9_15

exceptions. They offered evidence that region-specific characteristics have power to explain firm growth. In particular, these studies have concluded that industrial diversity, agglomeration economies, and employees' qualifications in a region explain firm growth.

For this reason, this paper aims at adding on the discussion about the factors that explain the high-growth firms' phenomenon. Particularly, our chief goal is to empirically evaluate if specific-region characteristics where the firm is located shape the probability of a firm being high-growth. To that, we use a sample of all active Portuguese firms registered in the database *Quadros de Pessoal* between 2002 and 2006. This database encompasses information about firms, their employees, and industries. It is also possible to know the firm's geographical location. The results indicate that employees' qualifications, industrial diversity, and services agglomeration in a region explain in a significant way the probability of firms being high-growth.

The remainder of the paper is organized as follows. Section 15.2 discusses the theoretical framework and previous empirical evidence on the relationship between firms' growth and geographical location. Section 15.3 describes the database used in the empirical analysis, presents a discussion on alternative definitions of high-growth firms, and presents some descriptive statistics on high-growth firms in Portugal and its distribution across Portuguese regions. Additionally, the econometric methodology and empirical explanatory variables are presented in Sect. 15.3. Section 15.4 presents and discusses the empirical results, while the main conclusions are summarized at Sect. 15.5.

15.2 The Role of Region-Specific Characteristics on Firm Growth

Internal and external factors have been identified as important factors that explain the differences on firms' growth rate (Dobbs and Hamilton 2007; Hermelo and Vassolo 2007). The impact of high-growth firms on a given economy and the specificity of this type of firms have been fostering some empirical studies.

Some studies focus attention on explanatory factors specific to the firm, as size and age. These variables have been extensively scrutinized to explain the process of firm growth. Through the survey of studies in different countries, industries, and time periods, it is possible to list the following results.

- High-growth firms tend to be young and small, contradicting Gibrat's law. Although the findings on the age's effect are consensual, the results on firms' size are more ambiguous (Henrekson and Johansson 2010; Hözl 2011).
- High-growth firms tend to belong to a business group. The connections between firms offer a set of facilities and allow their growth (Falkenhall and Junkka 2009; O'Regan et al. 2006).

- The firm level of human capital has a positive impact on high-growth (BERR 2008; Falkenhall and Junkka 2009).

The geographical location also seems to influence firm's performance. Location is intensely analyzed as an important factor in firms' formation rate. Nevertheless little is known about the impact of geographical location on firm growth (Acs and Armington 2004; Audretsch and Dohse 2007; Barbosa and Eiriz 2011). Audretsch and Dohse (2007) refer that there is a lack of theories and empirical evidence about the role that locational aspects have in firm growth. At empirical level, lack of detailed data prevents researchers from carrying out this analysis. Nevertheless, Audretsch and Dohse (2007) state that there are some reasons for geographical location have an impact on firm growth. Issues related to agglomeration, knowledge externalities in a location or region, as well as human capital are identified as important locational factors.

Agglomeration economies are a set of positive externalities resulting from spatial concentration of economic activity and consequently knowledge spillovers (Glaeser et al. 1992; Guimarães et al. 2000). According to Glaeser et al. (1992), the literature about the growth of cities differs along two models. The first argues that the transmission of knowledge occurs when there is some interaction between industries in a region. The Marshall-Arrow-Romer model posits that the concentration of firms with the same activity promotes the transmission of knowledge between them (Glaeser et al. 1992). Accordingly, the knowledge spillover is the most important to firm growth. There is no room for knowledge spillover across industries.

In fact, there are some reasons that encourage the location of firms in a cluster (Krugman 1991; Guimarães et al. 2000). The concentration of firms belonging to the same industry in a region allows the contact with a specialized labor market, with specific skills and it will be more likely for the existence of intermediary suppliers in the region as well as natural resources (Krugman 1991; Guimarães et al. 2000). Finally, the diffusion of information allows the firm to get a better production function than individual firms.

Limiting the impact of knowledge diffusion only at inside of the same industry could ignore an important source of knowledge across industries (Glaeser et al. 1992; Feldman and Audretsch 1999). According to Glaeser et al. (1992), the diversity of industries in a region leads to economic growth. Feldman and Audretsch (1999) conclude that the diversity of industries promotes the knowledge spillovers, the innovation in the firm and hence, economic growth. Nevertheless, some interaction across industries should occur in order to facilitate the exchange and creation of new ideas. Guimarães et al. (2000) consider that there are two important externalities related to agglomeration. The first is the size of the industry in the region and the second is the level of services agglomeration. These two externalities would impact significantly on firms' productivity, and would attract more firms to the region.

Empirical studies confirm the importance of diversification in a region (e.g., Glaeser et al. 1992; Figueiredo et al. 2009; Barbosa and Eiriz 2011). Glaeser et al. (1992) find that the diversity, instead of specialization, in the region is the chief driver of growth employment in the industries. Knowledge diffusion inside the same industry is less important to growth than the diffusion among industries. Figueiredo et al. (2009) and Barbosa and Eiriz (2011) found that firms located in regions with more industrial diversity tend to exhibit a higher growth rate. Investment in innovation inside industries tends to be less in regions more concentrated in an industry (Feldman and Audretsch 1999). In a similar vein, Guimarães et al. (2000) conclude that agglomeration is the main driving force for location choice of foreign firms, while Acs et al. (2007) conclude that the local services agglomeration are relevant for firm survival. Nonetheless, Acs et al. (2007) pointed out that that effect only occurs when looking at the number of firms, regardless of their sizes. The number of firms in a region appears to be the driving force of that effect and not the number of employees with experience in these industries.

On the other hand, the local level of human capital has been recognized as an important explanatory factor among theories of economic growth (Acs and Armington 2004). The characteristics and the number of employees, their costs, skills, and their capabilities are important issues scrutinized in the literature (North and Smallbone 1995; Acs and Armington 2004). Acs and Armington (2004) refer that the level of human capital and innovation activity in a region mainly explains differences in firm formation rates, after controlling for demand and business characteristics. These factors at regional level stimulate the creation of new firms in the region and explain high rates of new firm formation.

In particular, higher educational level in a region fosters the formation of specific skills, which are important for start-up activities (Armington and Acs 2002; Acs et al. 2007). Nonetheless, many service firms started with unskilled and lower educational level labor force, which appear to be important for their survival. Jointly these findings suggest that in a region, a diversified educational and skills level of labor force is required for firms' growth and survival.

Empirical studies show that the regional workforce qualifications are positively linked with firm formation rates (e.g., Armington and Acs 2002; Acs and Armington 2004) and firm growth (Audretsch and Dohse 2007). Armington and Acs (2002) find that that relationship occurs mainly in technologically advanced industries. In a study on Japanese manufacturing start-ups in the United States, Woodward (1992) concludes that they are mainly located in regions with more educated and productive employees. Nevertheless, the results show that availability of employees with specific knowledge is not crucial. According to Acs et al. (2007), firms' survival is positively linked with the availability of well-educated employees in the region, but this relationship does not occur during recession periods. Barbosa and Eiriz (2011) analyzed the impact of specialization versus skills diversity in a region on firms' growth. Firms located in regions with a higher diversity of qualifications tend to have a higher growth compared with firms located in regions where there is a great concentration of one type of skills.

15.3 Data, Empirical Variables, and Econometric Model

15.3.1 The Data

The data used in this study comes from the database *Quadros de Pessoal*, provided by the Portuguese Ministry of Employment. This database provides information about employees and firms' characteristics and firm's geographical location. Thus, we can obtain information on the number of employees in a firm, their level of qualifications and educational fields, firm's size, and age, and the geographical location of firm, at municipalities, districts, or NUTS regions. *Quadros de Pessoal* is a compulsory and annual survey of all Portuguese firms, allowing us to collect information about almost all active firms in Portugal.

This paper covers the period from 2002 to 2006, using the firm as unit of analysis. All industries and firms are considered, regardless the legal form or ownership (public or private). Some studies have, nonetheless, excluded some industries, like construction, hotels and restaurants, agriculture and retail trade, on the grounds of high seasonality (Hözl 2011; Garcia and Puente 2012). The geographical unit of analysis chosen was the NUTS III, which is more disaggregated than district but they are bigger than municipalities. These geographical units do not have any administrative organization, but they are important for statistical analysis and allocation of structural funds. They are functional because of aggregate interaction between municipalities, labor mobility and they usually have similar problems and challenges.

15.3.2 On the Identification of High-Growth Firms

There is no unique method to define high-growth firms. Previous studies have applied different methods and measures to define and identify this type of firms. One can find growth measures based on employment growth (Delmar et al. 2003; Oliveira and Fortunato 2006; Bos and Stam 2011; Garcia and Puente 2012), turnover growth (Teruel and Wit 2011), market share, sales or profits (Delmar et al. 2003; Moreno and Casillas 2007; Henrekson and Johansson 2010), and total assets (Serrasqueiro et al. 2010; Barbosa and Eiriz 2011).

The database *Quadros de Pessoal* allows us to identify and analyze high-growth firms in terms of employment or sales. Using sales to compute firm growth requires a measurement at constant prices, as sales are sensible to inflation and currency exchange rates, while employment does not require such correction. On the other hand, according to Henrekson and Johansson (2010), the number of employees has been intensely used as a measure of growth to identify high-growth firms. In particular, the number of employees appears to be a good indicator when the study aims at concluding about the impact of high-growth firms on job creation. According to Coad and Hölzl (2010) employment is useful and more efficient when we consider multi-industries and different countries in our analysis.

Nevertheless, Delmar et al. (2003) have pointed out that the number of employees is affected by labor productivity and by the degree of capital–labor substitution. A firm can grow considerably in assets and production, while the number of employees remaining unchangeable. In a similar vein, Teruel and Wit (2011) argue that employment in comparison with economic and financial indicators does not reflect properly firm's growth. Country-specific labor legislation can affect the number of high-growth firms if one uses employment to identify them. Countries with strong labor protection legislation tend to reduce the number of high-growth firms identified using employment as an indicator of growth.

Apart from the heterogeneity on the choice of growth indicators, the definition of high-growth firms is also not consensual. The OECD definition considers a firm as a high-growth firm if it attains an average growth of 20 % for 3 successive years and employs at least ten workers (OECD 2010). Conversely, Delmar et al. (2003) and Bjuggren et al. (2010) pointed out that the choice between a relative or an absolute measure of growth could be relevant if firms have different sizes. High-growth firms defined using a relative measure tend to be in a smaller number than those based in an absolute measure. To reduce the impact of firm size on identification of a high-growth firm, Birch (1979) suggests an indicator that combines both the relative and absolute growth. This indicator, known as the Birch index, is defined by the difference between the employment in the period t and the employment over a 3 years period:

$$\left(E_{i,t} - E_{i,t-3}\right)\left(\frac{E_{i,t}}{E_{i,t-3}}\right), \tag{15.1}$$

where $E_{i,t}$ is the employment of the firm i, at the time t. According to Garcia and Puente (2012) an indicator should reflect characteristics of the firm as innovation strategies, successful, the management, among others, and not favor any size class. Hözl (2011) emphasizes that it is more important to take into account the relative or absolute growth than to be concerned with the use of specific measures of growth.

Some studies define the 10 % of firms with the highest Birch index as high-growth firms (Schreyer 2000; Falkenhall and Junkka 2009; Garcia and Puente 2012). Nevertheless, Hözl (2011) refer that this imposition in relative terms is not useful when one aims at studying the prevalence of high-growth firms over time. For that reason, Hözl (2011) suggests the modified Birch index, in which high-growth firms should report an annual growth rate of 20 % over 3 years and a size, at the beginning of the 3-years period of 20 employees. Until 20 employees, the index will require a higher relative growth than the OECD criteria and above 20 employees, a lower relative growth is required. Hözl (2011) denotes this type of firms as high impact firms. The modified Birch index can be defined as:

$$\left(E_{i,t} - E_{i,t-3}\right)\left(\frac{E_{i,t}}{E_{i,t-3}}\right) \geq 25.15968, \quad \text{se } E_{i,t-3} \geq 8. \tag{15.2}$$

Based on that index, Hözl (2011) have concluded that overall job creation by high impact firms is higher than overall job creation by high-growth firms based

Table 15.1 Annual distribution of high-growth firms: 2002–2006

Year	High-growth firms	%	Total of firms
2002	2,651	0.92	288,678
2003	2,404	0.82	294,949
2004	2,296	0.76	300,850
2005	2,224	0.68	328,230
2006	2,469	0.75	330,967
Total	12,044	0.78	1,543,674

Source: Quadros de Pessoal. Authors' calculation

on the OECD criteria. Moreover, the persistence of being a high-growth firm is much higher when applying the modified Birch index in comparison with the OECD criteria. These results suggest that high-growth firms identified through the modified Birch index seem to have a more impact on the economy. For that reason we will use this indicator in this study. Table 15.1 presents the percentage of high-growth firms in Portugal (excluding Madeira and Azores islands) from 2002 to 2006.

The results show that the proportion of high-growth firms is quite small when compared with the total number of observed firms. In 2002, the percentage of high-growth firms has the highest value. Since 2003, the number of high-growth firms decreases. This trend continues until 2005, despite the increase in the number of observed firms.

On the other hand, Table 15.2 shows the distribution of high-growth firms across NUTS III regions. The results show that high-growth firms are located in all regions, even though one can observe an asymmetric distribution. The regional distribution shows a large percentage of high-growth firms in the *Grande Lisboa* area. During the sampled period, 33.4 % of the high-growth firms were located there. There is, also, a great concentration of high-growth firms located in *Grande Porto* area, but with a smaller proportion. The regional distribution across other regions is almost irrelevant.

Moreover, the results show that high-growth firms are mainly located in metropolitan areas, which seems to offer several advantages for doing business. This may well explain why the *Península do Setúbal* region, due their proximity with *Grande Lisboa*, has a higher percentage of high-growth firms, in comparison with other regions. In the same way, regions of *Tâmega* and *Ave*, due his proximity with *Grande Porto*, have a higher percentage of high-growth firms. Over time, we can observe a quite homogeneous evolution of the high-growth firms' distribution by NUTS III, suggesting that region-specific characteristics have not substantially changed to engender a significant change on high-growth firms' distribution across regions.

15.3.3 Econometric Model and Empirical Variables

The main objective of this study is to assess the role of regions' characteristics in shaping the probability of a firm being high-growth. Thus, the dependent variable, y_i, with $i=1, \ldots, n$ takes the value 1 if the firm is a high-growth firm, using the

Table 15.2 Regional distribution of high-growth firms

NUT III	2002	2003	2004	2005	2006	Total	%
Minho Lima	37	38	40	38	52	205	1.70
Cávado	86	83	79	79	96	423	3.51
Ave	126	115	121	101	134	597	4.96
Grande Porto	328	277	314	275	297	1,491	12.38
Tâmega	113	110	127	111	138	599	4.97
Entre Douro e Vouga	53	62	57	53	56	281	2.33
Douro	18	22	23	23	20	106	0.88
Alto Trás-os-Montes	23	22	15	20	11	91	0.76
Algarve	129	112	102	102	100	545	4.53
Baixo Vouga	106	75	67	78	88	414	3.44
Baixo Mondego	74	70	58	58	55	315	2.62
Pinhal Litoral	103	86	73	66	66	394	3.27
Pinhal Interior Norte	23	19	20	20	24	106	0.88
Dão Lafões	66	45	47	48	49	255	2.12
Pinhal Interior Sul	4	4	5	4	5	22	0.18
Serra da Estrela	8	5	8	3	5	29	0.24
Beira Interior Norte	20	21	18	14	11	84	0.70
Beira Interior Sul	12	12	7	6	11	48	0.40
Cova da Beira	9	9	15	12	14	59	0.49
Oeste	81	77	63	62	84	367	3.05
Médio Tejo	42	48	39	50	35	214	1.78
Grande Lisboa	885	813	726	758	846	4,028	33.44
Península de Setúbal	159	134	115	120	125	653	5.42
Alentejo Litoral	15	23	25	23	24	110	0.91
Alto Alentejo	12	18	22	17	24	93	0.77
Alentejo Central	35	22	30	21	18	126	1.05
Baixo Alentejo	19	18	16	17	21	91	0.76
Lezíria do Tejo	65	64	64	45	60	298	2.47
Total	2,651	2,404	2,296	2,224	2,469	12,044	100

Source: Quadros de Pessoal. Authors' calculation

definition based on Eq. (15.2), and 0 otherwise. We can see the dependent variable as being the result of latent variable, firm's growth index, $\boldsymbol{y}^*$, that is a function of explanatory variables, $\boldsymbol{x}_{i,t-3}$ and unobservable factors, $\boldsymbol{e}_{i,t}$. In this vein, the probability of high-growth would be given by

$$\boldsymbol{P}(y = \mathbf{1} \mid \boldsymbol{x}) = \boldsymbol{p}(\boldsymbol{y}_{it} * > 25.15968 \mid x) = \boldsymbol{\Phi}(\boldsymbol{x}_{i,t-3}; \boldsymbol{e}_{i,t}). \tag{15.3}$$

and it can be modeled through a probit model. In addition, the panel nature of the data suggests the use of fixed or random effects estimation methods. The choice between them should account for the imposed constraints on the relationship

Table 15.3 Explanatory variables: definition and expected effects

Variable	Operationalization	Expected effect
Service agglomeration	Share of total employment in the tertiary sector, by NUTS III	+
Qualification in the region	Sum of the squares of region qualification share, defined by the number of employees with each qualification with respect to total employment in the region	–
Industrial specialization	Sum of the squares of industry share in the region, defined as the number of employees in an industry and region by the employment in an industry	+
Location quotient	Ratio between the number of firms in an industry and region and the number of firms in the industry, divided by the ratio between the number of employees in the region and the total employment in the country	–

between the explanatory variables and the unobserved effects and the observed variability on the data. Random effects estimation implies that the unobserved effect is not correlated with the explanatory variables in all periods of the time, while fixed effects estimation relax this constraint on the relationship between the explanatory variables and the unobserved effects. However, fixed effects estimation—also called the *within* estimator—captures the effects engendered by the variability on the data within the observed units, while random effects estimation takes into account the overall variability. Comparing those estimators, Wooldridge (2003) refer, nonetheless, that panel estimation by fixed effects is usually a more efficient approach than estimation by random effects. Given that the explanatory variables in this study show greater variation between firms than within firms and over the time, a random effects estimation procedure is applied.

Based on data availability and theoretical and empirical arguments discussed previously, we consider the following explanatory variables, which aim at measuring region-specific characteristics: (1) qualification in the region; (2) service agglomeration; (3) industrial specialization; and (4) location quotient. In order to control for firm-specific characteristics, we added firm size and age as control variables. Table 15.3 describes the way each explanatory and control variable has been operationalized and indicates their expected effect, while Table 15.4 presents some descriptive statistics for each variable. All explanatory and control variables were measured at a 3-year lag.

Overall, all variables show some variability, indicating that Portuguese regions differ with regard to the operationalized specific characteristics. Employees' qualifications have low variability between regions, which suggests that, on average, the distribution of qualifications across regions is quite homogeneous. Nevertheless, the regions differ greatly with respect to the economic activities distribution. Concerning service agglomeration, we found that, the share of employees in the tertiary sector is high. On average, more than a half of employees in a region perform functions in the services sector.

Table 15.4 Descriptive statistics of dependent and explanatory variables

Variable	Observation	Mean	Std. dev.	Minimum	Maximum
High-growth	713,903	0.013	0.113	0	1
Qualification in the region	713,903	0.228	0.026	0.192	0.309
Industrial specialization	713,903	0.004	0.030	0.000	1
Location quotient	713,903	1.995	3.347	0.011	193.374
Service agglomeration	713,903	0.523	0.183	0.192	0.784
Age	713,903	2.124	1.023	0	7.602
Size	713,903	1.493	1.096	0	9.781

Source: Quadros de Pessoal. Authors' calculation

15.4 How Important Are Regional-Specific Characteristics?

In order to assess the effect of regional-specific characteristics on the probability of a firm being a high-growth firm, alternative probit models have been estimated. In all models, industry- (using two digits CAE) and year-dummies, age, and firm size have been included to control for firm- and industry-specific effects and for time-fixed effects. Given the nonlinear nature of the probit models, the coefficient estimates do not measure the substantial impact of a unit-change in an explanatory variable on the probability of the firm being high-growth. For that, marginal effects have to be estimated. Thus, coefficient estimates are present as long as the marginal effect of each explanatory variable.

Table 15.5 present estimates based on cross-sectional analysis, where explanatory variables are taken the value at the beginning of the growth period, while Table 15.6 shows the estimates for panel data with random firm-specific effects. Given the high correlation between services agglomeration and qualification in the region, these variables are alternatively included in the models. In the case of cross-sectional analysis, observations for a given firm are not identical and independently distributed over time, due to unobserved firm-specific characteristics. Therefore, the estimates of standard errors and variance–covariance matrix were corrected in order to account for the correlation of the intra-firm errors.

The results of cross-sectional and panel data show notable similarity in terms of statistical significance and coefficients' signals. Nevertheless, when estimates do not account for that a firm may be repeatedly observed over time—cross-sectional data—the marginal effects suggest a greater impact of the regional-specific characteristics on the probability of a firm being high-growth. This appears to suggest that no account for unobserved firm-specific effects overestimate the impact of the regional-specific characteristics on the probability of a firm being high-growth. For that reason, the discussion of the results is based on panel data estimates.

Overall, holding everything else constant, region-specific characteristics appear to have a substantive impact on the probability of a firm being high-growth. All but one explanatory variable are statistically significant and the signal

Table 15.5 Estimates and marginal effects on the probability of a firm being high-growth in Portugal: cross-sectional data

	Model 1		Model 2	
	Coefficient	Marginal effect	Coefficient	Marginal effect
Industrial specialization	−0.859*** (0.191)	−0.020*** (0.004)	−0.908*** (0.193)	−0.021*** (0.004)
Location quotient	0.002 (0.002)	0.000 (0.000)	0.003 (0.002)	0.000 (0.000)
Qualifications in the region	−1.082*** (0.006)	−0.025*** (0.006)	–	–
Services agglomeration	–	–	0.267*** (0.006)	0.006 (0.009)
Size	0.651*** (0.006)	0.015*** (0.000)	0.649*** (0.006)	0.020*** (0.000)
Age	−0.220*** (0.007)	−0.005*** (0.000)	−0.220*** (0.007)	−0.005*** (0.000)
Temporal dummies	Yes	Yes	Yes	Yes
Sectorial dummies	Yes	Yes	Yes	Yes
Constant	−2.870*** (0.077)		−3.252*** (0.049)	–
Pseudo-$R2$	0.33		0.33	
Number of observations	713,893		713,893	

Notes: Figures in parentheses are clustered standard errors
*, **, *** mean that coefficients are statistically significant at 10 %, 5 %, and 1 % level

of estimates agreed with the expected effect of the specific-region variables. Thus, geographical location seems to play an important role in firms' performance and how the firms grow.

Moreover, the results provide empirical evidence that firms located in regions with a less industry specialization, have a greater probability of being high-growth, holding everything else constant. These results are consistent with previous studies (e.g., Barbosa and Eiriz 2011), and show that firm growth process is significantly related with a greater diversity of industries in the region a firm is located.

Nonetheless, the results seem to cast some doubt on the importance of a firm belonging to an industrial cluster, where they have a set of favorable conditions to grow, like the existence of intermediate suppliers, natural resources, and specialized employees, as suggested by Krugman (1991) and Guimarães et al. (2000). The externalities of knowledge and the relationships that are established between firms from different industries seem to have a positive impact on the probability of being a high-growth firm. According to Feldman and Audretsch (1999), the proximity of complementary economic activities can promote innovation and thus firm growth.

The results also suggest that increasing the share of employment in the tertiary sector increases the probability of being a high-growth firm. There are different measures to analyze agglomeration; nevertheless we only assess the impact of the

Table 15.6 Estimates and marginal effects on the probability of a firm being high-growth in Portugal: panel data

	Model 1		Model 2	
	Coefficient	Marginal effect	Coefficient	Marginal effect
Industrial specialization	−0.648*** (−0.157)	−0.005*** (0.001)	−0.717*** (0.157)	−0.005*** (0.001)
Location quotient	0.003 (0.002)	0.000 (0.000)	0.005** (0.002)	0.000** (0.000)
Qualifications in the region	−1.674*** (0.339)	−0.012*** (0.002)	–	–
Services agglomeration	–	–	0.416*** (0.049)	0.003*** (0.000)
Size	0.840*** (0.008)	0.006*** (0.000)	0.838*** (0.008)	0.006*** (0.000)
Age	−0.287*** (0.008)	−0.002*** (0.000)	−0.288*** (0.008)	−0.002*** (0.000)
Temporal dummies	Yes	Yes	Yes	Yes
Sectorial dummies	Yes	Yes	Yes	Yes
Constant	−3.814*** (0.099)		−4.408*** (0.069)	
Pseudo-$R2$	0.38		0.38	
Number of observations	713,903		713,903	
Number of firms	270,616		270,616	

Notes: *, **, *** mean that coefficients are statistically significant at 10 %, 5 %, and 1 % level

concentration of business services. The relative importance of services agglomeration seems to indicate that the concentration of economic activities has impact on firm growth. At the same time, the results show the importance of complementary economic activities. The proximity of financial services, communication, and other business-related services seem to be important for a high-growth firm.

Looking at workforce qualifications in a region, the estimates suggest that the concentration of one type of skills affect negatively the probability of being a high-growth firm. In a different framework, Barbosa and Eiriz (2011) have attained a similar finding, establishing that a firm located in a region with diversity of qualifications seems to be important to grow. The results allow us to point out the importance not only of the availability at the region of top-educated employees, like some studies have been concluded (e.g., Audretsch and Dohse 2007) but also the mix of them with less-educated employees for firm growth. Thus, the concentration of skills and capabilities linked with high qualifications in a region appear not enough to foster high-growth firms. More interestingly, the diversity of employees' skills and capabilities appears to be the regional-specific characteristics with the greatest impact on the probability of being a high-growth firm, reinforcing the importance of human capital in a region.

15.5 Conclusion

In this chapter, the impact of region-specific characteristics on the probability of a firm being high-growth has been assessed. Using the modified Birch index, proposed by Hözl (2011), to identify Portuguese high-growth firms, the results suggest that firms located in regions that exhibit industrial diversity and services agglomeration have a greater probability of being high-growth. Moreover, the diversity of employees' skills and capabilities in a region explain in a significant way the probability of firms being high-growth. Several empirical studies refer the importance of high qualifications. However, the results show that regions with different types of employees enhance the probability of a firm here located to be of high-growth.

The major contribution of this chapter is to highlight the relevance of region-specific characteristics to engender high-growth firms, adding to the strand of the literature that mainly focuses on firm-specific characteristics and their impact on firm growth. In further research it would be interesting to analyze if the results are robust to the use of different growth measures and definitions to identify high-growth firms. Another interesting and potentially fruitful extension of our research would be to evaluate whether the relevance of region-specific characteristics on the probability of being a high-growth firm changes over time and business cycle. It would contribute to a better understanding of the conditions under which regions may have an important role in the formation of high-growth firms.

References

Acs ZJ, Armington C (2004) The impact of geographic differences in human capital on service firm formation rates. J Urban Econ 56(2):244–278

Acs ZJ, Armington C, Zang T (2007) The determinants of new-firm survival across regional economies: the role of human capital stock and knowledge spillover. Pap Reg Sci 86(3):367–391

Armington C, Acs ZJ (2002) The determinants of regional variation in new firm formation. Reg Stud 36(1):33–45

Audretsch DB, Dohse D (2007) Location: a neglected determinant of firm growth. Rev World Econ 143(1):33–45

Barbosa N, Eiriz V (2011) Regional variation of firm size and growth: the Portuguese case. Growth Change 42(2):125–158

Barringer BR, Jones FF, Neubaum DD (2005) A quantitative content analysis of the characteristics of rapid-growth firms and their founders. J Bus Ventur 20(5):663–687

BERR (2008) High growth firms in the UK: lessons from an analysis of comparative UK performance, BERR economics paper no. 3. Department for Business Enterprise and Regulatory Reform, London

Birch D (1979) The job generation process. MIT program on neighbourhood and regional change, vol 302. MIT, Cambridge

Bjuggren CM, Daunfeldt S, Johansson D (2010) Ownership and high-growth firms. Ratio working paper, no. 147. The Ratio Institute, Stockholm

Bos JWB, Stam E (2011) Gazelles, industry growth and structural change. Working papers, no. 11-02. Utrecht School of Economics, Utrecht

Coad A, Hölzl W (2010) Firm growth: empirical analysis. Papers on economics and evolution, no. 1002. Max Planck Institute of Economics, Germany
Delmar F, Davidsson P, Gartner WB (2003) Arriving at the high-growth firm. J Bus Ventur 18(2):189–216
Dobbs M, Hamilton RT (2007) Small business growth: recent evidence and new directions. Int J Entrepreneurial Behav Res 13(5):296–322
Falkenhall B, Junkka F (2009) High-growth firms in Sweden 1997–2007 characteristics and development patterns. The Swedish Agency for Growth Policy Analysis, Stockholm
Feldman MP, Audretsch DB (1999) Innovation in cities: science-based diversity, specialization and localized competition. Eur Econ Rev 43(2):409–429
Figueiredo O, Guimarães P, Woodward D (2009) Localization economies and establishment size: was Marshall right after all? J Econ Geogr 9(6):853–868
Garcia PL, Puente S (2012) What makes a high-growth firm? A dynamic probit analysis using Spanish firm-level data. Small Bus Econ 39(4):1029–1041
Glaeser E, Kallal M, Shleifer A, Scheinkman J (1992) Growth in cities. J Polit Econ 100(6):1126–1152
Guimarães P, Figueiredo O, Woodward D (2000) Agglomeration and the location of foreign direct investment in Portugal. J Urban Econ 47(1):115–135
Henrekson M, Johansson D (2010) Gazelles as job creators: a survey and interpretation of the evidence. Small Bus Econ 35(2):227–244
Hermelo FD, Vassolo R (2007) The determinants of firm's growth: an empirical examination. Abante 10(1):3–20
Hözl W (2011) Persistence, survival and growth. A closer look at 20 years of high-growth firms in Austria, WIFO working paper, no. 403
Krugman P (1991) Increasing returns and economic geography. J Polit Econ 99(3):483–499
Moreno AM, Casillas JC (2007) High-growth SMEs versus non-high-growth SMEs: a discriminant analysis. Entrep Reg Dev 19(1):69–88
North D, Smallbone D (1995) The employment generation potential of mature SMEs in different geographical environments. Urban Stud 32(9):1517–1534
OECD (2010) Structural and demographic business statistics. Publicação OECD
Oliveira B, Fortunato A (2006) Firm growth and liquidity constraints: a dynamic analysis. Small Bus Econ 27(2–3):139–156
O'Regan N, Ghobadian A, Gallear D (2006) In search of the drivers of high growth in manufacturing SMEs. Technovation 26(1):30–41
Schreyer P (2000) High-growth firms and employment. OECD science, technology and industry working papers, no. 2000/3
Serrasqueiro Z, Nunes PM, Leitão J, Armada M (2010) Are there non-linearities between SME growth and their determinants? A quantile approach. Ind Corp Change 19(4):1071–1108
Teruel M, Wit G (2011) Determinants of high growth firms: why have some countries more high-growth firms than others? EIM working paper, no. H201107
Wooldridge JM (2003) Introductory econometrics: a modern approach. Thomson, Mason
Woodward DP (1992) Locational determinants of Japanese manufacturing start-ups in the United States. South Econ J 58(3):690–708

Chapter 16
Regional Industrial Policy in Norway and Spain

Arnt Fløysand, Stig-Erik Jakobsen, and José Luis Sánchez-Hernández

Abstract This chapter discusses the connection between changing ideas for regional policy formulation in Norway and Spain taking on a "scalar politics" framework. The analysis demonstrates that regional industrial policies are rooted in processes of downscaling in Norway and upscaling in Spain, while rescaling of regional policy away from being primarily a nationally controlled project is a universal concern. Another trend is that the policy instruments have become more homogeneous across communities and regions over the years. Thus, it seems that the Fordism and post-Fordism left more scope for contextual policies than the recent phase of "contextualism".

Keywords Hegemonic ideas • Scalar politics • Regional development • Norway • Spain

16.1 Introduction

In this chapter, we trace the connection between changing "meta-rationales", or hegemonic ideas, for policy formulation and the regional industrial political instruments of national authorities. We begin the discussion by elaborating on industrial development and policy trends in Western countries since 1945. We explore three phases—Fordism, post-Fordism, and a current phase we have termed "contextualism"—and we identify their hegemonic ideas for industrial policy formulation. Viewed in

A. Fløysand (✉)
Department of Geography, University of Bergen, Fosswinckelsgt 6, 5007 Bergen, Norway
e-mail: Arnt.Floysand@geog.uib.no

S.-E. Jakobsen
Bergen University College, PO Box 7030, 5020 Bergen, Norway
e-mail: sjak@hib.no

J.L. Sánchez-Hernández
Department of Geography, Universidad de Salamanca, Calle Cervantes 3, 37002 Salamanca, Spain
e-mail: jlsh@usal.es

R. Baptista, J. Leitão (eds.), *Entrepreneurship, Human Capital, and Regional Development*, International Studies in Entrepreneurship 31,
DOI 10.1007/978-3-319-12871-9_16

combination, the phases reveal how hegemonic ideas and national policy strategies have moved from a basis in nomothetic principles and standardized policy formulas to one of idiographic principles and design of regional development policies that is currently becoming more sensitive to context.

We are particularly interested in the scalar politics of this shift, the ways in which it links to the broader production of regional industrial policy and the effects of its national–regional development over time and space. To explore this, we introduce new literature on the political economy of scale. The benefit of this is that it enables analyses that account for the structure of various dimensions of political phenomena, and the embedding of political practice in spatialities and geographical framings at the same time. We concur with MacKinnon's approach to scale, which can be understood as an "open" political economy approach informed by a critical realist position that sees scales as "real" material entities that are known and understood through particular political representations and discourses (Mackinnon 2011). An "open" approach provides us with an inclusive concept of scale, which views scales as historically created, and highly interrelated social dimensions that frame institutional scope, political practices, and mental constructs.

The next step in the chapter is to present findings on the scale and scope of former and present regional industrial policies in the real world. We do this by focusing on the main characteristics of regional industrial politics in Norway and Spain in the period since 1945. In this empirical part of the chapter, our concern is the correspondence of these politics with hegemonic ideas and related policy instruments, and the degree to which the concept of scalar politics can explain our observations. These findings demonstrate that the regional industrial policy of Norway leaves the hegemonic growth pole paradigm of Fordism generally undisturbed, while Spain has rapidly adapted to a growth pole strategy after the failure of its import substitution policy. The ideas of post-Fordism, in terms of flexible specialization and restructuring, fit rather well in both cases. However, in the contemporary contextualist phase, we find that both countries have recently emphasized development from below and the use of context-sensitive instruments, but that this is to a certain degree standardized from above through buzzwords and success stories.

Accordingly, we believe there are reasons to argue that the hegemonic ideas of Fordism and post-Fordism have left enormous scope for national influence on regional industrial policies in terms of focus and policy instruments, while the recent phase of "contextualism" tends to reduce national control over regional policy affairs. This phase represents a more direct connection between hegemonic ideas on a macro scale and policy implementation at the regional level.

The chapter develops these arguments as follows. Section 16.2 discusses the close interdependence between economic phases, hegemonic ideas and regional policies, and the concept of scalar politics outlined in this introduction. Section 16.3 describes the relation of the main characteristics of the regional industrial politics in Norway and Spain in the period since 1945 to hegemonic ideas and the related policy instruments. Section 16.4 applies the concept of scalar politics to a discussion of lessons from the case studies and suggests future avenues of research.

16.2 Hegemonic Ideas on Industry Development and Scalar Politics

16.2.1 Hegemonic Ideas and Regional Industrial Policies in Western Countries Since 1945

Hegemonic ideas are "meta-rationales" about the role of the state and its propensity and capacity for policy action (Laranja et al. 2008). These hegemonic ideas are manifested in dominant modes of policy regulation in the pursuit of particular goals. The capitalist mode of production in the period 1945–1975 has been termed *Fordism*. It has been characterized as a model stressing economic expansion and technological progress based on mass production through manufacturing of standardized products in huge volumes by operating special-purpose assembly lines. The leading sectors to be inspired were basic and heavy industries. The main policy instruments to kick off this form of industrialization were the market guided by national industry in developing regulatory strategies for industrial *growth poles* and increased capital and labor mobility to create comparative advantage and increased international trade. In a more moderate form, Fordism was closely related to the form and function of the *Keynesian welfare state* that was developed in many Western countries during the post-war period (Amin 1992). A Keynesian regulation regime implies a proactive state that tries to balance supply and demand to reduce the fluctuations and cyclical swings of competitive markets. The Keynesian welfare state also plays a key role in facilitating economic growth through its investment in infrastructure and stimulation of capacity development and mass production to ensure full employment (Jessop 1992).

The second phase, ranging approximately from 1980 to 2000, is often described as *post-Fordism*. It was linked to policies inspired by Schumpeterian thinking, which emphasizes *flexible specialization* of former industries (Amin 1992; Morgan 1997). Post-Fordism is about promoting organizational and market innovation in an open economy, with a focus on supply-side intervention to address the problems associated with a lack of economic growth. Changes in the international economy, such as the oil shocks of 1973 and 1979 and increased competition from foreign markets, made the old system of mass production uncompetitive in Western countries. Thus, post-Fordism has been accommodated with a new mode of regulation. Jessop (1992) has described this new policy regime as the *Schumpeterian workfare state*, which is more suited in form and function to an emerging post-Fordism. The top-down approach of the Keynesian welfare state is challenged by a broader perspective of development from below that includes development of various territorial resources (Pike et al. 2006). One important policy instrument has been *restructuring programmes* that should guide firms from mass production to flexible specialization. Industrial policies in this phase thus emphasize strengthening the capabilities of firms and developing their skills, knowledge, and networking abilities. Furthermore, there is an emerging tendency towards a shift from government to governance, where the latter involves vertical co-operation between tiers of government and horizontal co-operation between public and private entities (Jessop 1997). Thus, the dominant role of the strong national state in regional policy formulation and implementation is diminished in relative terms (Pike et al. 2006).

Over the past decade or so, a new and perhaps rather indistinct phase has been emerging. We have chosen the term *contextualism* as a label for this phase because theory, management, and policy become much more sensitive to the contribution of unique capabilities and local resources, whether tangible or intangible, to the competitiveness of firms and milieus in a globalizing economy (Breschi 2011). Contexts thus gain credibility as frameworks for understanding economic life and for promoting *innovation programmes*. Proponents of contextualism further developed neo-Schumpeterian ideas about *endogenous development*. The difference between this and earlier versions of Schumpeterianism is a focus on regions as the main geographical level and a very strong emphasis on regional differences (or what we can describe as a *neo-Schumpeterian region*). Cooke (1985) has long argued for the importance of understanding regional characteristics and complexities in economic policy, while Tödtling and Trippl (2005) underline that a one-size-fits-all policy does not work in a world of diverse regions. In fact, several recently published voluminous handbooks have elaborated on new theories and concepts that allegedly explain regional industrial (under)development (Boschma and Martin 2010; Cooke et al. 2011). This development is also addressed in a new OECD report on regional policy (OECD 2010), which observes an ongoing shift towards a new paradigm for regional policy characterized by an emphasis on endogenous local assets, place-based approaches, proactive strategies and the involvement of different levels of government, and a variety of stakeholders in the organization of the initiatives (i.e., governance). In line with this, Lagendijk (2011) argues for a shift in regional development policy from an initial emphasis on regional implementation of national politics (that is, the fine-tuning and adaptation of programmes and instruments developed at the national level) to a greater focus on policies designed at and oriented to the regional and local levels. The idea of "smart specialization," recently introduced as the main strategy for regional development within the European Union, is also linked to context sensitivity, regional capabilities, and utilization of specific regional advantages (McCann and Ortega-Argilès 2011). In summary, suggesting contextualism as a label for this rather indistinct phase stresses the importance of externalities, knowledge, learning, networking, clustering, and diversification. Such an approach has contributed to a certain adjustment or contextualization in the politics of regional development.

The three phases will guide us in the presentation of the regional industrial politics of Norway and Spain in the period since 1945. What we can already note is that geography in terms of territory (regional industrial policy, growth poles, state, and regions) has a significant position in these matters. Thus, before we enter the empirical investigation we turn to recent debates within political geography about scale and scalar politics. The scale dimension is highly relevant to our discussion of hegemonic ideas on macro scale, national policy formulation, and regional policy implementation.

16.2.2 Scalar Politics

Throughout the long-standing debate on how to understand and conceptualize scale, the concept has been subject to different interpretations (Herod 2011). A central issue within the literature has been the "rescaling" of political influence from the national scale to other scales such as global, regional, and local (Haarstad and Fløysand 2007; Brenner 2009; Underthun et al. 2011). A related issue discussed under the heading of rescaling is how the political production of scale is linked to the broader production of economic regions (Mackinnon 2011). In the latter settings, a political-economic perspective on scale and scalar production has dominated the geography literature. This perspective stresses the relational production of scales through capital accumulation, the "spatial fixes" of capital and socio-spatial struggle (Harvey 1989; Brenner 1999; Brenner 2001; Swyngedouw 1997). The emphasis on the "spatial fixes" of capital, which implies a relatively material conception of scale, has been subject to post-structural critiques that have stressed the fluidity and impermanence of scales as social constructs (Mackinnon 2011). These post-structural critiques have attempted to show that scales are not ontologically given, discrete objects, but constructed relationally through political action. At the same time, such political actions are always under the influence of path-dependent structures of dominant scale constructions. MacKinnon attempts to find a compromise between the various positions, arguing that:

> Rather than distinguishing between a post structural concern with the fluidity of scale and the alleged political-economic emphasis on fixity, it seems more productive to suggest that each highlights different dimensions of the construction of scale, emphasizing material and discursive processes, respectively. (Mackinnon 2011, p. 26)

The advantage of such a political-economic approach is its sensitivity to the historical construction and transformation of scale through discursive processes, and a view to the ways in which scales are recreated through political practice (Brenner 2001; Mansfield 2005; Mackinnon 2011). A remaining question is how such material and discursive dynamism of scalar politics can be captured in empirical research. MacKinnon introduces the concept of "scalar politics", or four related key elements, to cope with this coexistence of discursive and material elements in the real world. In brief, a scalar political approach "replaces the implication that the politics of scale are fundamentally about scale with the idea that particular political projects and initiatives have scalar aspects and repercussions" (Mackinnon 2011, p. 29). Second, it advocates that we "focus attention on the strategic deployment of scale by various actors, organizations and movements" (Mackinnon 2011, p. 29). Third, a scalar political approach should underline "the influence and effects of pre-existing scalar structures, created by past processes of social construction" (Mackinnon 2011, p. 30). Finally, it should stress "the closely related question of the creation of new scalar arrangements and configurations, occurring at the point of interaction between inherited and emergent projects and scales" (Mackinnon 2011, p. 31).

What seems clear from the discussion above is that "scalar politics" are about both discursive processes underlying a particular political project and material structures of scale in terms of former, present, and future scalar repercussions of political action. In the following, we reflect upon such scalar aspects linked to the relations between hegemonic ideas (discourse) and regional policies (political projects). We do this by focusing upon the regulation of industrial activities in Norway and Spain since World War II. Just after World War II, such economic regulation regimes were formed in the domain of the national state, and as such were primarily on a national scale. This preexisting scalar structure does not mean that localized or globalized processes were insignificant, or that processes on a national scale can be seen as isolated from the local or the global. From the very beginning, national strategies have been formed by global ideas of local origin, and as it will be demonstrated, these strategies have created new projects challenging the inherited national state project. However, the local context is also of vital importance. Despite exposure to similar hegemonic ideas, regional policies in the two countries have been quite dissimilar.

16.3 Regional Industrial Policies in Norway and Spain

16.3.1 Introduction

In this section, we present findings on the scale and scope of former and present regional policies in Norway and Spain. The processes we are concerned with are how the hegemonic ideas (discourse) and the regional policies (material outcomes) described above have been applied in the national regional policies of the two countries. The purpose of this is to illustrate how the theory of scalar politics applies to the evolution of regional policy in Norway and Spain and to tease out certain aspects that to some extent explain the differences and similarities between the countries. The main reason for selecting Norway and Spain for comparison is their rather peripheral position in a discourse of hegemonic ideas taking place in the leading world economies and institutions. Moreover, both economies are resource dependent and internationally oriented. Seafood, hydropower-fuelled metallurgic and forest industry products and, since the 1970s, oil and gas are the most important goods exported from Norway, while Spain has extensively relied on food (e.g., wine, olive oil, fish) and sun and beach tourism for foreign visitors as income sources.

The sources on which we rely are the academic literature and key documents related to the regional industrial policies in the two countries. In the case of Norway, this concerns writings and analysis of regional policy trends and more specific analyses of programmes such as the restructuring programmes, cluster programmes, and the RIS programmes (for instance Reginn, Mobi, and VRI). In Spain, the setting for the discussion is the Development Plans (*Planes de Desarrollo*) of the 1960s, the Industrial Restructuring Programme (*Política de Reconversión Industrial*) of the 1980s and the implementation of European Regional Policy after the accession in 1986, namely the LEADER and URBAN programmes, focused on rural and urban areas, respectively.

16.3.2 Norway: From Welfare State Building to Innovation Programmes

16.3.2.1 Fordism and a Strong Rural Periphery (1945–1970s)

In Norway, the hegemonic ideas and policy instruments linked to the Fordist phase were interpreted in a very particular way. First, the regional policy became one of many instruments intended to support the building of the Norwegian welfare state and a mode of regulation that involved state engagement in managing conflicts between capital and labor. Second, it was closely linked to the Keynesian idea of state involvement in terms of a countercyclical policy to ensure growth in periods of economic recession. Third, and most important for the particularity of the Norwegian regional industrial policy at the time, the state was seen as the distributor of welfare to underdeveloped regions (Cruickshank et al. 2009).

To consider the latter argument first, during the 1960s and early 1970s there was an ongoing debate on the importance of stabilizing the settlement pattern and ensuring consistent economic growth in all parts of the country. A broad political consensus that rural areas should be included in the development of welfare state services and support was established as a basic principle of regional policy (Cruickshank et al. 2009). It is indisputable that the development of this demographic consensus and the regional relocation of jobs in the public sector have been extremely important for the regional industrial policy. The political aim was to avoid depopulation of peripheral settlements and municipalities. Consequently, there was a state-driven industrialization of the periphery combined with incentives to ensure private investment in these areas. Several large export industry firms were established in rural areas during the 1950s, 1960s, and 1970s. Some of these were state owned, while others were based on private investment (Grønlund 1994). Efficient utilization of natural resources was vital for national economic growth, and many of these plants were located close to mineral or water resources (hydropower) in rural Norway, forming "one-company towns" in rural areas. Thus, even if the Fordist phase forced the authorities in Norway to provide infrastructure suitable for industrial growth, no Norwegian version of the growth pole strategy inspired by the work of Perroux and his "pole de croissance" ever developed. A "minor" version was tested during the mid-1960s, but proved unsuccessful (Hansen 1987). Instead of stimulating urban concentration through growth poles, the regional industrial policy became strongly influenced by a national policy that argued for the status quo in terms of the urban–rural settlement pattern.

In addition, the dominant development path in Norway was not the Fordist mode of capital-intensive, large-scale industrial production. Instead, this was complementary to the main form of production, which was small-scale industrial production characterized by local ownership and low capital intensity (Wicken 2009). Many of these small industrial plants were directly and indirectly linked to exploitation of natural resources. In this respect, it was important that fishermen and farmers were given influence and legitimacy in policy. This ensures a fair overall regional distribution of the economic development (Arbo 2004; Cruickshank et al. 2009).

The success of Norwegian regional policy during the Fordist phase was grounded partly in the nature of the post-war boom and a general economic upswing. The real test of the regime came with the collapse of the post-war boom, the oil-price shock of the early 1970s and an emerging crisis of the Fordist mass-production regime (Therborn 1986). Growing pressure from newly industrialized countries in low-cost areas and the internationalization of national economies may explain the crisis that made some of the Keynesian forms of state intervention less efficient. As a small, open economy, Norway certainly was exposed to these megatrends in the global capitalist system. However, it can be argued that the regional redistribution practices of the Keynesian era could be maintained for a longer period in Norway than in most other European countries because of the profits from North Sea oil that began to fuel the Norwegian economy in the late 1970s (Grønlund 1994). The Norwegian variant of the Keynesian welfare state model was "a strong corporate state" emphasizing both national economic growth and regional redistribution of resources (Aarset and Jakobsen 2009).

Nevertheless, many of the industrial plants in the rural areas encountered problems in the late 1970s and early 1980s because of increased international competition. Some one-company towns were also in a negative "lock-in" situation (Dale 2002). They were highly specialized local firms, unable to handle the new technological and organizational challenges of faster-paced capitalism characterized by increased fluctuations (Martin and Sunley 2006; Hassink 2010).

16.3.2.2 Post-Fordism and Restructuring Programmes of One-Company Towns (1980s–1990s)

The "restructuring instrument" was established by the Norwegian government in 1983 in direct response to the challenges facing the one-company towns established in the Fordist phase (NOU 1983). The goals of the instrument were to promote new jobs, diversify local industry, and add value in trade and industry. The instrument was intended to stimulate industrial and commercial development and strengthen the local economic and social foundation of this development. Originally, the national authorities (Ministry of Local Government and Regional Development) decided which areas should be granted "restructuring status" and a "restructuring programme". During the first part of the 1980s, the organization and strategies of the restructuring programmes were still Keynesian in nature. A strong state provided the local communities with comprehensive funds to reorganize their local industry to make it better adapted to meet the challenges of markets in the future. Gradually, there was a shift in the profile of this instrument towards neo-Schumpeterian ideas on restructuring.

Obviously, regional industrial politics inspired by flexible specialization and the Schumpeterian welfare state in the post-Fordist phase have their own distinct flavour in various countries; there is no single dominant form. In the regional industrial policy of Norway in this period, there was an intensified focus on local resources and endogenous growth (Bukve et al. 1995). In other words, "the new localism" of

Norway was given a form of "a national strategy for regional development based on enhanced regional and local control and responsibility" (Grønlund 1994, p. 161). Demographic changes that influenced regional policy also took place. Immigration into the larger cities increased and the ambitions of preserving settlement patterns were softened. New ideas about developing robust regions and lifting the settlement goal from municipalities to regions accompanied the development of a more coherent regional policy strategy during the 1990s (Cruickshank et al. 2009). This new strategy included ways both to develop rural areas and to stimulate further growth in urban and central areas.

During the end of the post-Fordist phase, there was an emergence of innovation policy as a new policy area in Norway, despite the fact that the policy area is significantly older (Remøe 2005). Innovation policy as an explicit area had long been anchored in a type of technology-push policy. Such linear models strongly influenced the formulation of innovation policy in the early 1980s, despite growing recognition that innovation was the result of a dynamic interplay between separate, interacting factors and actors (Jakobsen and Onsager 2008). The link between innovation policy and regional policy during this period largely concerned the communication of relevant research from research institutions to small and medium-sized enterprises in rural areas. The 1990s also witnessed the establishment of regional research institutions and competence centers "to create contact and support between SMEs and national R&D institutions, in addition to providing various common services to regional firms" (Asheim and Isaksen 1997, p. 320). The spread of R&D from the national milieu to firms in other regions is an important instrument for regional growth, but there was also a need for an alternative approach. Nonetheless, it was not until well into the 1990s that an approach grounded in an understanding that innovation is an interactive process began to take shape. Informed by these neo-Schumpeterian ideas, Asheim and Isaksen argued in their 1997 paper for a differentiated Norwegian regional innovation policy that met the specific challenges of various regions.

Practices for regional restructuring in the late 1990s were clearly consistent with neo-Schumpeterian policies. The focus of the restructuring programme in this period was on stimulating endogenous growth by mobilizing local resources (Jakobsen and Høvig 2014). There was a strong focus both on entrepreneurship (start-ups) and on innovation in existing firms. Furthermore, establishing networks between actors with complementary resources was a critical factor. Innovation, entrepreneurship, and networking had all become the new buzzwords of regional policy in Norway in the post-Fordist phase, legitimizing various supply-side initiatives to facilitate restructuring, innovation, and growth (Jakobsen 2004).

16.3.2.3 Contextualism and Innovation Programmes (2000–)

The increased emphasis on networking and regional capabilities in the final phase of post-Fordism resulted in the introduction of several programmes to foster innovation. The Arena programme, introduced in 2002, was the first Norwegian cluster programme to strengthen the development of regional clusters. The need for a tailor-made policy addressing the specific challenges, problems, and opportunities in each region is at the core of the cluster idea. Within the Norwegian Arena programme, there is a clear intention that each regional project must address the specific challenges and possibilities that have been identified for the selected regional cluster. In 2006, a second Norwegian cluster programme was introduced. While the Arena programme places particular weight on emerging clusters, the Norwegian Centre of Expertise (NCE) is a programme for mature and internationally oriented clusters. The Arena programme can stimulate regional cluster development for up to five years in each project, while the NCE programme is directed towards financial support for a period of 10 years.

Another important initiative in the regional policy of the last decade is the development of regional innovation systems (RIS). The VRI (Programme for Regional R&D and innovation), introduced in 2007, has been a key instrument in attempts to realize this ambition. The VRI programme is a Research Council of Norway initiative, targeting research and innovation at the regional level in Norway through cooperation between R&D institutions and regional firms. Thus, the VRI programme can be interpreted as a national initiative to facilitate the development of innovation systems at the regional level. An RIS is made up of two subsystems embedded in a common regional socio-economic and cultural setting. The first subsystem is the knowledge application and exploitation subsystem (firms, etc.), while the second subsystem is the knowledge generation and diffusion subsystem (including R&D institutions and other knowledge providers) (Tödtling and Trippl 2005). Lack of interaction between firms and R&D institutions has been identified as the main failure of the Norwegian system (Jakobsen and Onsager 2008). The importance of the regional level is partly based on the observation that knowledge spillovers, which are essential in processes of interactive innovation, tend to be spatially bounded and decrease with distance. It is also a fact that regions differ with respect to industrial specialization, institutional architecture, and patterns of innovation (Tödtling and Trippl 2005). Innovation activity is thus a territorial phenomenon.

Despite being introduced as a new initiative towards research and innovation at the regional level, the VRI also represented the continuation of working methods, networks, and structures of the three previous innovation programmes: VS2010, Competence Brokering and ICC. VS2010 was established in 2001, and was part of a tradition of Norwegian development programmes for firms based on involvement of employees and their representatives in processes of change ("the Nordic Model"). Originally, such programmes included only intra- and intercompany processes. However, gradually there was increasing involvement of researchers, and VS2010 also emphasized building broader regional partnerships, including "helpers" in the public sector and R&D institutions (Arnold et al. 2005). VS2010 merged into VRI and brought ideas from the Nordic model and action research into the more regionalized and system-oriented new Competence Brokering programme, introduced in 2004. The double aim was originally to promote R&D in small and medium-sized businesses with little or no experience in R&D and to strengthen research institutes as partners for innovation in private businesses. ICC was introduced in 2003, and had the objective of equipping university colleges to serve regional businesses. Both programmes were merged into VRI in 2007.

One important effect of the VRI programme is that regional authorities have strengthened their position in regional policy formulation. The VRI provided an arena for county administrations to take an active leadership role in regional R&D, and they have seized the opportunity. County administrations are using the VRI to learn about challenges, solutions, and organizational models for facilitating regional innovation. The requirements that initiatives are to be partly financed regionally and that priority areas and activities should reflect regional political priorities have further strengthened counties' positions (Jakobsen et al. 2012). In 2003, county municipalities in Norway had already been granted greater authority to manage regional policy tools through "the responsibility reform," and the VRI fits well with the ambitions of this reform.

The "Triple Helix Model", with R&D institutions in an enhanced role in innovation processes (Etzkowitz and Leydesdorff 2000), has been integrated into some of the clusters and RIS initiatives. However, it never reached the stage of involving triple helix systems and regional independence per se, as witnessed in Spain, for example.

16.3.3 Spain: From Growth Poles to Neo-Schumpeterian Regions

16.3.3.1 Fordism and Growth Poles (1959–1970s)

In the first phase of Fordism, Franco's regime was isolated by the international community and its government deployed a national self-sufficiency economic policy (autarky) based on the rigid supervision of external trade and currency exchanges, along with the substitution of foreign imports by national production. Nevertheless, this economic model led the country close to bankruptcy by the end of the 1950s, and was thus replaced by a new industrial policy similar to those of other Western European capitalist countries in the early 1960s. It relied on increasingly open trade with the rest of the world. Such a radical shift was also because of the steady integration of Franco's regime into the wider international community after the signature of a bilateral co-operation agreement with the United States in 1953 and the subsequent accession to the United Nations Organization in 1955.

The *Plan de Estabilización* of 1959 (Stabilization Plan) is the starting point for this new period in Spanish economic policy. Rapid economic growth, the development of a strong tourism sector, an increase of foreign industrial investment, a massive exodus of rural populations to growing industrial cities and regions and the outmigration of many Spaniards to Western European countries (such as France, Germany, Belgium, and Switzerland) are the most prominent features of this period, which lasted until Franco's death in 1975. From the geographical perspective, this process of huge social and economic modernization deepened previous imbalances between the more industrialized regions (Madrid, Catalonia, Basque Country, Asturias, Cantabria, and Valencia) and those more dependent on agriculture, tourism, and public administration, mostly located in central and southern Spain and in the two archipelagos (Nadal and Carreras 1990).

Regional policy conceived, designed, and put into practice by the Spanish government to cope with this unbalanced process of regional development closely followed Fordist principles along with the tools currently used in France. In brief, each of the three *Planes de Desarrollo Económico y Social* (Social and Economic Development Plans, 1964–1967, 1968–1971, and 1972–1975) enacted in Spain during this period, usually labelled "desarrollismo" (developmentalism) in Spanish economic literature, included the instruments termed *Polo de Desarrollo* (Development Pole) and *Polo de Promoción Industrial* (Industrial Promotion Pole). These instruments of regional policy were granted to cities (such as Vigo, La Coruña, Oviedo, Burgos, Valladolid, Logroño, Zaragoza, Sevilla, and Huelva) that previously hosted an industrial base perceived as strong enough to catalyze a cumulative process of growth and diversification with new large factories that were expected to generate a multiplier effect in the local and regional economies. Tax reduction, lower interest rates, and public co-funding were the most common incentives granted to new companies located in these growth poles, along with huge investments in transport infrastructure to attract industrial facilities.

The design and management of Development Poles was highly centralized and scrutinized by the Spanish government (Presidencia del Gobierno 1963), so their operation was made homogeneous all over the country to promote industrial development in less favored regions or in areas close to the main industrial cores and thus avoid agglomeration diseconomies. This is the case for the Development Poles granted to small cities highly accessible by road or railway from Madrid (Aranda de Duero, Guadalajara, Toledo, Manzanares, and Alcázar de San Juan), which were included in this strategy to avoid industrial overconcentration in Madrid and, simultaneously, to strive for a more balanced industrial location pattern in the underpopulated regions surrounding the capital city.

Moreover, the goal of more balanced regional development was founded on industrial growth as the most important driving force, in line with the overarching ideas about economic growth in Western countries. Specifically, it is easy to trace the strong influence of French economists like François Perroux and Jacques Boudeville. Their concept of growth poles was widely used in France as a framework for a regional policy highly concerned with the risk of over-agglomeration in the Île-de-France, which was addressed by the allocation of large industrial factories to cities like Bordeaux, Grenoble, Toulouse, Nantes, or Lille.

Development Poles are the best known and most researched tools for regional development in Spain before it turned to democracy. However, additional instruments were operated during this second phase of Franco's dictatorship. First, industrial parks were built by the government in those small and medium-sized cities that were not granted Development Pole status: these hard infrastructure projects had the same goal of fostering industrial location as a highway for economic growth and job creation outside the most dynamic Spanish regions. Second, in transport policy there was substantial investment to build a tight network of roads, motorways, and railways to achieve three complementary goals: connecting the domestic market, increasing the accessibility of industrial regions, and opening faster linkages with European markets.

For many years, Development Poles have been assessed in a rather critical or skeptical way that emphasizes their limitations in terms of capital investment, job creation, or firm growth during their period of operation or immediately thereafter (Lorca et al. 1981). Nonetheless, a longer-term perspective that accounts for the contribution of those cities to the industrial wealth of Spain during the 1990s and 2000s imposes a full revision of those standpoints. Most of the former Development Poles have become important industrial centers that control large regions that, without such an instrument, would never have taken part in the rapid industrialization process that was experienced by the Spanish economy during this period.

16.3.3.2 Post-Fordism and Industrial Restructuring (1980s–1990s)

In 1970, Spain was the tenth largest industrial producer in the world. However, the oil shock in 1973 strongly affected the Spanish economy, which lost 21 % of its industrial employment between 1978 and 1984 (Segura 1989). Not surprisingly, the industrial crash mostly affected Spanish provinces with greater specialization in iron, steel, coal mining, forging, shipbuilding, textiles, footwear, electrical appliances, and other electrical equipment. Its geographical implications are now well known. Factory closures, rising unemployment, urban deprivation, and a loss of attractiveness to new investors, entrepreneurs, and companies are all factors that fell under the category of *industrial decline* in contemporary academic literature and public policies, both in Europe and in the United States (Bluestone and Harrison 1982).

The geography of industrial decline in Spain encompasses three types of territories severely affected by the crisis (Pascual 1993): regions in the northern coast (Asturias, Cantabria, and the Basque Country), metropolitan peripheries in Madrid and Barcelona, and an array of one-company towns highly dependent on corporate decisions or highly specialized in heavy industries (Cádiz, Sagunto, Vigo, and Ferrol). These cities and regions were granted specific restructuring instruments, the *Zonas Industriales en Declive* (Declining Industrial Areas) and the *Zonas de Urgente Reindustrialización* (Areas for Urgent Reindustrialization).

The new Spanish democratic governments dealt with this decline, suddenly serious after 1977, in a much more complex manner than that employed under the typical previous Fordist recipe for industrial growth, that is, tax reduction and infrastructure provision. First, and in accordance with the conceptual framework of post-Fordism in Table 16.1, the core objective of economic growth was replaced by a new main focus on industrial restructuring to make companies and factories more competitive against new producers from emerging Asian countries such as Korea, Singapore, and Taiwan. With this new focus, public financial resources were mostly spent on the reduction of productive capacity to match the shrinking demand, the technological updating of older factories, and the merging and acquisition process

Table 16.1 Hegemonic ideas, industrial policy instruments, and scalar repercussions in Norway and Spain under Fordism, post-Fordism, and contextualism

Period	Hegemonic ideas	Industrial policy instruments	Scalar repercussions
Fordism (1945–1980)	Growth	Growth poles (Spain)	Concentration
		Keynesian welfare state (Norway)	Decentralization
Post-Fordism (1980–2000)	Flexible specialization	Restructuring programmes (Spain and Norway)	Revitalization of cities and metropolitan regions
		Schumpeterian workfare state (Norway)	Revitalization of rural towns
Contextualism (2000–)	Endogenous development	Innovation programmes (Spain and Norway)	Commodification of place
		Neo-Schumpeterian region (Spain)	Regionalization

designed to build economically competitive and financially strong industrial corporations (Navarro 1989, 1990).

Second, an ambitious reindustrialization programme was developed for those areas deeply affected by the restructuring process described above, which resulted in serious redundancy problems and many factory closures. This reindustrialization was supposed to diversify the local/regional industrial base, linked to mature sectors, through the location of new companies operating either in modern, emerging and technology-intensive industries or in advanced producer services, the latter usually being weak in most prominent Spanish industrial regions and areas (Méndez and Caravaca 1993).

Third, additional funding was allocated to address the effects of redundancy on the worst-hit local communities. Workers laid off from factories under restructuring, which used to pay higher wages and hire a very large staff, were allowed to retire if they were old enough. Younger workers were included in the so-called *Fondos de Promoción de Empleo* (Job Promotion Funds) to receive additional training, improve their competences and skills, and have priority to be appointed to new jobs created by the new companies established during the reindustrialization process.

Fourth, technological modernization and innovation lie at the core of the whole restructuring and reindustrialization process. In addition to the previous instruments, the first technological parks in Spain date back to the late 1980s and were located in the regions most affected by the industrial crisis and the subsequent restructuring policies (Ondátegui 2008). These new industrial spaces strictly follow the international design standards influenced by Silicon Valley and other innovative districts, which contrast strongly with those of the old declining industrial brownfields. These technological parks are intended to have an impact on the development of alternative economic bases for these regions and cities, and to be much more strongly connected to the most dynamic sectors of the third industrial revolution:

electronics, computers, new materials, telecommunications, aeronautics, and later biotechnology. Technology is thus acknowledged to have a key role in regional industrial growth (a sort of technology-driven or technology-push strategy for regional development). This explains another substantial novelty of Spanish regional industrial policy from the 1980s onwards: the design, funding, and operation of the first National Research and Development Frameworks (Sanz 1997), and the increase in the budgets of universities and public research institutions to build a triple helix model (university, public sector, and private sector) of regional development.

Finally, another set of changes in the governance model of this policy of restructuring, reindustrialization, and technological innovation should be mentioned. The Spanish government assumed responsibility for the design and funding of the restructuring plans and Urgent Reindustrialization Areas, in this respect following the centralized tradition of economic and territorial planning inherited from the Franco dictatorship and the French Jacobin model that inspired the Development Poles during the Fordist phase. However, between 1980 and 1990, Spain departed from the centralized tradition and established the *Estado de las Autonomías* (Autonomous Communities), a very decentralized model in which autonomous regions were granted the authority to manage economic policy, spatial planning, and vocational training.

This shift has great implications for the realm of governance. Regional governments have taken an increasingly active leadership role in the whole process of reindustrialization, and especially in the promotion of technological innovation, technology parks, vocational training programmes, and urban/territorial planning related to the reuse of derelict industrial brownfields and the construction of new spaces for economic activities. This involvement of regional authorities in the instruments applied within their territories must be underlined as a first but clear step towards a more contextualized mode of regional policy implementation, closer to the currently prevailing framework explained in the next subsection. Indeed, regional governments have steadily included local factors in the formulation of the objectives and instruments of these reindustrialization policies; for instance, they have given priority to activities related to local human and natural resources, or activities more likely to take advantage of the region's geographical position and economic tradition.

Moreover, Spain's accession to the European Common Market in 1986 provided national authorities with an additional opportunity to benefit from European industrial restructuring programmes (RESIDER, RECHAR, and RETEX). In recent years, these programmes have funded a number of technological interventions in those regions heavily dependent on those industries and a wide array of vocational training programmes for unemployed and disadvantaged groups because of resources supplied by the European Social Fund (YOUTH, NOW, HORIZON).

The latter two circumstances (political decentralization and membership of the European Union) are critical to understanding the overall transformations of Spanish regional policy during what we have termed the contextualist phase, discussed in the next subsection. In any case, a short assessment of this second phase confronts the same discrepancy between short-term analyses, which are used to find significant shortcomings in the outcomes of all these tools for restructuring and reindustrialization, and more nuanced overviews that, from a wider temporal perspective, emphasize that the areas benefiting most from these policies now represent major industrial centers in Spain (Nadal 2003).

16.3.3.3 Contextualism and Neo-Schumpeterian Regions

As suggested above, the institutional framework for the design, funding, and operation of regional policy in Spain has been thoroughly modified since the late 1980s, consistent with the emerging contemporary contextualist phase. First, regional policy in Spain must meet the general rules of the European Union regarding competition and free markets, and the particular rules of the various programmes and initiatives launched by the European Commission. This dependence on European guidelines operates on three geographical and political scales. On a national scale, the main decisions and projects regarding territorial planning, transport, and communication infrastructure provision (highways, high-speed trains and optic fiber networks), and knowledge creation, dissemination, and transference to the private sector (research and development frameworks, higher education, and scientific research bodies), mostly rely on support from Structural Funds or the Cohesion Fund (with their different names since 1986), allocated after bargaining between Spain and the European Commission. Regional governments have also drawn on European resources to fund a large proportion of their programmes for transport infrastructure, technological innovation, rural development, vocational training, and urban renewal. Moreover, local authorities—either in rural areas or in larger municipalities—have relied on the budget of well-known European programmes such as LEADER (1991–2006) or URBAN (1994–2006) to fund a bewildering number of interventions focused on rural development and urban regeneration, respectively.

Second, administrative and political decentralization has progressed a long way in Spain during the past two decades. The very concept of local development policies supported by the European Union is based on the engagement or involvement of local actors in goal design, the choice of the governance schemes, and the most efficient strategies to meet the shared objectives (Esparcia Pérez and Escribano Pizarro 2012). Terms such as competitiveness, innovation, entrepreneurship, knowledge, sustainability, co-operation, and endogenous development must inform the whole process and practices of every programme, plan, and project launched under the European Commission's financial umbrella. Such a bottom–up approach has been sympathetically adopted by local and regional authorities in Spain, usually eager to capitalize on any conceptual, ideological (and financial) endorsement of their policy of defining particular and differentiated development models and pathways for their localities and territories (Plaza and Velasco 2001). In other words, the guidelines passed by the European authorities are thus quickly adapted to particular contexts defined by the cultural, environmental, geographic, social, and economic features of each and every rural and urban area in Spain.

From a geographical perspective, LEADER and URBAN are accurate case studies of regional policy in Spain because they are designed to meet the demands of the two principal forms of human settlement: cities and rural areas. Furthermore, from the perspective of the argument in this article, their conception, design, and practices represent the current contextualist phase of regional policy in Western countries. LEADER's goal is the promotion of endogenous economic development in rural areas located in Europe's less favored regions. Regeneration of deprived small cities or metropolitan neighbourhoods affected by the industrial decline and the subsequent loss in terms of quality of life is the main goal of URBAN. Both programmes aim to foster innovative, competitive, inclusive, and sustainable economic activities capable of strengthening each target territory's ability to build a self-sustainable and independent path of economic development that no longer depends on public money transfers at the conclusion of the programme. This core idea is consistent with neo-Schumpeterian discourses, usually critical of state intervention on the demand side and more confident in each territory's responsibility for its own social and economic future.

Nevertheless, URBAN's and LEADER's notion of innovation is far more complex than the linear model that prevailed in the post-Fordist phase. Innovation is actually conceptualized as a permanent task or attitude on the part of authorities, society, and economic actors. This socio-economic innovation is not a straightforward process that begins in basic research, moves on to applied research, and finally becomes embodied in new and marketable products and processes. On the contrary, socio-economic innovation is interactive and involves a wide network of actors on different geographical scales (local, regional, national, and often international) and in different societal realms (cultural, political, economic, and technological). Regional innovation systems are supported by regional and national governments, the private sector being far less involved in Spain, and provide consultants and partners for local or foreign investment projects, whatever the size, in any sector of the economy (Buesa 2012).

This stands in sharp contrast to the former regional industrial policy of Fordism and post-Fordism. Instead of focusing on industry as the main engine of regional development, contemporary policies embodied in LEADER and URBAN set the sectorial focus aside and give preference to a horizontal and territorialized strategy, more connected with the mobilization of local/regional material and non-material resources. Industrial location programmes are now included in more context-sensitive strategies intended to create favorable conditions for entrepreneurship and firm location in every economic sector. Accordingly, the scope of tools has been stretched to include training programmes for employees and the unemployed, with a specific focus on entrepreneurship, financial resources at low interest rates, provision of digital infrastructure, and public consultancy bodies and local development agencies that advise local companies in their efforts to innovate or internationalize their markets. In addition to this focus on the local socio-economy, territorial marketing campaigns are launched to attract foreign investors and to broadcast an appealing image of the city/rural area.

The particular outcomes of these complex policies in each territory are thus not as easily predictable as in the Fordist phase (more industry) or under post-Fordism (more modern industry), but rather contingent on local resources, opportunities, and constraints. Moulaert and Nussbaumer (2005) have criticized this change in the field of regional policy, arguing that it simply attempts to adjust territorial "org-ware" to the demands of global capitalism and its accumulation goals at the local level, instead of improving social and economic conditions in cities and rural settlements.

Local actors' networks (Local Action Groups, Local Development Agencies) in charge of promoting and managing URBAN and LEADER programmes are a clear demonstration of the wide diffusion of influential academic ideas about public–private partnerships and inclusive governance so often repeated in specialized publications and conferences and in official reports about territorial planning. Those steering networks need prior support from regional and national governments to apply for EU funding, another trait of the contextualist phase, whereby a trans-scalar approach (from the local to the international level) is imperative in the design of a collective project for any given territory granted LEADER or URBAN resources.

As for the two previous phases, it is rather difficult to present a balanced assessment of these contextualized regional policies that LEADER and URBAN adequately represent in Spain. Both have obviously contributed to a thorough renovation of infrastructure and public services in urban spaces and to positive economic diversification in rural areas. Notwithstanding this, their success in the development of a sustainable, innovative, competitive, and solid productive system has been seriously challenged by the profound impact of the current economic downturn that has exposed the shortcomings of the Spanish economic model after 25 years of EU membership and generous funding. Of course, this preliminary conclusion needs a more detailed and careful analysis that, for instance, accounts for the differences between urban areas, more affected by high unemployment, and rural areas, whose diversified economy and weaker connection with the housing bubble have lessened, to some extent, the impacts of the Great Recession.

16.4 The Scalar Politics of Regional Industrial Policy in Norway and Spain

In the previous section, we reviewed how Norwegian and Spanish regional policy has been influenced by the hegemonic ideas of Fordism, post-Fordism, and what we have termed contextualism. Table 16.1 (see Section 16.3.3.2) summarizes the main characteristics of the three phases and how they are represented in the regional industrial politics of Norway and Spain in the period since 1945. There is no doubt that the Norwegian and Spanish experience of the translation of hegemonic ideas to regional policy instruments provides lessons on the importance of context and particularity.

Nevertheless, we believe that revisiting the concept of scalar politics may be fruitful in explaining the similarities in and differences between the regional industrial policies in Norway and Spain in a more generic way. First, it is very clear from both cases that particular political projects and initiatives have scalar aspects and repercussions (Mackinnon 2011, p. 29). For example, growth through industrialization was an indisputable principle in both countries under Fordism, but while growth poles became the key policy tool in Spain they were absent in Norway. During the post-Fordist phase, restructuring programmes were the leading idea in both countries, which launched nationwide restructuring programmes for declining industries, but while this took place in the bigger cities in Spain, in Norway the scene was mainly rural one-company towns. Finally, in the prevailing contextualist phase, both countries seem to have adapted to the dominant idea of endogenous development in terms of regional development programmes engaging a trans-scalar network of stakeholders. The stakeholders combine a fashionable set of buzzwords to weave together the capabilities of local resources and actors to meet the challenges of the knowledge economy and competition in globalizing markets.

Overall, the most significant difference in scalar repercussions of the regional industrial policies in the two countries is the decentralization–concentration divide. Following MacKinnon's scalar approach, this divide can partly be understood through an analysis of "the strategic deployment of scale by various actors, organizations and movements." Until very recently, regional industrial policy has been characterized by a particular rural "gaze" in Norway. The politics of scale behind this has been the efficient lobbying of the farmers' and fishermen's organization for rural development, making the idea of urban growth centers very controversial. In Spain, the Franco regime used regional industrial policies not only for the purpose of consolidating power in Madrid and its surrounding urban areas, but also for coupling industrialization and urbanization. During the restructuring period, rural areas were set aside in the agenda of territorial planning and the debate and resources were focused on recovering industrial competitiveness. It is only in recent years that rural areas have gained political momentum in Spain because of their status of quality food suppliers (Baylina and Berg 2010), but the huge investment has been in soft and hard infrastructure and innovation fully designed in and for cities.

In both countries, these and the other aspects of former regional industrial policies constitute what MacKinnon underlines as "the influence and effects of pre-existing scalar structures, created by past processes of social construction" (Mackinnon 2011, p. 30). This is very prominent in both countries during the post-Fordist phase. In Norway, the first restructuring programme addressed the problems that one-company towns in rural areas encountered as international competition forced them to restructure production, while the restructuring programmes had an urban bias in Spain because large factories and industrialized areas were mostly located in cities and metropolitan regions. Industrial crises and urban decline were just two sides of the same coin.

Finally, to recall our theoretical discussion, a scalar approach should stress "the closely related question of the creation of new scalar arrangements and configurations, occurring at the point of interaction between inherited and emergent projects and scales" (Mackinnon 2011, p. 31). During the development of Fordism, post-Fordism, and contextualism, Norway and Spain have slowly upgraded their economies and societies from a peripheral to a more central position within the European economy. The Civil War (1936–1939) in Spain and World War II (1939–1945) in Norway seriously damaged their industry and infrastructure. Despite their contrasting political and ethical standpoints, the Labour Party in Norway and Franco's dictatorship in Spain developed a regional industrial governance system very dependent on a strong state in the form of infrastructure provision and state-controlled companies. This pattern was maintained during post-Fordism. The two nations launched restructuring programmes in a way that kept the regulation of regional industrial policy affairs in the domain of the nation state. Accordingly, the instruments used in regional industrial policies were primarily on a national scale. At the end of the post-Fordist phase, and certainly in the current phase of contextualism, this has been changing. In Norway we have seen that regional industrial policy has become increasingly rescaled, with some of the responsibilities for the design and implementation of initiatives being transferred from the national to the regional level (Isaksen and Remøe 2001; Remøe 2005; Jakobsen et al. 2012). Seen in isolation, the Norwegian case looks like an example of downscaling of policy responsibility. In 2003, the county municipalities in Norway were granted greater authority to manage several regional policy tools. This "responsibility reform" was intended to give regional and local actors increased flexibility to distribute allocated funds in line with their own strategic priorities (Norwegian Ministry of Local Government and Regional Development 2004–2005). The regionalization going on in Spain seems to confirm the Norwegian case. However, a more thorough understanding of the Spanish case forces us to reconsider this conclusion. What is new in Spain is that the neoliberal agenda underpinning the construction of a common market in Europe limits the former "developmental state". As a full member of the European Union, Spain has been most strongly influenced by this ideological position. Well aware that the huge decentralization process undertaken in Spain, currently evolving as a quasi-federal state, is also a result of internal processes, we argue that in terms of the scalar politics of regional industrial policy the national scale has been losing influence in favor of both upscaling (Brussels) and downscaling (Comunidades Autónomas). Thus, Spain is much closer to the development of neo-Schumpeterian regions than Norway.

16.5 Conclusion

In this chapter, we have traced the connection between three broad economic evolution phases in two developed countries during the post-war period, the changing meta-rationale or hegemonic ideas for policy formulation during these phases and the regional industrial political instruments of these two countries. We have argued that the economic evolution of developed countries during the post-war period can be divided into three broad phases: Fordism, post-Fordism, and the recent period for which we propose the label of contextualism. Each of these phases is rooted in a set of hegemonic ideas on policy regulation, for example, economic growth and growth pole deployment during the Fordist phase, flexible specialization and industrial restructuring during the post-Fordist phase, and endogenous development and innovation programmes in the current contextualist phase. In line with the concept of "scalar politics" developed by Mackinnon (2011), we reason that politics of scale in the case of regional industrial policy is an instrumental scalar practice that has unintended scalar aspects and repercussions. To establish these arguments empirically, we used the experiences of Norway and Spain. In short, comparing the regional industrial policies of these countries through the phases demonstrates that their policies in terms of structure, strategy, and goals are shifting from divergence to convergence. Recalling the concept of "scalar politics", these shifts are examples of the particularity of such rescaling, regional policy being rooted in processes of downscaling in Norway and upscaling in Spain. However, a universal trend can also be observed in terms of a rescaling of regional policy away from being primarily a nationally controlled project. Another shared pattern that emerges is that the policy instruments in use have become more, rather than less, homogeneous across communities and regions in the two countries over the years. However, more case studies are needed to check whether these observations are a global tendency in the current regional industrial policy or just a coincidence in the cases of regional industrial policy in Norway and Spain.

Acknowledgements This chapter was supported by the Spanish National Research and Development Framework 2008–2011 under Grant number CSO2011-29168-C03-03—Project title: *Worlds of production and location patterns of food industry in Spain*; and the Research Council of Norway (the VRI programme).

References

Aarset B, Jakobsen S-E (2009) Political regulation and radical institutional change: the case of aquaculture in Norway. Mar Pol 33:280–287

Amin A (1992) Post-Fordism: models, fantasies and phantoms of transition. In: Amin A (ed) Post-Fordism. A reader. Blackwell, Oxford, pp 1–40

Arbo P (2004) Kan innovasjon planlegges? In: Arbo P, Gammelsæter H (eds) Innovasjonspolitikkens scenografi. Nye perspektiver på næringsutviklin. Tapir Akademisk Forlag, Trondheim, pp 245–267

Arnold E, Muscio A, Nählinder J, Reid A (2005) Mid-term evaluation of the VS2010 programme: a report to the Research Council of Norway Conclusions and recommendations from the report. Technopolis, Mechelen

Asheim BT, Isaksen A (1997) Location, agglomeration and innovation: towards regional innovation systems in Norway? Eur Plann Stud 5:299–330

Baylina M, Berg NG (2010) Selling the countryside: representations of rurality in Norway and Spain. Eur Urban Reg Stud 17:277–292

Bluestone B, Harrison B (1982) The deindustrialization of America. Plant closings, community abandonment and the dismantling of basic industry. Basic Books, New York

Boschma R, Martin R (eds) (2010) The handbook of evolutionary economic geography. Edward Elgar, Cheltenham

Brenner N (1999) Beyond state-centrism? Space, territoriality, and geographical scale in globalization studies. Theor Soc 28:39–78

Brenner N (2001) Limits to scale? Methodological reflections on scalar structuration. Progr Hum Geogr 25:591–614
Brenner N (2009) Open questions on state rescaling. Cambridge J Regions Econ Soc 2:123–139
Breschi S (2011) The geography of knowledge flows. In: Cooke P, Asheim B, Boschma R, Martin R, Schwartz D, Tödtling F (eds) Handbook of regional innovation and growth. Edward Elgar, Cheltenham, pp 132–142
Buesa M (2012) El sistema nacional de innovación en España: un panorama. Información Comercial Española 869:7–42
Bukve O, Glosvik Ø, Teigen H (1995) Kommunalt tiltaksarbeid. Rapport 6/95. Vestlandsforskning, Sogndal
Cooke P (1985) Regional innovation policy: problems and strategies in Britain and France. Environ Plann C Govern Pol 3:253–267
Cooke P, Asheim B, Boschma R, Martin R, Schwartz D, Tödtling F (eds) (2011) Handbook of regional innovation and growth. Edward Elgar, Cheltenham
Cruickshank J, Lysgård HK, Magnussen ML (2009) The logic of the construction of rural politics: political discourses on rurality in Norway. Geogr Ann B Hum Geogr 91:73–89
Dale B (2002) An institutional approach to local restructuring: the case of four Norwegian mining towns. Eur Urban Reg Stud 9:5–20
Esparcia Pérez J, Escribano Pizarro J (2012) La dimensión territorial en la programación comunitaria y el nuevo marco de políticas públicas: desarrollo rural territorial, reforma de la PAC y nuevo LEADER. Anales de Geografía de la Universidad Complutense 32:227–252
Etzkowitz H, Leydesdorff L (2000) The dynamics of innovation: from national systems and 'mode 2' to a triple helix of university-industry-government relations. Res Pol 29:109–123
Grønlund IL (1994) Restructuring one-company towns: the Norwegian context and the case of Mo i Rana. Eur Urban Reg Stud 1:161–185
Haarstad H, Fløysand A (2007) Globalization and the power of rescaled narratives: a case of opposition to mining in Tambogrande. Peru' Polit Geogr 26:289–308
Hansen JC (1987) Fornorsking av modeller for regional utvikling. Sosiologi i dag 3–4:131–147
Harvey D (1989) The condition of postmodernity: an enquiry into the origins of cultural change. Basil Blackwell, Oxford
Hassink R (2010) Locked in decline? On the role of regional lock-ins in old industrial areas. In: Boschma R, Martin R (eds) The handbook of evolutionary economic geography. Edward Elgar, Cheltenham, pp 450–470
Herod A (2011) Scale. Routledge, London
Isaksen A, Remøe SO (2001) New approaches to innovation policy: some Norwegian examples. Eur Plann Stud 9:285–302
Jakobsen S-E (2004) Virker virkemidlene? Teori og praksis for omstillingsarbeidet. In: Lindkvist KB (ed) Ressurser og omstilling—et geografisk perspektiv på regional omstilling i Norge. Fagbokforlaget, Bergen, pp 199–236
Jakobsen S-E, Høvig ØS (2014) Hegemonic ideas and local adaptations: development of the Norwegian restructuring instrument. Norwegian J Geogr 68(2):80–90
Jakobsen S-E, Onsager K (2008) Innovasjonspolitikk for regional næringsutvikling. In: Isaksen A, Karlsen A, Sæther B (eds) Innovasjoner i norske næringer. Et geografisk perspektiv. Fagbokforlaget, Bergen, pp 269–288
Jakobsen S-E, Byrkjeland M, Båtevik FO, Pettersen IB, Skogseid I, Yttredal ER (2012) Continuity and change in path-dependent regional policy development: the regional implementation of the Norwegian VRI programme. Norwegian J Geogr 66:133–143
Jessop B (1992) Post-Fordism and the state. In: Amin A (ed) Post-Fordism. A reader. Blackwell, Oxford, pp 251–279
Jessop B (1997) Capitalism and its future: remarks on regulation, government and governance. Rev Int Polit Econ 4:561–581
Lagendijk A (2011) Regional innovation policy between theory and practice. In: Cooke P, Asheim B, Boschma R, Martin R, Schwartz D, Tödtling F (eds) Handbook of Regional Innovation and Growth. Edward Elgar, Cheltenham, pp 597–608

Laranja M, Uyarra E, Flanagan K (2008) Policies for science, technology and innovation: translating rationales into regional policies in multi-level setting. Res Pol 37:823–835
Lorca A, Martínez A, García L (1981) Una evaluación de la política de "Polos de Desarrollo". La España de Las Autonomías, vol I. Espasa-Calpe, Madrid, pp 608–673
Mackinnon D (2011) Reconstructing scale: towards a new scalar politics. Progr Hum Geogr 35:21–36
Mansfield B (2005) Beyond rescaling: reintegrating the 'national' as a dimension of scalar relations. Progr Hum Geogr 29:458–473
Martin R, Sunley P (2006) Path dependence and regional economic evolution. J Econ Geogr 6:395–437
McCann P, Ortega-Argilès R (2011) Smart specialisation, regional growth and applications to EU cohesion policy. Document de treball de l'IEB 2011/14, Barcelona
Méndez R, Caravaca I (1993) Procesos de reestructuración industrial en las aglomeraciones metropolitanas españolas. Ministerio de Obras Públicas y Transportes, Madrid
Morgan K (1997) The learning region: institutions, innovations and regional renewal. Reg Stud 35:491–503
Moulaert F, Nussbaumer J (2005) The social region. Beyond the territorial dynamics of the learning economy. Eur Urban Reg Stud 12:45–64
Nadal J (ed) (2003) Atlas de la industrialización de España, 1750–2000. Fundación BBVA-Crítica, Barcelona
Nadal J, Carreras A (eds) (1990) Pautas regionales de la industrialización española (siglos XIX y XX). Ariel, Barcelona
Navarro M (1989) Crisis y reconversión de la siderurgia española, 1978–1988. Junta del Puerto de Pasajes-Ministerio de Obras Públicas, Madrid
Navarro M (1990) Política de reconversión: balance crítico. Ediciones Universidad Complutense de Madrid, Madrid
Norwegian Ministry of Local Government and Regional Development (2004–2005) St.meld. no. 25 (2004–2005). Om regionalpolitikken. Norwegian Ministry of Local Government and Regional Development, Oslo
NOU (1983) 10: Problemer og muligheter på ensidige industristeder. Industridepartementet, Oslo
OECD (2010) Regional development policies in OECD countries. Organisation for Economic Co-operation and Development, Paris
Ondátegui J (2008) Las tecnópolis en España. Thompson-Civitas, Madrid
Pascual H (1993) Reconversión y reindustrialización en España: los nuevos dinamismos espaciales. Secretariado de Publicaciones de la Universidad de Valladolid, Valladolid
Pike A, Rodriguez-Pose A, Tomaney J (2006) Local and regional development. Routledge, London
Plaza B, Velasco R (2001) Política industrial de las Comunidades Autónomas, 1980–2000. Círculo de Empresarios Vascos, Bilbao
Presidencia del Gobierno (1963) Plan de Desarrollo Económico y Social para el período 1964–1967. Comisaría del Plan de Desarrollo Económico, Madrid
Remøe SO (2005) Governing fragmentation: the case of Norway. In: Remøe SO (ed) Governance of innovation systems, vol 2, Case studies in innovation policy. OECD, Paris, pp 217–244
Sanz L (1997) Estado, ciencia y tecnología en España. Alianza Editorial, Madrid
Segura J (1989) La industria española en la crisis (1978–1984). Alianza Editorial, Madrid
Swyngedouw E (1997) Neither global nor local: 'Glocalization' and the politics of scale. In: Cox K (ed) Spaces of globalization: reasserting the power of the local. Guilford, New York, pp 137–166
Therborn G (1986) Why some people are more unemployed than others. Verso, London
Tödtling F, Trippl M (2005) One size fits all? Towards a differentiated regional innovation policy approach. Res Pol 34:1203–1219
Underthun A, Kasa S, Reitan M (2011) Scalar politics and strategic consolidation: The Norwegian Gas Forum's quest for embedding Norwegian gas resources in domestic space. Norwegian J Geogr 65:226–237
Wicken O (2009) The layers of national innovation systems: the historical evolution of a national innovation system in Norway. In: Fagerberg J, Mowery DC, Verspagen B (eds) Innovation, path dependency, and policy. Oxford University Press, Oxford, pp 33–60

Chapter 17
Entrepreneurship, Job Creation, and Growth in Fast-Growing Firms in Portugal: Is There a Role for Policy?

Elsa de Morais Sarmento and Alcina Nunes

Abstract Economies that thrive most on their ambitions, innovative and productive firms are due to grow and develop. Our motivation is thus to uncover who are these fast-growing firms and where they operate. These interrogations provide the foundation for an exploration into what are the different choices for policy, and an opportunity to engage afresh with why and if they ought to receive support in the first place, infusing the discussion as to when and how it could be provided and what could the intended results be. We use the dataset *Quadros de Pessoal* to provide a stronger two-fold measurement, according to the employment and turnover growth criteria. We find among Portugal's distinctive characteristics its high share of SMEs in the population of fast-growing firms, the narrowing down of the difference between measurements according to the employment and turnover criteria and the disproportionate amount of employment generated by the largest segment of fast-growing firms. We find that gazelles are outstanding job creators, having a disproportionately larger impact in job creation than high-growth firms. Accordingly, it is the rapid growth of a few large firms, combined with the entry of a higher number of firms of a higher average size that generates positive net job creation in Portugal. A more thorough understanding of fast-growing firms ought to lead to adjustments in government policies to heighten their exceptional contribution to economic growth. We provide a conceptual framework for tapping into how to design policies for firms which are growing at a faster pace and a roadmap for tackling some of its most controversial issues.

Keywords High-growth firms • Firm turbulence • Gazelle • Job creation

E. de Morais Sarmento (✉)
African Development Bank, Tunis-Belvedère, Tunisia

Universidade de Aveiro, Aveiro, Portugal
e-mail: elsa.sarmento@gmail.com

A. Nunes
GEMF—Grupo de Estudos Monetários e Financeiros, Faculdade de Economia da Universidade de Coimbra, Coimbra, Portugal

Instituto Politécnico de Bragança, Bragança, Portugal
e-mail: alcina@ipb.pt

R. Baptista, J. Leitão (eds.), *Entrepreneurship, Human Capital, and Regional Development*, International Studies in Entrepreneurship 31,
DOI 10.1007/978-3-319-12871-9_17

17.1 Introduction

Following the work of Birch (1979), the current thinking for over three decades was that small businesses (both young and old) were the engine behind job growth. In the present day, job creation and employment growth are still central indicators of labor market performance, thus bringing small businesses under the limelight and placing them at the core of the policy-making debate. However, recent academic research has established that not only small size, but a combination of characteristics of small size and young age make these firms a key source of job creation (Henrekson and Johansson 2010; Haltiwanger, et al. 2013; Van Praag and Versloot 2008; Acs et al. 2008; Storey 1994; Birch 1981, 1987). The implicit rational behind researching into this theme has been to put to good use the learning about these firms' behavior and characteristics so as to intensify the amount of fast-growing firms and its impact on job creation. This interest has been demonstrated by the findings uncovered by empirical data exploration originating from several regions and countries (Brown and Mawson 2013; Lawless 2013; Anyadike-Danes et al. 2013; Dalton et al. 2011; Biosca 2010; Salas et al. 2010; Acs and Mueller 2008; Stam 2005; Schreyer 2000; Brüderl and Preisendörfer 2000; OECD 2002, 2008, 2009, 2013b; Picot and Dupuy 1998).

Unlocking the growth potential of the private sector has continuously been at the core of discussions on how to boost economic recovery, but has intensified recently due to the economic slowdown hitting Europe, especially since 2009. Predominantly following downturn periods, decision-makers avidly seek the appropriate levers to restore competitiveness, accelerate economic growth, and distribute its benefits equitably at the regional level. Recognizably, major labor market reforms in the Euro area are essential to spur job creation, lower unemployment, and help prevent further sliding into cycles of long-term deterioration of potential output growth (ECB 2012; Tilford and Whyte 2011; McKinsey Global Institute 2010). Accordingly, authorities' statements and research findings in various countries have reinforced the catalytic role assigned to Small and Medium Enterprises (SMEs) in stimulating economic recovery and job creation, whose importance does not qualify at all as small, as its firm dimension may suggest (e.g., Goldman Sachs 2013; European Parliament 2011; Swedish Agency for Growth Policy Analysis 2011; CPA Australia/CGA-Canada 2010; OECD 1997; Schreyer 1996). However, the concern implicit in targeting young and small businesses with adequate support aimed at generating jobs is related to the higher uncertainty of these new ventures' outcomes.

In Portugal, over 99 % of firms are SMEs[1] and in particular newcomers are born with quite a small size (Sarmento and Nunes 2010a). In 1995, around 40 % had fewer than five employees and 60 % fewer than ten. A decade later, in 2005, 64 % of these newly created employer enterprises were dead, of which 14% had not survived

[1] According to the European definition, (SME's are considered firms below the 250 employees' threshold).

into their first year and 46 % into their first 5 years in business[2] (Sarmento and Nunes 2010c). In fact, 78 % did not manage to endure 18 years of activity. One of the explanations is bestowed by the level of firm turbulence, given by the sum of employer enterprise births and deaths, which is remarkable in Portugal. During the period 1987–2005, it amounted to 29 %, with over a quarter of all jobs being either destroyed or created over a typical 12-month period. Furthermore, smaller businesses exhibit the highest churn and failure rates, thus not only creating but also destroying more jobs. Differences in survival rates across firm size-classes become particularly evident from the early stages of a firm's life and are statistically significant for Portugal (Nunes and Sarmento 2012). Moreover, only a minority of new businesses grows phenomenally. On average during the period 1987–2005, Portuguese employer enterprises achieved an employment growth rate of 24.2 %, during their first year but only managed to sustain 3.7 % of growth ten years later. After 18 years in business, that firms cohort's employment growth fell to −1.2 % (Sarmento and Nunes 2010c).

To restrict the attention to those firms that truly generate jobs, academics, policy-makers but also recently practitioners, started focusing on a very small subset of firms, the so-called "high-growth firms" (e.g., OECD 2013a, b; Europe INNOVA 2011; Stangler 2010; Mitusch and Schimke 2011). These firms are dynamic players in economic growth, known to play a significant role in job creation and prosperity in many countries, through productivity enhancements derived from technology development and innovative behavior (NESTA 2009; European Cluster Observatory 2009; Autio et al. 2007; OECD 2002; Birch et al. 1997; Storey 1994; Baldwin et al. 1996). At the regional level, in tandem with the direct effects of fast-growing firms on employment and job creation, indirect effects can materialize through structural change, increased competition, attractiveness, and spillovers, thus leading to productivity increases, higher employment levels, and long-term economic development (Fritsch 2011; Bos and Stam 2011). Furthermore, the amount of fast-growing firms operating in individual countries and regions and the swiftness of its emergence provides a clear indication of how well national and local authorities are laying the foundations for growth among their new and established businesses.

International comparative evidence on firm growth has revealed that European countries have on average a lower share of high-growth businesses than the United States and a much larger share of static firms. These differences have been shown to be significant in accounting for variations in productivity across these economies (Biosca 2010). But in Europe, enterprises with growth potential have already started being targeted by many European governments (e.g., BIS 2011) and the banking sector for specific support (Financial Times 2014; Santander 2013). In Europe, the European Commissions' Strategy 2020 already assigns the contribution of high-growth firms a political objective (European Commission 2010).

[2] In Portugal, the estimated median duration of a newborn enterprise lies between 5 and 6 years, which is below that verified in other countries (Nunes and Sarmento 2012).

But the narrow focus on exceptionally fast-growing firms has been questioned, through at least three main lines of arguments. Firstly, we do not still know enough about firm growth, despite the extensive existing body of economic literature on the theory of the firm. For instance, Gibrat's law (Gibrat 1931), which posits that both small and large firms will on average perform at the same rates of growth has been refuted by empirical evidence, whilst no consensual alternative theory has been posited.[3] Hence, the linkages between theory and reality checks in what concerns firm formation, growth, and decline are recognizable, rudimentary, and conflicting. Nonetheless, the growth process of these exceptional performers is perceived to be nonlinear and known to be more of an unstable kind (Levie and Lichtenstein 2010), contrary to the way depicted by the traditional life cycle theory of the firm (e.g., Churchill and Lewis 1983; Greiner 1972). One way of approaching these outbursts of sudden growth stems from identifiable "trigger points" that reconfigure the firm to induce rapid and transformative growth through a catalytic process. According to Storey (1994), these triggers can catapult moderate performing firms into high performing ventures, whereby they become "flyers". Brown and Mawson (2013) offer an analogous insight of this process, by employing the concept of "growth triggers"[4] for looking into Scottish enterprises growth paths. They observe that most high-growth firms appear to have a "stepped" growth approach pattern, with periods of low or modest growth being combined with periods of high growth. In fact, moving away from growth rates towards analyzing growth trajectories might yield a more thorough understanding of the interplay between performance, growth, and business survival.

Secondly, recent research challenged the universally accepted assumption that firm growth is a sign of success in itself, pointing out that unprofitable growth can also lead to future profits via increased market shares (Davidsson et al. 2005; Steffens et al. 2009). Moreover, Davidsson et al. (2010) have also shown that profitable but low-growth firms are more likely to reach the desirable state of high-growth and profitability compared with high-growth and low-profitability type of firms. Similarly, dormant firms, such as "sleeping gazelles" (Bornhäll et al. 2013), which enjoy high profitability but do not generate new jobs, might also provide a good target for policies focused on cost-effectiveness and maximized impact on job creation.

Thirdly, the debate of whether it is the entry of many new firms or the rapid growth of a few well performing firms that generates employment growth and job creation. This discussion is still being fuelled by new evidence for high-growth (HG) firms (e.g., Lawless 2013; Davidsson and Delmar 2006; Storey 1994).

Most types of growth are beset with complex intricacies that also rely on a combination of territorial elements, which can favor or hinder growth. The question of why some businesses grow more than others in certain environments and regions can be partially answered by analyzing the presence of elements such as infrastructure,

[3] There are, however, other theorizations. For instance, Wennekers and Thurik (1999) put forward an economic development typology based upon new enterprise formation and growth.

[4] A growth trigger is a "systematic change to the structure and workings of a firm which provides a critical opportunity for altering that firm's growth trajectory" (Brown and Mawson 2013).

specialized labor, clusters, innovative ecosystems, scientific and technological environments, and institutional settings in a given territory. However, answering the question of which combination of economical–political, institutional, and territorial instruments can offset this gap is considerably more challenging in both theoretical and practical terms. It is demanding, and often impossible to create external elements which can mimic and compensate for the gaps that a high-growth environment provides. One must usually hope that firm adaptation to the local environment conveys the necessary speed of growth to overcome the barriers to faster growth so as to offset the advantages made available by more competitive territories. In order to address all these issues, we need a strong conceptual framework of analysis, able to deliver a rational, an approach method and a toolbox of different policy options, based on more in-depth, comprehensive, and multidimensional analysis of longitudinal data (Garnsey et al. 2006; Delmar et al. 2003; Chandler and Lyon 2001; Davidsson and Wiklund 2000), which is able to uncover empirical regularities, allowing a better response to the many challenging questions, such as those related to which types of firms ought to receive support in order to maximize job creation.

In this paper, we use *Quadros de Pessoal* data (an employee–employer linked longitudinal dataset of Portuguese employer enterprises) within the period 1985–2007, to provide estimates of the amount and incidence of high-growth and gazelle firms, its regional distribution to a geographical level of disaggregation of NUTS II, but also its employment and job creation. The microdata comprehensiveness of the dataset provides the platform for uncovering high-growth firms' features which have not been examined to such a detail before. By applying the Eurostat and OECD's methodology of the "Manual of Business Demography Statistics" (Eurostat/OECD 2007), we obtain a specific dataset for high-growth and gazelle enterprises active since 1990 and 1992, respectively, whose results can be directly compared to those from other datasets to which this same methodology has been applied to (e.g., OECD 2008, 2009, 2011, 2013b; Eurostat 2008; NESTA 2009; Anyadike-Danes et al. 2009). Two parallel accounts are provided, according to the turnover and employment criteria.

Our motivation is to uncover who are these fast-growing firms (high-growth and gazelles) and where they operate and the incidence of regional employment, and subsequently, what types of firms create most jobs. These interrogations provide the foundation for an exploration into what are the different choices for policy, thus disentangling its *raison d'être*, and an opportunity to engage afresh with why and if they ought to receive support in the first place, infusing the discussion as to when and how it could be provided and what could the intended results be (the "so what" question).

The following section intent is to describe the dataset, concepts, and methodology adopted. Section 17.3 introduces fast-growing firms in Portugal, describing its most common characteristics while profiling them at the firm, employment, and regional level, according to four distinct groups of fast-growing employer enterprises: high-growth, and gazelles categories, measured by employment and turnover. Section 17.4 provides an account of employment and job creation for high-growth and gazelles by employment. Section 17.5 conveys a conceptual framework that aims to facilitate policy-making design and support for fast-growing firms, while Sect. 17.6 offers concluding remarks.

17.2 Data and Methodology

Despite the consistency of findings concerning the importance of fast-growing firms,[5] no internationally accepted definition exists either for high-growth or gazelle firms (Anyadike-Danes et al. 2013; Nordic Council of Ministers 2010; Biosca 2010; Henrekson and Johansson 2009, 2010; Hölzl 2009; Ahmad 2008). The literature offers several definitions inspired by the work of David Birch (Birch 1987; Birch et al. 1995). In this particular area, definitions, ceilings, and calculation methods adopted for measurements matter as "summary statements which gloss over the detail of the definitions may seriously mislead researchers and policy-makers alike" (Anyadike-Danes et al. 2013, p. 5). This chapter follows the methodology adopted by the Eurostat/OECD 2007, which has been accepted internationally and used widely in the business demography field (OECD 2008, 2009; Salas et al. 2010).

The main data source in Portugal for the universe of employer enterprises (enterprises with more than one employee) is *Quadros de Pessoal*. This annual mandatory survey, conducted by the Portuguese Ministry of Labour and Social Security, provides a rich and comprehensive matched employer–employee-establishment dataset. According to the registrars of the Portuguese Social Security, it is composed of all active enterprises with at least one paid employee. The database obtained from the cleaning of *Quadros de Pessoal*, adheres to the Eurostat and OECD methodology "Manual on Business Demography Statistics"

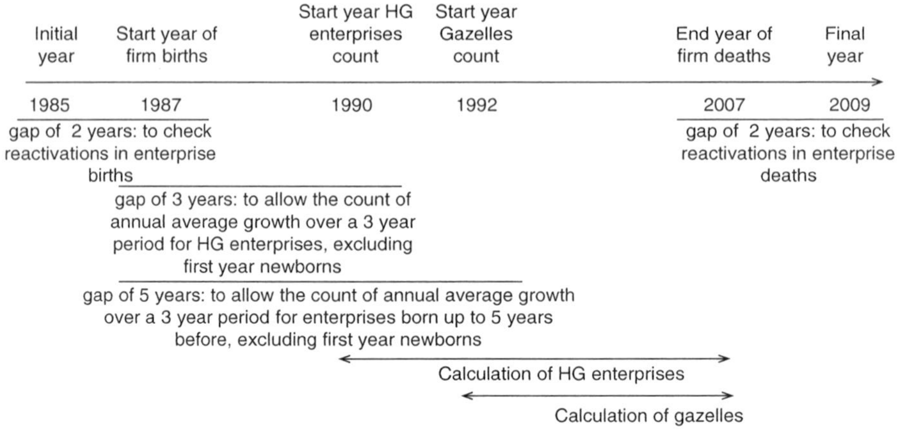

Fig. 17.1 The application of the Eurostat/OECD (2007) methodology and the timings required for the calculation of high-growth and gazelle firms

[5] In this chapter, we shall use the term "fast growing" firm to include both "high-growth" and "gazelle" enterprises.

(Eurostat/OECD 2007). It focuses on employer enterprises, which are known to be an important source of job creation. The derived dataset from the application of this methodology consists of an annual average of 215,903 active employer enterprises, with an annual average of 36.803 births and 23,743 enterprise deaths over a 20-year period (1987–2007 and 1985–2005, respectively).

Although the dataset covers the period 1985–2009, 2 years at the beginning and end of the period are lost due to the application of the Eurostat/OCDE's (2007) methodology, when calculating enterprise births and deaths. It is recommended looking 2 years into the past from the reference period, to check for reactivations, before enterprise births are actually considered (Eurostat/OECD 2007). Thus, enterprise births were only calculated from 1987 onwards, instead of 1985, the starting year of the dataset (Fig. 17.1).

A high-growth enterprise is any employer enterprise with ten or more employees in the beginning of the observation period, with an average annualized growth greater than 20 % *per annum*,[6] over a 3-year period.[7] Enterprise growth can be measured according to two distinct definitions, either by the number of employees (employment) or by turnover.

Given the methodology employed, enterprise births start being calculated in 1987 but high-growth firms' birth rates can only be calculated 3 years later, in 1990, to allow for the count of the annual average growth over a 3-year period, excluding first year newborn. The reason is that, in order to fully comply with the methodology, growth rates have to be always identified from the same base population, which means excluding enterprises born in the first year from the growth measurement. Consequently, the data on high-growth enterprises should be cleaned so as to remove firms that were born in year $t-3$ (in our case, 1987), when measuring growth from $t-3$ to t.

Gazelle enterprises are a subset of high-growth enterprises. Gazelles, measured by employment (or turnover), are all employer enterprises employing at least ten employees at the beginning of the 3-year period, which have been employers for a period up to 5 years, with an annual average growth in employment (or turnover) greater than or equal to 20 % over a 3-year period. In other words, they reflect high-growth enterprises born 5 years or less before the end of the 3-year observation period. Moreover, the data on gazelles should also be cleaned by removing firms that were born in year $t-5$, when measuring growth from $t-5$ to t.

[6] A minimum of 20 % growth a year for 3 consecutive years represents a minimum of 72.8 % growth over 3 years $((1.2\times1.2\times1.2)-1=0.728)$. According to this methodology, a firm which might have grown 72.8 % (either in turnover or in employment) within a single year with no growth in the following two does not qualify as high-growth.

[7] Settling the period over which growth is measured is determinant for defining what makes a high-growth firm. If the measurement period is too short (e.g., a year), firms with short-term contracts or seasonal employees might be classified as such even though their employment growth is temporary. Also, firms can live short lives and die before the start of the new measurement period, thus not being accounted for. Conversely, the period for defining high-growth firms should be long enough such that changes of a transitory nature are not erroneously accounted for as high growth. The OECD definition thus recommends a 3-year growth threshold.

A size threshold of ten employees,[8] for both turnover and employment, is set at the start of the observation period, to avoid the small size-class bias contained in the above definition of high-growth and gazelles. In setting the employment threshold, the methodology needed to balance two competing criteria, if the threshold was set too low, it would cause a disproportionate number of small enterprises appearing in the statistics, but on the other hand, would reduce disclosure problems related to the statistical confidentiality of the microdata. If it was set too high, disclosure problems could increase, in particular for smaller economies where large enterprises are less numerous than smaller-sized ones.

The employment measurement of high growth and gazelle firms is generally preferred and is more widely used (e.g., NESTA 2009, 2011; Anyadike-Danes et al. 2009; OECD 2002), as it refers to a real variable whereas turnover is nominal, thus suffering more influence from national and structural factors, such as inflation and a country's fiscal system. Moreover, in our data, the turnover criteria shows a higher degree of volatility than employment, when we account for both enterprises and employment in high-growth and gazelles. According to the OECD (2011), greater country discrepancies are also uncovered when the turnover definition is used, particularly at sectoral level analysis. In our analysis, when possible, we shall provide an account along these two dimensions.

The application of the Eurostat/OECD (2007) methodology also required identifying and excluding mergers and acquisitions from the dataset. As a result, most of the growth reported here is mainly organic growth (growth through new appointments in a firm) and not to acquired growth (growth through acquisitions and/or mergers). Lastly, only employer enterprises classified in sectors from sections A to Q of the Portuguese Economic Classification of Economic Activities (CAE-Rev.2.1) were considered for the purposes of this research. This includes Manufacturing sector, Agriculture, and Services.

17.3 Fast-Growing Firms in Portugal: High-Growth and Gazelles

This section introduces fast-growing firms in Portugal at the firm, employment, and regional level, according to four distinct groups of fast-growing employer enterprises: high-growth and gazelles categories, measured by two different growth criteria, employment and turnover.

[8] In 2007, more than 81 % of Portuguese employer enterprises had fewer than ten employees. The OECD definition thus excludes an average of approximately 175,512 firms (of a total of 215,905 firms) with fewer than ten employees from being classified as high-growth firms over the period.

17.3.1 Profiling Fast-Growing Firms in Portugal

This section presents a characterization of high-growth and gazelles, according to the employment and turnover criteria, for its amount, employment, incidence, and size-class. During this 17-year period, ranging from 1990 to 2007, Portuguese high-growth firms and gazelles, when measured by turnover, decreased both in number and their amount of employees. However, a different picture arises when the employment criteria is used, whereby both number and employees of high-growth firms' increase over time (Table 17.1).

In 1990, 8,557 high-growth firms by turnover and 1,453 according to the employment criteria operated in Portugal (24.6 % and 4.2 % of the enterprises with over ten employees, respectively). By 2007, the number of high-growth firms by turnover decreased 40 %, while those by employment definition increased by around 10 %. Thus, in 2007, only 9.5 % of all Portuguese employer enterprises (with more than ten employees) had a turnover in line with that of high-growth firms. If instead of turnover, the employment metrics is used, the percentage of high-growth firms drops by 6.5 percentage points (p.p) to only 3 %. Similarly, the number of gazelles is also higher when measured by turnover. Over the period, the proportion of gazelles by employment was kept around 30 % of that by turnover. In 2007, firms classified as gazelles constitute only 2.2 % of the total number of Portuguese employer enterprises as accounted by the turnover criteria and 0.7 % by the employment criteria. These shares are significantly lower than those at the beginning of the period considered in this study. In 1992, reported gazelles were 1,726 and 420 in number, by turnover and employment, respectively. The amount of gazelles (by turnover) suffered a considerable decline up to 2007 (−31 %), although not as large as that of high-growth firms, the same happening with gazelles accounted for by the employment definition, which declined by around 14 %. Gazelles (employment definition) represented 23 % of high-growth firms in 2007 and 34 % in 1992, respectively.

The gap between the two measurement criteria narrowed considerably, hinting at an overall slower growth of turnover and profitability over time relative to employment growth (Table 17.1). A similar pattern was observed for gazelle firms, indicating that more firms grew faster in employment than in turnover.[9]

In 1990, the share of high-growth according to employment criteria was 17 % of that accounted by the turnover criteria, whereas in 2007 this share increased to 31 %. Put differently, in 2007 there were relatively more high-growth firms accounted by the employment criteria than 17 years ago. However, its share on the population of firms with more than ten employees decreased when compared to 1990 (3 %), although keeping a somehow stable performance since 2003.

[9] Some authors have pointed out that growth is first consummated in terms of turnover and only later on feeds into employment. From the visible fluctuations of our data, we have no account of that phenomenon, but it is an issue worth looking at in subsequent work.

Table 17.1 Number and incidence of high-growth and gazelle enterprises, according to the employment and turnover definition (% in active employer enterprises employing more than ten employees and its employment)

	High-growth								Gazelles							
	By employment				*By turnover*				*By employment*				*By turnover*			
	Enterprises		Employment		Enterprises		Employment		Enterprises		Employment		Enterprises		Employment	
	No.	%	No.	%	No.	%	No.	%	No.	%	No.	%	No.	%	No.	%
1990	1,453	*4.2*	134,331	*7.4*	8,557	*24.6*	532,866	*29.2*								
1991	1,370	*3.8*	132,390	*7.2*	7,885	*22.1*	488,411	*26.7*								
1992	1,231	*3.3*	110,471	*6.0*	7,556	*20.4*	513,731	*28.0*	420	*1.1*	28,512	*1.6*	1,726	*4.7*	68,619	*3.7*
1993	1,007	*2.7*	92,613	*5.3*	6,405	*17.4*	384,010	*21.8*	336	*0.9*	22,192	*1.3*	1,574	*4.3*	68,493	3.9
1994	1,017	*2.7*	108,766	*6.4*	5,177	*13.9*	325,282	*19.0*	342	*0.9*	31,866	*1.9*	1,254	*3.4*	52,413	*3.1*
1995	948	2.6	108,433	*6.3*	4,412	*11.9*	275,119	*16.1*	267	*0.7*	28,090	*1.6*	963	2.6	45,871	*2.7*
1996	1,043	*2.8*	118,724	*7.0*	3,880	*10.5*	245,748	*14.5*	286	*0.8*	28,592	*1.7*	836	*2.3*	38,320	*2.3*
1997	1,171	*3.0*	139,456	*7.9*	4,586	*11.7*	256,267	*14.5*	286	*0.7*	27,422	*1.6*	1,011	*2.6*	40,845	*2.3*
1998	1,387	*3.4*	164,941	*8.9*	5,150	*12.5*	330,966	*18.0*	412	*1.0*	42,642	*2.3*	1,353	*3.3*	67,788	*3.7*
1999	1,466	*3.4*	191,704	*10.0*	5,422	*12.4*	335,700	*17.5*	433	*1.0*	50,533	*2.6*	1,392	*3.2*	68,871	3.6
2000	1,623	*3.5*	196,627	*9.9*	5,737	*12.5*	316,615	*16.0*	345	*0.8*	35,210	*1.8*	1,211	*2.6*	49,951	*2.5*
2001	1,827	*3.7*	207,052	*9.9*	5,894	*12.0*	327,354	*15.7*	402	*0.8*	41,039	*2.0*	1,272	*2.6*	55,166	*2.6*
2002	1,640	*3.3*	165,879	8.2	5,723	*11.5*	303,128	*15.0*	390	*0.8*	31,686	*1.6*	1,402	*2.8*	63,360	*3.1*
2003	1,370	*2.8*	142,951	*7.0*	4,878	*9.9*	286,725	*14.1*	335	*0.7*	32,778	*1.6*	1,310	*2.7*	55,722	*2.7*
2004	1,308	*2.7*	152,610	*7.3*	4,271	*8.7*	268,591	*12.9*	365	*0.7*	37,154	*1.8*	1,336	2.7	57,261	*2.8*
2005	1,339	*2.6*	135,622	*6.2*	4,858	*9.4*	248,396	*11.3*	394	*0.8*	33,996	*1.5*	1,918	*3.7*	64,403	2.9
2006	1,463	*2.8*	159,660	*7.2*	5,079	*9.8*	261,463	*11.7*	407	*0.8*	28,080	*1.3*	1,532	*3.0*	46,280	*2.1*
2007	1,595	*3.0*	175,259	*7.6*	5,127	*9.5*	280,861	*12.1*	363	*0.7*	33,998	*1.5*	1,186	2.2	46,968	*2.0*

	Difference between the two criteria (% turnover–% employment, p.p.)															
	High-growth								Gazelles							
	Enterprises		Employment								Enterprises		Employment			
1990	*20.5*		*21.9*						1992		3.5		*2.2*			
2007	*6.6*		*4.6*						2007		*1.5*		*0.6*			
	Average size															
	High-growth								Gazelles							
	By employment				*By turnover*					*By employment*				*By turnover*		
1990	92				62				1992	68				40		
2007	110				55				2007	94				40		
	By size class															
	By employment				*By turnover*				*By employment*				*By turnover*			
SC	*10–19*	*20–49*	*50–249*	+250	*10–19*	*20–49*	*50–249*	+250	*10–19*	*20–49*	*50–249*	+250	*10–19*	*20–49*	*50–249*	+250
1990	18	32	97	643												
2000	19	31	95	980												
2003	18	32	94	736												
2007	18	32	97	779												

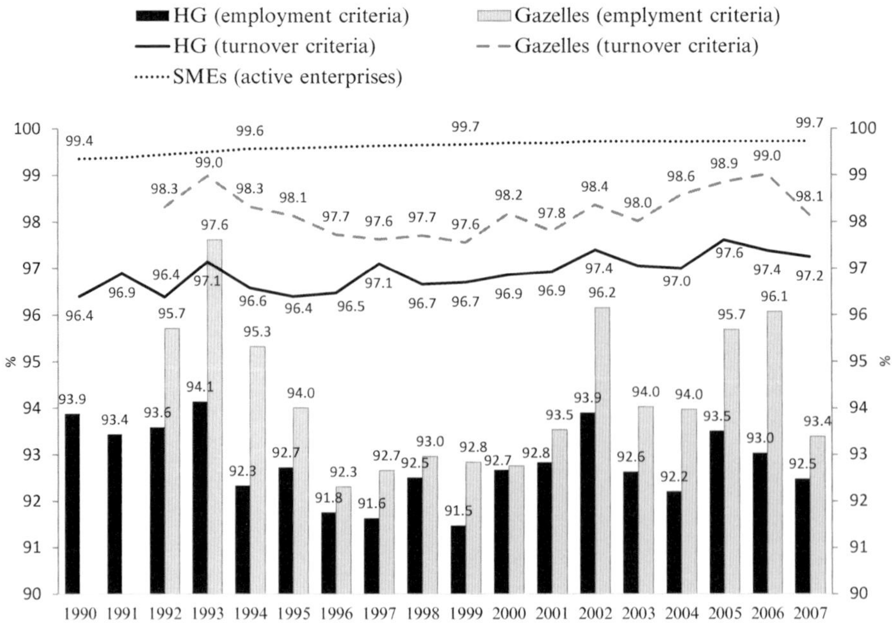

Fig. 17.2 SME's share in high-growth firms, gazelles' and active employer enterprises (%)

Employment in high-growth firms (by turnover) decreased almost by half, from 532,866 employees in 1990 (29 % of employment in active firms with more than ten employees) to 280,861 (12 %) by 2007, while employment, as measured by the employment criteria, increased from 134,331 (7.4 %) in 1990 to 175,259 employees (7.6 %) by 2007. Employment in gazelles, when measured by the turnover criteria, also faced a considerable decline (68,610 employees in 1992 to 46,968 in 2007) but conversely, when measured by the employment criteria it increased to 33,998 workers in 2007 (28,512 employees in 1992). Throughout the period, a minimum of 92 % of all Portuguese high-growth companies are SMEs, below the threshold of 250 employees (Fig. 17.2). However, the share of SMEs in Portugal scores higher, averaging over 99 % during the 17 years considered.

Although high-growth firms are larger on average than gazelles, both types of firms are of a much larger size than the average employer enterprise firm in Portugal (Table 17.1).[10] Throughout this period, all three types of fast-growing firms verify an average size increase, with the exception of high-growth firms by turnover, which display in 2007 a lower average size (55 employees) than that verified in 1990 (62 employees). Due to their smaller average size (that also stems from their young age), gazelles qualify more easily as SMEs, thus weighing considerably more in the number of active employer enterprises, where they are relatively more abundant than their high-growth counterparts. They also score higher when compared to

[10] Please refer for instance to Sarmento and Nunes (2010c) for more information.

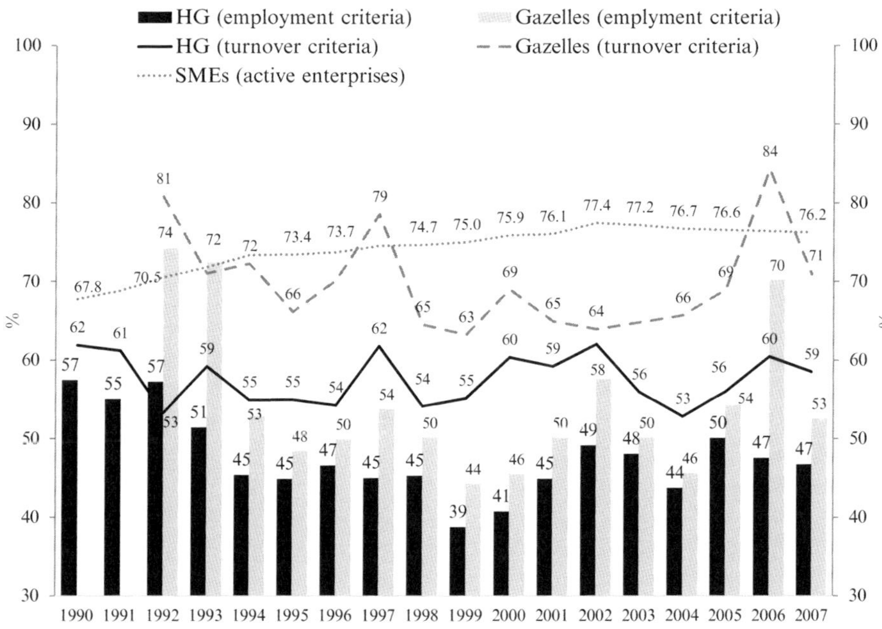

Fig. 17.3 SME's employment share in high-growth firms, gazelles' and active employer enterprises (%)

high-growth firms' share of employment (employment criteria), which is kept below 50 % in most years. As a matter of fact, the turnover criteria always yields a higher share of SMEs for gazelles.

The comparison between the two criteria shows that when accounted by the turnover criteria, SME's and employment share in the population of both high-growth and gazelles is relatively higher. This means it is easier for a smaller firm to grow 20 % in turnover than the same amount in employment over the period.[11] In some of years (namely 1992, 1993, and 2006), gazelle SMEs (by employment criteria) managed to create over 70 % of all the employment generated by the overall gazelle firm population (Fig. 17.3).

The same peaks are also verified by the turnover criteria, whereby in those same years, gazelle SMEs generated 81 %, 79 %, and 84 % of all gazelle employment, hinting at the fact that these firms withstand considerably better the downturns of the economic cycle than other types of firms. In 1990, 0.6 % of high-growth firms (by employment) of the largest size-class (+250 employees), generated 42.6 % of the employment in high-growth firms. After 1999, 0.3 % of these largest gazelles generated over half of total employment in high-growth firms (61.3 % in 1999 and 53 % in 2007).

[11] This means that if a firm which started with the minimum required of ten employees and has to grow a minimum of 20 % during the following 3 years, it has to recruit at least two extra workers in the first year, 2.4 in the second and 2.88 in the third, ending up with a minimum required of around 17 workers at the end of the 3-year period.

17.3.2 Regional Outlook

Empirical evidence shows that fast-growing firms are randomly distributed across size and regions (OECD 2013a). However, academic research has not yet provided unequivocal evidence on the locational characteristics and determinants of high-growth firms, besides those on the general findings on the turnover and mobility of firms (e.g., Bartelsman et al. 2005; Sutton 1997; Caves 1998), the streams of the literature focusing on regional variations in general entrepreneurial attitude and activity (e.g., Bosma and Schutjens 2011; Barbosa and Eiriz 2011), those on the linkages related to the benefits of clustering or agglomeration of complementary economic activity and supporting institutions (e.g., Gilbert et al. 2006, 2008; Lechner and Dowling 2003; Porter 1998) and that in which geographic proximity facilitates the access and absorption of localized knowledge spillovers (e.g., Audretsch and Feldman 1996; Jaffe et al. 1993).

However, it is now widely acknowledged that regional disparities in entrepreneurship are noteworthy, significant, and often persistent, which can frequently surmount differences at the country level (Bosma and Schutjens 2007; Fritsch and Mueller 2006; Tamásy 2006). Fast-growing firms are no exception (OECD 2013a). In this section, we will examine in greater detail, the regional incidence and distribution of high-growth and gazelle enterprises and that of its employment by NUT II regions in Portugal.

We find high-growth firms and gazelles scattered in every region of Portugal, but to different degrees. In 2007, the region which concentrates over 46 % of high-growth firms (by both criteria) is the capital region of Lisbon. Over time, both high-growth and gazelles have become more concentrated in the Lisbon area, and less represented in almost every Portuguese NUT II region, in particular in Centro, Algarve, and Alentejo. This contrast becomes sharper when the employment definition is used. The capital/periphery divide has also widened over time, employment-wise, for high-growth firms, except for the increases in the regions with the smallest share of high-growth and gazelles in the country, the Archipelagos of Madeira and Açores (Fig. 17.4) and for gazelles located in Alentejo and Algarve, according to the turnover definition, also regions with modest shares of fast-growing firms (Fig. 17.4).

Furthermore, in 1990, the weight of the NUT II region of Lisbon in the regional distribution of high-growth firms, according to the employment definition (34.6 %) was close, though smaller, of that accounted for with the turnover criteria (33.2 %). After 17 years, this gap widened substantially and the high-growth count with the employment definition is became 6.4 p.p. larger, indicating that there were comparatively more high-growth firms growing faster in employment than in turnover in Lisbon. Similarly to other countries, Portuguese urban areas seem to be more conducive to high-growth firms, which contribute to deepen regional inequality. This might be caused by the increasing servicitization of the Portuguese economy and specialization in services, which has also pushed high-growth firms into becoming relatively more labor intensive. Lisbon also concentrates the bulk of the public sector

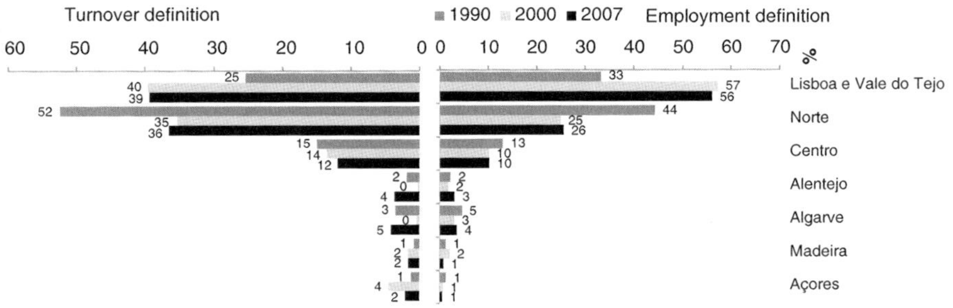

Fig. 17.4 Regional distribution of gazelles' employment by NUTII, share in the country's total employment (by employment and turnover criteria)

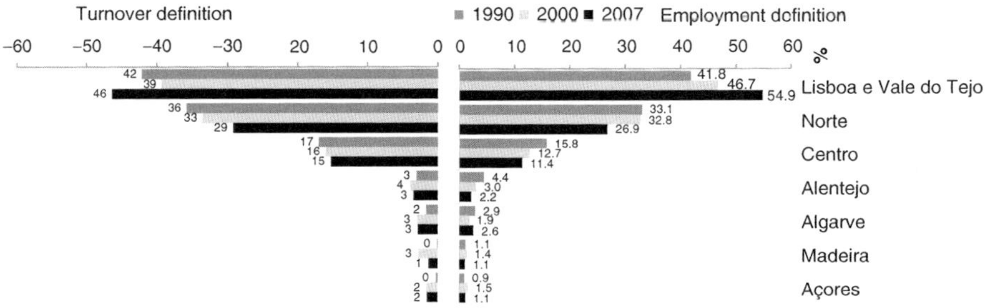

Fig. 17.5 Regional distribution of high-growth firms' employment by NUTII, share in the country's total employment (by employment and turnover criteria)

administration, being particularly intensive in services, such as financial and real estate activities[12] (Sarmento and Nunes 2010a, 2012).

On the other hand, the loss of prevalence of high-growth firms in other regions, namely in the Norte region becomes quite noticeable. In 1990, 33 % of high-growth firms (by employment) and a greater amount by turnover[13] (36 %) emerged in the North, where manufacturing activities were still more prevalent than in other regions. After 17 years, in 2007, Norte lost 1.7 p.p. of its regional weight in high-growth firms and 6.2 p.p. of total employment, according to the employment criteria, and even more according to the turnover criteria (−6.6 p.p. employment-wise), attaining in 2007 an employment share in the country of slightly over a quarter (27 % and 29 %, according to employment and turnover definitions, respectively) (Fig. 17.5).

The regions of Centro, Algarve, and Alentejo got into a similar downward spiral over time, especially when accounted by the employment criteria. High-growth firms

[12] Caution must be employed when interpreting these results, as this might also be due substantially to the fact that a considerable amount of firms' headquarters are located in the Lisbon area and that we are using enterprise and not establishment data.

[13] The turnover definition tends to heighten the manufacturing sector.

in peripheral regions, such as the Archipelago of Madeira increased substantially their representativeness in the country, more than doubling its share, to around 3 %, while the Azores also shows a noteworthy increase, from 0.1 % to 2 % from 1990 to 2007, according to the turnover criteria. However, when accounted by the employment criteria, these regions' weight of high-growth firms' employment in the country's total has not experienced substantial changes between 1990 and 2007. Yet, when accounted by the turnover criteria, both Madeira and the Azores increased their share in national high-growth employment by 1.2 p.p.

Now turning to the regional distribution of gazelles, Norte displays the sharpest decrease of all regions, losing its prevalence as the region with the highest gazelle employment in the country at the start of the 1990s. In 1992, Norte generated 44.3 % of gazelles according to employment definition and 52.3 % according to the turnover.

After Portugal's accession to the European Union (EU) in 1986, the manufacturing sector, in which Norte was particularly specialized, was severely hit by the restructuring of many firms. By 2000, this region's share of gazelles was considerably reduced to a quarter (25 %), by the employment criteria, and to 35.2 %, according to the turnover. It is only in 2007 that signs of a mild recovery in these regions' quota of gazelle's employment can be found.

Another aspect worth highlighting is that the share of gazelles lost by the Norte and Centro seems to have been relocated to Lisbon and Vale do Tejo, where their share of employment accounted by the employment criteria surpasses that accounted by turnover's, and where the gap between both measurements escalates over time (8 p.p. in 1992 to 17 p.p. in 2007, the latter difference being twice as high as that of high-growth firms), indicating a relatively faster growth in employment terms than in turnover's, related to a higher concentration of services in Lisbon.[14] When analyzed from the employment definition perspective, Algarve is the sole region that manages to recover slightly its share of gazelles in 2007 (3.1 %), whereas Centro faces loses initially, but manages to stabilize around a quota of 10 % after 2000.

The perspective of high-growth and gazelle's employment share within the region where they are located, also confirms the loss of importance of these types of firms in all regions, except that of Lisbon (Tables 17.2 and 17.3). Within the region's employment, Lisbon displays a higher proportion of high-growth firms' later in 2007 (10.5 %) than initially in 1990 (7.6 %). On the other hand, in five other regions, high-growth firms' share of regional employment in 2007 was reduced by almost

[14]During this period, high-growth firms and gazelles have been emerging considerably more in service and commerce sectors. According to the employment criteria, we observed a clear shift in the distribution of high-growth firms away from manufacturing (34 % in 1995, down to 20 % in 2007) to services and commerce (49 % in 1995 up to 56 % in 2007), as well as construction (15 % in 1995, up to 20 % in 2007). A similar pattern is observed for gazelles, although the drop in manufacturing sector is higher, it falls sharply by over a half in 13 years (42 % in 1995 to 20 % in 2007). A significant number of high-growth firms in Portugal operated in the construction sector, which was particularly hit by variations in the business cycle. This sectoral rebalancing reflects trends already perceived in the overall population of employer enterprises (Sarmento and Nunes 2010b, c).

Table 17.2 Share of high-growth firms' employment (employment definition) in total employment (in firms with over ten employees) and in the region's employment, by NUTII regions

Regions	Lisbon e Vale do Tejo		Norle		Centro		Alentejo		Algarve		Madeira		Açores	
	Total employment (+10 empl)	Employment within the region	Total employment (+10 empl)	Employment within the region	Total employment (+10 empl)	Employment within the region	Total employment (+10 empl)	Employment within the region	Total employment (+10 empl)	Employment within the region	Total employment (+10 empl)	Employment within the region	Total employment (+10 empl)	Employment within the region
Share in (%)														
1990	3.1	7.6	2.4	33.1	1.2	15.8	0.3	4.4	0.2	2.9	0.1	1.1	0.1	0.9
1991	3.3	8.2	2.3	31.3	1.0	14.4	0.3	4.6	0.1	2.1	0.1	1.3	0.0	0.5
1992	2.5	6.3	2.1	35.2	0.8	14.0	0.2	3.9	0.1	2.1	0.1	1.3	0.1	1.5
1993	2.2	5.5	1.5	29.4	1.0	18.1	0.3	5.1	0.1	2.2	0.1	2.4	0.1	1.4
1994	2.9	7.6	1.8	28.7	1.0	15.4	0.3	4.7	0.1	1.7	0.2	2.5	0.0	0.7
1995	3.0	7.6	1.9	29.9	1.0	16.2	0.2	3.1	0.1	1.3	0.1	1.5	0.1	1.2
1996	3.3	8.6	2.1	30.0	1.0	13.8	0.2	3.3	0.1	1.9	0.1	2.0	0.1	1.6
1997	3.4	9.1	2.8	35.8	0.9	11.8	0.3	4.1	0.1	1.8	0.1	1.2	0.1	1.9
1998	4.0	10.5	2.7	30.7	1.1	11.9	0.4	5.0	0.2	1.8	0.3	3.5	0.2	2.2
1999	5.4	13.9	2.9	29.4	1.0	10.4	0.3	3.3	0.2	1.7	0.1	0.8	0.1	0.8
2000	4.6	11.9	3.3	32.8	1.3	12.7	0.3	3.0	0.2	1.9	0.1	1.4	0.1	1.5
2001	4.4	11.1	3.2	32.1	1.4	13.7	0.3	3.1	0.3	2.9	0.2	2.0	0.2	2.1
2002	4.1	10.6	2.2	26.6	1.1	13.3	0.2	2.8	0.2	2.7	0.2	2.7	0.1	1.7
2003	3.8	9.8	1.5	20.7	0.8	11.8	0.3	4.2	0.2	3.2	0.2	3.3	0.2	2.2
2004	3.8	9.7	2.0	27.9	0.6	7.8	0.3	4.6	0.2	2.2	0.2	3.4	0.2	2.2
2005	3.6	9.2	1.3	20.8	0.7	11.2	0.2	2.5	0.1	1.7	0.1	1.9	0.2	3.3
2006	4.4	11.3	1.5	21.1	0.7	9.6	0.2	2.5	0.1	1.9	0.1	1.8	0.1	1.3
2007	4.2	10.5	2.0	26.9	0.9	11.4	0.2	2.2	0.2	2.6	0.1	1.1	0.1	1.1
Number of employees in high-growth firms														
1990	56,182		44,433		21,244		5,940		3,830		1,710		696	
2000	60,573		41,455		19,094		6,128		2,734		1,458		1,617	
2007	46,410		38,836		15,516		4,276		2,358		2,203		1,338	

Table 17.3 Share of high-growth firms' employment (turnover definition) in total employment (in firms with over ten employees) and in the region's employment, by NUTII regions

Regions	Lisbon e Vale do Tejo		Norle		Centro		Alentejo		Algarve		Madelra		Açores	
	Total employment (+10 empl)	Employment within the region	Total employment (+10 empl)	Employment within the region	Total employment (+10 empl)	Employment within the region	Total employment (+10 empl)	Employment within the region	Total employment (+10 empl)	Employment within the region	Total employment (+10 empl)	Employment within the region	Total employment (+10 empl)	Employment within the region
Share in (%)														
1990	12.3	42.2	10.5	35.8	5.0	17.0	0.5	3.0	0.9	1.7	0.0	0.1	0.1	0.3
1991	12.1	45.2	8.7	32.8	4.1	15.3	0.4	3.0	0.8	1.5	0.3	1.3	0.2	0.9
1992	13.2	47.2	9.6	34.2	3.6	12.8	0.4	2.2	0.6	1.6	0.4	1.3	0.2	0.7
1993	10.8	49.7	6.6	30.3	3.3	15.3	0.4	2.7	0.6	1.6	0.1	0.2	0.0	0.2
1994	8.5	44.7	6.3	33.0	2.8	14.5	0.3	3.1	0.6	1.5	0.3	1.8	0.3	1.4
1995	6.7	41.6	5.8	36.2	2.6	16.4	0.2	2.3	0.4	1.3	0.3	1.7	0.1	0.6
1996	6.3	43.3	4.7	32.4	2.6	17.8	0.2	2.8	0.4	1.1	0.2	1.7	0.1	0.8
1997	5.1	35.1	6.0	41.1	2.2	15.4	0.2	3.6	0.5	1.7	0.2	1.7	0.2	1.5
1998	7.8	43.5	6.2	34.4	2.4	13.6	0.2	3.5	0.6	1.1	0.5	2.7	0.2	1.2
1999	7.6	43.4	5.7	32.5	2.5	14.2	0.3	4.2	0.7	1.9	0.4	2.5	0.2	1.2
2000	6.3	39.3	5.4	33.5	2.6	16.0	0.5	3.9	0.6	3.0	0.4	2.8	0.3	1.6
2001	7.0	44.5	4.5	29.0	2.5	16.2	0.5	3.7	0.6	3.1	0.3	2.2	0.2	1.3
2002	5.7	38.1	5.2	34.6	2.5	16.4	0.5	3.7	0.6	3.1	0.4	2.5	0.2	1.6
2003	6.9	48.8	3.8	27.3	2.1	14.8	0.4	3.0	0.4	2.9	0.3	2.4	0.1	0.8
2004	5.7	44.0	4.2	32.8	1.5	11.6	0.3	4.2	0.5	2.7	0.3	2.5	0.3	2.1
2005	5.6	49.2	2.8	24.7	1.5	13.3	0.3	3.3	0.4	2.5	0.3	2.5	0.5	4.5
2006	5.6	47.4	2.9	24.8	1.6	13.2	0.3	3.2	0.4	2.5	0.3	2.3	0.8	6.5
2007	5.6	46.4	3.5	29.2	1.9	15.3	0.3	3.5	0.4	2.8	0.2	1.3	0.2	1.5
Number of employees in high-growth firms														
1990	224,759		90,579		90,579		16,229		8,867		486		1,446	
2000	124,499		50,675		50,675		12,363		9,367		8,731		5,040	
2007	130,297		42,914		42,914		9,781		7,946		3,622		4,352	

a half compared to 1990 (Algarve, −6.1 p.p.; Açores, −5 p.p.; Madeira, −2.1 p.p.; Alentejo, −5.5 p.p.; Centro, −2.7 p.p), with Norte suffering a more modest decrease of −0,5 p.p.. Comparing 2007 shares of regional employment, high-growth firms' employment in Lisbon (10.5 %) is almost twice as higher as that of the Norte (6.1 %) and the Algarve (6 %). The regions where high-growth employment is lower in the regions' employment are Madeira and Azores (1.1 % by employment and 1.3 % in Madeira, and 1.5 % in Açores).

Lisbon increased its share of gazelles in the region's employment, surpassing both Norte and Centro over time. In 2007, gazelles' employment share in most regions' employment was below 1.1 %, except for Lisbon which held a share twice as large (2.1 %) and Algarve, with the second highest percentage (1.6 %) (Table 17.4). In 1992, Algarve held the highest share of gazelles in the region's employment (3.8 % according to employment and 6.9 % to the turnover criteria). Despite declining over time to 1.6 % and 3.2 % in 2007, by employment and turnover criteria respectively, its performance was enough to confirm these regions' second and first highest positions in the regional ranking, respectively (Table 17.5).

In 2007, Madeira and Centro are featured as the regions with the smallest share of the region's employment in gazelles (0.4 % in Madeira, according to the employment criteria and 1.5 % in Centro according to the turnover).

Finally, considering the enlarged European Union region, the latest evidence that uses the same methodology we have applied in this paper, points to Portugal being ranked within the middle (bottom) of the ranking of the OECD's Entrepreneurship Monitor 2013 (OECD 2013b), when the indicator "high-growth enterprises rate" is used. In what concerns high-growth firms measured by employment growth, Portugal ranked 11th amongst 16 countries, in the manufacturing sector and 11th amongst 14 countries in the service sector in 2010. Considering the measurement by turnover growth, it scored 7th amongst 11 countries in manufacturing and 6th amongst ten countries in services. In what concerns gazelles, the positioning is comparatively better for the manufacturing sector, 7th in 16 countries and 2nd in ten countries, by the employment and turnover criteria, respectively. In what regards services, it was positioned as 11th amongst 15 countries and 8th amongst ten, by the employment and turnover criteria, respectively.

17.4 Employment and Job Creation

It is well documented in the empirical literature, the disproportionate contribution of young and small firms to the generation of employment, earnings, productivity growth, and overall wealth creation (Henrekson and Johansson 2009; Acs and Mueller 2008; Van Praag and Versloot 2008; Birch et al. 1995; Storey 1994). However, the claim that small businesses generate a large percentage of new jobs has been openly criticized by Davis et al. (1996). Previous findings need to be evaluated in the light of different definitions of small businesses coexisting in the literature, being applied to databases with dissimilar characteristics, but also has to take

Table 17.4 Share of gazelles' employment (employment definition) in total employment (in firms with over ten employees) and in the region's employment, by NUTII regions

Regions	Lisbon e Vale do Tejo		Norle		Centro		Alentejo		Algarve		Madelra		Açores	
	Total employment (+10 empl)	Employment within the region	Total employment (+10 empl)	Employment within the region	Total employment (+10 empl)	Employment within the region	Total employment (+10 empl)	Employment within the region	Total employment (+10 empl)	Employment within the region	Total employment (+10 empl)	Employment within the region	Total employment (+10 empl)	Employment within the region
Share in (%)														
1992	0.5	1.3	0.7	1.9	0.2	1.3	0.0	1.0	0.1	3.8	0.0	1.4	0.0	1.7
1993	0.4	1.1	0.4	1.2	0.2	1.1	0.0	1.0	0.1	7.8	0.0	2.8	0.0	0.0
1994	0.8	2.1	0.7	2.0	0.2	1.1	0.0	1.1	0.1	4.3	0.0	1.2	0.0	0.1
1995	0.8	2.0	0.6	1.7	0.2	1.1	0.0	0.4	0.0	1.1	0.0	1.0	0.0	0.6
1996	0.8	2.2	0.6	1.6	0.2	1.2	0.0	0.5	0.0	1.3	0.0	1.3	0.0	0.7
1997	0.9	2.3	0.4	1.1	0.1	0.8	0.0	0.9	0.0	1.9	0.0	1.0	0.1	6.0
1998	1.0	2.5	0.6	1.6	0.2	1.5	0.1	1.3	0.2	9.3	0.2	10.2	0.1	5.1
1999	1.5	3.9	0.6	1.8	0.3	1.6	0.0	0.9	0.1	6.6	0.0	1.7	0.0	1.0
2000	1.0	2.6	0.4	1.3	0.2	1.1	0.0	0.8	0.1	2.3	0.0	0.7	0.0	2.6
2001	1.1	2.7	0.5	1.5	0.2	1.1	0.1	1.5	0.1	3.2	0.0	0.7	0.0	3.2
2002	1.0	2.4	0.3	1.0	0.2	1.2	0.0	0.7	0.0	1.6	0.0	0.9	0.0	0.5
2003	1.0	2.4	0.4	1.1	0.2	0.9	0.0	0.5	0.1	1.9	0.1	2.4	0.0	1.4
2004	1.1	2.9	0.3	1.0	0.1	0.9	0.0	1.0	0.1	2.5	0.0	1.8	0.0	0.7
2005	0.9	2.4	0.4	1.1	0.1	0.7	0.0	0.6	0.0	1.0	0.0	1.3	0.1	3.3
2006	0.6	1.5	0.4	1.3	0.1	0.7	0.0	0.8	0.1	1.7	0.0	1.3	0.0	1.6
2007	0.8	2.1	0.4	1.1	0.2	0.9	0.0	1.1	0.1	1.6	0.0	0.4	0.0	0.7
Number of employees in gazelles														
1992	9,494		12,632		3,706		1,317		631		375		357	
2000	20,169		8,797		3,580		1,049		615		257		743	
2007	19,062		8,714		20		1,217		1,051		197		280	

Table 17.5 Share of gazelles' employment (turnover definition) in total employment (in firms with over ten employees) and in the region's employment, by NUTII regions

Regions	Lisbon e Vale do Tejo		Norle		Centro		Alentejo		Algarve		Madelra		Açores	
	Total employment (+10 empl)	Employment within the region	Total employment (+10 empl)	Employment within the region	Total employment (+10 empl)	Employment within the region	Total employment (+10 empl)	Employment within the region	Total employment (+10 empl)	Employment within the region	Total employment (+10 empl)	Employment within the region	Total employment (+10 empl)	Employment within the region
Share in (%)											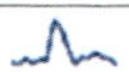	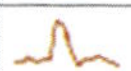	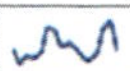	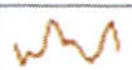
1992	0.9	2.4	2.0	5.4	0.6	3.6	0.1	1.9	0.1	6.9	0.0	3.1	0.0	2.6
1933	1.6	4.1	1.4	3.9	0.5	3.4	0.1	1.5	0.2	11.4	0.0	2.7	0.0	0.0
1994	1.2	3.2	1.0	2.8	0.5	3.0	0.1	1.6	0.2	9.0	0.1	4.2	0.0	1.6
1995	0.9	2.4	1.2	3.3	0.4	2.4	0.0	0.4	0.1	4.0	0.0	2.8	0.0	1.2
1996	1.0	2.5	0.7	2.1	0.4	2.3	0.0	0.8	0.1	3.1	0.1	3.4	0.0	1.9
1997	0.8	2.2	0.8	2.2	0.4	2.5	0.1	1.6	0.1	3.5	0.1	3.2	0.1	5.5
1998	1.4	3.6	1.3	3.6	0.4	2.7	0.1	1.3	0.2	9.3	0.3	12.8	0.1	4.9
1999	1.5	4.0	1.1	3.1	0.4	2.5	0.1	1.4	0.2	10.6	0.2	11.7	0.0	2.7
2000	1.0	2.6	0.9	2.6	0.3	2.0	0.1	1.4	0.1	3.7	0.1	2.8	0.0	2.9
2001	1.2	3.1	0.8	2.4	0.3	2.1	0.1	2.4	0.1	3.1	0.0	2.0	0.0	2.3
2002	1.6	4.1	0.9	2.6	0.4	2.3	0.1	1.8	0.1	4.2	0.1	3.5	0.0	1.0
2003	1.3	3.4	0.8	2.3	0.4	2.3	0.1	1.5	0.1	3.7	0.1	3.2	0.0	0.5
2004	1.3	3.3	0.7	2.0	0.4	2.3	0.1	2.1	0.2	7.0	0.1	4.3	0.1	1.4
2005	1.1	2.9	1.1	3.4	0.4	2.2	0.1	2.0	0.1	2.9	0.1	3.5	0.1	4.3
2006	0.7	1.8	0.7	2.2	0.3	1.9	0.1	2.0	0.1	2.6	0.1	3.1	0.1	5.4
2007	0.8	2.0	0.7	2.2	0.2	1.5	0.1	1.8	0.1	3.2	0.0	2.0	0.0	2.0
Number of employees in gazelles														
1992	17,412		35,914		10,271		2,399		1,249		829		545	
2000	19,754		17,588		6,749		1,708		1,090		2,228		834	
2007	18,456		17,109		5,598		2,384		1,700		963		758	

into account that smaller firms destroy more jobs due to their higher failure rates. Thus, when job destruction is accounted for, a significantly smaller share of net new jobs are created by these firms. A number of studies have also maintained that high-growth firms account for a significant percentage of net job creation (Anyadike-Danes et al. 2013; Salas et al. 2010; NESTA 2009; Anyadike-Danes et al. 2009; OECD 2002; Schreyer 2000). In this section, we will approach high-growth and gazelle employment and job creation according to the employment criteria, in order to understand which types of firms engender more job creation.

For the count of job creation several precisions need to be made, namely flows of gross job creation and loss must be distinguished from net job creation (the difference between job gains and job losses). Although obtaining net job creation is commonly the target, information on gross flows can also be of interest to policy, as simultaneous job creation and destruction shows evidence of labor market churning, which is part of firm dynamics and the process of market adjustment.[15]

In Portugal, much of this churning is size related. Within the period 1990–2005 the average enterprise churn rate for the overall economy was 28 %, where small enterprises under 50 employees displayed a churn of 29 %, while large enterprises over 250 employees showed a turbulence rate of 5.5 %. However, it is also important to disentangle the relative importance of birth rates, the decline of larger firms and the survival and growth of existing firms and its contribution to employment growth. Within the period 1987–2005, an average of over 20 % of all jobs in active employer enterprises were being created and destroyed within a single year. For the largest firms (+250), we observe that the percentage created by firm rotation (entries and exits) was low (3 %, with the share of job creation due to entry of new firms being 2.6 %), thus existing firms created most jobs (97 %). In the overall economy, 83.9 % of new jobs were created by existing firms and 16.1 % by firm rotation within a year. The percentage of job creation due solely to the entry of new firms recorded 6.7 %. Thus, small firms contributed the most for net job creation through firm rotation, while in larger firms the majority of job creation originated from established firms.

Secondly, when analyzing net job creation, beyond taking into consideration the aggregate level of employment, one should also consider the relative importance of firm characteristics and the role played by particular groups of firms, as net job creation may differ substantially across levels and collections of firms. For instance, even though total employment may decrease, certain groups of firms (e.g., large) may enjoy net job growth. Thus, one of the most common appraisal indicators is net job creation rates for different firm characteristics, notably different size-classes to account for the contribution of small and large firms.

[15]The challenge arises from the number of firms being a stock variable, measured at a single point in time whilst job creation, as a flow is measured between two different points in time. Consequently, this relationship also depends on the length of the measurement period.

Thirdly, net job creation rates are percentage ratios relating net job gains to the total number of employees.[16] However, a large job creation rate does not necessarily mean a large absolute contribution to the total number of net jobs created.[17] Thus, a size-class with a high net job creation rate but with a small share of initial employment, may still cause a minor impact on overall job creation, whereas a size-class with a large share of employment may contribute more substantially to overall net job creation, even with a small rate of net job creation.

It might be useful to consider more in detail the way in which high-growth firms are measured in the Eurostat/OECD (2007) adopted methodology. In this paper, job creation is not being measured in three-year spans, that is, each firm's employment growth is not being accounted from its first relative to its third year of growth. In other contemporary high-growth research, job creation is measured otherwise, within 3-year spells where growth is measured, for instance, between the first and third year for firms which were already selected precisely because they were already growing fast. It is then obvious that job creation has to be positive, as no job destruction is accounted for. Furthermore, in this "static" 3-year measurement, firms do not "leave" the group of high-growth firms. Clearly, beyond obtaining a positive count of jobs, it will also tend to be large, as the best performing firms are being measured precisely during the periods they perform the best, leading to the conclusion that high-growth firms are responsible for a disproportionately high share in employment relative to its share in total enterprises.

On the other hand, in our methodology, as reported in Sect. 17.2, firms have to comply with a sequence of 3 years of annualized average growth of 20 % (in either employment or turnover) in order to qualify for the category of high-growth firm or gazelle. After being classified as a high-growth or gazelle in a given year, if in the following year that particular firm does not add up to 20 % of annualized growth (making it three successive years of growth), they are removed from the group of fast-growing firms. Another aspect worth mentioning is that when a given firm does not manage to grow at this rate and withdraws from this fast-growing "group," it removes its employees from this count, which represents a kind of "job destruction" given the way the data is conveyed, which will only be cancelled out if incoming high-growth firms or gazelles to the group bring along an equivalent amount of employees to during that same year. Because not every firm is able to sustain indefinitely this rhythm of rapid growth, net job creation might be negative in a given year, if the amount of employment of excluded high-growth firms (that were not able to sustain that amount of growth the following year) is greater than the amount of employment brought forward by incoming firms (included that year in the count of high-growth firms).

Given our methodology, job creation is dependent not only on the amount of turnover of firms that qualify (and leave) each year the pool of high-growth and

[16] In the case of the present data, it refers to employees in employer enterprises in the size-class of over ten employees.

[17] As absolute contributions are the product of net job creation rates and the share that a category occupies in total employment.

gazelles, but also on their relative size as compared to the firms which leave the group. In other words, incoming and outgoing fast-growing firms' average size also matters. Despite the waves of new incoming firms, if outgoing firms are on average larger employers than incoming, negative job creation might occur. Consequently, net job creation results from the interaction of both quantity and size of firms entering and leaving the group of fast-growing firms each year. Thus, with our methodology and such an indicator as net job creation, periods of negative job creation can occur, whereby the outflow of high-growth firms with larger average employment is greater than that brought in by incoming firms.

For fast-growing enterprises, the debate concerning whether it is the high growth of a few number of firms or the entry of many new incumbents that engenders employment growth is ongoing and is still being fuelled by new evidence (Lawless 2013; Davidsson and Delmar 2006). In what concerns gazelles, Henrekson and Johansson (2009) point to a complementarity between these two views, whereby employment in the average new firm is as important as the net job contribution of these firms. Put differently, a continuous entry of new firms is necessary to achieve net job creation, given that only a small subset of gazelles manages to achieve sustained growth (Parker et al. 2010; Henrekson and Johansson 2009).

We find this to be the case of Portuguese employer enterprise data, according to the criteria we use for accounting high growth. Particularly due to the high turbulence related to firm churning, especially in sectors such as services (Sarmento and Nunes 2010a, 2012), both the amount and relative size of firms that go in and out of the category of fast-growing firms each year cannot be neglected by the analysis. We should also draw the attention to the fact that the method by which fast-growing firms are selected matters to the results and hardens comparability between different studies. Different definitions and methodologies used for classifying fast-growing firms in specific settings and countries can yield diverse results and caution must be employed not to overstate their relative importance.

In Fig. 17.6, we portray net job creation in active employer enterprises with over ten employees, along with that of high-growth firms and of gazelles. Given the employment and job creation focus of this section, we will privilege the usage of the employment definition to account for high-growth and gazelles, which despite being more demanding on the firm, yields better results for international comparability across countries, being more "resistant" and less biased towards other influencing factors such as taxation systems, which can blur turnovers.

Given the longitudinal perspective of this research, net job creation is measured by the difference between gross job creation and gross job destruction in consecutive years. Gross job creation (or destruction) is the sum of employment gains (loss) for all (new and existing) employer enterprises whose employment level is greater (smaller) than that of the previous year.[18] We observe high-growth and gazelle's net job creation accompanies the major upward and downward job creation cycles, but its peaks are more softened, especially in the case of gazelles, which seem to suffer from a lower volatility and exposure to the business cycle. The negative peaks have

[18] More static analysis account for net job creation as the difference between job gains and job losses in any given year.

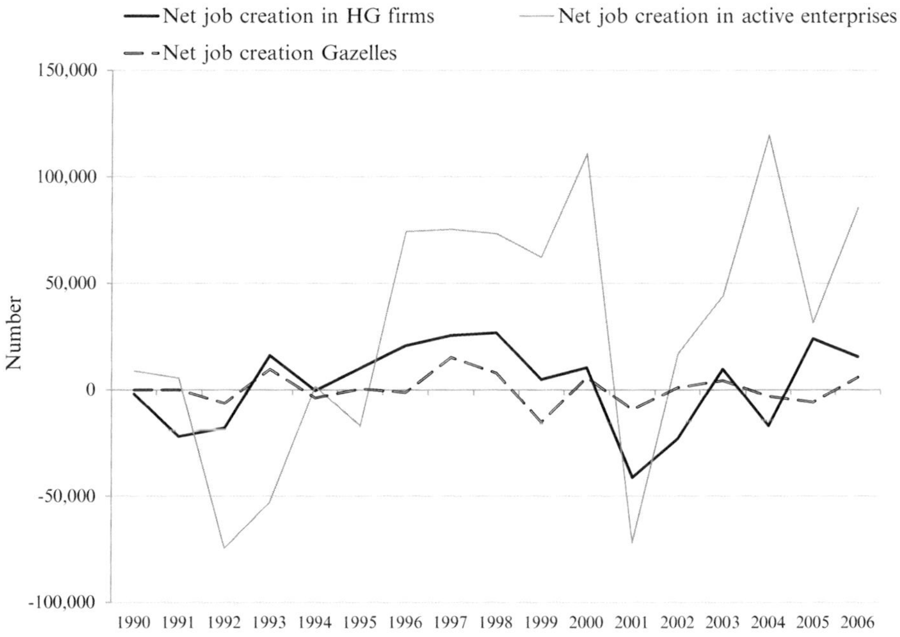

Fig. 17.6 Net job creation in high-growth firms and gazelles (employment definition) and in active enterprises with over ten employees (number of employees), 1991–2007

been shown to be related to periods of economic downturn[19] (e.g., Sarmento and Nunes 2010b, 2012).

In order to facilitate this investigation, we group the study period into subperiods (1991–1995, 1996–2001, 2002–2007, and 2003–2007), due to the substantial volatility surrounding the two main years of economic slowdown, 1993 and 2000 (Table 17.6). During the first sub-period, high-growth enterprises were responsible for the destruction of 20 % of employment of firms with over ten employees, as the number of firms that managed to sustain that rate of growth decreased visibly between 1991 and 1995, with the exception of 1994, where there was a net increase of ten firms. Due to the methodology used, the effect of crisis of 1993 is still observable during the following 3 years, and only from 1996 onwards is the count of both high-growth and gazelles (by employment) positive, the same happening for turnover one year later, in 1997. Thus, the number of firms able to sustain the rhythm of growth of 20 % in three consecutive years in order to qualify for the category high-growth firms decreased considerably over this period, bringing about considerable job destruction. Gazelles, however, managed to create 80 net jobs from 1992 to 1995, showing a better endurance to the economic slowdown.

Between 1996 and 2001, a recovery period mediating between the two downturn periods, net job creation in fast-growing firms amounted to 111,568 jobs, over a quarter (29.4 %) of the total net job creation in firms with more than ten employees.

[19] Business cycles could explain part of the dynamism of European firms (Biosca 2010).

Table 17.6 Net job creation in high-growth firms and gazelles (employment definition) and in active enterprises with over ten employees (number of employees), 1991–2007

	Unit	1991–1995	1996–2001	2002–2007	2003–2007
Active employer enterprises (>10 employees)					
Net job creation	No.	−128,574	379,479	225,186	297,158
Share active enterprises (>10 employees) employment in total employment	%	79.1	74.4	71.7	71.8
High-growth (by employment)					
Net job creation	No.	−25,898	98,619	−31,793	9,380
Share in active enterprises (>10) net job creation	%	20.1	26.0	(14.1)	3.2
Gazelles (by employment)		1992–1995	1996–2001	2002–2007	2002–2007
Net job creation	No.	80	12,949	−7,041	2,312
Share in active enterprises (>10) net job creation	%	(0.1)	3.4	(3.1)	0.8

Note: Shares between brackets have either a negative numerator or denominator

High-growth firms, which represented an average of 3.3 % of total active firms with over ten employees throughout this period, engendered 26 % of overall net job creation and accounted for the bulk of the net job creation (88 %) as compared to gazelles (22 %), which represented 0.8 % of all firms, creating 3.4 % of total net job creation. In contrast, the following period 2002–2007 depicts net job destruction for both types of firms if the year of 2002 is included in the count, which indicates that a combination of more numerous and possibly larger fast-growing firms exited these categories (Table 17.6).

Because of the methodology and the count of 3 years of successive growth, the impact of the 2000 crisis is shown to be more prominent in the year 2002, as several firms were not able to maintain their growth trajectories. Over the sub-periods, it is observable that although gazelle job creation rates are lower than high-growth's, due to being less abundant in the economy, they display nonetheless better resilience to the business cycle, not only by creating but also by destroying a lesser amount of jobs.

In order to provide a perspective of these firms' importance for the Portuguese economy, Table 17.7 displays a summary of their shares in the number of enterprises, employment, and job creation.

Within the extended period, high-growth firms represented 3.1 % of all active enterprises with over ten employees and 7.5 % of its employment, but generated 7.9 % of its jobs, which corresponds to 4 % of all active employer enterprises job creation. Gazelles displayed a more striking performance, even though they created a lesser amount of jobs, given they are less abundant than high-growth firms in the economy. Gazelles represented less than 1 % of all active enterprises with over ten employees and less than 2 % of its employment, but generated a considerable higher proportion of job creation, 7 %, which corresponds to 3.5 % of all job creation by

Table 17.7 Share of high-growth and gazelles (by employment) in the number of enterprises, employment, and job creation, during 1990–2007 and 1992–2007, respectively

	Share in			
	Active enterprises (>10 employees)	Employment in active enterprises (>10 employees)	Job creation in active enterprises (>10 employees)	Job creation (all active enterprises)
	%			
High-growth	3.1	7.5	7.9	4.0
Gazelles	0.8	1.7	7.0	3.5
Fast-growing firms	3.9	9.2	14.9	7.5

all active employer enterprises. Thus taken together, fast-growing firms, roughly 4 % of firms with over ten employees, employing 9 % of its workforce, created 15 % of all jobs (and 7.5 % when firms of all size-classes are considered).

Next, we attempt to disentangle the effects of size in job creation for fast-growing firms, dividing firms into two main groups, SMEs and large firms. We have first computed a shift-share analysis of job creation by size-class to later arrive at the summary of shares for the most relevant economic variables, shown in Table 17.8.

In Portugal, over the period 1990–2007, 98 % of enterprises (10–249 employees) were SMEs. When all active employer enterprises are considered (1–250), this proportion raises to 99.6 %. In what concerns high-growth firms, 93 % are SMEs (10–249) and only 7 % stand as large enterprises. We observe that this small number of large high-growth firms employing more than 250 employees (over 100 enterprises during the extended period, weighing 52 % in overall high-growth employment), were responsible for 95 % of the total jobs created by high-growth firms from 1990 to 2007. This amounts to 38,706 jobs or 65 % of all jobs created by active enterprises with over ten employees and more than half of all jobs created by all employer enterprise firms. This is striking when compared to the universe of Portuguese active employer enterprises with over ten employees, which only accomplished a mere 11 % of job creation and 7 % when all active enterprises are considered.

Four main reasons lie behind this ravishing performance of the largest high-growth firms. Their number and relative abundance over time, coupled with size and age characteristics. Firstly, their average size (803 employees) is disproportionately higher than that of high-growth firms in other size-classes (55 for high-growth SMEs) and greater than that of active firms of the same size-class (763 workers in all employer enterprises). Secondly, employment in the largest size-class of high-growth firms, as compared to remaining smaller size-classes of firms increased considerably over time during this period. Furthermore, by the late 2000s the biggest size-class of high-growth firms were more abundant than at the start of the 1990s (the share of firms with over 250 employees increased 10 p.p. from 43 % in 1990 to 53 % in 2007). Fourthly, high-growth firms are on average older than gazelles. Their ability to thrive has already been put to test as they have stood for longer in the market. According to the age-survival relationship found in previous research,

Table 17.8 High-growth firms, gazelles, and active firms share in enterprises, employment, and job creation, by size-class

	Average in the period	Size class	Share in number of enterprises (%)		Share in employment (%)		Share in job creation (%)		Absolute contribution to overall jobs created (no. of jobs)		Share in overall jobs created (%)	Average number of jobs created (no. of jobs created/no. of firms)		Average size (no. of employees)	
			SMEs (×250)	Large (×250)	SMEs (×250)	Large (×250)	SMEs (×250)	Large (×250)	SMEs (×250)	Large (×250)		SMEs (×250)	Large (×250)	SMEs (×250)	Large (×250)
High growth	1990–2007	>10	93	7	47	53	5	95	2,222	38,706	High growth:	5	401	55	803
Active employer enterprises			98	2	66	34	89	11	458,784	59,553	>10 7.9	32	69	45	763
		A1	99.6	0.4	75	25	93	7	960,726	68,159	A1 4.0	20	79	30	
Gazelles	1992–2007	>10	94	6	53	47	39	61	13,406	20,592	Gazelles:	118	1,030	52	764
Active employer enterprises			98	2	67	33	81	19	392,337	91,775	>10 7.0	27	107	46	762
		A1	99.7	0.3	75	25	89	11	861,534	104,269	A1 3.5	17	122	30	
Active employer enterprises	1996–2007	>10	98	2	65	35	92	8	641,930	57,991	100.0	48	75	47	770
		A1	99.6	0.4	74	26	95	5	1,241,628	67,336	100.0	28	87	30	

larger firms exhibit higher average survival rates (Nunes and Sarmento 2012). Thus, taken as a size-class, its job creation ability has been above the average of other size-classes and also above that of the largest size-class of gazelles, making them extremely resilient to job destruction and hence a massive net positive contributor to job creation.

But within younger firms,[20] size seems to also matter. Despite gazelle's large average size (764 employees), similar to that of the average large firm (762), their average size as a size-class is substantially higher than that of other gazelle's size-classes (52). Considered from a size-class perspective, largest firms amass 47 % of gazelle's employment over the extended period. The larger gazelles with over 250 employees (6 % of all gazelles, corresponding to an average of 20 enterprises over the extended period) are responsible for 66 % of gazelles' job creation, contributing with 20,592 jobs (22 % of all jobs created by active enterprises with over ten employees and 20 % of jobs created by all active enterprises). This performance is overwhelming when compared to active employer enterprises in the period 1992–2007, which only managed to create 19 % of jobs in overall jobs created by firms with over ten employees and 11 % when job creation in all active enterprises is considered.

Despite the smaller amount of gazelles (averaging 22.5 % of that of high-growth firms within the period 1992–2007), they managed to create 58 % of high-growth firms' jobs, and 37 % of all job creation of fast-growing firms, thus engendering relatively more jobs per firm than high-growth enterprises (1,148 new jobs created on average compared to 203 for all high-growth firms). This seems to be attributed to these younger firms capacity not only to foster faster job creation, but to better endure unfavorable business cycles, thus triggering less job destruction than their high-growth counterparts.

Six main findings arise from the analysis of these empirical facts. Firstly, net job gains are significantly smaller than gross job gains. Secondly, fast-growing firms are outstanding job creators, being 3.9 % of all firms over ten employees, but employing 9.2 % of the workforce and being responsible for 15 % of jobs and 7.5 % of those created by all active enterprises.

Thirdly, from the group of fast-growing firms, gazelles are the most outstanding job creators. They are less relatively abundant and smaller than high-growth, thus their absolute share in job creation is lower, though close, to that of high-growth firms. Nonetheless, their impact is strikingly higher. Their job creation ability is disproportionately higher given their smaller weight in the share of firms and employment. Gazelles constitute only 0.8 % of all firms, with an employment share of 1.7 %, but manage to create 7 % of jobs in active enterprises with over ten employees, which represents four times its employment share.

[20] The pool of high-growth firms contain on average older firms than the pool of gazelles. This is also verified for Portugal using another information source applying a similar methodology (Informa D&B 2011). Stylized facts of firm dynamics also indicate that established firms, are on average, of a bigger size than new entrants.

Fourthly, net job creation tends to be the highest among the largest high-growth and gazelle firms (over 250 employees), contrary to what is verified in the universe of active employer enterprises. Thus, the largest high-growth firms and gazelles are responsible for the bulk of job creation. In fact, a very few firms, a total of 120 high-growth firms and gazelles on average in the period, generated 44 % of the total jobs created by large firms in the extended period (65 % by high-growth firms and 23 % by gazelles), corresponding to a share of 9.5 % of the total job creation in enterprises with over ten employees (compared to a share of 9.7 % for all high-growth firms) and 4.3 % for gazelles (7 % for all gazelles).

This evidence for fast-growing firms challenges the standard assumption of the negative relationship between size and net job creation, whereas most job creation is attributed to small firms. This however still holds true when the overall set of enterprises is considered, where 99.6 % of enterprises are SMEs, responsible for 95 % of all job creation.

Fifthly, considering the largest size-class, high-growth firms create comparatively more (net) jobs than gazelles (95 % and 61 % respectively). This group of the largest high-growth firms, not as young as gazelles, but of a larger average size[21] are of critical importance as a source for job creation in the Portuguese economy.

Sixthly, when comparing the contribution to job creation of these two types of fast-growing firms, we find that is not firm age per se that drives the bulk of net job creation, but rather firm size along with the turnover of firms that are able to attain and sustain high growth[22]. Thus, for the group of employer enterprise firms with over ten employees, size seems to bring about a relatively more significant impact in job creation than age. As mentioned, the discrepancy between average firm sizes for the largest size-class of both gazelles and high-growth is staggering. Another fact which can also help explaining this phenomenon can be traced back to the characteristics of Portuguese entrepreneurial fabric, which displays a smaller average size as compared to most of their European and American counterparts (Sarmento and Nunes 2010a; OECD 2008, 2009) and a sustained decreasing average firm size over the last two decades (Sarmento and Nunes 2010a, c). In this setting, firms with a larger than average size, such as large fast-growing firms, can bring about a more significant impact on job creation.

Another factor worth pointing out is whether the relative impact of the largest size-class of high-growth and gazelles in job creation would be reduced if we considered all firms and not only, those with more than ten employees also depend on the amount of high-growth and gazelles in the population of micro-firms. It is acknowledged that attaining higher rates of growth in employment is relatively easier for smaller than for larger firms (e.g., for firms with one employer, the hiring of another already qualifies them as high-growth). However, there are many methodological issues that make these firms' inclusion problematic, hindering comparabil-

[21] High-growth average firm size is larger than that of gazelles' throughout the period.

[22] We cannot fully evaluate size *vis-à-vis* with age, as the methodology we employ restricts the analysis to firms with over ten employees. This excludes 20–30 % of Portuguese employer enterprises from the analysis.

ity at the international level, and arguing for their exclusion from the pool of firms where fast-growing firms are drawn. A last remark to mention that if we took the more positive stance of the turnover criteria, bearing in mind that the turnover criteria always yield a greater amount of employment for Portuguese firms, the impact of these fast-growing firms in job creation would have been even higher.

17.5 High-Impact Growth and Policy Design

As already mentioned, there is wide agreement surrounding the significant generation of broader social benefits, arising from the activities of high-growth and gazelles, in terms of both employment and earnings and the spread of its benefits to the economy as a whole. This evidence has turned high-growth and gazelles into a row model that many aim to follow. Accordingly, several authors have advocated the adoption of selective assistance interventions, focused on firms that have the potential of becoming high growth and impacting the real economy. In view of this line of argument, one might be led to think that all that remains to be done is to provide fast-growing firms with the conditions, means, and support to ensure that their growth is sustainable and more widespread.

In this quest, policy-makers are often left to figure out for themselves the right kind of policy-mix and geographical scale of intervention that better supports these fast-growing firms, some even without a clear understanding if these are worth pursuing or not, given the usual market failure rational behind policy intervention and the potential for deadweight loss. But how close should policy zoom into these firms for an optimal policy fit and maximum impact is a matter still under considerable debate.

This section intends to tackle these issues and contribute to the discussion by shedding some clarity onto the process of policy design for fast-growing ventures. The challenge is to translate our present (limited) knowledge on these issues into a conceptual framework for conceiving policy support, which remains sufficiently robust to be used within a policy context. This is approached through a conceptual modular framework, divided into six building blocks of questions that ought to be answered sequentially: "why," "what," "who," "when," and "how" to provide support, to finally arrive at the "so what" fundamental question.

By definition, fast-growing enterprises create more jobs, being crucial for change and renewal of productive sectors (Schreyer 2000). But is there an economic rational or some form of policy justification to provide specific support to successful enterprises? Why should high-growth firms and gazelles be offered more (targeted) support than other ventures, when they appear to need it the less? These overperforming firms present a major challenge to policy-makers, as high-growth firms are themselves the product of a dynamic growth process of a market, whereas gazelles are in a constant state of change. Thus, what makes a clear target for policy?

Knowledgeable policy-makers demand to use the best available evidence in order to make evidence-based decisions or, at best, informed-based decisions. By looking into the empirical evidence for an answer, one realizes that no matter how carefully empirical studies are laid out, most suffer from data and methodological constraints[23] and are often by themselves not able to provide an insight on how to connect observable facts with the best policies, and thus lead firms, regions, and national economies into the best growth path (Anyadike-Danes et al. 2013; Basu 2013). Furthermore, there is a considerable scope for human subjective reasoning, as linking data and statistical procedures with policy entails invariably a leap of imagination.

It is also common to ascertain that beyond data, theory must be employed to make policy prescriptions. Moreover, in order to decide appropriately, one also needs reason and "that is often a stumbling block" (Basu 2013, p. 17). In such a case, what is the role of theory in all this process? Are there instances where theory can be made expendable, cases where spotting regularities in data, coupled with reasoned intuition can lead into useful policy prescriptions? Hitherto, one of the main roles of theory has been to allow consistency checks on our intuitive beliefs.

And is entrepreneurial success determined internally by the assembled resources of the firm, or is it environmentally determined? Or is it derived from the interaction of both internal and external factors? Different theories contend different approaches.

Consequently, how to address all these innumerable and conflicting demands? Primarily, we have to acknowledge the limitations of the present exercise. No matter the size of the population from which we draw our analysis, since it is impossible to draw even the smallest samples from tomorrow's businesses, and given that the policies we craft today are due for future implementation, there is actually no scientific way to go from today's evidence regularities into tomorrow's policy. We are then left to rely heavily on reasoned intuition, common sense, and good judgement to bring about clairvoyance to informed decision-making.

17.5.1 Why "Type" of Questions

Thereby, we start by acknowledging the importance of asking the "why" type of questions, a fundamental ingredient of human understanding. In our view, when considering policy and/or support design, the "why" type of questions have to be addressed right from the start and well ahead before dwelling into other considerations.

However, providing answers to these interrogations is neither easy nor straightforward. Thus, for the time being, what can we pinpoint that can still be

[23] This can be due to data paucity, data quality constrains, and a variety of methodological issues, amongst which diversity of measurements which can disregard gross job flows in favor of a narrower emphasis on net job contribution and regression-to-the-mean effects (Haltiwanger and Krizan 1999).

put to good use from a policy perspective? Firstly, there is still no consensus surrounding the validity of market failure arguments in support of high-growth ventures. In most common frameworks of policy action, support to firms is justified where a problem of some kind arises in a given market, usually related to market failures. These can be derived from situations such as low skill levels, low supply of capital, informational barriers, and low investment levels in areas where R&D has a public good nature. Many caution that there is no market failure rational behind these types of policy interventions and that those focused on fast-growing firms amount to "picking winners," which should not be the primary aim of government support. Gazelles might even make a stronger case to receive some type of support, given that market failures are more susceptible to arise from the additional risk derived from their activity and investment decisions, as they usually engage in more uncertain activities. But gazelles are by definition successful. They are the living proof of far better achievements at handling risk, which growth and expansion entails, than most other firms. Thus, what does often legitimize support is the realization of market failures arising from the specific needs of these firms not being adequately addressed by the market and the private sector due to asymmetric and incomplete information, as well as moral hazard issues.

Secondly, policy support can also be legitimized by system failures, such as the lack of interaction with innovative systems, academic and knowledge networks or situations where impairments of some kind limit the absorption of new scientific knowledge. Thirdly, it can also be legitimized by broader macroeconomic goals such as employment creation or productivity growth related to competitiveness issues. These do not necessarily need to go together. They are often mutually exclusive in terms of policy options and design. The underlying motivation is that the market might be generating a suboptimal level of fast-growing enterprises and thus employment and wealth creation, leading to inefficient allocation of resources, stemming from market failures or suboptimal levels of value creation, this time derived from system failures. An obvious outcome of policy support is the increase in the number and incidence of high-impact firms that can spur faster growth in key economic variables. The ultimate outcome can be more employment or new value creation through production growth, achieved by increased innovation and productivity.

As current practice is concerned in this particular field, high-growth firm policy has been promoted enthusiastically, despite the known weaknesses lying at the base of its evidence and the lack of impact studies demonstrating clear positive effects in firm growth and performance and its relation to macroeconomic variables such as employment or job creation. Somehow, policy-making has been running ahead of evidence, frequently driven by government policy rhetoric, political headlines, benchmarking, and "arms race" competitions with other countries (or regions), thus implemented based on the assumption that more is better than less, that higher rates of ambitious entrepreneurship are preferable to feeble ones and that some regions can instantaneously become more attractive to capital and investment. These motivations are particularly emphasized when output indicators, such as unemployment rates behave unfavorably. The lack of a clear economic rational, such as when policy support only stems from a coordinated reaction of some regions/countries to others, might explain the absence of the positive estimated aggregate effects on GDP and employment levels.

In the early days, since its inception in 1990, entrepreneurship promotion efforts were geared towards increasing the rate of entrepreneurship, rather than targeting specific types of entrepreneurs or firms. By then, distinction was not made between high or low rhythms of growth. Today, in contrast, several countries (e.g., Denmark; Finland; Sweden; France; Netherlands; UK, and Scotland in particular, Germany, Canada, US, and New Zealand)[24] have geared some of its policies towards nurturing an increasing number of fast-growing firms, especially gazelles, which can yield higher and faster job creation rates. Some already have mechanisms in place (Stam et al. 2012; Europe INNOVA 2011; Lilischkis 2013). But most of these policies still draw on the standard arsenal conceived for intervening at the national level, through mechanisms such as industrial policy, whereas employing regional and local policies for engendering and stimulating higher growth firms is still found to be uncommon (OECD 2013a). These facts point to the need of undergoing a preliminary mapping of existing policies, and uncovering those which are already affecting fast-growing enterprises, either positively or negatively, and directly or indirectly. It might be the case that only some fine-tuning on instruments and/or targets is required for policies or programs in progress.

In Denmark, policy design starts by approaching the business cycle. Depending on how well the economy is progressing, the emphasis shifts between fostering productivity or job creation. During the last few years, the emphasis has been on job creation, although in reality the end effect may well be on both. After the support is provided, Danish authorities also conduct surveys in order to track and assess real progress in performance and job creation.

In connection to the way Danish authorities approach this matter, more fundamental questions arise, concerning for instance whether the lack or underperformance of fast-growing firms is the consequence or the cause of the economic performance of a region or an economy. The case of Portugal shows that the country has some of the highest rates of new firm formation relative to the existing stock of firms and some of the highest death rates of its European counterparts, particularly in the services sector (Sarmento and Nunes 2010a, b, 2012). The available evidence for Portuguese micro-firms seems to point to the fact that high growth does not seem to grant better survival chances. Gazelles seem more prone to dying than high-growth

[24] The Gazelle growth program, for instance, assists the best Danish growth companies to expand to international markets. For Finland, consider the VIGO programme Lilischkis (2013) and for Sweden Bornefalk and Du Rietz (2009). For France, see Betbèze and Saint-Étienne (2006), for Germany consider the IMProve project, for instance. For Scotland consider Brown and Mawson (2013) and for Canada, Herman and Williams (2013). For the United States, consider the initiative Start-up America and for New Zealand see Ministry of Business, Innovation and Employment (2013) and New Zealand Government (2013).

firms, showing that rapid growth based on short-run factors, such as the business cycle does not grant longevity or sustained growth.[25] Firms' behavior and performance thus seem to a large extent to be a by-product of the economy's own economic performance and its subdued pattern of structural reforms (e.g., OECD 2012).

The fact that job creation in fast-growing firms stems from a long line of empirical research, proven to be consistent among different settings and countries, provides a starting point and a reasoning for considering some form of policy intervention, or at least of looking into ways of synergizing with existing policies so as to include these firms.

After identifying the exact market failure to be addressed, or in case there is none, after devising a sufficiently robust economic rational, the raison d'être, for policy support in favor of fast-growing firms, policy design should focus on clarifying sequentially other five types of questions, "what" is the purpose, "who" to support, to later address the combination of "when" and "how" to intervene in the market with the right support propositions.

17.5.2 What Are the Intended Results?

In case a decision is taken to formally support fast-growing firms, a policy and strategy is known to be able to facilitate high impact entrepreneurship through delivered outputs and outcomes of policy support. From a macroeconomic perspective, decisions have to be made whether in the particular situation of a region/country, priority is given to job creation and employment or to productivity increases, faster growth, and value creation. These two different options lead to different outputs and outcomes for non-high-growth firms and entrepreneurs and for firms who are already growing at a faster rate. From a more microeconomic perspective, a fundamental choice has to be made ahead, if the intended purpose is to increase the quantity or improve the quality of entrepreneurial ventures. This entails deciding on the intervention reach (if broad or more targeted) and determining whether policy support will aim at facilitating entry, new firm operation, business growth, awaking dormant firms, or support the repetition of period of high-growth.

Consequently, different policies, strategies, and combinations of instruments ought to be devised according to the desired results of policy support but need to be tailored to target audiences, which often overlap. As its distinction and specific linkages to the remainder modules of this framework is not always obvious, we propose to look at the actors in more detail in the next section.

---

[25] From the 87 % of Portuguese micro-firms existing between 1991 and 2009 in the Bank of Portugal's *Central de Balanços* database, only ten grew into large firms (Banco de Portugal 2010).

17.5.3 Who to Support?

When applying the "who" to support criteria for arriving at a suitable policy design, several successive layers of selectivity questions have to be thought through. In the first place, are fast-growing enterprises/ambitious entrepreneurs[26] the most appropriate target for reaching the desired economic goals? Further down the road, the answer to this question makes a difference for the chosen policy-mix, as a more general "enabling" policy might be able to deliver the intended results and be better suited to bring about the intended benefits, which can be more widespread to the general entrepreneurial fabric. We propose a segmentation criteria to be made on the basis of firm growth or growth prospects according to pretested variables, instead of the most commonly used age or size. Then, further selection layers can be applied according to most prevalent characteristics of firms, such as age, size, industry, and technology intensiveness. The way to slice across the population of enterprises to obtain different groups of firms with a given range of characteristics considered useful to target, is highly dependent on the policy purpose.

Secondly, it is relevant to distinguish between targeting the entrepreneur or the firm. We have chosen to include both. One of the possibly ways to tackle who to support is to start by segmenting actors based on their growth pattern and secondly age, so as to distinguish fast-growing ventures from static and former fast-growing firms and among them, young from old (in order to isolate gazelles from high-growth firms).

Thirdly, whether the former or the latter, or both, are chosen to receive support, a detailed characterization is needed for identifying exactly who, amongst all actors, will be targeted for support. If the objective is targeting a firm/entrepreneur that has a potential or is already engaged in some kind of high-growth, some sort of definition of "what" constitutes high-growth is also required. As mentioned earlier, there are no universal definitions for entrepreneurship, let alone for high-growth entrepreneurship. At the international level, the most commonly used has been the OECD/Eurostat's (2007), but other countries and authors have devised and employed a diverse array. For instance, in Denmark, the threshold for a high-growth enterprise is not ten employees, but five, as firms are considered too small. In the Netherlands, the OECD definition was not fully adopted as the size of the firm is taken at the end of the three year period of growth. Parker et al. (2010) makes use of the definition of a firm belonging to the group with the highest rate of growth of a population, in a particular period (e.g., the so-called "ten-percenters"). Given the economic circumstances and specificities of a country, its policy objectives and the type of entrepreneurial fabric, existing definitions might still need to be subject to fine-tuning and updating.

---

[26] Stam et al. (2012) labels an "ambitious entrepreneur" as someone who engages in the entrepreneurial process with the aspiration to create as much value as possible. Schoar (2010) contends that only a small percentage of entrepreneurs are likely to succeed in scaling-up their businesses towards increasing profits and creating jobs, putting forward a distinction between "subsistence" and "transformational" entrepreneurs.

Fourthly, after the first round of actor identification, it is imperative to define the correct support thresholds to discern exactly who of a given category of entrepreneurs/firms is actually eligible for support (often a combination of age, size, industry, technology intensiveness, and growth patterns). Though opportunities to take advantage of fast-growing firms exist in every region, there might also be instances where a regional dimension needs to be added to the selection of variables, mostly due to the fact that resources are limited and that areas of intervention must be established either to pilot programs or to guarantee better effectiveness, especially when a more direct and targeted approach is the chosen tactic.

But there might well be no universal criteria to determine whether firm A deserves better support than firm B. There are many elements of discretionary choice involved. Indeed, what constitutes a meaningful measure of the potential success of a firm can actually be a function of different types of considerations, such as the nature of the firm's activity (e.g., manufacturing versus services, innovative versus non-innovative), its governance structure, along with other economic and financial indicators, such as its capital and equity structure.

There has been a tension for long between advocates of the promotion of start-ups and those wanting to focus on the growth potential of established firms. Our evidence suggests that both start-ups and young firms (such as gazelles) and established businesses have rapid growth potential. For the largest 120 high-growth and gazelles (on average each year) identified by this research as the leading job contributors in Portugal, they ought to be analyzed in terms of their ability to sustain growth in a number of relevant variables (in this case job creation) and the probability of being replaced by other fast growers of the same average size. Given these firms have already achieved a considerable size (especially for more established high-growth firms), there is the need to acknowledge they might not be able to grow indefinitely, once they reach the plateau of maturity in their sector or market. For these firms and for past overperformers, policy should aim at making sure the environment is set right for them to at least withstand their employment levels, while looking into fast-tracking other variables, such as their capacity to attract foreign investment or increase export capacity.

Simultaneously, a parallel winning strategy could be investigating potential replacements for fast-growing firms which discontinue high-growth trajectories. One way to go about could be looking into a combination of sectors and regions for medium-sized firms (such as those in the size-class just below that of the extraordinarily performing larger firms). This can be done through the analysis of business microdata and through matching processes based on some of the verified determinant success characteristics found in their predecessors. In fact, the focus on medium-sized enterprises is not a novelty[27] and had already been brought to the attention of the Portuguese Government in 2010 by the *Conselho para a Promoção da*

[27] In France, medium-sized enterprises have for long been recognized as the engines of growth (e.g., GE Capital 2013; KPMG 2013 and 2012; KPMG and CGPME 2012) and the Government has tailored specific initiatives in support of these enterprises (Ernst and Young 2013).

Internacionalização.[28] Actively profiling firms and prospecting the market in a given range of preestablished categories, in search for future fast-growing candidates among medium-sized firms might prove itself as a cost-effectiveness strategy. Another appealing strategy, which is not mutually exclusive of others already mentioned, is to search for dormant fast-growing enterprises and trigger them into employment growth (or the chosen variable for achieving the preestablished policy goals).

There is evidence that "sleeping gazelles" do exist in several countries. In Sweden, they represent a much larger share than high-growth firms (Bornhäll et al. 2013). These are mostly small and young firms which have historically sustained high profitability, regardless of recessions and government changes, but which are reluctant to grow in employment. An eventual calibration of existing policies, that focuses on these more abundant "dormant" firms for specific support might yield superior and faster results for job creation, as many of the fast-growing firms as defined in this paper, may be found unlikely to repeat rapid growth. In this case, policy-making should be geared towards removing barriers to growth for small business, this being an old debate in Portugal. In parallel, research should be directed towards a better understanding of what needs to be improved in order to create a better business environment that impacts on job creation.

17.5.4 When to Offer Support?

The prior conceptual analysis behind policy design needs to accommodate more than the recurring "why" and "how" types of questions. It must also involve "when" interrogations. Matters of "when" and "how" are in fact closely linked, as the set of preestablished instruments of intervention are also constructed based on the actors, the predecided outputs and outcomes of business support and the specific moment of intervention.

But knowing the right instance with sufficient accuracy, the exact stage of a firm's growth path where support interventions are made more useful is not entirely an easy matter, because of the scope for bad allocation, deadweight loss, and the consequent waste of public money and resources in ineffective and inefficient policies remains considerable.

We can however distinguish between two main approaches, considering whether the unit of analysis is the entrepreneur or the firm. When focusing on the firm, deciding when to offer support relates to knowing at what exact stage of the growth cycle support should be provided, if before a high-growth period (i.e., for firms which have never experienced high growth before, such as newborn enterprises, start-ups, enterprises with moderate growth), if during a high-growth period (for high-growth firms, gazelles[29] and dormant high-growth firms) or if after a high-growth period

[28] Since 2011, it has been replaced by the *Conselho Estratégico de Internacionalização da Economia* or CEIE.

[29] This is particularly important for gazelles, as its growth tends to be highly concentrated over a short period of time.

(for former fast-growing firms). This question is crucial, as it influences the set to tools that can be made most efficient and effective to deliver the relevant kind of support. Alternatively, support might be provided at identified trigger points of firm growth, such as in the case of Scotland (Brown and Mawson 2013).

17.5.5 How to Provide Support?

There are a number of mediating questions that also need to be posed and answered before a policy is outlined. What determines the likelihood of a firm achieving high growth? And how does this inform the optimal design of interventions that aim to accelerate business growth? The vast majority of research has focused on explaining the importance of age, size, sector, access to finance, and other barriers to business. Limited consideration have been given to the interactions of these with managerial and leadership capabilities and aspirations of their management, which are often the catalytic agent of change towards high growth. As concerns the fast-growing group of firms, researchers may well have been looking in the wrong places, and policy-makers might well be adopting an ex-post model to solve an ex-ante dilemma. We then start by acknowledging these limitations, including the fact that policy on its own can be insufficient to create or restore high growth to firms. Policy support can only contribute to the probability of their success, as there are other factors, environmental, societal, and cultural laying beneath the surface of perceptible performance determinants, shaping mindsets and behaviors.

Amid the current crisis, countries are showing a growing interest in cutting costs and allocating resources more efficiently, while doing better at targeting support, especially towards firms with a greater potential to impact the real economy. The right question to pose is thus how to provide support more effectively? In order to address this single question fully, one has to slice and dice this conundrum into smaller parts, to include other sub-questions, starting by going back to the initial aim[30] of policy support, in order to understand whether the focus should then be on supporting firms to achieve a high-growth path, or to support current fast-growing firms, or else going further and refine these questions according to precise economic sectors or even getting more specific as to the firm characteristics intended as support targets (all approaches looking for minimal interference in the market's natural selection process).

Once these first sub-questions are cleared out, moving onto more strategic considerations imply bearing in mind the answers given to the former enquiries and

[30] The aim and focus of the intervention also influences the choices of targets made later on, and the former also influences subsequently the type of resource allocation. Traditional SME focused policies are mostly supported by public funds, with a little support going to many agents, thus privileging quantity instead of quality. Focusing on fast-growing firms entails a somehow different focus, on quality and on the allocation of relatively more funds to a fewer number of firms, possibly through a mix of public and private funding.

combining them with the choice of the most appropriate moment for intervention, for increased effectiveness. Next, comes considering whether the intervention strategy ought to be proactive and *ex-ante*, engendering high-growth entrepreneurship before its inception (e.g., leadership and entrepreneurship programs in schools or screening for potential fast-growing firms and intervening at trigger points before growth realizes) or *ex-post*, that is after high-growth has taken place or is about to take place (e.g., selection of the fittest to scenario, or support the comeback into growth). Or else reactive, where interventions are laid out as a reaction to a given phenomenon, such as an economic crisis, the realization of competitiveness issues, or even after seeing firms in action, by reacting to the high-growth phenomena itself (or its absence), by helping to realize the creation of new value, support survival, or simply maintain jobs.

And should this support be generic (broad) or customized and in either case delivered directly, through a direct interaction with the agent or indirectly (an example being the easing of the environment and context in which firms operate)? Insofar as the enabling environment for bringing about growth is concerned, it has to be looked at in two ways, the sector and the supporting space (e.g., region), both of which are decisive. Clearly no intervention by itself can transform the growth prospects of firms, as beyond the individual characteristics of management, mentioned above, other factors, such as the characteristics of the territory, its ecosystem and its resource base shape behaviors and decisions and may constitute an imperceptible barrier to growth (or an element of stimulation). However, it is crucial to start by assessing if businesses are able to take full advantage of the ecosystem where they operate.

Subsequently, comes the identification of the instruments which are able to shape the emergence of fast-growing enterprises, followed by the mapping of existing policies and the interplay between them and its effect on fast-growing firms and finally, the articulation, complementarity and additionality between existing and new policies devised to target these firms. Thus, the first piece of ground work is indeed to conduct a policy and instrument mapping to understand what is going on and what factors are already affecting fast-growing ventures at the different levels of policy delivery (wider region, country, region, and locally).

Previous policy support for fast-growing firms has been largely around transactional forms of assistance commonly applied to most SME support (OECD 2010), usually being reactive and taking an ex-post outlook. Typically, firms self-select into these programs simply because support is available from public funding at very little cost. Because SME support policies are usually designed to work in favor of all firms and not necessarily for the benefit of the fastest growers, and as most SMEs are born small and remain relatively small, the current approach may not make a significant contribution to the economy. Besides, with most SME policies, a wide number of (small) firms must be reached for commensurate effects. Moreover, because small firms in particular are highly volatile, they must be carefully monitored on the scale required to allow for maximum returns on the spending. Administratively, the bureaucratic management of these programs also poses a great deal of challenges, a fact acknowledged by Birch (1979) many decades ago, beyond being costly.

In effect, poorly designed policies may even put a break on the fastest growing firms, because of the failure to address the bottom line issue, growth. Firm growth and in particular new firm growth, this being the case of gazelles, which can verify considerably fast-growth trajectories, is a heterogeneous phenomenon. Because of the inherent nonlinearity of their growth trajectories, which are neither life cycle-based (uninterrupted or linear) nor totality random (idiosyncratic), the appropriateness of quantitative approaches used by investors or policy-makers to judge firms or evaluate their potential according to uniform standards (such as growth rates in employment or turnover) can be questioned to a great extent.

A more targeted approach to the design of a stimulus policy in favor of high-growth can thus be expected to be more effective in achieving policy-makers' goals to strengthen local economic development based on high-impact entrepreneurial activity. However, this also compels practitioners and policy analysts to focus on conveying robust policy designs, which enable such fine targeting. This field of research needs to develop a more informed conceptualization of this phenomenon, rooted in the most advanced methods of longitudinal data analysis, with substantial cross-fertilization between quantitative and qualitative research methods in support of both more holistic and dynamic types of analysis across multiple organizational contexts, as well as further enable the exploration of the many nuances that have emerged from recent empirical work, thus helping to promote a more thorough understanding of the high-growth process.

But governments usually prefer supporting broader and indirect "enabling policies", instead of more targeted approaches, whereby they can be accused of giving leeway to certain economic agents in disregard of others. Moreover, designing and monitoring more targeted policies can be more demanding and can fall more easily under the scrutiny of the public opinion. As a matter of fact, targeting fast-growing firms for policy support is distinct from simply supporting entrepreneurship or new venture creation. What the dynamic character of these fast-growing firms seems to suggest quite strongly is that the traditional policy-mix of "static" policies, aimed indiscriminately at all firms in the SME size-class, might not necessarily work well for firms which have laid the foundations for growth, or who are starting to grow at a faster rate, or even for those already enduring high-growth rhythms. For greater effectiveness for fast-growing firms support, the specific needs of these types of enterprises have to be accounted for. Fast-growing firms require novel forms of more customized support, along with design sophistication and the adoption of nuances to particular cases, and lastly but not the least, a complementary and productive interplay between existing policies (e.g., industrial, entrepreneurship, SMEs, innovation, regional).

Policy support which artificially generates more fast-growing in a closed environment, such as a constrained national market can cannibalize existing enterprises' market segments and customers. Similarly, it one can also question whether these polices lead to an additional number of new jobs or just reallocate jobs from established static firms to new, more dynamic ventures. Existing evidence indicates that fast-paced firms contribute with a net positive effect to the rate of ambitions entrepreneurship and national economic growth (Stam et al. 2011; Stam and Van Stel 2011). But it does not follow from the previous statement that policy designed to support to stimulate ambition entrepreneurship or fast-growing firms necessarily leads to enhanced aggregate economic performance.

During a policy design phase, these issues may prompt further questioning about the right policy-mix and whether other types of interventions ought to be included and combined, such as internationalization support, more effective at unlocking external markets and providing greater scope for growth. Gazelles and high-growth firms are known to be more likely than other firms to export their products and services. By creating new markets and industries, these firms can diversify an economy and reduce its vulnerability to shocks. Whether additional policies should also be combined (e.g., innovation and cluster policy), highly depends on the sector and the innovative and technological intensiveness character of the firm. During the last decades, industrial policy has increasingly been aiming at integrating all these business support interventions, designed to stimulate firms based on the central assumption that they are at the core of productivity, innovation, and economic growth. In fact, historically, many policy objectives have been measured against different industry and enterprise indicators.

The delivery of policies can be done at a single-level (a region, a country) or multi-level (e.g., wider region/country/ region/ district). The geographical area of policy delivery and its scalability also ought to be considered. Some countries have this figured out at the national level (e.g., Stam et al. 2012; Lilischkis 2013), while the European Union is still in search of the best fit for interventions across its regions (Europe INNOVA 2011).

But how does this success spill over to local environments? It is often the case that the share of high-growth firms is greater in the capital cities, as they concentrate the networks of services and clusters these businesses needed for thriving on growth. Framework conditions should be such that firms can be created and sustained in any region, thus levelling out regional inequality. And is there scope for local policies, designed and delivered at the sub-national level for fast-growing firms? Many cross-sectorial policies already draw extensively on local business ecosystems (skills, resources, and initiative of local actors, notably universities), which can differ substantially from region to region. So far, local interventions are uncommon for fast-growing firms, as they put a great deal of demand on the existing local administrative organizational structure, requiring response to many kinds of specific challenges and entailing leveraging local and regional assets, including gaining access to upper levels of regional administrative bodies. On the other hand, local governments often see a limited role for themselves when it comes solely at picking winners. What can be observed in the countries for which there is evidence available, is a blend of national and regional policies in favor of fast-growing firms (Bosma and Stam 2012). Often, nationally designed policy programs are fitted differently in distinct regions, leaving room for adaptation to the local characteristics and the type of specialization within the region.[31] The chosen set of policies ought to complement each other in terms of intervention sphere, but the same applies to its geographic domain

[31] This has also been the principle applied by the European Union, where policies designed at the supranational level can be left to be adapted regionally, making use of the principle of subsidiarity.

of intervention, so that they do not foster unnecessary local competition that undermines the overall growth and development goals (e.g., the creation jobs in one region at the expense of another). Examples of targeted local policies aimed at fostering fast-growing firms are business accelerator programs, targeted industrial policies, and regional clusters, which have been found relevant important, to root these firms within a given region.

We have so far distinguished three main characteristics of firms, based on growth (non-high-growth, high-growth, and former high-growth). Within each of these 3 categories, further distinctions can be made based on age (young and established) and within each of the former two, a third categorization can also be introduced based on size (SMEs and large firms). These categories can be used to make for the main types of entrepreneurial ventures under analysis. At the early stages of a business life cycle (the prospective entrepreneur or the newborn firm), contributing to engender high-growth ventures has to be at the top of the considerations. Fostering a culture that is more risk-taking and tolerable to failure can create more start-ups with potential for growth. Entrepreneurship policy is one obvious candidate, at the disposal of most countries. The nuance that needs to be introduced is to aim at high quality, ambitious entrepreneurs, who are able to realize the creation of jobs and value, thus focusing on quality rather than on quantity.

Portugal already has a considerable turnover of firms and a substantial turnover of jobs, especially in the smallest size and youngest segments. Creating the conditions for businesses to grow and persist in the market, thus decreasing its failure rate, especially for SMEs, which have higher rates of mortality, seems critical to maintaining employment levels and the creation of value added. Portugal can use its SME policy to make sure the subset of (potentially) best performing SMEs is targeted, along with its fast-growing firms, putting a special emphasis on young firms, as they are the most probable to fail. Gazelles specifically need legal systems that respect intellectual and property rights, tax policy, and incentives for R&D spending and commercialization.

For the largest segment of fast-growing firms, the champions of growth, which consist of an annual average of 120 high-growth and gazelles over the period, support needs to be more customized, tailored to the combination of their specific characteristics (age, sector, region, market, degree of technological intensity, etc.). Because of their considerable impact on job creation and its small number, policy support does not incur in the huge management costs of most SME assistance schemes. However, because it has to be better targeted and due to the possibly considerable amount of resources involved, it has to be properly designed, implemented and monitored. It needs to start by looking at the interplay between existing policies, and specifically at innovation and internationalization instruments, to perceive how these might be affecting affecting these large firms.

Portugal has made in the past decade substantial efforts in easing the environment and context in which firms operate, namely in cutting bureaucracy and red tape. However, its framework conditions have to keep on improving in order to keep up with the global race for investment attraction.

Similarly to other countries, industrial policy in Portugal has tried to agglutinate and provide coherence to the efforts mentioned previously. But on its own, it might not suffice to impact on the ability of a firm's achieving high growth, leaving some ends loose. Significant disparities exist at the regional level, making it necessary to consider if regionally targeted interventions through regional policy or more decentralized local instruments can be made more useful for fast-growing firms, as there are currently none devised at the local level for these firms.

17.5.6 And Then, So What?

Ultimately, these types of programs are designed to help generating firm growth and job creation, which might otherwise not have happened (e.g., Goldman Sachs 2013). The mobilization of financial funding and technical resources needed to carry out such programs often calls for an evaluation, to look at if any evidence exists that indicates the program delivered what was supposed to and to look more closely into its relevancy, efficiency, effectiveness, additionally and impact, intending to link up individual objectives and firm-level achievements to larger impacts at the regional and national level.

However, evaluations of high-growth policy programs do not abound, either at the national, regional, or local level, remaining unclear what policy instruments are successful for high-growth firms, and in particular for SMEs (Lilischkis 2013). There are nonetheless some impact evaluation studies on SME support in various countries.[32] That of Morris and Stevens (2009) is one of the very few that focuses on evaluating high-growth SME programs. There are also other evaluations of policy-related programs at the local level, which might nevertheless provide useful insights for designing support policies at a sub-national level, such as the effects of the SBIR program (Lerner 1999) and that of a firm's location in a science park (Siegel et al. 2003), which focus on local and microeconomic results.

17.6 Conclusion

Economies that thrive on their most ambitions, innovative and productive firms are due to grow and develop. Some of the most stimulating of ambitious enterprises are those included in the sub-group whose growth is extremely fast. Consequently, having current information about the incidence of fast-growing enterprises within a country or region, its characteristics, and growth patterns is essential for drawing conclusions about the economic foundations of a country, the best strategies towards economic growth and the rational for policy intervention.

When it comes to establishing descriptive features of past business facts, the main aspiration is to gain access to the whole population of firms. We have used a linked dataset in this analysis, which contains all the population of Portuguese

[32] The European Investment Bank (2005) has conducted an evaluation on SME loans in the enlarged European Union and the World Bank (Acevedo and Tan 2011) on SMEs programs in Latin America and the Caribbean.

employer enterprise firms over an extended period of time, 1985–2009. The strict application of the Eurostat/OECD (2007) methodology provided a time span of roughly 17 years of firm activity and organic growth analysis, between 1990 and 2007 for high-growth firms and 1992–2007 for gazelles.

In 2007, high-growth firms represented 3 % of all employer enterprises with over ten employees (by the employment criteria and 9.5 % by turnover), responsible for 7.6 % (12 %) of the employment. Gazelles are a smaller share of firms, 0.7 % (2.2 % by turnover) employing 1.5 % (2 %) of the work force. Overall, the evidence suggests that high-growth firms and gazelles are not a homogeneous group of firms. There is also evidence of significant differences of high-growth firms across regions, with more than half concentrated around the metropolitan area of Lisbon and another quarter in the North. Over the years, high-growth firms and gazelles tended to gravitate towards the Lisbon district. Similarly to other countries, Portuguese urban areas seem to be more conducive for fast-growing firms, which can contribute to deepen regional inequality.

We also find that job creation in fast-growing companies in Portugal, accompanies the cycles verified in the overall economy, but that they accommodate better periods of economic downturn, especially in the case of gazelles, which display a smaller volatility during recession spans. We can also conclude for the acceptance of the proposition that a relatively small proportion of firms are responsible for a disproportionate share of job creation. Gazelles are the most prolific category of job creating firms. Although small enterprises are overrepresented in the population of high-impact firms, a few with over 250 employees generate a disproportionate share of all new net jobs within this period. In particular, a small number of the largest high-growth firms, (over 100 firms on average during the extended period), were responsible for over 50 % of the total jobs created from 1990 to 2007. When analyzing these two types of firms' contribution to job creation, we find that is not firm age per se that drives the bulk of net job creation, but rather firm size along with the turnover of firms that are able to attain high growth.

However, there is evidence that smaller firms employing less than ten employees across all sectors also account for a disproportionate large share of job creation, relative to their overall share of employment. Because of the methodology we employed focuses on employer enterprise firms with over ten employees, we have not gathered evidence of job creation by smaller firms, and the same applies to the self-employed. Thus, the strict definition used in this paper underestimates[33] the economic dimension of high-impact firms in Portugal. We believe that extending the definition to include the smallest subset of firms along with complementing it with other evidence, such as that provided by GEM's (2012) and the intrapreneurship[34] phenomenon, may provide a more accurate, not only of existing, but also of potential (high-growth) entrepreneurs and ventures.

---

[33] An analysis of Swedish firms suggests that the strict application of the Eurostat/OECD definition excluded about 95 % of all surviving firms, creating 39 % of all new jobs during the period (Daunfeldt et al. 2012).

[34] Consider, for instance, Felício et al. (2012) and *Câmara de Comércio Americana em* Portugal (2012).

Furthermore, when considering net job creation measurement rates for fast-growing companies, additional methodological caution must be employed, as its results can be misleading, as well as the kind of policy advice they provide. When considering other studies and the international evidence available, we find that methodology, definitions, and terminology matter. Identifying high-growth and non-high-growth businesses and their economic impact will be highly dependent on the set of variables, the calculations, the criteria used to measure growth, and the corresponding thresholds adopted. What we consider more relevant though is the definition of "high-growth" firm or "gazelle" to be aligned with the specific context or objective of the investigation or policy goal, be it job creation, productive growth, regional policy development, competitiveness, or simply managerial performance.

An additional limitation of our study, as in most of the past research, is that we do not look into the path or growth trajectory followed by fast-growing firms, which would allow to capture the interplay between growth and survival. Similarly, we do not provide an insight into the dynamics of job creation over a firm's life cycle. We only look into high-growth after firms got there. Moreover, our analysis treats all jobs as equal and does not tell much about its persistence. We have also been absent-minded in what respects the role of the owner/entrepreneur's managerial capabilities in firm growth dynamics.

We consider that a more thorough understanding of fast-growing firms ought to lead to adjustments in government policies to heighten their exceptional contribution to economic growth. In this research, we have confirmed, there is some evidence upon which to rest the rationale for a range of policy initiatives in support of fast-growing firms, given the ability of these firms to counteract unfavorable business cycles and create more jobs at a faster rate and the survival problems affecting Portuguese firms and the resulting job losses it brings about. We have also acknowledged that policy can facilitate the impact of high-growth entrepreneurship. This line of argument can be regarded as a variant to the more general argument of SME as job creators, but with the advantage of identifying a clear target for SME assistance policy. We provided evidence that during the period 1990–2007, 93 % of Portuguese high-growth firms and 47 % of gazelles (as measured by the employment criteria) can be classified as SMEs, making them a clear target for SME policy. In supporting small high-growth ventures, policy-makers will not be starting from a blank slate but should, where necessary, catalyze and link together local resources, infrastructure, and networks that are already serving small businesses to create the right ecosystems where these types of firms can flourish and grow.

Beyond the standard advice to pursue policy options that are likely to generate faster growth among smaller and younger firms, we gather Portugal ought to focus specifically on its highest impact firms, the champions of employment growth, that is, biggest sized high-growth and gazelle firms, which are large enough to attract financing for institutional and industry investors with a lower level of effort. For the group of largest firms, a prior assessment of the most appropriate framework conditions ought to be conducted, together with an analysis of the interplay of different policies, namely innovation, internationalization and access to finance, possibly accompanied by a more targeted approach that takes into consideration their specific needs. Considering a specific strategy for mid-sized[35] high-growth firms and gazelles should also be a burning item on the agenda. These are already fast growers, which can contribute even more to net job creation if they manage to upscale their activities. Lastly, dormant high-growth and sleeping gazelles, along with static firms with growth potential, should be particularly targeted and awoken from their deep sleep to join their counterparts in enjoying the benefits of high-growth.

If a country's economic potential is to be realized in the decades ahead, it is up to policy-makers to exercise greater urgency and precision in designing policies in support of high-growth. This is even more pressing in Portugal, given that on the demand side, the present public sector capacity for stimulus measures, such as increasing public procurement, is severely constrained. There has to be necessarily a stronger emphasis on the supply side, which can only bear positive effects, if the market produces the right type of firms, able to improve employment prospects in the long run. This is only possible by means of a selective economic policy intervention, which relies on a selection of the fittest system, without incurring in market selection distortion costs. Providing this support effectively and efficiently should be the cornerstone of all the effort put in devising the right policies, requiring new ways of working together across the public and private sectors, and a greater openness to risk and to innovation in ideas and models. Global forward-looking national strategies, with integrated policy designs are preferred to the piecemeal program/project solutions often adopted. Over the long term, the most effective actions are those which mobilize all levels of government, the national, regional, and the local, as well as the private sector, the education sector, the venture capitalists, and all other primary actors, all of whom share a stake of the responsibility for laying the foundations of entrepreneurial excellence, and on whose collaboration rests the formation of the right ecosystem for the emergence of fast-growing enterprises in every region.

However, the job creation narrative in particular has not yet fast-tracked into a confined set of robust conclusions for policy. Whether the formation of typical start-ups should be discouraged and the focus put on encouraging the formation of high-quality entrepreneurs and the subset of business with growth potential still remains to be fully validated by concrete evidence. And even if the argument to stop subsidizing start-ups is accepted, it does not have any implications for the second line of reasoning. However, given the high turnover of firms in Portugal, related to a combination of size and age to a great extent, the growth argument might be stronger than the two former as the primary policy variable of support to strengthen the natural market selection of the best firms, a sort of a survival of fittest scenario, where policy intervention would play the role of helping to provide a favorable environment and the needed resources to help enduring market vicissitudes.

[35] In France, medium-sized enterprises have for long been recognized as the engines of growth (e.g., GE Capital 2013; KPMG 2012, 2013; KPMG and CGPME 2012) and the Government has tailored specific initiatives in support of these enterprises (Ernst and Young 2013).

Despite the wide recognition that fast-growing firms are a fundamental part of the process of economic development, and the agreement that support policies at different spatial and thematic levels have to concur for overreaching common goals and be mutually supportive and synergetic, we do not yet possess enough insight into its rational, effectiveness and efficiency, and in particular of how to design enabling policies and blend them with more customized direct policies aimed at locally hatching the capacity to generate more employment growth. Moreover, given the lack of evaluative studies focusing on support policies to fast-growing firms, it is still unclear which types and combinations of policy instruments are the most effective. However, we have attempted at providing a conceptual framework for tapping into the issue of how to design policies for firms who are growing at a faster pace and a roadmap to tackling some of its most controversial issues.

In this chapter, we do not intend to claim we have found causal implications from the data which lead straight into policy conclusions. What we do extensively in this paper is to uncover static and dynamic features of particular sets of fast-growing firms. Our findings take us to the edge of what we currently know, but we are still not able at the present moment to provide evidence on how they hinge on causality. In fact, when it comes to drawing on causality for designing the best policies, there is a role for a myriad of other factors, such as reasoned intuition, background, and experience, but also a shot of skepticism, the realization that for all our best efforts, we may well be found wrong.

Therefore, in what regards Portugal we can only attempt to make cautious recommendations based on what we have observed from our data, learned from other countries, and from the past and current policy-making practice. The available international evidence points to Portugal engendering a lesser amount of fast-growing firms in both manufacturing and service sectors. But what has distinguished particularly the country over time is the high amount of SMEs in its population of fast-growing firms, the disproportionate amount of employment generated by the largest category of high-growth firms and gazelles, the narrowing down of the difference in the two criteria adopted for classifying growth (employment and turnover), showing that in the 1990s and 2000s decades it has become relatively harder to grow in turnover employment, and the overall low survival rates of Portuguese employer enterprises relative to other countries. How to make these firms' growth trajectories more enduring, while providing policy with a rational and a role for contributing to engender high impact entrepreneurs and firms without distorting the market, should be among the leading policy concerns. We thus propose that the first layer of the segmentation criteria for firm support is made on the basis of growth or growth prospects and not on the most commonly used age or size. Considering growth as the first layer of selectivity for firm support will allow a better targeting and more effective allocation of scarce public funds.

High-growth is a stage in the development of enterprises with the potential and ambition to grow. Portugal can become a breeding ground for dynamic companies with the talent to achieve high growth along several dimensions, but which can especially spur job creation. The country may however need to be prepared to do more and especially better, at preparing the ground for next generation of aspiring firms and innovation leaders to engender the ambition and desire to compete and succeed on a global scale. We may have to concede that achieving high-growth standards might not be a question of "how many" but of "which", more a question of quality than of quantity. Shifting the support paradigm from a "survive" to a "strive" mentality and establishing an *a priori* credible compromise for growth might be a determining factor for achieving and sustaining firm expansion and economic growth.

Acknowledgment The authors would like to thank *Gabinete de Estratégia e Planeamento* of the Portuguese Ministry of Labor and Social Security for the provision of the data.

References

Acevedo GL, Tan HW (eds) (2011) Impact evaluation of small and medium enterprise programs in Latin America and the Caribbean. World Bank, Washington, DC

Acs ZJ, Mueller P (2008) Employment effects of business dynamics: mice, gazelles and elephants. Small Bus Eco 30(1):85–100

Acs ZJ, Parsons W, Tracy S (2008) High impact firms: gazelles revisited. Research summary 328. Office of Advocacy, U.S. Small Business Administration, Washington, DC

Ahmad N (2008) A proposed framework for business demography statistics. In: Congregado E (ed) Measuring entrepreneurship: building a statistical system, vol 16. Springer, New York, pp 113–174. doi:10.1007/978-0-387-72288-7_7

Anyadike-Danes M, Bonner K, Hart M, Mason C (2009) Measuring business growth: high-growth firms and their contribution to employment in the UK. NESTA research report, Oct 2009. NESTA, London

Anyadike-Danes M, Hart M, Du M (2013) Firm dynamics and job creation in the UK—taking stock and developing new perspectives White Paper 6. Enterprise Research Centre, Warwick Business School, Coventry

Audretsch DB, Feldman MP (1996) R&D spillovers and the geography of innovation and production. Am Econ Rev 86(4):253–273

Autio E, Kronlund M, Kovalainen A (2007) High-growth SME support initiatives in nine countries: analysis, categorization and recommendations. Edita, Finland

Baldwin JR, Dupuy R, Picot G (1996) Have small firms created a disproportionate share of new jobs in Canada? A reassessment of the facts, vol 71, Analytical studies branch. Statistics Canada, Ottawa

Banco de Portugal (2010) Estrutura e dinâmica das Sociedades não financeiras em Portugal. Estudos da Central de Balanços. Banco de Portugal, Lisboa

Barbosa N, Eiriz V (2011) Regional variation of firm size and growth: the Portuguese case. Growth and Change 42(2):125–158

Bartelsman E, Scarpetta S, Schivardi F (2005) Comparative analysis of firm demographics and survival: evidence from micro-level sources in OECD countries. Ind Corp Change 14(3): 365–391

Basu K (2013) The method of randomization, economic policy, and reasoned intuition. Policy research working paper 6722. World Bank, Washington, DC

Betbèze JP, Saint-Étienne C (2006) Une stratégie PME pour la France. Conseil d'Analyse Economique, La Documentation française

Biosca AB (2010) Growth dynamics, exploring business growth and contraction in Europe and the US. NESTA and FORA Research Report. NESTA, London

Birch DL (1979) The job generation process. MIT program on neighborhood and regional change, 302. Massachusetts Institute of Technology, Cambridge

Birch DL (1981) Who creates jobs? Public Interest 65:3–14
Birch DL (1987) Job creation in America: how our smallest companies put the most people to work. Free Press, New York
Birch DL, Haggerty A, Parsons W (1995) Who is creating jobs? Cognetics, Boston
Birch DL, Haggetty A, Parsons W (1997) Corporate almanac. Cognetic, Cambridge
BIS (2011). The plan for growth. Department of Business, Innovation and Skills. BIS—Department for Business, Innovation and Skills, HM Treasury, England
Bornefalk A, Du Rietz A (2009) Entrepreneurship policies in Denmark and Sweden—targets and indicators. Swedish Network for European Studies in Economics and Business, Stockholm, http://www.snee.org/publikationer_search_eng.asp
Bornhäll A, Daunfeldt S, Rudholm N (2013) Sleeping gazelles: high profits but no growth. HUI Working Papers 91. HUI Research, Stockholm
Bos J, Stam E (2011) Gazelles, industry growth and structural change. Research Memoranda 18. Maastricht Research School of Economics of Technology and Organization (METEOR), Maastricht
Bosma N, Schutjens V (2007) Patterns of promising entrepreneurial activity in European regions. Tijdschrift voor ecconomische en sociale Geografie 98(5):675–686
Bosma N, Schutjens V (2011) Understanding regional variation in entrepreneurial activity and entrepreneurial attitude in Europe. Ann Reg Sci 47(3):711–742
Bosma N, Stam E (2012) Local policies for high-employment growth enterprises. In: Report prepared for the OECD/DBA international workshop on high-growth firms: local policies and local determinants, Copenhagen
Brown R, Mawson S (2013) Trigger points and high-growth firms: a conceptualisation and review of public policy implications. J Small Bus Enterprise Dev 20(2):279–295
Brüderl J, Preisendörfer P (2000) Fast-growing businesses: empirical evidence from a German study. Int J Sociol 30(3):45–70
CPA Australia/CGA-Canada (2010). Report of the forum on SME issues: unlocking the potential of the SME sector. CPA Australia/CGA-Canada
Câmara de Comércio Americana em Portugal (2012) Intrapreneurship Portugal. CCAP, Lisboa
Capital GE (2013) PME-ETI: sommet pour la croissance, les secrets de ces entreprises de taille moyenne qui font la France. EPCE, França
Caves RE (1998) Industrial organization and new findings on the turnover and mobility of firms. J Econ Lit 36(4):1947–1982
Chandler GN, Lyon DW (2001) Issues of research design and construct measurement in entrepreneurship research: the past decade. Entrepren Theory Pract 25(4):101–113
Churchill NC, Lewis VL (1983) The five stages of small business growth. Harv Bus Rev 61(3):30–50
Commission E (2010) Europe 2020: a strategy for smart, sustainable and inclusive growth: communication from the Commission. Research report. European Commission, Brussels
Dalton S, Friesenhahn E, Spletzer J, Talan D (2011) Employment growth by size-class: comparing firm and establishment data. Monthly Labor Review 1–12 Dec
Daunfeldt S, Halvarsson D, Johansson D (2012) A cautionary note on using the Eurostat-OECD definition of high-growth firms HUI Working Papers 65. HUI Research, Stockholm
Davidsson P, Delmar F (2006) High-growth firms and their contribution to employment: the case of Sweden 1987-96. In: Davidsson P, Delmar F, Wiklund J (eds) Entrepreneurship and growth of the firm. Edward Elgar, Chelten, pp 7–20
Davidsson P, Wiklund J (2000) Conceptual and empirical challenges in the study of firm growth. In: Sexton D, Landström H (eds) The Blackwell handbook of entrepreneurship. Blackwell Business, Oxford, pp 26–44
Davidsson P, Achtenhagen L, Naldi L (2005) Research on small firm growth: a review. In: European Institute of Small Business
Davidsson P, Achtenhagen L, Naldi L (2010) Small firm growth. Found Trends Entrepren 6(2):69–166

Davis SJ, John CH, Scott S (1996) Job Creation and Destruction. The MIT Press, Cambridge. MA
Delmar F, Davidsson P, Gartner W (2003) Arriving at the high-growth firm. J Bus Ventur 18:189–216
ECB (2012) Euro area labour markets and the crisis, vol 138, Occasional paper series. European Central Bank, Frankfurt
Ernst & Young (2013) L'efficacité des aides publiques aux entreprises, Quelles priorités pour la compétitivité française? Ernst & Young, France
Europe INNOVA (2011) Gazelles, high-growth companies. Final Report, Consortium Europe INNOVA Sectoral Innovation Watch: European Commission
European Cluster Observatory (2009). Priority sector report: knowledge intensive business services. Center for Strategy and Competitiveness, Stockholm School of Economics, Europe INNOVA Initiative.
European Investment Bank (2005) Evaluation of SME global loans in the enlarged Union. Evaluation report, operations evaluation. EIB, Luxemburg
European Parliament (2011) Glasgow: Directorate General for Internal Policies. Directorate General for Internal Policies, Policy Department B: Structural and Cohesion Policies, EPRC, Glasgow
Eurostat/OECD (2007) Eurostat-OECD manual on business demography statistics. OECD, Paris
Entrepreneurship indicators: Employer business demography and high-growth enterprises in Europe, 21st Meeting of the Wiesbaden Group on Business Registers — International Round Table on Business Survey Frames, Session 6A: Entrepreneurship indicators, Business Demography and SMEs (Nov 2008), Paris
Felício JA, Rodrigues R, Caldeirinha VR (2012) The effect of intrapreneurship on corporate performance. Manage Decis 50(10):1717–1738
Financial Times (2014) British business bank to target SMEs with potential. Accessed Jan 5, 2014. http://www.ft.com/intl/cms/s/0/8fe98c74-6969-11e3-89ce-00144feabdc0.html#axzz2pueHPul2
Fritsch M (2011) The effect of new business formation on regional development: empirical evidence, interpretation, and avenues for further research. In: Fritsch M (ed) Handbook of research on entrepreneurship and regional development (Chapter 4). Edward Elgar, Cheltenham, pp 58–106
Fritsch M, Mueller P (2006) The evolution of regional entrepreneurship and growth regimes. In: Fritsch M, Schmude J (eds) Entrepreneurship in the region (Chapter 11). Springer Science, New York, pp 225–244. doi:10.1007/0-387-28376-5_11
Garnsey E, Stam E, Heffernan P (2006) New firm growth: exploring processes and paths. Ind Innov 13(1):1–20
GEM (2012) GEM Portugal 2012: estudo sobre o empreendedorismo. Global Entrepreneurship Monitor, Portugal
Gibrat R (1931) Les inegalités économiques. Recueil Sirey, Paris
Gilbert B, McDougall P, Audretsch D (2006) New venture growth: a review and extension. J Manag 32:926–950
Gilbert BA, McDougall P, Audretsch DB (2008) Clusters, knowledge spillovers and new venture performance: an empirical examination. J Bus Ventur 23(4):405–422
Goldman Sachs (2013) Stimulating small business growth, Progress Report on the Goldman Sachs 10,000 Small Businesses UK Programme. Goldman Sachs 10,000 Small Businesses in a joint collaboration with the University of Oxford, Aston Business School, University of Leeds, Manchester Metropolitan University and UCL
Greiner LE (1972) Evolution and revolution as organizations grow. Harv Bus Rev 76(3):37–46
Haltiwanger J, Krizan CJ (1999) Small business and job creation in the United States: the role of new and young businesses. In: Acs ZJ (ed) Are small firms important? Their role and impact (Chapter 5). Kluwer Academic, Boston, pp 79–97
Haltiwanger JC, Jarmin RS, Miranda J (2013) Who creates jobs? Small vs. large vs. young. Rev Econ Stat 95(2):347–361. doi:10.1162/REST_a_00288

Henrekson M, Johansson D (2009) Competencies and institutions fostering high-growth firms. Found Trend Entrepren 5(1):1–80
Henrekson M, Johansson D (2010) Gazelles as job creators—a survey and interpretation of the evidence. Small Bus Econ 35(2):227–244
Herman D, Williams AD (2013) Driving Canadian growth and innovation: five challenges holding back small and medium-sized enterprises in Canada. Centre for Digital Entrepreneurship and Economic Performance, Canada
Hölzl W (2009) Is the R&D behaviour of fast-growing SMEs different? Evidence from CIS III data for 16 countries. Small Bus Econ 33(1):59–75
Informa D&B (2011) Crescimento do tecido empresarial 2006–2009. 1º Conferência sobre crescimento empresarial e empresas de elevado crescimento em Portugal, Lisboa
Jaffe AB, Trajtenberg M, Henderson R (1993) Geographic localization of knowledge spillovers as evidenced by patent citations. Q J Econ 108(3):577–598
KPMG (2012) Voyage au cœur des entreprises de taille intermédiaire (ETI): une stratégie de conquêtes. KPMG, France
KPMG & CGPME (2012). Panorama de l'évolution des PME depuis 10 ans. Cahier Préparatoire. KPMG, France
KPMG (2013) Les ETI, leviers de la croissance en France, cinq ans après leur création, quel bilan et quelles perspectives? KPMG, France
Lawless M (2013) Age or size? Determinants of job creation. Research Technical Paper 2/RT/13. Central Bank and Financial Services Authority of Ireland, Dublin
Lechner C, Dowling M (2003) Firm networks: external relationships as sources for the growth and competitiveness of entrepreneurial firms. Entrepren Reg Dev 15(1):1–16
Lerner J (1999) The government as a venture capitalist: the long-run effects of the SBIR program. J Bus 72(3):285–297
Levie J, Lichtenstein BB (2010) A terminal assessment of stages theory: introducing a dynamic states approach to entrepreneurship. Entrepren Theory Pract 34:317–350
Lilischkis S (2013) Policies in support of high-growth innovative SMEs. Discussion paper for the 2013 ERAC mutual learning seminar on research and innovation policies, Brussels
McKinsey Global Institute (2010) Beyond austerity: a path to economic growth and renewal in Europe. McKinsey, Chicago
Ministry of Business, Innovation and Employment (2013) High-growth business in New Zealand. Research evaluation and analysis branch. Ministry of Business, Innovation and Employment, Wellington
Mitusch K, Schimke A (2011) Gazelles—high-growth companies. Task 4 Horizontal Report 5 (Final Report). Europe INNOVA Sectoral Innovation Watch for DG Enterprise and Industry, European Commission
Morris M, Stevens P (2009) Evaluation of the growth services range: statistical analysis using firm-based performance data. Ministry of Economic Development, Government of New Zealand, New Zealand
NESTA (2009) The vital 6 per cent: how high-growth innovative businesses generate prosperity and jobs. NESTA Research Summary (Oct 2009). NESTA, London
NESTA (2011) Vital growth: the importance of high-growth business to the recovery. NESTA Research Summary (March 2011). NESTA, London
New Zealand Government (2013) Information and communications technology. The New Zealand Sectors Report 2013. Ministry of Business, Innovation, and Employment, Wellington
Nordic Council of Ministers (2010) Nordic entrepreneurship monitor 2010. NCM, Copenhagen
Nunes A, Sarmento EM (2012) Business demography dynamics in Portugal: a non-parametric survival analysis. In: Bonnet J, Dejardin M, Madrid-Guijarro A (eds) The shift to the entrepreneurial society: a built economy in education, sustainability and regulation (Chapter 18). Edward Elgar, Cheltenham, pp 260–272. doi:10.4337/9780857938947.00027
OECD (1997) Small business, job creation and growth: facts, obstacles and best practices. Organization for Economic Cooperation and Development, Paris

OECD (2002) High-growth SMEs and employment. Organization for Economic Cooperation and Development, Paris

OECD (2007) OECD framework for the evaluation of SME and entrepreneurship policies and programmes. Organization for Economic Cooperation and Development, Paris. doi:10.1787/9789264040090-en

OECD (2008) Measuring entrepreneurship: a digest of indicators. OECD-Eurostat Entrepreneurship Indicators Programme. OECD Statistics Directorate, Paris

OECD (2009) Measuring entrepreneurship: a collection of indicators (2009 edn) OECD-Eurostat Entrepreneurship Indicators Programme. OECD Statistics Directorate, Paris

OECD (2010) High-growth enterprises: what Governments can do to make a difference. OECD Studies on SMEs and Entrepreneurship. Organization for Economic Cooperation and Development, Paris. doi:10.1787/9789264048782-en

OECD (2011) Entrepreneurship at a Glance 2010, Paris

OECD (2012) OECD economic surveys: Portugal 2012. Organization for Economic Cooperation and Development, Paris. doi:10.1787/eco_surveys-prt-2012-en

OECD (2013a) Key findings of the work of the OECD LEED programme on high-growth firms—interim report. Centre for Entrepreneurship, SMEs and Local Development, CFE/LEED, Paris

OECD (2013b) Entrepreneurship at a glance 2013. Organization for Economic Cooperation and Development, Paris. doi:10.1787/entrepreneur_aag-2013-en

Parker SC, Storey DJ, Van Witteloostuijn A (2010) What happens to gazelles? The importance of dynamic management strategy. Small Bus Econ 35(2):203–226

Picot G, Dupuy R (1998) Job creation by company size class: the magnitude, concentration and persistence of job gains and losses in Canada. Small Bus Econ 10(2):117–139

Porter ME (1998) Clusters and competition: new agendas for companies, governments, and institutions. In: Porter ME (ed) On competition. Harvard Business School Press, Boston, pp 197–299

Santander (2013) Growth Britain: unlocking the potential of our SMEs. Santander report 2013

Salas OA, Francolí, Gascón JFJM, Stoyanova A (2010) High-growth firmsand gazelles in Catalonia, Generalitat di Catalunya

Sarmento EM, Nunes A (2010a) Getting smaller: size dynamics of employer enterprises in Portugal. In: Lechman E (ed) Enterprise in modern economy—SMEs and entrepreneurship, vol 2. Gdańsk University of Technology Publishing House, Poland, pp 118–138

Sarmento EM, Nunes A (2010b) Entrepreneurship performance indicators for active employer enterprises in Portugal. Temas Económicos 9/2010. Gabinete de Estratégia e Estudos, Ministério da Economia, da Inovação e do Desenvolvimento, Portugal

Sarmento EM, Nunes A (2010c) Business demography in Portugal. Statistical publications. Gabinete de Estratégia e Estudos, Ministério da Economia, da Inovação e do Desenvolvimento, Lisboa

Sarmento EM, Nunes A (2012) The dynamics of employer enterprise creation in Portugal over the last two decades: a size, regional and sectoral perspective. Notas Económicas 36:6–22

Schoar A (2010) The divide between subsistence and transformational entrepreneurship. Innov Pol Econ 10:57–81

Schreyer P (1996) SMEs and employment creation: overview of selected quantitative studies in OECD Member Countries. OECD Science, Technology and Industry Working Papers, 1996/04. OECD, Paris. doi:10.1787/374052760815

Schreyer P (2000) High-growth firms and employment. OECD Science, Technology and Industry Working Papers, 2000/3. OECD, Paris. doi:10.1787/861275538813

Siegel D, Westhead P, Wright M (2003) Science parks and the performance of new technology-based firms: a review of recent UK evidence and an agenda for future research. Small Bus Econ 20(2):177–184

Stam E (2005) The geography of gazelles in the Netherlands. Tijdschrift voor Economische en Social Geografie 96(1):121–127

Stam E, Stel A (2011) Types of entrepreneurship and economic growth. In: Szirmai A, Naudé W, Goedhusys M (eds) Innovation, entrepreneurship and economic development (Chapter 4). Oxford University Press, Oxford, pp 78–95

Stam E, Hartog C, Van Stel A, Thurik R (2011) Ambitious entrepreneurship and macro-economic growth. In: Minniti M (ed) The dynamics of entrepreneurship. Evidence from the global entrepreneurship monitor data (Chapter 10). Oxford University Press, Oxford, pp 231–250
Stam E, van Bosma N, Witteloostuijn A, de Jong J, Bogaert S, Edwards N, Jaspers F (2012) Ambitious entrepreneurship: a review of the state of the art. Studie Reeks 23. Vlaamse Raad voor Wetenschap en Innovatie, Flemish Council for Science and Innovation, Brussels
Stangler D (2010) High-growth firms and the future of the American economy, vol 2, Kauffman Foundation research series: firm formation and economic growth. Kauffman Foundation, Kansas City
Steffens P, Davidsson P, Fitzsimmons J (2009) Performance configurations over time: implications for growth- and profit-oriented strategies. Entrepren TheoryPract 33(1):125–148
Storey D (1994) Understanding the small business sector. Routledge, London
Sutton J (1997) Gibrat's legacy. J Econ Lit 35:40–59
Swedish Agency for Growth Policy Analysis (2011) Entrepreneurship and SME-policies across Europe—the cases of Sweden, Flanders, Austria and Poland. Report 2010/31, Swedish Agency for Growth Policy Analysis
Tamásy C (2006) Determinants of regional entrepreneurship dynamics in contemporary Germany: a conceptual and empirical analysis. Reg Stud 40(4):364–384
Tilford S, Whyte P (eds) (2011) Innovation, how Europe can take off. Centre for European Reform, London
Van Praag MC, Versloot PH (2008) The economic benefits and costs of entrepreneurship: a review of the research. Found Trends Entrepren Res 42(2):65–154
Wennekers S, Thurik R (1999) Linking entrepreneurship and economic growth. Small Bus Econ 13(1):27–55

Index

R. Baptista, J. Leitão (eds.), *Entrepreneurship, Human Capital, and Regional Development*, International Studies in Entrepreneurship 31,
DOI 10.1007/978-3-319-12871-9

Printed in Poland
by Amazon Fulfillment
Poland Sp. z o.o., Wrocław

80783115R00240